D1757085

EC
BANKING LAW

Interests in Goods
by Norman Palmer and
Ewan McKendrick
(1993)

The Law of Insurance Contracts
second edition
by Malcolm A. Clarke
(1994)

EC Banking Law
second edition
by Marc Dassesse, Stuart Isaacs QC
and Graham Penn
(1994)

EC BANKING LAW

BY

MARC DASSESSE
Professor, Free University of Brussels (U.L.B.), Member of the Brussels Bar

STUART ISAACS QC
of Gray's Inn, Barrister

GRAHAM PENN
Partner, Cameron, Markby Hewitt London Visiting Professor, University College University of London

SECOND EDITION

FOREWORD BY
THE RT. HON. SIR LEON BRITTAN

LONDON   NEW YORK   HAMBURG   HONG KONG
LLOYD'S OF LONDON PRESS LTD.
1994

Lloyd's of London Press Ltd.
Legal Publishing Division
27 Swinton Street
London WC1X 9NW

USA AND CANADA
Lloyd's of London Press Inc.
Suite 308, 611 Broadway
New York, NY 10012 USA

GERMANY
Lloyd's of London Press GmbH
59 Ehrenbergstrasse
2000 Hamburg 50, Germany

SOUTH EAST ASIA
Lloyd's of London Press (Far East) Ltd.
Room 1101, Hollywood Centre
233 Hollywood Road
Hong Kong

©

Marc Dassesse, Stuart Isaacs QC, Graham Penn
1994

First published in Great Britain, 1985
Second edition 1994

British Library Cataloguing in Publication Data
A catalogue record for this book is
available from the British Library

ISBN 1–85044–207–X

Text set in 10/12 pt Linotron 202 Times by
Mendip Communications Ltd., Frome, Somerset
Printed in Great Britain by
Bookcraft Ltd., Midsomer Norton, Avon

FOREWORD

Banking is an industry which has changed out of all recognition in the past decade or so. The two factors which have been most responsible for this change are new technology and the development of banking legislation. The first is characterised by dramatic leaps forward and rapid obsolescence. The second has been a much more evolutionary process, gradually gathering pace during the life of the Single Market programme. When change is gradual it is always much harder to decide when to attempt to draw the various threads of change together into a volume such as this. I believe, however, that now is precisely the right time for the publication of *EC Banking Law*, for the European Single Market in banking is virtually complete, at least on the statute books, and political attention is now turning to the question of implementation. There will certainly be amendments and changes to this body of legislation in the future but these will not come for some time, and when they do will build on the principles outlined here.

I was fortunate enough to be the European Commissioner responsible for financial services between 1989–92 when most of the legislation described in this volume was put in place. It was clear at the time how important this would be for Europe. But it was less clear how much of an impact it would have beyond Europe. We have not only created a model for others, like the US, to follow but we have also created a model approach to market opening which gives the European banking industry the strongest basis on which to thrive at home and seek access to new markets abroad. I am sure that *EC Banking Law* will therefore remain an invaluable tool for both practitioners and students of banking for many years to come.

LEON BRITTAN

PREFACE

It is not without some relief on our part that this second edition of *EC Banking Law* sees the light of day. If the growth in the EC's interest in the banking sector between the publication of *Banking and the Competition Law of the EC* in 1978 and the first edition of this book, published in 1985 as *EEC Banking Law*, was great, the development of EC banking law since then has been positively exponential. On more than one occasion over the past few years, our preparation of this edition has been delayed because of the need to take into account the imminent adoption of new Community legislation in the field. In the result, the scope of the book has expanded considerably. It has also been substantially reorganised, primarily to reflect the increased importance in the sector of the freedom of establishment and the freedom to provide services and of the need for supervision of credit institutions but also to follow more closely the scheme of the EC Treaty itself.

The new Second Banking Directive adopted in 1989 has had a marked impact and is dealt with at length. We also consider in detail the new Investment Services Directive, Consolidated Supervision Directives, Own Funds, Capital Adequacy and Solvency Ratio Directives, the Large Exposures Directive, the Capital Movements Directive and the Bank Accounts Directive—each at varying times the reason for publication being deferred. In the area of competition law, there have also been far reaching developments in the decisions of the Commission and case-law of the European Court of Justice: the time when it was an open question whether the Community's rules on competition applied in the banking sector at all, let alone to agreements on interest rates, has gone for good. The book contains new Parts which deal with banking secrecy, consumer protection in the field of financial services and the particular position of non-EC banks and their subsidiaries. If only for the sake of our respective practices, we look forward to less frenetic activity in the Community in the years to come.

We should like to thank for their assistance in the research and preparation of this edition Annabelle Ewing (LLB. HONS.), Brussels; Neil Calver and Sarah Moore, barristers, of 4–5 Gray's Inn Square; and Sarah Smith, senior assistant at Cameron Markby Hewitt. Our thanks also go to our publishers for including the book in *Lloyd's Commercial Law Library* and for their patience.

We also express our appreciation to the Rt. Hon. Sir Leon Brittan, who has found the time to write the Foreword to this edition and who, as Commissioner in charge of financial institutions during a critical period, has been so instrumental in the evolution of Community law in the field.

We have stated the law in force on 1 July 1993 but have endeavoured as far as possible to take into account later developments to 31 December 1993.

MARC DASSESSE
Brussels

STUART ISAACS QC
Gray's Inn, London

GRAHAM PENN
Tower Hill, London

January 1994

TABLE OF CONTENTS

Chapter 14: The Supervision of Capital Adequacy—I: Own Funds

Chapter 15: The Supervision of Capital Adequacy—II: Solvency Ratio for Credit Institutions

PART THREE. BANKING SECRECY

Para.

PART SIX. CONSUMER PROTECTION IN THE FIELD OF FINANCIAL SERVICES

CONTENTS

TABLE OF CASES

EUROPEAN COMMISSION DECISIONS

NATIONAL COURT CASES

TABLE OF INTERNATIONAL CONVENTIONS, LEGISLATION ETC.

[Paragraph numbers printed in **bold** indicate where the text is set out in full]

PART ONE

FREEDOM OF ESTABLISHMENT AND FREEDOM TO PROVIDE SERVICES

CHAPTER 1

FREEDOM OF ESTABLISHMENT

THE RIGHT OF ESTABLISHMENT

1.1 The rules on the right of establishment are contained in articles 52 to 58 of the EC Treaty.[1] Article 52 provides that:

Within the framework of the provisions set out below, restrictions on the freedom of establishment of nationals of a Member State in the territory of another Member State shall be abolished by progressive stages in the course of the transitional period. Such progressive abolition shall also apply to restrictions on the setting up of agencies, branches or subsidiaries by nationals of any Member State established in the territory of any Member State.

Freedom of establishment shall include the right to take up and pursue activities as self-employed persons and to set up and manage undertakings, in particular companies or firms within the meaning of the second paragraph of Article 58, under the conditions laid down for its own nationals by the law of the country where such establishment is effected, subject to the provisions of the Chapter relating to capital.

The provisions of article 52 are intended to ensure that all nationals of Member States who establish themselves in another Member State receive the same treatment as nationals in that State and prohibit, as a restriction on freedom of establishment, any discrimination on the ground of nationality.[2] However, although the provisions are directed mainly to ensuring that foreign nationals and companies are treated in the host Member State in the same way as nationals of that State, they also prohibit the Member State of origin from hindering the "secondary" establishment in another Member State of one of its nationals or companies.[3]

The freedom of establishment is not confined to the right to create a single establishment within the Community but entails the right to set up and maintain any number of establishments within the Community.[4]

---

1. The Treaty establishing the European Economic Community ("the Treaty") was signed on 25 March 1957 between Belgium, France, Italy, Luxembourg, the Netherlands and West Germany and entered into force on 1 January 1958. By the Treaty of Accession signed on 22 January 1972, Denmark, Ireland and the United Kingdom became Member States as from 1 January 1973. By the Treaty of Accession signed on 28 May 1979, Greece became a Member State as from 1 January 1982. By the Treaty of Accession signed on 12 June 1985, Portugal and Spain became Member States as from 1 January 1986. The Treaty has been amended in several important respects by the Single European Act and the Treaty on European Union.
2. Eg, case 221/85 *Commission* v. *Belgium* [1987] ECR 719, case 198/86 *Conradi* v. *Direction de la Concurrence et des Prix des Hauts-de-Seine* [1987] ECR 4469.
3. Case 81/87 *R* v. *H.M. Treasury and Commissioners of Inland Revenue, ex parte Daily Mail and General Trust PLC* [1988] ECR 5483, 5510.
4. Case 143/87 *Stanton* v. *Inasti* [1988] ECR 3877; case C–106/91 *Claus Ramrath* v. *Minister of Justice* [1992] 3 CMLR 173; case C–351/90 *Commission* v. *Luxembourg* [1992] 3 CMLR 124.

THE PERSONS WHO MAY BENEFIT FROM THE RIGHT OF ESTABLISHMENT

1.2 Therefore, in order to benefit from the rules on the right of establishment, it is necessary to be a national of a Member State. The reference in article 52 to "nationals of a Member State" who wish to establish themselves "in the territory of another Member State" must not be interpreted narrowly so as to exclude from the benefit of the rules on the right of establishment a particular Member State's own nationals who are resident in another Member State.[5]

Article 58 of the Treaty provides that companies or firms formed in accordance with the law of a Member State and having their registered offices, central administrations or principal places of business within the Community are to be treated, for the purposes of the chapter on the right of establishment, in the same way as natural persons who are nationals of Member States. A literal reading of article 58 would enable a construction of the word "national", in the context of a body corporate, as a company formed in accordance with the law of a Member State which has either (a) its registered office, or (b) its central administration, or (c) its principal place of business within the Community. A literal interpretation of article 58, therefore, would make it comparatively easy for non-EC countries to gain access to the Community and thereafter obtain the benefits which the principles of freedom of establishment and freedom to provide services afford throughout the Community, without themselves affording similar or equal opportunities or market access. Article 58 cannot, however, be read in isolation from article 52, insofar as freedom of establishment is concerned, since both require that the rights set out in those articles are only available to nationals which are "established" in the territory of any Member State. The Commission's General Programme for the Abolition of Restrictions on Freedom of Establishment issued by the Council on 18 December 1961 indicates that "establishment" in this sense means that an institution has a real and continuous link with the economy of the Member State in which it claims to be established. The precise meaning of the phrase "real and continuous link with the economy" of the relevant Member State is difficult to discern. It is not clear, for example, how long an institution needs to have been present in a Member State and what volume of business it needs to have transacted there before it becomes "established".[6]

In case 270/83 *Commission* v. *France*,[7] the Court stated, with regard to companies:

it is their registered office . . . that serves as the connecting factor with a particular State, like nationality in the case of natural persons. Acceptance of the proposition that the Member State in which a company seeks to establish itself may freely apply to it a different treatment solely by reason of the fact that its registered office is situated in another Member State would thus deprive [Article 58] of all meaning.

1.3 Where an undertaking of one Member State maintains a permanent presence in another Member State in which it provides services, the undertaking comes within the scope of the provisions of the Treaty on the right of establishment even if that presence has not taken the form of a branch or agency but consists merely of an office managed by

---

5. Case 115/78 *J. Knoors* v. *Secretary of State for Economic Affairs* [1979] ECR 399; case C–61/89 *Bouchoucha* [1992] 1 CMLR 1033.
6. OJ No. 2 of 15 January 1962, p. 32; OJ English Spec.Ed., 2nd Series, IX, p. 3.
7. [1986] ECR 273, 304.

the undertaking's own staff or by an independent person authorised to act for the undertaking on a permanent basis, as would be the case with an agency.[8]

In practice, the country where a company's registered office is located will usually coincide with its place of incorporation. For this reason, any company which is incorporated under the laws of a Member State may normally take advantage of the right of establishment. A subsidiary incorporated under the laws of a Member State of a parent company incorporated outside the Community will also be able to benefit from that right.

However, the provisions of articles 52 and 58 confer on companies incorporated under the law of a Member State no right to transfer their central management and control and their central administration to another Member State while at the same time retaining their status as companies incorporated under the legislation of the first Member State.[9] In this context, "companies or firms" means:

companies or firms constituted under civil or commercial law, including cooperative societies and other legal persons governed by public or private law, save for those which are non profit-making.[10]

Therefore, companies not formed under the law of a Member State and companies which, though formed under the law of a Member State, do not meet the other requirements laid down in article 58 are excluded from the right of establishment under the Treaty.

1.4 It is generally accepted that, in order to determine the precise scope of the additional requirements laid down in article 58, its provisions must be read in conjunction with Title 1 of the General Programme.[11] Under the heading "Beneficiaries", Title 1 says that:

The abolition of restrictions on freedom of establishment . . . shall be carried out . . . for the benefit of:

. . .

Companies set up in conformity with the laws of a Member State . . . and whose registered office, central administration or principal place of business is located within the Community . . . for their establishment for the purpose of pursuing a non-wage earning activity in the territory of a Member State;

. . .

The abovementioned companies, on condition that, in case only their registered office is located within the Community, . . . their activities show an effective and continuous link with the economy of a Member State . . . excluding the possibility that this link might depend on nationality, particularly the nationality of the partners or the members of the managing or the supervisory bodies, or of the persons holding the capital stock, for the opening of agencies, branches or subsidiaries in the territory of a Member State.

In other words, where a company is incorporated under the laws of a Member State, it will be treated as an EC-based company and accorded the right of establishment under the Treaty if either its central administration or principal place of business is within the Community, or its registered office is within the Community *and* its activities show an effective and continuous link with the economy of a Member State. Having the central

---

8. Case 205/84 *Commission* v. *Germany* [1986] ECR 3755. The Court held that such an undertaking could therefore not avail itself of the provisions of the Treaty relating to freedom to provide services with regard to its activities in the Member State in question.

9. Case 81/87 *R* v. *H.M. Treasury and Commissioners of Inland Revenue, ex parte Daily Mail and General Trust PLC* [1988] ECR 5483, 5512.

10. Art. 58, second para.

11. See para. 1.2 above.

administration or principal place of business within the Community does not of course mean that the greater part of the company's economic activities or turnover must be in or its profits must be derived from the Community. Certain Member States, however, have in the past objected to this approach and would prefer a requirement that directors and shareholders of companies incorporated in the EC are also "established" in the Community. Given the general approach of the European Court of Justice to construing EC legislation in a purposive manner, with the objectives of the legislation having precedence over the wording, it is likely that such a restrictive approach would contravene EC law. Until the question comes before the European Court for a ruling, however, it may cause some practical difficulties for non-EC investors or directors of institutions incorporated in the Community.

It is possible, for example, that a wholly-owned French-incorporated subsidiary of a Japanese company will not be deemed "established" in the Community until it has been trading at a certain volume for a certain period of time, and even then may not be "established" because it is wholly owned by a non-EC national. Unless an institution is "established" in one Member State, it will be unable to take advantage of the opportunities which will be afforded by the more specific legislation implementing the principles of freedom of establishment elsewhere in the Community and freedom to provide services throughout the Community. In either case, the nationality of the directors and shareholders is irrelevant.

THE DIFFERENT FORMS OF ESTABLISHMENT

1.5 The concept of establishment involves the actual pursuit of an economic activity through a fixed establishment in another Member State for an indefinite period.[12] Article 52 envisages two forms of establishment.[13] The primary form includes the right to take up and pursue activities as self-employed persons and to set up and manage undertakings in a Member State under the conditions laid down by that State for its own nationals. Here, what is involved is the complete transfer of a person's economic activities from one Member State to another. For companies and perhaps firms, as opposed to individuals, this form of establishment is of no practical relevance because the complete transfer of a company's activities from one country to another will almost invariably also involve a change in the company's nationality. Community law confers no right on a company incorporated under the legislation of a Member State and having its registered office there to transfer its central management and control to another Member State.[14]

1.6 The subsidiary form of establishment involves the right of nationals of any Member State who are already established in the territory of a Member State to set up agencies, branches or subsidiaries. This form of establishment is of much greater importance than the primary form of companies which are already in existence. However, article 52 imposes a significant limitation on this secondary form of establishment in that it is only available to nationals (including companies) of a Member State who are already established within the Community.

---

12. Case C–246/89 *Commission* v. *United Kingdom* [1991] ECR I–4585; case C–221/89 *R* v. *Secretary of State, ex p. Factortame* [1991] ECR I–3905.

13. See case 270/83 *Commission* v. *France* [1986] ECR 273.

14. Case 81/87 *R* v. *H.M. Treasury and Commissioners of Inland Revenue, ex parte Daily Mail and General Trust PLC* [1988] ECR 5483.

THE DIRECT EFFECT OF ARTICLE 52

1.7 Under the Treaty, it was originally envisaged that the restrictions on both the right of establishment and the freedom to provide services would be progressively abolished during the 12-year transitional period, which came to an end on 31 December 1969.[15] In 1961, the Council issued General Programmes for the Abolition of Restrictions on Freedom of Establishment and for the Abolition of Restrictions on the Freedom to Provide Services[16] with the object of abolishing restrictions in accordance with the timetable laid down in the Treaty. The General Programmes made specific provision for the abolition of restrictions in the banking sector but they were in fact largely ineffective in achieving their objective of abolishing restrictions by the end of the transitional period.

However, in two important judgments in 1974,[17] the Court of Justice held that the right of establishment and the freedom to provide services were not dependent upon the implementation of the general Programmes but flowed directly from the provisions of the Treaty itself once the transitional period had ended on 31 December 1969.

1.8 In *Reyners*[18] the plaintiff was a Dutch national residing in Belgium who held a diploma giving him the right to take up the profession of *avocat* in Belgium. Under Belgian law, however, he was excluded from the profession by reason of his nationality. In proceedings started before the Belgian Conseil d'Etat for the annulment of the relevant provisions of the Belgian legislation, he alleged that they infringed, *inter alia*, article 52 of the Treaty, upon which he was entitled to rely. The Conseil d'Etat asked the Court of Justice for a preliminary ruling on several questions, including the question whether article 52, since the end of the transitional period, was a directly applicable provision upon which the plaintiff could rely despite, in particular, the absence of implementing directives.

The Court of Justice's reply was clear[19]:

Since the end of the transitional period Article 52 of the Treaty is a directly applicable provision, despite the absence, in a particular sphere, of the directives prescribed by Articles 54(2) and 57(1) of the Treaty.

In its judgment, the Court stressed that the General Programme on establishment and the directives provided for by the Treaty were intended to accomplish two functions: first, to eliminate obstacles in the way of attaining freedom of establishment during the transitional period; second, to introduce into the law of the Member States a set of provisions intended to facilitate the effective exercise of that freedom.[20]

However[21]:

The rule of equal treatment with nationals is one of the fundamental legal provisions of the Community.

As a reference to a set of legislative provisions effectively applied by the country of establishment to its own nationals, this rule is, in its essence, capable of being directly invoked by the nationals of all the other Member States.

---

15. Arts. 52 and 59.
16. JO No. 2 of 15 January 1962, p. 32; OJ English Spec. Ed., 2nd Series, IX, pp. 3 and 7.
17. Case 2/74 *Reyners* v. *Belgian State* [1974] ECR 631 on the freedom of establishment; case 33/74 *Van Binsbergen* v. *Bestuur van de Bedrijfsvereniging voor de Metaalnijverheid* [1974] ECR 1299 on the freedom to provide services.
18. [1974] ECR 631.
19. *Ibid.*, at 656.
20. *Ibid.*, 651, point 21.
21. *Ibid.*, 651, points 24 to 27, emphasis added.

In stating that the freedom of establishment shall be attained at the end of the transitional period, Article 52 thus imposes an obligation to achieve a specific result, the fulfilment of which *had to be made easier by, but not made dependent on*, the implementation of a programme of progressive measures.

The fact that this progression has not been adhered to leaves the obligation itself intact beyond the end of the period provided for its fulfilment.

1.9 Therefore, since 31 December 1969, the right of establishment conferred by article 52 of the Treaty has had direct effect. The implementing directives issued by the Council pursuant to articles 54(2) and 57 of the Treaty have only residual value insofar as they prescribe measures intended to make easier the effective exercise of the right of freedom of establishment.[22]

The exception to the freedom of establishment provided for by the first paragraph of article 55 of the Treaty, which exception covers activities which in a Member State are connected with the exercise of official authority, is restricted to those of the activities referred to in article 52 which in themselves involve a direct and specific connection with the exercise of official authority.[23]

22. *Ibid.*, 652, point 31.
23. Case 3/88 *Commission* v. *Italy* [1989] ECR 4035.

CHAPTER 2

FREEDOM TO PROVIDE SERVICES

THE RIGHT TO PROVIDE SERVICES

2.1 The rules on the freedom to provide services are contained in articles 59 to 66 of the Treaty. Article 59 provides that:

Within the framework of the provisions set out below, restrictions on freedom to provide services within the Community shall be progressively abolished during the transitional period in respect of nationals of Member States who are established in a State of the Community other than that of the person for whom the services are intended.

The Council may, acting by a qualified majority on a proposal from the Commission, extend the provisions of the Chapter to nationals of a third country who provide services and who are established within the Communty.[1]

THE PERSONS WHO MAY BENEFIT FROM THE RIGHT TO PROVIDE SERVICES

2.2 The persons who may benefit from the rules on the freedom to provide services are the same as those who have the right of establishment. This follows from article 66 of the Treaty, which provides that the provisions of articles 55 to 58 in the chapter of the Treaty dealing with the right of establishment are applicable to the matters covered by the chapter on the freedom to provide services.

"SERVICES"

2.3 In order to determine whether "services" exist within the meaning of article 59, it is first necessary to consider whether the services in question are cross-border in nature.

A service may be of such a nature even if provided in only one Member State. For example, in *Société Générale Alsacienne de Banque SA* v. *Koestler*,[2] the Court of Justice regarded the services in question, which consisted of a bank having orders carried out on a stock exchange and in current account transactions in conjunction with the opening of a credit, as cross-border in nature because the recipient of the services, before the termination of the contractual relations between the parties, took up residence in a Member State other than that where the services were provided.[3] Also, *Bond van*

---

1. Second para. as amended by art. 16(3) of the Single European Act. To date, the Commission has not made any such proposal.
2. Case 15/78 [1978] ECR 1971.
3. *Ibid.*, at 1979–1980, point 3.

Adverteerders v. *Netherlands*[4] concerned the transmission by operators of cable networks established in a Member State of television programmes supplied by broadcasters established in other Member States and containing advertisements intended especially for the public in the Member State where the programmes were received. The Court stated that the services in question were cross-border services for the purposes of article 59 because the suppliers of the services were established in a Member State other than that of certain of the persons for whom they were intended.

In the case of banking services provided by correspondent banks, it may be a difficult question whether the services in question are, in any given case, cross-border in nature. It is clear from *Société Générale Alsacienne de Banque SA* v. *Koestler*[5] that a service is cross-border in nature whenever a bank in one Member State opens a current account for a customer resident in another Member State, even if the customer operates the account by visiting the bank in person.[6]

2.4 Once it is established that the services in question are of a cross-border nature, it is then necessary to establish whether they are services normally provided for remuneration within the meaning of article 60,[7] insofar as they are not governed by the other Treaty provisions relating to freedom of movement for goods, capital and persons.[8] In particular, article 60 of the Treaty states that "services" include activities of an industrial character; activities of a commercial character; activities of craftsmen; and activities of the professions.[9] Services provided for oneself—and thus not for "remuneration"—fall outside the ambit of article 60. The concept of "remuneration" is not expressly defined in the Treaty but the Court has stated that its essential characteristic lies in the fact that it constitutes consideration for the service in question, and is normally agreed upon between the provider and recipient of the service.[10]

2.5 Most banking services are clearly "services" within the meaning of the Treaty because they will normally be provided, directly or indirectly, for a charge. It was implicit in the Court of Justice's decision in *Züchner* v. *Bayerische Vereinsbank*[11] that the Bayerische Vereinsbank's services in issue were "services" within the meaning of the Treaty. Also, the nature of certain banking services as "services" within the meaning of the Treaty was expressly considered by the Court in *Société Générale Alsacienne de Banque SA* v. *Koestler*[12]:

---

4. Case 352/85 [1988] ECR 2085, in particular at 2131, point 15.
5. Case 15/78 [1978] ECR 1971.
6. See Peter Troberg, "Questions fondamentales concernant la libération des activités transfrontalières dans la Communauté," *Revue du Marché Commun*, no 278, June 1984, p. 274, in particular at 284. See also in the insurance context Claude J. Berr and Hubert Groutel, [1987] RTDE 82, who describe the freedom to provide private services, at its most basic, as a situation where an insurer in one Member State waits for the client in another Member State to contact him of his own initiative.
7. Case 352/85 *Bond van Adverteerders* v. *Netherlands* [1988] ECR 2085, 2130, point 13.
8. Art. 60.
9. See case 159/90 *Society for the Protection of Unborn Children* v. *Grogan* [1993] 1 CMLR 197.
10. Case 263/86 *Belgium* v. *Humbel* [1988] ECR 5365, 5388. Troberg, in the article referred to in fn. 6 above, makes the point that where a customer in one Member State instructs his bank in that Member State to provide a guarantee to a beneficiary in another Member State, a cross-border service is involved even though, in Troberg's view, the service is provided by the bank to the customer in his own Member State (because it is the customer who pays the bank's charges and not the beneficiary of the guarantee). This view is, it is submitted, no longer tenable in the light of case 352/85 *Bond van Adverteerders* v. *Netherlands* [1988] ECR 2085, which leads here to a need to distinguish between two services, one provided by the bank to its customer and the other provided by the bank to the beneficiary of the guarantee. Further, it need not always be the case that the remuneration will be paid by the customer rather than by the beneficiary of the guarantee.
11. Case 172/80 [1981] ECR 2021.
12. Case 15/78 [1978] ECR 1971, 1979–1980, point 3.

There is in fact no doubt that services such as those at issue which consist in a bank having orders carried out on a stock exchange and in current account transactions in conjunction with the opening of a credit constitute the provision of services within the meaning of the first paragraph of Article 60 of the Treaty which refers generically to all activities of a commercial character.

Article 61(2) of the Treaty provides that the liberalisation of banking services connected with movements of capital must be effected in step with the progressive liberalisation of capital movements. However, the importance of the distinction between banking services connected with movements of capital and other banking services has greatly diminished since the entry into force of the Capital Movements Directive.[13]

In determining whether particular banking services are ordinary banking services, to which articles 59 and 60 of the Treaty apply, or banking services connected with the movement of capital, which are only to be liberalised in step with the progressive liberalisation of movements of capital, or actual movements of capital, so as not to be considered as "services" at all within the meaning of article 60, it is necessary first to decide whether or not the parties have entered into a contract for the movement of capital.[14] For the purposes of article 61(2) of the Treaty, "connected" banking services are assumed to be those in which the movement of capital is either necessary or normal in order to complete the transaction but which are merely incidental to the main purpose of movement of capital. In *Société Générale Alsacienne de Banque SA* v. *Koestler*, the Court of Justice was correct to categorise the operations in question, namely the carrying out of time-bargains and the maintenance of a current account relating thereto, as ordinary banking services to which articles 59 and 60 of the Treaty applied and not as banking services connected with movements of capital.[15]

The freedom to provide services includes the freedom, for the recipients of services, to go to another Member State in order to receive a service there, without being obstructed by restrictions, even in relation to payments.[16]

THE RIGHT TO PROVIDE SERVICES IS NOT DEPENDENT ON THE RIGHT OF ESTABLISHMENT

2.6 It may sometimes be necessary or desirable for the provider of a service to pursue his activity in the territory of a Member State other than the Member State in which he is established. To cover this situation, the third paragraph of article 60 of the Treaty expressly states that, without prejudice to the provisions of the chapter of the Treaty relating to the right of establishment:

the person providing a service may, in order to do so, temporarily pursue his activity in the State where the service is provided, under the same conditions as are imposed by that State on its own nationals.

Despite the apparently clear wording of these provisions, they do not have the

---

13. Directive 88/361 of 24 June 1988, OJ L178/5 of 8 July 1988. See, generally, Part Four below.

14. See the discussion of the distinction between ordinary banking services and banking services connected with movements of capital in the Opinion of A.G. Reischl in *Société Générale Alsacienne de Banque* at pp. 1984–1985. As already stated, the entry into force of the Capital Movements Directive has much reduced the importance of the distinction.

15. *Ibid.*

16. Joined cases 286/82 and 26/83 *Luisi and Carbone* v. *Ministero del Tesoro* [1984] ECR 377 and see Part Four below. The Court of Justice held, *inter alia*, that tourists, persons receiving medical treatment and persons travelling for the purposes of education or business are to be regarded as recipients of services.

consequence that all national legislation applicable to the nationals of a Member State and usually applied to the permanent activities of undertakings established therein may similarly be applied in its entirety to the temporary activities of undertakings established in other Member States. So in *Webb*,[17] the Court of Justice held that article 59 of the Treaty did not preclude the Netherlands, whose legislation required agencies for the provision of manpower to hold a licence, from requiring an agency established in the United Kingdom and pursuing its activities in the Netherlands to obtain a licence there even though the agency already held a licence under English legislation.

2.7 What a Member State cannot do is to require the provider of a service established in another Member State who wishes to pursue his activity in its territory actually to establish himself there also.[18] Article 59 would otherwise be deprived of any useful effect because it is essential to the distinction between the freedom to provide services throughout the Community and the right of establishment that the former need not involve the creation of a base in a different Member State from that in which the provider of the service is established.[19]

2.8 Also, as one of the fundamental principles of the Treaty, the freedom to provide services may only be made subject to restrictions of a very limited nature. As the Court stated in *Commission* v. *France*,[20] the freedom may be restricted[21]:

only by provisions which are justified by the general good and which are applied to all persons or undertakings operating within the territory of the State in which the service is provided in so far as that interest is not safeguarded by the provisions to which the provider of a service is subject in the Member State of his establishment. In addition, such requirements must be objectively justified by the need to ensure that professional rules of conduct are complied with and that the interests which such rules are designed to safeguard are protected.[22]

THE DIRECT EFFECT OF ARTICLE 59

2.9 Shortly before the judgment in *Reyners*, the Court of Justice in *Van Binsbergen* held that article 59 had direct effect once the transitional period ended and, accordingly, that the freedom to provide services was not dependent on the implementation of the General Programme for the Abolition of Restrictions on the Freedom to Provide Services issued by the Council in 1961.

The facts of *Van Binsbergen* are straightforward. The plaintiff was involved in proceedings before the Dutch Centrale Raad van Beroep (court of last instance in social security matters) and had entrusted the defence of his interests to a Mr. Kortmann, a Dutch national established in the Netherlands. During the course of the proceedings, Mr. Kortmann transferred his residence to Belgium, whereupon the Centrale Raad van

17. Case 279/80 [1981] ECR 3305.
18. *Ibid.*, 3325. See also joined cases 110 and 111/78 *Ministère Public and Chambre Syndicale des Agents Artistiques et Impressarii de Belgique ASBL* v. *Willy van Wesemael and Others* [1979] ECR 35; case C–106/91 *Ramrath* v. *Minister of Justice* [1992] 3 CMLR 173.
19. *Van Binsbergen*; case 76/81 *Transporoute et Travaux* v. *Ministry of Public Works* [1982] ECR 417.
20. Case 220/83 [1986] ECR 3663. Also, case 252/83 *Commission* v. *Denmark* [1986] ECR 3713, 3748; case 205/84 *Commission* v. *Germany* [1986] ECR 3755, 3802–3803; case 206/84 *Commission* v. *Ireland* [1986] ECR 3817, 3849.
21. Case 220/83 [1986] ECR 3663, 3708.
22. By way of illustration, in case C–106/91 *Ramrath* v. *Minister of Justice* [1992] 3 CMLR 173 a person who was established and authorised to practise as a company auditor in his home Member State and who took employment with an authorised auditor in another Member State was held not to have to be permanently present in the latter Member State.

Beroep advised him that he could no longer act for the plaintiff because, under Dutch law, only persons established in the Netherlands could appear before it as legal representatives.

The Court of Justice held that this requirement of Dutch law constituted a restriction incompatible with articles 59 and 60 of the Treaty. In language echoed in *Reyners*,[23] the Court referred to the objectives of the General Programme on services and the implementing directives provided for by the Treaty as being to abolish, during the transitional period, restrictions on the freedom to provide services and to introduce into the law of the Member States a set of provisions intended to facilitate the effective exercise of that freedom, in particular by the mutual recognition of professional qualifications and the co-ordination of laws with regard to the pursuit of activities as self-employed persons.[24] Such directives also had the task of resolving the specific problems resulting from the fact that, where the provider of the service is not established on a habitual basis in the State in which the service is to be performed, he may not be fully subject to the professional rules of conduct in force in that State.[25]

However[26]:

As regards the phased implementation of the chapter relating to services, Article 59 . . . expresses the intention to abolish restrictions on freedom to provide services by the end of the transitional period, the latest date for the entry into force of all the rules laid down by the Treaty.

The provisions of Article 59, the application of which was to be prepared by directives issued during the transitional period, therefore became unconditional on the expiry of that period.

The provisions of that Article abolish all discrimination against the person providing the service by reason of his nationality or the fact that he is established in a Member State other than that in which the service is to be provided.

Therefore, as regards at least the specific requirement of nationality or of residence, Articles 59 and 60 impose a well-defined obligation, the fulfilment of which by the Member States cannot be delayed or jeopardised by the absence of provisions which were to be adopted in pursuance of powers conferred under Articles 63 and 66.

The Court accordingly held that the first paragraph of article 59 and the third paragraph of article 60 had direct effect and could therefore be relied upon before national courts, at least insofar as those provisions sought to abolish any discrimination against a person providing a service by reason of his nationality or of the fact that he resided in a Member State other than that in which the service was to be provided.

2.10 The only exception to the freedom to provide services concerns those activities referred to in articles 59 and 60 which in themselves involve a direct and specific connection with the exercise of official authority by the host Member State.[27]

THE POSSIBLE APPLICATION TO SERVICES OF THE CASSIS DE DIJON PRINCIPLE BY WAY OF THE CODITEL DECISION OF THE COURT OF JUSTICE

2.11 The Court's judgment in the *Coditel* case,[28] which built upon its existing case-law in the field of the free movement of goods and, in particular, its earlier decision

---

23. [1974] ECR 631.
24. [1974] ECR 1299, 1311, point 21.
25. *Ibid.*, at point 22.
26. *Ibid.*, at points 23 to 25.
27. Case 3/88 *Commission v.* Italy [1989] ECR 4035.
28. Case 262/81 *Coditel SA* v. *Ciné-Vog Films SA* [1982] ECR 3381; also joined cases 60–61/84 *Cinéthèque* [1985] ECR 2605.

in the celebrated *Cassis de Dijon* case,[29] is generally recognised as having had a significant influence on the development of the new approach to harmonisation taken by the Commission to solve the problems involved in the creation of a truly single financial market.

2.12 In *Cassis de Dijon*, the Court decided that goods lawfully produced in one Member State might be sold in any other, even if they did not conform to local regulations, unless it was established that the regulations were strictly necessary, having regard to the reasons of general good set out restrictively in article 36 of the Treaty, [30] in particular public security and the protection of health, or to preserve other mandatory requirements not provided for by article 36 but accepted by the Court, such as the protection of consumers, the loyalty of commercial transactions or the effectiveness of fiscal supervision. However, if these reasons and requirements had already been taken into consideration in the original Member State in measures recognised as equivalent, even if not identical, to the measures in force in the importing Member State, the importing Member State's measures might not be relied upon to oppose the free trade in the imported products.

2.13 The significance of *Coditel* lies in the Court's application of the considerations underlying article 36 to the field of the freedom to provide services. In that case, the Court was concerned with the position, in relation to prohibitions contained in article 85(1), of a contract whereby the owner of the copyright in a film granted the exclusive right to show it within the territory of a Member State and for a specified period. Could such a grant fall outside the scope of article 85 by virtue of the special character attributed to that right by article 36 or by its protected status under national law? In the course of giving its ruling, the Court stated that[31]:

The distinction, implicit in Article 36, between the existence of a right conferred by the legislation of a Member State in regard to the protection of artistic and intellectual property, which cannot be affected by the provisions of the Treaty, and the exercise of such right, which might constitute a disguised restriction on trade between Member States, *also applies in the context of the movement of services.*

Just as it is conceivable that certain aspects of the manner in which the right is exercised may prove to be incompatible with Articles 59 and 60 it is equally conceivable that some aspects may prove to be incompatible with Article 85. . . .

That being so, it became possible to foresee the application of the *Cassis de Dijon* approach to the services field and, in particular, to the field of banking services.

THE GERMAN INSURANCE CASE[32]

2.14 The other ruling of the Court of Justice which is of importance to the development of the Commission's new approach is the *German Insurance* case, to

---

29. Case 120/78 *Rewe-Zentral* v. *Bundesmonopolverwaltung für Branntwein* [1979] ECR 649.
30. Art. 36 states that:
  The provisions of Arts. 30 to 34 shall not preclude prohibitions or restrictions on imports, exports or goods in transit justified on grounds of public morality, public policy or public security; the protection of health and life of humans, animals or plants; the protection of national treasures possessing artistic, historic or archaeological value; or the protection of industrial or commercial property. Such prohibitions or restrictions shall not, however, constitute a means of arbitrary discrimination or a disguised restriction on trade between Member States.
31. [1982] ECR 3381, 3401. Emphasis added.
32. Case 205/84 *Commission* v. *Germany* [1986] ECR 3755.

which reference has already been made in the context of the freedom of establishment.[33] There, the Court ruled that Germany was in breach of its obligations under Community law in providing under its domestic Insurance Supervision Act, as amended, that insurance undertakings wishing to provide services in Germany in relation to certain direct insurance business through salesmen, representatives, agents and other intermediaries, had to be established in its territory; and that, for services provided in connection with Community co-insurance where the risks were situated in Germany, the lead insurer had to be established and authorised there. The Court laid down two main principles: first, that the exercise of the freedom to provide services in another Member State could not be made conditional upon having a permanent base in that Member State since such a requirement would in effect negate the very freedom to provide services on a cross-border basis, which is distinct from the freedom of establishment. Accordingly, the German supervisory authorities could not make the provision of insurance services in Germany by insurers based in other Member States conditional upon the opening by them of a branch in Germany, even if the supervision of foreign insurers providing cross-border services in Germany was thereby made more difficult for the German authorities in the absence of such a permanent base. Second, a distinction had to be drawn between the users of financial services when assessing the extent to which a Member State might insist, in the absence of harmonisation at the Community level, on the observance of local regulations designed to protect the consumer by an institution based in another Member State providing such services in its territory. The Court held that the host country could not invoke such provisions to restrict the provision of financial services directed at commercial undertakings having no need of specific protection. It further highlighted, with regard to services directed at private consumers in need of protection, those areas which required harmonisation in order to afford sufficient consumer protection, namely insurance services, technical reserves, conditions of insurance contracts and co-operation between supervisory authorities.

2.15 The exception to the freedom to provide services provided by the first paragraph of article 55 of the Treaty, which exception covers activities which in a Member State are connected with the exercise of official authority, and article 66 is restricted to those of the activities referred to in article 59 which in themselves involve a direct and specific connection with the exercise of official authority.[34]

REVERSE DISCRIMINATION UNDER COMMUNITY LAW

2.16 It is convenient at this point to refer briefly to the position under Community law with regard to so-called reverse discrimination, that is, discrimination by a Member State against its own nationals. Despite the distortions of competition which it may entail for local undertakings, under the present case-law of the Court of Justice reverse discrimination is not considered to be contrary to Community law.[35] The issue of

33. See fn. 8 above.
34. Case 3/88 *Commission* v. *Italy* [1989] ECR 4035.
35. See the opinion of A.G. Rozès in joined cases 314–316/82 *Procureur de la République and Comité National de Défense contre l'Acoolisme* v. *Waterkeyn and Others. Procureur de la République* v. *Jean Cayand and Others* [1982] ECR 4337; case 355/85 *Driancourt (Public Prosecutor)* v. *Cognet Centre Leclerc* [1986] ECR 3231; joined cases 80 and 159/85 *Nederlandse Bakkerij Stichting and Others* v. *Edah BV* [1986] ECR 3359; case 98/86 *Ministère Public* v. *A. Mathot* [1987] ECR 809. *Cf.* case C–61/89 *Bouchoucha* [1992] 1 CMLR

reverse discrimination has particular relevance to the banking sector and will be discussed further in the context of the Second Banking Directive.[36]

1033. However, in certain Member States, such as France, it has been held that reverse discrimination is contrary to the principle of equality before the law enshrined in the national constitution, with the result that nationals may, on that basis, dispute the right of the national authorities to put them at a disadvantage on their home market *vis-à-vis* competitors based in other Member States. See Cass. Crim., 16 June 1983 (two cases), JCP 1983, II, 20044 and also Dalloz, 1984, p. 43. As the issue of reverse discrimination becomes more acute, this approach may well become more widespread.

36. See Chap. 4 below.

CHAPTER 3

HARMONISATION AS A PRECONDITION TO THE FULL IMPLEMENTATION OF THE FREEDOM OF ESTABLISHMENT AND THE FREEDOM TO PROVIDE SERVICES: THE INITIAL APPROACH

GENERAL

3.1 As it is one of the traditionally most strictly regulated sectors of the economy, the harmonisation of the banking sector at the Community level has presented considerable problems. The special position of banks was emphasised by the original provisions of article 57(2) of the Treaty under which directives aimed at harmonising national rules concerned with "the protection of savings, in particular the granting of credit and the exercise of the banking profession" required unanimity in the Council whereas, in almost all other cases, the Council was required to act only by a qualified majority.[1] As observed by Clarotti[2]:

It was apparent from the start that the abolition of discriminatory restrictions on the freedom of establishment and the freedom to provide services would not have been enough to bring about a true common market for credit institutions. The differences in banking regulations, in the broadest sense of the term, between the Member States were such that the mere fact of treating a credit institution from another Member State in the same way as a domestic credit institution, in accordance with the principles set out in Articles 52 and 59 of the Treaty, could not ensure the existence of a common market.

The Commission's initial approach towards harmonisation was to launch an ambitious programme intended to lead to the full harmonisation of banking structures and banking supervision. It is necessary to refer in this context to the Banking Directive 1973, which is now largely of historical interest, and the First Banking Directive of 12 December 1977.

THE BANKING DIRECTIVE 1973

3.2 On 28 June 1973 the Council adopted a directive to implement the General Programme in respect of banks and other financial institutions.[3] It applies not only to banks, including merchant and discounting banks, but also to various savings and loan

---

1. Art. 57(2) has now been amended by, *inter alia*, art. 16(2) of the Single European Act so as to require unanimity only for directives whose implementation "involves in at least one Member State amendment of the existing principles laid down by law governing the professions with respect to training and conditions of access for natural persons".
2. Paolo Clarotti "Progress and Future Developments of Establishment and Services in the EC in Relation to Banking" (1984) XXII *Journal of Common Market Studies* 199, 200.
3. Directive 73/183, OJ L194/1 of 16 July 1973.

institutions and certain insurance syndicates. The undertakings to which the directive applies are set out in full by category of undertaking in an annex to the directive.

In the light of the Court of Justice's decisions in *Reyners* and *Van Binsbergen*—both decided within the 18-month period laid down in the directive for the implementation of its provisions by the Member States—the 1973 Directive became superfluous with regard to implementing the freedom of establishment and freedom to provide services provided for by articles 52, 59 and 60 of the Treaty because, after the expiry of the transitional period, such freedoms became sanctioned by the Treaty itself with direct effect. Also, the limitations contained in the Directive could not thereafter remain valid. For example, the Directive excluded from its scope the activities of certain kinds of brokers, such as discount brokers, *courtiers en banque* and financial intermediaries. That exclusion became of no effect.

However, the 1973 Directive has not lost all interest. It contains useful provisions concerning the use of the words "bank", "banker", "savings bank" and any other equivalent term by non-EC undertakings which provide services in a Member State.[4] Those undertakings are permitted to provide services under names which include such terms provided that the names are their original ones and that the undertakings leave no doubt as to their status under the national law to which they are subject.

The Directive also provides a mechanism for co-operation and regular meetings between the Commission and the banking supervisory authorities in each Member State.[5]

FIRST BANKING DIRECTIVE OF 12 DECEMBER 1977[6]

3.3 On 12 December 1977, the Council adopted a First Directive on the co-ordination of laws, regulations and administrative provisions relating to the taking up and pursuit of the business of credit institutions, with the object of establishing common guidelines on various matters relating to the supervision of credit institutions in the Community. The preamble to the Directive stresses that it was only one step on the road to full co-ordination. It recognised the necessity, given the extent of the existing differences between the laws of the Member States as regards the rules to which credit institutions are subject, to proceed by successive stages but with the eventual aim of introducing uniform authorisation requirements throughout the Community.

In the words of the Court of Justice in *Commission* v. *Italy* and *Commission* v. *Belgium*[7]:

Council Directive 77/780 constitutes the first step in the harmonisation of banking structures and the supervision thereof. The purpose of such harmonisation is to permit the gradual attainment of freedom of establishment for credit institutions and the liberalisation of banking services. In that respect the directive introduces certain minimum conditions for the authorisation of credit institutions which all Member States must observe. In order to facilitate the taking up and pursuit of business as a credit institution the directive aims in particular to reduce the discretion enjoyed by certain supervisory authorities in authorising institutions.

3.4 For a long time, until the adoption of the Second Banking Directive of 15

---

4. Art. 6.
5. Art. 7.
6. Directive 77/780, OJ L32/30 of 17 December 1977.
7. [1983] ECR 449, 455; [1983] ECR 467, 476.

December 1989,[8] the First Banking Directive remained the only basis for the expansion of banking activities throughout the Community, allowing banks to exercise their freedom of establishment throughout the Community on the condition of strict adherence, as a rule, to all regulations applying to credit institutions created in accordance with the laws of the host Member State.[9]

1. "Credit institutions"

3.5 The Directive applies to the taking up and pursuit of the business of credit institutions[10] and provides a definition of a "credit institution" as[11]:

an undertaking whose business is to receive deposits or other repayable funds from the public and to grant credits for its own account.

The fact that the funds received have to be repayable excludes from the scope of the Directive institutions such as insurance and collective investment undertakings whose business does not involve the receipt of funds which are repayable to the public. The fact that the undertaking has also to grant credits also limits the types of institution coming within the scope of the Directive. A number of financial institutions presently given the appellation of "banks" take deposits but do not grant credit, or take deposits, but not from the public, or do not lend. For example, in the United Kingdom, the requirements of the Banking Act 1987 are that an institution must obtain authorisation from the Bank of England before it may accept a deposit in the course of carrying on a business which is, for the purposes of that Act, a deposit-taking business.[12] A number of qualifications and exemptions are, however, made to this general principle. For example, institutions which are active only in the interbank markets do not require authorisation from the Bank of England[13] and would not qualify as credit institutions under EC law, because they are not receiving funds "from the public". Also outside the scope of the Directive are intermediaries in the banking sector and commercial undertakings which, although they may receive repayable funds and grant credit facilities, do not do so as their usual business.

In principle, the central banks of Member States, post office giro institutions and other specialised institutions such as the National Savings Bank and credit unions in the

---

8. See Chap. 4 below.

9. For an interesting account of the limitations of the First Banking Directive see Fine "The Second EEC Banking Directive: A Practical Overview" [1988] 5 IJBL 197.

10. Art. 2(1).

11. Art. 1, first indent.

12. Second Consolidated Supervision Directive, art. 1.

13. The term "holdings" is not defined and is difficult to interpret in the context of this definition of financial institution. The Proposal for the Second Consolidated Supervision Directive contained the definition of "financial institution": "an undertaking other than a credit institution whose principal activity is to acquire and hold participations or to exercise one or more of the operations included in numbers 2 to 12 of [the Second Banking Directive]." This definition is rather more comprehensible than the final definition as it does at least provide an indication of what is meant by "holding" by reference to participations—see OJ C315/15 of 14 December 1990. The term "participation" is defined in the Second Consolidated Supervision Directive to mean the ownership, direct or indirect, of 20% or more of the voting rights or capital of an undertaking—see art. 1. This revises the definition of participation found in the First Consolidated Supervision Directive, so making it consistent with art. 33 of the Seventh Council Directive of 13 June 1983 on consolidated accounts (OJ L193 of 18 July 1983) and with art. 42 of Council Directive 86/635/EEC of 8 December 1986 on the annual accounts and consolidated accounts of banks and other financial institutions (OJ L372 of 31 December 1985); *cf.* fn. 16 below.

United Kingdom are within the definition of a credit institution but they are expressly excluded from the scope of the Directive.[14]

The Directive's definition of a credit institution is retained for the purposes of the Second Banking Directive[15] and later Community legislation in the field[16] and the institutions expressly excluded from the scope of the First Banking Directive are also excluded from the Second Banking Directive.[17]

2. Requirement of authorisation

3.6 The First Banking Directive obliges Member States to require credit institutions having their head offices in one Member State to obtain authorisation to carry on business before commencing their activities even if they do not intend to set up or carry on activities in another Member State.[18] The Member State in which a credit institution has been so authorised is defined in the Second Banking Directive as the "home Member State" for the purposes of that Directive.[19] Credit institutions which were already carrying on business in a Member State at the time when the Directive came into force on 15 December 1979 are deemed to have been authorised.[20] However, such institutions remain subject to the provisions of the Directive which concern the carrying on of the business of credit institutions. In this way, their activities are subject to the supervision of the competent authorities of the Member States in which they have their head offices and they may, in appropriate circumstances, be prohibited by the competent authority from carrying on their business. Member States may also require the branches of credit institutions having their head offices in another Member State to obtain authorisation to carry on business before commencing activities upon their territory.[21] However, in terms of establishment this ability has now been removed by the Second Banking Directive.[22]

Authorisation is defined by the First Banking Directive to mean[23]:

an instrument issued in any form by the authorities by which the right to carry on the business of a credit institution is granted.

Therefore, authorisation in the form of listing in an official register or by a system of licensing or by statute would be sufficient. This definition is retained for the purposes of the Second Banking Directive[24] under which, as will be seen, certain minimum conditions for authorisation are laid down. Once given, authorisation by the home Member State may only be withdrawn in the circumstances now specified in the Second Banking Directive.

14. Art. 2(2), as replaced by art. 1 of Council Directive 86/524(EEC) of 27 October 1986, OJ 1986 L309/15.
15. Art. 1(1) of the Second Banking Directive.
16. Eg, Council Directive 83/350/EEC of 13 June 1983 on the supervision of credit institutions on a consolidated basis (OJ 1983 L193/18); Council Directive 89/299/EEC of 17 April 1989 on the own funds of credit institutions (OJ 1989 L124/16).
17. Art. 2(2) of the Second Banking Directive.
18. Art. 3.
19. Art. 1(7).
20. Art. 10.
21. Art. 4(1).
22. See Chap. 4 below.
23. Art. 1, second indent.
24. Art. 1(2) of the Second Banking Directive.

The First Banking Directive also gives a definition of a "branch" which is retained in substantially the same terms in the Second Banking Directive.[25]

3. Relations with third countries

3.7 Under the First Banking Directive, Member States retained full competence to permit or refuse the establishment within their territory of branches of credit institutions having their head offices outside the Community. However, if a Member State permitted the establishment of such a branch, it was obliged not to accord it more favourable treatment than that accorded to branches of credit institutions having their head offices in another Member State.[26] The provisions of article 9(1) did little to address the issues arising as a result of non-EC credit institutions doing business in the Community and, in fact, approached the issues from the wrong direction. A simple provision to the effect that the national supervisory authorities of one Member State should not be biased in favour of non-EC credit institutions is no answer to a situation where non-EC credit institutions are able to be more competitive than EC credit institutions in the same market because their overall capital or compliance costs are lower. This is an issue considered in more detail below.[27]

4. Advisory Committee

3.8 The First Banking Directive provided for the establishment of a Banking Advisory Committee composed of representatives of the banking supervisory authorities of the Member States and the government departments responsible for banking policy and representatives of the Commission.[28] One of the major tasks of the Committee has been to assist the Commission with the preparation of later legislation in the banking field.

5. Co-operation between the supervisory authorities

3.9 The mechanisms for co-operation between the various interested bodies set up under the Banking Directive 1973 were carried through in the First Banking Directive not only through the Banking Advisory Committee but also as between the competent authorities of the Member States. Article 7(1) provides expressly that those authorities must collaborate closely in order to supervise the activities of credit institutions operating in one or more Member States other than that in which their head offices are situated. They must supply each other with *inter alia* all information likely to facilitate the monitoring of such institutions.[29]

6. Appeals procedure

3.10 Article 13 of the First Banking Directive, which it is submitted has direct effect under Community law, lays down that:

25. Art. 1, third indent defines a "branch" as "a place of business which forms a legally dependent part of a credit institution and which conducts directly all or some of the operations inherent in the business of credit institutions; . . ." Art. 1(3) of the Second Banking Directive refers to "transactions" instead of "operations".
26. Art. 9(1).
27. See Part Eight below.
28. Art. 11.
29. Art. 7(1), as amended by art. 14(1) of the Second Banking Directive.

Member States shall ensure that decisions taken in respect of a credit institution in pursuance of laws, regulations and administrative provisions adopted in accordance with this Directive may be subject to the right to apply to the courts. The same shall apply where no decision is taken within six months of its submission in respect of an application for authorisation which contains all the information required under the provisions in force.

7. Conclusion

3.11 The First Banking Directive has now largely been superseded by the impact of the Second Banking Directive in the field of freedom of establishment. However, the First Banking Directive made certain lasting achievements and remains of relevance in several important respects. Besides laying down various co-ordinated rules, Clarotti comments that it changed the picture of the institutional pattern in the following respects[30]:

— It has introduced a banking regulation in countries where there was no regulation at all (United Kingdom) or has brought an important reform of the existing regulation (Netherlands, Luxembourg, Denmark).

— It has created an institutional co-operation among the supervisory authorities . . . which has expanded beyond the EEC borders . . .

— It has made it mandatory for supervisory authorities of two or more Member States to collaborate in the monitoring . . . of a credit institution having business in two or more Member States.

— It has created an embryo of home country control . . .

— It has set up a first step towards a common policy *vis-à-vis* the third countries.

— It has given a common wide definition of a "credit institution" submitting all of these to the same regulations with the consequence of making it more difficult to maintain discriminatory treatment between the different types of credit institutions, and ensuring in that way more equal conditions of competition.

— It has underlined also the principle that all credit institutions should be allowed to carry out all operations related with this industry thus giving support to the trend towards the despecialisation of credit institutions, advocated by many circles.

— It is a positive ancillary step in the direction of the economic and monetary union.

30. Paolo Clarotti "The harmonisation of legislation relating to credit institutions" (1982) CMLRev 245, 266–267.

CHAPTER 4

THE SECOND BANKING DIRECTIVE OF 15 DECEMBER 1989: THE NEW APPROACH

THE NEW APPROACH EMBODIED IN THE SECOND BANKING DIRECTIVE

4.1 As indicated in Chapter 3, the First Banking Directive was held out at the time to be the first step on the road to full harmonisation of banking structures and their supervision. However, it is fair to say that the Community's record on harmonisation in the sector for the two decades which followed was "dismal".[1] Detailed harmonisation proved impracticable and, as already seen, the First Banking Directive remained for a long time the only basis for the expansion of banking activities throughout the Community.

This approach had two important consequences. First, it continued to make it extremely onerous for a bank to set up a branch in another Member State, in particular because of the requirement to allocate (at least in principle) the same endowment capital to the branch as that required for a locally incorporated bank.[2] Second, it continued to require the branch to comply in relation both to the local supervisory authorities and to its local customers with all national regulations applicable to the local banking institutions. Branches were therefore unable to benefit from any competitive advantage resulting from a more flexible regulatory system applicable to the home country, especially as regards "financial techniques" such as, for example, the use of variable interest rate mortgages or foreign currency mortgages, which are banned in some Member States and allowed in others; and the issue of zero coupon bonds or deep discount bonds. The result has been that branches opened in one Member State by a bank of another Member State have in general tended towards wholesale banking operations and not to the servicing of the local clientèle of private individuals and small and medium enterprises.

4.2 The freedom to provide banking services on a cross-border basis proved to be illusory, at least in the area of retail banking services, despite the leading decision in *Van Binsbergen* referred to earlier, which had stated that the freedom to provide services had become unconditional since 1 January 1970 regardless of whether directives designed to facilitate the exercise of that freedom had been adopted by that date.

---

1. See George S. Zavvos, "Banking Integration and 1992" (1990) *Harvard International Law Journal* Vol. 31, No. 2, p. 463, at p. 468.
2. Until the implementation of the Second Banking Directive, the United Kingdom was the only Member State which did not insist on branches of foreign banks having a separate endowment capital. This exemption, coupled with the City of London's traditional role as a principal world financial centre, made the United Kingdom, and particularly London, an attractive centre for foreign banks to establish branches.

Obstacles to the exercise of the freedom to provide services

4.3 Three sets of obstacles were responsible for frustrating the actual exercise of the freedom to provide banking services.

First, given that under article 61(2) of the Treaty the liberalisation of banking services is linked to the progressive liberalisation of the free movement of capital, until the entry into force on 1 July 1990 of the Capital Movements Directive Member States were free to maintain in force exchange regulations which prohibited individuals and undertakings from freely transferring or holding financial assets which were not directly related to the exercise of commercial operations.[3]

Second, national regulations aimed at consumer protection and general public policy considerations often involve a prohibition on the solicitation of investment business, the sale of financial services or the supply of credit by foreigners without the prior approval of the authorities of the host country. In practice, this approval necessarily presupposes the existence of a branch in the host country where the person concerned seeks to exercise the freedom to provide services.

Third, local fiscal regulations frequently constitute an obstacle to the freedom to provide financial services. For example, the grant of credit facilities by a bank established in one Member State to an individual or undertaking resident in another Member State is generally rendered impossible where the individual or undertaking is required to retain a withholding tax on the interest paid to the foreign bank. Also, tax advantages may be accorded to certain types of credits such as mortgage loans or certain types of investments if effected by local lenders or in local financial assets.[4]

The achievement of the Second Banking Directive

4.4 In 1984, one of the EC officials most closely involved with this issue, Paolo Clarotti, the Head of the Banks and Credit Institutions Division at DG XV, commented on the lack of progress towards freedom of establishment and freedom to provide services in the banking sector since the entry into force of the First Banking Directive as follows:

One has to come back to the starting point: no progress can be made, either within the field of the right of establishment or in respect of the free provision of services, until the harmonisation process has reached such an extent that home country control is possible, with a continuing role for the supervisory authorities of the host country only during the transitional period. . . . For the time being . . . while some progress has been made towards full freedom of establishment (as a result of the coming into force of the 1977 Directive), very little progress has been made towards freedom to provide services. The road to a common banking market is still very long. . . . The main problem, apart from the abolition of explicit discrimination, which should be considered as practically achieved throughout the Community, seems to be for increased transparency in the exercise of discretionary powers by the competent authorities. A full re-examination and, if necessary, harmonisation of apparently uniform rules which are especially disadvantageous to foreign banks are the only means by which to open the possibilities for a true and proper right of establishment and free provision of services for banks in all the Member countries.[5]

The road was to prove long indeed. A detailed examination of the changed political,

---

3. This issue was considered by the Court of Justice in case 203/80 *Casati* [1981] ECR 2595 and is discussed in detail in Part Four below.
4. A more detailed analysis of this subject is in Part Seven.
5. Paolo Clarotti, (1984) *Journal of Common Market Law Studies*, Vol. XXII, No. 3, p. 199, at pp. 210 and 212.

institutional and economic climate which led to the adoption of the Second Banking Directive on 15 December 1989 falls outside the scope of this book. However, those factors must be borne in mind in order to understand the difference in approach between the First and Second Banking Directives and the new policies embodied in the Second Banking Directive.[6]

The great achievement of the Second Banking Directive is formally to remove most of the regulatory obstacles to the effective exercise of the freedom of establishment and the freedom to provide services on a cross-border basis not already removed by the First Banking Directive. Its entry into force on 1 January 1993, at a time when the obstacles resulting from the link between most banking services and movements of capital and current payments have been removed following the entry into force of the Capital Movements Directive on 1 July 1990, has no doubt brought the Community much closer to a single market for banking services.

The Court of Justice's contribution

4.5 Reference has already been made in Chapter 2 to the contribution of the Court of Justice to the new approach. The Community has followed no particular economic model in designing its harmonisation measures. It is arguable that the case-law of the Court of Justice has been more influential than economic theory.[7] The influence of the *Cassis de Dijon* and *German Insurance* cases emerges clearly from the Commission's 1985 White Paper for achieving a single market in financial services by 1 January 1993.[8] As Clarotti points out:

> The fundamental thing about this document is the new approach set out in it in order to achieve the intended objective: the abandonment of prior harmonisation and standardisation of all existing regulations and its replacement by a harmonisation of only the essential aspects of such regulations, accompanied by two fundamental principles: mutual recognition, "home country control" . . . to which may be added a third, namely a single licence valid throughout the Community.[9]

THE GUIDING PRINCIPLES

1. The principle of mutual recognition

4.6 Mutual recognition involves the bank supervisors of the various Member States being required to consider from the date of entry into force of the Second Banking Directive that their respective national regulations, although not identical, offer equivalent guarantees for the supervision of banks. The principle rests on the notion of a sufficient level of minimum co-ordination having by then been achieved, in particular by the Own Funds Directive and the Solvency Ratio Directive. The consequence of mutual recognition is that the supervisors refrain from applying their own regulations to banks from other Member States operating on their territory, whether through

---

6. For an analysis of these factors, see in particular George S. Zavvos, "Banking Integration and 1992" (1990) *Harvard International Law Journal*, Vol. 31, No. 2, at p. 470 *et seq.*
7. George S. Zavvos, "Banking Integration and 1992" (1990) *Harvard International Law Journal*, Vol. 31, No. 2, 463, at 471.
8. Completing the Internal Market—White Paper from the Commission to the European Council, EUR-PARL-Doc (Com. No. 310 (1985)).
9. P. Clarotti, "Un Pas Decisif vers le Marché Commun des Banques" [1989] *Revue du Marché Commun*, 1989, 453, 454 (our translation).

branches or the provision of cross-border services. In effect, such banks are subjected for all their activities throughout the Community to the control of the supervisory authorities of their own Member State.

However, it is clear that, for the principle of mutual recognition—just like that of "home country control"—to be workable, there must be co-operation between the supervisory authorities of the bank's country of origin and those of the other Member States where it operates, whether through branches or the provision of cross-border services. Such co-operation is provided for in the Second Banking Directive along lines which have developed from the co-operation provisions of the First Banking Directive.[10]

2. The principle of "home country control"

4.7 The principle of "home country control" is the corollary of mutual recognition. It is considered in detail in Chapter 13. Once the supervisory authorities of the host country refrain from exercising their own supervision over banks from other Member States on the ground that such banks are subject to supervision by the supervisory authorities of their home country, possibly under different conditions but with equivalent guarantees, the supervisory authorities of the home country must be recognised as having the right to exercise their supervision over their "own" banks not only in respect of activities carried on at home but also in respect of activities carried on in other Member States, whether through branches or the provision of cross-border services. In other words, a bank remains subject to the exclusive control of the supervisory authorities of its home country, wherever in the Community it operates and by whatever means.

Thus the principle of home country control has two aspects: on the one hand, it is a means for achieving the liberalisation of banking services in the Community; on the other hand, it is a means of ensuring the unity and consistency of banking supervision throughout the Community.[11]

3. The principle of the single banking licence

4.8 The principle of the single banking licence is the logical result of the other two principles. Once a bank from one Member State operating in other Member States, whether through branches or the provision of cross-border services, becomes in principle subject to the exclusive control of the supervisory authorities of its home country for the entirety of its operations in the Community, only those authorities are competent to license that bank to carry on its activities. The licence, once granted, is valid not only for the operations carried out in the home country but also in respect of those carried out elsewhere in the Community.

These three principles have far-reaching implications in the context of the freedom of establishment and the freedom to provide services. Before discussing each of these aspects, it is necessary to consider the matters common to both which arise from the provisions of the Second Banking Directive.

---

10. See Part Two below.
11. See Wilfried Wilms, "Wegwijs in de Europese Bankwetgeving" (1990) *Tijdschrift voor rechtspersonen & vennootschap*, 224, at 235.

THE SINGLE BANKING LICENCE

1. Not limited to the two functions that characterise a credit institution, even though it can only be held by a credit institution

4.9 The single banking licence is only available, under article 18 of the Second Banking Directive, to a credit institution as defined by the First Banking Directive; and also to a financial institution assimilated to a credit institution. Yet the scope of the single banking licence may differ depending on the home Member State which grants it—and this in a situation where the institutions concerned may be in competition with each other in the same market.

The explanation for this superficially surprising state of affairs is to be found in the fundamental choice made when the scope of the Second Banking Directive was being defined. Instead of attempting to produce a revised definition of a credit institution to take account of the profound changes in the banking sector since the adoption of the First Banking Directive in 1977, it was decided—rightly, it is submitted—to leave the definition contained in the First Banking Directive unchanged[12] and to provide, as an Annex to the Second Banking Directive, a list of agreed activities which credit institutions (as defined by the 1977 Directive) licensed in one Member State might provide in all other Member States as long as they are authorised to do so by the home Member State.

4.10 As appears from the Annex, the list of "agreed activities" is extremely broad, being modelled on the "universal bank" model typical of the German banking industry. Perhaps the most significant feature of the list is the inclusion of all forms of transactions in securities.

The list may be updated periodically to include new services developed by the market by a simplified procedure which does not require any amendment to the Second Banking Directive itself.[13]

It is understood that, at the Council meeting at which the Second Banking Directive was adopted, the Commission confirmed that the use of the powers conferred on it would be limited to technical adaptations required in order to adapt the terminology of the list in the Annex, such adaptations being limited to operations which are characteristic of the activity of banking and which are performed by credit institutions; and that in no case would these adaptations affect the definition of credit institutions in article 1 of the Directive.

2. Distortion of competition amongst "credit institutions" and "non-credit institutions" carrying out the same activities

4.11 The grant of the single licence under the Second Banking Directive is conditional upon its holder being a credit institution as defined by the 1977 Directive. But the activities covered by the licence are not limited to the two activities which characterise the definition of a credit institution. This means that institutions which perform one or more of the activities listed in the Annex but which fall outside the definition of a credit institution cannot avail themselves of the benefit of the single

---

12. At the same time, it was provided that Member States must "prohibit persons or undertakings that are not credit institutions from carrying on the business of taking deposits or other repayable funds from the public": art. 3. These provisions closed off a loophole left open by the First Banking Directive.

13. Art. 22.

licence under the Second Banking Directive for those activities. They therefore face a competitive handicap if they wish to carry out these activities Community-wide in competition with credit institutions.

The problem is particularly acute in relation to activities which overlap the banking and insurance sectors. Over the last few years, the insurance sector has in fact showed a marked tendency to develop new insurance products which are in effect savings products, for example single premium policies and unit-linked policies. These new "insurance products" find themselves in direct competition with some of the activities listed in the Annex to the Second Banking Directive which, under the single licence which it creates, can only be performed Community-wide by credit institutions (if so allowed under their national regulations).

The risk of distortions of competition thereby created has certainly been a powerful incentive to achieve as quickly as possible a similar single licence for life assurance companies, to allow them to sell their savings products Community-wide, on a level playing-field with the banks, under a single insurance licence. Similar distortions of competition are potentially created for activities which overlap the banking and securities industries. This issue, of great importance for the financial sector in the United Kingdom, is discussed separately later.[14]

3. Distortion of competition amongst credit institutions licensed under different national laws—the problem of reverse discrimination in the banking sector

4.12 One writer has commented that "the Second Banking Directive's approach of divorcing the scope of the 'passport' from the ambit of regulation . . . [also] does . . . violence to competitive neutrality amongst [credit institutions]".[15]

Banks based in Member States which allow them to carry out all or a wide range of the services in the agreed list in the Annex to the Second Banking Directive will be able to provide those services in the territory of another Member State, even though the locally licensed banks in that other Member State may not be allowed by their own national regulations to provide some of these services.

4.13 This risk of reverse discrimination is, moreover, not confined to the range of products which can be offered by banks of one Member State in competition, on their own market, with banks from other Member States. It cuts across the whole range of provisions of the Second Banking Directive and is of particular importance in the field of banking supervision. This is because, in line with the general philosophy which underlines all "1992" financial legislation, the Second Banking Directive only lays down a minimum level of harmonisation which must be met by each Member State. The Member States remain in general free to lay down more onerous or far-reaching requirements than the minimum laid down by the Directive if they so wish. But Member States which take this course may not exclude from their home market banks licensed in other Member States provided that these latter Member States have complied with the minimum requirements laid down by the Second Banking Directive.

For example, the Directive provides that the authorities of the home country must establish a minimum initial capital requirement of at least five million ECU, as a rule,

---

14. See para. 4.16 below.
15. Paul Tillett, "Banking Regulation in 1992", in *1992: The Legal Implications for Banking*, editor Ross Cranston, 1989, Institute of Bankers/Centre for Commercial Law Studies, 43, at 50.

for its credit institutions but allows them to set a higher capital threshold.[16] Such authorities cannot oppose the establishment in their territory of branches of banks having their head offices in another Member State in which only the minimum capital provided for by the Directive is required. If the French authorities were to impose a minimum capital requirement of, say, eight million ECU for French banks and the United Kingdom authorities were content to require only the minimum capital of five million ECU, the French authorities could not prevent the setting up in France of branches of United Kingdom banks or the provision of cross-border services in France by United Kingdom banks, despite the fact that the level of their capital funding in their home country was below that required by French law for French banks.

4.14 The problem of reverse discrimination extends beyond the field covered by the Second Banking Directive. For example, the fact that the savings products sold by a bank of Member State A in the territory of Member State B (for example, UCITS) may be more attractive than similar products sold by the banks of Member State B and subject to the tax rules of Member State B, because of the more lenient tax rules to which they are subject in Member State A (for instance in relation to withholding tax on dividends and/or interest received by the UCITS), may also result in reverse discrimination against the banks of Member State B.

4.15 Some writers have suggested that the risk of reverse discrimination created by the Second Banking Directive might be held by the Court of Justice to be contrary to Community law on the basis of article 3(f) of the EEC Treaty, which includes amongst the objectives of the Community "the institution of a system ensuring that competition in the common market is not distorted."[17] It is submitted, however, that the Court of Justice would be unlikely to uphold that argument.

Consequently, it appears likely that the minimum harmonisation achieved in limited areas by the Second Banking Directive will, in the longer term, be complemented by a much greater and market-induced harmonisation. Member States which impose more stringent requirements on their own credit institutions than those laid down by other Member States which keep to the minimum requirements laid down by the Directive will inevitably come under pressure from the institutions to bring the requirements imposed on them more in line with those of "more competitive" Member States.[18] These downward pressures will not be limited to the areas covered by the Directive but will extend to other areas which affect the overall competition of services provided by one credit institution *vis-à-vis* similar services provided on the same market by credit institutions based in another Member State.

4. Special position of United Kingdom credit institutions in relation to the provision of investment services

4.16 As already stated, even though the agreed list of activities annexed to the Second Banking Directive is very broad, and includes in particular the whole range of

16. Art. 4 (*a contrario*); see also the ninth recital of the preamble to the Directive.

17. J. Pardon, President of the Legal Committee of the European Banking Federation, in the transcript of a conference on "L'integration financière" held in April 1988 at the Institut Français des Relations Internationales.

18. Or else face the risk that local credit institutions may create local subsidiaries in other Member States in order to service their home markets, at least with respect to certain types of products. The Second Banking Directive seeks to limit this risk of regulatory arbitrage but it is highly doubtful whether the mechanism set in place will be effective for this purpose; see below.

securities services, a credit institution of one Member State can only provide those services pursuant to the Directive in another Member State if it is authorised to provide them in its home Member State pursuant to the licence granted by its supervisory authorities.[19]

This approach could potentially create considerable distortions of competition for United Kingdom credit institutions wishing to provide investment services in other Member States pursuant to the Directive. The reason for these difficulties lies in the functional nature of supervision in the United Kingdom, according to which the jurisdiction of a supervisor is determined not by reference to the nature of the institutions to be supervised but by reference to the services provided, by whatever institution. This contrasts with the institutional approach generally adopted in continental Europe and, more to the point, in the relevant EC Directives. Thus:

in the U.K., a bank may provide any service so far as the Banking Act is concerned—so long as it continues to fulfil the prudential criteria—but it cannot engage in securities business (a listed activity under the Directive) unless it is authorised to do so under the Financial Services Act.[20]

4.17 On the assumption that a credit institution is licensed under the United Kingdom Financial Services Act 1986 to provide securities business services, the question arises whether it is entitled to do so in the other Member States under the single licence, even though not subject, in relation to those activities, to the supervision of the United Kingdom banking supervisory authorities—"the only banking authorities" for the purposes of the Directive—but to that of the securities industry regulators. If this question were to be answered in the affirmative, it could on the face of it produce results in direct contradiction of the philosophy of home country control, which presupposes that a bank of one Member State is supervised by the "competent authorities," as defined by the Directive, for all the activities that it carries out in another Member State. It was presumably with a view to preventing those difficulties, which may possibly also arise in other Member States, that a joint declaration of the Council and the Commission on article 1(5) of the Second Banking Directive (defining "the competent authorities") is understood to have been included in the minutes of the meeting of the Council at which the Directive was adopted. It is understood that it provides, in substance, that, where in one Member State there is more than one supervisory authority responsible for the supervision of a credit institution in respect of the carrying out of the activities listed in the Annex to the Directive, the various supervisory authorities of that Member State will agree with the competent authorities of other Member States on a co-ordination procedure appropriate to meet the needs of the Directive.[21]

4.18 An additional difficulty lay in the fact that most of the large deposit-taking institutions in the United Kingdom, such as the main clearing banks, usually carry out their securities activities through separate subsidiaries which, again, are subject to the

---

19. Being the supervisory authorities "which are empowered by law or regulations to supervise credit institutions": Second Banking Directive, art. 1(5), referring to art. 1 of the 1983 First Consolidated Supervision Directive, since replaced by art. 1 of Council Directive 92/80 of 6 April 1992 on the supervision of credit institutions on a consolidated basis (the Second Consolidated Supervision Directive) discussed in Part Two below.

20. Paul Tillett, "Banking Regulation in 1992", in *1992: The Legal Implications for Banking*, editor Ross Cranston 1989, Institute of Bankers/Centre for Commercial Law Studies, 43, at 49.

21. See, further, Part Two.

supervision not of the banking regulators but of the securities industry regulators.[22] These investment services subsidiaries will also normally fall outside the scope of the Second Banking Directive because they fall outside the definition of credit institutions.

Therefore, the risk exists that "universal banks" based on the German model generally adopted in continental Europe will enjoy the benefits of the single passport to, say, provide securities services in the United Kingdom through a branch or the provision of cross-border services, whereas the United Kingdom securities industry will, because of its different structure, be unable to do the same in continental Europe. The purpose of the Investment Services Directive, considered below insofar as it complements the Second Banking Directive, is essentially to remove this risk by creating a separate but equal single licence for the non-bank securities houses.

5. Non-credit institutions entitled to the single licence: the "assimilated" financial institutions

4.19 During the preparation of the Second Banking Directive, it became apparent that in some Member States banks were obliged, for a number of reasons, to carry out certain activities such as leasing or credit-card operations through separate corporate vehicles. Because those separate subsidiaries would not themselves have come within the definition of a credit institution within the Directive, the danger existed that banks established in those Member States would be prevented from exercising in other Member States under the provisions of the single licence any such activity even though included in the list of agreed activities.

To mitigate this risk, article 18(2) of the Directive provides that the benefit of the single licence is extended to "any financial institution", which expression is defined as "a subsidiary of a credit institution or the jointly owned subsidiary of two or more credit institutions, the memorandum and articles of association of which permit the carrying on of (one or more of) the activities [listed in the Annex]".

The financial institution must, in addition, fulfil *each* of the following conditions:

— the parent undertaking or undertakings must be authorised as credit institutions in the Member State by the law of which the subsidiary is governed;
— the activities in question must actually be carried on within the territory of the same Member State;
— the parent credit institution must hold 90% or more of the voting rights attached to shares in the capital of the subsidiary;
— the parent credit institution must satisfy its supervisory authorities regarding the prudent management of the subsidiary and must have declared, with the consent of the Member State's competent authorities, that it jointly and severally guarantees the commitments entered into by the subsidiary;
— the subsidiary must effectively be included, for the activities in question in particular, in the consolidated supervision of the parent credit institution.

The subsidiary's compliance with these conditions must be verified by the supervisory authorities of the parent credit institution. These authorities must supply the financial

---

22. See Stanisla M. Yassukovitch, "The European financial services industry after 1992—Regulation and the competitive challenge", *Butterworths Journal of International Banking and Financial Law* (1989), p. 201; also, Richard Novirnsky and Robin Brooks, "Financial services must take account of the new European rules", *FT Business Law Supplement*, p. 9, 12 April 1990.

institution with a certificate of compliance, which must form part of the notification to the authorities of the host Member State that is required when a credit institution—including, for the purposes of the Directive, an "article 18(2)" financial institution—wishes to open a branch or to provide services on a cross-border basis in another Member State.

In addition to these necessarily stringent conditions, the Directive provides, in line with the general principle of home country control which underlies it, that the competent authorities of the parent credit institution must ensure the Community-wide supervision of the "article 18(2)" financial institution under the same conditions as those laid down by the Directive (and by the 1977 Directive) for the supervision of credit institutions proper when they operate in other Member States.[23]

6. Position of credit institutions (and assimilated financial institutions) prohibited by national law from operating abroad

4.20 In some Member States, certain categories of credit institutions are prohibited by statute or regulations from operating abroad or from carrying out abroad some of the activities which they may carry out at home. In particular, in Germany, it is understood that some local savings banks may only operate within the specific part of Germany allocated to them under the terms of their licence.[24] In the United Kingdom, the Building Societies Act 1986 prohibits building societies from operating directly outside the United Kingdom, except where they are authorised to do so by Treasury Order. The Treasury has so far only made orders allowing societies to operate in the Channel Islands and the Isle of Man, territories which are outside the United Kingdom and, for the purposes of the Directive, outside the Community.

4.21 The draft of the Second Banking Directive initially proposed by the Commission provided in article 18 that "the activities listed in the Annex may be carried on within the territory [of any Member State] . . . by any credit institution authorised and supervised by the competent authorities of another Member State." It thereby gave to any credit institution the *right* to exercise in other Member States all activities which it was authorised to carry out in its home Member State provided that they were included in the list of agreed activities.[25] However, in view of opposition from some Member States, in particular Germany, to the granting of this right of exit to all credit institutions, an initial attempt at compromise was made whereby a list of exceptions to the right, or at least to its unconditional exercise, would have been drawn up. However, the Commission abandoned this approach when it became apparent that the proposed list of exceptions was in danger of becoming so long as to become the rule and of altogether depriving certain credit institutions of their right of establishment under the Treaty.

The eventual compromise was to leave to the Court of Justice the task of deciding whether and, if so, to what extent, a Member State might under its national law restrict or prohibit a local credit institution from operating in another Member State through a branch or the provision of cross-border services. Article 18(1) therefore reads:

---

23. Art. 18(2), third paragraph.
24. The so-called regional principle. One of the reasons for these restrictions is often that the liabilities of the institutions in question are guaranteed by the regional authorities where they are authorised to operate.
25. P. Clarotti, "Un Pas Décisif vers le Marché Commun des Banques" [1989] *Revue du Marché Commun* 453, 461.

The Member States shall provide that the activities listed in the Annex may be carried on within their territories . . . by any credit institution authorised and supervised by the competent authorities of another Member State . . . provided that such activities are covered by the authorisation . . .

In view of earlier pronouncements of the Court of Justice, it is submitted that it is unlikely that national rules or regulations which prohibit or restrict a local credit institution from carrying out in other Member States activities which it is licensed to carry out in its home country will generally be held to be compatible with Community law. In particular, in *R* v. *H.M. Treasury and Commissioners of Inland Revenue, ex parte Daily Mail and General Trust plc*[26] the Court held that:

. . . freedom of establishment constitutes one of the fundamental principles of the Community and that the provisions of the Treaty guaranteeing that freedom have been directly applicable since the end of the transitional period. These provisions secure the right of establishment in another Member State not merely for Community nationals but also for the companies referred to in Article 58.
Even though those provisions are directed mainly to ensuring that foreign nationals and companies are treated in the host Member State in the same way as nationals of that State, they also prohibit the Member State of origin from hindering the establishment in another Member State of one of its nationals or of a company incorporated under its legislation which comes within the definition contained in Article 52. . . .

As already stated,[27] these geographical restrictions are often explained by the fact that the liabilities of these credit institutions are guaranteed by a local public body. However, it is submitted that such a justification cannot constitute a valid reason for restricting the right of a credit institution to exercise the freedom of establishment or the freedom to provide services on a cross-border basis given to it under the Treaty. In any event, the guarantee of a state or public body cannot under Community law be a valid substitute for the minimum level of own funds required for all credit institutions, whether in public or private hands.[28] On the other hand, where a state or public body withholds its guarantee in relation to liabilities arising out of operations carried out in other Member States or deposits in a currency other than the local currency, it may be laying itself open to a charge of discrimination forbidden by the Treaty.

4.22 A more delicate question, in particular against the background of the recent BCCI affair, is whether the supervisory authorities of a Member State may restrict the establishment of branches or the provision of cross-border services by a local credit institution, whether publicly owned or not, outside its territory, on the ground that they lack adequate means properly to supervise these extraterritorial activities. Such an argument will clearly carry more weight as a result of the proposed directive on deposit guarantee schemes, which makes the authorities of the home Member State primarily responsible, through the national guarantee scheme, for the reimbursement of all deposits, including those received in other Member States through local branches there or the provision of cross-border services.

26. Case 81/87 [1988] ECR 5483, at 5510, points 15 and 16. See also, with regard to restrictions on the "export" of services by self-employed persons, joined cases 154 and 155/87 *RSVZ* v. *Wolf* [1988] ECR 3897; and, with regard to restrictions on the "export" of services by a commercial company, case 49/89 *Corsica Ferries France* v. *Direction Générale des Douanes Françaises* [1989] ECR 4441 and the commentary thereon by Giuliano Marenco, "La notion de restriction aux libertés d'établissement et de prestation de services dans la jurisprudence de la Cour", *Gazette du Palais* (France), 3–5 May 1992, p. 4 *et seq.*, at no. 24.
27. See fn. 24 above.
28. See the Own Funds Directive considered in Part Two below.

7. Activities covered and activities not covered by the single banking licence— differences in status

4.23 In essence, three situations may be distinguished. First, where a credit institution is licensed under its national laws to conduct an activity which is included in the list annexed to the Directive. Second, where a credit institution's licence under its national laws excludes the pursuit of an activity which is included in the list annexed to the Directive. Third, where a credit institution is licensed under its national laws to conduct an activity which is excluded from the list annexed to the Directive.

The first situation is the only one in which the credit institution will be able to avail itself of the single licence created by the Directive if it wishes to exercise in another Member State one or more of the agreed activities which it is also licensed, under its own national laws, to carry on at home. Accordingly, the activities that may be exercised fall into two categories. First, there are the traditional "commercial banking" activities such as deposit taking, lending (including consumer credit, mortgage credit, factoring with or without recourse and the financing of commercial transactions including forfaiting), trade financing, money transmission services (including credit cards and travellers cheques), guarantees and commitments and financial leasing. Second, the agreed list includes securities activities and some merchant banking activities: trading for one's own account or for the account of customers in short- and long-term securities, including money market instruments, financial futures and options; participation in securities issues and the provision of services related to them; portfolio management and advice; advice to undertakings on capital structure and industrial strategy; advice and services related to mergers and acquisitions.

In determining whether a credit institution falls into this first category, the question arises whether it is necessary that the terms of its national licence must specifically include the exercise of a given activity or whether it is sufficient that the national licence does not prohibit the carrying out of the activity. In various Member States, banks are traditionally allowed to carry out certain activities in, for example, the field of securities services, which are not always expressly covered by the terms of their national licence. Also, it will be recalled that in the United Kingdom a bank may carry on any activity provided it meets the prudential criteria imposed by the banking regulators but that it will need a licence from the securities industry regulators if it wishes to provide investment services to its customers.[29]

It is submitted that where a bank does not need a specific authorisation in its home Member State in order to carry on an activity listed in the Annex, it would be unreasonable to deny it the benefit of the single licence for the pursuit of that activity in another Member State. However, it is also submitted that where a bank does require a specific authorisation in its home Member State to carry on an activity covered by the Annex, it would not be unreasonable to deny it the benefit of the single licence for the pursuit of that activity in another Member State, even if the specific authorisation required must be given not by the bank's banking regulators but by another regulator such as, in the United Kingdom, the financial industry's regulators for the provision of investment services.[30]

---

29. Paul Tillett, "Banking Regulation and 1992", in *1992: The Legal Implications for Banking*, editor Ross Cranston, (1989) Chartered Institute of Bankers/Centre for Commercial Law Studies, 43, at 49.

30. In his article cited in fn. 29 above, Tillett also concludes, at p. 49, that "It would be reasonable to deny the 'passport' to services for which a bank needs, but does not possess, specific authorisation in its home State".

4.24 In the second situation, the bank concerned finds itself effectively prevented from carrying on in another Member State, whether through a branch or the provision of cross-border services, the activity which its regulators do not permit it to carry on at home.

This situation must, it is stressed, be distinguished from that in which a bank finds itself prevented under its national licence from carrying on activities in another Member State which it is authorised to carry on at home. It must also be distinguished from a situation where the bank's national licence allows it to carry on outside its home country some of the activities listed in the Annex but prohibits it from exercising those activities at home. If Member State A's authorities do not allow its banks, say, directly to carry on leasing activities on its territory but allow them to carry on those activities in other Member States, the banks concerned are, it is submitted, entitled to the benefit of the single licence when carrying on those activities in other Member States.

4.25 In the third situation, the bank concerned has no right under the Directive to carry on in other Member States the activities which it is authorised under its national laws to carry on at home. Such activities by definition fall outside the scope of the single licence created by the Directive. However, this does not mean that the bank is necessarily prevented from exercising such activities in another Member State, whether through a branch or the provision of cross-border services. Indeed, the freedom of establishment and the freedom to provide financial services are conferred by the Treaty and not by the Directive. The Directive and the single licence which it creates are only intended to facilitate the exercise of such freedoms. Hence recital 13 to the Directive states that:

the carrying on of activities not listed in the Annex shall enjoy the right of establishment and the freedom to provide services under the general provisions of the Treaty.

The same position prevails where institutions not authorised as credit institutions in their home Member States wish to carry out activities in another Member State which they may exercise at home, whether or not such activities are included in the Annex. Here, too, the right of the institutions concerned to exercise those activities exists under the general provisions of the Treaty and subject to the limitations permitted by the Treaty. As recital 15 to the Directive states:

Whereas the host Member State may in connection with the exercise of the right of establishment and the freedom to provide services require compliance with specific provisions of its own national laws or regulations on the part of institutions not authorised as credit institutions . . . provided that, on the one hand, such provisions are compatible with Community law and are intended to protect the general good and that, on the other hand, such institutions . . . are not subject to equivalent rules under the legislation or regulations of their home Member States.

4.26 The question which then arises is what is the difference between an activity which a bank of one Member State may carry out in other Member States under the single licence (because the activity is included in the agreed list in the Annex) and an activity which the bank may carry out at home, which is not included in the list but which it may nevertheless carry on in other Member States "under the general provisions of the Treaty".

Also, to say that the activities exercised "under the general provisions of the Treaty" may not benefit from the mutual recognition granted by the Directive to activities listed in the Annex in turn raises the question what is the precise content of the concept of mutual recognition and what are its limits.

It is submitted that a distinction must be drawn in this regard between, on the one hand, the right to carry on an activity in another Member State ("the mutual recognition of authorisation") and, on the other hand, the manner in which that right may be exercised ("the mutual recognition of financial techniques").

MUTUAL RECOGNITION

1. Mutual recognition of authorisation

4.27 The recitals to the Directive and the Directive itself draw a distinction between, on the one hand, the position of a credit institution which carries on in another Member State an activity which it is authorised to carry on at home and which is included in the Annex and, on the other hand, the position of a credit institution which carries on in another Member State an activity which it is authorised to carry on at home but which is not included in the Annex.

Recital 4 says:

Whereas the approach which has been adopted is to achieve only the essential harmonisation necessary and sufficient to secure the mutual recognition of authorization and of prudential supervision systems, making possible the granting of a single licence recognized throughout the Community and the application of the principle of home Member State prudential supervision.

Recital 12 says:

Whereas, by virtue of mutual recognition, the approach chosen permits credit institutions authorized in their home Member State to carry on, throughout the Community, any or all of the activities listed in the Annex by establishing branches or by providing services.

And recital 13 says:

Whereas the carrying-on of activities not listed in the Annex shall enjoy the right of establishment and the freedom to provide services under the general provisions of the Treaty.

These recitals are reflected in article 18 of the Directive, which is the key provision relating to the freedom of establishment and the freedom to provide services under the Directive. Article 18(1) provides:

The Member States shall provide that the activities listed in the Annex may be carried on within their territory . . . by any credit institution authorised and supervised by the competent authorities of another Member State . . . provided that such activities are covered by the authorization.

Accordingly, these provisions have the effect of excluding from the benefit of mutual recognition of authorisation activities not listed in the Annex.

4.28 The Directive itself is silent as to the powers of the host Member State to forbid the exercise by credit institutions on its territory of activities which do not enjoy the benefit of the mutual recognition of authorisation. However, some indication is given by recital 15 which, in fact does no more than restate the general and overriding principles of Community law which apply:

Whereas the host Member State may, in connection with the exercise of the right of establishment and the freedom to provide services, require compliance with specific provisions of its own national laws or regulations on the part of institutions not authorized as credit institutions in their home Member States and with regard to activities [carried on by duly authorized credit institutions but] not listed in the Annex provided that on the one hand such provisions are compatible with Community law and are intended to protect the general good and that, on the other hand, such institutions [not authorized as credit-institutions in their home Member States] or such activities are not subject to equivalent rules under the legislation or regulations of their home Member States.

Therefore, the difference between activities covered by the mutual recognition of authorisation and those not covered appears to be as follows.

In the case of activities carried on by a credit institution which are not included in the agreed list, the host Member State retains the right to prohibit the exercise of such activities by the foreign bank "in the interest of the general good", even if the foreign bank is validly authorised to carry on such activities in its home Member State. As always, however, the discretion retained by the host Member State is subject to the limitations imposed by the general rules of the Treaty, for example the prohibition of discrimination on grounds of nationality or place of residence and of restrictions which are disproportionate to the purpose which they seek to achieve. In such respects, the host Member State's discretion is subject to the control of the Court of Justice.

4.29 In the case of activities included in the agreed list, the authorities of the host Member State may not prohibit the pursuit of such activities provided that they are authorised by the home Member State of the bank concerned. This is so even if the local banks of the host Member State are not allowed to carry out such activities and even if the reason the local banks are so prohibited is the general good. In other words, a Member State may no longer invoke its own legislation justified by the general good to prohibit the pursuit on its territory of activities which are authorised in the home Member State and covered by the Annex. In the result, in this situation, the question whether the "general good" justification is compatible with the limitations imposed by the general rules of the Treaty is irrelevant. In effect, the harmonisation of the conditions for authorisation for the pursuit of such activities brought about by the Directive means that Member States may no longer lay down rules which derogate therefrom.[31]

2. Mutual recognition of financial techniques

4.30 The Second Banking Directive gives a credit institution authorised in one Member State an absolute right to carry on an activity included in the Annex in any other Member State. However, it does not follow that the institution also has the absolute right to carry on that activity in the host Member State in the same manner as that which prevails in its home Member State. Two examples may help clarify the distinction.

First, the receipt of deposits from the public is one of the activities included in the Annex. A United Kingdom bank therefore has the absolute right under the Directive to receive deposits from the public in France, through a branch there or the provision of

---

31. A comparison may be made in this respect with the Court of Justice's judgments in case C–208/88 *Commission* v. *Denmark* [1990] ECR 4445 and case C–367/88 *Commission* v. *Ireland* [1990] ECR 4465 where the Court stressed that Member States were not entitled to lay down additional requirements to those laid down at the time by the relevant directive on personal allowances for travellers since an *exhaustive* harmonisation had been achieved by the directive. See also case C–246/91 *Commission* v. *France*, judgment of 5 May 1993, point 7. On the occasion of a conference at the Centre for European Policy Studies in Brussels in December 1992, Peter Troberg, a leading DG XV Commission official, indicated, however, that the Commission's legal service has taken the view that, pursuant to the Treaty a branch may only carry out activities which the locally incorporated credit institutions are authorised to carry out (national treatment). The implication is that the Directive goes beyond what is required by the Treaty in allowing a branch to carry out all activities (within the scope of the Annex) authorised pursuant to its home State authorisation.

cross-border services. Assume that French law provides that banks may not pay interest on current account credit balances. Does the prohibition apply only to French banks or does it also apply to the banks of other Member States operating in France?

Second, another of the activities included in the Annex is lending, including the granting of mortgage credit. A United Kingdom bank can therefore grant mortgage credit to a customer in Belgium, including an expatriate. However, until recently Belgian law required that the lender charge a fixed rate of interest for the whole duration of the loan whereas United Kingdom banks are accustomed to charging a variable rate of interest. Could the Belgian authorities, after the entry into force of the Second Banking Directive, have required the United Kingdom bank to apply a fixed rate of interest in line with Belgian law? In this regard, Belgian law has now been amended, doubtless in order to avoid any possible risk of reverse discrimination should the answer to that question have been no, as, it is submitted, would have been the case.

Lobbying by Member States

4.31 The potential implications of the concept of mutual recognition of financial techniques, in particular for those Member States which severely restrict the freedom of credit institutions in devising new products or adapting existing products to meet new market needs, led to active efforts on the part of those Member States, both at the Council and European Parliament levels, during the process of adoption of the Second Banking Directive to secure changes in their favour to the text initially proposed by the Commission. However, the success of those efforts is, it is submitted, open to grave doubt.

The proposal for a Second Council Directive submitted by the Commission to the Council on 23 February 1988[32] made no express reference to the right of a credit institution to carry out activities covered by the single licence in the same manner, that is, using the same financial techniques, as that prevailing in its home Member State. However, recital 14 of the proposal stated that:

Member States *should* ensure that there are no obstacles to the activities benefiting from mutual recognition being undertaken *using the financial techniques of the home Member State*, as long as the latter are not in violation of the legal provisions governing the public good in the host Member State.[33]

The amended proposal submitted by the Commission to the Council after the European Parliament's first reading of the original proposal included an amendment which made express reference to the mutual recognition of financial techniques in the body of the Directive, in article 18, being the key provision relating to freedom of establishment and freedom to provide services.

At the same time, article 14 of the original proposal was amended so as to provide that the Directive was to be viewed "in conjunction with the proposed mortgage credit Directive[34] and the provisions for mutual recognition of financial techniques to be contained therein". One of the most far-reaching of those obligations was an obligation on the part of the host Member State to authorise its own local mortgage credit institutions to use financial techniques being used by mortgage credit institutions from

32. Com(87)715 Final, OJ C84/1 of 31 March 1988.
33. Emphasis added.
34. Com(84)730 Final, OJ C42/4 of 14 February 1985; amended proposal, OJ C161/4 of 19 June 1987.

other Member States active on its territory when failure to do so would put its own institutions at a competitive disadvantage.[35]

The final amendments to the draft Directive

4.32 However, the amended proposal for a Second Banking Directive submitted by the Commission to the Council was further amended when the Council adopted its Common Position prior to the draft Directive's second reading in the European Parliament. It is these amendments which are reflected in the final text of the Directive as adopted by the Council on 15 December 1989. They were threefold.

First, recital 16 (which corresponds to recital 14 of the original proposal) was amended so that the Directive was no longer linked to the mutual recognition of financial techniques in the mortgage sector. The previous reference to the proposed mortgage credit directive was moved to recital 11, which deals with future harmonisation of financial and investment services and where separate measures for mortgage credit harmonisation are referred to in order to facilitate mutual recognition of "the financial techniques peculiar to that sphere".

This new approach no doubt reflected the Commission's intention, later confirmed by it in answer to a Written Question in the European Parliament, to shelve its plans for the proposed mortgage credit directive and to proceed in this field only by way of the Second Banking Directive.[36] If the Second Banking Directive meets the needs of the mortgage market, no further action will be necessary. Only if it appears that there is a greater need for *minimum* harmonisation of financial techniques to meet the specific character of the mortgage credit sector may the proposed mortgage credit directive be revived. This seems rather unlikely, despite the efforts made at the time by the European Community Mortgage Federation to prevent the plans for a separate mortgage credit directive being halted. Indeed, any need for greater minimum harmonisation of financial techniques for the mortgage credit sector, as opposed to the banking sector as a whole, is unlikely to become apparent until after the Second Banking Directive has been in force for some time. As a result, pressure has been applied by mortgage credit lenders on their national authorities in the Member States most at risk from reverse discrimination because of the rigidity of their regulations.

For example, the Belgian legislation which prohibited variable rate mortgages has been amended under pressure from the local mortgage credit institutions, which were fearful of being handicapped by the prohibition if it had remained in force after the single banking licence of foreign lenders on the Belgian market has become a reality. This example highlights two trends. It confirms that the approach underlying the Second Banking Directive "will provide a major impetus towards market-induced alignment" not only of the Member States' supervisory systems but also of the "financial techniques" which they allow.[37] It also indicates that even though a Member State may oppose the use of "foreign" financial techniques if they are contrary to its own

35. Art. 5.
36. Answer by the Commission on 15 May 1990 to Written Question 440/90 of Mr. Willy Rothley, no. 90 C171/91, OJ C171/43 of 12 July 1990: "Once the general content of the Second Banking Directive had been finalised, a reassessment was made of what remained to be done to promote mortgage credit in the Community, on the basis of a new text which eliminated duplication. Since the remaining disparity was minimal, it was suggested that the Commission awaits the result of the Second Banking Directive and its practical effects for mortgage credit and if necessary refers new proposals to the Council."
37. See René Smits, "Banking Regulation in a European Perspective", (1989) *Legal Issues of European Integration*, 61, at 69.

legislation justified by the "general good"[38]—an argument which might possibly be made to justify the Belgian requirement of fixed rate mortgages[39]—the local credit institutions have little confidence in the ability of their local authorities to enforce effective compliance by banks from other Member States operating on their market.

The scope for prevention of qualifying activities

4.33 The second amendment made at the time of the adoption of the Directive also concerns recital 16. Whereas recital 14 of the original proposal (to which recital 16 of the Directive corresponds) began with the words "Member States should ensure . . .", recital 16 begins with the words "Member States *must* ensure . . .".[40] Perhaps unwittingly, this amendment seems to have cleared up any remaining doubt as to whether and, if so, to what extent, a host Member State may legitimately prevent the pursuit of a qualifying activity or control the manner in which the activity in question is carried on. As a result of the amendment, it is now clear, in terms of the recital, that activities which benefit from the single licence must be allowed to be carried on in the host Member State "in the same manner," that is using the same financial techniques as in the home Member State, subject only to the host Member State invoking its national legislation prohibiting the use of such techniques on the ground of the "general good". As will be seen, that concept is subject to specific limitations imposed by Community law.

For completeness, it must be noted that recital 16 also substitutes for the expression "using the financial techniques of the home Member State" in recital 14 of the original proposal the expression "in the same manner as in the home Member State". It is submitted that this change is without real significance.

4.34 The third amendment made at the time of the adoption of the Directive concerns article 18(1). Whereas the Commission's amended proposal contained an amendment to article 16(1) of the original proposal (to which article 18(1) of the Directive corresponds) whereby express reference was made to the mutual recognition of financial techniques, the Council reverted to the text of the original proposal, which contained no such reference. This is somewhat surprising in view of the second amendment discussed above. However, it is submitted that, even in the absence of an express provision in the body of the Directive, in line with the case-law of the Court of Justice,[41] the general principles of the Treaty itself require the host Member State to authorise qualifying activities to be exercised on its territory "in the same manner" as in

---

38. See para. 4.35 below.

39. The success of any such argument is, however, far from a foregone conclusion. A.G. Van Gerven has commented extrajudicially that "good arguments . . . may . . . be made in support of the contention that the prohibition on variable rates is not necessary for the protection of the borrower. In fact, it may be stated that such a prohibition is unnecessary in order to achieve the desired objective in that whilst it protects the borrower against possible rate increases it also takes away from him the benefits of possible rate cuts. It can also be maintained that the obligation to apply a fixed rate increases the interest rate risk of credit institutions, which in turn will have a general effect on the level of rates available to the borrower. Finally, assuming that such a prohibition is necessary in order to achieve the intended objective, it is difficult to see why this might not equally be achieved by a less severe system whereby, for example, credit institutions would be obliged to offer potential borrowers the choice of a fixed or variable rate mortgage and to provide along with the offer sufficient information to enable them to make an informed choice" (our translation): Advocate General Van Gerven, "La deuxième directive bancaire et la jurisprudence de la Cour de Justice", (1991) *Revue de la Banque* (Belgium) Vol. 1, 39, at 45 *et seq.*

40. Emphasis added.

41. Ever since *Reyners* and *Van Binsbergen*, it has been settled Community law that directives are not creative of the freedom of establishment or the freedom to provide services but are only intended to facilitate

the home Member State, subject only to the right of the host Member State to insist on compliance with its own legislation when the same is properly justified by the general good or relates to an area which, by way of exception to the general rule of home country control, remains within the jurisdiction of the supervisory authorities of the host Member State.

3. Right of the host Member State to invoke its legislation justified by the general good

4.35 The right of the host Member State to demand compliance with its legislation justified by the general good—a right specifically referred to in recital 16—is expressly provided for by article 21, which concerns the powers of the host Member State *vis-à-vis* credit institutions from other Member States having a branch or providing services on its territory.

According to article 21(5):

The foregoing provisions shall not affect the power of host Member States to take appropriate measures to prevent or to punish irregularities committed within their territories which are contrary to the legal rules they have adopted in the interest of the general good. This shall include the possibility of preventing offending institutions from initiating any further transactions within their territories.

However, the Directive contains no definition of what constitutes the "general good."

Approach of the Economic and Social Committee

4.36 The Opinion of the Economic and Social Committee ("the ESC") given in September 1988,[42] suggested that the authorities of the host Member State would retain the right to require compliance by a bank from another Member State with all national legislation of an overriding, binding nature, that is, those mandatory rules which the parties may not contract out of, including legislation designed to prevent distortion of competition or to promote consumer protection. On this basis, the authorities of the host Member State would be able to insist on compliance with all local legal provisions relating to such matters as price advertising and, more generally, as the transparency of the conditions of sale or for the provision of services, the regulation of sales or the provision of services tied to financial inducements, the regulation of misleading advertising and the prohibition of the door-to-door sale of certain products.[43] They would equally retain the power to require compliance with:

legal provisions . . . designed to protect the interests of the party deemed to be more vulnerable or less well informed. Although it is true that they can constitute an obstacle to the free provision of services, the interests in question require the continuation in force of the substantive laws of the Member States designed to protect the more vulnerable or less well informed party to a contract.[44]

The view of the ESC was that the only solution was to implement in all Member States, at the latest by the time of the entry into force of the Second Banking Directive,

---

the exercise of such freedoms, conferred by the Treaty and subject only to the restrictions compatible with the Treaty.

42. OJ C318/42 of 12 December 1988, at paras. 1.6.3.1 to 1.6.3.3.
43. *Ibid.*, at paras. 1.6.3.1 and 1.6.3.2.
44. *Ibid.*, para. 1.6.4.3.

the provisions of the Convention on the law applicable to contractual obligations signed by the Member States[45]—a wish which has since been fulfilled, at least partially, in that the Convention is presently in force between nine Member States.[46] Those provisions are designed in particular to ensure that the consumer is not denied the protection of those mandatory legal rules applicable in the State where he has his habitual residence.[47]

This approach assumes, of course, that observance of all mandatory legal provisions of the Member State of the consumer's residence can be insisted upon even where they involve restrictions on the free provision of services on a cross-border basis or on the freedom of establishment by banks having their head office in another Member State.[48]

4.37 If such was indeed the import of the Second Banking Directive, it would have marked only a limited step towards the liberalisation of the provision of financial services throughout the Community, particularly in the area of retail banking. Generally speaking, all national provisions designed to ensure fairness in commercial dealings and the protection of the consumer are in the nature of mandatory rules which cannot be contracted out of and which the national courts must apply even where the contract is governed by the law of another Member State.

This approach, if upheld, would mean that in practice banks established in one Member State which seek to provide their services to individuals or SMEs established in another Member State—the two categories of customers most likely to benefit from the Second Banking Directive—would have to ensure that their services comply, in all respects, with the applicable local legislation. The cost of so doing would render the freedom to pursue such activities wholly illusory, particularly in relation to the provision of cross-border retail services.

Guidance from the Court of Justice

4.38 As already indicated, the ESC's analysis is based upon the assumption that, so long as there is an absence of harmonisation of all mandatory legal provisions in the Member States in such areas as the fairness of commercial dealings and consumer protection (a somewhat fanciful objective), the Member States retain exclusive and unlimited sovereignty to determine what provisions of their national laws constitute mandatory rules justified by the "general good" within the meaning of that expression in the Directive.

45. The so-called "Rome Convention," signed on 19 June 1980, which provides that it will enter into force among the Member States which have ratified it once seven ratifications have been made. This occurred in January 1991, following ratification by the United Kingdom.

46. Member States have also signed two protocols (not yet in force) authorising the Court of Justice to interpret the Rome Convention.

47. Art. 5 of the Convention.

48. J. Pardon, President of the Legal Committee of the European Banking Federation, in the transcript of a conference held in April 1988 at the Institut Français des Relations Internationales on "L'Intégration Financière", at p. 23; also, J. Pardon, "La loi applicable aux contrats bancaires dans l'espace financier européen de 1993", Association européenne pour le droit bancaire et financier, 11 May 1990, Luxembourg. See also more generally, on what by all accounts is an extremely complex issue, J. Biancarelli, "L'intérêt général et le droit applicable aux contrats financiers", *Revue Banque* (France), 1992, p. 1090; B. Sousi-Roubi, "La Covention de Rome et la loi applicable aux contrats bancaires", Rec. Dalloz-Sirey, 1993, p. 183; W. Van Gerven and J. Wouters "Free movement of financial services and the European Contracts Convention" in *EC Financial Markets Regulation and Company Law* (ed. M. Ardenas); René Smits, *Establishment and Services, Banking and EC Law*, p. 33.

However, it is submitted that such an assumption is not consistent with the general principles of Community law.

4.39 According to the case-law of the Court of Justice, any recourse to the provisions or principles of national law for the purpose of interpreting the scope of an expression contained in Community legislation can only be had with the unity and effectiveness of Community law in mind.[49] Any such interpretation must therefore be made under the eventual supervision of the Court of Justice, which thereby ensures that Community law is interpreted and applied on a uniform basis.

In order to determine whether a national legal provision amounts to a mandatory rule justified "in the interest of the general good" within the meaning of the Second Banking Directive, regard must be had to the concept of the "general good" not as it is variously defined in the different Member States but as it will be defined in due course by the Court of Justice.[50]

This submission is supported by the answer given on 24 January 1990 on behalf of the Commission by Sir Leon Brittan, the Commissioner then in charge of financial institutions, to a Written Question in the European Parliament.[51] Asked to what extent host Member States would be able to demand compliance by a foreign bank with local national regulations on the ground that the regulations in question were justified by the "general good", the answer given was that:

The extent to which host countries will be able to impose a specific national rule, justified by the general good, is limited by the conditions laid down in various rulings of the Court of Justice of the European Communities.[52] Restrictions are allowed only in particular circumstances if they apply without discrimination to all persons and undertakings in that host country, if the interest safeguarded by those rules is not already covered by similar provisions in the home country and if the requirements are objectively justified. It will ultimately be up to the Court of Justice to

49. Eg, case 28/67 *Mölkerei-Zentrale* [1968] ECR 143, case 14/68 *Walt Wilhelm* v. *Bundeskartellamt* [1969] ECR 1, case 11/70 *Internationale Handelsgesellschaft mbH* v. *Einfuhr-und Vorratstelle für Getreide und Futtermittel* [1970] ECR 1125.

50. In this regard, it is interesting to note that the expression "general good" was substituted during the process of adoption of the Directive for the expression "public good." This latter expression was used in the Commission's original proposal and recalled the concept of *ordre public* used in the legal systems of civil law Member States to define national laws regarded by national legislators or courts as of such paramount importance that they must be applied by the courts notwithstanding any attempt by the parties to a contract to exclude their application. In those countries, a distinction is generally drawn between *ordre public* and *ordre public international*. Only local laws falling into the more restrictive category of *ordre public international* will, as a rule, take precedence over the proper law of the contract when that law is the law of another country and there are objective reasons for their application, that is, there is an objective international nexus. A pragmatic approach to the question of the extent to which a Member State may demand compliance with its local laws on the ground that they are justified by the general good could be to limit that right to the laws which are viewed by its courts as falling into the *ordre public international* category.

51. Written Question 916/89 of Sir James Scott-Hopkins, OJ 139/14 of 7 June 1990. See also the comments of A.G. Van Gerven in "La Deuxième Directive Bancaire et la Jurisprudence de la Cour de Justice," (1991) *Revue de la Banque* (Belgium) 39, at 43 and fn. 1 thereto. However, see P. Clarotti, "Le Deuxieme Directive de Coordination en matière d'établissements de crédit," [1989] *Revue du Marché Commun*, No. 330, p. 453, at 463, who takes the view that "all national legislation of [general interest] such as criminal, tax and social legislation must be complied with by foreign banks, even from other Member States, when they operate by whatever means in the territory of a given country". Clarotti acknowledges that, on the other hand, the case-law of the Court "gives certain guidelines for the application of these rules of [general interest]" (our translation). However, in our submission, these guidelines are the precise reason not all national laws of general interest are in the "general good" within the meaning of the Directive. In order to be such, the provisions of national law in question must in addition meet the criteria laid down by the Court of Justice. See also Vasseur, "Les problèmes juridiques de l'Europe financière", *Revue Banque* (France), September 1988 (Supplément Banque et Droit), at 40.

52. Eg, case 205/84 *Commission* v. *Germany* [1986] ECR 3755.

examine whether any national rules restricting the freedom of banking services are compatible with these strict conditions.

Role reserved to the national courts and to the Court of Justice

4.40 Article 21(6) of the Directive expressly provides for a right of appeal in the host Member State against:

any measure . . . involving penalties or restrictions on the exercise of the freedom to provide services

which right would, it is submitted, also extend to restrictions on the freedom of establishment under the Directive.[53]

The existence of such a right of appeal will enable the undertaking concerned to request that the local court to which the right of appeal lies make a reference to the Court of Justice under article 177 of the Treaty for a preliminary ruling in order to establish whether or not the restrictions invoked by the host Member State are justified in the interest of the general good within the meaning of the Directive.

4.41 In the light of the case-law of the Court of Justice, and in particular its 1986 decisions concerning the freedom of establishment and the freedom to provide services of insurance companies, it is likely that the Court will interpret the expression "general good" in a far more restrictive manner than that suggested by the ESC.

In particular, it is submitted that the Court of Justice would in general hold that the following types of measures fall outside the category of justified restrictions:

— Consumer protection provisions imposed on an undertaking operating through the provision of cross-border services which do not take account of comparable and possibly stricter provisions to which the undertaking is subject in its home country.[54]

— Consumer protection provisions invoked against undertakings operating through the provision of cross-border services in respect of services provided to industrial or commercial undertakings or, perhaps, to individuals acting in a professional capacity.

— Measures which restrict the ability of foreign based banks to advertise their services, or the more competitive terms upon which those services are offered, on the market of another Member State. In this regard, the judgment of the Court of Justice in case 362/88 *GB-INNO-BM* v. *Confédération du Commerce Luxembourgeois*[55] is of importance. There, the Court ruled that national legislation which prohibited the inclusion, in advertisements relating to a

53. Art. 21(6) refers to any measures adopted pursuant to paras. 3, 4 and 5 of the same art. Para. 3 refers in turn to the situation where the "foreign" credit institution concerned "fails to take the necessary steps" to comply with the instructions issued by the competent authorities of the host Member State when they ascertain "that an institution *having a branch* or providing services within [the] territory [of the host Member State] is not complying with the legal provisions adopted in that State pursuant to the provisions of the Directive involving powers of the host Member State's competent authorities (*cf.* art. 21(2)—emphasis added).

54. The case may also arise where the consumer-oriented legislation makes it (potentially) impossible to provide certain banking services on a cross-border basis, see the Commission's answer of 21 February 1992 to Written Question no. 3037/91 of 13 January 1992 by MEP G. de Vries, relating to the Dutch law on the registration of personal data which empowers the authorities to prohibit the exportation of personal data (OJ C141/35 of 3 June 1992).

55. Case C–362/88 [1990] ECR 667. This principle has since been reaffirmed by the Court in case C–126/91 *Yves Rocher GmbH*, judgment of 18 May 1993, not yet reported.

special purchase offer, of a statement showing the duration of the offer or the previous price, and which was likely to prevent individuals from shopping in another Member State, could not be justified under Community law. In the Community law on consumer protection, consumer information is one of the main requirements and consequently national legislation which denies consumers access to certain information cannot be justified by mandatory requirements based on consumer protection. In the light of this ruling, it seems likely that the proviso to article 21(11) of the Second Banking Directive, whereby "nothing in this Article shall prevent credit institutions with head offices in other Member States from advertising their services through all available means of communication in the host Member State, *subject to any rules governing the form and the content of such advertising adopted in the interest of the general good*"[56] will be restrictively interpreted.[57]

— Measures which, in relation to the giving of credit or the making of loans, make it compulsory to charge a minimum interest rate. These measures are usually justified by the supervisory authorities as ensuring the solvency of the financial institutions concerned. As already seen, the Second Banking Directive gives such responsibility exclusively to the authorities of the home country.

— Measures which, in relation to deposits, impose a maximum rate of interest. These measures cannot be justified on the ground of consumer protection. Also, it follows from the Court's case-law that the concept of the general good does not permit a Member State to justify, under article 36 of the Treaty, restrictions designed to protect the national currency.[58] In such circumstances, the Member State's proper course of action is to follow the procedures laid down elsewhere in the Treaty concerning the taking of co-ordinated Community action in the event of monetary difficulties.[59]

Scope and limits of the obligation of the competent authorities of the host Member State to indicate to the foreign bank the national provisions existing in the interest of the general good

4.42 The uncertainty left by the Second Banking Directive as to the precise definition of the general good and, in consequence, as to the limits of the mutual recognition of financial techniques may in part be reduced by the provisions of article 19(4) of the Directive, whereby:

Before the branch of a credit institution commences its activities [in another Member State], the competent authorities of the host Member State shall, within two months of receiving [from the

---

56. Emphasis added.

57. On the other hand, a Member State may validly continue to invoke national rules which prevent certain selling methods, such as the door-to-door selling of financial products: see case 382/87 *Buet* [1989] ECR 1203, where the Court upheld a French provision which prohibited the door-to-door sale of foreign language books in France. The prohibition would have to apply in a non-discriminatory manner. It would appear to be difficult to justify in the interest of the general good national rules which, eg, prohibit the door-to-door selling of securities except for the sale of bonds issued by the Member State concerned, without also giving the benefit of this exception to bonds issued by other Member States (at least under a system of fixed exchange rates). Note in this regard that, under the Investment Services Directive, "the door-to-door selling of transferable securities . . . should remain a matter for national provisions" (recital 8).

58. See case 95/81 *Commission* v. *Italy* [1982] ECR 2187.

59. The compatibility with EC law of measures imposing a *maximum* rate of interest in relation to bank deposits is considered further in Part Five below.

competent authorities of the home Member State notice of such intention] . . . if necessary indicate the conditions under which, in the interest of the general good, those activities must be carried on in the host Member State.

According to Advocate General Van Gerven:

if one reads this article together with article 21(5), whereby the host Member State is allowed to take measures to prevent or sanction conduct contrary to national provisions adopted in the interest of the general good, it may be asked to what extent a host Member State may still intervene in relation to a credit institution whose branch has infringed the provisions in question but which has not been previously notified of them by the competent authorities of the [host] Member State.[60]

In other words, the host Member State, upon receipt of the notice of the home Member State's authorities referred to in article 19(4), could be precluded from relying upon its national provisions, even if these are properly justified on the ground of the general good, where the branch concerned has not been notified of those provisions in accordance with the requirements of the Directive. Against this, Advocate General Van Gerven has pointed out that such an interpretation would have serious consequences in that it would mean that imperative provisions of national law could be disregarded in the absence of a formal notification.[61]

4.43 Indeed, it is submitted that such an interpretation of the notification procedure provided for by article 19(4) would not be correct, for the following reasons.

First, it would run counter to the very reasoning which underlies the fact that the Directive does not allow the host Member State automatically to invoke national measures allegedly justified as in the interest of the general good. As Clarotti observes, the Commission refused to define the national measures which were so justified, and the Council finally agreed with the Commission's approach, for two basic reasons:

. . . on the one hand, because it would have been inappropriate to attempt to delimit a concept created by the case-law of the Court; on the other hand, because it would in any event have been too difficult and would have run the risk of not taking every possible circumstance into account. There is therefore some discretion given to the authorities of the host country . . . subject to review by the Court . . .[62]

Second, it would create an inconsistency between the position of banks operating through a branch and those operating through the provision of cross-border services. This is because the obligation imposed on the authorities of the host Member State by article 19(4) only applies where the foreign bank intends to open a branch.

Third, it would create an inconsistency between banks which were already carrying on their activities through a branch in another Member State at the date of entry into force of the Directive and those which opened a branch after 1 January 1993. The notification obligation does not apply to banks which were carrying on business through a branch in another Member State at that date. Article 23 provides that such branches "shall be presumed to have been subject to the procedure laid down in Article 19(1) to 19(5)". This means that the authorities of the home Member State do not have to give notice in respect of those branches to the authorities of the host Member State, which is the starting point of the two-month period which the authorities of the host Member

---

60. "La Deuxième Directive Bancaire et la Jurisprudence de la Cour de Justice" (1991) *Revue de la Banque* (Belgium), 39, at 46. Our translation.

61. *Ibid.*

62. "La Deuxième Directive de Coordination en matière d'établissements de crédit" [1989] *Revue du Marché Commun* 453, at 462.

State have within which to notify the foreign bank of the local provisions applicable to the branch and justified in the interest of the general good.

Fourth, it would result in the authorities of the host Member State being required to notify the branch of the foreign bank of local provisions applicable to it which are enacted after the date on which it opens for business.

4.44 On the other hand, Advocate General Van Gerven is undoubtedly correct in saying that, independently of the question whether the notification obligation imposed by article 19(4) is properly to be interpreted in the wide sense indicated above, those provisions appear to be particularly effective from the viewpoint of a single internal market, for several reasons:

In the first place, . . . they imply a saving of [energy] for credit institutions in so far as they will no longer have to engage in research themselves in legal systems with which they are unfamiliar to identify the provisions which their branches will have to comply with in carrying out their respective activities.

. . .

They also imply, in the event of any dispute, that the onus of proving that the application of the contested provisions is justified in the interest of the general good rests on the competent authority of the host Member State.

. . .

Finally, and above all, the nature of the procedure provided for by article 19(4) is such as to start a dynamic process of harmonisation of the various national laws in question. The competent authorities may be expected to draw up one or more lists of the national laws justified in the interest of the general good which lists will serve as models for the individual notifications which will be required to be given to the credit institutions wishing to set up a branch. It is also probable that the Commission will take steps to coordinate efforts amongst the competent authorities in order to clarify and harmonise the criteria for the determination of what constitute provisions justified by the general good. In this way, a harmonised concept of the general good will be defined by speedier and more effective means than could be achieved by the Court of Justice through infringement proceedings or preliminary rulings.[63]

Measures specific to the activities listed in the Annex[64] with which the authorities of the host Member State may require compliance and which do not require to be justified as being in the general good

4.45 As will be seen,[65] the principle of home country control enshrined in article 13 of the Directive is subject to various exceptions, albeit of a (presumably) temporary nature.

By article 14(2):

host Member States shall retain responsibility, in cooperation with the competent authorities of

---

63. Our translation. So far as the first reason given by the A.G. is concerned, the authorities of the host Member State are not of course required to notify the branch of all legislation with which it must comply but only those provisions which are considered to be in the general good and which are designed to regulate access to and the exercise of the specific activities of credit institutions, such as those in the agreed list in the Annex to the Directive. So far as the third reason is concerned, the experience of the first few months since the entry into force of the Directive suggests that the A.G. may have been over-optimistic. The lists of national laws justified in the interests of the general good drawn up by the authorities of the host Member States are usually so all-embracing as to be meaningless. This makes the second reason (onus of proof) all the more important in practice. See also C. Cruickshank and W. M. Harris-Burland, "Framework Commentary: Banking", in "Banking and Financial Services", *Butterworths European Law Service* (1992), p. L.2 XII: ". . . the existence of such a list implies that, in the event of disputes, the onus will be on the host Member State to establish that the contested provision is in fact justified by the general good."

64. See the comment in fn. 63, above.

65. Part Two, below.

the home Member State, for the supervision of the liquidity of the branches of credit institutions pending further coordination. Without prejudice to the measures necessary for the reinforcement of the European Monetary System, host Member States shall retain complete responsibility for the measures resulting from the implementation of their monetary policies. Such measures may not provide for the discriminatory or restrictive treatment based on the fact that a credit institution is authorised in another Member State.

Also, the host Member States' authorities retain, under article 14(3), shared responsibility for the supervision of the risks arising out of open positions on the financial markets; and, under article 21(1), the right to require information from local branches "for statistical purposes".

It follows that, in those areas which remain within their jurisdiction, the competent authorities of the host Member State may require banks of other Member States operating in its territory, whether through branches or the provision of cross-border services, to comply with national laws specific to the activities of credit institutions listed in the Annex without having to justify them as being in the general good. But it is essential that the measures in question fall within the very limited areas reserved by article 14 to the authorities of the host Member State and that they do not lead to discriminatory or restrictive treatment of the foreign banks.

Difficulties of categorisation

4.46 In order to determine whether the authorities of the host Member State may, in accordance with the Directive, require compliance by the foreign bank with a particular national measure, it is necessary to determine whether the measure is justified by the general good; or else results from the implementation of monetary policy; or else relates to the liquidity of the branch on its territory.

However, it is not always easy to distinguish between measures designed to ensure bank solvency from those designed to regulate monetary policy. In France, for example, it is understood that national law prohibits banks from paying interest on current accounts. The question arises whether a United Kingdom bank operating under the Directive through a branch in France and not subject to any such prohibition at home could pay interest on the current accounts held at its French branch. If the French measure is regarded, as a matter of Community law (and so subject to review by the Court of Justice), as a measure designed to ensure the solvency of French credit institutions, the answer to the question would be yes. The authorities of the host Member State, in this case France, would not have jurisdiction over the branch of the foreign bank in such matters. If, on the other hand, the French measure is regarded, as a matter of Community law, as a measure resulting from French monetary policy, the answer would be no, because the authorities of the host Member State retain exclusive responsibility in that field and hence have jurisdiction in that field not only over locally incorporated (French) banks but also over French branches of foreign credit institutions. The categorisation, for the purposes of Community law, of national laws or government-supported agreements on interest rates is considered in more detail in Part Five.

It may also be difficult to distinguish between measures designed to ensure bank solvency and consumer protection measures. In some Member States, for example Italy, it seems that banks are prohibited from extending mortgage credit for more than a defined percentage of the value of the property in question. In others, for example the United Kingdom, no such restriction exists. The question arises whether a United

Kingdom bank operating under the Directive through a branch in Italy could extend mortgage credit of up to 100% of the value of a property in Italy to a customer of the branch. The answer depends on whether Community law would consider the Italian measure to be a means of ensuring the solvency of Italian banks, by preventing the granting of insufficiently guaranteed credit, in which case it cannot be imposed on the Italian branch of the United Kingdom bank; or else a means to protect borrowers from falling into excessive debt or a means of limiting, for monetary reasons, the volume of mortgage credit extended, in which case it must be complied with by the Italian branch of the United Kingdom bank.

CHAPTER 5

FREEDOM OF ESTABLISHMENT UNDER THE SECOND BANKING DIRECTIVE: SPECIFIC ISSUES

1. NOTIFICATION PROCEDURE—COMPATIBILITY WITH THE EC TREATY

5.1 As already stated, the Directive provides for a notification procedure whereby a bank intending to open a branch in another Member State must give notice thereof to its home authorities, which must then notify the authorities of the host Member State.

This notification procedure has been viewed in some quarters with reserve, at least from the viewpoint of principle, with regard to its compatibility with the unconditional character of the freedom of establishment. Smits observes that the Commission "has not dared to go to the full length of its self-proclaimed ideal of a single Community banking licence" in that:

the setting up of branches will still be subject to a system of prior notification to the home- and host-State supervisors. This seems to be a bureaucratic obstacle which we could easily do without.

Yet it is a great step forward from the present situation. It is significant from a legal point of view that the new system, though not impeccable, and perhaps even contrary to article 8a,[1] is an improvement over the Treaty system as it has been applied thus far: . . . if there is to be an area without internal frontiers, any distinction between setting up a branch inside or outside the Member State of incorporation should disappear . . .[2]

2. LIMITS IMPOSED BY THE HOME MEMBER STATE ON THE FREEDOM OF ESTABLISHMENT THROUGH THE SETTING UP OF BRANCHES

5.2 In *Commission* v. *France* (tax credits for insurance companies),[3] the Court recalled that the freedom of establishment might be exercised either through the setting up of subsidiaries or by the setting up of branches in another Member State. However, the single licence created by the Second Banking Directive is only valid when the freedom of establishment is exercised through the setting up of branches. Indeed, if a bank in one Member State exercises its freedom of establishment in another Member State through the setting up of a local subsidiary, that subsidiary will, in all respects, be supervised by the authorities of the host Member State. This being so, the Directive

---

1. Art. 8a provides that "The Community shall adopt measures with the aim of progressively establishing the internal market over a period expiring on 31 December 1992 . . . The internal market shall comprise an area without internal frontiers in which the free movement of goods, persons, services and capital is ensured in accordance with the provisions of this Treaty."

2. "Banking Regulation in an European Perspective", (1989/1) *Legal Issues of European Integration*, 61, at 70 and fn. 37 thereto; also R. Smits, *Establishment and Services, Banking and EC Law*, p. 65, *et seq.*

3. Case 270/83 [1986] ECR 273.

favours, in that perspective, establishment through branches and so influences the choice of the legal form of establishment which must normally be able to made freely by credit institutions. According to Advocate General Van Gerven, the scope of the Directive is thereby considerably reduced, taking into account the fact that implantations of credit institutions through subsidiaries are much more numerous than through branches.[4]

However, it is suggested that this pessimism is unfounded. The reinforcement of the requirement of banks to possess adequate own funds, together with the suppression by the Second Banking Directive of the requirement that branches (but not subsidiaries) be endowed with their own funds will lead credit institutions in time to prefer the extension of their operations in the Community through branches rather than subsidiaries and may even lead them to make branches out of their existing subsidiaries. This said, however, Advocate General Van Gerven's comments are, from the viewpoint of principle, fully justified.

3. "REGULATORY ARBITRAGE"

5.3 Recital 8 to the Directive provides that:

The principles of mutual recognition and of home Member State control require the competent authorities of each Member State not to grant authorization or to withdraw it where factors such as the activities programme, the geographical distribution or the activities actually carried on making it quite clear that a credit institution has opted for the legal system of one Member State for the purpose of evading the stricter standards in force in another Member State in which it intends to carry on or carries on the greater part of its activities; whereas, for the purposes of this Directive, a credit institution shall be deemed to be situated in the Member State in which it has its registered office; whereas the Member States must require that the head office be situated in the same Member State as the registered office.

This concern to prevent regulatory arbitrage, both in terms of supervisory standards and in terms of permitted activities and financial techniques, is reflected to some limited degree in article 7 of the Directive, under which there must be prior consultation with the competent authorities of the other Member State involved on the authorisation of a credit institution which is:

— a subsidiary of a credit institution authorised in another Member State; or
— a subsidiary of the parent undertaking of a credit institution authorised in another Member State; or
— controlled by the same persons, whether natural or legal, as control a credit institution authorised in another Member State.

5.4 It is clear that the scope of the provisions of article 7 is potentially very wide. Their compatibility with the provisions of the Treaty dealing with the freedom of establishment, in particular articles 52 and 58, is open to question. It might also be claimed that they effectively represent a retreat from the logic of the very principles of

---

4. "La deuxième directive bancaire et la jurisprudence de la Cour de Justice," (1991) *Revue de la Banque* (Belgium), 39, at 42. As rightly pointed out by Sir Leon Brittan, however, the extension of the "single licence" concept to locally incorporated subsidiaries would, in the present state of (incomplete) harmonisation of Community law, encounter "very serious and perhaps insurmountable difficulties": "Internal market for financial institutions: Legal implications for their secondary establishment", *Butterworths Journal of International Banking and Financial Law* (1993), 3 at 5.

mutual recognition and home country control relied upon by the Council in recital 8 to justify the measures envisaged by that recital. On closer examination, however, the implications of the inclusion of those provisions are less dramatic.

In the final analysis, it seems highly unlikely that such a refusal will be made, except in BCCI-like circumstances, since it is for the home Member State to take any decision concerning the refusal of authorisation, albeit with some provision for co-operation with the authorities of the other Member State. This is on the basis that it may be contrary to such a Member State's own interests to refuse such a request for authorisation. The shift towards placing responsibility on the home Member State's deposit guarantee system for deposits taken in other Member States through branches or the provision of cross-border services can be expected to lead to a more critical appraisal by the home Member State of where its own interests lie when considering whether to authorise a credit institution, a large part of whose activities is directed at one or more other Member States. Such a situation is almost inevitable in the case of a credit institution whose home Member State represents, for geographical reasons, a small domestic market: in order for the credit institution to be viable, the domestic market must necessarily be complemented by the provision of services directed at other Member States, without any "regulatory arbitrage" being involved.

The essentially protectionist rationale for the inclusion of recital 8 is in any event contradicted by article 21(11) of the Directive according to which duly authorised banks with head offices in other Member States *must* be allowed to advertise freely and by whatever means in the host Member State, subject to the host Member State's rules governing advertising based upon the general good.

CHAPTER 6

FREEDOM TO PROVIDE SERVICES UNDER THE SECOND BANKING DIRECTIVE: SPECIFIC ISSUES

1. NOTIFICATION PROCEDURE—COMPATIBILITY WITH THE EC TREATY

6.1 Here, too, a notification procedure is provided for under article 20 of the Directive, albeit a less complex one than that provided for in the case of the freedom of establishment. The technical details of the procedure are considered below.[1]

This procedure, viewed from the point of principle, must be viewed with even greater reserve than that applicable to the freedom of establishment. As Smits has commented, with some justification[2]:

This system . . . represents a step backwards from the present situation. Nowadays, lots of banks provide cross-border services which are included in their reporting to the home Member State's supervisors, without separate notifications flying around Europe. Prior notification of the planned exercise of a right deriving from the Treaty would seem to be inconsistent with the Treaty. Moreover, [one] can see no benefit ensuing from the notifications required from thousands of banks. . . . Such notification is contrary to fundamental EEC law and only amounts to a lot of futile paperwork. We should cut the red tape and save the trees.

It is submitted that the ulterior motive for this paradoxical re-regulation of the provision of cross-border banking services, both at the retail and wholesale levels, concomitantly with the coming into force of the Single Market, is first and foremost the wish to monitor, for tax purposes, the movement of funds throughout the Community which involve a resident of a Member State. A similar trend has accompanied the

---

1. See Part Two below.
2. "Banking Regulation in an European Perspective", 1989/1, *Legal Issues of European Integration*, at 72; also R. Smits, *Establishment and Services, Banking and EC Law*, p. 65 *et seq.* It must be borne in mind that, even though banks which were already providing cross-border services at the time the Directive came into force are not required to comply with the notification procedure, they may, in practice, experience difficulties in case of disputes to prove that they were indeed providing cross-border services in a particular Member State prior to 1 January 1993. *Quaere* also whether the test of proportionality should not be applied to the sanctions that a Member State may apply when the notification procedure has not been properly observed. In particular, it is submitted that it would be disproportionate to allow the borrower or guarantor to plead in such circumstances that the contract is void, see *EC Times* (Brussels) 5 July 1993, p. 3 "Notification requirements of S.B.D. remain unclear". In an attempt to minimise these uncertainties, it has recently been suggested that the notification procedure provided for by the Directive does not apply if the credit institution is not actively present on the territory of the host Member State where it is providing cross-border services (an "active" presence being taken to mean, for example, a mailing campaign directed at potential customers in the host Member State or visits by delegates of the credit institutions). A paradoxical result of this distinction, if accepted, is that a credit institution which restricts itself to the "passive" provision of cross-border services will be subject to fewer restrictions, that is, it will enjoy a *fuller* passport under the Treaty than the passport given to the same institutions pursuant to the Second Banking Directive when it provides services on a cross-border basis in a more active way.

liberalisation of life assurance services in the Community pursuant to the Second and Third Life Insurance Directives.

2. SIMULTANEOUS EXERCISE OF THE FREEDOM TO PROVIDE SERVICES AND THE FREEDOM OF ESTABLISHMENT—IS "CUMULATION" PROHIBITED?

6.2 The theory of prohibition of "cumulation" may be summarised as follows: an economic operator has the choice between two different ways of operating in another Member State—either by establishing a branch there or by providing cross-border services from the head office—but it would not be able to operate by means of simultaneously exercising the two freedoms.[3]

Many large banks having their head offices in one Member State are already present in one or more other Member States and are operating there through branches. If the theory of prohibition of cumulation as outlined above were to be applied, a bank having its head office in Member State A and a branch already set up in Member State B would be unable to provide its services in Member State B, whether from its head office or from a branch in Member State C. Such an approach would impose a tremendous restraint on the new possibilities opened up by the Second Banking Directive: it is precisely by taking advantage of the differences between the services provided in the home Member State and those offered by local banks in the host Member State that the provision of services in the banking sector throughout the Community may expand.

6.3 It is submitted, contrary to the views expressed by some writers,[4] that the Court of Justice's decision in the *German Insurance* case[5] has by no means legitimated the theory of prohibition of cumulation and a leading Commission official has, for his part, firmly opposed it:

There exist two different freedoms [freedom of establishment and freedom to provide services] and therefore any economic operator may benefit therefrom, *even simultaneously*, on the condition that it does not use the one (provision of services) to evade the regulations relating to the other (the right of establishment).[6]

Also, article 23 of the Second Banking Directive expressly says that article 20 (which provides that a bank of one Member State must notify its intention to provide cross-border services to the authorities of the home Member State, which must in turn inform the authorities of the host Member State):

shall not affect rights acquired by credit institutions providing services before the entry into force of the provisions adopted in implementation of this Directive.

6.4 It is submitted that one of the reasons for the inclusion of these provisions was to dispel any suggestion that, as a result of the coming into force of the Directive, banks could no longer combine, as often done in the past, the exercise of the freedom of

---

3. See P. Clarotti, *Revue Banque* (France), September 1988 Supplément Banque et Droit, p. 140.

4. In particular J. Biancarelli, "1992: Quel droit bancaire," *Revue Banque* (France), September 1988 (Supplement), *Banque et Droit*, p. 78. See also Van Gerven A.G. in "La Deuxième Directive Bancaire et la Jurisprudence de la Cour de Justice," (1991) *Revue de la Banque* (Belgium), 39, at 42, who considers, however, that the rule allegedly laid down by the Court was formulated in terms "whose generality is surprising" (our translation).

5. Case 205/84 *Commission* v. *Germany* [1986] ECR 3755.

6. P. Clarotti, *Revue Banque* (France), (1988) (Supplément Banque et Droit), p. 140 (our emphasis; our translation).

establishment in one Member State by the opening of a local branch with the exercise of the freedom to provide services in that same Member State, either from their home base or from a branch in another Member State. Therefore, it is submitted that a different view must be taken from Advocate General Van Gerven's opinion that a credit institution established in one Member State may only combine the exercise of the freedom of establishment and the freedom to provide services in another Member State insofar as the activities carried out through the branch and those carried out through the provision of cross-border services differ.

In support of his opinion, the Advocate General emphasises the importance for him of the notification procedure by the authorities of the home Member State to the authorities of the host Member State for activities which the bank intends to pursue in the host Member State, whether through a branch or the provision of cross-border services, from which "emerges clearly the importance of indicating from the outset which activities are intended to be carried out through the provision of cross-border services and which through a branch"[7]. In practice, such an approach would amount to a ban on the freedom of establishment and the freedom to provide services being exercised together in relation to the same activity, even where it cannot be shown that the undertaking concerned has used one or the other of those avenues in order to avoid the application to it of the laws of the State of establishment. There may be many reasons, relating for example to the bank's commercial organisation, its internal structure or its product range, why a bank may decide to offer its services for the same activity in a given Member State sometimes through a branch which it operates in the host Member State and sometimes from its head office or a branch in another Member State. For example, it would not be unusual for United Kingdom expatriates in, say, Brussels, to continue to do some business with their United Kingdom branch of a United Kingdom bank or with the expatriates' department of the bank's head office even though they might also do business with the bank's Brussels branch.

Finally, such an approach would also reflect the very restrictions in the area of "cumulation" previously in force in the insurance sector under the regime of the Second Life Directive and Second Non-life Directive which have now been abolished as from 1 July 1994 as a result of the Third Life[8] and Non-Life Insurance Directives.[9]

---

7. See the article by Advocate General Van Gerven referred to in fn. 4. (our translation).
8. Directive 92/96/EEC of 10 November 1992.
9. Directive 92/49/EEC of 18 June 1992.

CHAPTER 7

PROVISION OF INVESTMENT SERVICES BY CREDIT INSTITUTIONS UNDER THE INVESTMENT SERVICES DIRECTIVE[1]

1. GENERAL REMARKS

7.1 The list of activities contained in the Annex to the Second Banking Directive encompasses a broad range of financial services, including dealing in shares and debentures, advice on takeovers, portfolio management and custodian services, in addition to the core banking activities of deposit-taking and the provision of credit. The list reflects the "universal bank model" which is usually followed in continental Europe, where both core banking activities and other financial services are provided by a single corporate entity.

As a result, under the Second Banking Directive a continental "universal bank" is able to carry out commercial banking *and* investment banking activities throughout the Community within a single corporate structure and subject to a single regime of financial regulation applied by the supervisory authorities of its home Member State. In contrast, most of the large United Kingdom deposit-taking institutions, such as the main clearing banks, carry out their securities activities through separate subsidiaries, which are subject to the supervision of the securities industry regulators and not the banking supervisors.[2] These investment services subsidiaries will normally fall outside the scope of the Second Banking Directive. Therefore, the danger exists that universal banks could benefit from the single passport created by that Directive by, for example, providing a wide range of financial services in the United Kingdom whereas the investment services subsidiaries of a United Kingdom bank could not do the same elsewhere in the EC.

Conversely, in relation to funding requirements, the tightening up of the capital requirements imposed on credit institutions by the Solvency Ratio Directive gave rise to concern on the part of continental "universal banks" that they might end up in a less favourable position than United Kingdom investment services subsidiaries which, not being credit institutions, are not subject to the capital requirements laid down for credit institutions by that Directive.

7.2 The Investment Services Directive and the Capital Adequacy Directive[3] were proposed in order to meet these concerns. Their combined purpose is to create a

---

1. Council Directive 93/22/EEC of 10 May 1993 on investment services in the securities field, OJ L141/27 of 11 June 1993.
2. See Stanislas M. Yassukovitch, "The European financial services identity after 1992—Regulation and the competitive challenge", (1989) *Butterworths Journal of International Banking and Financial Law*, p. 201; also Richard Novirnsky and Robin Brooks, "Financial services must take account of new European rules", *FT Business law supplement*, p. 9 at p. 12, April 1990.
3. Council Directive 93/6/EEC of 15 March 1993 on the capital adequacy of investment firms and credit institutions, OJ L141/1 of 11 June 1993.

separate but equal single licence for the non-bank securities firms while ensuring that they do not have a competitive advantage in terms of funding requirements *vis-à-vis* credit institutions when such institutions are providing investment services.

It was for this reason that it was initially envisaged that the Investment Services Directive and the Capital Adequacy Directive would come into force on 1 January 1993, being the date of entry into force of the Second Banking Directive and the date by which credit institutions are required under article 10(1) of the Solvency Ratio Directive "permanently to maintain" an 8% ratio.

These concerns also explain why the Investment Services Directive is modelled as closely as possible on the Second Banking Directive and why only certain provisions of the Investment Services Directive and of the Capital Adequacy Directive are applicable to credit institutions when they provide investment services.

7.3 However, the timeframe originally intended has not been fulfilled. Indeed, the Investment Services Directive and the Capital Adequacy Directive were only adopted in mid-1993, and will only come into force on 1 January 1996, a full three years after the entry into force of the Second Banking Directive.

This situation is bound to create legal uncertainties and distortions of competition between, on the one hand, universal banks whose authorisation under the First and Second Banking Directives includes one or more investment services and, on the other hand, United Kingdom-type investment services companies providing investment services only.

The review of these difficulties, however foreseeable, and of the provisions of the Investment Services Directive and of the Capital Adequacy Directive which do not specifically concern credit institutions fall outside the scope of this book.

7.4 The limited examination which follows is itself necessarily subject to the very considerable uncertainties which still surround the way in which many of the—arcane—provisions of the Investment Services Directive will be interpreted by the Commission and implemented by the Member States.

Only certain provisions of the Investment Services Directive apply to credit institutions when providing one or more of the "investment services" listed in Section A of the Annex to that Directive.[4]

The substance of these provisions in terms of the supervision and funding requirements of credit institutions when providing investment services is considered separately in Part Two. It is only intended here to draw attention to the way in which the Investment Services Directive brings about for credit institutions, when providing investment services, several important exceptions, sometimes of doubtful validity, to the basic Treaty principles which underlie the single licence created by the Second Banking Directive.

---

4. Paradoxically, Section A of the Annex includes in such "investment services" the case where an institution—whether a credit institution or an investment services firm—deals "for its own account" in securities. This definition seems hard to reconcile with the definition of the provision of a service under the Treaty, which does not include services provided to oneself: see art. 60. For further consideration of this issue, as well as the distortions of competition which may continue to exist between credit institutions (of the "universal" type) and investment services firms see M. Dassesse, A. Ewing and E. Marx "The EC Investment Services Directive", *Butterworths European Law Services*.

2. RESPECTIVE JURISDICTION OF THE HOME MEMBER STATE AND THE HOST MEMBER STATE IN RESPECT OF CONSUMER CONDUCT OF BUSINESS RULES AND OF PRUDENTIAL RULES

7.5 The principle of home country control under the Investment Services Directive has suffered very significant erosion during the protracted revisions of the Commission's initial proposal.

This is best illustrated by article 11. Under article 11(1):

Member States shall draw up [consumer protection] rules of conduct which investment firms shall observe at all times.

and the provision goes on to list the objectives of such rules. However, article 11(2) provides that:

without prejudice to any decisions to be taken in the context of harmonisation of the rules of conduct, their implementation and the supervision of compliance with them shall remain the responsibility of the Member State in which a service is provided.

The blurring of the respective jurisdictions of the home country and the host country is further shown by article 10. Whereas article 10, first paragraph, provides that:

Each home Member State shall draw up prudential rules which investment firms shall observe at all times ... [which] rules shall require [in particular] that an investment firm ... be structured and organised in such a way as to minimize the risk of clients' interests being prejudiced by conflicts of interest between the firm and its clients or between one of its clients and another,

the last sentence of the same article provides that:

nevertheless, where a branch is set up the organisational arrangements may not conflict with the rules of conduct laid down by the host Member State to cover conflicts of interest.

7.6 As in other fields covered by the Investment Services Directive, investment firms, and credit institutions when providing investment services, may well end up facing the problem of having to abide by two—sometimes conflicting—sets of rules, one imposed by the home Member State which has authorised the firm, and the other imposed by the authorities of the host Member State where the service is provided. Sometimes, a third set of requirements, namely those imposed by the home Member State of the market on which a securities transaction is carried out, may also have to be complied with.

The magnitude of the difficulties potentially created by these provisions will be fully appreciated when it is borne in mind that an investment firm will end up providing a service in another Member State even when it provides a service from its home base to a client resident in another Member State, at the latter's initiative. Even though in such a case the investment firm has taken no initiative whatsoever to provide a service in another Member State, it risks being subject to two conflicting sets of rules, namely those of the Member State where it is established and those of the Member State where the client is habitually resident. It is submitted that the end result of such a situation—at least for retail operations—is likely to be one of two things: either the rules of the Member State of residence of the client (that is, the host Member State) will be ignored or the institution will refuse to do business with the client. This latter result is, to say the least, paradoxical in view of the purpose of the Investment Services Directive.

3. JURISDICTION OF THE HOST MEMBER STATE IN TERMS OF MEMBERSHIP OF A COMPENSATION SCHEME

7.7 Another significant exception to the principle of home country control is brought about—hopefully for a short time only—by article 12. Pursuant to that provision:

> Before doing business with them, a firm shall inform investors which compensation fund or equivalent protection will apply in respect of the transactions envisaged, what cover is offered by whichever system applies, or if there is no fund or compensation.

> The Council notes the Commission's statement to the effect that it will submit proposals on the harmonization of compensation systems covering transactions by investment firms by 31 July 1993 at the latest. The Council will act on those proposals within the shortest possible time with the aim of bringing the systems proposed into effect on the same date as this Directive.

Also, in terms of recital 38 of the Directive:

> ... until the date on which [a unified compensation system] is brought into effect, host Member States will be able to impose application of their compensation systems on investment firms, including credit institutions, authorized by other Member States when the other Member States have no compensation systems or where their systems do not offer equivalent levels of protection.

Pursuant to article 2, article 12 is of application to credit institutions when providing "investment services" as defined by the Investment Services Directive.

However, it is to be anticipated that article 12 is only meant to apply to credit institutions in respect of their "securities obligations" (that is, accounting for securities held or received for the account of their customers in connection with the provision of investment services) and not in respect of their "monetary obligations" (that is, accounting for the proceeds of the sale of securities or for monies received with a view to acquiring securities) as the latter come within the ambit of the Second Banking Directive and the proposed directive on deposit guarantees.[5]

4. THE ISSUE OF CONCENTRATION

7.8 One of the most controversial provisions of the Investment Services Directive is undoubtedly article 14(3) and (4), which concerns the issue of concentration. This is the right for the Member State of the investor's residence to insist that a securities transaction be executed on a regulated market, which in practice is likely to be the local regulated market, when the securities concerned are traded on a regulated market in that Member State, subject to the right of the investor:

> not to comply with [this] obligation and have the transactions ... carried out away from a regulated market. Member States may make the exercise of this right subject to express authorization, taking into account investors' differing needs for protection and in particular the ability of professional and institutional investors to act in their own best interests. It must in any case be possible for such authorization to be given in conditions that do not jeopardize the prompt execution of investors' orders.[6]

In order to secure a compromise between the Member States which opposed concentration and the Member States supporting it (the so-called Club Med countries),

---

5. As will be seen in Part Two, under the proposed directive on deposit guarantees, the host Member State must give to the local branch of a bank based in another Member State the option to join the local deposit guarantee scheme, but cannot require it to do so.

6. Art. 14(4).

article 14(3) provides that a Member State may only insist on concentration, without prejudice to the above waiver, if each of three conditions are met, namely:

— the investor must be habitually resident or established in that Member State;
— the investment firm must carry out the transaction either through a main establishment, through a branch situated in that Member State or under the terms of the freedom to provide services in that Member State;
— the transaction must involve an instrument dealt in on a regulated market in that Member State.

However, of those three conditions two are in Community law terms identical. Where an investment firm in Member State A provides an investment service, whether solicited or unsolicited, to an investor resident in Member State B, that firm will always be acting "under the terms of the freedom to provide services in that [latter] Member State."

No doubt to allay the fears of some Member States that some of the Club Med countries might impose conditions on the right of waiver which would in effect make the provision of investment services on a cross-border basis impracticable, a recital has been added to the preamble, as follows:

Whereas a Member State may not limit the right of investors habitually resident or established in that Member State to avail themselves of any investment service provided by an investment firm situated outside that Member State and acting outwith that Member State.

In practice, the right of Member States to insist on "concentration" may well turn out to have little substance if SEAQ International is designated by the United Kingdom authorities as a "regulated market" which, in turn, assumes that the rules governing SEAQ International can be demonstrated to comply, or can be amended so as to comply, with the requirements for a "regulated market" under article 1(13) of the Investment Services Directive.

5. THE ISSUE OF DIRECT BANK ACCESS TO STOCK EXCHANGES

7.9 Another contentious issue addressed by the Investment Services Directive is whether a Member State may refuse direct access by a bank of another Member State to its stock market, at least when it imposes similar restrictions on its "own" banks. This issue is all the more important when it is borne in mind that, at the same time, a Member State may, pursuant to the provisions on concentration, insist (without prejudice to the right of waiver of the investor) that a transaction carried out by an investment firm established in another Member State in securities traded on a regulated market of the Member State of the investor, be executed on a regulated market which, in practice, is likely to be the regulated market of the Member State of the investor.

Here too, a compromise solution was reached. Pursuant to article 15(3):

... those Member States which, when this Directive is adopted, apply laws which do not permit credit institutions to become members of or have access to a regulated market, unless they have specialised subsidiaries, may continue until 31 December 1996 to apply the same obligation in a non-discriminatory way to credit institutions from other Member States for purposes of access to those regulated markets.

[Spain, Greece and Portugal] may extend this period until 31 December 1999. One year before that date, the Commission shall draw up a report ... The Council may, acting by a qualified majority ..., decide to review those arrangements.

7.10 It will, however, be recalled that the freedom of establishment and the freedom to provide services flow directly from the Treaty itself and are not created at the discretion of the Council by the adoption of directives. Directives are there only to facilitate the exercise of those freedoms, not to restrict it. Therefore, whatever the merits of the political compromise reflected by article 15(3), the justification—and possibly the validity in terms of EC law—of the restrictions which it allows Member States to continue to impose for several years in terms of direct bank access to stock exchanges[7] is questionable. Nowhere in the Investment Services Directive is any justification to be found, whether in terms of investor protection or "coherence" of the local stock exchanges.[8] Similarly, no justification is offered as to why restrictions on direct bank access—which must be assumed to be objectively justified until 1997[9]—will suddenly cease to be so justified after that date, unless revived by the Council acting by a qualified majority on a proposal from the Commission.

7. A necessary condition to allow banks to provide some of the services which they are authorised to provide Community-wide under the Second Banking Directive, especially when the same Member State insists on execution of securities transactions on the local regulated markets.

8. To make a parallel with the language of case 204/90 *Bachmann* v. *Belgium* [1992] ECR 249, considered below.

9. In the case of Greece, Spain and Portugal, 1999.

PART TWO

THE SUPERVISION OF CREDIT INSTITUTIONS UNDER EUROPEAN COMMUNITY LAW

CHAPTER 8

INTRODUCTION

8.1 This Part considers the structure of the supervision of credit institutions in the EC with particular reference to consolidated supervision; the minimum standards of prudential supervision set by the Second Banking Directive; capital adequacy; and large exposures. However, before embarking on this analysis it is appropriate, briefly, to consider the context in which the supervision rules are to be implemented, and the approach which has been taken to date to establish minimum supervisory standards.

1. THE BANKING AND FINANCIAL SERVICES MARKET

8.2 The supervisory rules presently being proposed and implemented by the EC, although of particular import within the Community itself, are being negotiated and enforced not merely from the perspective of the establishment within the EC of a single market in banking and financial services, but also with the international nature of the present-day banking industry very much in mind. It would not be an over-statement to say that the banking and financial services industries throughout the world have been revolutionised in the past 30 years. The traditional banking business of relationship-oriented domestic lending to maturity which prevailed before the 1960s has been replaced by the truly international capital markets of the 1990s in which a borrower of sufficient standing can arrange its funding through any number of banks or securities houses established in any number of countries in any combination of currencies through a variety of different financial instruments which combine to produce a financial package which meets as precisely as possible the borrower's individual funding requirements. The regulatory consequences of the internationalisation and deregulation of the banking and financial services industry are both obvious and awesome. This book is concerned principally with the supervision of deposit-taking institutions, although it will be obvious to all who practise in the financial sector that the boundary between banking, in the sense of deposit-taking, and securities business is becoming less and less distinct and, particularly in the EC, there is considerable overlap between the two industries.

Fundamental principles of banking supervision: analysing risks

8.3 The fundamental principle lying at the core of banking supervision is the protection of depositors' cash and, therefore, the maintenance of confidence in the banking industry so as to ensure a continuing flow of investment from investors to end-users requiring capital to finance their business. The importance of ensuring the integrity and efficiency of bank supervisors in a capitalist society is manifest. The financial environment today is, however, so complex, and the means of distributing capital so numerous and varied, that the task of analysing the risks undertaken by banks and establishing rules to retain the risks within prudent bounds has become increasingly difficult. The internationalisation of the banking industry, together with the change in the nature of the business carried out by banks, now means that it is impossible for a bank supervisory authority to supervise adequately the activities of a bank incorporated in its jurisdiction unless it can obtain free and extensive access to information regarding the credit institution's activities in other jurisdictions. In order to access this information, close co-operation between national supervisory authorities is imperative. The risks which a credit institution incurs in its daily business depend not only on the domestic economic environment of its place of incorporation but also on the political, economic and legal risks and consequences which doing business in other countries and other currencies entails. As evidenced by the recent collapse of the Bank of Credit and Commerce International ("BCCI") the difficulty of achieving adequate prudential supervision is compounded by the setting up of subsidiaries (or, in some cases, branches) in other jurisdictions which, without the adoption of an internationally co-ordinated approach to consolidated supervision and an orderly division of supervisory responsibilities which leaves no gaps, could result in large areas of potential risk being insufficiently supervised. This difficulty is compounded if the independent legal status accorded to foreign subsidiaries is allowed to prevail over the economic consequences of moral pressure felt by the parent companies as well as more tangible economic risks inherent in investment in a subsidiary.

Questions for national regulators

8.4 The global nature of the business of banking gives rise to difficult questions to be faced by the national regulators: should their supervision apply to foreign banks operating in their country but not to the foreign branches of domestic banks (the "national treatment" principle), or should it extend to the foreign branches of the domestic banks incorporated in the same country as the regulator (the "home country principle")? To what extent should national regulators be responsible for the supervision of foreign subsidiaries of domestic banks? To what extent should national regulators be obliged to protect the investments of depositors who have placed funds with foreign branches or subsidiaries of domestic institutions and, equally, should they assume responsibility to those depositors who have invested in domestic branches and subsidiaries of foreign institutions? This last question, of course, queries how far the role of the national supervisor as lender of last resort should be extended. Prudential supervision these days requires far more than a knowledge of the domestic economy and domestic financial markets: it requires an ability to analyse and legislate for risks incurred in disparate and diverse markets throughout the world (which implies that supervisory authorities must be capable of obtaining accurate and plentiful information regarding all activities in which banks are engaged worldwide) and an ability to negotiate a common approach with other national supervisors so as to ensure equal supervisory treatment in increasingly competitive international and domestic markets, and the protection of depositors in an increasingly integrated banking environment.

Deregulation

8.5 In tandem with the effect of globalisation, the emphasis of the banking industry in recent years, starting with the partial deregulation of the banking industry in the United States of America in the 1970s, has been on deregulation, so permitting institutions whose business has traditionally concerned the taking of deposits and lending on the strength of the deposit base to expand into more esoteric and sophisticated forms of financing and funding such as the selling and underwriting of equities and securities. The best and most dramatic example of deregulation in the financial markets is, perhaps, the so-called "Big Bang" in the London markets in October 1986. As a consequence of the deregulation of the financial services in the United Kingdom, banks were able for the first time to take equity stakes in, and indeed buy outright, the business of financial intermediaries, for example, stockbroking firms, and to trade in the equities and securities markets on their own account. The risks inherent in this type of business are, of course, rather different from those inherent in a traditional banking business, not least because they are market driven: counterparty failure, traditionally the yardstick whereby banking risk is measured, is a far less accurate means of assessing the risk of taking positions in the equity markets or underwriting securities. There are, therefore considerable dangers attached to a decision by a bank to engage in securities and other non-banking financial business.

Differences in types of risk

8.6 A failure by a bank to comprehend the differences between the types of risk associated with traditional banking business on the one hand and securities trading and underwriting on the other can obviously result in serious trading losses and loss of investment. Equally, a failure by bank national supervisors to regulate these activities in a manner which reflects an understanding of the different businesses and markets, yet which ensures that all such activities are carried out in a prudent manner, may result in severe and unwarranted disruption to the whole financial sector.

2. THE APPROACH TAKEN TO ESTABLISHMENT OF MINIMUM SUPERVISORY STANDARDS

8.7 The desire to establish minimum supervisory standards and competitive equality insofar as regulatory requirements were concerned has been approached by two supra-national bodies, namely the Commission and the Committee on Banking Regulations and Supervisory Practices, set up under the auspices of the Bank for International Settlement in Basle, Switzerland (hence its common appellation the "Basle Committee") and it is the work of both bodies that has shaped the supervisory regime which will apply within the single market in the Community, in the field of banking and financial services.

In keeping with the overall objectives of the Treaty, in particular the concepts of freedom of establishment and freedom to provide services, the Commission has been concerned to create an environment in which all banking institutions within the EC, whether involved in domestic lending or in the international financial markets, should be able to offer their services throughout the Community on the same, or a similar, supervisory foundation. As already indicated in Part One, to create such an environment without ceding all supervisory powers to a supra-national regulator requires either a harmonisation of the supervisory rules of each Member State, or minimum harmonisation of essential authorisation and supervisory standards such as capital adequacy, coupled with recognition by each Member State of the adequacy of the rules of other Member States insofar as the authorisation and supervision of banking institutions are concerned. The former approach would, if achieved in its entirety, eliminate the possibility of regulatory arbitrage[1] and so create the "level playing field" required to ensure that competition between banks incorporated in different Member States is carried out on a common foundation. The latter approach does not entirely eliminate the possibility of different national rules continuing to apply to banking supervision and, accordingly, the potential for distorting competition remains, albeit in a diluted form. This approach is, however, more astute and takes account of the various sensibilities of national regulators.

It has already been seen[2] that, although the Commission initially proposed to create a single market on the first basis mentioned above, the approach eventually adopted was the second basis, namely minimum harmonisation of certain fundamental authorisation and supervisory standards and mutual recognition. Needless to say, whichever approach was adopted, the basic objectives of banking supervision, that is to ensure the financial stability and viability of banks and the protection of consumers (notably depositors), were as much the concern of the policy formulators and regulators as ensuring the free entry into the single market and the removal of anti-competitive barriers, howsoever arising.

CONCLUSION

8.8 Whether or not the new supervisory regime established in the Community will create the stable financial system which its architects envisage remains, of course, to be seen. Consideration is given below to the difficulties and inconsistencies which can already be seen to exist or lie latent in the proposed structure. One serious practical drawback of the proposed regime, however, is its limited application. Only credit institutions incorporated in the EC and, in certain limited circumstances, their financial services subsidiaries, are entitled to benefit from and, perhaps more importantly in this context, will be subject to the burdens of, the "passport" to the European financial sector. Credit institutions incorporated in non-EC countries will not be entitled to establish branches or offer services throughout the EC on the basis of an authorisation given by one Member State, and therefore arguably they are at a competitive disadvantage to EC credit institutions.[3] However, unless minimum capital adequacy standards are applied globally (and, in particular, unless there is not a significant divergence between the capital adequacy requirements of the major non-EC industrial powers such as the USA, Canada, Japan and (perhaps in the fullness of time) the Russian Federation, and those prevailing in the EC), it is quite possible that non-EC credit institutions operating on the basis of local authorisation in one Member State may be in a position to compete on much keener terms than EC credit institutions active

1. The concern to prevent regulatory arbitrage is reflected to a limited degree in article 7 of the Second Banking Directive. For a discussion of regulatory arbitrage generally see paras. 5.3–5.4, above.
2. See Chaps. 3 and 4, above.
3. The position of non-EC banks and their subsidiaries is considered in detail in Part Eight.

in the same Member State. The dynamics of the financial markets may become less, rather than more, stable. The Commission is, of course, aware of this danger and consideration is given below to the adequacy of its response. Equally, the supervisory authorities in the major industrialised countries are alive to the dangers which an unstable financial sector could pose to the world economy and, as noted earlier, have been moving in the past two decades in any event towards a consensus in the approach to banking supervision. The EC solution may offer no real solution, however, to credit institutions incorporated in less scrupulous countries.

CHAPTER 9

THE BASLE COMMITTEE AND THE FIRST BANKING DIRECTIVE

9.1 It became clear by the end of the 1970s that the banking industry in many countries had changed its nature and business so fundamentally during the previous decade, and appeared set on continuing its divergence of activities, that the existing regulatory and supervisory regime of most national regulators was insufficient to cope, both from the perspective of ensuring the continuing stability and viability of the international finance system as a whole, and from the narrower perspective of safeguarding the interests of depositors, and had itself to adapt accordingly. Furthermore, it was evident that diverse national supervisory standards were creating distortions and anti-competitive practices within the international markets. The process of adaptation was to be achieved first by each national bank supervisory authority recognising, evaluating and providing adequate prudential supervision for the new types of business in which those institutions subject to its supervision were engaging, and second, by co-ordinating and consolidating the activities of the various national regulators, and reaching a consensus on minimum standard capital and liquidity requirements for banks which were active in international or cross-border lending.

The desire to establish minimum supervisory standards and competitive equality insofar as regulatory requirements were concerned has been approached, by two supra-national bodies, namely the Commission and Basle Committee and it is the work of both bodies that has shaped the supervisory regime which has applied within the single market throughout the EC in banking and financial services from 1 January 1993.

THE COMMISSION'S APPROACH VERSUS THAT OF THE BASLE COMMITTEE

9.2 The Commission has, of course, been keen to establish a single market throughout the Community in banking and financial services, and, in keeping with the overall objectives of the Treaty, in particular the concepts of freedom of establishment and freedom to provide services, has been concerned to create an environment in which all credit institutions within the EC, whether involved in domestic lending or in the international financial markets, should be able to offer their services throughout the Community on the same, or a similar, supervisory foundation.

9.3 The Basle Committee comprises representatives of the central banks and supervisory authorities of the Group of Ten (G10) countries, namely Belgium, Canada, France, Germany, Italy, Japan, the Netherlands, Sweden, Switzerland, the United Kingdom and the United States, together with Luxembourg. Hence, certain Member States of the EC were already examining the issues of cross-border supervision of banks before the Commission began to consider the issue in detail. There is one major difference between the ideological aims of the Basle Committee and the Commission: the Basle Committee is concerned only with the adequate supervision of banks which are active in the international, cross-border banking markets. The Commission, on the other hand, is concerned with *all* banks in the EC, whether or not they do business internationally. This difference in emphasis accounts for the slight divergence in approach taken by these two bodies on certain supervisory issues.

Initially, there was a sharp contrast between the approach of the Basle Committee and that of the Commission as concerning the issue of achieving international (or, in the case of the Commission, EC-wide) co-ordination between supervisory regimes. The approach of the Basle Committee was manifestly pragmatic in its efforts to establish broad parameters for cross-border supervision which did not limit the powers of the national supervisory bodies, and its recommendations bore all the hallmarks of a political compromise. Not surprisingly, the initial approach of the Commission was founded firmly in the theory of creating a single market in banking and financial services which was to be achieved on the basis of full harmonisation of the laws of each Member State and, as such, was politically naïve and impractical.

CO-OPERATION BETWEEN THE BASLE COMMITTEE AND THE COMMISSION

9.4 From the outset, however, the two bodies worked in tandem, as is evident if one compares the Concordat agreed by the Basle Committee in 1975 (the "1975 Concordat"), together with the Agreement of May 1983 (the "1983 Agreement") which superseded that, with the stated aims of the First Banking Directive.[1] The 1975 Concordat and 1983 Agreement were, it is fair to say, concerned with a much narrower issue than the First Banking Directive, in that they sought only to address the question of cross-border supervision of banking institutions, in particular the division of responsibilities between various national regulators insofar as banks engaged in activities in more than one country were concerned and, latterly, the question of supervision on a consolidated basis. The First Banking Directive, on the other hand, states in its preamble that, *inter alia*, the eventual aim of the EC "is to introduce uniform authorisation requirements throughout the EC for comparable types of credit institutions",[2] and that eventually, after proceeding through the requirements laid down by successive, more specific, directives, "the result of this process should be to provide for overall supervision of a credit institution operating in several Member States by the competent authorities in the Member State where it has its head office, in consultation, as appropriate, with the competent authorities of the other Member States concerned".[3] The intended approach of the EC was, therefore, clear even at this relatively early stage. The preferred method of cross-border supervision was evidently based on the home country principle, as opposed to the national treatment principle. In order to ensure competitive equality and freedom of market access, however, it was envisaged that this principle be brought into effect by harmonising the laws of each Member State.

1. Directive 77/780/EEC: OJ L322/30 of 17 December 1977, see Chap. 3 above.
2. First Banking Directive, 8th recital.
3. *Ibid.*, 3rd recital.

9.5 As indicated in Chapter 3, the operative provisions of the First Banking Directive are minimalist in their terms and seek only to set down a general programme designed to bring about homogeneous standards of regulation. The First Banking Directive envisaged that this would be achieved through a series of specific directives covering, for example, minimum standards for the authorisation of a credit institution to be established in a Member State,[4] and a basis on which minimum capital, liquidity and gearing requirements might be agreed.[5] The First Banking Directive also provided for the co-operation and collaboration of the various national supervisors and regulators in the Community in order to supervise the activities of credit institutions operating in one or more Member States other than that in which their head office is situated.

4. *Ibid.*, art. 3.
5. *Ibid.*, art. 6.

CHAPTER 10

CONSOLIDATED SUPERVISION

INTRODUCTION

10.1 As indicated in the preceding Chapter, the 1975 Concordat sought in broad terms to establish co-operation between the national supervisors of the countries represented on the Basle Committee to enable national regulators to obtain information on the financial status and performance of overseas branches of banks subject to their supervision, and so obtain a clearer picture of the overall soundness of such banks. At the time of its publication, however, some members of the Basle Committee were reluctant to concede the necessity for consolidated supervision, so bringing into account the performance of subsidiaries and other entities in which banks had significant shareholdings or, indeed, entities which held significant shareholdings in banks, and the 1975 Concordat was limited in its practical efficacy: the need for information passing between national supervisors and for the establishment of common supervisory standards was identified: the means of achieving the identified aims were not specified or, indeed, agreed. A sharp recession in many western economies and a secondary banking crisis in the United Kingdom which had a "knock-on" effect in a number of other industrialised countries caused the national regulators represented on the Basle Committee to accept the principle that "banking supervisory authorities cannot be fully satisfied about the soundness of individual banks unless they can examine the totality of each bank's business worldwide through the technique of consolidation".[1] Consolidation is necessary, in the context of prudential supervision, essentially for two reasons. First, because financial difficulties affecting subsidiaries, or other institutions in which banks have made a significant investment, may affect the financial standing and soundness of the parent institution, this factor being frequently termed the "contagion risk". Second, equity investments are generally of a long term nature, and illiquid. Substantial holdings of equities of other institutions, therefore, represent significant amounts of capital which will not generally be available should the parent institution experience liquidity problems.

The Basle Committee Agreement 1983

10.2 The "1983 Agreement" consists of a series of recommendations agreed by the Basle Committee in respect of the responsibilities of national banking supervisors for monitoring the prudential conduct and soundness of the business of banks' foreign establishments. As such, it recommends certain divisions of responsibility between the "host" regulator (that is, the national supervisory body of the country in which the

---

1. See Basle Agreement of May 1983; para. 1.

foreign establishment, branch or subsidiary, is situate) and the "parent" regulator (that is, the national supervisory body of the country in which the relevant bank or bank parent has its head office), and emphasises the need for a continuing dialogue and co-operation between the host and parent regulators. The 1983 Agreement is clear in stating that the concept of consolidated supervision is not intended to inhibit or derogate from the supervisory powers and responsibilities of the host country, although it was recognised that full implementation of the consolidation principle may well lead to the extension of the responsibility of the parental supervisor. This statement represented an acceptance in the long term of the principle of home country control for supervisory requirements, rather than the principle of national treatment, although in a much more diluted form than proposed in the First Banking Directive. It was also stressed that the technique of consolidated supervision is merely one of a number of devices through which supervisory bodies could monitor the risk exposure of parent banking institutions, and should not be applied to the exclusion of unconsolidated supervision of subsidiary undertakings by parent and host regulatory bodies, as appropriate.

The first part of the 1983 Agreement is concerned with establishing the parameters for consolidated supervision, and in so doing engages in a brief analysis of the status in law of branches, subsidiaries and joint ventures (considering, for example, questions such as their independent legal status, or absence of such, and their true place of incorporation). This analysis enables one to identify the areas in which supervision may be lacking. For example, the host country supervisor may consider that the subsidiary of a bank within its jurisdiction is not, according to its national laws, a bank, whereas the parent regulatory authority takes the opposite view. Similar problems may arise if the parent institution is a non-bank holding company, or indeed if there is an intermediary non-bank holding company within a network of banks, or if minority shareholdings exist. The Basle Committee sought to identify all the potential *lacunae* which might exist because of such factors, and to make appropriate recommendations for implementation by its members. The 1983 Agreement then concludes with a discussion of the appropriate division of responsibilities between host and parent supervisory bodies on matters such as the liquidity, solvency and foreign exchange exposure of overseas bank branches and subsidiaries.

THE FIRST CONSOLIDATED SUPERVISION DIRECTIVE

10.3 Within a month of the publication of the 1983 Agreement, the Council Directive on the supervision of credit institutions on a consolidated basis (the "First Consolidated Supervision Directive")[2] was published. The First Consolidated Supervision Directive, like the First Banking Directive, was adopted with the unanimous approval of the Member States in accordance with the provisions of article 57(2) of the Treaty. The draft Directive was first submitted to the Council by the Commission on 28 September 1981 and it was adopted less than two years later, a fact which reflects the preparatory work achieved first by those participants in the 1983 Agreement of the Basle Committee who were also Member States and, looking more

---

2. 83/350/EEC, OJ L193/18 of 18 July 1983.

particularly at the ramifications and intended aims of the Directive within the EC, by the Banking Advisory Committee. Within the EC itself, the danger of *lacunae* in cross-border banking regulation had already been highlighted by the experience of the West German supervisory bodies insofar as the supervision of Luxembourg-incorporated subsidiaries of West German banks was concerned. The necessity for national regulators to liaise with and pass information to each other, regardless of national secrecy laws, was then further emphasised by the Banco Ambrosiano affair (and has since been emphasised even more graphically in the BCCI affair), the impact of which could have been lessened had an effective system of consolidated supervision and access to relevant information across national frontiers existed at the time.

The First Consolidated Supervision Directive follows on from the theme established in the 1983 Agreement and extends it in the context of the political ideal of facilitating freedom of establishment within the EC and creating a single market in banking services throughout the Community. In this context, the single market would be achieved eventually by providing for the overall supervision of a credit institution which was part of a banking group to be carried out by the national supervisory body in the home of the parent credit institution (the "home supervisory authority"), in consultation, where appropriate, with the competent authorities of other Member States (the "host supervisory authorities"). The First Consolidated Supervision Directive was, to this extent, more forthright in its aims of establishing home country control than the 1983 Agreement. Similarly, the consensus of opinion which existed at that time within the EC on the question of the necessity for cross-border consolidated supervision of groups containing credit institutions, being founded on much more focused political aims than existed at the time among the G10 nations, enabled the Council to be more specific than the Basle Committee in identifying which types of banking entities should be subject to consolidated supervision.

Application

10.4 The First Consolidated Supervision Directive applied to all credit institutions, as defined in the First Banking Directive, and also affected financial institutions, defined as undertakings not being credit institutions but whose principal activity is to grant credit facilities (including guarantees), to acquire participations or to make investments.[3] "Participation" is defined in article 1 as the ownership by a credit institution, directly or indirectly, of 25% or more of the capital of another credit or financial institution. In introducing a new category of undertaking, to which consolidated supervision would extend, through the concept of a "financial institution", the draftsmen of the Directive were seeking to avoid those gaps in supervision, also identified by the Basle Committee, which arise when a non-bank company appears within a corporate structure headed by a credit institution. The Directive did not seek to require consolidation in cases of a corporate structure headed by a non-bank holding company. This omission is addressed in the Second Council Directive relating to the Supervision of Credit Institutions on a Consolidated Basis,[4] which now replaces the First Consolidated Supervision Directive.

3. First Consolidated Supervision Directive, art. 1.
4. 92/30/EEC, OJ L110/52 of 29 April 1992.

THE SECOND CONSOLIDATED SUPERVISION DIRECTIVE

10.5 The Second Council Directive relating to the supervision of credit institutions on a consolidated basis (the "Second Consolidated Supervision Directive") was adopted by the Council on 6 April 1992 and repealed the First Consolidated Supervision Directive with effect from 1 January 1993. The political impetus driving the adoption of this legislation was considerably increased in the wake of the collapse of the Bank of Credit and Commerce International SA, a scandal which emphasised the urgent need for a co-ordinated approach to banking supervision in a non-unified market and which highlighted with unwelcome clarity the pitfalls which could befall the single market if a home country supervisor exercises inadequate supervision over the credit institutions subject to its control. The political impact of the BCCI scandal is evidenced by the late introduction of a further preamble to the Second Consolidated Supervision Directive,[5] emphasising that consolidated supervision must protect, in particular, the interests of depositors. No amendment, however, was made to the substantive text of the Directive as a consequence of the BCCI affair although proposals have since been made to extend the ambit of EC banking legislation and the provisions relating to consolidated supervision to address some of the weaknesses exposed by the BCCI affair. The Directive provides that not only EC credit institutions which have participations in other credit or financial institutions are to be compulsorily supervised on a consolidated basis, but also that EC credit institutions which are subsidiaries of "financial holding companies" are also to be supervised on the basis of the consolidated financial situation of their parent.[6] A financial holding company is defined in the Second Consolidated Supervision Directive as a financial institution the subsidiary undertakings of which are either exclusively or mainly credit institutions or financial institutions, one at least of these being a credit institution.[7] The Second Consolidated Supervision Directive also introduces the concept of the "mixed-activity holding company", which is defined in article 1 as "a parent undertaking other than a financial holding company or a credit institution, the subsidiaries of which include at least one credit institution". The definition of "financial institution" contained in the First Consolidated Supervision Directive has been amended to mean an undertaking other than a credit institution whose principle activity is to acquire holdings[8] or to exercise one or more of the operations included in numbers 2 to 12 of the Annex of the Second Banking Directive. The relevant provisions of the Second Banking Directive are considered in more detail

---

5. Second Consolidated Supervision Directive, 11th recital.

6. Second Consolidated Supervision Directive, art. 3(2). Article 3(2) makes clear, however, that the consolidation of the financial holding company shall not in any way imply that supervisory authorities are required to play a supervisory role in relation to the financial holding company.

7. Second Consolidated Supervision Directive, art. 1.

8. The term "holdings" is not defined and is difficult to interpret in the context of this definition of financial institution. The Proposal for the Second Consolidated Supervision Directive contained the following definition of "financial institution": "an undertaking other than a credit institution whose principal activity is to acquire and hold participations or to exercise one or more of the operations included in numbers 2 to 12 of the Second Banking Co-ordination Directive." This definition is rather more comprehensible than the final definition as it does at least provide an indication of what is meant by "holding" by reference to participations—see OJ C315/15 of 14 December 1990. The term "participation" is defined in the Second Consolidated Supervision Directive to mean the ownership, direct or indirect, of 20% or more of the voting rights or capital of an undertaking—see art. 1. This revises the definition of participation found in the First Consolidated Supervision Directive, so making it consistent with art. 33 of the Seventh Council Directive of 13 June 1983 on consolidated accounts (OJ L193 of 18 July 1983) and with art. 42 of Council Directive 86/635/EEC of 8 December 1986 on the annual accounts and consolidated accounts of banks and other financial institutions (OJ L372 of 31 December 1985); *cf.* fn. 18, below.

in Chapter 12. For present purposes, it is sufficient to note that the operations referred to in numbers 2 to 12 of the Annex to the Second Banking Directive include operations commonly carried out by universal banks, including trading in securities and derivatives. The acceptance of deposits is not included in these operations.[9]

General principles

10.6 The general principles of the First Consolidated Supervision Directive are set out in article 3(1) which required, save in the circumstances set out in article 3(2), that any credit institution which had a participation in another credit or financial institution should be subject to supervision on the basis of the consolidation of its financial situation with that of the institution in which it had such participation. Supervision on a consolidated basis was the remit of the national supervisory body of the country in which the credit institution which had the participation had its head office. No attempt was made in the First Consolidated Supervision Directive to establish a common definition for supervision on a consolidated basis; article 3(1) referred merely to the fact that supervision should be carried out according to the national procedures of the national supervisory body of the head office institution. The absence of a common definition of what was meant to be covered by consolidated supervision, and in particular the absence of a consensus on what information was required to effect a form of consolidated supervision which met with prudent supervisory standards, clearly created an opportunity for disagreement and divergence of interpretation between Member States as to how much co-operation and information they could expect to receive from other Member States.

THE PRINCIPAL AREAS OF CONSOLIDATED SUPERVISION

10.7 The principal areas of consolidated supervision identified by the Second Consolidated Supervision Directive are set out in article 3. This article provides that:

(i) every credit institution which has a credit or financial institution as a subsidiary or which holds a participation in such institutions shall be subject to supervision on the basis of its consolidated financial statements. Although the extent of the consolidated supervision is a matter for the determination of the supervisory authority charged with the supervision of the consolidated group, supervision applied to the consolidated group must encompass at least solvency, the adequacy of funds to cover market risks and control of large exposures, together with confirmation of the existence of adequate internal control mechanisms in all institutions included in the scope of the consolidated supervision of a credit institution[10];

(ii) every credit institution the parent company of which is a financial holding company shall be subject to supervision on the basis of the consolidated financial situation of that financial holding company. Again, as a minimum,

---

9. Deposit-taking is the first listed activity in the Annex to the Second Banking Directive, and is the activity which essentially distinguishes credit institutions, or banks, from investment services firms.

10. Art. 3(1), (5) and (6) of the Second Consolidated Supervision Directive. Compliance with the requirements of the Solvency Ratio Directive is required to be supervised and controlled on the basis of the consolidated or sub-consolidated financial situation of each EC credit institution by art. 3(5) of the Second Consolidated Supervision Directive.

the consolidation should extend to solvency, funds for market risk and large exposures, together with an enquiry into the existence of adequate internal control mechanisms in all relevant credit and other institutions.[11] This consolidated supervision shall not, however, imply in any way that the relevant national bank supervisors have a supervisory role in relation to the financial holding company itself. Member States are obliged to adopt any measures necessary, where appropriate, to include financial holding companies in consolidated supervision.

Article 3(3) of the Second Consolidated Supervision Directive provides for Member States to decide, in certain specified cases, that a credit institution, financial institution or auxiliary banking services undertaking (which is not defined) which is a subsidiary or in which a participation is held (presumably of or by a credit institution or a financial institution included in the consolidated supervision of a credit institution) need not be included in the consolidation. The circumstances in which consolidated supervision may be waived are:

(a) bank secrecy laws of, or other legal impediments to the transfer of the necessary information from, a non-EC Member State in which the relevant undertaking is situate. This exemption on its own amply demonstrates the fragility of the system which is being implemented in the EC. The health and stability of the EC financial markets can clearly adversely be affected, particularly in the present-day global financial markets, if non-EC banks operating within the EC fail or if a third country subsidiary or joint venture of an EC credit institution fails. It is almost impossible to determine the viability of a financial institution without complete disclosure of all relevant financial information relating to both holdings held by that institution and any subsidiary companies relative thereto. Reference is made later in this Chapter to the continuing need for banking regulators across the world to agree, for the sake of the health of the international financial system, to transmit between each other the information which they hold on banks subject to their supervision or which are active in their jurisdictions. Within the Community, regulators need to be vigilant to ensure that non-EC banking groups whose financial viability has not been demonstrated clearly to all relevant regulatory authorities do not gain access to the entire EC market and thus increase exponentially the damage which could potentially be caused by the collapse of such a banking group; or

(b) because the undertaking concerned is, in the opinion of the appropriate national supervisor, of only negligible interest with respect to the objective of monitoring credit and in all cases if the balance sheet total of the undertaking that should be included is less than the smaller of (i) 10 million ECU or (ii) 1% of the balance sheet total of the parent undertaking or the undertaking which holds the participation; or

(c) if, in the opinion of the appropriate national supervisor, the consolidation of the financial situation of the undertaking that should be included would be inappropriate or misleading as far as the objective of the supervision of credit institutions is concerned. This final category may, theoretically, impact on the

11. *Ibid.*, art. 3(2) and 3(5) and (6).

overall adequacy of consolidated supervision if different regulatory authorities take different views on where consolidation is appropriate. Until a consensus is reached between all regulators, the possibility of a regulatory gap continues to exist. In addition, it should be remembered that the solvency ratio of a credit institution which is part of a financial services group will be calculated on the basis of its consolidated financial situation. If differing views are held by the various competent authorities within the EC as to when it is appropriate or not misleading to consolidate the accounts of an associate or subsidiary for the purposes of consolidated supervision, not only will potential gaps in supervision arise but credit institutions incorporated in Member States with a more cautious regulatory regime may find themselves at a competitive disadvantage against credit institutions incorporated elsewhere in the EC.[12] It is important, therefore, both from the perspective of protecting depositors throughout the EC and in terms of trading equality, that a consensus is reached as regards the objectives and prudent extent of consolidated supervision.

Parent undertakings

10.8 Where a credit institution is a parent undertaking and, therefore, subject in any event to supervision on a consolidated basis, Member States are given a discretion to waive any requirement for supervision of the institution on a solo basis; equally any subsidiary of a credit institution subject to authorisation and supervision by the same national supervisory authority as its parent undertaking and which is included in the consolidated supervision of the parent credit institution may also, at the discretion of the national supervisory authority, be exempted from solo supervision.[13] Solo supervision is rendered somewhat otiose in these situations as the supervised institutions would only be providing the same or less information as would be required to be provided for the consolidated supervision of the parent undertaking in any event. Equally, where a parent undertaking is a financial holding company which has its head office in the same Member State as the subsidiary credit institution then, provided that it is subject to the same supervision as that exercised over credit institutions, in particular as regard solvency, control of large exposures and adequacy of funds to cover market risks, solo supervision of the credit institution subsidiary may be waived by the national supervisory authority concerned. In fact, it may be the exception rather than the rule that solo supervision will be waived in these circumstances as it is unlikely that, in a number of Member States, a financial holding company would be subject to the

12. As discussed in Chap. 14 below, investments in unconsolidated subsidiaries and associates of credit institutions are required, pursuant to the Own Funds Directive, to be deducted from total capital if the investment concerned exceeds certain thresholds. Thus, there is not an immediately obvious competitive disadvantage to banks which have consolidated financial institution subsidiaries, as deduction from capital may have the same net effect, in capital ratio terms, as consolidation. Whether or not this is the case depends, however, on: first, whether the capital ratio of the consolidated entity equals that of the parent, or is lower, thus resulting in a lower consolidated ratio which might need to be compensated for by the raising of further capital; second, whether the consolidated entity's operations fall within the "trading book" definition contained in the Capital Adequacy Directive (see Chap. 16 below), and third on whether the parent credit institution is situate in a Member State, such as the UK or Ireland, which generally imposes higher capital ratio requirements on credit institutions subject to its consolidated supervision than the minimum 8% capital ratio contained in the Solvency Ratio Directive. In other words, as long as national differences remain in the sphere of the constitution of capital and attribution of capital ratios, competitive tensions will remain in the EC financial sector.

13. Second Consolidated Supervision Directive, art. 3(7).

same supervisory standards as its credit institution subsidiaries. Even though the Capital Adequacy Directive entails the analysis of solvency ratio requirements on a functional rather than an institutional basis, as discussed in Chapter 16 below, initial capital requirements remain higher for credit institutions than for other financial services entities, and the political desire to protect the interests of depositors with credit institutions by the insistence on, for example, higher capital requirements, remains as a prime cause for relatively stricter supervisory standards. In any case where solo supervision is waived, however, the supervisor concerned must ensure that the capital within the banking group is distributed adequately.

Subsidiaries

10.9 Where a credit institution is a subsidiary of another credit institution incorporated in a different Member State, solo supervision of the subsidiary credit institution is, *prima facie*, required of its national supervisory authority.[14] This is consistent with the concept of home country supervisory responsibility as it ensures that the supervisory authority which granted the authorisation for the subsidiary credit institution continues to be primarily responsible for its supervision. Notwithstanding this, consolidated supervision for the banking group headed by the parent credit institution will be the province of the national supervisory authority which authorised the parent.[15] Adequate provision for the passing of information between the two national supervisory authorities must still be made in order to ensure the efficacy of the supervision and regulation over the banking group and, unless and until there is full harmonisation of the supervisory requirements of all Member States in the banking sector, the possibility of a gap in supervision arising from different supervisory treatments in different jurisdictions still remains, although much reduced by the provisions of EC legislation in the banking and financial services sector. It is possible, however, for the national supervisory authority of the subsidiary credit institution to delegate its responsibilities to the national supervisory authority of the parent institution pursuant to a bilateral agreement, provided that the Commission is made aware of these arrangements.[16] The abrogation by a supervisor of its supervisory functions may give some comfort to the authority responsible for consolidated supervision, as (provided that it has the same rights of access to information as it would have had had it been the "home" supervisory authority of the subsidiary institution) a consistent regulatory approach can be adopted throughout the banking group. In order to protect national sovereignty and sensitivities, however, the authority responsible for consolidated supervision cannot impose solo supervision on a credit institution incorporated outside its own jurisdiction but within the Community. It seems unlikely that national supervisory authorities would want, at least in the short term, to cede their authority to a foreign supervisor. Furthermore, supervision by a foreign supervisor is unlikely to be welcomed by the subsidiary credit institution itself, or by the wider investment community, which may have quite legitimate concerns that the foreign supervisor will not understand or make allowances for the business culture, market practices or legal requirements which exist in the subsidiary's place of incorporation. The provisions of article 3(9) are unlikely, therefore, to be used in practice in the

14. *Ibid.*, art. 3(8).
15. *Ibid.*, art. 4(1).
16. *Ibid.*, art. 3(9).

immediate future, but clearly signal the ideal of consistent "one-stop" supervision of banking groups which would be the inevitable result of a fully-integrated internal banking market within the EC, at least insofar as EC banking groups are concerned.

WHICH NATIONAL REGULATOR IS RESPONSIBLE FOR CONSOLIDATED SUPERVISION?

10.10 The division of supervisory responsibilities between the different national supervisory bodies in the various Member States in which credit or financial institutions subject to cross-border consolidation are situate is provided for in article 4 of the Second Consolidated Supervision Directive. The national regulators are referred to throughout the Directive as "competent authorities" and article 4 provides that:

(i) Where the parent undertaking is a credit institution, supervision on a consolidated basis shall be exercised by the competent authorities that gave the parent undertaking its banking licence (that is, the national regulatory authority in the country where the parent undertaking has its head office[17]).

(ii) Where the parent of a credit institution is a financial holding company, supervision on a consolidated basis shall be exercised by the competent authorities which authorised the credit institution. So, for example, if an English bank subsidiary of a German non-bank holding company is authorised to accept deposits by the Bank of England, the Bank of England will be responsible for reviewing the consolidated accounts of the group, including the German parent, and not the national regulator in Germany.

(iii) Where, however, credit institutions authorised in more than one Member State have for their parent the same financial holding company, supervision on a consolidated basis shall be undertaken by the competent authorities of the credit institution authorised in the Member State where the financial holding company has been established. Thus, to adapt the example above, if the German non-bank holding company also had a German bank subsidiary, consolidated supervision of the group would be carried out by the German competent authorities and not the Bank of England.

(iv) If a financial holding company holds participations in a number of credit institutions, but there is no credit institution subsidiary in the Member State where the financial holding company has been set up, the competent authorities of the Member States concerned (including the Member States where the financial holding company has been set up) will seek to reach a common agreement as to which amongst them will exercise supervision on a consolidated basis. In the absence of such agreement, consolidated supervision will be exercised by the competent authorities of the credit institution with the biggest balance sheet; if this is the same for two or more credit institutions, supervision will be undertaken by the competent authority of whichever credit institution was first authorised pursuant to the criteria for

17. In the recitals of the Second Banking Directive, it is stated that a credit institution shall be deemed to be situated in the Member State in which it has its registered office and that the Member States require that the head office be situated in the same Member State as the registered office. This does not address the question which supervisory authority within the EC is the most appropriate "home country" supervisory authority, as the market where most business is transacted may be in yet different Member States.

authorisation specified in the First Banking Directive. To address the apportionment of supervisory responsibilities in this manner may have resolved political sensitivities at the time but appears difficult to justify when considering it in the light of the objectives of consolidated supervision. In particular, for how long do the different supervisors argue amongst themselves before deciding which of them is the most appropriate to undertake the task of carrying out consolidated supervision or before agreeing to revert to the backstop formula provided by the Directive. Even the backstop approach appears quite arbitrary: the fact that an EC-incorporated bank has a larger balance sheet than an affiliated bank incorporated in a different Member State or that it was authorised earlier than an affiliated credit institution does not make the supervisory authority of the first Member State the obvious first choice to carry out consolidated supervision. The first supervisory authority may have a larger deposit base to be concerned about or longer experience in dealing with one particular member of that banking group. It is possible, however, that the business of the affiliated bank may be far more complex and sophisticated than the business of the first bank. This is particularly true in Europe where the sophistication of the financial markets varies enormously between Member States. It would hardly be sensible, for example, to give the Greek supervisory authorities the task of supervising on a consolidated basis a banking group which consisted of a Spanish financial holding company having a Greek bank subsidiary with a large balance sheet engaged in traditional medium and long-term lending and associated simple derivative products such as forex and interest rate swaps, and an English investment bank subsidiary having a smaller consolidated balance sheet, engaging in traditional bank finance but also having a sophisticated derivative products business, securities underwriting and equities trading businesses and a stockbroking subsidiary. The quantities stated on balance sheets are a crude indicator of what is required in terms of prudential supervision and, indeed, misleading if they are to be used as the basis on which to apportion supervisory responsibility. Equally, long familiarity with one institution does not necessarily imply competence to supervise on a consolidated basis that institution and an affiliate engaged in rather more esoteric forms of banking. The EC approach assumes, contrary to the facts, that the financial markets in each Member State are all at the same stage of development and that the financial regulators are all equally capable, sophisticated and *au fait* with the international capital markets and banking environment. In order to safeguard the financial system and save face for the less sophisticated regulators, the approach to consolidated supervision in the Community will need to involve, in the immediate future, a considerable degree of behind-the-scenes assistance from the more sophisticated regulators (or, at least, regulators who have more experience in sophisticated financial products) where the burden of consolidated supervision falls on those supervisors who have less experience of the newer financial products. Indeed, a criticism which can be levelled at the whole of the EC legislation in the financial services sector is its inadequate approach to issues of quality of supervisory standards. It remains an option, of course, for the regulators of subsidiary credit institutions to suspend or withdraw authorisation of the subsidiary if in any way concerned about the viability of the subsidiary, and it is the responsibility of the supervisory of the subsidiary credit institution to pass on all pertinent information to the supervisory authority responsible for consolidated supervision. As will be seen below, the Second Consolidated Supervision Directive does go to some lengths to ensure that the right information of the right quality is passed to supervisory authorities with responsibility for carrying out consolidated supervision. Information in itself has no use, however, unless it can be meaningfully interpreted and analysed.

(v) Where Member States have more than one competent authority responsible for the prudential supervision of credit institutions and financial institutions, Member States are required to take the requisite measures to organise co-ordination between such authorities. So, in the United Kingdom for example, where securities business is regulated under the Financial Services Act 1986, the Bank of England, as lead regulator of all credit institutions subject to its supervision, would need to ensure proper disclosure of information by the Securities and Investment Board or any relevant self-regulatory organisation insofar as the same regulates any aspect of the business of the credit institution concerned or any financial subsidiary of the credit institution concerned.

THE EXTENT OF CONSOLIDATION

10.11 The extent of consolidation is considered in article 5 of the Second Consolidated Supervision Directive, which should be contrasted to article 4 of the First Consolidated Supervision Directive, with the former being both more specific and more extensive.

Article 4 of the First Consolidated Supervision Directive required mandatory consolidation where a credit institution held a participation[18] of more than 50% in another credit institution or financial institution,[19] although it was left to the individual Member State charged with effecting the consolidated supervision to determine whether, in the particular circumstances of the institutions concerned, full or *pro rata* consolidation should be required.[20] In cases where a credit institution held a participation of less than 50% in another credit or financial institution, the First Consolidated Supervision Directive contrasted situations where effective control by the credit institution existed, and those where it did not.[21] It was for the national supervisory body of the country in which the participating credit institution had its head office to decide whether or not effective control existed in any particular situation. If it decided that effective control did exist, then that national supervisory body would determine the appropriate method of consolidation. If of the view that effective control did not exist, the national supervisory body of the participating credit institution might

---

18. Defined in art. 1 of the First Consolidated Supervision Directive as the ownership by a credit institution, directly or indirectly, of 25% or more of the capital of another credit or financial institution: *cf.* fn. 8 above.

19. Defined in art. 1 of the First Consolidated Supervision Directive as an undertaking, not being a credit institution, whose principal activity is to grant credit facilities (including guarantees), to acquire participations or make investments.

20. *Ibid.*, art. 4(1).

21. *Ibid.*, art. 4(2).

nonetheless decide whether and how consolidation was to be effected, but before consolidating it was required to advise the national supervisory bodies otherwise charged with the supervision of the credit or financial institutions in which the participating credit institution had an interest.[22]

Article 5 of the Second Consolidated Supervision Directive provides that, unless proportional consolidation is appropriate competent authorities charged with the exercise of consolidated supervision must require full consolidation of credit institutions and financial institutions which are subsidiaries of the parent undertaking.[23]

Proportional consolidation

10.12 Proportional consolidation of institutions in which a credit or financial institution is a majority shareholder may be permitted in cases where, in the opinion of the competent authorities, the responsibility of the undertaking holding the participation is limited to its share of the capital, because of the liability of other shareholders or members whose solvency is considered satisfactory, and whose commitment and responsibilities to the institution in question are clearly established.[24] This partial exemption is rather curious in that it involves a national supervisory authority having to make a judgement as to the solvency of an undertaking which is not itself (or, at least, is not necessarily) subject to the supervisory authority's jurisdiction. It also takes no account of the very real economic effects on a deposit-taking institution which may result from the failure of institutions in which the deposit-taking institution holds a significant shareholding: to estimate damage in terms of loss only of the value of an equity participation is a little naïve. The consolidated balance sheet of a parent credit institution forms the basis of the calculation of the capital adequacy ratio of the credit institution's group. Equity interests held by credit institutions in unconsolidated associates[25] are required to be deducted from the capital of the credit institution for

22. *Ibid.*, art. 4(3).

23. Defined in art. 1 of the Second Consolidated Supervision Directive as a parent undertaking within the meaning of art. 1(1) of Council Directive 83/349/EEC, OJ L193 of 18 July 1983. For an example of the implementation of the Second Consolidated Supervision Directive, see, for example, the Bank of England's Notice on "the Implementation in the United Kingdom of the Directive on the Consolidated Supervision of Credit Institutions", BSD/1993/1 February 1993. This states that the Bank of England will require consolidation (i) where a credit institution incorporated in the UK is itself the parent of companies which conduct one or more of the activities listed in the Annex to the Notice (essentially, those items listed on the Annex to the Second Banking Co-ordination Directive, other than deposit-taking); and (ii) when the UK credit institution is not a parent company but is part of a group or sub-group whose business wholly or mainly comprises the activities listed in the Annex to the Notice, and the parent of which is a financial institution. To qualify as a financial institution, the exclusive or main business of the parent company must be either to carry out one or more of the activities listed in the Annex, or to acquire holdings in companies undertaking these activities. The Bank of England will interpret the phrases "mainly" and "main business", to mean the balance of business, that is, it will generally require consolidation when companies carrying out the activities listed in the Annex to the Notice comprise the majority (over 50%) of the group or sub-group balance sheet. In determining the balance of business, the Bank of England will additionally take account of off-balance sheet activities of group companies and of fee-based services. Where such a balance of business test proves inconclusive, the Bank will take into consideration the number of subsidiaries which fall into the financial and non-financial categories. As a general rule, the presumption will be in favour of consolidation.

24. Second Consolidated Supervision Directive, art. 5(1). Article 5(1) also provides that the liability of other shareholders and members must be clearly satisfied, if necessary, by means of formal, signed commitments.

25. The failure to consolidate, for supervisory purposes, the accounts of a subsidiary with the accounts of its parent can only be justified if the business of the subsidiary is substantially different from that of its parent and the parent's accounts can, notwithstanding the exclusion still be said to present a true and fair view of the financial condition of the parent.

capital adequacy purposes so as to ensure that multiple use of the same capital is not made through an unconsolidated banking group. This deduction is made in an amount equal to the book value of the equity investment, an approach which can be justified in broad terms in the case of associates whose business is substantially different from that of the credit institution because the likelihood of the credit institution suffering losses other than the value of its investment (that is, suffering further losses by reason of the so-called "contagion risk") is relatively low. The credit institution in this situation is unlikely to have had any managerial involvement in the failed institution and, although the quality of its investment abilities may be doubted, the reputation and integrity of its core business will not necessarily be compromised or tainted. If, on the other hand, a credit institution holds a majority shareholding in another institution, the danger of suffering from the effects of contagion risk will generally be greater and are more likely to cost, in real terms, more than the value of the equity investment. The circumstances in which proportional consolidation, as opposed to full consolidation, may be justified ought, in this context, to be narrowly defined and any assessment of the financial condition of other shareholders carried out on a very conservative basis. The Second Consolidated Supervision Directive does not address how a supervisory authority can satisfy itself as to the viability of other shareholders which are not subject to its supervision and whose financial information may not be capable of independent verification in a satisfactory manner.

Specific cases

10.13 In addition to the cases set out above, the competent authorities responsible for effecting consolidated supervision shall determine whether and how consolidation is to be carried out in the following cases:

   (i) where, in the opinion of the competent authorities, a credit institution exercises a significant influence over one or more credit institutions or financial institutions, but without holding a participation or other capital ties in these institutions. This category expressly acknowledges the dangers to a credit institution of contagion risk but extends it from the situation where a credit institution has a capital investment in the affected institution to the situation in which the credit institution has lent its name to another credit or financial institution and is involved to a material extent in the management and strategy of the other institution. It is difficult to envisage such a situation arising in practice, at least in a deliberate manner, as it implies the involvement of a bank with an unassociated finance company to an extent which is normally considered improper for a credit institution, unless acting in an advisory capacity as, for example, investment banks may act as corporate finance advisers to commercial banks. Revocation of authority, rather than consolidation, ought to be the relevant issue in such circumstances, for both concerned;

  (ii) where two or more credit institutions or financial institutions are placed under single management other than pursuant to a contract or clauses of their constitutory documents; and

 (iii) where two or more credit institutions or financial institutions have administrative, management or supervisory bodies with the same persons constituting a majority.[26]

All three circumstances set out above point to situations in which de facto as opposed to de jure involvement exists between financial services entities, and point to the desire of supervisory bodies to ensure effective supervision of banking entities in the face of devious business practices. The national discretions may, of course, leave open the possibility for national differences in supervisory requirements to develop insofar as consolidated supervision is concerned. The fifth recital to the Second Consolidated Supervision Directive contains a reminder that supervisory authorities are empowered by both the First Banking Co-ordination Directive and the Second Banking Co-ordination Directive to refuse or withdraw banking authorisation in the case of certain group structures considered inappropriate for carrying on banking activities, in particular because such structures could not be supervised effectively.[26a]

SUPERVISION OF MIXED-ACTIVITY HOLDING COMPANIES

10.14 Consolidated supervision of mixed-activity holding companies and their subsidiaries is not required by the Second Consolidated Supervision Directive, although provision is made to require mixed-activity holding companies and their subsidiaries to supply, either directly or through credit institution subsidiaries, any information which would be relevant for the purposes of supervising credit institutions which are subsidiaries of such mixed-activity holding companies.[27] This implies that each Member State must enact legislation empowering not only the competent supervisory authority in its own jurisdiction to require production of information, but also the competent supervisory authorities in other Member States, which amounts to a far greater ability for foreign supervisors to exert authority within the borders of other Member States than previously seen. Curiously, and unlike other similar provisions, national authority, as a first approach, does not appear to have been preserved in this circumstance. Provision is also made for competent authorities to carry out or arrange to have carried out on-the-spot inspections to verify information received from mixed-activity holding companies and their subsidiaries.[28] If the mixed activity holding company or one of its subsidiaries is an insurance undertaking, the procedures specified in article 7(4) of the Second Consolidated Supervision Directive may be employed to gain the information referred to in article 6. If on-the-spot verification of non-insurance mixed-activity holding companies or subsidiaries is required in a Member State other than that in which the supervised credit institution is incorporated, the procedures set down in article 7(7) of the Second Consolidated Supervision Directive must be followed.[29]

---

26. Art. 5(4) of the Second Consolidated Supervision Directive. The Bank of England, for example, will normally require consolidation of companies over which the parent or another group company exercises "dominant influence". In determining whether or not dominant influence exists, the Bank of England will generally make use of the definition provided by the contemporary UK accounting standards (at present, the Accounting Standard Board's Financial Reporting Standard 2 (FRS 2), "Accounting for Subsidiary Undertakings").

26a. First Banking Co-ordination Directive, art. 8(1) and Second Banking Co-ordination Directive, arts. 5 and 11.

27. *Ibid.*, art. 6(1).

28. *Ibid.*, art. 6(2).

29. *Ibid.*, art. 6(2).

ACCESS TO SUPERVISORY INFORMATION

10.15 The free flow of pertinent, reliable and accurate information on the financial activities of a credit institution and its foreign branches and subsidiaries is fundamental to an effective system of consolidated supervision. Access to information assumes an even greater importance in the context of the Single European Market, where banking and financial services can be provided freely across borders and supervision of banking businesses is largely devolved on one supervisory authority only, namely the home supervisory authority of the Member State in which the relevant credit institution is incorporated. The system of supervision and consolidated supervision will work only if barriers to the retrieval of relevant information, for example national banking secrecy laws, are dismantled at least to the extent that will permit access to banking supervisory authorities. Article 7 of the Second Consolidated Supervision Directive contains measures intended to facilitate the transfer of information between the various competent authorities in Member States to ensure that consolidated supervision can be meaningfully achieved, at least within the EC. Such measures include an obligation on Member States to restrict the ambit of national legislation (which would include confidentiality laws) to ensure that information necessary to achieve consolidated supervision can be obtained. This will encompass information regarding any relevant credit institution, financial institution, ancillary banking services undertaking and subsidiaries of mixed-activity holding companies which may be relevant to the supervision of a credit institution subsidiary of the same mixed-activity holding companies.

The requirement on competent authorities to exchange information

10.16 Where a parent undertaking which is itself a credit institution is incorporated in a different Member State from its EC credit institution subsidiary or subsidiaries, the competent authorities in the relevant Member States are obliged to communicate to each other all information which may allow or aid the exercise of supervision of the banking group on a consolidated basis.[30]

As in the First Consolidated Supervision Directive,[31] it is emphasised, presumably to placate national sensitivities, that the collection and possession of information regarding financial institutions, ancillary banking services or mixed-activity holding companies, does not imply that a supervisory function is being exercised over these enterprises by the competent authorities charged with supervising the related credit institutions.[32] The concept of professional secrecy, originally enshrined in the First Banking Directive,[33] also applies to all information passed between competent authorities for the purpose of achieving consolidated supervision.[34] It should be noted, however, that the provisions on the exchange of information contained in article 7 of the Second Consolidated Supervision Directive are expressly limited to transfers of information from one supervisory authority to another (supervisory authorities including, for these purposes, non-bank regulatory organisations such as securities

---

30. *Ibid.*, art. 7(2).
31. See Zavvos, "The Integration of Banking Markets in the EEC—The Second Banking Co-ordination Directive" [1988] 2 JIBL 53.
32. Second Consolidated Supervision Directive, art. 7(3).
33. First Consolidated Supervision Directive, art. 5(2).
34. Second Consolidated Supervision Directive, art. 7(5).

industry and insurance industry regulators). There is no scope provided in the Second Consolidated Supervision Directive for information received by a supervisory authority in its capacity as such to be passed on to another supervisory authority for anything other than supervisory purposes; the provisions do not, for example, sanction the passing on of confidential information acquired in a supervisory capacity to the tax authorities in a different Member State, although if information passed gives rise to concern as to the propriety of a credit institution's *modus operandi*, it may, presumably, be used to form a basis for revocation of authorisation. Even if the impropriety amounts to a criminal act, however, there is no right or obligation, under this piece of EC legislation, to disclose the information to a prosecuting authority.

The requirement for co-operation between authorities

10.17 Where a credit institution, financial holding company or mixed-activity holding company also controls one or more insurance subsidiaries or investment services subsidiaries, the competent authorities of the credit institution and the authorities responsible for the supervision of the insurance and investment services subsidiaries are obliged to co-operate closely and to provide each other with any information likely to simplify their task and to ensure supervision of the activity and overall financial situation of the undertakings they supervise.[35] The extent of the co-operation envisaged is not enlarged upon in the Second Consolidated Supervision Directive. Differences of opinion may still occur between what an authority seeking information deems is pertinent information, and what the authority receiving a request for information deems is pertinent. The convergence between banking and insurance institutions is very much a live issue in the EC and abroad at the present time. There are, however, many difficulties involved in the supervision of bank assurance or "allfinanz" entities, not least because the risks undertaken in the two sectors are fundamentally different, requiring distinct forms of risk analysis for each business which do not relate easily to the other. In the insurance sector there is, further, the distinction between life and non-life assurance, to which equally different rules of risk evaluation and liquidity apply. Simply comparing general banking risks with general insurance risks, however, the divergence in risk analysis is as obvious as it is fundamental: the risk of non-performance of a traditional bank asset such as a loan is easily quantifiable and, indeed, capital standards imposed on banking businesses assume that the asset has a par value to which a risk weighting is ascribed. The assumption, generally, is that the asset will perform and the risk weighting process goes little beyond an analysis, in relatively crude terms, of the creditworthiness of the counterparty from whom performance of the asset is due. By contrast, the assessment of risk in the context of a contract of insurance must be carried out on the basis of the likelihood of the insured event occurring, which will involve a very sophisticated analysis of the factors affecting the particular risk involved, beyond credit analysis to far more esoteric risks.

The requirement to list financial holding companies

10.18 Article 7 of the Second Consolidated Supervision Directive provides further that competent authorities responsible for carrying out consolidated supervision of

---

35. *Ibid.*, art. 7(4). Insurance companies will not normally be included in the consolidated supervision of credit institutions, as the business of insurance companies is fundamentally different from that of financial institutions.

groups containing EC credit institutions must establish lists of financial holding companies of the type referred to in article 3(2) of the Directive (that is, financial holding companies which are parents of credit institutions where the supervision of the credit institution must be carried out on the basis of the consolidated financial condition of the holding company). The lists must be communicated to the other Member States and the Commission.[36] In this way, a central depository of information on the participants in the European financial market can be developed and information concerning financial groups be pooled. The requirement to compile and submit such lists to the Commission amounts to an attempt to fill any gaps in the supervisory process which may arise as a result of the creation of pan-European financial services groups.

Verification procedure

10.19 Where the competent authorities of one Member State wish in specific cases to verify the information concerning a credit institution, a financial holding company, a financial institution, an ancillary banking services undertaking, a mixed-activity holding company, a subsidiary of a mixed-activity holding company other than a credit institution or finance institution, or a non-consolidated subsidiary of a credit institution or a financial holding company, in each case situated in a different Member State from the enquiring competent authority, the enquiring competent authority must ask the local competent authority to have the verification carried out. The local competent authority which receives such a request must, within the framework of its competence, act upon it by carrying out the verification itself, by allowing the enquiring authority to carry it out or by allowing an auditor or expert to carry it out.[37] The provisions of article 6(1) of the Second Consolidated Supervision Directive may be compared with the provisions of article 7(7) just cited above. It appears that by article 6(1) Member States are obliged to implement domestic legislation by which mixed-activity holding companies and their subsidiaries subject to the same jurisdiction can be compelled to provide information requested of them by the bank supervisory authority in that Member State, if the credit institution concerned is incorporated in that Member State, and also by the bank supervisory authorities in other Member States which have the responsibility for supervising the credit institution on a consolidated basis. The language of the Directive is not phrased in terms that, in the latter case, the foreign supervisory authority must make its request for information of the domestic supervisory authority and then wait for the results to come via the conduit so established; rather, it is phrased in terms of providing direct and enforceable access. As against this, however, article 7(7) provides that if the foreign supervisory authority wishes to verify any of the information it has obtained through direct means, it must, in the first instance, apply to the domestic supervisory authority to arrange for this verification to be carried out. It is difficult to understand why, if the domestic supervisory authority is not thought to be necessary to the purpose of obtaining information, it should be necessary to the process of verifying that information, particularly when considered in the light of the fact that the institutions whose information is required to be verified in these circumstances, namely mixed-activity holding companies and their non-bank subsidiaries, are not themselves subject to any bank supervisory regime within their domestic territory.

The obligation contained in article 7(7) is intended to ensure that all relevant

36. *Ibid.*, art. 7(6).
37. *Ibid.*, art. 7(7).

information required for consolidated supervision can be obtained even from recalcitrant local supervisory authorities who, if unwilling themselves to verify information emanating from institutions in their jurisdiction, must at the end of the day permit access to the supervisory authority within the Community which has overall authority for consolidated supervision of an EC banking group. As stated above, it is difficult to see why, if the local supervisory authority has no jurisdiction over entities from whom information is sought by foreign supervisors which do (or ought to) have the legal right to require the production of information, the local supervisory authority should be involved in the verification process.

The provisions relating to the giving of information are then swept up by article 7(8), which requires Member States to ensure, without prejudice to their provisions of criminal law, that penalties or measures aimed at ending observed breaches or the causes of such breaches may be imposed on financial holding companies and mixed-activity holding companies, or their effective managers, that infringe laws, regulations or administrative provisions enacted to implement the Second Consolidated Supervision Directive. In certain cases, such measures may require the intervention of the courts. The competent authorities in each Member State are required to co-operate closely to ensure that the above-mentioned penalties or measures produce the desired results, especially when the central administration or main establishment of a financial holding company or of a mixed-activity holding company is not located at its head office.

CONSOLIDATED SUPERVISION OF NON-EC CREDIT INSTITUTIONS

10.20 Article 8 of the Second Consolidated Supervision Directive concerns the method of ensuring the supervision on a consolidated basis of credit institutions having a head office in a third country and of credit institutions situated in a third country whose parent undertaking, whether a credit institution or a financial holding company, has its head office in the Community. The proposals in this instance expand on those set out in article 6 of the First Consolidated Supervision Directive by widening the net of consolidated supervision to financial holding companies. In the First Consolidated Supervision Directive, consolidated supervision is not limited to participations in EC credit and financial institutions, but an exemption contained in article 3(2) applies to credit or financial institutions located outside the EC where there are legal impediments to the transfer of the necessary information. Article 6 was intended to go some way towards alleviating this problem by providing that each Member State would conclude a bilateral agreement on the basis of reciprocity with the national regulatory body of third countries in which parent undertakings of EC credit institutions are based, or in which credit institutions whose parent undertakings are established in the EC are incorporated.[38] This approach did nothing to eradicate potential differences between the supervisory treatment by third countries of credit institutions established in different Member States. The Second Consolidated Supervision Directive provides for the Commission to negotiate with third countries to establish a procedure for consolidated supervision of banking and financial services groups which comprise both EC and non-EC credit institutions. The Commission may engage in negotiations either

38. First Consolidated Supervision Directive, art. 6(a).

at the request of a Member State or on its own initiative.[39] In this way, it should be possible to agree an EC-wide basis of co-operation on the issue of consolidated supervision with any particular third country and so ensure that some Member States do not receive more favourable treatment than others and that all Member States receive the information necessary for their supervisory bodies to carry out the supervisory responsibilities in a proper manner.

The principle of consolidated supervision was carried a stage further by the implementation of the Council Directive of 8 December 1986 on the annual accounts and consolidated accounts of banks and other financial institutions (the "Bank Accounts Directive").[40] The Bank Accounts Directive brings a degree of harmonisation to the content, format and layout of accounts of credit institutions in different Member States and therefore should significantly aid cross-border supervision.[41]

NON-EC BRANCHES AND SUBSIDIARIES

10.21 The Second Consolidated Supervision Directive applies only to credit institutions, financial institutions, financial holding companies and mixed-activity holding companies incorporated in the EC. No attempt is made through EC legislation to claim extraterritorial effect for its regime. Non-EC branches of EC credit institutions are caught within the EC regulatory system to the extent that they are one and the same legal entity as the head office institution. In addition, local banking supervision rules may apply to local branches of EC banks outside the EC; for example they may be obliged to hold endowment capital, a requirement which can no longer be imposed on branches of EC credit institutions within the EC. Equally, subsidiaries of EC credit institutions incorporated outside the EC will, on ordinary accounting principles, be required to be consolidated with their parent institutions. The difference between such subsidiaries and those incorporated in the EC is that the provision of the information necessary to practise consolidated supervision is not assured through binding legislation and different approaches to bank regulation may result in a shortfall in the supervisory process.

10.22 Branches within the Community of non-EC incorporated credit institutions are subject to whatever local rules the local supervisor wishes to impose although, obviously, the local supervisor will have no obligation to carry out consolidated supervision of the head office of the branch and its subsidiaries.

Subsidiaries incorporated in the Community of non-EC incorporated credit institutions are subject to and (subject to proving that they are "established" in the sense that such term is employed in article 58 of the Treaty of Rome and subject also to any fetters on their activities which may be imposed through the reciprocity provisions contained in article 9 of the Second Banking Directive[42]) benefit from the rules relating to the single banking market. The supervisory authority which authorised its

39. Second Consolidated Supervision Directive, art. 8(1).
40. 86/635/EEC, OJ L372/1 of 31 December 1986: see Chap. 32.
41. The harmonisation achieved by the Bank Accounts Directive covers the layout, terminology and components of the balance sheet and the profit and loss account of credit institutions; the valuation rules; the contents of the notes on the accounts; the provisions related to consolidated accounts; and the rules concerning publication and auditing. The contents of this Directive are discussed in detail in Chap. 32.
42. As to establishment and reciprocity, see Part Eight, below.

establishment will have to satisfy itself as to the quality of information received, if requested, from the parent's supervisory authority but, absent bilateral treaties ensuring the provision of regulatory information between the EC and non-EC supervisory authorities, will generally have little in terms of legal redress if information sought is not provided, other than to revoke the subsidiary's authorisation if the failure to provide information, or the content of the information provided, gives rise to a concern that the interests of depositors with the EC subsidiary may be prejudiced.

CONSOLIDATED SUPERVISION OF MARKET RISKS

10.22.1 Article 9(1) of the Second Consolidated Supervision Directive provides that Member States must implement its provisions before 1 January 1993. Notwithstanding the provisions of article 3(5) of the Directive, which requires consolidated supervision of credit institutions to extend to the supervision of solvency, the adequacy of capital to cover market risks and control of large exposures, article 9(2) of the Directive permits supervisory authorities to extend consolidated supervision to financial institutions principally exposed to market risks in accordance with methods to be determined by those authorities in the light of the particular nature of the risks involved. National treatment of consolidated supervision in these circumstances is sanctioned until the Capital Adequacy Directive is implemented. Until 1996, therefore, disparities are likely to be found among the supervisory standards imposed by the Member States in the sphere of consolidated supervision.[43] For example, in some jurisdictions, offsetting of market positions held in different group companies is permitted, whereas the same practice is prohibited or limited in other jurisdictions. The ability to offset market positions across group companies can reduce overall capital requirements assessed on a consolidated basis. Article 7(10) of the Capital Adequacy Directive provides that, for the purposes of calculating the capital requirements set out in Annex I to that Directive (position risk) and Annex VI (large exposures) on a consolidated basis, national supervisory authorities may permit net positions in the trading book of one institution (that is, a credit institution or a financial institution) to offset positions in the trading

---

43. For example, the Bank of England has stated in its Notice on the implementation of the Second Consolidated Supervision Directive (BSD/1993/1) that it will use an interim system for the consolidated capital adequacy treatment of group undertakings principally exposed to market risk. In the view of the Bank of England, the various capital adequacy regimes applied to companies supervised in connection with the Financial Services Act 1986 provide close approximations to the risk measurement framework that will be introduced for such companies by the Capital Adequacy Directive, and that the Bank of England will accordingly design a series of reports designed to make use of these risk measurement frameworks. The assessment of capital cover will be determined by the supervisory authority responsible for such companies under the Financial Services Act 1986. If the Bank of England is informed of a capital deficiency, it will deduct the deficiency from the group's consolidated capital, in addition to the investment in the group company as shown in the group's statutory accounts. Where the report shows the group company to have adequate capital cover, only the value of the investment will be deducted from the group's consolidated capital. Exposures to group companies which are subject to this treatment will, with the Bank's agreement, attract a zero weighting for the purposes of the calculation of the reporting bank's consolidated capital adequacy. The Own Funds Directive, and the Bank of England's Notice implementing the Own Funds Directive, as amended, require only deductions of investments in *unconsolidated* subsidiaries and associated from Tier 1 and Tier 2 capital (ie, unconsolidated in group accounts, as opposed to for the purposes of consolidated supervision). A UK incorporated bank will, nonetheless, be required to meet the consolidated capital adequacy ratio required of it by the Bank of England pursuant to the Solvency Ratio Directive. Group companies which are principally exposed to market risks but which are not supervised in connection with the Financial Services Act 1986 will be included in the reporting institution's consolidated returns according to the system of risk measurement based on the Solvency Ratio Directive.

book of another institution incorporated in the same Member State according to the rules set out in Annex I and Annex VI respectively. In addition, supervisory authorities may allow foreign-exchange positions subject to Annex III of the Capital Adequacy Directive in one institution to offset foreign exchange positions subject to Annex III in another institution in accordance with the rules set out in Annex III. So, for example, a long position in a specific bond held by a credit institution may be offset against a short position in the same bond held in a financial institution subsidiary incorporated in the same EC Member State for the purposes of calculating the consolidated capital requirement for specific risk in respect of that bond.[44] Supervisory authorities may permit offsetting of the trading book and of foreign exchange positions of undertakings located in third countries, subject to the simultaneous fulfilment of the conditions specified in Article 7(11) of the Capital Adequacy Directive. Article 7(11) of the Capital Adequacy Directive specifies the following conditions:

(i) the undertakings in the third countries must have been authorised in such countries and either satisfy the definition of credit institution given in Article 1 of the First Banking Co-ordination Directive, or are recognised third country investment firms;

(ii) such undertakings comply, on a solo basis, with capital adequacy rules equivalent to those laid down in the Capital Adequacy Directive; and

(iii) no regulations exist in the countries in question which might significantly affect the transfer of funds within the group. Such regulations would include exchange control restrictions and other restrictions preventing or inhibiting the repatriation of profits or other transfers of funds.

It would obviously be easier to feel comfort in relying on article 7(11) if international standards could be agreed among bank regulators and regulators of securities houses on the capital adequacy requirements for investment business. Until then, reliance on article 7(11) will be a matter for national discretion and the judgment of each supervisory authority in the Member States.

Offsetting of market positions, large exposures on the trading book and foreign exchange positions may also be permitted, at the discretion of a national supervisory authority, within a group of financial services entities that have all been authorised in the Member State in question, provided that first, there is a satisfactory allocation of capital within the group, and secondly that the regulatory, legal or contractual framework in which the institutions operate is such as to guarantee mutual financial support within the group.[45]

44. Art. 7(7) of the Capital Adequacy Directive permits Member States to waive the application of the capital adequacy requirements of this Directive, on an individual or subconsolidated basis, to an institution which, as a parent undertaking, is subject to supervision on a consolidated basis and to any subsidiary of such an institution which is subject to supervision and authorisation by the same supervisory authority as the parent and is included in the supervision on a consolidated basis of its parent institution. The same right of waiver may be granted where the parent undertaking is a financial holding company, that has its head office in the same Member State as a regulated credit or financial institution, provided that the parent financial holding is subject to the same supervision exercised over credit institutions or investment firms, and in particular the capital adequacy requirements of the Directive. In addition, art. 7(9) of the Capital Adequacy Directive permits supervisory authorities of subsidiary creditor financial institutions to delegate their supervisory function in respect of capital adequacy and large exposures to the supervisory authority of the parent, in accordance with a bilateral agreement. If the waivers contained in art. 7(7) or the delegation of authority contained in art. 7(9) are exercised, the offsetting of positions between the institutions concerned as described in art. 7(10) will not be permitted.

45. Capital Adequacy Directive, art. 7(12).

Lastly, each Member State has a discretion to permit the offsetting of market positions, large exposures on the trading book and foreign exchange positions between institutions within a group that satisfy the two conditions referred to above and any institution included in the same group that has been authorised in another Member State, provided that the latter institution is obliged to fulfil the capital adequacy requirements of articles 4 and 5 of the Capital Adequacy Directive on a solo basis.[46]

Capital for the purposes of determining fulfilment of the capital adequacy requirement on a consolidated basis will be determined in accordance with the Own Funds Directive, subject to recognition of the validity of the specific capital definition contained in Annex V of the Capital Adequacy Directive for the purpose of supporting trading book assets.[47]

THE RESPONSE OF THE BASLE COMMITTEE

10.23 In June 1992 the Basle Committee published a paper setting out four minimum standards (the "Basle Standards") for the supervision of international banking groups and their cross-border establishments. This paper represents the response of the international college of regulators constituting the Basle Committee to, in particular, the collapse of BCCI and the faults in the system of cross-border regulation of international banking groups which were exposed by the BCCI scandal. The intention of the June 1992 paper is to expand the principles of the Basle Concordat and to reduce these enlarged principles to agreed minimum standards that will have rather more force, albeit they will still not be legally binding, than the guidelines contained in the 1983 Agreement. The supervisory authorities represented on the Basle Committee have undertaken to implement in their own jurisdictions the measures necessary to ensure that their own supervisory arrangements will meet the Basle Standards as soon as possible. The Basle Committee itself will monitor its members' experience in implementing the standards with a view to determining what further refinements are needed as part of its on-going efforts to enhance co-operation in the supervision of international banks.

The Basle Committee also reviewed the supplement to the 1983 Agreement published in April 1990 and entitled "Information flows between banking supervisory authorities." This paper provided practical guidance for on-going contact and collaboration among supervisory authorities. The Basle Committee reports, in the June 1992 paper setting out the Basle Standards, that the nature and extent of information-sharing possible among supervisory authorities must continue to be determined largely on a case-by-case basis and cannot, for the present, usefully be expressed in minimum standards. Nevertheless, the Basle Committee believes that supervisory authorities should undertake a positive commitment to co-operate, on a best efforts basis, with supervisory authorities from other countries on all prudential matters pertaining to international banking groups and, in particular, in respect of the investigation of documented allegations of fraud, criminal activity or violations of banking laws. Furthermore, the Basle Committee and its members have undertaken to continue their efforts to reduce impediments to the sharing of information among supervisory authorities.

46. *Ibid.*, art. 7(13).
47. *Ibid.*, art. 7(14) and 7(15).

10.24 In the EC, the provision of information required for effective supervision of EC banking groups is intended to be ensured through mandatory laws enacted pursuant to article 7 of the Second Consolidated Supervision Directive. There is, therefore, an immediate difference, at least in theory, between the standard and quality of consolidated supervision one might expect of banking groups incorporated in the EC and the standard and quality of consolidated supervision which can be exercised in practice outside the EC or over non-EC banking groups. The normative consensus absent within the G10 countries and the extended international banking community is explicitly contained in EC legislation and should, in theory, ensure that national sensitivities and regulatory regimes do not impede the free flow of accurate and sufficient information by which the performance of EC banking groups and, therefore, the health of the EC banking system, can be judged. If one takes a closer look, however, at the actual situation and comparative competence of the supervisory authorities in the EC Member States, one is entitled to be a little sceptical of the efficacy of the Community structure, at least in the short term. It is instructive, in this regard, to compare the requirements of the Basle Standards in terms of consolidated supervision with the intended effect of and the division of supervisory responsibility established by the Second Consolidated Supervision Directive.

The Basle Standards are to be applied by individual supervisory authorities in their assessment of their relations with supervisory authorities in other countries. The paper in which the Basle Standards are set out emphasises, in particular, that a host supervisory authority into whose jurisdiction a bank or banking group is seeking to expand ought to determine, through a deliberate process, whether that bank or banking group's home supervisory authority has the necessary capabilities to meet the Basle Standards. The Basle Standards are as follows:

1. All international banking groups and international banks should be supervised by a home supervisory authority that capably performs consolidated supervision.

    To meet this minimum standard, the host supervisory authority should assure itself that the home supervisory authority: (a) receives consolidated financial and prudential information on the bank or banking group's global operations, has the reliability of this information confirmed to its own satisfaction and assesses the information as it may bear on the safety and soundness of the banking group, (b) has the capability to prevent corporate affiliations or structures that either undermine efforts to maintain consolidated financial information or otherwise hinder effective supervision of the bank or banking group, and (c) has the capability to prevent the bank or banking group from creating foreign banking establishments in particular jurisdictions.

2. The creation of a cross-border banking establishment should receive the prior consent of both the host supervisory authority and the home supervisory authority of the bank and, if different, banking group. In reviewing proposals for inward (in the case of a host supervisory authority) and outward (in the case of a home supervisory authority) expansion, host and home supervisory authorities should, at a minimum, give weight (a) to the strength of the bank's and banking group's capital and (b) the appropriateness of the bank's and banking group's organisation and operating procedures for the effective management of risks, on a local and consolidated basis respectively. In judging

these criteria, a host supervisory authority is cautioned to be particularly concerned with the level of support that the parent is capable of providing to the proposed establishment. The paper also recognises, in its discussion of this minimum standard, the fact that the activities of international banking groups frequently cut across different areas of supervisory competence and may be managed on a basis which makes the allocation of supervisory responsibilities recommended in the 1983 Agreement inappropriate to the particular operations or business of a bank or banking group. If either host or home supervisory authority concludes that the present allocation of supervisory responsibilities is inappropriate to any particular circumstance, it is obliged to initiate consultations with the other supervisory authority so that the two reach an explicit understanding on which of them is in the best position to take primary responsibility either generally or in respect of specific activities. Inaction on the part of either supervisory authority will be taken as an acceptance of the division of responsibilities established in the 1983 Agreement. Thus each supervisory authority is responsible for making a deliberate choice between accepting its responsibilities under the 1983 Agreement or initiating consultations or an alternative allocation of supervisory responsibilities for the case at hand.

3. Supervisory authorities should possess the right to gather information from the cross-border banking establishments of the banks or banking groups for which they are the home supervisory authority.

4. If a host supervisory authority determines that any one of the foregoing minimum standards is not met to its satisfaction, that authority can impose whatever restrictive measures it deems necessary to satisfy its prudential concerns consistently with the aforementioned minimum standards, including the prohibition of the inward expansion into its jurisdiction. The result of this approach is that, if a bank or banking group is not subject to the level of supervision and supervisory co-operation required by the Basle Committee's minimum standards, and the relevant home supervisory authority is not actively working to establish the necessary capabilities, that bank or banking group will only be permitted to expand its operations into jurisdictions whose authorities are adhering to the minimum standards if the host country authority itself accepts the responsibility to supervise the local establishments of the bank or banking groups in a manner consistent with the minimum standards. It is difficult to see how this can be achieved in practice if the failure relates to inadequate access to relevant information: if the host supervisory authority is deprived of access to information regarding the stability or financial condition of the bank or banking group, it is difficult for it to establish a clear picture of the financial health of the institution subject to its solo supervision.

THE RESPONSIBILITIES OF THE HOST SUPERVISOR UNDER THE BASLE STANDARDS

10.25 In the context of the non-EC banking community, the responsibilities of host supervisory authorities, which appeared to be on the wane in the shadow of the ascendency of the home supervisory authority, have been reasserted with unusual vigour. In order to protect depositors within its own jurisdiction, a host supervisory authority adhering to the Basle Standards is now obliged to assess the quality and calibre of the home supervisory authority and, in effect, deny foreign banks access to its market and, hence, the international banking community, if not satisfied as to the quality of supervision practised by the home supervisory authority or by the adequacy and sufficiency of the information received by it with regard to the operations of a foreign banking entity. The home supervisory authority remains principally responsible for the consolidated supervision of the banking group but its activities will, to an extent, be shadowed by the host supervisory authority. Indeed, the host supervisory authority is capable of rendering the question of consolidated supervision completely academic, at least as regards activities in its own jurisdiction, by refusing inward expansion into its territory if it is not satisfied as to the quality of the supervision practised by the home supervisory authority.

10.26 The Basle Standards are, to a large extent, inconsistent with the concept of the single banking market and, in particular, the single banking licence, because of the emphasis in the EC banking legislation on, first, minimum agreed standards of prudential supervision, and secondly, on the power of home supervisory authorities. The emphasis as regards supervisory responsibility in the EC banking regime is clearly placed on the home supervisory authority of a credit institution or, where a credit institution is the subsidiary of another credit institution incorporated in the EC, on the home supervisory authority of the parent credit institution. Once authorisation is obtained from the competent authorities in the Member State where a credit institution has its head office, it may offer the services listed in the Annex to the Second Banking Directive throughout the EC, provided that such activities are covered by the terms of its own authorisation. One of the results of this approach is that a credit institution duly authorised in one Member State (assuming, again, that it is established there within the meaning of article 58 of the Treaty of Rome and is not affected by any reciprocity directions issued by the Commission under article 9 of the Second Banking Directive) may offer services, either directly or through a locally established branch, in host Member States which credit institutions incorporated in the host Member States are not permitted to offer on the terms of their own, local authorisation, and that there is little that the host supervisory authority can do to prevent this. Some safeguards are built in for host Member States; for example, a host supervisory authority may require a credit institution to comply with specific provisions of domestic law with regard to activities *not* listed in the Annex to the Second Banking Co-ordination Directive, provided that these provisions are compatible with EC law and are intended to protect the "general good", and that such activities are not subject to equivalent rules in the jurisdiction of the home supervisory authority. Equally, host supervisory authorities currently retain responsibility for the monitoring of the liquidity of, and compliance with domestic monetary policy by, branches of EC credit institutions in their jurisdiction. The dominant purpose of the EC legislation, however, is to implement articles 52 and 59 of the Treaty of Rome, the freedom to provide services without interference, so far as possible, from arbitrary domestic regulations. The supremacy of the home supervisory authority under EC law is evidenced by the provisions of article 19 of the Second Banking Co-ordination Directive, which governs the establishment by an EC credit institution of branches in other Member States. The lead role in this process is given emphatically to the home supervisory authority: it is to its home supervisory authority that a credit institution notifies its intention to establish a foreign branch within the EC; it is to its home supervisory authority that a credit institution forwards details of the programme of operations for the proposed branch, including the type of business envisaged to be engaged in and the organisation of the branch; it is the home supervisory authority which judges the merits and adequacy of the proposal to establish the foreign branch within the EC.

Limitations on host regulatory authorities' powers

10.27 Apart from with respect to breaches of conditions set locally under the general good exemption, a host regulatory authority is limited in the action which it can take should a local branch of a credit institution incorporated elsewhere in the EC fail to comply with the local supervisory requirements. Although it may request the credit institution to regularise the situation, the sanction for non-compliance lies with the home supervisory authority, which will inform the host supervisory authority of the action which it has taken in respect of the breach but otherwise owes no duties to the host authority. It is only if the breach of local rules is persistent and continuing that a host supervisory authority can take matters into its own hands to prevent or punish further irregularities.

As regards the establishment by an EC credit institution of a subsidiary credit institution in another Member State, safeguards are provided in article 7 of the Second Banking Co-ordination Directive, which requires that the supervisory authorities in the two Member States concerned should consult with each other prior to the authorisation of the subsidiary. Article 7 is silent on what this consultation is intended to cover or achieve, but clearly the need to be assured of the viability of the subsidiary and the ability to practise effective consolidated supervision of the banking group so established will be paramount. It should be remembered that insofar as EC-incorporated credit institutions are concerned, the aim of the EC legislation in this area is to achieve consistent minimum standards for the authorisation and supervision of such credit institutions. Provided that the supervisory authority in the Member State in which it is proposed to establish a subsidiary applies the minimum standards of authorisation to the subsidiary, as it is required to do by EC law, and assuming, again as one ought to be entitled to do as compliance will be required by law, that a procedure exists for the transfer of information to the parent credit institution and its supervisory authority, it appears that there is little to prevent EC credit institutions from establishing subsidiaries across the EC. It is, however, naïve to assume that what one is required to do by law one is actually carried out in practice. Thus although, when considering whether to permit a subsidiary of a credit institution established in another Member State to be incorporated in its own jurisdiction, an EC supervisory authority theoretically has the ability to refuse authorisation, it must take care in so doing that it is not, impliedly, stating that the supervisory authority of the parent institution is not capable of carrying out consolidated supervision (and therefore has not met the mandatory EC minimum supervisory standards). Equally the supervisor of the parent credit institution will have difficulty in arguing, without implying that the other supervisory authority is operating in breach of EC law, that the local subsidiary should not be established either because the local supervisor is not applying the minimum authorisation requirements, that it is not capable of supervising the subsidiary on a solo basis, or that the supervisor of the parent institution believes that it will not receive the information necessary to practise an efficient form of consolidated supervision over parent and subsidiary. As stated earlier, EC law runs the risk of assuming compliance without a proper assessment of the quality of compliance. The ability to practise effective consolidated supervision over EC banking groups is intended to be assured in law for the supervisory authority of the parent credit institution. Whether or not it will be depends ultimately on the manner in which the EC legislative requirements are enacted, not the number of laws that may be enacted in this regard.

THE EC CONSOLIDATED SUPERVISION PROVISIONS AND THE BASLE STANDARDS COMPARED

10.28 Comparing the system of the single banking licence (which, it should be remembered, can extend to fully consolidated financial subsidiaries of credit institutions incorporated in the same jurisdiction as the parent credit institution, by virtue of article 18(2) of the Second Banking Co-ordination Directive) with the Basle Standards, it is immediately apparent that, at least insofar as the establishment of foreign branches of EC credit institutions within the EC is concerned, the two approaches are irreconcilable as, under EC law, the competence of other EC supervisors is assumed on the basis that all Member States are required to adopt minimum standards of supervision. Taking the first-stated minimum standard first, the Basle paper requires a host supervisory authority to evaluate the efficacy and sophistication of the home supervisory authority, its ability to carry out effective consolidated supervision, its ability to prevent banks from creating corporate structures which undermine the efficacy of consolidated supervision and its ability to prevent banks subject to its supervision from creating banking establishments in particular jurisdictions if not satisfied as to its capacity to exercise meaningful consolidated supervision in respect of activities carried on in such jurisdictions. This minimum standard, in particular, sits very uneasily with EC legislation. The concept of mutual recognition of supervisory standards presupposes that the supervisory authorities in each Member State have common, minimum standards with regard to the initial authorisation of credit institutions and, in particular, precludes any Member State from imposing higher supervisory standards on any credit institution incorporated in another Member State or from questioning the capabilities of the supervisory authorities in other Member States. There is nothing explicitly stated in the operative provisions of EC legislation, as opposed to legislative recitals, that, for example, the establishment of corporate structures which occlude the financial operations of banking groups should be declared illegal in the Member States. Combined with this, the Second Consolidated Supervision Directive places a clear obligation on the home supervisory authority to impose adequate consolidated supervision on a banking group the parent credit institution of which is incorporated in its jurisdiction, and attempts to ensure that the information needed to assure adequate supervision is provided by supervisory authorities of subsidiary credit or financial institutions within the EC notwithstanding national frontiers and legislation. Provision is even made in article 3(9) of the Second Consolidated Supervision Directive for the supervisory authority of a credit or financial institution which is the subsidiary of a credit institution incorporated in a different Member State to delegate its responsibilities to the supervisory authority of the parent institution, provided that the Commission is kept informed of the existence and content of any such arrangement. This right to abrogate prudential supervision in favour of a home country authority presents a contrast to the aims of the new Basle paper and can only be justified on the basis that, in the EC, all regulators are assumed to be equally competent and sophisticated and the freeflow of all relevant and pertinent information is assured.

Foreign branches of EC-incorporated credit institutions

10.29 As far as foreign branches within the EC of an EC-incorporated credit institution are concerned, the provisions of article 19 of the Second Banking Co-ordination Directive prevent host country authorities from analysing the competence of other supervisory authorities within the EC and limit the supervisory responsibilities of host supervisors to a few specialist areas. It is possible, however, that the host supervisory authority will have a significant regulatory role to play, for example if the branch wishes to carry out an activity which is not comprised in the Annex to the Second Banking Co-ordination Directive or which is included in the Annex but which is not covered by the home country authorisation. Equally it should be remembered that host supervisory authorities will, at least in the short term, retain primary responsibility for the supervision of the liquidity of branches in their jurisdiction and on exposure to market risks. Both these responsibilities are fundamental to an adequate system of comprehensive supervision. In the case of activities not included in the Annex or covered by its own authorisation, the local branch cannot rely on its home authorisation but will be subject to local rules. The home supervisory authority would want to assure itself in these circumstances as to the quality of host country supervision in respect of this particular activity, the adequacy of the local rules governing the carrying out of this activity and the reliability of the information regarding this activity which is reported back to it. Alternatively, it may wish to prohibit the local branch from carrying out such an activity, but in so doing must take care to ensure that it does not itself overstep its authority and, in particular, infringe the credit institution's rights under EC law generally.

Pure consolidated supervision

10.30 Insofar as pure consolidated supervision is concerned, covering situations where a credit or financial institution incorporated in one Member State is the subsidiary of a credit institution incorporated in a different Member State, the principle of mutual recognition of supervisory standards will equally prohibit the supervisory authority of the subsidiary institution from questioning the capability of the supervisory authority of the parent institution or assuming a greater supervisory role than that devolved upon it by EC legislation. The division of supervisory responsibilities in the context of consolidated supervision within the EC is clearly specified in the Second Consolidated Supervision Directive and it would be extremely difficult, not to say politically mischievous, for one supervisory authority unilaterally to propose a different sharing of supervisory responsibilities if not satisfied as to the competence of a different supervisory authority in a particular case. As discussed earlier in this chapter, however, the division of supervisory functions in the manner specified in the Second Consolidated Supervision Directive may not always result in the most logical or prudent split of such functions.

Cross-border banking establishments

10.31 The second Basle Standard is that the creation of a cross-border banking establishment should receive the prior consent of both the host supervisory authority and the bank's or, if different, banking group's home supervisory authority. It is immediately obvious that, at least insofar as the establishment of foreign branches of an EC credit institution within the EC is concerned, this standard is also inconsistent with EC law pursuant to which, by virtue of article 19 of the Second Banking Directive, a credit institution specifically is *not* obliged to obtain the consent of the host supervisory authority in the Member State in which it intends to establish a branch. A host supervisory authority is not even given the choice to consent or object to the establishment of the branch; the most that it can do is impose conditions on the carrying out of certain operations pursuant to the general good exemption. Use of the general good exemption will, it is presumed, be strictly limited to ensure that national prejudices or sensitivities do not hinder the development of the single market. Insofar as the establishment of subsidiary credit or financial institutions is concerned, again the theory of mutual recognition of supervisory standards ought in practice to preclude any Member State from claiming that the authorisation or supervisory standards of another Member State are inadequate. In any event, responsibility for consolidated supervision is firmly imposed on the supervisory authority of the parent credit institution and the regulator of the subsidiary credit institution, rather than satisfying itself that the parent's supervisory authority has the ability to access the information needed to ensure effective consolidated supervision of the overall banking group, is bound to implement whatever measures are necessary to ensure first that there are no legal impediments to the exchange of information between it and the parent's supervisory authority and secondly that it can communicate all information which may allow or assist in the exercise of consolidated supervision. The ability of the parent's supervisory authority to interpret this information and act appropriately is not considered at all.

The rights to gather information

10.32 The third Basle Standard, namely the right to gather information, is, as stated above, expressly provided for in the Second Consolidated Supervision Directive, but with the emphasis on ensuring the transmission of information upwards to the home supervisory authority rather than upwards and downwards.

The prevention of establishment

10.33 As for the fourth of the Basle Standards, with the exception of the general good exemption, discussed above, this proposal is also contrary to the ideology of the single banking market and the Treaty of Rome. In particular, a host supervisory authority has no jurisdictional basis on which it may prohibit the establishment within its territory of a branch of a credit institution incorporated in another Member State, unless either the credit institution is not "established" in its place of incorporation for the purposes of article 58 of the Treaty of Rome or it is a subsidiary of a non-EC institution against which reciprocal action has been invoked by the Commission pursuant to the Second Banking Co-ordination Directive.

CONCLUSION

10.34 When considering the import of the 1992 Basle paper, a distinction should be drawn between credit institutions incorporated in the EC and those incorporated in third countries. It must also be borne in mind, in particular, that banking supervision in the EC is now based on a legally-binding framework which asserts the supremacy of the home supervisory authority and, through the principle of mutual recognition of minimum standards, significantly reduces the influence of host supervisory authorities. Even as regards dealings with credit institutions from third countries, it should be remembered that the objective of the Commission is to ensure equal treatment abroad for all credit institutions incorporated in the Community. The most efficient way to achieve this is by way of a concerted effort by the Commission to represent all the Member States in seeking to agree provisions relating to minimum standards of supervision and the passing of information between EC and non-EC supervisory authorities, rather than to leave individual Member States to make their own arrangements.[48]

The success of the EC regime will depend, it is submitted, very much on the willingness of the European Court of Justice and the Commission to insist on the less sophisticated regulators within the EC acquiring the skills of their more sophisticated colleagues, and the willingness of the more sophisticated to assist in this process. The proposed regime assumes, rather naïvely, that all regulators are starting from the same point in terms of experience and expertise. It would be incorrect to assume that, just because minimum supervisory standards exist, they will be consistently and diligently applied across the EC. Equally, it is dangerous to assume that the quantity of assets supervised bears a direct correlation to the quality of supervision required. The Community approach has deprived EC bank regulators of the opportunity to second guess or prejudge their counterparts in other Member States, because to permit them so to do would be to deny the fundamental premise of the single banking market and the principles of mutual recognition. If sanctions do not exist in the national arena, however, they must be created at the supranational level, which means either relying on the Court of Justice to insist on compliance by recalcitrant Member States or supervisory authorities, or devolving more power on the Commission or even a supranational regulator to ensure the overall soundness of the EC banking and financial services sector. The question of consolidated supervision of international banking groups, whether within or outwith the EC, is too important to the world's economy to leave to chance. EC credit institutions may, as a consequence of EC law, establish branches in other EC Member States on the basis of their home country authorisation and incorporate subsidiaries in other Member States provided the subsidiary meets EC-wide authorisation standards. In the case of branches, host country authorities are effectively emasculated, notwithstanding quite legitimate concerns which they may have as regards the competence, in practice, of the home supervisory authority.

10.35 It is far more important to the long-term health and efficacy of the EC system of consolidated supervision, however, that international agreement is reached with other major economies, in particular on the practice of consolidated supervision and the division of responsibilities between supervisory authorities. Equally importantly, the provision of relevant and accurate supervisory information must be assured within

48. Second Consolidated Supervision Directive, art. 8.

and outwith the EC. In the case of banks not incorporated in the EC, those supervisory authorities which are members of the Basle Committee will be expected to apply the Basle Standards, so making it more difficult for non-EC banks from jurisdictions in which a relatively lax supervisory regime is in place from expanding into the EC. But what of those EC supervisory authorities who are not members of the Basle Committee? Generally, these are the supervisory authorities in Member States with less sophisticated financial markets. Care will need to be exercised that these Member States do not provide a partially open door to less-well regulated banks from outside the EC. The dangers can be over-emphasised: if banks from non-EC countries wish to establish a presence in the Community and gain the advantage of a single banking licence, they will have to incorporate a subsidiary in the EC and thus comply, through the subsidiary, with the minimum authorisation requirements. The EC supervisory authority must assure itself, however, that it is able to access information regarding the financial condition of the parent institution and the adequacy of the supervision, solo and consolidated, practised by the supervisory authority responsible for the parent institution. Those Member States which are not members of G10 could, if caution is not exercised, become the weak link in the chain intended to ensure the stability of the EC financial markets.

10.36 It is obvious that there are supervisory authorities within the EC which are less sophisticated than others or which do not have the manpower necessary to supervise all the banks which they have authorised, at least on a consolidated basis. Rather than decreasing the regulatory burden on these institutions, however, EC legislation increases the burden where the credit institutions authorised by such supervisory authorities head banking groups and, moreover, renders the other interested supervisory authorities within the EC largely impotent in terms of legal (as opposed to political) redress. This approach patently did not work in the BCCI situation and yet is now embodied within a legislative framework. This suggests that, until the trauma of the creation of the single market has been overcome, there could be many difficult times ahead for depositors with EC credit institutions and their supervisors.

CHAPTER 11

MUTUAL RECOGNITION OF SUPERVISORY STANDARDS UNDER THE SECOND BANKING DIRECTIVE

11.1 As indicated in Chapter 3, the original aim of the Community, as manifested by the preamble to the First Banking Directive, was to establish a single market in banking services throughout the EC by harmonising the national laws of each Member State insofar as they concerned the establishment of credit institutions and the setting of common standards of prudential supervision, notably as regards capital adequacy and solvency, liquidity and gearing ratios. Directives such as the First Consolidated Supervision Directive[1] and the Bank Accounts Directive[2] were individual examples of attempts to achieve a certain degree of minimum harmonisation of national supervisory regimes. It soon became apparent, however, that the harmonisation approach belied a political naïvety on the part of the Commission and did not cater for the widely different bases of supervision used by the various national regulators, each of which was partial to and jealous of its own supervisory regime.

THE FINANCIAL INTEGRATION WHITE PAPER

11.2 In April 1983, the Commission published a White Paper on financial integration within the Community, calling for more work on the part of Member States to achieve a better allocation of savings and investment in the EC. This paper was followed by the White Paper presented by the Commission at the Meeting of the Council of Ministers in Milan in 1985. The second White Paper proposed the completion of the internal market throughout the EC by the end of 1992, and for the removal within the same time period of all fiscal, technical and physical barriers to free competition within the internal market. The premise of the White Paper was that the aim of achieving full harmonisation of national legislation should be abandoned as it had proved, on the basis of the results achieved up to that time, to have been cumbersome, impractical and insensitive to the requirements of many Member States. In place of the policy of full harmonisation, the Commission proposed to adopt as its main tool for integration in the banking sector the mutual recognition of supervisory standards. The principle of mutual recognition could itself only be made to work on a practical level, acceptable to all the Member States, if a minimum harmonisation of prudential standards throughout the EC could be established. The principle of mutual recognition would then be founded upon the acceptance by the supervisory authorities of each Member State of the adequacy of supervision of the credit institutions of other Member States, based on the minimum agreed standards. The term "minimum harmonisation" in this context did

---

1. Discussed in detail in Chap. 10, above.
2. See Chap. 33, below.

not equate to an endorsement of the lowest common denominator, so that all Member States slip to the standards of the most lax national supervisory body; rather, it implied that all Member States must mutually agree a minimum standard of prudential supervision which ensured the protection of depositors and provided a safeguard for the financial system throughout the EC as a whole.

11.3 Even following the implementation of the agreed minimum standards, national regulators will still possess a discretion, as discussed below, to set higher standards if they so wish, although such action would clearly adversely affect the competitiveness of credit institutions subject to the supervision of the stricter regulator. No national regulator, however, is entitled to require other national regulators to apply more than the minimum agreed standards and, assuming that these standards are met, must recognise the competence of the other national regulators to authorise and supervise credit institutions within their jurisdiction.

11.4 In addition to the concept of mutual recognition, the Commission proposed that, once a credit institution had been authorised by one Member State to carry on its banking business, it should be free to provide the authorised services throughout the EC, without any requirement to obtain a banking licence in any other Member State in which it set up a branch or provided services. The supervision of such an institution would be the responsibility of the competent authority which first authorised it, the final outright acceptance of the principle of home country supervision. This aspect of the ideals of freedom of establishment and freedom to provide services within the banking sector consequent on authorisation in one Member State is frequently referred to as the "single banking licence". Again, it depends for its efficacy on establishing certain minimum criteria for authorisation applicable in all Member States, upon which the mutual recognition of a duly authorised credit institution might prudently be based. The First Banking Directive had already established some minimum requirements which merely needed to be expanded upon.[3]

THE SINGLE EUROPEAN ACT

11.5 The proposals of the Commission in the 1985 White Paper were endorsed by the Member States and then incorporated into the 1986 Single European Act. The Single European Act also established a voting method based on a qualified majority, which could be implemented in certain cases, including the establishment of the principle of mutual recognition based on agreed minimum supervisory standards. The qualified majority voting procedure has greatly facilitated and accelerated the implementation of legislation in the banking sector.

THE SECOND BANKING DIRECTIVE

11.6 The draft legislation proposed by the Commission in the banking sector since the 1985 White Paper, and the implementation of such legislation by the Council and the European Parliament, have all been founded on the principle of mutual recognition. The principal piece of legislation implementing the Commission's proposals in the banking sector is the Second Banking Directive.[4]

---

3. The minimum requirements are discussed at para. 3.6, above.
4. Directive 89/646/EEC, OJ L386/1 of 30 December 1989, discussed in detail in Chap. 4, above.

Before considering in detail the relevant provisions and the aims of the Second Banking Directive, it would be profitable to recall at this point those aims of the Treaty which the Commission's White Paper set out to realise. In the context of the banking sector, the relevant articles of the Treaty are articles 52 to 55, 58 and 59, which are discussed more fully in Part One. What should be borne in mind at this stage, however, are the concepts of freedom of establishment anywhere within the EC, and the freedom to provide services throughout the EC. The Second Banking Directive is merely instrumental in achieving these aims and, given the traditionally teleological approach of the Court of Justice, the particular provisions of the Treaty must never be ignored when considering any issues concerning those freedoms specifically cited in the Treaty.

The principles stated above apply just as much to credit institutions as to any other institution, and should be remembered when considering the terms of the Second Banking Directive and, in particular, the concept of the single banking licence.

CHAPTER 12

THE MINIMUM STANDARDS OF PRUDENTIAL SUPERVISION SET BY THE SECOND BANKING DIRECTIVE

12.1 The Second Banking Directive sets minimum standards of prudential supervision in three areas:

— minimum capital for authorisation of credit institutions;
— control of major shareholders in credit institutions;
— participations by credit institutions in the non-bank sector.

1. MINIMUM CAPITALISATION REQUIREMENTS

12.2 Article 4 of the Second Banking Directive establishes a minimum capitalisation standard for all credit institutions by providing that no competent authority shall grant authorisation in cases where the initial capital of the applicant undertaking is less than 5 million ECU.[1] Again, it should be remembered that this is a minimum, not an absolute, standard and it is open to Member States to require greater initial capital. For example, in the United Kingdom, initial capital of at least £1 million was required for authorisation of a deposit-taking institution by the Bank of England,[2] an amount which had to be increased before 1 January 1993 in order to meet the requirements of article 4. The Bank of England also sets a second standard, however: only authorised institutions with paid-up share capital of more than £5 million may use a name which indicates that the institution is a bank, banker or carrying on a banking business.[3] This second standard is higher than the sterling equivalent of 5 million ECU, but the Second Banking Directive does not impose any obligation on the Bank of England to reduce this requirement.

12.3 Article 5 provides that no competent authority shall authorise a credit institution until it has established the identity of those shareholders or members of that institution which have qualifying holdings, and the amounts of those holdings, and has satisfied itself as to the suitability of these shareholders or members in the context of ensuring the sound and prudent management of the institution concerned. "Qualifying holding" is defined to mean a direct or indirect holding in an undertaking which represents 10% or more of the capital or voting rights or which makes it possible to exercise a significant influence over the management of the undertaking in which a holding subsists. The emphasis, therefore, in common with the traditional EC approach to all aspects of corporate control, is on *de facto* rather than *de jure* control.

1. Second Banking Directive, art. 4(1).
2. Banking Act 1987, Sched. 3, para. 6. For a more detailed analysis of the UK requirements, see Penn, *Banking Supervision* (Butterworths) 1989.
3. Banking Act 1987, s. 67. See Penn, fn. 2, above.

12.4 In addition, article 10 provides that the qualifying capital (for prudential supervision purposes) must not fall below the threshold of 5 million ECU at any time.[4]

Article 10 contains a partial exemption for credit institutions already in existence at the time the Second Banking Directive was implemented whose qualifying capital was, at that time, less than the 5 million ECU prescribed by article 4. In such a case, the relevant home supervisory authority might allow the credit institution concerned to continue to trade, provided that its qualifying capital did not fall below the highest level of qualifying capital achieved by the relevant credit institution between the date of publication of the Second Banking Directive and 1 January 1993. This exemption means that a tiering of credit institutions could potentially arise: save in certain restricted circumstances, all credit institutions authorised in the EC after 1992 will have a qualifying capital base of at least 5 million ECU, whereas those already authorised may have less qualifying capital, but will nonetheless be entitled to compete with the newly-authorised institutions, and will not be required to raise their qualifying capital to 5 million ECU, assuming they are otherwise complying with the criteria set down in the Own Funds Directive and the Solvency Ratio Directive, even after 1992. In order to prevent abuse of this exemption, paragraph 3 of article 10 provides that if control of a credit institution benefitting from the exemption is taken by a legal or natural person "other than the person who controlled the institution previously" (that is, presumably, other than the person who controlled the institution at the time of publication of the Directive), then the qualifying capital of the institution must be increased to at least the prescribed 5 million ECU.

12.5 If two or more credit institutions benefiting from the exemption should merge, then "in certain specified circumstances" (which are not specified in the Directive) and with the consent of the relevant home supervisory authority or authorities, the qualifying capital of the resultant institution must not fall below the total of the qualifying capital of the pre-merger institutions as at the time of the merger, but need not necessarily exceed or amount to 5 million ECU. Thus, change of control of a credit institution exempted from the provisions of article 10(1) by the provisions of article 10(2) will result in the credit institution being obliged to increase its qualifying capital of 5 million ECU, unless the change of control arises consequent upon the merger of the exempt institution and one or more other such exempt institutions, the combined qualifying capital of which, immediately before the merger, was less than 5 million ECU.

If the qualifying capital of a credit institution falls below the minimum level set out in paragraphs (1), (2) and (4) of article 10, the home supervisory authority may, if the circumstances justify, allow the credit institution a limited amount of time to rectify its situation, or to cease its activities. There seems little justification for permitting credit institutions with a capital base of less than 5 million ECU as at 1 January 1993 to continue *ad infinitum* with a smaller capitalisation than their competitors. It is to be hoped that, before long, all EC credit institutions will be obliged to comply with a uniform minimum capital base and that the "grandfathering" provisions will be repealed.

---

4. Second Banking Directive, art. 10(1).

2. CONTROL OF MAJOR SHAREHOLDERS IN CREDIT INSTITUTIONS

12.6 The nature and identity of the shareholders in a credit institution are clearly matters of concern to any bank supervisor, as they constitute the authors of the institution's business stratagem and the persons from whom assistance would be sought and required should the credit institution run into financial difficulties. Looking at the banking system from a more global perspective, the danger of systemic collapse increases rateably with the incidence of cross shareholdings by banks in other banks active in the same market and, therefore, prone to the same business risks. From a legal perspective, as well as a commercial perspective, cross-shareholdings between banks can also give rise to conflicts of interest, especially at times of crisis. On the other hand, cross-shareholdings, if adequately controlled, may benefit credit institutions and increase their efficiency, and so are not to be absolutely prohibited or discouraged. In order to ensure the stability of the banking system, therefore, in the context of the single internal market, it is important to ensure that all national supervisory authorities adopt minimum common standards with regard to major shareholdings in EC credit institutions.

12.7 Article 11 of the Second Banking Directive sets out these minimum standards, by reference to the concept of a "qualifying holding". A "qualifying holding" is defined to mean a direct or indirect holding in an undertaking which represents 10% or more of the capital or voting rights or which makes it possible to exercise a significant influence over the management of the undertaking in which a holding subsists. The emphasis, therefore, is firmly on substantive control.

Paragraph (1) of article 11 provides that Member States shall require any person who proposes to acquire, directly or indirectly, a qualifying holding in a credit institution first to inform the home supervisory authority of that institution, telling it of the size of its proposed holding. Similarly, any person who proposes to increase his qualified holding so that the proportion of the voting rights or the capital held by him would reach or exceed the threshold of 20%, 33% or 50% or so that the credit institution would become its subsidiary, must notify the relevant home supervisory authority of its proposal. The home supervisory authority then has a maximum of three months from the date of notification to oppose any such plan if, in view of the need to ensure sound and prudent management of the credit institution concerned, they are not satisfied as to the suitability of the notifier. If the home supervisory authority does not object to the proposal, it may nonetheless fix a maximum period for its implementation.[5]

12.8 If the notifying institution is itself a credit institution authorised in a different Member State from that in which the target credit institution is authorised, or if it is the parent or controller of a credit institution authorised in a different Member State and if, as a result of the proposed acquisition, the target credit institution would become a subsidiary or subject to the control of the notifying institution, then the assessment of the acquisition must be the subject of prior consultation with the two relevant home supervisory authorities in accordance with the provisions of article 7.[6]

12.9 The disposal of qualifying holdings is dealt with in paragraph (3) of article 11. Paragraph (3) mirrors paragraph (1) *mutatis mutandis* by reference to disposals, directly or indirectly, of qualifying holdings in a credit institution. Similarly, the relevant home supervisory authority must be informed if any person wishes to reduce its qualifying

5. *Ibid.*, art. 11(1).
6. *Ibid.*, art. 11(2).

holding in a credit institution so that its proportion of the voting rights or capital falls below the threshold figure of 20%, 33% or 50%, or so that the credit institution would cease to be its subsidiary.

Paragraph (4) requires credit institutions themselves to inform their national supervisory authorities of any acquisition or disposal of holdings in their capital of which they are aware which cause the total holdings of the owner of such capital to exceed or fall below the thresholds referred to in paragraphs (1) and (3) respectively, and to report at least annually on all shareholders and members with qualifying holdings, and the sizes of such holdings.

12.10 Where the influence of a person with a qualifying holding is likely to operate to the detriment of the prudent and sound management of the credit institution concerned, the relevant home supervisory authority is to be empowered to take appropriate measures to remedy the situation. These measures may include, for example, injunctions, sanctions against directors and managers or the suspension of voting rights of the person with the qualifying holding in question. Similar measures may be taken against a person acquiring a qualifying holding, or increasing it beyond any of the three threshold percentage levels specified in paragraph (1) of article 11, who has failed to notify the relevant home supervisory authority of its proposal to make such acquisition. If, notwithstanding the objections of the home supervisory authority, a person acquires or increases a qualifying holding, then the home supervisory authorities are to be empowered to suspend the voting rights attached to such holding or increased holding, or to nullify any votes cast by virtue of such holdings, or to annul the holdings.[7]

12.11 The Second Banking Directive is silent as to the nefarious characteristics that the owner of a qualified holding would need to possess which would entitle the home supervisory authority of any relevant credit institution to invoke such draconian measures. It is a question which is likely to depend much on the particular supervisory regime. Clearly, any such characteristics could not include the nationality of the owner of the holding if it were an EC national, as attempts to prevent the acquisition of shareholdings on the grounds of nationality alone would be a clear breach of EC law. The use of such measures will, therefore, ordinarily be left to the discretion of the individual national supervisory authority, acting within general principles of EC law.

The list of financial holding companies required to be maintained pursuant to Article 7(6) of the Second Consolidated Supervision Directive[8] should assist in the policing of qualifying shareholdings in EC credit institutions and, through the Articles in the Second Consolidated Supervision Directive which facilitate the provision of information necessary to the supervisory process, adequacy of information on significant shareholders incorporated in the EC[9] ought, eventually, to be assured. Difficulties are likely to remain, however, insofar as obtaining information about shareholders incorporated outside the EC unless bilateral agreements ensuring the full provision of relevant information are entered into between the EC and non-EC countries.

---

7. *Ibid.*, art. 11(5).
8. See para. 10.18, above.
9. See paras. 10.15 to 10.19, above.

3. PARTICIPATIONS BY CREDIT INSTITUTIONS IN THE NON-BANK SECTOR

12.12 Participations taken in peripheral and unconnected businesses are limited by national supervisory authorities to same extent, because of the overriding concern to protect depositors' funds and to ensure the stability of the financial markets by containing the risks to those known (and, therefore, able to be calculated and guarded against) within the markets. Again, the creation of a single market requires a minimum harmonisation of the national supervisory laws regarding equity holdings in non-financial institutions, to ensure the stability of the internal markets in banking and financial services as a whole. The risks associated with such participations are essentially the same two which underline the need for the consolidation of accounts as an important element of prudential supervision, namely the need to take account of the effect of the collapse, or financial difficulties, of one company impacting on the reputation and financial soundness of its shareholders, or contagion risk, and secondly the fact that an equity investment, particularly if it constitutes a large proportion of the issued share capital of the issuer of the equities, is generally an illiquid asset, the purchase of the shares normally being made for long-term investment. Added to these risks is the risk of exposure to a different sphere of economic activity and different trading risks which, on the one hand, may allow the spreading of risk overall by diversification but which, on the other hand, may infect the integrity of the core financial businesses should trading losses be suffered in these other sectors.

12.13 The Second Banking Directive addresses this issue in article 12, which provides that no credit institution may have a qualifying holding the amount of which exceeds 15% of capital qualifying for the purposes of calculating its solvency ratio (or "qualifying capital") in an undertaking which is neither a credit nor a financial institution, nor an undertaking whose business is a direct extension of banking or concerns services ancillary to banking.[10] Exposure to the non-banking sector is limited further by providing that the *total* amount of a credit institution's qualifying holdings in undertakings other than credit institutions, financial institutions or ancillary businesses may not exceed 60% of that credit institution's qualifying capital.[11] Member States are, however, given a discretion whether or not to apply the individual and total limits set out above to holdings in insurance companies.[12] Similarly, shares held temporarily during a financial reconstruction or rescue operation or during the normal course of underwriting, or on behalf of others, are not included in calculating the limits set out above.

If the individual or total limits for qualifying holdings established by paragraphs (1) and (2) of article 12 are exceeded by any credit institution, the relevant home supervisory body must require the institution concerned either to increase its qualifying capital base or to take equivalent measures.[13] Compliance with the limits is to be ensured by means of supervision and monitoring on a consolidated basis.[14]

Those credit institutions which, on the date of entry into force of the provisions

---

10. *Ibid.*, art. 12(1).
11. *Ibid.*, art. 12(2).
12. Art. 12(3)—cf. the USA. The US Bank Holding Company Act of 1956 s. 4(c)(6), 12 U.S.C. s. 1843(C)(6) (1988) prohibits bank holding companies from controlling more than 5% of any class of voting stock of a company engaged in non-bank activities.
13. Second Banking Directive, art. 12(5).
14. *Ibid.*, art. 12(6).

implementing the Second Banking Directive, exceeded the individual or total limits set out above were given 10 years from the date of entry into force in order to comply with the requirements.[15]

12.14 Finally, some discretion is allowed to the individual Member States by paragraph (8) of article 12 which provides that home supervisory authorities need not apply the limits set down in paragraphs (1) and (2) of article 12 if they require instead that 100% of the amount by which a credit institution's qualifying holdings exceed those limits must be covered by capital which is excluded from the calculation of that institution's solvency ratio. This discretion does not, however, prejudice the aim of the principal provisions of article 12, namely to ensure that the strength of a credit institution's capital base is not prejudiced by investments in more speculative undertakings, and so to ensure the stability of the institution and the protection of depositors' funds.

---

15. *Ibid.*, art. 12(7).

CHAPTER 13

HOME COUNTRY CONTROL AND HOST COUNTRY CONTROL

13.1 The concept of the single banking licence is introduced in the Second Banking Directive primarily through the provisions of article 18(1), which provides that a Member State shall provide that the activities listed in the Annex may be carried on within its territory, either by the establishment of a branch or by way of the provision of services, by any credit institution authorised and supervised by the competent authorities of another Member State, in accordance with the Second Banking Directive, provided that such activities are covered by the authorisation.

In order to ensure the objective of the freedom to establish branches of credit institutions set out in article 18(1), article 6(1) abolishes the necessity for a foreign branch of a credit institution authorised in the one Member State (the "home country") to obtain authorisation in the Member State in which the branch is established (the "host country"). Similarly, the host country can no longer impose an obligation on branches of foreign banks to have endowment capital.[1]

PRIOR CONSULTATION

13.2 Article 7 of the Second Banking Directive requires the prior consultation of the authorities of one Member State with the authorities of the other Member State involved in the authorisation of a credit institution which is:

1. a subsidiary of a credit institution authorised in the other Member State;
2. a subsidiary of the parent undertaking of a credit institution authorised in the other Member State; or
3. controlled by the same persons, whether natural or legal, as control a credit institution authorised in another Member State.

THE EFFECT OF AUTHORISATION

13.3 Once authorisation is obtained in one Member State, therefore, according to the requirements for authorisation of that Member State (which must not be less, in those areas in which minimum standards have been prescribed by the Second Banking

1. Art. 6(2) contains transitional provisions permitting host Member States to insist upon branches of foreign EC credit institutions having endowment capital until the provisions of art. 6(1) have been implemented subject, however, to the fact that such branches may not be required to have endowment capital exceeding 50% of the initial capital required by the host country for the authorisation of its own credit institutions of the same nature.

119

Directive, than the minimum prescribed criteria), then the duly authorised credit institution may offer any of the services listed in the Annex throughout the EC, provided that these are activities which are authorised by its own terms of authorisation. The corollary of this is that a credit institution may offer on the strength of its home country authorisation services in a host country which credit institutions authorised by the competent authorities in that host country are unable to offer because, although such services are listed in the Annex, they are not covered by the terms of the host country authorisation.

Although the emphasis of the Second Banking Directive is clearly on home country control, so that the competent authority which originally authorised a credit institution remains (subject to the terms of the Second Consolidated Supervision Directive) the principal supervisor of that credit institution and all its branches and operations throughout the EC, some safeguards are built in for host countries. For example, a host Member State may require a credit institution to comply with specific provisions of its own national laws or regulations with regard to activities *not* listed in the Annex, provided that these provisions are compatible with EC law and are intended to protect the general good, and that such activities are not subject to equivalent rules under the legislation or regulations of the home Member State of the credit institution concerned.[2] This tempers the right of freedom to provide services, as set out in article 59 of the Treaty, which remains relevant insofar as activities not listed in the Second Banking Directive are concerned.[3] The basic freedoms provided for in the Treaty remain, but so do the protections similarly provided for (albeit these are suspended in the case of activities listed in the Annex). It is likely that the "general good" exception will be restrictively interpreted by the European Court of Justice, and clearly that national laws which have the effect of discriminating against nationals of other Member States will offend against EC law, and be ineffective.

THE POSITION FOR UNLISTED ACTIVITIES

13.4 Thus, if a credit institution wishes to engage in activities not listed in the Annex to the Second Banking Directive, but nonetheless authorised by the home country supervisor, a host country supervisor may impose additional requirements of licensing and supervision on that credit institution before allowing it to engage in those activities on its territory, assuming also that the activities are permitted to credit institutions authorised in the host Member State. These additional criteria may be imposed, however, only if (i) credit institutions authorised in the host Member State are also subject to them; (ii) the imposition of the additional host country control and supervision, on top of the supervision of the home country supervision, can be justified on the grounds of public policy; (iii) the likelihood of causing harm to the public justifies the licensing requirement or the imposition of the additional restrictions.

THE ESTABLISHMENT OF BRANCHES

13.5 The mechanics for the establishment of branches are provided for in article 19. Again, once a credit institution has obtained authorisation in one Member State, it

---

2. Second Banking Directive, preamble, 15th recital.
3. *Ibid.*, 13th recital.

establishes its presence on other Member States through a notification procedure. A credit institution which wishes to set up a branch in another Member State is required, in the first instance, to notify its home supervisory authority, which is obliged to ensure that the notifying credit institution provides to it the following information (set out in article 19(2)):

(a) the Member State in which the credit institution intends to set up a branch;
(b) a programme of operations for the proposed branch, setting out, *inter alia*, the type of business envisaged and the structural organisation of the branch;
(c) the address in the host Member State from which documents may be obtained;
(d) the names of those responsible for the management of the branch.

It is the home supervisory authority, and not the host supervisory authority, which judges whether or not the proposed administrative structure and the financial situation of the applicant credit institution is adequate in the context of the activities in which it is envisaged the proposed branch will engage. The home supervisory authority is obliged to transmit to the host supervisory authority the information received from the applicant credit institution within three months of receiving it, together with details of the capitalisation of the applicant and its solvency ratio and details of any deposit-guarantee scheme intended to ensure the protection of depositors with the proposed branch. The home supervisory authority is obliged to inform the applicant when it has transmitted the information provided by the applicant with regard to the proposed branch. If it refuses to communicate this information to the relevant host country supervisor, it is obliged to give reasons for its refusal to the applicant again within three months of receipt of the information referred to above.

13.6 The decision of the home country supervisor to refuse to communicate the information supplied is subject to a right of the applicant to challenge the decision in the courts of the home Member State. For example, in England any refusal by the Bank of England to transmit such information would be expected to be subject to judicial review, although this remains to be seen. The present ambit of the judicial review procedure may need to be extended to ensure that English credit institutions are assured of an opportunity to challenge decisions of the Bank of England or, equally, any failure by the Bank of England to take a decision or follow a particular course of action, and also to ensure that adequate remedies are available. It should be remembered that the system of administrative law in the United Kingdom, although developing fast, is yet in its infancy and is much less well-developed than continental systems. In no public entity is the present lack of judicial control of administrative action perhaps more obvious than in the Bank of England, still perceived as an august and unchallengeable institution.[4] With the Bank of England lobbying hard for its independence from the government of the day, the question of its accountability to those it supervises and the public is one which requires urgent and extensive examination.

Within two months of receiving the information supplied by the home country supervisor, the host country supervisor is obliged to prepare for the supervision of the proposed branch in accordance with article 21 and, if necessary, to indicate the conditions under which, in the interest of the general good, those activities must be carried on in the host Member State.[5] The proposed branch may be established and

4. But see *R.* v. *H.M. Treasury and the Bank of England, ex p. Centro-Com, The Times*, 23 September 1993 where, however, the substantive challenge to the Bank of England, acting on behalf of the Treasury, failed.
5. Second Banking Directive, art. 19(4).

commence its activities upon the earlier of (i) receipt of any communication from the host country supervisory authority or (ii) the expiry of the two month period referred to above.[6]

THE "GENERAL GOOD" EXCEPTION

13.7 Again, therefore, the concept of "general good" is raised as a potential barrier to or qualification on the freedom to establish branches in host Member States, and this time is not restricted to the provision of services falling outside the list in the Annex. As before, it is to be expected that the Court of Justice would construe this exception very strictly, so as to ensure that the overall objectives of the Treaty are not obscured or avoided by nationalistic prejudices. As will be discussed below, however, some supervisory responsibility for foreign branches remains with host country regulators, and it is possible that the "general good" exception is intended to apply to similar areas of prudential supervision which are adjudged to be best regulated, for reasons of determining risk and protecting national economies, by the host regulator. The "general good" exception cannot be invoked, however, to allow a host Member State to impose additional authorisation criteria on branches of credit institutions duly authorised elsewhere in the EC, nor can it restrict the types of services which such branches may offer, provided that they are services listed in the Annex.

CHANGES IN PARTICULARS

13.8 If there is any change proposed in any of the particulars communicated by a credit institution to its home supervisory authority pursuant to paragraphs 2(b), (c) and (d) of article 19, or in the deposit guarantee scheme covering the depositors with the branch, the credit institution is obliged, by paragraph 6 of article 19, to give written notice of the change in question to the home and host supervisory authorities at least one month before making the change so as to enable the home supervisory authority to take a decision whether or not to communicate the request to open the branch to the host supervisory authority, and to allow the host supervisory authority to take a decision whether or not, if the branch is established, it will impose conditions pursuant to article 19(4) under which, in the interest of the general good, the branch must carry on its activities.

THE AVOIDANCE OF CROSS-BORDER LEGAL ISSUES

13.9 The reference throughout this article to deposit guarantee schemes covering depositors in foreign branches raises another issue which is not yet settled under EC law, namely to what extent, if at all, should domestic deposit guarantee schemes protect depositors with foreign branches or should the depositors be protected by schemes set up in their own jurisdiction, so avoiding complex cross-border legal issues? This issue is more fully considered in Chapter 31. Equally, it is not at all obvious under the scheme of home/host country control as to which central bank should act as lender of last resort.

6. *Ibid.*, art. 19(5).

The theory of home/host country control implies that the correct person should be the home supervisory authority, especially if it has responsibility for consolidated supervision throughout the EC. This role could, however, impose enormous financial burdens on those supervisory authorities in the more advanced Member States, whose credit institutions are more likely to expand their operations throughout the EC, and would be to ignore local political and economic conditions which may equally cause branches to fail.

The thrust of the Second Banking Directive is that the principle of home country control should operate in tandem with the concept of the single banking licence, to the intent that the national supervisory body which originally authorised a credit institution should have principal responsibility for regulating and supervising the activities, and particularly the solvency, of that credit institution throughout the EC. It is recognised, however, that until and unless full harmonisation is reached on certain fundamental issues, in particular with regard to such sensitive areas as monetary policy, host supervisory authorities must retain some supervisory control.[7] The Second Banking Directive was published simultaneously with the Solvency Ratio Directive[8] and shortly after publication of the Directive harmonising the components of capital for credit institutions (the "Own Funds Directive"). Harmonisation has yet to be achieved, however in regard to the supervision of the liquidity, market, interest-rate and foreign-exchange risks run by credit institutions.[9] Accordingly, the host supervisory authorities will retain responsibility for the supervision of the liquidity of local branches of credit institutions authorised on other Member States, and for monetary policy, and the supervision of market risk must be the subject of close co-operation between home and host supervisors.

13.10 These principles are set out in articles 13 and 14 of the Second Banking Directive. Article 13 establishes the principle of home country prudential supervision in respect of credit institutions and their branches established in the EC. Home country supervisors are obliged to require that every credit institution subject to their supervision has sound administrative and accounting procedures and adequate internal control mechanisms. Article 14 provides that host country supervisors shall retain responsibility, in co-operation with the relevant home country supervisor, for the supervision of the liquidity of branches of credit institutions within their territory, pending further co-ordination. Host country supervisors retain complete responsibility for the measures resulting from the implementation of the host Member State's monetary policies, but may not impose discriminatory or restrictive treatment on branches of foreign credit institutions solely on the basis that these are branches of a credit institution authorised in another Member State. Home country supervisors and host country supervisors are obliged to collaborate to ensure that risks arising out of open positions, resulting from transactions carried out on financial markets of the host country, are adequately covered. Usually, the host country supervisor will have a far greater appreciation of the liquidity and sensitivity of its national financial markets (and the effect of unforeseen volatility of the financial markets on the worth and stability of credit institutions was clearly seen in the stock market crash in October 1987). The treatment of such risks, however, for the purposes of capital adequacy, remains the

---

7. *Ibid.*, 10th recital.
8. 89/647/EEC, OJ L386/14 of 30 December 1989.
9. Second Banking Directive, 7th recital.

subject of much discussion and disagreement.[10] Host country supervisors may require branches in their territory to provide the same information as they require from credit institutions authorised by them in order to discharge its supervisory functions in regard to liquidity, monetary policy and market risks.[11]

13.11 In order to enable home country supervisors to carry out their duty of prudential supervision, host Member States are obliged to ensure that home country supervisors may, having first informed the host country supervisor, carry out either themselves or through an intermediary on-the-spot verification of the information which may be relevant to the home supervisor's task. Host Member States also have the right to carry out on-the-spot verification of branches established within their territory for the purpose of discharging their limited supervisory duties.[12]

By article 21 of the Second Banking Directive, host Member States may, for statistical purposes only, require all credit institutions having branches within their territory to report periodically on their activities within their territory to the host supervisory authorities.[13] If an institution with a branch or providing services in a host Member State fails, in the view of the host supervisory authority, to comply with the requirements of the host supervisory authority (derived from powers given pursuant to the Second Banking Directive) then the host supervisory authority shall require the institution concerned to put an end to the irregular situation.[14] Except in cases of emergency,[15] the sanction for failure to comply with this order lies initially, however, with the home country supervisor in accordance with the principle of home country control of supervision. The host supervisory authority can merely inform the home supervisory authority of the irregularity, and it is left to the home country supervisor to take all appropriate measures at the earliest opportunity in order to cure the irregularity. The home supervisory authority will then inform the host supervisory authority of the action which it has taken.[16] If the institution concerned persists in violating the national rules of the host Member State, despite the action taken against it by its home supervisory authority or because that action has proved inadequate, then at this point the host supervisory authority can, after informing the home supervisory authority, takes measures to prevent or to punish further irregularities and, insofar as is necessary, to prevent that institution from initiating further transactions within its territory.[17]

This procedure may be contrasted with the powers which host supervisory authorities

---

10. See the discussion of the Capital Adequacy Directive, in Chap. 16. Both this Directive and the Investment Services Directive, when in draft, were the subject of much acrimonious debate and deadlocked discussion, principally because of the difference in culture between the two most powerful Member States active in the securities markets. The UK approach to securities regulation has traditionally been one of extensive market regulation, but low capital requirements, whereas the Germanic approach to regulation is the total opposite, requiring a high capital threshhold and involving relatively little market regulation. The major securities markets follow the English approach, but on the European level, a significant amount of work was required to be done in the political arena to reconcile the two camps and provide a system of supervision which protects investors but allows European firms to compete in the global markets. High capital requirements obviously inhibit competitiveness, and in a market-driven environment, are difficult to justify. Liquidity is a more important criterion to the stability of these markets, together with a close, comprehensive and daily monitoring of position, market, rate and settlement risks.

11. Second Banking Directive, art. 21(1).

12. *Ibid.*, art. 15.

13. *Ibid.*, art. 21(1).

14. *Ibid.*, art. 21(2).

15. *Ibid.*, art. 21(7)—the circumstances which would constitute an emergency are not defined.

16. *Ibid.*, art. 21(3).

17. *Ibid.*, art. 21(4).

have to take appropriate measures to punish or prevent irregularities which are contrary to rules adopted in the host country in the interest of the general good. In these circumstances, the host supervisory authorities retain the principal right to impose sanctions on the offending institution.[18]

However, any measure taken by a home supervisory authority or by a host supervisory authority consequent on the occurrence of irregularities against the host authority's powers of supervision or contrary to the rules of the host Member State adopted in the interest of the general good, which involves penalties or restrictions on the exercise of the freedom to provide services must be properly justified and communicated to the institution concerned, and shall be subject to a right of appeal in the courts of the relevant Member States.[19]

WITHDRAWAL OF AUTHORISATION

13.12 If a home country supervisor withdraws its authorisation from a credit institution which has branches or provides services in other Member States, then it is obliged to notify the withdrawal to the relevant host supervisory authorities. The host supervisory authorities are then to take appropriate measures to prevent the institution concerned from initiating further transactions within the relevant territories and to safeguard the interests of depositors.[20]

CREDIT INSTITUTION SUBSIDIARIES

13.13 The principle of home country supervision applies only to branches of credit institutions authorised in a Member State; it does not apply to subsidiaries of credit institutions which are themselves credit institutions. As a subsidiary company has a legal existence independent of its parent, it requires separate authorisation from the supervisory authority in the Member State in which it has its registered office and, therefore, head office.[21] The Second Consolidated Supervision Directive[22] is intended to ensure that groups containing a credit institution are supervised on an adequate and prudential basis. The subsidiary credit institution itself will, needless to say, obtain the full benefits of the single banking licence (assuming it is "established" in its place of incorporation) once it has obtained its authorisation.[23]

13.14 It was thought appropriate, however, to extend the principle of mutual recognition to activities listed in the Annex when they are carried on by financial

---

18. *Ibid.*, art. 21(5).
19. *Ibid.*, art. 21(6).
20. *Ibid.*, art. 21(9).
21. *Ibid.*, 8th recital.
22. See Chap. 10, above.
23. Second Banking Directive, art. 7—there must be prior consultation with the competent authorities of the other Member State involved in the authorisation of a credit institution which is (i) a subsidiary of a credit institution authorised in another Member State, or (ii) a subsidiary of the parent undertaking of a credit institution authorised in another Member State, or (iii) controlled by the same persons, whether natural or legal, as control a credit institution authorised in another Member State. These requirements are intended to ensure that there is adequate capitalisation and supervision across the whole group.

institutions[24] which are subsidiaries of credit institutions, provided that such subsidiaries are covered by the consolidated supervision of their parent undertakings and meet certain strict conditions.[25] This extension of the single banking licence was implemented in order to overcome the difficulties of national laws in certain Member States which at present prohibit credit institutions from engaging directly in some of the activities listed in the Annex, notably leasing, factoring and trading of securities, but which allow these same activities to be carried out by non-bank subsidiaries of banks. Such parent credit institutions would be placed at a considerable competitive disadvantage if credit institutions authorised in other Member States whose authorisation did encompass such activities were able, by virtue of the single banking licence, to offer the same throughout the EC, whereas they, authorised under a more restrictive regime, would not only themselves be prevented from engaging in these activities, but also their non-bank subsidiaries would not be able to benefit from the opportunities afforded by a single banking licence. (Although, if articles 52 and 59 of the Treaty are interpreted literally, even non-banking subsidiaries, as with all other persons, should be entitled to freedom of establishment and the freedom to provide services throughout the EC, subject to certain safeguards.)

Article 18(2) implements the principle of freedom of establishment insofar as financial institutions which are subsidiaries of credit institutions are concerned. A financial institution may carry out in any other Member State certain of the activities listed in the Annex (principally the activities numbers 2 to 12 in the Annex) either by the establishment of a branch or by way of the provision of services, provided that the financial institution is either a subsidiary of a credit institution or the jointly-owned subsidiary of two or more credit institutions, whose memorandum and articles of association permits the carrying on of those activities, and which fulfils each of the following conditions:

1. the parent undertaking or undertakings must be authorised as credit institutions in the Member State by the law of which the financial institution subsidiary is governed;
2. the activities in question must actually be carried on within the territory of the same Member State;
3. the parent undertaking or undertakings must hold 90% or more of the voting rights attaching to shares in the capital of the subsidiary;
4. the parent undertaking or undertakings must satisfy their home supervisory authority regarding the prudent management of the financial institution subsidiary and must have declared, with the consent of the home supervisory authority, that it (or they, if more than one, jointly and severally) guarantee(s) the commitments of the financial institution subsidiary;
5. the financial institution subsidiary must be effectively included, for the activities in question in particular, in the consolidated supervision of the parent undertaking, or of each of the parent undertakings, in accordance with the Consolidated Supervision Directive, in particular for the calculation of the solvency ratio, for the control of large exposures and for the purposes of

---

24. A "financial institution" is defined in the Second Banking Directive as an undertaking other than a credit institution the principal activity of which is to acquire holdings or to carry on one or more of the activities listed in points 2 to 12 of the Annex (ie, excluding the taking of deposits from the public).
25. Second Banking Directive, 14th recital.

limiting holdings by credit institutions in undertakings which are neither credit nor financial institutions.

Again, the supervisory burden falls upon the home supervisory authority, this time of the parent credit institution or institutions. It is the home supervisory authority which must satisfy itself as to compliance with the conditions set out above and, if satisfied, it will issue a certificate of compliance to the financial institution subsidiary. This certificate must be produced in any notification which the subsidiary makes to the home supervisory authority of its intention to set up branches or provide services elsewhere in the EC. The home supervisory authority is then responsible for the continuing prudential supervision of the subsidiary.[26]

13.15 There is a curious dislocation between the provisions of the Second Consolidated Supervision Directive and the provisions of article 18 of the Second Banking Directive. In order to benefit from the extension of the principle of the single banking licence, a financial institution must effectively be included, at least for the Annex activities, in the consolidated supervision of its parent credit institution. In particular for the purpose of article 3(1) of the First Consolidated Supervision Directive, any credit institution which had a participation in another credit or financial institution is to be subject to supervision on a consolidated basis with that of the institution in which it has its participation.[27] Article 19 of the Second Banking Directive is consistent with this approach, albeit more restrictive. Article 3(1) of the Second Consolidated Supervision Directive contains similar provisions. By article 3(3) of the Second Consolidated Supervision Directive, however, a financial institution involved in activities which are principally subject to market risks, and which is itself subject to a particular supervisory regime, may be excluded from the consolidated supervision exercised over any credit institution which has a participation in the same. This exemption applies pending further co-ordination of the capital requirements relating to market risks.

Article 3(3) of the Second Consolidated Supervision Directive envisages a situation entirely contrary to the criterion on consolidated supervision stated in article 18 of the Second Banking Directive. The Second Consolidated Supervision Directive appears to have been drafted with the Investment Services Directive in mind, which sets lower capital and solvency ratio requirements for financial institutions engaged in financial business other than the taking of deposits from the public, and contemplates a different supervisory regime tailored to suit those particular business activities. There is, therefore, a direct conflict between the provisions of the Second Banking Directive and the provisions of the Second Consolidated Supervision Directive.[28]

NOTIFICATION TO HOME SUPERVISORY AUTHORITY

13.16 Finally, the provision of services cross-border, in reliance on the single banking licence, is provided for by article 20 of the Second Banking Directive. Any

---

26. *Ibid.*, art. 18(2), third paragraph. The home supervisory authority is to ensure the supervision of the financial institution subsidiary in accordance with arts. 10(1), 11, 13, 14(1), 15 and 17 of the Second Banking Directive and arts. 7(1) and 12 (as substituted) of the First Banking Directive.

27. See paras. 10.3 and 10.4, above.

28. The circumstances in which consolidated supervision may be waived is considered in detail at para. 10.7, above.

credit institution wishing to provide its services in another Member State for the first time is to notify its home supervisory authority of the activities listed in the Annex which it intends to offer. Within one month of receipt of this notification, the home supervisory authority is to forward it to the host supervisory authority, that is, the Member State in which the activities are to be offered. No allowance is made in the Directive for host supervisory authorities to object to the provision of these services, whether or not on the grounds of general good.

THE FREEDOM TO PROVIDE SERVICES

13.17 Drawing on all the provisions in the Second Banking Directive regarding freedom of establishment and freedom to provide services, the following examples may be given:

1. Assume bank A is authorised and established in country A (a Member State), and its authorisation empowers it to trade in securities. Bank A wishes to establish a branch in country B (a Member State). The supervisory authority for banks incorporated in country B does not allow banks which it authorises to trade in securities. Nonetheless, unless country B can invoke the "general good" exception, bank A is entitled to establish a branch in country B through the notification procedure prescribed in article 19, which branch may trade in securities without any restrictions on this activity save those imposed by the supervisory authority in country A.

2. Assume bank B is established and authorised in country B. It cannot trade in securities, because its authorisation prohibits carrying on this type of activity. However, it has a wholly-owned non-bank subsidiary, B Co., established and authorised in country B which carries on securities business. B Co.'s activities are supervised on a consolidated basis with those of bank B by the home supervisory authority in country B. If the home supervisory authority in country B is satisfied with the management of B Co., and provided that bank B has guaranteed performance of all B Co.'s obligations, B Co. may apply to the national supervisory authority for a certificate of compliance on the basis of which it can establish branches or provide its services throughout the EC.

3. Assume bank B has another securities-trading subsidiary, C Co., which is established and incorporated in country C (a Member State). Even though C Co. is a wholly-owned subsidiary of bank B and carries on an activity specified in the Annex to the Second Banking Directive, it cannot obtain the benefits of a single banking licence, because it does not fulfil all the criteria set out in article 18, paragraph 2.

CHAPTER 14

THE SUPERVISION OF CAPITAL ADEQUACY—
I: OWN FUNDS

INTRODUCTION

14.1 The legislation enabling the harmonisation of minimum standards on capital adequacy throughout the EC is currently contained principally in two Directives: Council Directive 89/299/EEC, of 17 April 1989 on the own funds of credit institutions[1] (the "Own Funds Directive") and Council Directive 89/647/EEC of 18 December 1989 on a solvency ratio for credit institutions[2] (the "Solvency Ratio Directive"). To these two directives will be added the Capital Adequacy Directive.[3] All three Directives are concerned essentially with establishing the components of capital on which banks and securities houses may rely to support their assets, and the minimum ratio which such capital must bear to the assets which it supports. Identification of the types of capital which ought to qualify for the purposes of measuring the minimum ratio is, therefore, critical and has been the subject of much argument among bank and securities firms' regulators for some years. The consensus now reached in EC legislation, after much political wrangling, is to apply the same capital regime to banks and securities houses alike, apart from initial capital requirements (which are higher for banks), assessing the capital requirement in both cases by reference to the nature of the asset which such capital is intended to support. This categorisation depends essentially on whether or not the asset is tradeable in nature and a viable market exists in which it can be traded. The EC approach to the measurement and adequacy of capital is examined in the following three chapters. This chapter concentrates on the Own Funds Directive and the complementary provisions of the Capital Adequacy Directive.

14.2 The function of capital and the determination of an adequate level of capital cover to support the day-to-day operations of a business are essential aspects of every form of economic activity. Capital is intended primarily to provide a permanent fund capable of absorbing on-going losses and permitting a business to carry on trading in times of economic adversity. In return for providing funding of this nature, an investor would expect to receive some kind of return. Traditionally, permanent capital carries no fixed funding costs (for to do so would deprive the investment of one of its most fundamental characteristics), but provides a return based on the profit of the entity in which the investment is made. A clear distinction is drawn, therefore, between the creditors of an entity, whose claims must be met on an on-going basis out of turnover or capital, and capital investors, whose claims, if any, can be met only of out distributable profits and whose investment is wholly at risk in the event of an insolvency of the entity

1. OJ L124/16 of 5 May 1989.
2. OJ L386/14 of 30 December 1989.
3. 93/6/EEC, OJ L141/1 of 11 June 1993.

in which the investment is made. In the case of a credit institution, the distinction between investors in that institution and creditors of such institution has a greater political sensitivity than in an ordinary trading concern because creditors will consist primarily of depositors. Capital may exist, however, in a variety of different guises depending on local laws, local accountancy policies and the appetite and sophistication of investor markets.

THE BASIC CATEGORIES OF CAPITAL

14.3 Three basic categories of capital existing today are equity capital, debt capital and hybrid capital, the latter combining elements of the other two. Debt capital in fact provides little protection to ordinary creditors as it carries fixed funding costs which generally cannot be suspended without breaching the terms on which the debt is provided. The capital will cease to be available if the issuer becomes insolvent and the providers of the capital will ordinarily rank *pari passu* with creditors in any insolvency. Hybrid capital, for example preference shares and subordinated debt, may provide some support to a business in that funding costs, although *prima facie* payable, may be suspended if there is insufficient cash to meet them and ensure the continuing viability of the issuer; hybrid capital thus may absorb on-going losses and provide a layer of insulation for ordinary creditors. Such forms of capital are, however, rarely available when the entity in which the investment is made is insolvent: the investor's rights of repayment are generally accelerated on the occurrence of an insolvency. Even within the category of equity capital, numerous different forms of equity investment exist, the common factor in all being that the investment is locked in, even in an insolvency situation. It is not possible, however, to define capital on an international basis otherwise than by defining an investment by reference to the characteristics which must be evidenced in order for it to constitute capital or a type of capital. Different local laws may permit a type of investment to constitute capital in one country, yet the same investment cannot exist according to the laws of a different country: the fact that the investment is not recognised in one jurisdiction should not prejudice its inclusion in the capital of an entity incorporated elsewhere provided that it performs the universally-accepted function of capital.

THE APPROACH TO THE AVAILABILITY OF CAPITAL IN THE EC

14.4 A particular factor in the types and amount of capital available in different jurisdictions is the degree of sophistication and depth of the investor base available to institutions in such jurisdictions. It is no accident that the most innovative creators of new forms of capital, the American investment bankers, are practising their art in the deepest, broadest and most sophisticated domestic capital market in the world. The sophistication of the market tends to be matched (although rarely simultaneously) by the sophistication of the regulators of the market. Thus species of capital acceptable to the regulators in one jurisdiction may not be acceptable to regulators in less sophisticated or market-driven jurisdictions. Within the EC, there are considerable disparities between the Member States in their approach to the definition and measurement of capital, a fact that is not surprising given the overwhelmingly different economic philosophies which prevail in the Member States. The tensions which result from these different approaches to the function and availability of capital were particularly evident within the EC during the negotiation of the Own Funds and Solvency Ratio Directives and even more so in the posturing which surrounded the frequently deadlocked negotiations on the Capital Adequacy Directive, and the Investment Services Directive. The differences between the Member States went to the most fundamental levels of the theories of markets and functions of capital. At one end of the spectrum is the United Kingdom, with its essentially market-driven economy and numerous and varied providers of capital: banks, mutual funds, pension funds, private individuals, insurance companies, and so on. The basis of the United Kingdom economy has been essentially a market culture, with funding being provided mostly in the form of private capital through open, relatively unregulated markets. The dependence on equity capital has, consequently, resulted in considerable powers for shareholders, reflected in legislation. Numerous markets (not all of them recognised exchanges) and market intermediaries exist to introduce those seeking capital to those seeking to provide it. The primary markets have themselves over time developed secondary markets and derivative products, an evolutionary process which has been markedly accelerated over the last ten years as a result of a combination of the globalisation and deregulation of the capital markets and the considerable advances made in computer technology, which have improved the analysis and understanding of market risk and opportunity.

14.5 At the other end of the spectrum of EC market economies is Germany. German businesses have traditionally turned to German banks as providers of both debt and equity capital, with the result that German banks have substantial shareholdings in German corporates (resulting in a very concentric economic model). German banks have thus developed as "universal banks", providers of debt and equity funding alike, with a significant amount of economic power and a highly developed role as financial intermediaries. German investors have traditionally preferred fixed income investments to more speculative, purer forms of capital such as ordinary share capital; this preference is evidenced by the relatively few species of capital issued by German corporates. As well as providing capital, German universal banks have also been the primary distributors of capital, unlike in England where a multitude of financial intermediaries co-exist to broke capital investment. The strength and power of the German universal banks and their regulator, the Bundesbank, was evident in all discussions in the EC on the capital adequacy issue.

14.6 Most other Member States occupy the ground between the United Kingdom and Germany. Most other Member States do not have market-driven economies to the extent of that of the United Kingdom, not because they have powerful local banks but because until recently the State has owned any economic entity, banks included, of any size, or has, at the least, had a strongly interventionist approach to government. Debt markets tend, therefore, to be more developed than equity markets. Markets have not been needed to source capital in the manner seen in the United Kingdom because the capital has been sourced in different ways through government activity. Furthermore, most placing and trading of capital has traditionally taken place in such jurisdictions on recognised exchanges, with relatively little over-the-counter activity.

14.7 As well as an awareness of the different ways in which capital may be sourced, this Chapter should be read in the context of the functions which capital is intended to perform and, in the light of those, of the amount and nature of the capital support necessary for a particular economic activity. As stated earlier, capital is intended to provide a cushion to absorb day-to-day losses of a business activity and so enable a business to trade as far as possible without prejudicing creditors. The risk of doing business should, in other words, fall primarily on the investors in the business (who equally benefit from the fruits of its success) and not on the ordinary creditors of the business. The extent to which the insulation provided by capital is needed depends on the nature of the business and, more particularly, its assets and liabilities. Banks fund their businesses from a number of different sources, share capital, interbank lines and deposits being the most important. Share capital is, predominantly, a permanent form of investment with few or no fixed financing charges (financing charges will generally only exist on hybrid species of share capital such as preference shares which, equally, may not be a permanent type of investment). Interbank lines are withdrawn as swiftly as they can be provided. Deposits are generally provided on a short-term basis. Bank assets, on the other hand, have traditionally been loans with medium or long term maturities and have generally been illiquid. The mismatch in maturity of deposits and bank assets is compensated for by an insistence on a relatively high ratio of capital to assets. The interests of the depositors are further protected by deposit guarantee schemes, whereby the banking industry effectively insures (to a certain amount) depositors of other banks operating (traditionally) in the same jurisdiction against the failure of those other banks. Further protection is also afforded by the placing of mandatory exposure limits against particular counterparties or economic or geographic sectors. The first lines of the defence of depositors' interests is, however, the capital to asset ratio.

THE MOVE TOWARDS DISINTERMEDIATION

14.8 Recent years have seen a marked change in the business activities of banks. In the last decade, a market of some depth (albeit most participants are banks) has developed in the trading of loan assets, to the extent that, today, not only is nearly every Eurocurrency loan agreement drafted on the basis that loan participations are assignable but also a mechanism for assignment is actually provided for in the documentation. The effect of the process of disintermediation is, however, that banks are encroaching more and more into the province of the securities houses, arranging and placing debt and equity issues rather than taking debt onto their own books. Equally, banks are investing in and selling financial services products far removed from the traditional bank lending products; for example a number of banks now offer life assurance products through affiliates or subsidiaries, or act as financial intermediaries in arranging for such products to be provided to their customers by independent third parties. The result of this encroachment is that the EC capital adequacy regime, represented by the Own Funds Directive, the Solvency Ratio Directive and the Capital Adequacy Directive, has been developed on a functional rather than an institutional basis and will eventually apply to credit and financial institutions alike, apart from minimum capital requirements which, because of the perceived political need to protect the interests of private depositors, are set at higher levels for credit institutions than for financial institutions. In other words, apart from initial capital requirements the EC capital adequacy regime will determine capital requirements not by reference to whether or not an institution takes deposits, but by reference to the nature of the assets of that institution and the particular risks inherent in holding those assets. This regime will not come into operation, however, until 1 January 1996. Until then, credit institutions will be obliged to comply with the requirements of the Own Funds and Solvency Ratio Directives, the provisions of which, as will be seen, may in a number of important cases be far from functional and bear little resemblance to the risks incidental to the business of banking.

The measurement of capital and the establishment of common capital adequacy ratios have been the subjects of much debate among bank and securities houses regulators over the past decade, as markets have been deregulated and access to capital provided on a global scale. The Basle Committee, in particular, has been examining the issue of capital adequacy of banks involved in the international banking markets and in July 1988 it published an agreement (the "Basle Agreement") between the governors of the central banks represented on the Committee, setting out agreed constituents of capital (or "qualifying capital"), a formula for measuring the risk in terms of required capital support of particular assets (or risk-weightings), and a proposed treatment of off-balance sheet assets for the purpose of the measurement of capital adequacy.[4] These components are combined to calculate the ratio of qualifying capital of a bank to its risk-weighted assets (on and off-balance sheet), which was set at a minimum of 8% for banks subject to the supervision of those countries represented on the Basle Committee. In April 1993, the Basle Committee published further papers proposing revisions to the Basle Agreement to take account of the different capital adequacy requirements that are presented by the holding of liquid, tradeable assets.[4A]

The Basle Committee's initial approach to measuring capital adequacy against risk-weighted assets was followed in the EC by the adoption of the Own Funds Directive and the Solvency Ratio Directive. The Solvency Ratio Directive also establishes a minimum capital adequacy/risk asset weighting ratio of 8% for EC credit institutions (with the eventual exception of the trading book of credit institutions, to which the lower capital ratios stipulated by the Capital Adequacy Directive will apply) and proceeds on a basis broadly compatible with that established by the Basle Committee by the original Basle Agreement. But, as discussed below, there are some differences between the EC's definition of qualifying capital (or "own funds") and its calculation of the solvency ratio and the corresponding treatment of such matters in the Basle Agreement. As explained further below, there are more fundamental differences between the treatment of foreign exchange risk for capital adequacy purposes proposed by the Basle Committee in its 1993 proposals, and the capital adequacy requirements for foreign exchange risk contained in the Capital Adequacy Directive. Equally, the 1993 Basle Committee's proposals regarding capital adequacy requirements for equity positions held by banks are considerably shorter than the requirements currently contained in the Capital Adequacy Directive.

---

4. The first major result of the work of the Basle Committee was in fact the Basle Agreement published in 1983 entitled "Principles for the Supervision of Banks' Foreign Establishments." This report proposed, amongst other things, a regime for international co-ordination of bank supervision. In December 1987 the Basle Committee published its first report on the regulation of bank capital and it was following a consultation procedure on this report that the Committee published in July 1988 its Convergence Agreement. The work of the Basle Committee is considered in greater detail in Chap. 9, above.

4a. See "The Prudential Supervision of Netting, Market Risks and Interest Rate Risk", published by the Basle Committee on Banking Supervision in April 1993.

THE MEASUREMENT OF BANK CAPITAL

14.9 The essential question for a bank supervisor when considering the question of the constitution of the capital base of the banks which it supervises is what investments in those banks should properly be considered as capital, in the context of being available to support the banks' interests in times of crisis, and being able to fund the banks' business generally.[5]

The highest quality capital is, of course, ordinary shares or common stock issued by a company and fully paid up. Ordinary shares are not redeemable at the holder's option, so are available as a source of capital for as long as the issuer requires; the shareholder has, normally, no contractual right to receive dividend income and, therefore, there are few, if any, servicing or fixed finance costs, and the shareholder's rights to receive a dividend in the event of the liquidation of the issuer are, normally, subordinated to the rights of all creditors of the issuer to receive repayment of indebtedness. In the case of credit institutions, a large equity base demonstrates to potential depositors the willingness of equity investors to put their own funds at risk on a permanent basis to support the depositors' funds. The issued share capital of an institution is also a very public form of investment, so making it easier to gauge the true value and worth of the issuer.

14.10 The other principal high quality capital item is disclosed reserves because, as with equity capital, the amount involved is highly visible in the accounts of the institution concerned; it is permanent in that it represents funds which belong solely to the institution, and it is capable of being written down against current or future trading losses.

Both ordinary shares and disclosed reserves also have the advantage, within the international banking framework, of being features which are common to most countries' legal and accounting systems.

14.11 Less pure forms of investment are often found which, though containing some characteristics of the two examples of high quality capital referred to above, do not fulfil all the traditional criteria of capital. An example of a high quality yet less visible form of capital is undisclosed reserves which, although they have passed through the profits and loss account of the institution concerned, have not been published and the value of which is, therefore, difficult to gauge. Accounting systems in certain Member States, notably Germany and Belgium, have historically permitted the creation of undisclosed reserves by allowing banks to undervalue certain assets or overstate liabilities through the profit and loss account in order to set aside funds to absorb the fluctuations in the return on assets inherent in a banking business. Undisclosed reserves most closely resemble retained earnings or disclosed reserves, the principal difference being their lack of transparency. The trend towards fuller and more extensive disclosure of bank

---

5. In 1980 the Bank of England published a paper entitled "The Measurement of Capital" which identified four important purposes for which capital is required, namely: (i) to cushion against losses; (ii) to demonstrate to potential depositors the willingness of shareholders to put their own funds at risk on a permanent basis; (iii) to provide resources free of fixed financing costs; and (iv) to be a suitable form of finance for the general infrastructure of the business in question. The Bank of England published a further paper in May 1988 entitled "Banking Act 1987—Section 16: Statement of Principles" para. 2.4 of which outlines the various papers published by the Bank and which covered its general approach for the assessment of capital adequacy. That Statement of Principles was in turn revised by a statement published by the Bank of England simultaneously with the Banking Act Report for 1992/93. The former position in the UK is discussed in Penn, *Banking Supervision* (Butterworths), 1988, p. 48, which also includes the s. 16 Statement of Principles; see App. I, below.

assets and liabilities has ensured that the use of unpublished reserves is becoming obsolete, and indeed the concept does not even exist in the majority of Member States. Even in those Member States whose accounting rules do permit the creation of such funds, the supervisory treatment differs. For example, in Germany banks may only include undisclosed reserves as a component of capital if they have been taxed; in Belgium, banks are actually prohibited from including such reserves in capital at all.

14.12 The second type of reserve established by credit institutions is the revaluation reserve. There are two basic types: the first type arises from a formal revaluation of the premises owned by credit institutions, which revaluation is carried through the balance sheet. The revaluation of fixed assets is designed to accommodate significant changes in the market value of such assets relative to their original book value and has traditionally been permitted in a number of Member States, notably Belgium, France, Italy, the Netherlands and the United Kingdom. Equally, however, because revaluation reserves represent unrealised and therefore, to an extent, illusory gains, some national regulators have traditionally declined to permit the inclusion of such reserves in bank capital for the purpose of calculating the capital adequacy ratio. Examples of G10 countries where the regulators are more cautious are the USA, Switzerland, Canada and Japan. The second type of revaluation reserve is the so-called "latent" revaluation reserve which arises from the implicit revaluation of long-term holdings of equity securities valued at historic cost on the balance sheet. Revaluation reserves can be used to absorb losses on an on-going basis and, therefore, fulfil one of the principal criteria for the constitution of quality capital. They are, however, subject to market volatility until actually realised and, frequently, to a tax charge on gains made on realisation, and any inclusion of such items in capital is normally discounted so as to take into account these factors. The danger of over-reliance on such types of capital is evidenced by the difficulties which Japanese banks have encountered in the past few years. Japanese banks have traditionally invested both in each other's shares and in the shares of corporates. While the Japanese stock market was performing well in the early 1980s, these shareholdings carried substantial unrealised gains. The last few years have, however, seen an equally dramatic fall in stock prices, wiping out or substantially reducing the gains. The Japanese bank regulators were unusual in permitting unrealised gains in market investments to be included in the calculation of the capital ratio. The result of the falling stock market has been the substantial erosion of the capital base of numerous Japanese banks and corresponding deterioration in their capital adequacy ratio. These banks are then caught in a "no win" situation: if they sell large amounts of stock to realise the gain that is still there (albeit falling), they force down the price of the stock, thus requiring the sale of more stock to maintain the capital ratio, and so on.

14.13 In more recent times, new types of instruments combining features of debt (such as servicing fees) with features of equity (such as providing for some degree of permanence) have been developed in various forms, classified generally as "hybrid capital instruments". Examples include perpetual debt instruments in the United Kingdom, *titres subordonnés à durée indéterminée* in France, and *Genußscheine* in Germany. To these types of investment have been added investments of limited duration, such as term subordinated debt and dated preference shares, which are more characteristic of debt than equity in that they are unavailable to support losses once the issuer becomes insolvent.

Equity, of course, is traditionally a more expensive form of financing a business than debt. There was a temptation, therefore, for credit institutions incorporated in jurisdictions whose supervisors permitted it to bolster balance sheets with hybrid capital instruments priced mid-way between debt and equity, at the expense of more pure forms of capital. This enabled the issuing institution to pursue its business more cheaply, and so offer keener margins, than institutions with a more solid capital base, a result which could ultimately have prejudiced the stability of the international markets as globalisation of the business of banking increased. The Basle Agreement sought to counter the potential competitive inequality caused by the different capital requirements imposed on banks in different jurisdictions, and to ensure the continued stability of the international financial markets, by setting common standards for the composition of capital that can prudently be used as a measure against which the risk of those assets that it is intended to support is calculated.

THE BASLE AGREEMENT: CONSTITUENTS OF CAPITAL

14.14 The Basle Agreement provides that the capital of banks active in the international markets should be categorised, for the purposes of prudential supervision, into two types. The first type of capital or "core capital" is pure capital of the type described above, namely permanent shareholders' equity (issued and fully paid-up ordinary shares/common stock and perpetual non-cumulative preference shares[6]) and disclosed reserves (created or increased by appropriations of retained earnings or other surplus, eg, share premiums, retained profit, general reserves and legal reserves[7]). Perpetual non-cumulative preference shares are shares which cannot be redeemed at the option of the holder or on a predetermined date and in relation to which the holder has no right to recoup in the future a dividend that is not paid when accrued. Their inclusion as "core capital" is a little surprising since it could be argued that they are not free of fixed financing costs,[8] nor are they common to all legal systems whose central bank authorities were represented, at the appropriate time, on the Basle Committee.[9] Core capital is also referred to in the Basle Agreement as "Tier 1 capital".

The second category of capital, "supplemental capital" or "Tier 2 capital", consists of less pure types of capital which nonetheless provide some support for the operations of the institution in question on a going-concern basis. The Basle Agreement itemises the following types of supplemental capital:

(i) *undisclosed reserves*—these are eligible for inclusion in Tier 2 capital at the

6. Perpetual, non-cumulative preference stock is an American invention and a form of capital frequently issued in the US markets. Banks incorporated in most Member States are also permitted to issue such stock but, apart from UK banks (which, even then, have tended to issue in the US rather than the Euromarkets), few European banks have issued such stock as European capital markets and investors are as yet unreceptive to it. France, eg, prohibits the issue of such stock in its domestic markets. See in addition the Paper issued by the Basle Committee on 27 September 1990 entitled "Interpretation of the Capital Accord".

7. See the Consultative Paper issued by the Basle Committee on 21 February 1991, entitled "Proposals for the inclusion of general provisions/general loan-loss reserves in capital" and the Amendment to the Basle Accord in respect of the inclusion of general provisions/general loan-loss reserves in capital, published on 6 November 1991.

8. Consequently, such investments may not fulfil all the purposes required by the Bank of England's "Measurement of Capital" paper; see fn 5, above, although, as stated in fn 6, UK banks have issued such stock.

9. It was the US which fought hardest for the inclusion of non-cumulative preference shares as qualifying within Tier 1 or core capital. The inclusion of such investments follows the approach previously taken by the regulators in both the US and the UK and also reflects the approach adopted in the US/UK Agreed Proposal on Primary Capital and Capital Adequacy Assessment of January 1987.

discretion of the home supervisory authority. Such reserves should have the same high quality and character as a disclosed capital reserve, unencumbered by any provision or known liability and freely available to meet unforeseen future losses;

(ii) *asset revaluation reserves*—these include permitted actual revaluations of fixed assets from time to time in line with the change in market values of the assets over time, which revaluations are reflected on the face of the balance sheet; and hidden values, latent revaluation reserves. Both types may be included in Tier 2 provided that the assets in question are prudently valued, fully reflecting the possibility of price fluctuation and forced sale. In the case of latent revaluation reserves, a discount of 55% will be applied to the difference between the present market value and the historic cost book value to reflect the potential volatility of this form of unrealised capital and the notional tax charge on it;

(iii) *general provisions/general loan loss reserves*—these are provisions or reserves held against future, presently unidentified losses which are freely available to meet losses which subsequently materialise. Provisions ascribed to an identified deterioration of particular assets or known liabilities are excluded.[10]

(iv) *hybrid (debt/equity) capital instruments*—the Basle Agreement provides that, in order for these to qualify for inclusion in supplementary capital, hybrid capital instruments should meet the following requirements:
  — they are unsecured, subordinated and fully paid-up;
  — they are not redeemable at the initiative of the holder or without the prior consent of the supervisory authority of the issuing institution;
  — they are available to participate in losses without the issuer being obliged to cease trading (unlike conventional subordinated debt);
  — although they may carry an obligation to pay interest that cannot permanently be reduced or waived, they should allow for deferral of service obligations (as with cumulative preference shares) where the profitability of the issuer would not support payment.

Hybrid capital instruments issued in conjunction with repackaging arrangements are to be treated as subordinated term debt, on the grounds that the instruments (by carrying an above-market coupon, but also a step-down in interest rates after a specified period) are effectively being amortised.

(v) *subordinated term debt*—this category includes conventional, unsecured, subordinated debt capital instruments with a minimum original fixed term to maturity of over five years, and limited life redeemable preference shares. During the last five years to maturity, these instruments are to be amortised at a rate of 20% *per annum* to reflect their diminishing value as a component of capital. Also, in order to constitute Tier 2 capital, this type of debt should not be capable of prepayment without the prior written consent of the home supervisory authority of the issuing institution.

10. The Basle Committee accepted at an early stage the difficulty in distinguishing between general provisions and specific provisions and attempted to clarify this distinction in its report dated February 1991. In the report, the Basle Committee emphasised the need for general provisions and loan-loss reserves to be freely available to meet future, unidentified, losses and, therefore, reserves which are "earmarked" in any way should be excluded. The resultant Amendment to the Basle Agreement, published on 6 November 1991, reflects this thinking and restricts the eligibility of such general provisions and loan-loss reserves to 1·25% of weighted risk assets.

14.15 Having categorised capital components into Tier 1 and Tier 2 elements, the Basle Agreement then provides that, in order to maintain overall quality and balance to the capital base of a bank, the sum of Tier 1 and Tier 2 elements will be eligible for inclusion in the capital base subject to the following limits:

   (i) the total of Tier 2 elements will be limited to a maximum of 100% of the total of Tier 1 elements;

  (ii) subordinated term debt and items akin to it will be limited to a maximum of 50% of the Tier 1 elements;

 (iii) where general provisions/general loan loss reserves include amounts reflecting low valuations of assets or latent but unidentified losses already present in the balance sheet, the amount of such provisions or reserves will be limited to a maximum of 1·25% or, exceptionally and temporarily, up to 2% of the risk assets.[11]

The following deductions are required to be made from capital:

   (i) goodwill, which should be deducted from Tier 1 capital immediately it arises;

  (ii) from total capital, investments in unconsolidated banking and financial institutions;

 (iii) from total capital, and at the discretion of the relevant supervisory authority, capital investments in other banks and financial institutions.

14.16 The Basle Committee recommended that member countries should ensure that, by the end of 1992, a bank subject to their home country supervision should have a minimum base of qualifying capital consisting of the elements set out above equal to 8% of the total risk-weighted assets of that bank. At least one half of this 8% should be Tier 1 capital. Investments in a bank which do not fall within the established categories of Tier 1 and Tier 2 capital do not qualify as capital for the purpose of calculating the capital adequacy of a bank, nor do those elements of Tier 2 capital which, when combined with all other types of Tier 2 capital, causes the sum of Tier 2 capital to exceed the total of qualifying Tier 1 capital.

THE OWN FUNDS DIRECTIVE AND THE BASLE AGREEMENT COMPARED

14.17 The Own Funds Directive adopts the same approach to categorising capital as devised by the Basle Committee, and was conceived in conjunction with the Basle recommendations. With seven Member States also represented on the Basle Committee, it was imperative to ensure that the approach to the measurement of capital agreed by the Basle Committee was compatible with the approach taken by the Commission and the EC. There are, however, some differences in the classification of types of capital as between the Basle Agreement and the Own Funds Directive. It should also be remembered that the capital requirements stipulated in the Own Funds Directive may eventually not apply insofar as the "trading book" of a credit institution is concerned, a fact which, once the Capital Adequacy Directive comes into force on 1 January 1996, will result in considerable divergence between the capital adequacy regime prevailing for EC credit institutions and the capital adequacy regime applying to

11. See the paper "Interpretation of the Capital Accord", and fn. 10, above.

other banks active in the international capital markets unless the proposals contained in the Basle Committee's papers of April 1993 are implemented before or simultaneously with the Capital Adequacy Directive.

It should be remembered that the objective of the Basle Committee and that of the Commission and the EC are not identical. The Basle Committee is concerned primarily with the stability and efficiency of the international banking markets; the principal objective of the EC is to establish a single market throughout the EC in banking and investment services and is concerned, therefore, not just with banks which already engage in cross-border banking activities, but also with the domestic banking systems within Member States. The preamble to the Own Funds Directive reminds of the objective that credit institutions throughout the EC should engage in direct competition with each other, and that such an intention can be fulfilled only if definitions and standards pertaining to "own funds" (or qualifying capital) are equivalent throughout the Member States: the adoption of common basic standards is in the best interests of the EC in that it will prevent distortions of competition and will strengthen the EC banking system.[12]

14.18 The Own Funds Directive sets out only a description of types of qualifying capital or the characteristics which capital is required to meet, and their qualifying amounts, leaving it to the discretion of each Member State as to which species of capital should be eligible for inclusion in the capital adequacy ratio or to adopt lower ceilings for qualifying amounts[13] and, as with the Basle Agreement, Member States have the ability to introduce stricter criteria than the minimum set out in the Directive.[14] As with the Basle Agreement, the Own Funds Directive distinguishes two types of capital on the basis of quality. The types of capital which, in the terminology of the Basle Agreement, constitute Tier 1 capital, or core capital, are referred to in the Own Funds Directive as "original own funds". Tier 2 capital, or supplemental capital is called "additional own funds" in the Own Funds Directive.

THE OWN FUNDS DIRECTIVE: CONSTITUENTS OF CAPITAL

14.19 The types of capital which may qualify as own funds of a credit institution are listed in article 2(1) of the Own Funds Directive, and constitute the following:

1. capital within the meaning of article 22 of the Consolidated Accounts Directive (Directive 86/635/EEC) insofar as it has been paid up, plus share premium accounts but excluding cumulative preference shares. Capital within the meaning of article 22 of the Consolidated Accounts Directive is, essentially, ordinary shares/common stock and perpetual, non-cumulative preference shares;

2. reserves within the meaning of article 23 of the Consolidated Accounts Directive and profits and losses brought forward as a result of the application of the final profit and loss account. Article 23 of the Consolidated Accounts Directive itself refers back to article 9 of Directive 78/660/EEC (Fourth Council Directive on the annual accounts of certain types of company), which defines reserves as legal reserves, insofar as required by national law, reserves

---

12. Own Funds Directive, 4th recital.
13. *Ibid.*, 5th recital.
14. *Ibid.*, 6th recital.

for own shares, insofar as required by national law, reserves provided for by the articles of association of the company concerned and "other reserves". Member States may, at their discretion, allow interim profits to be included in reserves, provided that they have been verified by persons responsible for the auditing of the accounts and the amount has been evaluated in accordance with the provisions of the Consolidated Accounts Directive, and provided also that the amount is net of any foreseeable charge or dividend.[15] This insistence that profits be audited before they may be included in core capital marks one relatively important difference between the requirements of the Basle Agreement (which requires no such verification) and the strictures of the EC legislation;

3. revaluation reserves within the meaning of article 33 of Directive 78/660/EEC (which does not include latent revaluation reserves);
4. funds for general banking risks;
5. value adjustments within the meaning of article 37(2) of the Consolidated Accounts Directive;
6. other items within the meaning of article 3 of the Own Funds Directive (essentially, general loan loss reserves and hybrid debt instruments—see below);
7. the commitments of the members of credit institutions set up as co-operative societies and the joint and several commitments of the borrowers of certain institutions organised as funds, as referred to in article 4(1);
8. fixed-term cumulative preferential shares and subordinated loan capital as referred to in article 4(3) of the Own Funds Directive.

The list of items available for inclusion in the eligible capital base of a credit institution is, therefore, similar to the inventory contained in the Basle Agreement, the major differences being the inclusion in the Own Funds Directive of the fund for general banking risks (as to which see further below) and the exclusion from the Own Funds Directive of latent revaluation reserves relative to equity holdings. Article 2(3) provides that the items 1 to 5 above must be available to a credit institution for unrestricted and immediate use to cover risks or losses as soon as these occur. The amount must be net of any foreseeable tax charge at the moment of its calculation or be suitably adjusted insofar as such tax charges reduce the amount up to which these items may be applied to cover risks or losses.

DEDUCTIONS FROM OWN FUNDS

14.20 Items of deductions from own funds are set out in items 9 to 13 of article 2(1) of the Own Funds Directive. Again, the list provided is not exhaustive and Member States

15. See, eg, the terms on which UK banks are permitted to include interim profits in their capital computations, contained in the Notice issued by the Bank of England in August 1992 entitled "Verification of Interim Profits in the Context of the Own Funds Directive" (BSD/1992/5). Essentially, if interim profits have been verified by a UK bank's external auditors, in a manner which covers the areas set out in the Notice in this regard, such profits may be included in Tier 1 capital. If the interim profits have not been externally audited but have been verified by the UK bank's internal audit department, applying the criteria set out in this regard in the Notice, they will be eligible for inclusion in Tier 2 capital only. If interim profits are not verified internally or externally, they cannot be included in eligible capital. As before, interim losses will be immediately deducted from Tier 1 capital.

may require the deduction of additional items at their discretion, albeit there is an underlying premise that Member States are obliged to consider increased convergence with a view to a common definition of own funds.[16]

The items provided for in points 9 to 13 are as follows:

9. own shares at book value by a credit institution;
10. intangible assets within the meaning of article 4(9) ("assets") of the Consolidated Accounts Directive;
11. material losses of the current financial year[17];
12. holdings in other credit and financial institutions amounting to more than 10% of their (that is, the investee institution's) capital, subordinated claims and hybrid capital instruments which a credit institution holds in respect of credit and financial institutions in which it has holdings exceeding 10% of the capital in each case.

    An exemption from this deduction is provided for where shares in another credit or financial institution are held temporarily for the purpose of a financial assistance operation designed to rescue that credit or financial institution;
13. holdings in other credit and financial institutions of up to 10% of their capital, the subordinated claims and hybrid capital instruments which a credit institution holds in respect of credit and financial institutions other than those referred to in point 12 in respect of the amount of the total of such holdings, subordinated claims and hybrid capital instruments which exceed 10% of that credit institution's own funds calculated before the deduction of items falling within items 12 and 13.

14.21 The first three deductions are self-explanatory and are the same as those items which the Basle Agreement requires to be deducted from Tier 1 capital (although what is meant by "material losses" in item 11 is not immediately obvious). Under the Own Funds Directive also these items are to be deducted from "original own funds"—see article 6(1)(a). Items falling within points 12 and 13 are to be deducted, both under the Basle Agreement and the Own Funds Directive, from the total of original, or Tier 1, own funds and additional, or Tier 2, own funds. At first sight, items 12 and 13 are difficult to decipher—the English version of the Directive is not as felicitously drafted as one would wish. The intention of these two provisions, however, is relatively clear and that is a desire to avoid "double gearing" or "double counting" of capital through cross-shareholdings between credit institutions. Again, the overall intention is to establish solid capital bases for all EC credit institutions which are insulated, so far as is possible, from any dangers of systemic collapse. Substantial shareholdings or capital investments in other credit institutions can have a dual impact on the calculation of the adequacy of capital. First, if the institution which makes the investment does not deduct that investment from its own capital base, the same figure is, in fact, incorporated into the capital base of two institutions although, obviously, is only available to support the losses of one. Secondly, the greater the incidence of cross-shareholding, the greater the possibility of systemic collapse becomes. On the other hand, provided that the

16. See the Own Funds Directive, art. 2(2).

17. Why the word "material" was used is not entirely clear, and it will be interesting to see how many supervisory authorities ignore it. One would have thought that any trading loss ought to be deducted from capital for capital adequacy purposes. Introducing a concept of materiality appears contrary to basic principles of prudential supervision and, being a subjective test, may give rise to differences of view among EC supervisory authorities.

investment made is prudent and of a size which is not disproportionate to the value of the capital base of the investing institution, then some cross-shareholding is to be encouraged as, within these prudent limits, the overall soundness of the credit institutions concerned may actually be strengthened.[18] Hence the Own Funds Directive permits cross-shareholdings, consistently with the Second Banking Directive, but, unlike the Basle Agreement, which has no *de minimis* threshold for deductions from capital in such circumstances except as may be established in the discretion of an individual supervisory authority, requires their deduction from total capital only if specified thresholds are crossed. A deduction from capital is required under the Own Funds Directive when investments in the capital instruments of other credit and financial institutions are in excess of 10% of the investee institution's capital base, in which case the whole amount of the investment is deducted from the investor institution's capital. In addition, if the total amount of investments in the capital of other credit and financial institutions are in excess of 10% of the investor credit institution's own funds, the excess over the 10% threshold is required to be deducted.

In recognition of the difficulty of agreeing a definition of capital common to all legal and accounting systems, article 3(1) of the Own Funds Directive sets out a "menu" of characteristics of capital, to the intent that any form of capital satisfying the criteria specified in the definition may, at the discretion of a Member State, be included within the own funds, or qualifying capital, of a credit institution incorporated in that Member State, notwithstanding that it is not specifically referred to in Article 2 of the Own Funds Directive. Capital, for these purposes, is required to have the following characteristics, whatever their legal or accounting designations:

(a) it is freely available to the credit institution to cover normal banking risks where revenue or capital losses have not yet been identified;
(b) its existence is disclosed in internal accounting records;
(c) its amount is determined by the management of the credit institutions, verified by independent auditors, made known to the competent authorities and placed under the supervision of the latter. With regard to verification, internal auditing may be considered as provisionally meeting the aforementioned requirements until such time as EC legislation making external auditing mandatory has been implemented.

Article 3(2) of the Own Funds Directive then sets out the criteria which hybrid capital instruments must meet if they are to qualify as additional own funds (or, in Basle terminology, Tier 2 capital). These criteria are more or less the same as those identified in the Basle Agreement and are as follows:

(a) such instruments may not be reimbursed on the bearer's initiative or without the prior agreement of the credit institution's supervisory authority;
(b) the debt agreement (if the capital instrument concerned is debt) must provide

---

18. This is a view which is not accepted by the Bank of England, which requires all investments by a UK-incorporated credit institution in unconsolidated subsidiaries and associates and all holdings by such an institution of shares in other banks' and building societies' capital instruments to be deducted from total capital, save for certain concessions allowed to primary and secondary market makers. See Bank of England, *Banking Supervision Division Notice on the Implementation in the United Kingdom of the Directive of the Own Funds of Credit Institutions*, BSD/1990/2, December 1990. The Bank of England, in adopting this approach, is following the lead of the Basle Agreement rather than EC legislation.

for the credit institution to have the option of deferring the payment of interest on the debt;

(c) the lender's claims on the credit institution must be subordinated to those of all non-subordinated creditors. It should be noted, therefore, that the terms on which the investment is made should ensure that all rights of set off which the lender might otherwise have against the issuer of the debt should be excluded (other than mandatory rights of set off applicable on insolvency) lest the investor prefer his claim over the claims of non-subordinated creditors;

(d) only fully paid-up amounts shall be taken into account;

(e) the documents governing the issue of the securities must provide for debt and unpaid interest to be such as to absorb losses, whilst leaving the credit institution in a position to continue trading. This in effect amounts to a requirement that the right to receive payments of interest and repayments of principal should be conditional on the issuer being solvent both before and after the payment in question is made. Solvency for these purposes should be defined by reference to the insolvency law prevailing in the issuer's country of incorporation. The difficulty of this approach, however, is in policing adherence to the terms of the instrument. If a principal repayment is mistakenly made or interest paid when contractually it was not due, it may be difficult to recover the amount paid, particularly if the issuer is declared insolvent prior to the recovery having been made. This problem will be compounded in a practical sense if the investors are numerous and dissipated over a wide area. Legal structures do exist to alleviate some of the issues raised in these circumstances but may not be available in all jurisdictions. For example, in the English jurisdiction, a trust may be imposed on the holder of the securities so that if a payment is made by mistake and in breach of the terms of the issue the holders are deemed to hold the receipt on trust for the issuer or its liquidator. There are a number of difficulties associated with this approach, however. For example, the terms of the trust must clearly be established in favour of beneficiaries who are identified or identifiable at the time of the creation of the trust, which raises the issue of when the trust is created. It may be agreed that the time of the creation of the trust is the date on which the wrongful payment was made, and that at that date the issuer's creditors can be identified as a clear and separate class. It may be some time, however, before the wrongful payment comes to light and in the meantime some of those creditors who fell within the class of creditors at the date of the wrongful payment may have been paid out and new creditors may have appeared on the scene. As the latter did not have a claim under the trust as at the date of its creation, should they be entitled to claim under the trust in a subsequent liquidation? Finally, to what extent may a liquidator of the issuer mount a tracing claim if the recipient of the wrongful payment has applied the received funds elsewhere? As an alternative approach, a trustee may be interposed between the issuer and the holders of the securities for the purposes of policing the transaction. A trustee in these circumstances, however, is appointed to safeguard the interests of the investors, not the creditors of the issuer, and may not be privy to all financial information pertaining to the issuer. All information which the trustee receives on the financial status of the issuer will have been produced by the issuer and is unlikely to be verified each and every time a payment on the investment falls due. Also, once a payment has actually been disbursed to the investors, the practical problems of recovering it still exist: the legal analysis remains that, as no debt was due, the payment has been received mistakenly and gratuitously by the investor. Payment pursuant to a mistake of fact gives rise in some jurisdictions to a restitutionary claim. A claim in restitution is little help, however, if investors are scattered across the globe: the costs of recovering the payments may exceed the amounts of the payments themselves;

In addition, perpetual cumulative preference shares may be accepted as components of additional own funds.

14.22 The inclusion of subordinated term debt and fixed-term cumulative preference shares as constituents of capital is dealt with in article 4(3) of the Own Funds Directive. These provisions state, in similar terms to the Basle Agreement, that Member States may include fixed-term cumulative preference shares and subordinated loan capital within the calculation of own funds provided that binding agreements exist in respect of these investments under which, in the event of a bankruptcy or liquidation of the credit institution which has issued the shares or, as the case may be, borrowed the loans, the claims of the shareholders and subordinated lenders rank after the claims of all other creditors and are not to be repaid until all other debts outstanding at the time have been settled. In addition, subordinated loan capital must fulfil the following criteria if it is to be included as a component of capital:

(a) only fully paid-up funds may be taken into account;

(b) the loans involved must have an original maturity of at least five years, after which they must be repaid; if the maturity of the loans is not fixed, such loans shall be repayable only subject to five years' notice unless the loans are no longer considered as own funds or unless the prior consent of the competent authorities (that is, the home supervisory authority of the borrowing credit institution) is specifically required for early repayment. The competent authorities may grant permission for the early repayment of such loans provided the request is made at the initiative of the borrowing credit institution, and the solvency of the borrowing credit institution is not affected thereby;

(c) the extent to which subordinated loans may rank as own funds must gradually be reduced at least five years before the repayment date. This equates to the "amortisation" of such instruments under the Basle Agreement;

(d) the loan agreement must not include any clause providing that, in specified circumstances other than the winding-up of the credit institution, the debt will become repayable before the agreed repayment date. In other words, the acceleration provisions found in most commercial term loan agreements are not appropriate to subordinated loans made to credit institutions for capital-raising purposes.

ORIGINAL OWN FUNDS AND ADDITIONAL OWN FUNDS

14.23 The categorisation of components of capital into original own funds and additional own funds is achieved by virtue of article 6 of the Own Funds Directive. The general approach of the Own Funds Directive in this regard is similar to that of the Basle Agreement, with one major difference, discussed below. In general, however, article 6(1) provides that:

(a) the total of items comprised within points 3 and 5 to 8 of article 2(1) (that is, additional own funds, excluding commitments of members of co-operative societies and borrowers of funds, fixed term cumulative preference shares and subordinated debt) may not exceed a maximum of 100% of original own funds minus the items comprised within points 9, 10 and 11. Apart from this overall limit, there is no equivalent in EC legislation to the restriction contained in the Basle Agreement which limits general loan loss reserves in Tier 2 to 1·25% of risk-weighted assets;

(b) the total of items comprised within points 7 and 8 of article 2(1) (that is, the commitments of members of co-operative societies, fixed term cumulative preferential shares and subordinated loan capital) may not exceed a maximum of 50% of original own funds minus those items comprised within points 9, 10 and 11;

(c) the total of items comprised within points 12 and 13 of article 2(1) is to be deducted from the total of original and additional own funds.

Thus, the value of subordinated debt and other capital of a less permanent nature is discounted, as in the Basle Agreement, and additional own funds, as in the Basle Agreement, may not exceed 100% of original own funds for the purposes of calculating a credit institution's solvency ratio. There is one further major difference, however, between the Basle Agreement as originally drafted and the Own Funds Directive, namely the treatment of funds for general banking risks.[19] Article 6(2) of the Own Funds Directive originally provided that this item[20] is to constitute a third category of capital. Provisionally, it was to be included in own funds without limit, so was treated as original, or Tier 1, own funds but was not to be included in Tier 1 capital once the basis of the limit of additional own funds had been fixed. The Commission was to have proposed within six months of the implementation of the Own Funds Directive a final treatment for funds for general banking risks either in original own funds or in additional own funds.

The category of a fund for general banking risks was not recognised at all in the Basle Agreement: the fund equates to an undisclosed reserve which, as discussed above, is permitted in only a few jurisdictions, notably Germany, Belgium and Switzerland. At its meeting held on 13 December 1990, the Basle Committee agreed to include funds for general banking risks within Tier 1 capital on the basis that, because the monies comprised within these funds had to pass through the profit and loss account of the reporting bank, and could not be directly charged to the fund, the balance on the fund represented a visible, published reserve of a kind akin to disclosed reserves, which were already treated as Tier 1 capital. The inclusion of funds for general banking risks within Tier 1 capital was, therefore, consistent with the existing items qualifying as Tier 1 capital, provided that the funds met certain specified criteria.[21]

19. Such funds exist in some Continental systems, but do not exist among UK banks which, rather, treat such funds merely as a component of retained earnings (and therefore original own funds) without creating a separate category for them.

20. The fund for general banking risks was introduced in the Bank Accounts Directive, 86/635/EEC.

21. The criteria are as follows: (i) allocations to funds must be made out of post-tax retained earnings, or out of pre-tax earnings adjusted for any potential tax liabilities; (ii) the funds and movements into or out of

14.24 The Commission was fully involved in the debate on the treatment of the fund for general banking risks taking place in Basle and, together with the Banking Advisory Committee, was in agreement with the Basle Committee's conclusion. Accordingly, on 26 July 1991, the Commission published a Proposal[22] to amend article 6(1) of the Own Funds Directive to include funds for general banking risks within original own funds, and to delete article 6(2), with the intention that these amendments should be implemented by Member States not later than 1 January 1993.

14.25 A procedure is laid down pursuant to article 8 of the Own Funds Directive to allow technical adaptations to be made to the Directive, where necessary, by the Council acting by a qualified majority on a Commission proposal. This procedure may be followed:

— to clarify the definitions to ensure uniform application of the Directive throughout the EC;
— to clarify the definitions to take account, in implementing the Directive, of developments in the financial markets; and
— to bring the terminology and wording of the definitions into line with that of subsequent acts concerning credit institutions and related areas.

In March 1992, a Council Directive was adopted which introduced the comitology procedure into the Own Funds Directive, permitting the Directive to be amended in future by technical adaptations made by a committee procedure or, in the absence of an agreement by the committee, by qualified majority voting of the Council of Ministers.[23]

THE CAPITAL ADEQUACY DIRECTIVE

14.26 The Own Funds Directive must also, however, now be read in conjunction with the Capital Adequacy Directive.[24] As mentioned above, the adoption of the Investment Services Directive and the Capital Adequacy Directive has taken place only after a protracted struggle between different interest groups arising from the divergent market practices and philosophies operating in the different Member States. This book concerns only the supervision of credit institutions. Its review of the provisions of the Investment Services Directive and of the Capital Adequacy Directive is given to the extent only that they impact on banking business. Both the Investment Services Directive and the Capital Adequacy Directive are, however, of considerable importance to credit institutions, not only as a consequence of the evolution in banking which has seen the growth of disintermediation but also because of the nature of banking business in certain Member States, notably Germany, where banks have traditionally engaged in securities-type business themselves rather than through financial services subsidiaries. EC banking legislation prior to the adoption of the Capital Adequacy Directive was perceived to pose a considerable competitive

---

them must be disclosed separately in the reporting institution's published accounts; (iii) the funds must be available to the reporting institution to meet losses for unrestricted and immediate use as soon as they occur; and (iv) losses cannot be changed directly to the funds but must be taken through the profit and loss account—see the Consultative Paper referred to at fn. 6, the Amendment to the Basle Agreement dated 6 November 1991 and the Bank Accounts Directive.

22. COM(91) 284 final, OJ C/239/5 of 14 September 1991.
23. 1992/16/EEC, OJ L75/48 of 21 March 1992.
24. See fn. 3, above.

disadvantage to such universal banks. Although the single banking licence will permit such banks to develop their securities business throughout the EC on the basis of their home country authorisation, the combination of the requirements of the Second Banking Directive, the Own Funds Directive and the Solvency Ratio Directive will require such banks to hold considerably more capital against their securities operations than financial services institutions. This competitive disadvantage is mitigated to some extent if financial services institutions are at least 90% owned subsidiaries of credit institutions, incorporated in the same jurisdiction as their parent, and wish to benefit from the single passport provided by article 18(2) of the Second Banking Directive. In such instances, the parent credit institution is obliged to guarantee the obligations of its financial services subsidiary, so the wish to use the article 18(2) route will have a direct impact on the parent institution's solvency ratio even if, under article 9(2) of the Consolidated Supervision Directive, different, more lenient capital adequacy requirements are applied to the subsidiary as its business involves mainly market risk. Nonetheless, significant local competitive advantage could be secured by financial services institutions which do not wish to take advantage of the article 18(2) single passport.

14.27 As with the agreement on capital adequacy requirements for banks, the discussion on the Capital Adequacy Directive took place simultaneously with a similar debate on a more global basis initiated by the International Organisation of Securities Commissions ("IOSCO") and the Basle Committee. A joint statement was published by the Basle Committee and IOSCO in January 1992 on the measurement of capital adequacy for financial services institutions (including credit institutions to the extent that they engage in securities trading), from which it appeared that consensus between the two regulatory bodies had been reached, notably as regards the so-called "building block" approach on position risk requirements for debt securities, discussed in the chapter on the Solvency Ratio Directive below. This announcement was followed, however, by a subsequent release that stated that the Basle Committee and IOSCO had been unable to reach a consensus on capital adequacy requirements for entities engaged in securities activities. In April 1993, the Basle Committee unilaterally published its own proposals for extending the Basle Agreement to cover capital requirements for banks engaged in securities trading. The Basle Committee's proposals of April 1993 address capital requirements for position risk, which is specifically addressed in the Capital Adequacy Directive, and interest rate risk, which as yet is not addressed by the Capital Adequacy Directive. As stated above, a majority of EC Member States is also represented on the Basle Committee. It will be imperative both to the success of the EC capital adequacy regime and the ability of EC credit institutions to compete in the international capital markets that some consensus is reached between the EC, the Basle Committee and IOSCO. The Capital Adequacy Directive, with this paramount political objective clearly in the minds of the negotiators from the various Member States, specifically provides for its revision within three years of the date of its implementation, if such revision is deemed necessary in the light of experience acquired in applying it, taking into account market innovation and, in particular, developments in international fora of regulatory authorities.[25]

25. See Capital Adequacy Directive, art. 14. The optimum position to be in by 1 January 1996, of course, would be for the EC, the Basle Committee and IOSCO to have reached a consensus the capital adequacy requirements for financial services institutions. It is apparent, however, from reports on the breakdown of the discussions between IOSCO and members of the Basle Committee, and from the exchanges of views between

Lower capital adequacy ratios

14.28 The Capital Adequacy Directive will permit credit institutions, together with financial institutions, to meet lower capital adequacy ratios on that part of their business which constitutes the "trading book". The definition of "trading book" is contained in paragraph 6 of article 2 of the Capital Adequacy Directive, which states that the trading book of an institution shall consist of:

(a) the proprietary positions in financial instruments which are held for resale and/or which are taken on by the institution with the intention of benefiting in the short term from actual and/or expected differences between their buying and selling prices, or from other price or interest-rate variations, and positions in financial instruments arising from matched principal broking, or positions taken in order to hedge other elements of the trading book;

(b) the exposure due to unsettled transactions, free deliveries and over-the-counter ("OTC") derivative instruments[25a] referred to in paragraphs 1 to 3 and 5 of Annex II to the Directive, the exposures due to repurchase agreements and securities lending which are based on securities included in the trading book as defined in paragraph (a) above and referred to in paragraph 4 of Annex II, those exposures due to reverse repurchase agreements and securities-borrowing transactions described also in paragraph 4, provided the competent authorities so approve, which meet either conditions 1, 2, 3 and 5 or conditions 4 and 5 as follows:

1. the exposures are marked to market daily following the procedures laid down in Annex II;
2. the collateral is adjusted in order to take account of material changes in the value of the securities involved in the agreement or transaction in question, according to a rule acceptable to the competent authorities;
3. the agreement or transaction provides for the claims of the institution to be automatically and immediately offset against the claims of the counterparty in the event of the latter's defaulting;
4. the agreement or transaction is an interprofessional one;
5. such agreements and transactions are confined to the accepted and appropriate use and artificial transactions, especially those not of short-term nature, are excluded; and

(c) those exposures in the form of fees, commission, interest, dividends and margin on exchange-traded derivatives which are directly related to the items included in the trading book referred to in paragraph 6 of Annex II.

Particular items shall be included in or excluded from the trading book in accordance

---

Richard Breedon, then Chairman of the Securities and Exchange Commission, and Sir Leon Brittan, at the XVIII Annual IOSCO Conference in October 1992, that there are considerable differences of opinion in the setting of minimum capital adequacy requirements, in particular for position risk in equities, between bank regulators and securities firms' regulators, and between the SEC and investment services regulators in the EC. The SEC, for example, currently sets capital adequacy requirements for specific risk in equity positions that are considerably higher than those in the Capital Adequacy Directive and the higher capital requirements proposed by the Basle Committee's paper of April 1993.

25a. Over-the-counter derivative instruments are defined in para. 10 of art. 2 of the Capital Adequacy Directive as the interest rate and foreign exchange contracts referred to in Annex II to the Solvency Ratio Directive and off-balance sheet contracts based on equities, but excluding contracts that are traded on recognised exchanges where they are subject to daily margin requirements, and foreign exchange contracts with an original maturity of 14 or fewer days.

with objective procedures, including, where appropriate, accounting standards in the institution concerned, such procedures and their consistent implementation being subject to review by the competent authorities.

Repurchase and reverse repurchase agreements

14.30 The expressions "repurchase agreement" and "reverse repurchase agreement" are defined in paragraph 17 of article 2 of the Directive as any agreement in which an institution or its counterparty transfers securities or guaranteed rights relating to title to securities where that guarantee is issued by a recognised exchange which holds the right to the securities and the agreement does not allow an institution to transfer or pledge a particular security to more than one counterparty at one time, subject to a commitment to repurchase them (or substituted securities of the same description) at a specified price on a future date specified or to be specified, by the transferor, being a "repurchase agreement" for the institution selling the securities and a "reverse repurchase agreement" for the institution buying them.

A reverse repurchase agreement is to be considered an interprofessional transaction for the purposes of the definition of the trading book when the counterparty is subject to prudential co-ordination at Community level or is a Zone A credit institution as defined in the Solvency Ratio Directive or is a recognised third-country investment firm, or when the agreement is concluded with a recognised clearing house or exchange.

Securities lending and securities borrowing

14.31 The expressions "securities lending" and "securities borrowing" are defined in paragraph 18 of article 2 as any transaction in which an institution or its counterparty transfers securities against appropriate collateral subject to a commitment that the borrower will return equivalent securities at some future date or when requested to do so by the transferor, being "securities lending" for the institution transferring the securities and "securities borrowing" for the institution to which they are transferred.

Securities borrowing is to be considered an interprofessional transaction when the counterparty is subject to prudential co-ordination at Community level, is a Zone A credit institution or is a recognised third-country investment firm or when the transaction is concluded with a recognised clearing house or exchange.

14.32 The treatment of reverse repurchase (or "reverse repo" agreements) and securities borrowing agreements serves as a useful indicator of the differentiation between the trading-book assets and the non-trading book assets of an institution. The reverse repo and securities borrowing markets are relatively new and are, unsurprisingly, much more developed in those Member States which have active stock exchanges with high trading turnovers. Reverse repos and securities borrowing agreements have a number of different functions: they may be used to fund long positions, to cover short positions (in both cases being used as a book-balancing exercise) or they may simply be used in an arbitrage situation. There has been concern among national regulators, however, that these instruments may be being utilised not to cover market risk positions or to profit from arbitrage opportunities, but as a means of obtaining security from counterparties or as a means of obtaining medium-term funding at a relatively lower cost because high grade securities are, effectively, being offered as security for the funding. The definition of trading book provides, therefore, that reverse repo agreements and securities borrowing agreements must fulfil certain criteria in order to fall within the trading-book, not least of which is the requirement that the transactions are confined to their "accepted and appropriate use". Artificial transactions, particularly those of a medium and long-term nature, will be excluded from the trading book and must be risk-weighted in accordance with the more stringent requirements of the Solvency Ratio Directive as the risk assumed by the "buyer" in a reverse repo transaction or a "borrower" in a securities borrowing transaction is more naturally categorised as a credit risk (albeit supported by high grade and tradeable collateral) than a market risk. In addition, as highlighted by the Basle Committee in its April 1993 paper entitled "The Supervisory Treatment of Market Risks", regulators will be vigilant in seeking to prevent "gains trading" by the use of instruments such as repos, through which banks can improve their short-term profitability by realising accrued profits and deferring the realisation of losses on securities that are not marked to market.

The language of the Directive is, in this context as in many others, imprecise, leaving much latitude for interpretation by the individual Member States: what exactly is meant, for example, by "accepted and appropriate use"? Presumably, the use of such instruments in particular situations must be agreed by relevant competent authorities to be accepted market use, in appropriate market circumstances, leaving it to each competent authority to gauge these requirements by reference to the market practices, procedures and risks within their jurisdiction. The use of such instruments has evolved over a very short period of time, making it difficult in some circumstances for regulators to understand their uses and to determine an appropriate regulatory treatment to cover the risks involved in dealing in or holding such instruments. The existence of these instruments arises through market initiatives and market forces, constantly changing and redefining themselves, which makes effective regulation providing adequate control of risk (without stifling market ingenuity) a challenge.

The regulators should in almost all instances revert to basic principles: what is a particular transaction intending to achieve? If in truth the transaction is intended, for example, to fund a long position over a short period of time, it is essentially a trade transaction and should be risk weighted as such. The risk to be guarded against is less counterparty failure and more position risk. The emphasis on position risk is underlined by the fact that most such transactions are marked-to-market on a daily basis and margin requirements are adjusted accordingly (both of these requirements being preconditions to reverse repos and security agreements with non-professional counterparties falling within the trading-book definition). If a reverse repo transaction is in fact intended not to provide a market hedge but as a form of security, it is not entered into for trading purposes and should not be risk-weighted as such. The risk in this type of transaction is more clearly focused on counterparty failure, although position risk is also, of course, a very relevant factor.

Briefly, although this is discussed in more detail in Chapter 15 below, the Solvency Ratio Directive applies relatively crude risk-weightings to assets the subject of the reverse repo agreements, depending on the nature of the counterparty. Even if reverse repos are entered into for the purpose of obtaining security, the downside for the buyer, in the event of a counterparty's insolvency, is in effect a market risk, that it will sell the securities which it holds for less than what it paid (or lent) and the margin which it holds to offset the position risk is insufficient to cover the shortfall. This analysis assumes that the buyer in a reverse repo transaction is permitted to terminate the agreement, and thus the obligation to sell the securities back to its counterparty, in the event of the counterparty's insolvency. The Solvency Ratio Directive does recognise the value of the securities held in one sense, in that it permits national supervisory authorities to reduce the risk weighting on a reverse repo transaction that does not fall within the trading book if the risk weighting of the issuer of the securities "purchased" is lower than the risk weighting of the "seller" of such instruments. Thus a reverse repo agreement in which a bank "puchases" Zone A government securities from a non-bank private entity may, at the discretion of the relevant supervisory authority and subject to the fulfilment of certain conditions, carry a risk weighting for the purposes of the Solvency Ratio Directive of 0% and not 100%, as would otherwise be required.

All well-drafted reverse repo agreements should provide for termination on insolvency, provided that this approach is permitted under applicable national laws. If termination on insolvency is permitted under relevant domestic law and it is clear that title in the "purchased" securities is fully vested in the "purchaser", free of any obligation to resell the securities to the seller, it appears inappropriate to apply a capital weighting against the transaction on the basis only of the counterparty's risk weighting. Unless the issuer of the securities is an OECD government or a bank incorporated in an OECD country, it is likely that the capital cost of the transaction, if weighted under the Solvency Ratio Directive, will be significantly greater than the risk weighting which would have applied had the transaction fallen within the trading book definition, notwithstanding that the asset with which the "purchaser" is left will ordinarily be in tradeable form and liquid. This result bears little relevance to the economic or legal risks associated with this type of transaction. A similar argument could be raised in regard to the treatment of securities borrowing agreements in the capital adequacy regime.

14.33 It should also be noted that, for the purposes of the trading-book definition of reverse repos and security borrowing, the Capital Adequacy Directive distinguishes between contracts made between institutions which are market professionals and contracts made between an institution and a non-professional. In the former case, reverse repos and securities borrowing agreements will fall within the trading-book definition provided only that the agreements concerned are "confined to their accepted and appropriate use and artificial transactions, especially those not of a short-term nature, are excluded".

In the case of dealings with non-professionals, three further requirements in addition to the criteria laid down for professional trades are imposed, namely that the exposure on the contract should be marked to market, that collateral should be adjusted in accordance with material changes in the value of the underlying security (collateral, in this case, presumably includes margin deposits) and that the agreement provides for the claims of the reporting institution to be automatically and immediately offset against the claims of the counterparty in the event of the latter's default. The first two of these conditions should be relatively easy to fulfil. The third criterion may, however, be more difficult to satisfy depending on the requirements of the insolvency laws in the jurisdiction of the defaulting counterparty.[26]

---

26. In England and Wales, eg, a contractual right of set-off is not capable of being exercised once one party to the contract is insolvent. Rule 4.90 of the Insolvency Rules promulgated under the Insolvency Act 1986 imposes, instead, a statutory obligation on all creditors of the insolvent to set-off their mutual credits, mutual debts and mutual dealings. A creditor may not exercise a statutory set-off, however, if he was aware at the time that the debt he is attempting to set off became due that to a notice convening a meeting of the creditors

14.34 An interprofessional transaction is defined as one made by an institution with a counterparty which is either subject to prudential co-ordination at a Community level (for example, an insurance company), is a Zone A credit institution or is a recognised third country investment firm. In addition, an interprofessional transaction includes transactions concluded with a clearing house or exchange.

Comment is made in Chapter 15 on the crudeness of the risk-weighting system adopted in the Solvency Ratio Directive. The same criticisms can be levelled at the capital treatment accorded to non-market counterparties of reverse repo agreements. A large corporate will usually run its own treasury operation, including a portfolio of liquid third party debt and equity holdings as well as cash. It is difficult to see why more stringent capital requirements ought to apply to a reverse repo agreement with a highly-rated corporate than to a reverse repo agreement with a bank incorporated in an OECD country whose debt has a lower independent debt rating than that applied to the debt of the corporate. The three additional criteria which must be satisfied in order for a reverse repo with a corporate to fall within the trading-book definition point essentially to counterparty risk in the context of a market trade and the legal implications of counterparty failure. Counterparty risk still exists even if the counterparty is an EC credit institution subject to the EC capital adequacy regime, and the legal risk will rarely differ between a bank and a corporate established in the same jurisdiction. It might be argued that it is easier to gauge the solvency of institutions subject to prudential consolidation or supervision requirements agreed internationally, either between EC Member States or through organisations such as the Basle Committee, than it is to assess the solvency of entities to which no common standards of supervision or capital adequacy apply. This agreement is, however, somewhat simplistic when applied to large corporations, particularly those whose shares or debt is quoted on a major stock exchange, as such corporates will generally be subject to reasonably standardised accounting practices and principles and are required to make considerable disclosures to enable third parties to evaluate their worth. If one adds to this an independent debt rating, the crude discriminatory treatment of reverse repo agreements concluded with corporates is difficult to justify.

Capital treatment of trading books

14.35 The separate capital treatment accorded by the Capital Adequacy Directive to the trading books of credit and financial institutions constitutes an official acknowledgement of the essential difference between credit risk and position or market

---

of the debtor for the purpose of considering a voluntary winding-up had been published, or that a petition for the winding-up of the insolvent was then pending. Statutory set-off on insolvency is mandatory under English law: see *National Westminster Bank Ltd* v. *Halesowen Presswork & Assemblies Ltd* [1972] AC 789, and cannot be excluded by contract. Under English law, therefore, it may be possible for a reporting institution to satisfy the criteria specified in the definition of trading-book if the provisions of Rule 4.90 are satisfied: whether or not they will be can only be determined on a case-by-case basis. Alternatively, the agreement concerned should be drafted to ensure that the termination right, and the contractual right to set-off claims, is exercisable at an instant of time before the counterparty is technically insolvent. Compare, here, contracts traded in on a recognised investment exchange or through a recognised clearing house and contracts concluded over-the-counter. A new insolvency regime for the former has been established pursuant to s. 155 *et seq.*, Companies Act 1989. Securities lending through Euroclear/Cedel and other recognised clearing exchanges will be subject to the new regime, ie the settlement procedures of the clearing house will prevail over Rule 4.90—s. 159, Companies Act 1989.

risk: less capital is required to be held against an asset that can be traded away than an asset which is intended to be held to maturity or for which no market exists.

Article 4(1) of the Directive contains the facilitative provisions of the capital adequacy regime, by providing that competent authorities shall require institutions (ie both credit and investment institutions) to provide own funds which are always more than or equal to the sum of:

   (a) the capital requirements for their trading-book activities, calculated in accordance with Annex I (position risk), Annex II (settlement and counterparty risk) and Annex VI (large exposures);

   (b) the capital requirements for all of their business activities which carry a foreign exchange rate risk, calculated in accordance with Annex III;

   (c) the capital requirements imposed by the Own Funds Directive for all of their business activities, excluding both trading-book business and their illiquid assets if the latter are deducted from the third "tier" of capital described in Annex V of the Capital Adequacy Directive;

   (d) capital requirements imposed under article 4(2), namely against risks arising in connection with the business of an institution that is outwith the scope of both the Capital Adequacy Directive and the Own Funds Directive and considered to be similar to the risks covered by the aforesaid Directives by adequate own funds.

Article 4(1) is then supplemented by the provisions of Annex V, in which the constituents of capital eligible to support the trading book are defined, as referred to above.

The definition of own funds

14.36 Annex V of the Capital Adequacy Directive provides, in the first instance, that the own funds of investment firms and credit institutions shall be defined in accordance with the Own Funds Directive.[27] Paragraph 2 of Annex V continues, however, to provide that competent authorities may permit those institutions (which is defined to mean credit institutions and investment firms[28]) which are required to set capital aside against position risks, settlement and counterparty risks, foreign exchange risk, other similar market risks and large exposures relative to such species of risk, to use an alternative definition of capital as prescribed in Annex V. The alternative definition prescribes eligible capital (or "Tier 3" capital) for the abovementioned market risks as follows:

   1. own funds as defined in the Own Funds Directive, excluding only items 12 and 13 in article 2(1) of such Directive for those investment firms which are required to deduct item 4 from this definition; and

   2. an institution's net trading-book profits net of any foreseeable charges or dividends, less net losses on its other business, provided that none of those amounts has already been included in item 1 above under item 2 or 11 of article 2(1) of the Own Funds Directive (below); and

   3. subordinated loan capital and/or the items referred to in paragraph 5 of Annex V, subject to the conditions set out in paragraphs 3 to 7 of Annex V; *less*

27. Capital Adequacy Directive (fn. 3, above), Annex V, para. 1.
28. *Ibid.*, art. 1.

4. illiquid assets as defined in paragraph 8 of Annex V.

Item 4 above is required to be deducted only if so required by the relevant competent authority.

Subordinated loan capital

14.37 Subordinated loan capital is defined for the purposes of the Capital Adequacy Directive in paragraph 3 of Annex V as having an original term to maturity of at least two years, being fully paid up and made available on terms that it shall not contain any right to early repayment other than on a winding-up of the issuer or with the approval of the issuer's supervisory authority. In addition, the terms of the debt issue should provide that neither the principal nor the interest on such subordinated loan capital may be repaid if such repayment would mean that the own funds of the institution in question would then amount to less than 100% of the institution's overall requirements. A reporting institution is obliged to notify its supervisory authorities of all repayments on subordinated loan capital as soon as its own funds fall below 120% of its overall requirements. Unlike the corresponding provisions on subordinated term debt contained in the Own Funds Directive, there is no requirement in Annex V to discount subordinated loan capital once it is in its final two years of issue.

Subordinated loan capital which satisfies the criteria specified in paragraph 3 of Annex V may not be included in eligible capital for the purposes of calculating the solvency ratio of an institution to the extent that it exceeds 150% of the original own funds[29] left to meet the capital requirements prescribed for market risk in Annexes I, II, III, IV and VI to the Capital Adequacy Directive. Furthermore, subordinated loan capital may approach the maximum figure of 150% only in particular circumstances acceptable to the relevant authorities. The Directive does not amplify what these circumstances might be and the existence of such latitude for supervisory authorities does, of course, permit competitive inequalities to arise between institutions incorporated in different Member States.

14.38 As an alternative to subordinated loan capital fulfilling the criteria set down in Annex V, Member States are permitted to allow institutions to substitute capital of the type described in items 3 and 5 to 8 of article 2(1) of the Own Funds Directive,[30] namely supplemental or Tier 2 capital. Supervisory authorities may also permit investment firms (but not credit institutions) to exceed the ceiling of 150% for subordinated loan capital described above if they judge it prudently adequate and provided that the total of such subordinated loan capital and Tier 2 capital does not exceed 200% of original own funds left to meet the capital requirements prescribed in Annexes I to IV and VI to the proposed Directive, or 250% of that amount where investment firms have deducted illiquid assets when calculating own funds.[31]

In the case of credit institutions, competent authorities may permit the ceiling of 150% of short-term subordinated term debt to be exceeded if they judge it prudentially adequate and provided that the total of such short-term subordinated loan capital and Tier 2 capital does not exceed 250% of the Tier 1 capital left to meet the capital requirements imposed in Annexes I to III and VI.[32]

29. *Ibid.*, art. 1, para. 23. See also Own Funds Directive.
30. *Ibid.*, Annex V, para. 5.
31. *Ibid.*, Annex V, para. 6.
32. *Ibid.*, Annex V, para. 7.

Illiquid assets

14.39 As stated above, illiquid assets may not benefit from the more relaxed capital requirements applied to the trading book and, at the discretion of the relevant national supervisory authorities, must be deducted from capital set aside to support the trading book. The definition of illiquid assets is, therefore, of no small importance. An inclusive definition of illiquid assets is provided in paragraph 8 of Annex V, which specifies that such assets include:

(a) tangible fixed assets (except to the extent that land and buildings may be allowed to count against the loans which they are securing);

(b) holdings in, including subordinated claims on, credit or financial institutions which may be included in the own funds of such institutions, unless they have been deducted under items 12 and 13 of article 2(1) of the Own Funds Directive (above) or under paragraph 9(iv) of Annex V. As an exception to this required deduction (which effectively requires the deduction by a credit institution and, save as stated below, an investment institution, of *any* holding in a credit or financial institution from capital supporting the trading book, without any *de minimis* threshold), competent authorities may waive this provision where shares in a credit or financial institution are held temporarily for the purpose of a financial assistance operation designed to reorganise and save that institution. This deduction may also be waived in respect of those shares which are included in an investment firm's (but not a credit institution's) trading book;

(c) holdings and other investments in undertakings, other than credit institutions and other financial institutions, which are not readily marketable;

(d) deficiencies in subsidiaries;

(e) deposits made, other than those which are available for repayment within 90 days, and also excluding payments in connection with margined futures or options contracts;

(f) loans and other amounts due, other than those to be repaid within 90 days;

(g) physical stocks, unless they are subject to the capital requirements imposed in article 4(2) and provided that such requirements are not less stringent than those imposed in article 4(1)(iii) of the proposed Directive.

14.40 It appears, therefore, that credit institutions which have a trading book can adopt one of two alternatives: either they can deduct illiquid assets from "Tier 3" capital permitted under Annex V, or they cannot make any deductions from "Tier 3" capital but must set capital comprised of Tier 1 and Tier 2 elements against the risks associated with the holding of such assets. The choice of which route to follow will be made by the supervisory authorities in each Member State which, although ensuring some consistency of approach in the domestic arena, may not result in credit institutions competing on equal terms. Capital of the type which falls within Tier 1 and Tier 2 will generally be more expensive to an issuer than capital falling within "Tier 3", particularly if supervisory authorities permit credit institutions to raise up to 250% of Tier 1 capital in the form of short-term subordinated debt to fund their trading book, rather than the lower limit of 150%.

The considerable degree of discretion left to national supervisory authorities not only to determine the manner in which illiquid assets should be treated (ie, whether deducted from "Tier 3" capital or weighted against Tier 1 and Tier 2 capital) but also the threshold limits for "Tier 3" capital, may well result in competitive inequalities arising within the Community single banking market.

In addition to distortions of competition between credit institutions, the attempt to treat credit and investment institutions identically in terms of the measurement of capital adequacy may also fail. For example, there are no circumstances in which credit institutions may treat holdings in other credit or financial institutions as liquid assets, qualifying for weighting against "Tier 3" capital, no matter how liquid is the market in those assets. Such holdings must either be deducted from total Tier 1 and Tier 2 capital of the reporting credit institution if the thresholds specified in items 12 and 13 of article 2(1) of the Own Funds Directive have been breached, or they will be risk-weighted in accordance with the Solvency Ratio Directive and must be covered in an appropriate amount by Tier 1 and Tier 2 capital. The only circumstance in which this capital treatment will not apply is if the investments are held for the purposes of a rescue of the issuing institution. The same holdings in the hands of an investment institution, if they fall within the definition of the trading book, may be supported by "Tier 3" capital.

The concern which the regulators are intending to address is apparent, namely that in order to avoid the risk of systematic collapse in the banking sector, cross-shareholdings between credit institutions should be avoided. As has previously been argued, however, there may actually be some benefit in banks taking small shareholdings in each other or buying bonds issued by other credit institutions, provided that the amount invested is relatively small as a proportion of both the investor and investee bank's capital base, and that there are no obvious objections to banks trading in each other's investments in any event. Furthermore, if the investment acquired is readily tradeable there seems no reason to impose higher capital requirements on the holding of such investment instrument than for any other form of tradeable security for which a liquid market exists.

14.41 The definition of illiquid assets also effectively excludes loan asset trading from benefiting from the lower, "Tier 3" capital requirements,[33] unless the loans concerned have a maturity of less than 90 days. The banking regulations are, therefore, continuing to take a cautious approach to the capital treatment of loans issued in assignable form, notwithstanding the enormous growth in the secondary loan market during the past decade. Although it is undoubtedly true that traded loans may carry more legal risk than traded securities, as the latter are frequently bearer, negotiable instruments which are freely transferable, traded on recognised exchanges and which carry few if any obligations on transfer, the steps made in recent years to streamline the procedures for the transfer of loan assets are numerous. Developments in this sphere include the creation of instruments such as transferable loan certificates which, in legal terms, cause the novation of a loan participation to a transferee on sale and thus ensure that all rights and obligations in the loan are enforceable by and binding on the transferee, resulting in little or no legal risk for the holder of the instruments. The transferable loan instrument which, in legal terms, permits the notified assignment, whether legal or equitable, of a loan participation, has also been developed to assist the trading of loan assets in a secondary market, free of legal risk.

It is probably true to say that the participants in the market for loan assets are primarily banks (and so the market is relatively small) and that although assets are traded, they are not generally traded with the frequency at which, say, bonds and

---

33. *Ibid.*, Annex V, para. 8.

equities are traded. In addition, the tax treatment accorded to loans and securities tends to differ in most jurisdictions, notably in the application of withholding tax rules. Loans by banks are frequently exempted from withholding tax requirements that would otherwise apply to interest payments on such loans, a factor which necessarily restricts the broadening of the secondary loan market as few borrowers will want to assume the additional costs associated with grossing up interest payments if loan participations are sold to non-bank entities and, equally, few lenders will want to receive interest payments net of withholding taxes. Different tax rules frequently apply to quoted, tradeable debt to ensure the viability of the debt markets and the depth of potential investors. Loan assets may not necessarily be held for resale but rather purchased to increase the credit quality of a credit institution's own assets and, where purchased for these reasons, it is entirely correct that the more permanent capital represented by Tier 1 and Tier 2 capital should be held against these investments. The Capital Adequacy Directive does not, however, for the present admit that there may be a fully-fledged market in the trading of loan assets.

14.42 The Capital Adequacy Directive requires competent authorities to ensure at all times that institutions maintain the minimum capital required by article 4(1) and to ensure that institutions subject to their supervision take appropriate measures to rectify the situation should their own funds fall below the requirement.[34] Competent authorities are required to ensure that institutions subject to their supervision set up systems to monitor and control the interest-rate risk on all of their business and that those systems are subject to overview by the competent authorities,[35] and institutions are themselves to require to satisfy their competent authorities that they employ systems which can calculate their financial positions with reasonable accuracy at any time.[36] All three of the foregoing provisions are written in somewhat vague terms effectively leaving it to the Member States and the competent authorities within Member States to interpret the requirements of the Directive in a subjective manner. The element of subjectivity is necessary not only for political reasons, at least to permit some form of consensus on the capital adequacy front, but also because of the very different degrees of sophistication which exist between Member States and their financial institutions. In addition, as stated earlier, the economic culture of the Member States varies enormously and computer systems which may predict market movements and enable market positions to be calculated with relative accuracy in, say, the derivatives market in one jurisdiction may be less appropriate in a different jurisdiction where different market forces are at play, or the market has less depth.

It has also been said on frequent occasions in recent years that the computer programs which have devised the new financial instruments in recent years and which track and predict market movements are now so complicated that few bankers and regulatory authorities actually understand them or their impact, particularly the impact of their default, on the markets. In this sort of scenario, regulators can either bluff their knowledge (which is hardly appropriate), outlaw the systems and instruments concerned or insist on a full explanation and analysis of the programs and instruments, requiring simplification of the process and the product if in any way unsure as to the potential risks. The choice of route will depend entirely on each regulatory authority. The esoteric world of derivatives, in particular futures, is particularly notorious for

34. *Ibid.*, art. 4(3).
35. *Ibid.*, art. 4(4).
36. *Ibid.*, art. 4(5).

being little understood by market users and regulators alike. The Capital Adequacy Directive provides little assistance or guidance to regulators concerned with ensuring that the capital requirements for derivative products are adequate, other than repeating the axiomatic statement that whatever procedures or rules are adopted for assessing capital adequacy should be sufficient to protect the safety and stability of the financial services sector.

Calculation of capital requirements

14.43 By article 4(6) of the Capital Adequacy Directive, competent authorities in Member States are permitted to allow institutions subject to their supervision to calculate the capital requirements for their trading book business in accordance with the Own Funds Directive rather than in accordance with the rules on position risk and settlement and counterparty risk contained in Annexes I and II of the proposed Capital Adequacy Directive, provided that:

    (i) the trading-book business of such institutions does not normally exceed 5% of its total business;

    (ii) their total trading-book positions do not normally exceed 15 million ECU; and

    (iii) the trading-book business of such institutions never exceeds 6% of their total trading-book positions, which never exceed 20 million ECU.

Article 4(7) provides that in order to calculate the proportion that trading-book business bears to total business, as referred to in article 4(6), the competent authorities may refer either to the size of the combined on and off-balance sheet business, to the profit and loss account or to the own funds of the institutions in question, or to a combination of those measurements. When the size of on and off-balance sheet business is assessed, debt instruments are to be valued at their market prices or principal values, equities at their market prices and derivatives according to the nominal or market values of the instrument underlying them. Long positions and short positions are to be summed regardless of their signs.

Finally, article 4(8) stipulates that if an institution should happen for more than a short period to exceed either or both of the limits imposed in paragraphs (i) and (ii) of article 4(6) or to exceed either or both of the limits imposed in paragraph (iii) of article 4(6), it shall be required to meet the capital requirements posed by article 4(1)(iii) rather than those of the Own Funds Directive in respect of its trading-book business and to notify its competent authority accordingly.

Proposals of the Basle Committee

14.44 As briefly referred to above, in April 1993 the Basle Committee published several discussion papers containing proposals to revise the Basle Agreement by incorporating provisions relating to, *inter alia*, the capital adequacy treatment of market risks and interest rate risk. The Basle Committee's proposals relating to the treatment of market risk are substantially based on the corresponding provisions of the Capital Adequacy Directive; in particular, it is proposed that lower capital requirements be agreed for securities and other assets held within the trading book and that less stringent criteria be imposed for the constituents of capital employed to support trading book assets. The concept of the trading book as outlined in the Basle Committee's proposals is essentially the same as the definition of the trading book contained in the Capital Adequacy Directive. The paper on market risk then proposes the recognition of "Tier 3 capital" for the purposes of supporting market risks *only*; in other words, unlike under the Capital Adequacy Directive, it is proposed that Tier 3 capital should not be eligible as capital required to support foreign exchange risk. Tier 3 capital as defined in the Basle Committee's discussion paper on market risk is essentially subordinated term debt that satisfies the requirements specified in Annex V of the Capital Adequacy Directive. There are, however, a number of important differences between the proposed definition of Tier 3 capital contained in the Basle Committee's discussion paper and the definition of own funds contained in Annex V of the Capital Adequacy Directive, notably the following:

(i) The Basle Committee is proposing that subordinated loan capital eligible for inclusion in Tier 3 capital should be subject to a "lock-in" clause which stipulates that neither interest nor principal may be paid (even at maturity) if such payment would mean that the capital allotted to the trading book for debt securities and equities would fall below a threshold 20% above the required capital laid down in the Basle proposals. The corresponding provision in the Capital Adequacy Directive requires an institution to notify its supervisory authorities of all repayments made on Tier 3 capital once its own funds fall below 120% of its overall (ie, trading book and non-trading book) capital requirement, but do not require suspension of payments of interest and repayments of principal unless and until such payment or repayment would result in such institution's capital amounting to less than 100% of its overall capital requirement. The Basle Committee's proposals are, therefore, more stringent than the basic requirements of the Capital Adequacy Directive in both the setting of the threshold at which a lock-in clause must be triggered and in the determination of what constitutes capital for the purposes of triggering the lock-in clause: Tier 1 and Tier 2 capital is effectively ignored. In both systems, the difficulty of policing the triggering of the lock-in clause is the same.

(ii) Tier 3 capital may be used by banks only to support market risks in the trading book for equities and debt securities. Tier 3 capital under the Capital Adequacy Directive may also be used to support foreign exchange risk, settlement and counterparty risk and large exposures risk arising from trading book assets, subject to the limits on the amounts of such capital contained in the Capital Adequacy Directive.

(iii) The Basle Committee proposes to limit Tier 3 capital to 250% of Tier 1 capital allocated to support securities trading book risks, which it states is consistent with the Capital Adequacy Directive. In fact, the principal ceiling limit on Tier 3 capital contained in the Capital Adequacy Directive is 150% of Tier 1 capital, although Member States are permitted, at their discretion, to permit the 150% ceiling to be exceeded by a credit institution if the relevant supervisory authority judges this to be prudentially adequate, and provided that the total of Tier 3 capital and Tier 2 capital of such credit institution does not exceed 250% of Tier 1 capital. The Capital Adequacy Directive is, therefore, *prima facie* more stringent than the Basle proposals on the amount of Tier 3 capital that may qualify for capital adequacy purposes.

(iv) The Basle Committee is considering retaining the principle currently contained in the Basle Agreement that Tier 1 capital should represent at least half of total qualifying capital, that is, that the sum of Tier 2 and Tier 3 capital should not exceed the total of qualifying Tier 1 capital. If the Basle Agreement is revised in this manner, much of the benefits introduced by Tier 3 capital will be lost, as although the more flexible Tier 3 capital will be available for inclusion in the measurement of capital adequacy, and accordingly funding costs can be reduced, the limits placed on amounts of Tier 3 capital eligible for inclusion will effectively reduce much of the cost savings as Tier 1 capital will need to be increased *pro tanto* with each increase in Tier 3 capital. It is, indeed, somewhat more concerning that the Basle Committee explicitly states that it is contemplating retention of the limitation of amounts of non-core capital because several members of the Committee "do not favour the use of Tier 3 capital for banks at all". This being the case, the difficulty of achieving international consensus on capital adequacy and the drift to a functional as opposed to an institutional approach to the measurement of capital becomes more apparent, and, of course, it should be remembered that the provisions of Annex V of the Capital Adequacy Directive, which provide for the use of Tier 3 capital, are not mandatory but are permissive only. It is entirely possible that considerable competitive disparities in the cost of funding banking and securities businesses could continue between the various EC Member States long after the implementation of the Capital Adequacy Directive, and EC credit institutions and securities firms may still find it more expensive to do business in third countries that impose higher local capital adequacy standards than the EC rules because of ideological differences in the assessment of capital adequacy.

CHAPTER 15

THE SUPERVISION OF CAPITAL ADEQUACY—II: SOLVENCY RATIO FOR CREDIT INSTITUTIONS

INTRODUCTION

15.1 The second principal directive implementing the capital adequacy regime for all EC-incorporated credit institutions is the Council Directive on a solvency ratio for credit institutions (the "Solvency Ratio Directive"), which was published on 18 December 1989, a couple of days after the Second Banking Directive.[1] The Solvency Ratio Directive complements the Own Funds Directive by analysing the asset side of a credit institution's balance sheet and applying risk-based weightings to asset values in order to determine how much qualifying capital, as determined initially by the Own Funds Directive, should be maintained to support assets held both on and off the balance sheet. As with the Own Funds Directive, the Solvency Ratio Directive must eventually be read in conjunction with the Capital Adequacy Directive.[2] It should be borne in mind, however, that the Capital Adequacy Directive will not be implemented in domestic legislation until 1 January 1996 at the earliest. Until implementation of the Capital Adequacy Directive, credit institutions must apply risk weightings to their assets in accordance with the Solvency Ratio Directive, regardless of whether a particular asset is intended to be held to maturity or, where the credit institution concerned is engaged in securities dealing, the asset is held for the purpose of trading only. As highlighted below, it is possible, therefore, that the delayed implementation of the Capital Adequacy Directive may result in credit institutions being placed at a competitive disadvantage to investment/financial institutions which do not take deposits.

The Solvency Ratio Directive, like the Own Funds Directive, follows the principles established in the Basle Agreement[3] in that it adopts the system of risk weighting assets according to perceived likelihood of counterparty failure. As with the Basle Agreement, the analysis of risk is rather crude on two principal counts. First, the only risk factor that is taken into account is counterparty failure. This restrictive approach to risk analysis can be justified for assets which are intended to be held to maturity, as counterparty failure is the obvious risk incidental to the holding of assets on such terms. It should be remembered, however, that credit institutions based in the EC, and particularly those structured on a universal bank basis, are just as likely to hold assets for trading purposes, incurring substantially different risks in so doing.

Second, even the analysis of credit risk is performed in a very crude manner which bears little relationship, in some cases, to the true credit risk associated with the holding

1. 89/647/EEC, OJ L386/14 of 30 December 1989, discussed in detail in Chap. 4, above.
2. 93/6/EEC, OJ L141/1 of 11 June, 1993.
3. The approach adopted by the Basle Agreement is discussed in more detail in Chap. 14, above.

161

of assets. For example, all assets which represent loans to non-bank, non-State entities are risk-weighted at 100%, regardless of the creditworthiness of the borrower concerned. By contrast, claims against industrialised countries are risk-weighted at 0%, disregarding any balance of payments or current account deficits, and claims against banks incorporated in OECD countries (or, to use the terminology of the Solvency Ratio Directive, Zone A countries) are risk-weighted at 20%, regardless of their balance sheet strength. On this basis, it is more expensive for a bank to lend to a global conglomerate whose debt carries the highest independent credit rating than it is for a bank to lend to another, financially-troubled bank, incorporated in an OECD country. More graphically, this approach means that, prior to the collapse of BCCI, but at a time when the majority of banks operating actively in the inter-bank market were sufficiently aware of the problems at BCCI, it was nonetheless cheaper in terms of capital cost for a bank to lend to BCCI than a blue chip corporate. In fact, blue chip corporates can generally borrow at cheaper rates in the money markets than lesser-known or dubious banks, and are frequently net lenders in the market.

As against this, bank regulators may argue that assessing the risk of lending to banks incorporated in an OECD country is rather easier than assessing the risk of lending to corporates because banks are subject to supervision which, although it may differ in its relative effectiveness and complexity from jurisdiction to jurisdiction, will generally be based on commonly held principles of minimum supervisory standards. Most industrialised nations, for example, now set minimum capital requirements for deposit-taking institutions and impose a minimum capital adequacy ratio on banks subject to their supervision. Within the G10 countries, there is the further assurance of an agreed minimum capital adequacy ratio for all banks incorporated in those countries. Equally, the initiatives displayed by the Basle Committee over the last two decades indicate the willingness (albeit born of necessity) of bank regulators in the developed nations to work together to agree minimum supervisory standards so that banks dealing with each other in the international financial markets can be reassured of the integrity of their market counterparties and, incidentally, of the safety and soundness of the markets in which they operate. A centralised system of regulation and supervision of banks, involving not only continuous monitoring of the performance and financial status of a bank, but also the imposition of capital and liquidity requirements, thus justifies the according of a lower risk weighting to a bank incorporated in an OECD country. Regulation and supervision does not, of course, guarantee the absence of bank failures nor, in a market economy, should they be intended so to do. Consequently, credit risk cannot be ignored, even for highly supervised banks, as is demonstrated by the 20%, rather than 0%, risk weighting allocated to claims against OECD banks.

15.2 Although the arguments set out above in favour of a reduced risk weighting for OECD banks have merit, they still may be criticised for their over-simplification and lack of sensitivity in an area where a true appreciation of risk factors is a prerequisite to an efficient and effective system of supervision. A number of criticisms to the according of straight 20% risk weighting for all OECD banks can be made. First, although there has been some measure of agreement among the G10 nations on a minimum capital adequacy ratio and on principles of consolidated supervision, the G10 nations do not constitute by any means all the OECD-member nations. Although some non-G10 OECD countries (for example, Australia) have voluntarily adopted the Basle Agreement, a large number of other OECD countries have not, or at least have not yet adopted it in full. The establishment through the Basle Agreement of a common definition of qualifying capital was crucial to the ability of banks and bank supervisory authorities to measure the soundness of a banking entity. In the absence of an internationally agreed definition of eligible capital, a bank which appears to be well capitalised according to local accounting and supervisory standards may fail to measure up to the standards set by the Basle Agreement. The likelihood of this happening is not insignificant, as evidenced by the difficulties which banks incorporated in G10 countries have faced in improving and restructuring their capital bases in order to meet the Basle Agreement requirements.[4]

15.3 Second, local laws and accounting practices and policies still differ significantly from jurisdiction to jurisdiction. It is impossible, therefore, to obtain a realistic appreciation of the financial soundness of a credit institution unless one appreciates the laws and accounting rules prevailing in the jurisdiction of its incorporation. The same criticism can, of course, be levelled in stronger terms against accounts produced by corporates which are not subject to any supervisory system. Accountancy, of course, is an art involving the expression of an opinion, not a science. The final opinion on a set of accounts will be tempered to an extent by the imposition of standard accounting policies and procedures, but without the protection of an external supervisor which can neutralise some of the excesses of interpretation and can enforce disclosure, the assessment of an institution's worth from a reading of its accounts can never be a reliable operation. The introduction of generally accepted accounting principles (GAAP), statements of standard accounting practice (SSAP) and financial reporting standards (FRS) and the like all contribute to the creation of some form of conformity in financial reporting and disclosure within particular jurisdictions but, as stated at the outset of this paragraph, differ from jurisdiction to jurisdiction in any event (for example United States GAAP is not identical to United Kingdom GAAP). Insofar as public reporting of accounts is concerned, much discretion still lies with the management of an institution, particularly as regards the valuing of assets, notwithstanding the oversight of an external auditor. The presence of a supervisory authority can introduce an element of restraint, as has been evident in recent years by, for example, the enforced provisioning against sovereign debt by the introduction of matrix provisioning requirements. In the case of corporates, disclosure obligations more incisive than those required by domestic laws may be imposed by the regulations of stock exchanges on which such corporates' stocks or bonds are listed, which again may enable potential creditors or investors to obtain a clearer picture of the financial situation of such corporates. Corporates generally, however, are not subject to the same kind of supervisory pressure as banks and it may be more difficult to assess, therefore, the true value of their assets as reported in their balance sheet. Absent these types of measures, however, it may be no easier to analyse the financial soundness of a credit institution on the basis of its financial reporting than it is to analyse the strength of any corporate, even though one is starting from the knowledge that a credit institution is required to meet a certain capital/assets ratio. Insofar as capital adequacy is concerned, it should also be remembered that this is only one, albeit an important, measure of financial soundness. Liquidity, for example, is just as important to a credit institution: a well-capitalised bank with no liquidity can just as easily fail as an undercapitalised bank,

---

4. For an interesting account of some of the difficulties which have been experienced in both EC and non-EC countries see: A. Murray-Jones and A. Gamble, *Managing Capital Adequacy* (Woodhead-Faulkner), 1991.

albeit perhaps with lower losses to depositors.[5] Financial reporting statements rarely provide any information of real value on the subject of liquidity, and consequently the maintenance by credit institutions of appropriate levels of liquidity is frequently found to be a prerequisite to continued authorisation.[6] In conclusion, therefore, although the presence of a supervisory authority is no assurance of better corporate governance and prudent business activity it may aid the prudent conduct of a credit institution's business.[7]

15.4 As has already been indicated above,[8] the establishment of minimum, internationally-agreed supervisory standards avails nothing if the standards are not strictly and diligently enforced or if a supervisory authority lacks the sophistication or resources necessary to supervise the operations of credit institutions which it has authorised. The latter point is particularly important in times of increasingly innovative financial products: the standards that have been agreed internationally or which, in the case of the EC, have been imposed by law, are merely crude skeletons onto which the intricacies of supervising particular businesses must be grafted: the skeleton is of no use if the muscle and skin grafts do not hold or do not fit, or are not attempted at all.

Everything depends, in the system developed in the EC and by the Basle Agreement, on the skill and diligence of the individual supervisory authorities: thus, one might argue that it is a bold (if not foolhardy) step to accord a 20% risk weighting to all credit institutions incorporated in an OECD nation without engaging upon any assessment of the sophistication or competence of the supervisory authorities in these countries. As indicated in the earlier chapter on consolidated supervision, the Basle Committee has already identified concerns regarding the actual, as opposed to assumed, capacity of bank supervisors and, in its paper published in June 1992, has advocated the prevention of expansion of banks across national borders if either home country supervisor or host country supervisor has doubts as to the other's capabilities. The collapse of BCCI has perhaps crystallised the concerns which a number of supervisory authorities clearly feel about the level of competence displayed by their fellow supervisors, even within the industrialised world and the EC. Just as these concerns remain, for the present, as dark mutterings under the breath, so they are ignored for the purpose of setting a risk weighting for claims against Zone A banks. There would be a certain irony, for example, if the supervisory authority in one Zone A country refused, in accordance with the Basle principles, to permit a bank incorporated in a different Zone A country from establishing a branch within its territory because of concerns which it had as to the adequacy of the supervision practised by the home country supervisory authority, yet still permitted credit institutions which it supervised to risk weight claims against that same bank at 20%.

15.5 Both the Basle Agreement and the combination of the Own Funds and Solvency Ratio Directives may be criticised on the ground that, in approaching the

---

5. Insofar as the position in the UK is concerned, the maintenance of adequate liquidity is a prerequisite criterion for initial and ongoing authorisation for credit institutions under the Banking Act 1987, see Penn, *Banking Supervision* (Butterworths), 1989, pp. 47–52.

6. In the UK, para. 4(1) of Sched. 3 to the Banking Act 1987 requires that an authorised credit institution conduct its business in a prudent manner, and in determining whether such business is conducted prudently the Bank of England will consider its liquidity which must be maintained at adequate levels. The Bank of England's general approach to liquidity is set out in a Bank of England paper dated July 1982 entitled "Measurement of Liquidity", amended by a paper issued in March 1988 entitled "Proposals for a Stock of High Liquidity".

7. See Penn, *above*, fn. 5, at p. 49.

8. See Chaps. 11 and 12, above.

supervision of credit institutions on an institutional basis without regard to the nature of the business carried on by those institutions or the quality of management of those institutions or their financial status, the resultant supervision fails to achieve its primary purpose, namely ensuring the financial stability of credit institutions and so protecting the interests of depositors. Factors such as political risk, settlement risk and market risk, all of which may substantially affect the value of assets, are largely ignored, although in practice they may give rise to serious problems in the context of the financial stability of a credit institution.

Notwithstanding the criticisms levelled above at the supervisory regime which has been established in respect of capital adequacy, it must be recognised that the new regime is merely a first step. The rules will undoubtedly change and, as they do, the level and application of supervisory standards will become more sophisticated and much more restrictive.

APPLICATION OF THE SOLVENCY RATIO DIRECTIVE

15.6 The Solvency Ratio Directive applies only to credit institutions as defined in the First Banking Directive.[9] Credit institutions which are affiliated to a central body in a Member State may be exempted from the provisions of the Directive, provided that all such affiliated credit institutions and their central bodies are included in consolidated solvency ratios in accordance with the Directive.[10] In addition, pending further harmonisation of the prudential rules relating to credit, interest rate and market risks, Member States may exclude from the scope of the Directive any credit institution specialising in the interbank and public-debt markets and fulfilling, together with the central bank, the institutional function of banking-system liquidity regulator, provided that (i) the sum of such institution's asset and off-balance sheet items included in the 50% and 100% risk weighting must not normally exceed 10% of total assets and off-balance sheet items, and shall not in any event exceed 15% before application of the weightings; (ii) its main activity consists of acting as intermediary between the central bank of its Member State and the banking system, and (iii) the competent authority applies adequate systems of supervision and control of its credit, interest rate and market risk.[11] Member States are obliged to inform the Commission of any exemptions granted, in order to ensure that they do not result in distortions in competition.

The Basle Agreement accords different risk weightings to claims on central governments and on credit institutions depending upon whether or not the countries concerned or the countries in which such banks are incorporated are full members of the OECD or have concluded special lending arrangements with the International Monetary Fund (IMF) associated with the IMF's General Agreement to Borrow. The Solvency Ratio Directive draws the same distinction for the purposes of risk weighting assets, but using different terminology, namely Zone A countries, which equate to OECD countries and countries which have concluded special lending arrangements with the IMF, and Zone B countries, which equate to non-OECD countries.[12] Similarly, under both the Solvency Ratio Directive and the Basle Agreement, a

9. Solvency Ratio Directive, 8th recital, art. 1(1).
10. *Ibid.*, art. 1(3).
11. *Ibid.*, art. 1(4).
12. *Ibid.*, art. 2(1).

distinction is drawn between claims on the banking sector and claims on the non-bank sector, the latter being accorded less favourable risk weightings. All claims on the non-bank private sector are, generally, risk weighted at 100%, except for specific items such as first ranking residential mortgages, which attract a 50% risk weighting so as to give some credit to the value of the collateral held in respect of such assets. The non-bank sector is defined in the Solvency Ratio Directive as all borrowers other than credit institutions, central governments, central banks, regional governments and local authorities, the EC, the European Investment Bank and multilateral development banks (defined to mean the International Bank for Reconstruction and Development, the International Finance Corporation, the Inter-American Development Bank, the Asian Development Bank, the African Development Bank, the Council of Europe Resettlement Fund, the Nordic Investment Bank and the Caribbean Development Bank, together, now, with the European Bank for Reconstruction and Development).

15.7 No attempt is made in the Solvency Ratio Directive to analyse the financial soundness of Zone A banks as opposed to banks incorporated in Zone B; rather, the assumption is implicitly made that banks incorporated in a Zone A country will generally be better supervised, and will tend to be supervised in accordance with standards which have been internationally accepted and are consistently applied, than banks incorporated in a Zone B nation. Accordingly, both long-term and short-term claims on Zone A banks are risk-weighted at 20%, whereas only short-term claims of Zone B banks will be risk weighted at 20%. Claims of a maturity of one year or more on Zone B banks will be risk weighted at 100%. There is some justification for discriminating in favour of Zone A credit institutions for supervisory purposes, the reasons being essentially the same as those set out at the beginning of this chapter in the discussion of the favourable treatment accorded to banks over corporates; the discrimination is, however, drawn on somewhat arbitrary grounds. For example, as stated above, not all OECD member nations subscribe to the Basle Agreement or international generally accepted accounting practices. Within Zone A nations themselves, furthermore, there is a considerable discrepancy in the standards of supervision and the capital adequacy and liquidity requirements imposed on credit institutions. As noted elsewhere in this book,[13] the Capital Adequacy Directive recognises the value of independent debt ratings as a pointer to the financial viability of a counterparty and permits a lower risk weighting to be accorded to trading book assets issued by entities which are not credit institutions, provided that such entities are sufficiently creditworthy (as independently determined) and, generally, a liquid market exists for the asset concerned. One might ask whether this approach should be applied to, or appropriate elements of this approach adjusted so as to result in a more sophisticated approach to the risk weighting of, all assets held by a credit institution and not simply those which fall within the trading book.

THE PRINCIPAL PROVISIONS OF THE SOLVENCY RATIO DIRECTIVE

15.8 The general principles of the Solvency Ratio Directive are specified in article 3, as follows:

1. The solvency ratio is a means of expressing qualifying capital (or own funds) as

---

13. See Chap. 16, below.

a proportion of risk-adjusted total assets and off-balance sheet items. The solvency ratio should be calculated on the basis of a credit institution's published audited accounts.[14]

2. The solvency ratios of credit institutions which are neither parent undertakings (as defined in the Consolidated Accounts Directive) nor subsidiaries of such undertakings are to be calculated on a solo basis.

3. The solvency ratios of credit institutions which are parent undertakings are to be calculated on a consolidated basis.[15]

4. Home country supervisory authorities may also require a parent undertaking which is a credit institution to calculate a sub-consolidated or solo solvency ratio in respect of that institution and any of its subsidiaries which are subject to their supervisory regime. Where this is not required, other measures must be taken by the home country supervisory authority to monitor the satisfactory allocation of capital within a banking group.

5. Where the subsidiary of a parent undertaking has been authorised by and is situate in a different Member State from its parent, its home country supervisory authority must require the subsidiary to calculate its sub-consolidated or solo solvency ratio. The subsidiary's supervisory authority may, however, delegate its responsibility for supervising the solvency of the subsidiary to the supervisory authority of the parent undertaking. Any such delegation of responsibility must be notified to the Commission.[16]

6. Home country supervisory authorities are required to ensure that the solvency ratios of the credit institutions subject to their supervision are calculated not less than twice each year, either by the credit institutions themselves, for onward communication to their supervisory authority, or by the supervisory authority, using data supplied by the credit institutions.

7. The valuation of assets and off-balance sheet items is to be effected in accordance with the Bank Accounts Directive.[17]

As stated in point 1 above, the qualifying capital (own funds) of a credit institution comprises the numerator of the fraction which produces the solvency ratio for each credit institution.[18] The denominator is comprised of the total of risk-adjusted assets and off-balance sheet items. The value of each balance sheet asset is multiplied by the risk weighting attributed to the counterparty under (primarily) article 6 of the Directive, to produce a risk-adjusted value.[19] Except as outlined in paragraphs 15.6 and 15.7 above, this book will not attempt to set out the risk weightings ascribed to various bank assets as specified in the Solvency Ratio Directive, and readers should refer, for specific details, to the Directive itself.

14. See also the Second Banking Directive discussed in detail in Chap. 4, above.

15. But note art. 9(3) of the Second Consolidated Supervision Directive, that supervisory authorities are not obliged to apply the Solvency Ratio Directive to subsidiaries whose business entails primarily market risk. Thus credit institutions which separate their trading book business and carry it on through a separate finance subsidiary may have a lower consolidated capital requirement than a universal bank which retains securities trading "in-house": see Chap. 10, above.

16. Solvency Ratio Directive, art. 3(6). See the comments in Chap. 10, above, regarding the consistency of this provision with the Basle Committee's Four Principles of Consolidated Supervision published in June 1992.

17. 86/635/EEC. This Directive is discussed in detail in Chap. 33, below. *See* especially paras. 33.5 to 33.15.

18. Solvency Ratio Directive, art. 4.

19. *Ibid.*, art. 5(1).

15.9 In the case of off-balance sheet items, the approach of the Basle Agreement has been adopted by the draftsmen of the Solvency Ratio Directive, that is a two-stage calculation is required. First, each off-balance sheet item is multiplied by a credit conversion factor, the amount of which will depend on whether the item in question is categorised as full risk (in which case 100% is taken into account), medium risk (in which case 50% is taken into account), medium/low risk (in which case 20% is taken into account) or low risk (treated as zero). The result of this calculation is then multiplied by the risk weighting attributed to the counterparty, as with balance sheet items. The result of this second calculation produces the risk-adjusted figure to be comprised in the amount constituting the denominator of the solvency ratio. This procedure is reviewed in detail later in this Chapter. With effect from 1 January 1993, EC-incorporated credit institutions have been required permanently to maintain a solvency ratio of at least 8%.[20]

RISK WEIGHTING OF DERIVATIVE INSTRUMENTS

15.10 In the case of interest-rate and foreign exchange-related off-balance sheet items, the method of calculating the appropriate risk weighting contained in the Solvency Ratio Directive follows that determined by the Basle Committee. The approach adopted in both the Solvency Ratio Directive and the Basle Agreement to calculating the risks incidental to holding these assets may be criticised as being somewhat insensitive to the actual risks incidental to the holding of these assets. Calculating the risks involved in the holding of derivative instruments, particularly those purchased over the counter ("OTC") as opposed to being exchange traded is, of course, an extremely difficult exercise, and at present there is little consensus both among the regulators and the regulated as to the manner in which such risks should properly be calculated. In the summer of 1993, a committee established by the G30 group of banks to examine the risks incidental to the holding of interest rate, currency and other OTC derivative instruments produced a report entitled "Derivatives— Practices and Principles", which attempted to remove some of the mystique and alleviate some of the fears expressed by regulators in relation to the creation, trading and holding of derivative instruments. The G30 report proposed the adoption of a number of industry practices to ensure both an understanding at managerial and board room levels of the risks associated in taking positions in derivatives instruments, and in selling such instruments to third parties, and that excessive exposures in such instruments are not assumed. In what has been criticised by a number of commentators as largely a self-serving report, however, the G30 committee did not advocate the introduction of additional or increased capital requirements to be held against derivatives exposures. In a separate development, the Basle Committee is continuing its own work on the analysis of such instruments.[21] It is likely to be some years, however, before the research from the Basle Committee is completed and consensus is reached

---

20. *Ibid.*, art. 10(1). See also the 9th recital to the Directive which states that the level of 8% has been adopted following a statistical survey of capital requirements in force at the beginning of 1988.

21. Recent publications emanating from the Basle Committee have included papers issued on the subject of netting *in forex* and interest rate swaps, but with no recommendations proposing any revised capital treatment for such derivatives. See "The Prudential Supervision of Netting, Market Risks and Interest Rate Risk", published in April 1993.

among regulators as to the most appropriate manner in which to risk weight OTC derivative instruments from a capital adequacy perspective.

The risks inherent in the holding of interest rate and currency swaps are entirely different from those applying to balance sheet assets. The risk involved in a lending transaction is obvious—failure to pay the debt in full results in the total or partial loss of that asset, or the expected income will not materialise when contractually due although some or all of it may be recovered in the future, thus resulting, at the least, in a short-term fall in expected available funds. Capital is required, therefore, to sustain this loss or cover the short term absence of funds and the amount of capital required will reflect the relatively illiquid nature of the asset. The most important source of risk, therefore, is the counterparty.

The asset concerned (that is, the loan) must be entered into the lender's accounts and balance sheet immediately it arises—a tangible outflow is seen. In their most simple form, interest rate and currency swaps are utilised to equalise an exposure resulting from a mismatch between the interest rate basis or currency of an income stream and the interest rate basis or currency of a payment obligation. For example, an entity which receives floating rate income but which is funded on a fixed rate basis has an obvious risk in basis exposure. Such an entity will accordingly seek a counterparty which has an equal but opposite exposure and so would be willing to swap its fixed rate income for the entity's floating rate income. The swap will then provide for a netted-out payment to be made on a series of payment dates. The need to manage basis risk and currency exposure has become more acute in recent years as a consequence of the movement away from government or central bank intervention in the management of interest and currency exchange rates, leaving the rates, by and large, to find their own level in the market.

Amounts due under an interest rate swap

15.11 Amounts from time to time due under an interest rate swap will be determined by reference to a notional principal amount which will normally be approximate, in the case of the example set out above, to the actual principal amount of fixed rate debt owed by the entity seeking the fixed rate counterparty. A swap will normally be structured, however, such that actual amounts are only payable one way on any payment date, depending on which way the market has moved; hence the characterisation of these instruments as contracts for differences. At each payment date, the floating rate arm of the swap will be reset by reference to the current rate of interest according to the index on which the floating rate is established. For the period up to the first payment date, the relevant floating rate will be that prevailing on the relevant index at the time the contract was struck. A payment is made at the end of each period by reference, therefore, to the rates of interest struck at the beginning of that payment period: in the case of the fixed rate arm of the swap, of course, the rate of interest will remain constant throughout the life of the swap. So, if in the example set out above the index on which the floating rate of interest is determined has fallen at the beginning of a payment period below the agreed fixed rate, the fixed rate payer will be obliged to pay an amount at the end of that period equal to the difference between the floating rate set at the beginning of the period and the fixed rate. If the floating rate increases above the agreed fixed rate, the converse applies and the floating rate payer must account to its counterparty for the difference. The floating rate payer thus effectively forgoes its opportunity of profiting from the interest rate differential which would occur in an increasing rate environment to obtain cover for itself in a declining rate environment.

Currency swaps

15.12 The same general principles apply to currency swaps, pursuant to which the parties agree to exchange payments in different currencies at an agreed strike rate. Currency exchange swaps differ from interest rate swaps, however, in that there is an actual exchange of principal (one currency for another) at the outset and on maturity (and, if the swap is amortising, throughout the life of the swap) and therefore the differential payment due on each payment date is calculated by reference to an actual rather than a notional principal amount.

The risks involved

15.13 The risks involved in these transactions can be categorised as counterparty risk, position risk and settlement, or delivery, risk. Of these, the most important is position risk as, indeed, the very essence of these contracts is their attempt to neutralise the effect of market movements on income versus payment obligations. The consequences, therefore, even of counterparty default will depend to an extent on the market position occupied by the non-defaulting party at the time of default. The approach of the Basle Agreement and the Solvency Ratio Directive to the analysis of this risk in terms of capital requirements is at first sight curious in that, as described in more detail below, capital is required to be held only against contracts under which the reporting credit institution (being the non-defaulting party) was "in the money" (ie, profiting) at the time of default. If the non-defaulting party is "in the money" at the time of default, the consequence of default is akin to a loss of opportunity—the profit which would have been made is no longer there (and who can say, even, if the contract had run to maturity that the same or any profit would eventually have been made). The failure to realise notional profits does not, however, constitute a drain on capital as such, if one ignores for present purposes the incidental expenses of engaging in this business. If the non-defaulting party was running a matched book, however, the loss of an in-the-money contract will result in an asymetrical market position, which ought to be rectified. A premium will generally be payable to the counterparty willing to replace an in-the-money contract to compensate for the fact that the counterparty will, by definition, be commencing the contract out of money. It is the cost of replacing a lost contract in the market, therefore, which generates a capital requirement. If the contract which was in the money is not replaced, and the book is left unmatched, there is no separate capital requirement in respect of the orphaned out-of-the-money contract although that contract represents a current actual loss to the reporting institution. The regulators' answer to this challenge would, presumably, be that the system of risk weightings contained in the Solvency Ratio Directive is intended to address only counterparty risk, not position risk. An out-of-the-money contract *ipso facto* carries no counterparty risk as all performance is due from the reporting institution. Any losses eventually incurred on a contract, to the extent not off-set by other income received in the relevant trading period, will in any event be deducted from total capital. In addition, a credit institution is under a general obligation to manage its business in a prudent manner, which means, in the case of over-the-counter derivatives such as interest rate and currency swaps, that matched books should be maintained at all times. If a lost swap were not immediately replaced, although a short term saving in capital might be achieved, it may be at the cost of eventually being penalised by the supervisory authority and, potentially, being prevented from entering into derivatives trading.

15.14 Because a swap transaction represents an exchange of payments over time, however, one cannot look only at the market position of a non-defaulting party at the time of counterparty default. A position which is in the money at the time of a counterparty's default may, if the contract cannot be terminated at that point, move out of the money during the remaining term of the contract. It is important, therefore, for strategic reasons if not capital adequacy reasons for a non-defaulting party to be able, so far as allowed by relevant local laws, to terminate a contract which its counterparty cannot perform to maturity. This issue gives rise to a number of legal questions of importance to bank supervisory authorities, including the following:

(i) at what point may a default be declared by a solvent party to a swap contract if the counterparty is insolvent or is giving rise to concerns as to its solvency? If the solvent party, for example, is out of the money at the time a winding-up petition is presented against its counterparty, the presentation of the petition does not render the counterparty incapable of performing the swap contract at that time because no amounts will be due from it; rather, payments will be due to it from the solvent party. Equally, even if the insolvent party were out of the money at the time of its becoming technically insolvent, insolvency does not necessarily constitute a repudiation of the contract and, indeed, in a number of legal systems, statutory provisions specifically provide for insolvency not to amount to repudiation so as to protect the assets of the insolvent for the benefit of its creditors. It is possible, in other words, that insolvency of a counterparty may not permit the solvent party to the contract to terminate the contract; on a worst case basis, the solvent party may be obliged to perform its side of the bargain but without receiving any benefit in return;

(ii) where a series of contracts has been entered into between two parties, there is the added danger that a liquidator, trustee in bankruptcy or similar officer may elect to "perform" only those contracts which benefit the insolvent (which by definition means that the solvent party is the one which is, in effect, required to render performance) and to disclaim the contracts under which the insolvent is making a loss. Otherwise, the solvent counterparty would seek to close out all the contracts and set off the losses and gains on termination. The right given to liquidators in many legal jurisdictions to disclaim onerous contracts and perform only those which will benefit the insolvent is particularly disadvantageous to market players. The decision to "perform" contracts may, however, be difficult for a liquidator to make if the contracts concerned have a medium or long term unexpired duration, as the market could just as easily move against the insolvent as continue to run in its favour. Once a liquidator affirms a contract, it is most unlikely that he will be given the opportunity to renounce his decision in the future. Of course, if a liquidator does affirm a swap contract, the counterparty will ordinarily rank *pari passu* with all other creditors insofar as concerns its right to payment on the contract out of the insolvent's assets.

Most interest rate and currency swaps are over-the-counter rather than exchange-traded contracts. Contracts entered into on exchanges may provide more protection to market players in the event of a counterparty insolvency for the reasons explained later in this Chapter. Standard market documentation does, however, exist for most types of interest rate and currency swaps[22] and attempts to avoid so far as possible the legal difficulties which arise on counterparty default, for example:

(a) where a party enters into more than one swap contract with a counterparty, or anticipates that it will be carrying out a number of trades over time, the trades will be documented on the basis of one master contract, so that each individual trade is expressed to form a part of the single, master contract and not to constitute a separate contract. This device will prevent a liquidator from disclaiming non-profitable contracts: he must either accept the whole of the master contract or disclaim it;

(b) equally, a master contract will provide that amounts payable in the same currency on the same day under different trades may be netted out so that only a net amount becomes payable from one party to the other;

(c) swap contracts will be drafted on terms which permit a party to the contract to terminate in the event that certain circumstances arise which cause concern as to the counterparty's solvency. These circumstances will generally relate to a period prior to formal insolvency because, as mentioned above, it may not be possible under certain legal regimes for a non-defaulting party to terminate a contract on the insolvency of its counterparty. Such a termination would, rather, amount to a repudiation by the solvent party which could render it liable for damages. Triggering events are linked, for example, to the presentation of a petition to wind up rather than the passing of a winding-up order or may even be linked to financial covenants. The occurrence of the event gives the solvent counterparty the right but not the obligation to terminate the contract;

(d) where trades between the same parties are documented in separate contracts, provision will usually be made in the contracts for the right to set off amounts due under each contract. Again, contractual rights of set-off will frequently be subject to mandatory set-off rules on insolvency and, if possible, contracts will therefore provide for termination of contracts to be effected prior to insolvency in order to ensure the ability to rely on contractual set-off rights;

(e) documentation will frequently include a mechanism by which the present value of unrealised future payments under prematurely terminated in-the-money contracts can be calculated and charged to the defaulting party (assuming it was the defaulting party that was out of the money). This calculation may amount simply to the cost of replacing the lost swap.

All the above legal factors will be of interest to supervisory authorities in their assessment of an appropriate risk weighting for off-exchange derivative contracts. Where the legal consequences of a default or insolvency are not certain, a higher risk weighting may be imposed than practitioners may perhaps expect or consider to be justified. For example, under the Basle Agreement and the Solvency Ratio Directive, the system of amalgamating trades into a single master contract for netting purposes

---

22. See, eg, the master interest rate and currency exchange agreement published by the International Association of Swap Dealers (ISDA), most recent version, 1992; master agreements are also produced by the British Bankers' Association, leg., BBAIRS, 2nd FRABBA.

("netting by novation") is recognised only for trades which call for delivery of the same currency on the same settlement dates. At the time of writing the Basle Committee is working on more extensive netting proposals but, in the absence of clear laws in a number of jurisdictions on the efficacy of more extensive forms of netting by novation in an insolvency situation, regulators will continue to tread the most cautious path.[23]

15.15 In the case of all contracts such as interest rate swaps, foreign exchange contracts and other contracts for differences or derivative instruments, the risks of the contract depend ultimately on the tenor of the particular contract and the volatility of the market rates (whether of interest or currency exchange) underlying, or the value (in the case of options or warrants) of, the particular instrument. As most of these instruments are matched by the credit institutions which enter into them (that is, they hedge their own risk under each contract by entering into an equal and opposite contract), the theoretical basis for calculating the credit risk associated with the contracts has consisted of an analysis of the behaviour of matched pairs of swaps under different volatility assumptions.

The Basle Agreement contains alternative methods of assessing the credit risk of interest rate and foreign exchange contracts: the current exposure (or "marking to market") method, and the original exposure method. The current exposure method requires banks to calculate the current replacement cost of each contract with positive value by marking to market such contract and then (except in the case of single currency floating/floating interest rate swaps) to add a factor (the "add-on") to reflect the potential future exposure over the remaining life of all such contracts. The add-on is calculated on the basis of the total notional and actual principal amount of each bank's book of such contracts, split by residual maturities:

Residual maturity	Interest-rate contracts	Exchange-rate contracts
Less than one year	nil	1%
One year and over	0·5%	5%

The original exposure method, used by a minority of central banks, ignores the first step of marking to market and instead estimates the potential future exposure only against each type of contract, and allots a notional capital weight accordingly. The credit conversion factors are applied to the notional or actual principal amount of each contract according to its nature and maturity:

Residual maturity	Interest-rate contracts	Exchange-rate contracts
Less than one year	0·5%	2·0%
One year and less than two years	1·0%	5·0% (ie 2·0% + 3·0%)
For each additional year	1·0%	3·0%

For interest rate contracts, the Basle Agreement contains a national discretion as to

23. See "The Prudential Supervision of Netting, Market Risks and Interest Rate Risk", published by the Basle Committee in April 1993, and in particular the paper entitled, "The Supervisory Recognition of Netting for Capital Adequacy Purposes", which contains the explicit acceptance by the Basle Committee of the analysis of interbank netting schemes contained in the Lamfalussy Report, published by the Bank for International Settlements in November 1990. The Basle Committee proposes, in the aforementioned paper, that the Basle Agreement should be revised to recognise, in addition to netting by novation, other forms of bilateral netting of credit exposures to the extent that such arrangements are effective under relevant laws and comply with the other minimum standards set forth in the Lamfalussy Report.

whether the conversion factors are to be based on original or residual maturity. For exchange rate contracts, the conversion factors are to be calculated according to the original maturity of the instrument.

15.16 The alternatives given in Annex II to the Solvency Ratio Directive are the same bases of calculation as given in the Basle Agreement, namely either the "marking to market" approach or the original exposure approach. These two approaches are to be used to measure the risks associated with the transactions listed in Annex III to the Solvency Ratio Directive, namely interest rate contracts (single currency interest rate swaps, basis swaps, forward-rate agreements, interest-rate options purchased and other contracts of a similar nature) and foreign-exchange contracts (cross-currency interest rate swaps, forward foreign-exchange contracts, currency futures, currency options purchased and other contracts of a similar nature). Annex II then sets out the steps in the calculation of the risk-adjusted value of such assets:

Marking to market   (a) mark to market the current replacement cost of all contracts with positive values;

(b) the potential future credit exposure is calculated (except in the case of single currency floating/floating interest rate swaps) by multiplying the notional principal amounts or values underlying a credit institution's aggregate book by the following appropriate percentage:

Residual maturity	*Interest-rate contracts*	*Exchange-rate contracts*
One year or less	0%	1·0%
More than one year	0·5%	5·0%

(c) the sum of the current replacement cost and (where relevant) potential future credit exposure is then multiplied by the risk weightings allocated to the relevant counterparties.

Original exposure approach (a) the notional principal amount of each instrument is multiplied by the relevant percentage, as follows:

Original maturity*	*Interest-rate contracts*	*Exchange-rate contracts*
One year or less	0·5%	2·0%
More than one year but not exceeding two years	1·0%	5·0%
Additional allowance for each additional year	1·0%	3·0%

(b) the figure thus obtained is then multiplied by the risk weighting allocated to the relevant counterparties.

* in the case of interest-rate contracts, credit institutions may, subject to the consent of their supervisory authorities, choose either residual or original maturity.

Interest-rate and foreign-exchange contracts traded on recognised exchanges where they are subject to daily margin requirements and foreign-exchange contracts with an original maturity of 14 days are excluded.

15.17 The approach taken to these instruments in both the Basle Agreement and the Solvency Ratio Directive is, therefore, substantially the same. It was noted above that exchange-traded interest rate and foreign-exchange contracts are excluded from the capital requirements of the Solvency Ratio Directive where they are subject to daily margin requirements. Exchange-traded contracts generally are less susceptible to the consequences of counterparty failure not only because of exchange-imposed margin requirements, which ensure daily marking-to-market of exposures and maintenance of collateral to absorb market movements, but also (and most fundamentally to credit risk) because normally the use of exchange will interpose a central clearer between market counterparties and, at the same time, restrict counterparties to members of an exchange. Trades transacted on an exchange will ordinarily be structured legally as two back-to-back trades between seller and exchange clearer and buyer and exchange clearer. Seller and buyer must normally transact as principals, even if engaging in a transaction for a client unable (through its not being a member) to access the exchange. Because clearing is carried out centrally, settlement and delivery risk, as well as counterparty risk, will also be reduced.[24] If an exchange member were to default on a contract, therefore, the direct loss would be felt not by its market counterparty, but by the exchange or the exchange's clearer subject to amenable local laws; all exchange contracts entered into by the defaulting counterparty may be terminated and netted out or set-off by the clearer itself. The fact that all members of an exchange must deal as principals assists in the set-off process as, if they were dealing as agents only on behalf of customers, the mutuality of dealing required by most legal jurisdictions as a prerequisite of set-off would not be satisfied.

Insolvency

15.18 The default and settlement rules of clearing houses are permitted to prevail over the statutory insolvency regimes in a number of industrialised countries.[25] More legal certainty pertains, therefore, to exchange-traded contracts than to over-the-counter derivatives, and this much is reflected in the treatment of counterparty risk. In the case of most sophisticated markets, the counterparty in an exchange-traded contract will be the exchange itself or its clearing house. This is recognised in terms of risk weighting, by, in effect, a nil capital requirement for counterparty risk, provided that the exchange rules call for daily margin requirements.

The calculation of the risk-adjusted value of foreign exchange contracts does not differentiate between currencies which are linked into an exchange rate mechanism, such as the European Monetary System, and in respect of which market risks are

24. Surprisingly, Annex II of the Capital Adequacy Directive does not explicitly recognise the reduction of settlement and delivery risk through sophisticated clearing systems; curiously, however, the 15th recital to the Capital Adequacy Directive states that it is important that monitoring of delivery/settlement risks should take account of the existence of systems offering adequate protection that reduces that risk.

25. Eg, the Companies Act 1989 has amended English insolvency law by recognising the default and settlement rules of recognised exchanges and permitting their application ahead of or instead of traditional English rules on the treatment of contracts on insolvency. The rules apply only to market contracts concluded on recognised exchanges which fall within the statutory definition and not to over-the-counter contracts, and are designed to protect the operation of the financial markets particularly in the City of London, not least the futures exchanges. The default and settlement rules of the exchanges are designed to establish the net sums owing between a defaulting member and (through the exchange clearer) other members and, if the member has been dealing also for its customers, between the defaulting member and its customers. The revisions made to insolvency law by the Companies Act 1989 permit these rules to be implemented in the insolvency of a member and require liquidators of an insolvent member to provide assistance to the exchange clearer in order to determine outstanding positions under exchange contracts. The net sums calculated by the clearer may then be proved in a liquidation or (with certain limited exceptions) may be set off against mutual debts. The power of a liquidator to disclaim onerous contracts is disapplied to exchange-traded contracts.

controlled within specified parameters, and currencies which float at unrestricted rates, in respect of which market risk is obviously that much greater. The theory of economic and monetary union, therefore, is studiously ignored on the practical level in the Solvency Ratio Directive. As will be seen, however, in the next chapter, this issue is addressed in the Capital Adequacy Directive.

Contracts for novation

15.19 As stated above, where there is a separate bilateral contract for novation, recognised by the relevant credit institution's supervisory authority, between the credit institution and its counterparty under which any obligation to each other to deliver payments in their common currency on a given date is automatically amalgamated with other similar obligations due on the same date, then it is only the netted-off amount which is required to be risk-weighted.[26] Where the documentation concerned does not novate agreements for the payment of obligations on the same date, but instead provides for acceleration and netting-off of due amounts in the event of the insolvency of the counterparty, then the gross amounts must be risk weighted, as the legal efficacy of insolvency close-out clauses such as described above is uncertain.[27]

The risk-asset weighting of derivative instruments is also the subject of the Capital Adequacy Directive, which applies a more sensitive (although many would query whether it is sensitive enough) analysis to position risk, settlement risk and delivery risk of derivatives.[28]

ON-BALANCE SHEET RISK WEIGHTINGS

15.20 The risk weightings to be attributed to assets are specified in article 6 of the Directive. Four categories of risk weighting have been devised, namely 0%, 20%, 50% and 100%. Article 6 specifies classes of assets within each band of risk weighting, but home supervisory authorities retain a discretion to fix higher weightings to particular assets as they see fit. Obviously, if one supervisory authority unilaterally fixes higher weightings to assets than provided for in the Directive, while the remaining national supervisory authorities adhere to the terms of article 6, credit institutions supervised by the first supervisory authority will be at a competitive disadvantage against credit institutions incorporated elsewhere in the EC, as a greater amount of capital will be required to achieve a solvency ratio of 8%.[29] The categories of risk weighting are broadly similar to those set out in the Basle Agreement (although the Basle Agreement also has a 10% risk weighting category which is applied at national discretion for certain claims on domestic public sector entities excluding central government, and loans guaranteed by such entities to the extent covered). For example, items such as cash and equivalent items and claims on Zone A central government and central banks are zero-risk weighted; items constituting claims on Zone A credit institutions (not being

26. Annex II, second para.
27. For an interesting discussion on the approach of the Basle Committee to the setting of capital requirements for derivative and hedging instrument, see Shea [1991] 6 JIBL 136.
28. The proposed Capital Adequacy Directive is considered in greater detail in Chap. 16.
29. The 8% solvency ratio is considered to be the minimum ratio by some supervisory authorities, eg, the Bank of England, which applies solvency ratios at levels much higher than 8% for the majority of institutions it authorises under the Banking Act 1987.

capital items referred to in the Own Funds Directive) are risk-weighted at 20%, as discussed above; loans secured on residential property occupied or let by the borrower are risk-weighted at 50%, claims on the non-bank sectors of Zone A and Zone B are risk-weighted at 100%, and claims on Zone B central governments and banks (except where denominated and funded in the national currency of the borrower) are also risk-weighted at 100%.

The classification of assets set out in article 6(1) is notable by its relative precision, particularly if one compares the classification here to the "definition by descrition" of capital contained in the Own Funds Directive, which contains much more latitude for interpretation. There appears, therefore, to be a curious dislocation between the drafting of the Own Funds Directive and the drafting of the Solvency Ratio Directive. The difference in style can, however, be explained away on the basis that the constituents of capital will differ in name and structure from jurisdiction to jurisdiction, whereas types of banking asset are relatively constant. Whereas capital can be described, for the sake of agreeing an international norm, only by distilling its essential characteristics, assets can be categorised relatively easily on a common basis in most jurisdictions: there are only a finite number of ways to describe a loan or a credit facility. As stated earlier, however, although much work has been done to achieve the classification of assets set out in article 6(1), the process still constitutes a somewhat crude system by which to accord risk factors. In contrast with the Own Funds Directive, relatively little scope is left to national supervisory authorities to apply more sensitive rules within the framework established by the Solvency Ratio Directive, which is regrettable particularly since the requirements have the immutable force of law which makes any unilateral adjustment perilous, no matter how sensible such adjustment might be considered to be. The comitology procedure, described at the end of this Chapter, is intended to permit amendments to the Directive without requiring the full legislative process to be followed through again, thus providing a partial answer to the concerns just raised. However, the comitology procedure itself is likely to be bureaucratic and burdensome and is unlikely to result in Member States being able to make swift amendments to the Directive to keep pace with market innovation. The EC legislation may ironically, inhibit EC credit institutions and result in their losing out to third countries able to react more swiftly to market change.

OFF-BALANCE SHEET RISK WEIGHTINGS

15.21 Off-balance sheet items are also risk weighted in accordance with the provisions of article 6(2) of the Solvency Ratio Directive. The imposition of capital requirements on off-balance sheet items reflects the concerns which have been felt by national supervisory authorities, particularly over the last decade, in relation to banks entering into transactions structured so that they do not need to be reflected in the bank's balance sheet according to traditional accounting methods but, if analysed in an economic manner as opposed to a technical manner, involve the bank undertaking real and significant risks. By not being required to enter these items on their balance sheets, banks were absolved of any obligation to set aside or ensure an appropriate level of capital to support the risk associated with the asset. The absence of the asset on the balance sheet, however, obviously does nothing to avoid the risk associated with the asset. The result of this practice, which emerged at a time when many banks' balance sheets were already under considerable strain as a consequence of non-performing debt such as LDC debt, was that banks whose balance sheets already barely met prudent capital adequacy targets were in fact in an even more precarious position as a result of undisclosed commitments and their associated risks.

The apportionment of risk weightings to off-balance sheet assets is achieved by a two-way process. First, the off-balance sheet items are accorded credit conversion factors which differ according to whether an asset is classified as full risk, medium risk, medium-low risk or low risk, as set out in Annex I to the Solvency Ratio Directive. The classification of off-balance sheet items by reference to credit conversion factors attempts to categorise the true nature of the credit risk associated with these assets. The full risk category covers items which are, in fact, loan substitutes, for example guarantees having the character of credit substitutes (which would encompass financial guarantees such as standby letters of credit and general guarantees of indebtedness), acceptances, transactions with recourse and sale and repurchase agreements. The credit conversion factor applied to these assets is 100%. Medium risk assets carry a credit conversion factor of 50% and include documentary credits issued and confirmed, performance and bid bonds, note issuance facilities and revolving underwriting facilities, and undrawn credit facilities with an original maturity of more than one year. Medium/low risk assets carry a credit conversion factor of 20% and include documentary credits in which the underlying shipment acts as collateral and other self-liquidating transactions; low risk assets carry a credit conversion factor of zero and include undrawn credit facilities with an original maturity of up to and including one year or which may be cancelled unconditionally at any time without notice.

Each off-balance sheet item is multiplied by the appropriate credit conversion factor, and the resultant figure is then multiplied by the appropriate risk weighting attributable to the counterparty to achieve a final risk weighting for capital adequacy purposes. In the case of asset sale and repurchase agreements and outright forward purchases, the weightings used are those applying to the assets in question and not to the counterparty in question. Thus, in the case of a repurchase agreement involving sovereign debt of a Zone A country between a credit institution and a non-bank private entity, the risk weighting of the transaction for the selling credit institution will be calculated on the basis of the 0% risk asset weighting accorded to the Zone A sovereign debt, and not 100% risk weighting of the counter-party. Reverse repurchase and securities borrowing agreements are treated by the Solvency Ratio Directive in effect the same as any other claim, with the risk weighting of the claim being determined by reference to the counter-party to the transaction rather than the assets the subject matter of the contract. If the assets concerned are high grade sovereign debt instruments or other such assets carrying a low risk weighting, however, the benefit of this lower risk weighting may, at the discretion of the relevant supervisory authorities, be realised by a credit institution if certain conditions are satisfied that permit recognition of the lower risk weighting of the collateral. Under the Capital Adequacy Directive, the treatment of reverse repo and securities borrowing transactions for capital purposes depends on whether they are held for trading purposes or as a means of taking security: if the latter is the case, the assets brought or borrowed are risk weighted according to the provisions of the Solvency Ratio Directive and not the proposed Capital Adequacy Directive, which will result in a higher risk weighting requirement.

15.22 Where off-balance sheet items carry explicit guarantees, they are to be weighted as if they had been incurred on behalf of the guarantor rather than the counterparty.[30] Thus the risk weighting of a transaction can be reduced by assiduous structuring and the imposition of, for example, a bank standby letter of credit to back a commercial credit. Where the potential exposure arising from off-balance sheet transactions is fully and completely secured to the satisfaction of the competent supervisory authority by collateral of the types referred to in article 6 paragraphs (1)(a)(7) and (1)(b)(11),[31] weightings of 0% and 20% will be applied, depending on the collateral in question. Thus, reverse repurchase and securities borrowing transactions the subject matter of which is central government securities issued by a Zone A country may benefit from a zero risk weighting, provided that the claim of the reporting credit institution is fully and completely secured against the government securities to the satisfaction of the credit institution's supervisory authority.

RISK WEIGHTING CLAIMS AGAINST LOCAL AUTHORITIES

15.23 Article 7 of the Solvency Ratio Directive permits Member States to fix a risk weighting of 0% to on- and off-balance sheet claims against their own regional governments and local authorities if there is no difference in risk between claims on these bodies and claims against their central governments because of the revenue-raising powers of the regional governments and local authorities and the existence of specific institutional arrangements the effect of which is to reduce the risk of default by these bodies.[32] Any Member State which believes this reduction to zero-risk weighting to be justified is obliged to notify the Commission, which will circulate this notice throughout the Community. Other Member States may then offer credit institutions subject to their prudential supervision the opportunity to apply a zero-risk weighting to any claims which they may have against the specified regional governments and local authorities or against claims guaranteed by them.[33] This approach attempts to ensure that competition between Community credit institutions is maintained at relatively equal levels, provided that the Member States do decide to accord all such claims the same risk-weighting. Failure by any Member State to do so will render it less attractive for credit institutions subject to supervision by that Member State to do business with such regional governments and local authorities.

CLAIMS COLLATERALISED BY SECURITIES

15.24 Article 8 of the Solvency Ratio Directive permits Member States to fix a risk weighting of 20% to claims which are secured, to the satisfaction of the supervisory authority concerned, by collateral in the form of securities issued by Zone A regional governments or local authorities, by deposits placed with Zone A credit institutions other than the lending institution, or by certificates of deposit or similar instruments issued by those credit institutions. This permits, for example, national supervisory

30. Solvency Ratio Directive, art. 6(4).
31. Ie, Zone A central government or central bank securities, securities issued by the EC, cash deposits placed with the lending institutions or similar instruments issued by and lodged with the latter, and asset items secured, to the satisfaction of the relevant supervisory authority, by collateral in the form of securities issued by the European Investment Bank or by multilateral development banks.
32. *Ibid.*, art. 7(1).
33. *Ibid.*, art. 7(2).

authorities to allow a syndicated loan to a non-bank private company to be risk-weighted at 20% on the books of a syndicate member where collateralised by a pledged deposit made with the agent bank where the agent is incorporated in a Zone A country (for example, an EC credit institution). The agent bank of course, may risk weight its claim against the borrower at 0%, if the collateral consists of a cash deposit or like security. The 20% risk weighting will be attributed only, of course, to the portion of the loan which is collateralised. In addition, if at any time the collateral is lost (if, for example, it is provided by a third party guarantor who becomes insolvent), the full risk weighting will apply to the loan. This national discretion also permits a 20% risk weighting to be accorded to reverse repurchase and securities borrowing agreements which involve certificates of deposit or other securities issued by Zone A credit institutions, provided that the securities are properly secured in favour of the buying institution.

Article 8 further permits Member States to apply a 10% risk weighting to claims on institutions specialising in the interbank and public debt markets in their home Member States and subject to close supervision by their national supervisory authority, where those claims are fully and completely secured, to the satisfaction of the home supervisory authority, by a combination of assets mentioned in article 6(1)(a)—that is, qualifying for a zero-risk weighting—and article 6(1)(b)—that is, qualifying for a 20% risk-weighting—and which are recognised by the home supervisory authority as constituting adequate collateral.

Any provisions adopted by a Member State pursuant to article 8 are to be notified to the Commission, which will circulate the information to the other Member States. The Commission is to examine the implications of these provisions on a periodic basis to ensure that they do not result in any distortions of competition. Within three years of the adoption of the Solvency Ratio Directive, the Commission is to submit a report to the Council together, where necessary, with any proposals it might consider appropriate.[34]

MINIMUM SOLVENCY RATIO REQUIREMENT

15.25 The minimum solvency ratio to be maintained by EC credit institutions is set at 8%,[35] although national supervisory authorities are free to impose higher rates as they consider appropriate.[36] As we indicated in an earlier chapter, the Bank of England has made clear its intention to continue its current practice of setting an individual solvency ratio requirement for each bank subject to its supervision, with an overall minimum requirement of 8%.[37] Credit institutions which are deemed, therefore, to engage in riskier business or to be less well managed (but obviously still managed on a prudent basis[38]), which are perceived to have greater than average exposure to particular sectors of the economy or particular counterparties or which, quite simply, are new institutions to the Bank of England and thus result in the Bank of England taking a very cautious

---

34. *Ibid.*, art. 8(3).
35. *Ibid.*, art. 10(1). See also 9th recital.
36. *Ibid.*, art. 10(2).
37. See Chap. 12, above.
38. As to the meaning of "prudent" in the context of banking supervision in the UK see Penn, fn. 5, above, at p. 48 *et seq.*

view, may be required to satisfy a higher solvency ratio requirement that those with more balanced exposures or better management or with a longer corporate history.

It may be argued that the system of risk-weighting is designed to create an adequate means of gauging the risks involved in all banking-type transactions with all categories of counterparty, and accordingly the minimum solvency ratio produced by this means should of itself equate to produce an adequate and constant standard for prudential supervision no matter what the particular characteristics of a credit institution and its business are, and that, accordingly, a higher individual ratio need not be set for particular credit institutions. This is certainly an argument used by some national supervisory authorities within the Community. Exposure to specific sectors of the economy, or to certain debtors or types of debtor, are seen as a distinct aspect of prudential supervision in themselves, to be legislated on in a specific manner, namely through the Large Exposures Directive,[39] which assumes the minimum 8% solvency ratio requirement.[40] The Large Exposures Directive will require extra capital to be raised if a credit institution engages in more business with a certain customer than thought prudent by the national regulators.

Given this safeguard, it may be thought that, as a starting point, all supervisory authorities should require only the minimum 8% threshold, and that those supervisory authorities, such as the Bank of England, which require more of specific institutions are penalising the credit institutions subject to their supervision unmeritoriously and inhibiting their competitiveness against other EC credit institutions. The answer to this charge is that it ignores the crudeness of the risk weighting system, which distinguishes between different types of counterparty only on a very rudimentary basis, makes no analysis of different economic spheres, and, more importantly, does not address the liquidity of a credit institution and makes no assessment of the quality of the management and internal risk-management ability of the reporting credit institution. As such it is a very imprecise means of establishing the prudent solvency ratio for individual banks, and indeed does not make any claims to be more than one element in determining the soundness of a credit institution. A more incisive means of ensuring the strength of individual banks and, consequently, the integrity of the system as a whole, is to set individual solvency ratios calculated by reference to each credit institution's particular strengths and weaknesses. For example, an exposure to a particular counterparty or economic sector may not be of such magnitude as to constitute a large exposure, as defined in the relevant legislation, but may still be of concern to a credit institution's supervisory authority. An ability to raise and lower specific solvency ratio requirements merely adds, in this context, a flexibility to the supervisory structure to ensure the overall stability of the system.

The risk of an imbalance in the competitive positions of EC credit institutions against each other, therefore, should only arise if one Member State requires less of its credit institutions by way of supporting capital than the others. This is a risk that is inherent in the entire structure for banking supervision after 1992[41] because of the manner in which

---

39. 92/121/EEC, OJ L29/1 of 5 February 1993.

40. The Large Exposures Directive is considered in detail in Chap. 17, below.

41. In July 1991, the British Bankers' Association published a report on the implementation to date of the Basle Agreement. One of the areas examined in the report was whether or not national supervisors party to the Basle Agreement were imposing an absolute solvency ratio of 8% on all banks subject to their supervision, or were treating the 8% figure merely as a "floor" to be increased depending on the circumstances of each bank. Insofar as concerns Member States of the EC, the findings were as follows: Ireland, Italy and the UK each intend to impose minimum ratios higher than 8% for some banks; Belgium,

supervisory authorities are treating the minimum requirement. The minimum solvency ratio requirement was intended as simply that: a minimum requirement. It was not intended as a replacement for qualitative assessment of a credit institution. It would, indeed, be ironic if competitive pressures at the end of the day forced out banks which are the subject of a supervisory regime more sensitive to the risks of that particular institution and the markets in which it operates, or resulted in credit institutions migrating to more lenient jurisdictions. That situation could well, however, materialise.

If the solvency ratio of any credit institution falls below 8%, the relevant home supervisory authority is required to ensure that the offending institution takes appropriate steps to restore its ratio to the minimum 8% as quickly as possible.[42]

IMPLEMENTATION

15.26 By article 121(1), Member States were to have adopted the measures necessary for them to comply with the provisions of the Solvency Ratio Directive by 1 January 1991, with the 8% minimum requirement being implemented with effect from 1 January 1993.

Paragraph 1 of article 11 provides that a credit institution which had not achieved the minimum 8% ratio by 1 January 1991 must gradually approach that level in successive stages, and may not allow its solvency ratio to fall below the level reached before it has achieved the minimum 8%. Any fluctuations should be temporary and the relevant home supervisory authorities should be apprised of the reasons therefor. Further, for not more than five years after 1 January 1993, Member States may fix a weighting of 10% for the bonds defined in article 22(4) of the UCITS Directive,[43] and may maintain that weighting when and if they consider it necessary to avoid grave disturbances in the operation of their markets. All such exceptions must be advised to the Commission.

Other exemptions are specified in paragraphs (3) and (4) of article 11 by reference to specific Member States. Finally, Member States may apply a 50% risk weighting to property leasing transactions concluded within 10 years of 1 January 1991 and concerning assets for business use situated in the country of the head office of any relevant credit institution and governed by statutory provisions whereby the lessor retains full ownership of the rented asset until the tenant exercises his option to purchase.[44]

15.27 Technical adaptations may be made to the Solvency Ratio Directive in certain areas by use of a comitology procedure akin to that laid down in the Second Banking Directive. The situations in which the comitology procedure may be used are specified in paragraph 1 of article 9 and include: a temporary reduction in the minimum 8% ratio or the risk-weighting prescribed in article 6, in order to take account of specific circumstances; the definition of Zone A; the definition of "multilateral development banks";[45] amendment to the definitions of the assets listed in article 6 to take account of

---

Denmark, France, Germany, the Netherlands, Portugal and Spain intend to impose the minimum 8% solvency ratio on all banks subject to their supervision. Banks incorporated in these latter countries, therefore, have potentially a competitive advantage over banks incorporated in the first three-named countries.

42. Solvency Ratio Directive, art. 10(3).

43. 85/611/EEC.

44. Solvency Ratio Directive, art. 11(5).

45. This definition was amended to include the European Bank for Research and Development. See Directive 91/31/EEC, OJ L17/20 of 23 January 1991.

developments in the financial markets; the lists and classifications of off-balance sheet items in Annexes I and III and their treatment in the calculation of the ratio as described in articles 5, 6 and 7 and Annex II; clarification of the definitions in order to ensure uniform application of the Solvency Ratio Directive throughout the Community; clarification of the definitions in order to take account of developments in the financial markets; and amendments necessary to permit the alignment of terminology on and the framing of definitions in accordance with subsequent acts on credit institutions and related matters.

15.28 The comitology procedure consists of the Commission operating in tandem with a committee composed of representatives of the Member States, chaired by a representative of the Commission. The Commission representative is to submit to this committee drafts of the proposed measures. The committee is to deliver its opinion on the proposed measures within a time limit set by the chairman according to the urgency of the particular measures; its opinion may be reached by majority vote pursuant to article 148(2) of the Treaty of Rome, with the votes of the representatives of the Member States being weighted in the manner set down in article 148(2). The chairman has no vote. The Commission is to adopt the proposed measures if they are in accordance with the opinion of the committee. If the committee does not agree with the proposed measures, or if it does not deliver an opinion, the Commission is obliged, without delay, to submit to the Council a proposal concerning the measures to be taken. The Council will then act on these by a qualified majority within three months of the referral from the Commission, failing which the Commission will adopt the proposed measures. If the Council decides against the proposed measures by a simple majority, the Commission has no power or authority to implement them.[46] The comitology procedure is intended, therefore, to foreshorten the legislative process to permit amendments to be made to the Solvency Ratio Directive and so ensure that it keeps pace with market innovations. It is, nonetheless, a bureaucratic process which is likely to take some time and its efficacy remains to be proved.

46. Solvency Ratio Directive, art. 9(2).

CHAPTER 16

THE CAPITAL ADEQUACY DIRECTIVE

INTRODUCTION

16.1 Some comment has already been made in preceding chapters to the Capital Adequacy Directive,[1] a piece of legislation which is intended to consolidate the capital adequacy requirements for credit institutions and financial institutions alike, on the basis of an analysis of the types of assets held by such institutions and the liquidity or marketability of such assets. It is not appropriate to discuss in this book all the potential ramifications of this legislation, and, in particular, its impact on non-bank financial institutions, but further comment is necessary because of its impact on the capital adequacy requirements of credit institutions.

At the time of writing, the capital adequacy requirements of credit institutions are contained in the Own Funds Directive and the Solvency Ratio Directive, the latter of which requires an overall solvency ratio of not less than 8%. The initial capital requirements for non-bank investment firms as contained in the Capital Adequacy Directive are considerably lower than the capital requirements imposed for credit institutions under the Second Banking Co-ordination Directive. Capital adequacy requirements for both credit institutions and financial institutions will, for the purposes of calculating the capital to assets ratio of such institutions, be determined according to a common set of rules. For assets that fall within the definition of the "trading book",[2] capital adequacy requirements for both credit institutions and financial institutions will be determined according to the Capital Adequacy Directive, which adopts the so-called "building block" approach to determine the capital adequacy requirement by aggregating separate capital requirements for position risk (which, as described below, is further categorised for capital adequacy purposes, into the specific risk and general risk entailed in holding an asset), settlement risk, risk arising from initial underwriting, and a catch-all category of "other risks". Capital required to support risks arising from trading book assets must satisfy the criteria specified in Annex V to the Capital Adequacy Directive, which contains a less rigorous definition of capital than that contained in the Own Funds Directive. The less rigorous definition of capital reflects the need for more flexible types of capital that are required by assets, the risks in respect of which are primarily risks arising from market movements, as opposed to longer-term risks such as counterparty risk. Conversely, capital adequacy requirements for all assets of credit institutions and financial institutions, other than assets falling within the trading book, will be determined according to the requirements of the Own Funds Directive and the Solvency Ratio Directive. The overall solvency ratio required of

1 93/6/EEC, OJ L141/1 of 15 March 1993.
2. Capital Adequacy Directive, art. 2(6). See also Chap. 14 above.

credit institutions will remain at 8%. The principal difference, therefore, between the capital requirements for credit institutions and financial institutions will be the initial capital requirements.

The reasons for the reduced initial requirements for non-deposit taking financial institutions are many: the business of investment firms involves essentially the taking of positions within various financial markets. Counterparty risk, although obviously present, is less important than market risk, especially as sophisticated settlement procedures have been established for most of these markets which should enable transactions to complete promptly. Market risk is perceived as being less capital and more liquidity intensive. In addition, there are certain safeguards for investors which are not available to depositors of credit institutions, particularly the requirements on investment firms to segregate investors' money from the firm's own money and the existence of compensation funds and effective conduct of business rules. Finally, these institutions trade globally, in competition with non-EC-incorporated institutions, and must be able to compete against foreign institutions. Traditionally, U.S. and Japanese investment houses have not been required to be highly capitalised (and it should be remembered that in both the United States and Japan, clear distinctions are drawn between banks and the type of business in which they can engage, and securities houses and investment banks). EC investment firms, therefore, would not be able to bear high capital and solvency requirements and still be able to compete on equal terms against the other major non-EC players in their market. The difficulty remains, however, that at present the universal banks within the EC are being penalised by having to apply the 8% solvency ratio requirement to the whole of their business, including those parts of their business which are active in financial products markets, as opposed to pure banking.

16.2 Article 3(3) of the Second Consolidated Supervision Directive permits national supervisory authorities to exclude a financial services subsidiary of a credit institution from the ambit of the regulations regarding consolidated supervision if the inclusion of such subsidiary would be inappropriate or misleading as far as the objective of the supervision of credit institutions is concerned. Article 9(2) of the Second Consolidated Supervision Directive, on the other hand, provides that until the Capital Adequacy Directive comes into effect, supervisory authorities should include in the consolidated supervision of credit institutions, financial institutions which are principally exposed to market risks, the methods of such consolidated supervision to be determined by the supervisory authority in question in the light of the particular nature of the risks involved. Until 1996, therefore, it is intended that, so far as possible, financial institution subsidiaries of credit institutions should be included in the calculation of consolidated solvency ratios and in consolidated supervision, but Member States have the latitude to apply locally agreed consolidation requirements for such institutions in assessing compliance with overall EC supervision guidelines. Notwithstanding this, article 3(5) of the Second Consolidated Supervision Directive provides that supervision of solvency and of the adequacy of funds to cover market risks and control of large exposures shall be exercised on a consolidated basis and that compliance by a credit institution with the minimum solvency ratio requirement of 8% shall be supervised on the basis of the consolidated or sub-consolidated financial situation of such credit institution. As a consequence of the functional approach to capital adequacy contained in the Capital Adequacy Directive, coupled with the provisions of the Second Consolidated Supervision Directive, the likelihood of financial services subsidiaries of credit institutions being able to compete on more favourable terms than deposit-taking credit institutions as a result of lower capital requirements, should be substantially reduced once the Capital Adequacy Directive has been implemented. Until the Capital Adequacy Directive comes into effect, however, some distortions in the respective competitive positions of universal banks and banks with separate financial services subsidiaries may arise.

There will also continue to be a disparity in the costs of doing business between independent financial institutions and universal banks or financial services subsidiaries of credit institutions because of the higher initial capital requirements imposed on credit institutions and the solo or consolidated (as applicable) solvency ratio requirement of not less than 8% imposed on credit institutions as a means of protecting the interests of depositors. The capital adequacy costs of independent financial institutions engaged principally in trading assets that fall within the trading book definition may well be lower than the capital costs incurred by a universal bank active in similar markets, but subject to the overall minimum solvency ratio requirement of 8%. Where an independent financial institution holds assets that do not fall within the trading book definition, the requirements of the Own Funds Directive and the Solvency Ratio Directive will apply, as stated above. This will result in a relatively high capital charge, compared to corresponding securities regulatory regimes in non-EC jurisdictions, a consequence which arises from the forcing together of banking supervision and regulatory requirements which look primarily to the political and social need to protect the interests of depositors, and securities regulation requirements. The two sectors of financial mediation are fundamentally different in a number of respects, and the attempt to reconcile the two sectors in one set of common rules has led to a number of anomolous results and a series of political disagreements, the most serious of which has been the failure of IOSCO and the Basle Committee to agree a common approach to the regulation of market risks on lines similar to that contained in the Capital Adequacy Directive.

16.3 The additional definition of capital contained in Annex V to the Capital Adequacy Directive was discussed in Chapter 14. As already indicated, the capital requirement is applied to assets falling within the trading book according to the "building block" approach which identifies the separate risks involved in holding such assets and ascribes as separate capital requirement to each such risk. The analysis involved is more complicated, therefore, than the somewhat rudimentary approach to risk analysis contained in the Solvency Ratio Directive, which, as previously stated, assumes that the assets of a credit institution, such as loans, will be held to maturity and that the principal risk involved in the holding of such assets is, therefore, the risk of default by the counterparties. The types of risk involved in the holding of trading book assets are identified in the Capital Adequacy Directive as position risk, settlement and counterparty risk, risks assumed over underwriting periods, and a catch-all category of "other risks". The Capital Adequacy Directive also contains capital adequacy requirements for foreign exchange risks, which will apply to all assets of credit and financial institutions denominated in a currency other than the domestic currency of the reporting institution.

THE PROVISIONS FOR DETERMINING POSITION RISK

16.4 Annex I of the Capital Adequacy Directive contains detailed provisions for determining capital adequacy requirements for position risk arising from the holding of trading book assets. The provisions are technical and somewhat elaborate, and it is not intended to set them out in full in this book. The following is a brief summary of the provisions of Annex I:

(a) The position risk associated with the holding of a trading book asset is determined according to two distinct measures: specific risk and general risk. Specific risk refers to the risk of price fluctuations in a particular asset by reason of the identity of the issuer of such asset, and will exist, obviously, whether a long or short position is held in that asset. General risk relates to price fluctuations in traded securities attributable simply to market conditions generally, rather than the specific identity of an issuer or the attributes of any particular security.[3] Capital requirements for specific risk and general risk will be calculated on the market price of an asset rather than its par value.[4]

(b) Specific risk and general risk are treated separately according to their particular characteristics. Some hedging techniques are recognised as effectively reducing risk; for example, long and short positions in the same security may be offset for the purposes of calculating the capital requirement for specific risk,[5] but no offsetting is permitted, for the purposes of calculating specific risk, between different securities as to do so would be incompatible with the identification of specific risk. Positions in derivative instruments such as options and warrants are treated essentially as positions in the underlying securities, subject to the application of the delta in the case of options.[6] No netting is permitted, however, between a convertible and an offsetting position in the instrument underlying it, unless the relevant supervisory authority adopts an approach under which the likelihood of a particular convertible's being converted is taken into account or have a capital requirement to cover any loss which conversion might entail.

(c) Interest rate futures, forward rate agreements ("FRAs") and forward commitments to buy or sell debt instruments will be treated as combinations of long and short positions. Thus, a long interest rate futures position will be treated as a combination of a borrowing maturing on the delivery date of the futures contract and a holding of an asset with a maturity date equal to that of the instrument or notional position underlying the futures contract in question. Both the borrowing and the asset holding will be risk weighted at 0% for the purpose of calculating the capital requirement for specific risk. Capital requirements for interest rate futures, FRAs, options and warrants that are traded on exchanges may, at the discretion of the relevant supervisory authority, be calculated according to the margin required by the relevant exchange if satisfactory to such supervisory authority.[7]

3. Solvency Ratio Directive, art. 3(3).
4. Capital Adequacy Directive, art. 4(2) and Annex IV.
5. Capital Adequacy Directive, Annex I, para. 1.
6. The delta of an option is defined in art. 2, para. 21 of the Capital Adequacy Directive as the expected change in an option price as a proportion of a small change in the price of the instrument underlying the option. See also Capital Adequacy Directive, Annex I, para. 5.
7. Capital Adequacy Directive, Annex I, paras. 4 and 5.

(d) Swaps will be treated for interest rate risk purposes on the same basis as on-balance sheet instruments. Thus, an interest rate swap under which an institution receives floating rate interest and pays fixed rate interest will be treated as equivalent to a long position in a floating rate instrument of maturity equivalent to the period until the next interest fixing date and a short position in a fixed rate instrument with the same maturity as the swap itself.[8]

(e) Institutions which mark to market and manage the interest rate risk on their derivative instruments on a discounted cashflow basis may use the sensitivity models to calculated their position risk in such derivatives as an alternative to the treatment set out above, subject to certain conditions, including that the relevant supervisory authority has approved the sensitivity model concerned and its use.[9] Even if sensitivity models are not used, some offsetting between derivative instruments may be permitted by local supervisory authorities if the conditions specified in paragraph 9 of Annex I are met.

(f) Offsetting of positions in the same security is required to establish capital requirements for specific risk. Net positions are then assigned a capital weighting depending on their maturity and the nature of the counterparty. Weightings range from 0% (central government items and certain derivative instruments) to 8%. Weightings for so-called "qualifying items" range from 0.25% for assets with maturities of up to six months, to 1.6% for assets with maturities in excess of 24 months.[10] The term "qualifying item" is defined in article 2 of the Capital Adequacy Directive[11] and includes, essentially, high grade, liquid non-government debt instruments, including long and short positions in debt instruments issued by investment firms (including certain non-EC investment firms) and corporate debt provided, in the latter case, first that such debt is listed on at least one regulated market in a Member State or on a stock exchange in a third country (provided that such exchange is recognised by the relevant supervisory authority of the institution holding such item), and secondly that the asset concerned be considered by the reporting institution to be sufficiently liquid and, because of the solvency of the issuer, to be subject to a degree of default risk, that is comparable to or lower than that accorded to assets falling within the 20% risk weighting band contained in the Solvency Ratio Directive. Although this judgment of the quality of an asset is principally to be made by the institution holding such asset, it is subject to oversight and, if necessary, reversal by such institution's supervisory authority. Supervisory authorities are also permitted to make independent determinations of qualifying items, subject to fulfilment of the same two criteria that institutions making such determination must demonstrate, together with an additional requirement that is not imposed on institutions, namely that, unless inappropriate to the circumstances, the default risk associated with an asset must have been evaluated as equal to or less than the 20% risk band of the Solvency Ratio Directive, by at least two credit rating agencies recognised by the relevant supervisory authority, or by only one credit rating agency so long

8. *Ibid.*, para. 7.
9. *Ibid.*, para. 8.
10. *Ibid.*, para. 14.
11. Capital Adequacy Directive, art. 2(12).

as such asset is not rated below the required debt rating by any other credit rating agency recognised by such supervisory authority.

The introduction of lower risk weightings for demonstrably high grade and liquid corporate debt is to be welcomed, and to some extent answers the criticisms made in respect of the crude approach to risk weighting of non-liquid assets contained in the Solvency Ratio Directive. Nonetheless, a number of criticisms can be made of the definition of qualifying items contained in the Capital Adequacy Directive. First, the definition links credit quality to the 20% band of risk weighting contained in the Solvency Ratio Directive. As discussed in Chapter 15, the 20% band comprises, primarily, assets constituting claims on banks incorporated in OECD countries and local governments, without undertaking a qualitative assessment of the counter-party concerned. Reliance is placed, instead, on the revenue raising powers of local governments, notwithstanding historical proof that local governments can become technically insolvent and suspend payment of their debts, and the supervisory process to which banks are subjected, notwithstanding, again, that it is obvious that there are clear disparities between the creditworthiness of banks, as shown, ironically, by the wide diversity in debt ratings given to banks by independent credit rating agencies. Perhaps a more useful indicator of the quality of a debt instrument, and an indicator that is part of the definition of a qualifying item, is an independent assessment of credit quality. In other words, the reference to the 20% risk weighting band contained in the Solvency Ratio Directive appears to be superfluous and in any event a less than reliable indicator of creditworthiness.

A second criticism that might be made of the definition of qualifying item is the latitude that is left for subjective judgement both at the level of each reporting institution subject to the requirements of the Capital Adequacy Directive, and at the national level. It is surprising in particular, that the judgement of the supervisory authorities must be reinforced by the independent assessment of credit rating agencies, yet no such additional requirements are imposed on the reporting institution's themselves, subject to the right of supervisory authorities to overturn any determination made by an institution. There is considerable scope for different interpretations of the requirements of the Capital Adequacy Directive with regard to the definition of qualifying items, which could result in disparities between capital adequacy requirements.

Thirdly, there is no analysis in the definition of qualifying item of what constitutes an adequate independent debt rating. As discussed above, reference to the Solvency Ratio Directive's risk weighting bands will not necessarily produce a reliable indicator of high grade liquid debt against which the debt of corporates may be compared. One might have expected the definition of qualifying item to include a requirement that, say, in the case of a short-dated debt instrument, such instrument must carry the highest short term debt rating of an independent credit rating agency and in the case of a long term instrument, that such instrument should have a debt rating in either of the two highest rating bands of an independent credit rating agency, or at least be investment grade.

Generally, the lower a debt rating on an instrument, the less liquid the market in that instrument will be. Many purchasers of such instruments, such as mutual funds, pension funds and insurance companies, are limited in the assets that they can purchase by regulations that expressly refer to the debt ratings assigned by independent credit rating agencies. In order to reduce to an extent the latitude for national discretion that is provided by the somewhat loose definition of qualifying item, and thus alleviate concerns of competitive inequality arising from differing national capital requirements, an argument can be made for introducing more concrete credit quality requirements into the definition of qualifying item by reference to more specific debt rating criteria. Such an approach might also assist in reducing capital requirements for debt instruments issued by special purpose entities in asset-backed transactions, where the identity of the issuer is in substance a subsidiary issue. The risks involved in owning an asset-backed security arise rather from the risk of default in the underlying asset than the identity of the issuer, particularly as most such issues are non-recourse. To date, the asset-backed securities market has relied heavily on independent credit rating agencies to provide an assessment of the credit quality of the underlying assets and the likelihood of receiving repayment in full of one's investment. One might expect similar reliance to be placed on such rating agencies if and when substantial markets in these assets are developed in the EC. A credit rating, of course, gives no indication of the liquidity of an asset, and there seems little alternative in gauging liquidity than to rely on the necessarily subjective judgement of the holder of such asset, subject to the overview of a supervisory body.

(g) Offsetting of positions in the same debt securities and of positions in different debt securities within the same maturity band is required when calculating capital requirements for general risk. Fixed rate debt securities will be allocated to a maturity band according to their residual term to maturity; floating rate securities will be allocated to a maturity band on the basis of their next repricing date. Offsetting of long and short positions in different maturity bands is also permitted for the purposes of calculating general risk, subject to the fulfilment of certain criteria.[12] In other words, the Capital Adequacy Directive provides for both "vertical offsetting" and "horizontal offsetting" within and among various maturity bands for the purpose of calculating the capital requirement associated with general risk arising from the holding of debt securities, subject to certain limits. In order to take account of the more volatile nature of zero coupon, deep discount and other debt securities with coupons below market rate, some adjustments are made in the setting of maturity bands for the calculation of risk weightings for such securities,[13] principally by shortening the periods of such maturity bands. Risk weights are determined for general risk of debt instruments on the basis of net positions in debt instruments and their maturities and an institution's capital adequacy requirement for general risk will be determined on the basis of matched positions within and across the three different maturity bands set out in paragraph 18 of Annex I to the Capital Adequacy Directive, and of the residual unmatched weighted positions in debt securities.

12. Capital Adequacy Directive, Annex I, paras. 15–23.
13. *Ibid.*, para. 18. See the table set out therein.

(h) As an alternative to calculating the capital requirement for general risk on the basis of the maturity of a debt security, as described in paragraph (g) above, the requirement can be calculated according to a duration based analysis of such risk, as described in paragraphs 24 to 30 of Annex I. The calculation of capital required will here be made on the basis of the modified duration of each asset, calculated by reference to the market value of such asset and its yield to maturity. Again, assets are assigned to different time bands or zones according to their modified duration, and duration-weighted long and short positions within each zone are matched within each zone, and then between zones, to calculate the overall capital requirement.[14]

(i) Insofar as equities are concerned, the starting point again for each reporting institution is to sum all its net long positions and net short positions in each holding. The total of the two net positions constitutes the institution's overall gross position, and the difference between the two constitutes the overall net position.[15] The capital requirement against general risk for an institution will be its overall net position multiplied by 8%.[16] The capital requirement against specific risk for equity holdings (long and short) will be, generally, 4% of the relevant institution's overall gross position, 2% in the case of a highly liquid portfolio that satisfies the criteria specified in paragraph 33 of Annex I, which includes requirements as to the perceived credit quality of the issuer (that is, its debt must fall within the definition of qualifying item), liquidity and size of the exposure in terms of the reporting institution's overall equities portfolio. The relaxation of the capital requirement for specific risk to 2% in the case of liquid portfolios is available only at the discretion of the supervisory authority of the reporting institution concerned.[17]

(j) Both general risk and specific risk must be calculated by an institution in their domestic currency. Currency conversion must be effected on a daily basis on all net positions, long or short, at the prevailing spot exchange rate.[18]

THE LIKELY IMPACT OF THE CAPITAL ADEQUACY DIRECTIVE

16.5 In the absence of agreement between the EC, the Basle Committee and IOSCO, it is difficult to predict what the impact of the Capital Adequacy Directive will be on EC credit and financial institutions both in their trade activity within the EC and in third countries. The Capital Adequacy Directive is notable for the large number of situations in which implementation of its overall requirements, frequently drafted in somewhat vague terms, is left to national supervisory authorities or even individual institutions, subject to regulatory oversight. In many respects, the Capital Adequacy Directive provides nothing more than a framework with even less definition than the Own Funds Directive. This is inevitable given the very different levels of sophistication and business activities of institutions engaged in investment services activities, and the increasing complexity of new financial instruments, and is a failing that is perhaps

14. *Ibid.*, paras. 27–30.
15. *Ibid.*, paras. 1 and 31.
16. *Ibid.*, para. 34.
17. *Ibid.*, paras. 32 and 33.
18. *Ibid.*, para. 3.

unavoidable in a piece of legislation that attempts to provide common rules for entities that, traditionally at least, have had fundamentally different capital requirements because of the different sources of their working capital and the assets to which such capital was applied. The strains in seeking a functional approach to regulation are apparent in the terms of the Capital Adequacy Directive, which leaves open to national regulators the possibility to impose stricter capital requirements on credit institutions than financial institutions in any number of instances, in the guise of the exercise of national discretion. For supervisory authorities that take a conservative approach to the protection of depositors, therefore, the Capital Adequacy Directive will not prevent them from imposing stricter standards on credit institutions within the framework of the Directive itself, without relying on the inherent right of all Member States to impose standards and requirements stricter than those laid down by any EC Directive in the sphere of the regulation of credit institutions.

THE POSITION AS COMPARED WITH THE PROPOSALS OF THE BASLE COMMITTEE

16.6 The analysis of capital requirements against position risk contained in the Basle Committee's proposals published in April 1993[19] is based on the same approach as that contained in Annex I to the Capital Adequacy Directive. There are, however, some fundamental differences between the Basle Committee's proposals and Annex I. The most significant being the Basle Committee's proposal that capital against the specific risk of a bank's overall gross position in equities should be 8%, double the corresponding capital requirement contained in Annex I. Like Annex I, the Basle Committee's proposals envisage the 8% requirement being relaxed if a bank can demonstrate that its equities portfolio is liquid and well diversified. The Basle Committee proposal warns, however, of the difficulty of defining liquidity and diversification in a sufficiently prudent manner, and at the time of writing has sought comments from the banking industry on addressing this dilemma. For the time being, all members of the Basle Committee have agreed that national supervisory authorities should determine their own criteria for liquid and well diversified portfolios, and may apply a lower capital requirement against specific risk for such portfolios, provided that the capital requirement is at least 4% of a bank's overall gross equity position. There is clearly a sharp difference of opinion between the formulators of the Capital Adequacy Directive and the members of the Basle Committee on appropriate capital standards for equity holdings. The Basle Committee's proposal is considerably more cautious than the requirements of the Capital Adequacy Directive, perhaps unsurprisingly as the Basle Committee comprises regulators of the banking industry. A general capital requirement of 4% against gross equity positions may be justifiable for a securities firm, which is unencumbered by political concerns for depositors rights, but may be considered too liberal for a bank. If, however, it is accepted that banks can invest in equity securities (the question whether or not it should being an entirely different one), regulators should assess the nature of the risk of that investment according to the attributes of the investment itself. In certain circumstances, the investment will be deducted from capital in any event, as required by the Own Funds Directive.

19. Published under the general title, "The Prudential Supervision of Netting, Market Risks and Interest Rate Risk". See also Chaps. 14 and 15.

Otherwise, the risk entailed in holding an equity instrument is essentially a market risk, although the price of a share will obviously be influenced by the perceived creditworthiness of the issuer, it will be affected by numerous other market related risks. If a market for an equity instrument exists, then it might be argued that the capital requirement for specific risk should reflect the existence of the market and the element of liquidity inherent in the asset, and thus should not be identical to the risk weighting applied to a debt instrument. If it is clear that no market exists for the equity instrument, a debt-type risk weighting is perhaps more apposite, although how the asset is then valued presents an entirely different problem, as par value will in most circumstances be meaningless.

Position risk arising from the underwriting of securities issues is the subject of paragraph 39 of Annex I to the Capital Adequacy Directive. This requires net positions in each issue to be calculated by deducting the underwriting positions that are subscribed or sub-underwritten by third parties on the basis of formal agreements. The net positions are then reduced by risk weightings that vary from 100% on the day on which the institution concerned becomes unconditionally committed to accepting a known quality of securities at an agreed price, to 25% on the fifth working day following the aforesaid commitment day. After the fifth working day, no reduction of an underwriting position for capital adequacy purposes is permitted.

SETTLEMENT AND COUNTERPARTY RISK

16.7 Annex II of the Capital Adequacy Directive adds the second element to the building block approach to assessing capital requirements for trading book assets by introducing a capital requirement for settlement and counterparty risk. This type of risk will arise where transactions in trading book assets are unsettled after their due delivery date. The basis of the capital calculation for settlement risks is, essentially, the difference between the agreed settlement price for the asset concerned and its current market value.[20] No capital is required to be set against this risk until the fifth working day after the due delivery date of a security has passed without settlement. The amount of capital required will depend on the number of days elapsed since the due settlement date. If settlement is not made by the end of the 45th day after the settlement date, capital equal to the full amount of the exposure is required to be set aside.[21]

16.8 Capital is required to be held against counterparty risk if free deliveries of securities are made, that is, (a) an institution pays for securities before receiving them, or delivers securities before receiving payment for them; and (b) in the case of cross-border transactions, one day or more has elapsed since such payment or delivery. A capital requirement of 8% of the value of the securities or cash owed, multiplied by the risk weighting of the counterparty, will be imposed on each free delivery.[22]

16.9 Annex II to the Capital Adequacy Directive also imposes additional capital requirements on repos, reverse repos, securities lending and securities borrowing agreements that fall within the trading book. In the case of repo agreements and

20. Capital Adequacy Directive, Annex II, paras. 1 and 2. Para. 2 of Annex II permits, at national discretion, an alternative method of calculating the capital requirement for settlement risk by multiplying the agreed settlement price of every transaction that is unsettled between five and 45 days after its due date by an appropriate factor, specified in column B of the table set out in para. 2.

21. *Ibid.*

22. *Ibid.*, paras. 3.1 and 3.2.

securities lending agreements, an institution is required to calculate the difference between the market value of the securities sold or lent and the amount borrowed or the market value of the collateral received, where the difference is positive. In the case of reverse repos and securities borrowing agreements, the difference between the amount the reporting institution has lent or the market value of the collateral and the market value of the securities it has received, where that difference is positive, is calculated. The capital requirement in each case will be 8% of the figure produced by the above calculation, multiplied by the risk weighting of the relevant counterparty.[23]

FOREIGN EXCHANGE RISK

16.10 The Capital Adequacy Directive prescribes capital requirements to be met in respect of foreign exchange risks incurred by credit institutions and financial institutions by reason of the holding of assets denominated in a currency other than the domestic currency of the institution concerned, whether or not such assets are comprised in the trading book. Capital is required, generally, to be held against foreign exchange risk if an institution's overall net foreign exchange position, calculated in accordance with Annex III to the Capital Adequacy Directive, is in excess of 2% of its total capital. The excess is multiplied by 8% to produce the capital requirement.[24] The overall net foreign exchange position of an institution is calculated by calculating such institution's net open position in each currency in which it holds assets, as specified in paragraph 3.1 of Annex III. Any positions that an institution has taken deliberately in order to hedge against the adverse effects of exchange rates on its capital ratio may, if of a structural and non-trading nature, and subject to the consent of the relevant supervisory body, be excluded from the calculation of net-open positions. The net-open position in each currency other than the reporting currency must then be converted at the prevailing spot rate into the reporting currency. The totals of net short open positions and net long open positions are then calculated, and the difference between the two constitutes the overall net foreign exchange position.[25]

Alternative methods for calculating foreign exchange risk may also be employed, subject to compliance with the parameters laid down in paragraphs 6, 7 and 8, as applicable, of Annex III. Lower capital requirements may also be permitted, subject to national discretion, for closely-correlated currencies, as determined by paragraph 6 of Annex III. The reduced capital requirement for closely-correlated currencies is a clear reference to the currencies in the Exchange Rate Mechanism and, in the future, to the European Monetary System.

16.11 In its paper entitled "The Supervisory Treatment of Market Risks" published in April 1993, the Basle Committee proposed an approach to the analysis of the capital requirement for foreign exchange risk that, again, is substantially the same as the approach taken in Annex III to the Capital Adequacy Directive. The Basle Committee's proposals differ, however, in a number of key respects. First, the Basle Committee proposes that its capital requirement calculations should apply not only to debt and equity instruments dominated in foreign currencies, but also to trading in gold and other precious metals. Secondly, the Basle Committee advocates the use of a

---

23. *Ibid.*, paras. 4.1 and 4.2.
24. Capital Adequacy Directive, Annex III, para. 1.
25. *Ibid.*, paras. 2, 3, 3.2 and 3.4.

five-year observation period if the simulation method of calculating foreign exchange risk is employed. The simulation method is described in detail in the Basle Committee's paper and in somewhat less detail in paragraph 7 of Annex III to the Capital Adequacy Directive, where it is presented as an alternative method of calculating the capital requirement for foreign exchange risk rather than calculating the overall net foreign exchange position. The simulation method anticipates actual exchange rates experienced in past observation periods being employed to revalue an institution's present foreign exchange position, including options in foreign currencies. The revaluations are used to calculate simulated profits and losses that would have arisen if the current foreign exchange positions had remained fixed for a defined holding period. The capital requirement is then set according to the worst or near to the worst loss that would have arisen during the holding period. The Basle Committee proposes that if the simulation method is used, a holding period of a rolling 10 working days and a rolling observation period of five years be employed. The level of confidence required in measuring the risk for purposes of setting the capital requirement is expressed in terms of a loss quantile. The Basle Committee has proposed a loss quantile of 95%, that is the level of confidence that includes 95% of the hypothetical losses that would have arisen during the holding period from the current set of open foreign exchange positions of an institution. This means, in terms of a capital requirement, that capital set aside for foreign exchange risk must be sufficient to exceed 95% of such hypothetical losses. The Capital Adequacy Directive allows an alternative loss quantile of 99% calculated over a 10-day rolling period on the basis of a three-year observation period. This shorter observation period may, depending on exchange rate volatility if measured over a five-year period, result in a lower capital requirement for foreign exchange risk under the Capital Adequacy Directive than could be achieved under the Basle Agreement. A scaling factor is the final element of the simulation method. The scaling factor is added to the chosen loss quantile to determine the toughness of the capital requirement. The Basle Committee is proposing a scaling factor equal to 3% of the overall net open foreign exchange position. The scaling requirement under Annex III to the Capital Adequacy Directive requires a scaling factor that will exceed at least 2% of the overall net foreign exchange position.

CONCLUSION

16.12 Insofar as trading book assets of credit institutions are concerned, therefore, the capital requirements will be determined by aggregating the different capital requirements specified for position risk, settlement risk, counterparty risk, additional risk requirements for instruments such as repos, and, in the case of an underwriting of a securities issue and underwriting risk. The capital adequacy requirement for all other assets will be determined in accordance with the Solvency Ratio Directive and the definition of capital contained in the Own Funds Directive. Further capital may be required if large exposures are incurred in relation to trading book assets. An additional capital requirement is then levied on all assets denominated in a foreign currency. As stated previously, the success of this proposed regime will depend in part on the negotiations still taking place in other international fora and, in any event, on the manner in which it is implemented by each Member State. Considerable room for disparate and different interpretations of the Directive's requirements exist, and until

Member States begin the implementation exercise, further comment or analysis will probably prove futile.

THE SUPERVISION OF LARGE EXPOSURES

INTRODUCTION

16A.1 As already indicated in Chapters 14 and 15, the minimum solvency ratio requirement of 8% on EC-incorporated credit institutions pursuant to the terms of the Solvency Ratio Directive is a figure reached by way of compromise, and presupposes a diversified asset base of a credit institution; otherwise the ratio may well have been fixed at a much higher figure.[1] In addition, the regulatory authorities in certain Member States have in any event interpreted the 8% requirement as truly a minimum criterion (as opposed to a flat percentage applicable to all credit institutions) that may be required to be exceeded by a credit institution if, for example, the regulatory authority concerned considers a higher ratio to be a prudent requirement.[2] This may occur because, among other reasons, a credit institution is considered to be over-exposed to a particular economic or geographical sector or to particular counterparties. The supervision of large exposures is intended to deal with concentration risk either by ensuring that such risks do not arise or, if they do, that adequate additional capital is dedicated to supporting losses that may be incurred if the asset, the subject of a large exposure, fails to perform.

Setting a minimum solvency ratio, in other words, is only stage one of an ongoing process and will not, in particular, be sufficient to provide a safe and sound banking environment to protect the interests of depositors if a credit institution's asset base is not diversified by its solvency ratio requirement.

The movement towards supervising large exposures commenced in 1986 when the Commission adopted a Recommendation[3] setting out guidelines on the monitoring and controlling of large exposures of credit institutions and that Recommendation was followed by a directive (the "Large Exposures Directive")[4] on the monitoring and controlling of large exposures of credit institutions. The Large Exposures Directive was formally adopted in December 1992 and Member States were required to implement it into their national law by 1 January 1994 at the latest.

The goals of the Large Exposures Directive are twofold. First, it is intended to harmonise the criteria applied by national supervisory authorities for determining the concentration of exposures. Secondly, the Commission claims that such harmonisation should prevent distortion of competition in so far as all credit institutions throughout

---

1. See, in particular the introduction to Chap. 15 at para. 15.1 and 15.2 above.
2. The Bank of England has adopted such a practice in relation to institutions authorised under the Banking Act 1987.
3. Commission Recommendation 87/62 EEC.
4. Directive 92/121 1992; OJ 1993 L29.

the Community will be subject to the same rules, and limits on large exposures will enable more credit institutions to grant assistance to a given customer. The Large Exposures Directive is, however, essentially based on regulatory necessity.[5]

The Large Exposures Directive will apply to all credit institutions that have obtained authorisation pursuant to article 3 of the First Banking Directive.[6] However, Member States will not need to apply the Large Exposures Directive to certain institutions listed in article 2 of the First Banking Directive such as, *inter alia*, central banks, national Post Offices and Giro institutions.[7]

THE REPORTING OF LARGE EXPOSURES

1. What is meant by the term "exposure"

16A.2 In describing the requirements set out in the Large Exposures Directive on the reporting of large exposures it is first necessary to define what the term "exposure" means. In defining what is meant by an "exposure", the Large Exposures Directive refers to the assets and off-balance sheet items of a credit institution, as defined in article 6 of the Solvency Ratio Directive.[8] The usefulness of the Solvency Ratio Directive in determining what constitutes an "exposure" should, if all things were equal, be limited to the identification of assets and off-balance sheet items contained in that Directive, without also applying the risk-weighted formulae ascribed by the Solvency Ratio Directive to such assets and items for the purpose of calculating its capital : assets ratio. The recitals to the Large Exposures Directive specifically state that the object of the Directive is not to adopt the classification of the risk weightings of assets set out in the Solvency Ratio Directive. The Commission, in its commentary accompanying the draft Large Exposures Directive, stressed that setting limits on an institution's maximum risk of loss with respect to a given client requires a prudent approach that takes account of exposures at their nominal value, without reducing these values by weighted percentages determined according to the perceived credit risk of the counterparty. As discussed below, the manner in which this principle has been applied in the operative provisions of the Large Exposures Directive may deprive the stated intention of the Directive of much of its impact.

It is important to note that certain foreign exchange transactions[9] or transactions for the purchase or sale of securities,[10] as well as assets entirely covered by own funds (ie, capital), may be excluded from the definition of exposures in certain circumstances.

---

5. The reporting of large exposures in the United Kingdom was first addressed on a statutory basis by section 38 of the Banking Act 1987. Section 38 has been supplemented by various Bank of England Notices (see BSD 1987/1 as amended by BSD 1992/2) the most recent of which was published by the Bank of England in October 1993 implementing, in the United Kingdom, the Large Exposures Directive (see BSD 1993/2). For a detailed account of the development of a large exposures policy in the United Kingdom see Penn, *Banking Supervision* (Butterworths, 1989), Chap. 10.

6. See art. 2 of the Large Exposures Directive.

7. Art. 2 of the Large Exposures Directive provides that Member States need not apply the Directive to those institutions listed in art. 2 of the First Banking Directive or to institutions defined in art. 2(4)(a) of that Directive which are "affiliated to a central body established in that Member State . . . provided that . . . the central body . . . is subject to global monitoring".

8. See art. 1.

9. Namely those incurred in the ordinary course of settlement during 48 hours following payment (see art. 1 of the Large Exposures Directive).

10. Namely those incurred in the ordinary course of settlement during the five working days following payment or delivery of the securities, whichever is the earlier (see art. 1).

2. What is a "large exposure"?

16A.3 An exposure of a credit institution to a client or group of connected clients is considered to be a large exposure where its value is equal to or exceeds 10% of the own funds of that credit institution (ie, capital eligible for inclusion in the calculation of the credit institution's solvency ratio).[11] Under the Large Exposures Directive, a group of connected clients means:

(i) two or more persons, whether natural or legal, who constitute a single risk because either one of them holds, directly or indirectly, power of control over the others; or

(ii) two or more persons who are so interconnected that if one of them were to face financial problems, the other or all of them would be likely to encounter repayment difficulties.

The concept of control includes, in particular, the holding of a majority of voting rights, the right to appoint or remove a majority of the directors, and the right to exercise a dominant influence over an undertaking pursuant to a contract.

The first limb of the definition, arguably, is subsumed by the second as it is the economic relationship between counterparties that matters whether or not accompanied by relationships recognised in or derived from legal principles.

3. The reporting of large exposures

16A.4 The supervision of large exposures is based on regular notifications by credit institutions to the competent regulatory authority. The Large Exposure Directive requires that a report of every large exposure (as defined above) shall be made by a credit institution to its supervisory authorities, *after* the exposure has been incurred. The Large Exposure Directive[12] allows two methods of reporting, which Member States may choose at their discretion:

(i) notification of all large exposures at least once a year combined with reporting during the year of all new large exposures and any increases in existing large exposures of at least 20% with respect to the previous communication;

(ii) notification of all large exposures at least four times a year.

It remains uncertain whether Member States will have the choice of transposing into national law either one of these methods only, or both methods.

Regulatory authorities in the various Member States are required, pursuant to the terms of article 3, to ensure that all credit institutions falling under its supervisory remit should have "sound administrative and accounting procedures and adequate control mechanisms for the purpose of identifying and recording all large exposures and subsequent changes to them . . . and for that of monitoring those exposures in the light of each credit institution's own exposure policies".

The Directive is silent however on whether a credit institution is required to agree its exposure policy with its national regulator and the level of input, if any, the regulator is to have with regard to such policy.[13]

---

11. Art. 3.
12. Art. 3, para. 2.
13. In the United Kingdom it is the practice for institutions authorised under the Banking Act 1987 to set out their policy on large exposures in a formal memorandum adopted by the institution's board of directors and agreed with the Bank of England.

LIMITS ON LARGE EXPOSURES

General limits

(a) Individual exposures

16A.5 The core rule of the Large Exposures Directive provides that credit institutions may not incur an exposure to a client or group of connected clients where its value exceeds of 25% of own funds[14] (ie, Tier 1 capital plus qualifying Tier 2 capital less mandatory reductions).[15] The Commission has stressed that this limit should be considered as a maximum ceiling for exposures of "impeccable quality" and that credit institutions should not reach or approach that limit except in the case of exposures of such quality.

(b) Aggregate large exposures

16A.6 Under the Large Exposures Directive credit institutions may not incur large exposures which in the aggregate exceed 800% of own funds.[16] This aggregate limit will mean that a credit institution can at most have 80 large exposures representing 10% of own funds each and maximum of 32 exposures that reach the individual ceiling of 25% of own funds.

Specific limits

16A.7 The Large Exposure Directive lays down a specific 20% limit applying to exposures to associated enterprises of the reporting credit institution (ie, parent undertaking of the credit institution and/or one or more subsidiaries of that parent undertaking).[17] This threshold is set at a lower level than the general threshold in order to address banking regulators' perennial fear of bank failures being caused by credit problems within the banking group rather than by external factors. If, however, an associated entity is included in the consolidated supervision of the reporting credit institution, pursuant to the provisions of the Consolidated Supervision Directive,[18] an exposure in excess of 20% to that entity may be fully or partially exempted from the Large Exposures Directive's threshold limit. This exemption places much faith in the efficacy of consolidated supervision, a placing of trust that, it might be argued, is far from justified at present.

Exceptions to the 20%, 25% and 800% limits

16A.8 The Large Exposures Directive provides that the threshold limits of 20%, 25% and 800% referred to above, must be observed at all times by EC credit institutions. They may, however, be exceeded in exceptional circumstances and, in such cases, the competent regulatory authorities must fix a deadline within which the credit institution must regularise its situation. Article 4(7) of the Large Exposures Directive also sets forth a long list of exemptions that are specifically authorised by the Directive.

---

14. Art. 4.
15. For a detailed account of the calculation of own funds see paras. 14.9 to 14.23, above.
16. Art. 3, para. 3.
17. *Ibid.*, para. 2.
18. See Chap. 10, above.

As stated above, Member States may fully or partially exempt from the application of those limits exposures incurred by a credit institution to its parent undertaking, to other subsidiaries of that parent or to its own subsidiaries, provided that these undertakings are subject to supervision on a consolidated basis.

Member States may fully or partially exempt a number of specific exposures from the application of the 20%, 25% and 800% limits, as provided in article 4(7). For example, exposures incurred to Zone A central governments and central banks (Zone A mainly includes EC Member States and countries that are members of the OECD) and to the European Communities may be exempted, and certain exposures to non-government counterparties may be reduced by applying a percentage factor to their book value.

The list of exemptions set out in article 4(7) of the Large Exposures Directive bears a striking resemblance to the list of assets subject to reduced risk weightings under the Solvency Ratio Directive.[19] By permitting full or partial exemptions for these assets, based on the application of percentage factors, without requiring additional capital to be held against the risk of their failure, the Large Exposures Directive is in effect permitting Member States to apply the concept of risk-weighting to large exposures. This is in contradiction to the principle stated in the recitals to the Large Exposures Directive that such an approach is incompatible with the supervision of large exposures. The supervision of large exposures is not merely concerned with counterparty risk; it is concerned with concentration risk. The Large Exposures Directive would fail to protect the depositors of a credit institution if, for example, the credit institution has an exempted large exposure to a sovereign lender which unilaterally announces suspension of all its debt obligations.

A relaxation of the large exposures limit is also available for underwriting exposures, the extent of the relaxation being dependent upon the amount of the exposure as a percentage of qualifying capital and the number of days since the underwriting date that the exposure has been in existence.

The various relaxations of the large exposure limits set out in the Large Exposures Directive must however be read in conjunction with the provisions applicable to such relaxations in the Capital Adequacy Directive. These provisions are discussed more fully in Chapter 16.

Discretion left to the Member States

16A.9 Under the Large Exposures Directive, Member States may impose more stringent rules than the limits laid down in article 4[20] (namely, the 20%, 25% and 800% threshold limits) and they may exercise discretion as regards either full or partial exemptions.[21] The objective of preventing distortion of competition between credit institutions established throughout the Community might be jeopardised if Member States were to adopt widely differing rules by means of the discretion afforded pursuant to article 4. As with the other Directives in the banking and financial services sector, full equality of opportunity cannot be achieved unless the principal rules on large exposure requirements are fully harmonised and national discretions largely eliminated.

19. See paras 15.20 and 15.21, above.
20. Art. 4(4).
21. *Ibid.*, paras 6 and 7.

SUPERVISION ON A CONSOLIDATED OR UNCONSOLIDATED BASIS

16A.10 If a credit institution is neither a parent undertaking nor a subsidiary, the obligations related to a reporting of, and limits on, large exposures must be supervised on an unconsolidated basis.[22] In other cases, these obligations must be supervised on a consolidated basis in accordance with the Consolidated Supervision Directive.[23]

The Consolidated Supervision Directive also lays down rules related to the supervision of subsidiaries and parent undertakings established in different Member States.[24]

TRANSITIONAL PROVISIONS

16A.11 Article 6 of the Large Exposures Directive adopts a pragmatic approach as regards credit institutions which have already incurred an exposure or exposures exceeding either the large exposures limit or the aggregate large exposures limit at the time of the Directive in the *Official Journal*. The Large Exposures Directive provides that the competent authorities will have to require these credit institutions to take steps to have such exposures brought into line with the provisions of the Large Exposures Directive within a period deemed by these authorities to be consistent with the principle of sound administration and fair competition.[25] This period must expire no later than 31 December 2001.[26]

This transition period is much longer than that provided for in other EC legislation in the banking and financial services sector. This may be due to the fact that the Large Exposures Directive represents the first attempt by the EC or any other international entity to agree minimum standards on this aspect of banking supervision. The Directives concerning the capital adequacy of credit institutions, for example, benefited from the breakthrough achieved by the Basle Accord.[27]

CONCLUSION

16A.12 Some EC Member States currently have no proper system in force for the supervision of large exposures. It is often the banks in those jurisdictions that carry what will, under the Large Exposures Directive, constitute large exposures. Locally-incorporated credit institutions in such jurisdictions are frequently state-owned and the large exposures concerned frequently involve exposures to the other state-owned entities. In this context the local supervisory authority does not perceive a large exposures problem to exist as the credit institution's exposure is, in effect, to the state and hence itself. The exemptions contained in the Large Exposures Directive will permit this treatment to be continued.

There is now, however, a trend in a number of EC Member States where the system prevails to sell off state-owned assets, including credit institutions and industrial

---

22. Art. 5.
23. Directive 92/30/EEC, discussed more fully in Chap. 10, above.
24. See paras 10.8 and 10.9, above.
25. Art. 6(2).
26. *Ibid.*, para. (4).
27. See Chap. 16, above.

concerns. For credit institutions, the sale of a state-owned entity to which it has an exposure will have at least a twofold impact. First, the risk-weighting of the exposure under the Solvency Ratio Directive will, in most cases, increase to 100%, which may require the credit institution either to increase its eligible capital or to sell the asset concerned, in order to maintain an adequate capital : assets ratio. Secondly, if the exposure is a large exposure previously accorded a full or partial exemption from the Large Exposures Directive requirements, that exemption may be lost, which may entail a further capital cost or, again, may require the asset to be sold in order to comply with the limits on exposures contained in the Large Exposures Directive. The credit institutions and the state entities that own them will in most situations not have the resources to support these large exposures and, equally, if private capital is to be attracted to the banks, investors will expect a clean balance sheet. Investors will hardly be enticed to subscribe for shares in a credit institution when it is clear that the subscription proceeds will need to be utilised to support existing exposures to industry from which the selling state is withdrawing its financial support, rather than used to develop new business. The multiplication of risk factors will create a product too speculative for most investors.

It might be expected, therefore, considerable activity in the secondary debt market and in the securitised debt markets as credit institutions sell down these loans whenever they are unable to sustain the cost of retaining them on their balance sheet or in circumstances where they are preparing for privatisation. Securitisation, in fact, may be the only alternative for any such credit institutions as it allows the non-investment grade assets to be credit enhanced to investment grade status and offered to a wider investment community.

PART THREE

BANKING SECRECY

CHAPTER 17

BANKING SECRECY UNDER THE FIRST BANKING DIRECTIVE

1. THE NEED FOR BANKING SECRECY AS A CONDITION FOR EFFECTIVE COMMUNITY-WIDE SUPERVISION

17.1 Banking secrecy usually tends to be associated with the issue of tax investigations into the financial affairs of a bank's customer. However, it is also a necessary element to make possible the efficient supervision of the credit institutions operating cross-border, especially by way of branches, in the Community.

Effective supervision requires the home country supervisor in Member State A to be able to supervise the operations conducted by one of "his" banks at the level of the bank's branch in Member State B, either directly or in co-operation with the competent authorities of the host Member State. However, difficulties may stand in the way of this necessary co-operation between the competent authorities of the home Member State and those of the host Member State as a result of the different standards that may exist there with regard to the use that can be made in each Member State of the information so collected for purposes other than the supervision of the credit institution concerned.

2. BANKING SECRECY UNDER THE ORIGINAL TEXT OF ARTICLE 12 OF THE 1977 BANKING DIRECTIVE

17.2 An early attempt to solve or at least limit these difficulties was made by article 12 of the 1977 Banking Directive, which deals with the professional secrecy by which the banking supervisors are bound.

As described at the time by Paolo Clarotti in a seminal commentary of the 1977 Directive[1]:

[Article 12] deals with the problems resulting from the fact that [the banking supervisors in the various Member States] are, on the one hand, subject to rules concerning professional secrecy, but also, on the other hand, are required to collaborate on a cross-frontier basis and possibly exchange information [see article 7 of the 1977 Banking Directive]. The general rule is that such information retains the degree of confidentiality that the authorities of the country of origin attribute to it. However, in order to avoid a conflict between rules of a binding nature, it was necessary to supplement the provisions by a certain measure of approximation of legislation. The objective of this is to limit the possible effects of too great a divergence between the rules relating to secrecy in different countries. Although there is no problem when information is given by the authorities of a country where professional secrecy rules are relatively lax to the authorities of a

---

1. "Progess and future development of establishment and services in the EC in relation to banking" [1984] *Journal of Common Market Studies* 199, at p. 218 (our emphasis). Also, "The Harmonisation of legislation relating to credit institutions" [1982] CMLRev. 245, at p. 265.

country where the rules are very strict, serious difficulties can arise *if the flow is reversed*. It is clear that this exchange of confidential information between competent authorities presupposes that each believes that the information will remain confidential . . . [If such a guarantee does not exist, it] could discourage some supervisory authorities, having to comply with strict secrecy obligations, from collaborating with other authorities whose obligations are less strict.

It was to avoid this danger that article 12 was inserted in the 1977 Directive. Before it was amended by article 16 of the Second Banking Directive, article 12 of the 1977 Directive read:

1. Member States shall ensure that all persons now or in the past employed by the competent authorities are bound by the obligation of professional secrecy. This means that any confidential information which they may receive in the course of their duties may not be divulged to any person or authority except by virtue of provisions laid down by law.
2. Paragraph 1 shall not, however, preclude communications between the competent authorities of the various Member States, as provided for in this Directive. Information thus exchanged shall be covered by the obligation of professional secrecy applying to the persons now or in the past employed by the competent authorities receiving the information.
3. Without prejudice to cases covered by criminal law, the authorities receiving such information shall use it only to examine the conditions for the taking up and pursuit of the business of credit institutions to facilitate monitoring of the liquidity and solvency of these institutions or when the decisions of the competent authority are the subject of an administrative appeal or in court proceedings initiated pursuant to article 13.

As envisaged by its draftsmen, that provision in effect[2]:

laid down that, no matter what the secrecy obligations that have to be observed by the supervisory authorities in their respective countries are, the latter, when receiving information from their counterparts in other countries, may use if for certain purposes. These are to examine the conditions for the taking up and pursuit of business and to facilitate the monitoring of conditions of pursuit of business . . . In other words, and to speak in practical terms, there is no question that such information could be given to eg the tax authorities. There is however a general exception, which can be readily understood, for cases which involve the criminal law.

3. THE HILLEGOM CASE AND ITS IMPLICATIONS

17.3 On 11 December 1985, in *Municipality of Hillegom* v. *Hillenius*,[3] the European Court of Justice was called on for the first time to determine the scope of professional secrecy of banking supervisors under article 12 of the 1977 Directive.

The case arose in the context of proceedings brought by the Dutch municipality of Hillegom against the then head of banking supervision at the Dutch Central Bank, Mr Hillenius. The purpose of these proceedings was to gather evidence from Mr Hillenius in order to establish that a foreign-owned bank which had failed a few months after the municipality of Hillegom had deposited substantial funds with it had been inadequately supervised by the Dutch Central Bank in that it had allegedly failed to act upon information received from banking supervisors in other Member States.

The main question before the Court was whether Mr Hillenius could refuse to give such evidence in reliance on article 12(3) of the 1977 Directive (and the Dutch implementing legislation) or whether, having regard to the last sentence of article 12(1) whereby banking supervisors may not divulge the information received in the course of

2. See Paolo Clarotti, "Progress and future development of establishment and services in the EC in relation to banking" [1984] *Journal of Common Market Studies* 199, at p. 219.
3. Case 110/84 [1985] ECR 39.

their duties "to any person or authority *except* by virtue of provisions laid down by law", he could be forced to answer on the basis of a general provision of the Dutch Civil Code.

In its submission before the Court, the Commission had suggested that a distinction should be made under article 12 between information collected by a national authority itself and information received from the supervisory authorities in other Member States. In the Commission's view[4]:

Article 12 . . . introduces two sets of rules. The first set of rules concerns information obtained in a Member State where legal provisions within the meaning of the last sentence of paragraph 1, determine the scope of the obligations to maintain the professional secrecy to which such information is subject. The second set of rules concerns information obtained in other Member States, which is *governed by Community rules* subjecting the use and disclosure of such information to the criteria laid down in paragraph 3. The use of information received from other *Member States* in civil proceedings[5] is therefore excluded . . .

Advocate General Sir Gordon Slynn rejected that distinction and took the view that:

Despite the force of this contention . . . it should not be accepted . . . This Directive is a first step in the harmonisation of national laws relating to credit institutions. National laws on confidential information, and as to the right or the duty to refuse to answer, vary and have not yet been harmonised. In the present state of things, however regrettably imprecise may be the result . . . Member States have a discretion under Article 12(1) of the Directive to retain or introduce exceptions to the prohibition on disclosure, which are not limited to the situation envisaged in Article 12(3). Such exceptions must, however, be compatible with the overall purpose of the Directive. Exceptions which would seriously inhibit the disclosure of information to the competent authority, or which might have a serious effect on the stability of credit institutions and which cannot be justified by other overriding considerations of public interest would not be compatible with the overall purpose of the Directive.

The Court of Justice clearly opted for this latter approach, albeit in less clear-cut terms[6]:

. . . It is . . . clear from the general reference to the provisions laid down by law in each Member State that at this initial stage, when the aim is only to eliminate the most obstructive differences between the legislative provisions of the Member States, the existing or future provisions of the Member States may contain exceptions to the duty to maintain professional secrecy. As regards the conflict which may arise between the interest in establishing the truth, which is fundamental to the administration of justice, and the interest in maintaining the confidentiality of certain kinds of information, it is for the courts to find a balance between those interests if the national legislature has not resolved the conflict in specific legislative provisions. In a case such as this, in which the relevant provision of national law is, according to the national court's interpretation, general in character, it is therefore for the national court to weigh up those interests . . . In weighing up those interests, the national court must in particular decide . . . what importance is to be attached to the fact that the information in question was obtained from the competent authorities of other Member States in accordance with Article 12(2) of the Directive.

On those grounds, the Court ruled:

The provisions laid down by law allowing confidential information to be divulged, as envisaged by Article 12(1) cited above, include general provisions not specifically intended to lay down exceptions to the ban on disclosing the kind of information covered by the Directive, but

4. Judgment, at para. 19. Our emphasis.
5. As opposed to *criminal* proceedings: see art. 12(3), opening sentence. The Court held in a later case (422/85 *Gaziano Mattiazzo* [1987] ECR 5413, at p. 5427) that the 1977 Directive "does not detract from the powers of the Member State to lay down rules on the legal status of credit institutions. [As a result], the classification of employees of credit institutions as 'public officials' or as 'persons responsible for a public service' for the purposes of the application of the criminal law of a Member State is not contrary to the provisions or the objective of [the 1977 Directive]".
6. Judgment, at paras. 32 to 34.

establishing the limits which the maintenance of professional secrecy places on the obligation to give evidence as a witness.

17.4 The Court's judgment is not authority for the proposition that Member States enjoy complete discretion in laying down the conditions under which the information collected by or exchanged between the supervisory authorities can be divulged, including disclosure to the revenue authorities. However, its failure to make an unequivocal pronouncement affirming the existence of such a limitation resulted in reluctance on the part of certain Member States having very strict confidentiality requirements to exchange information with other Member States having less strict requirements. This situation was all the more regrettable in view of the fact that the confidentiality of information exchanged under the 1983 Consolidated Supervision Directive and under the 1992 Consolidated Supervision Directive which replaced it from 1 January 1993 is also defined by reference to article 12 of the 1977 Directive.

It was partly in order to remove these obstacles and uncertainties that article 12 of the 1977 Directive was substantially amended by the Second Banking Directive.

4. ARTICLE 12, AS AMENDED BY ARTICLE 16 OF THE SECOND BANKING DIRECTIVE

1. Purposes of the amendment

17.5 As recalled by Clarotti,[7] the purpose of the amendment of article 12 by article 16 of the Second Banking Directive is twofold: first, to reinforce the obligation of professional secrecy imposed on the banking supervisors pursuant to article 12; second, to extend the possibilities for exchange of information between the banking supervisors and the supervisors of other financial institutions such as insurance companies and investment services firms, whether based in other Member States or in the same Member State.

However, it must be borne in mind that, as recalled by the same writer, the revised text of article 12 is a compromise, the result of long drawn out negotiations between Member States which have very different traditions in the field of banking secrecy. Hence, it is not devoid of ambiguities.

2. The reinforcement of the obligation of professional secrecy

17.6 The amended text of article 12 in effect reproduces the distinction unsuccessfully suggested by the Commission before the Court of Justice in the *Hillegom* case between, on the one hand, information collected by a national supervisory authority itself and, on the other hand, information received by that authority from the supervisory authorities in the other Member States, to which must be added information collected by the supervisory authority directly or through persons appointed by it when supervising branches in other Member States of credit institutions for which it is the home country supervisor.[8]

---

7. Paolo Clarotti, "La Deuxième Directive de Coordination en matière d'établissements de crédit" [1989] *Revue du Marché Commun* 453, at no. 16.

8. Art. 15 of the 1989 Banking Directive now makes it possible for the home country supervisor to carry out on-the-spot inspections of branches of "its" credit institutions in other Member States, either directly or through the intermediary of persons appointed by it, for the purposes of checking the information referred to

Cases where disclosure is allowed

17.7 In relation to the disclosure by the supervisory authorities of "own information" collected in accordance with the Directive, the effect of the amended version of article 12 would seem to be to reduce the discretion enjoyed by Member States in laying down by law the situations where information collected by their banking supervisors in furtherance of the relevant banking directives can be passed on to other authorities in that Member State. The amended text no longer provides the wide-ranging exception to confidentiality contained in the original version of article 12(1), whereby disclosure was allowed "by virtue of provisions laid down in law." However, the definitive answer to this question must await case-law of the Court of Justice.

Instead, the amended text of article 12(1) provides that:

... no confidential information ... may be divulged to any person or authority whatsoever, except in summary or collective form such that individual institutions cannot be identified, without prejudice to cases covered by criminal law.

Nevertheless, where a credit institution has been declared bankrupt, or is being compulsorily wound up, confidential information which does not concern third parties involved in attempts to rescue that credit institution may be divulged in civil or commercial proceedings.

Also, the amended text of article 12 provides a detailed list of situations where disclosure of information is permitted, such as:

— exchange of information with banking supervisors in other Member States mandated by the Directives concerning credit institutions, it being understood that such information "shall be subject to the conditions of professional secrecy indicated in paragraph 1" (see art. 12(2));

— exchange of information allowed for by article 12(5) between the banking supervisors on the one part and certain other authorities on the other part, whether in the same or in other Member States, such as the authorities responsible for the supervision of other financial organisations and insurance companies, for the supervision of financial markets, for the liquidation and bankruptcy of credit institutions, for statutory audits as well as the bodies which administer deposit guarantee schemes. Here too, the information received is subject to the conditions of professional secrecy indicated in paragraph 1 of article 12;

— the disclosure of information made, by virtue of provisions laid down by law by the Member States, "to other departments of their central government administrations responsible for legislation on the supervision of credit institutions, financial institutions, investment services and insurance companies and to inspectors acting on behalf of those departments", subject to the condition that such disclosures "may be made only where necessary for reasons of prudential control" (see article 12(7), first and second sentences).

It is submitted that the list of situations contained in the amended text of article 12 where disclosure is allowed must be viewed as exhaustive and not just as illustrative, although the list may be extended as a result of amendments presently under consideration under the proposed so-called BCCI Directive, as well as in consequence

---

in art. 7(1) of the 1977 Directive [as amended], being information of a supervisory nature, subject only to "having first informed the competent authorities of the host Member State".

of other Directives already in force, such as the Money Laundering Directive considered below. It is of interest, in this context, that the Council minutes relating to the adoption of the Second Banking Directive are understood to include a declaration to the effect that the "cases covered by criminal law", being one of the situations where disclosure is allowed under article 12(1), includes cases of criminal offences in the tax field. This declaration was no doubt inserted in the Council's Minutes at the request of those Member States which presently provide or which wish to be able to provide for the possibility of such disclosure by their banking supervisory authorities to their tax authorities. This declaration in turn raises the question whether a Member State may in effect circumvent the limitations imposed upon it by the amended text of article 12 as to the situations where disclosure is permitted by increasing the number of "cases covered by criminal law". It may be questioned whether the reference to cases covered by criminal law means that the supervisory authorities can take the initiative to inform the competent authorities of criminal conduct (including criminal offences in the tax field) which they have uncovered or whether they are only allowed to provide information to the competent authorities at the latter's request after the latter have uncovered, by their own investigations, the existence of the criminal conduct committed by the credit institution.

Special safeguards regarding disclosure of information received from authorities in other Member States, or collected by the home supervisors in other Member States

17.8 In relation to the disclosure of information received from authorities in other Member States or collected by the home supervisors in other Member States, a key provision is article 12(7), the last paragraph of which reads:

However, the Member States shall provide that information received under paragraphs 2 [from banking supervisors in other Member States] and 5 [from other authorities be it in the same or in other Member States] and that obtained by means of the on-the-spot verification referred to in Article 15(1) and (2) of [the Second Banking Directive 1989, i.e. supervision of branches in other Member States by the home banking supervisor] may *never* be disclosed in the cases referred to in this paragraph except with the express consent of the competent authorities which disclosed the information or the competent authorities of the Member State in which the on-the-spot verification was carried out.

It is understood, additionally, that the Council's Minutes relating to the adoption of the Second Banking Directive contain declarations to the effect that:

— the possibility of disclosure of information referred to in article 12(7) includes disclosure to Parliamentary commissions of inquiry (subject, in that case too, to the consent of the authorities of the host Member State, if applicable);
— Member States are never obliged to make use of the possibility of exchange of information offered by article 12, paragraph 5 (exchange of information between the banking supervisor of one Member State and certain other authorities, such as insurance company supervisors, of other Member States), and paragraph 7 (disclosure of information to departments of central government administrations responsible for legislation on supervision of credit institutions, financial institutions, investment services and insurance companies and to inspectors acting on behalf of those departments); and
— the procedure under article 22, paragraph 1, third indent, of the Second Banking Directive whereby technical adaptations may be made to the areas in

which the Member State's authorities *must* exchange information under article 7(1) of the 1977 Directive, as amended by the Second Banking Directive, only relates to information necessary for prudential supervision; and

— perhaps superfluously, the necessity for consent of the supervisory authorities of the Member States from which the information has been received, provided for by article 12(7), last paragraph, applies to information obtained by means of on-the-spot verification of the information referred to in article 15(1) of the Second Banking Directive.[9]

5. EXCHANGE OF INFORMATION BETWEEN THE BANKING SUPERVISORS OF A MEMBER STATE AND THE BANKING SUPERVISORS OF A THIRD COUNTRY

17.9 The detailed provisions of article 12 of the 1977 Directive, as amended, on the confidentiality of information obtained or received by banking supervisors would obviously be undermined if a Member State could provide information to a third country under conditions of confidentiality less rigorous than the ones laid down by Community law for exchange of information within the Community. Therefore, article 12(3) of the 1977 Directive, as amended, provides:

Member States may conclude cooperation agreements, providing for exchange of information, with the competent authorities of third countries only if the information disclosed is subject to guarantees of professional secrecy at least equivalent to those referred to in this Article.

6. BANKING SECRECY AND SUPERVISION ON A CONSOLIDATED BASIS

17.10 As already stated, the importance of the professional secrecy provisions contained in article 12 of the 1977 Directive is highlighted by the fact that both the 1983 Consolidated Supervision Directive and the replacement 1992 Consolidated Supervision Directive expressly provide that:

information received pursuant to this Directive and in particular any exchange of information between competent authorities which is provided for in this Directive shall be subject to the obligation of professional secrecy defined in Article 12 of the [1977 Banking Directive].[10]

The words "information received pursuant to this Directive *and in particular ...*" indicate, it is submitted, that the provisions on professional secrecy in article 12 of the 1977 Directive apply not only to exchanges of information between the competent authorities for the purposes of consolidation under the Consolidated Supervision Directive but also to other exchanges of information relevant for the purposes of supervision in accordance therewith. This is the case, for instance, for exchanges of information between companies referred to in article 7(1) of the 1992 Consolidated

9. Being the provision pursuant to which the competent authorities of the home Member State may "after having first informed the competent authorities of the host Member State, carry out themselves or through the intermediary of persons they appoint for that purpose on-the-spot verification [at branch level] of the information referred to in art. 7(1) [of the 1977 Directive, as amended by the Second Banking Directive]".

10. *Cf.* art. 7(5) of Council Directive 92/30/EEC of 6 April 1992 on the supervision of credit institutions on a consolidated basis, reviewed in, Part Two, above.

Supervision Directive which, under the heading "Measures to facilitate the application of this Directive" reads[11]:

> Member States shall take the necessary steps to ensure that there are no legal impediments preventing the undertakings included within the scope of supervision on a consolidated basis, mixed activity holding companies and their subsidiaries, or subsidiaries of the kind covered in Article 3(10), from exchanging amongst themselves any information which would be relevant for the purposes of supervision in accordance with this Directive.

In other words, provisions of national law may not preclude the companies subject to consolidated supervision from exchanging the information relevant for the purposes of consolidated supervision in accordance with the Directive. That information, in turn, can only be used by the competent authorities in accordance with the professional secrecy provision of article 12 of the 1977 Directive, as amended.

17.11 Also, it will be recalled that under the 1992 Consolidated Supervision Directive (as well as under the 1983 Consolidated Supervision Directive), the authorities which bear eventual responsibility for supervision on a consolidated basis do not have the right to make on-the-spot investigations in other Member States without the prior approval of the competent authorities of those other Member States. According to article 7(7) of the 1992 Consolidated Supervision Directive, the authorities of the other Member States, when in receipt of such a request, must "within the framework of their competence, act upon it either by carrying out the verification themselves, by allowing the authorities who made the request to carry it out, or by allowing an auditor or expert to carry it out." This situation contrasts with the situation existing with regard to branches under the Second Banking Directive. In that situation, under article 15(1) of the Second Banking Directive, the competent authorities of the home Member State of a credit institution need only "first inform" the authorities of the host Member State where a branch of that credit institution is located before carrying out "themselves or through the intermediary of persons *they* appoint for that purpose on-the-spot verification . . .".

With regard to relations with third countries, the position in terms of professional secrecy is also somewhat different when it comes to supervision on a consolidated basis. The 1977 Directive only contemplated the conclusion of bilateral agreements for exchange of information between individual Member States and third countries. However, article 8 of the 1992 Consolidated Supervision Directive provides that:

> (1) The Commission may submit proposals to the Council, either at the request of a Member State or on its own initiative, for the negotiation of agreements with one or more countries regarding the means of exercising supervision on a consolidated basis over:
> — credit institutions the parent undertakings of which have their head-offices situated in a third country, and
> — credit institutions in third countries the parent undertakings of which, whether credit institutions or financial holding companies, have their head-offices in the Community . . .
> . . .
> (3) The Commission and the Advisory Committee set up under Article 11 of [the 1977 Directive] shall examine the outcome of the negotiations referred to in paragraph 1 and the resulting situation.

This text differs substantially from article 6 of the 1983 Consolidated Supervision Directive, which provided *inter alia*:

> (1) Application of the principle of supervision on a consolidated basis to credit institutions

---

11. A similar provision was inserted into the 1983 Consolidated Supervision Directive, in art. 5(1).

whose parent companies have their head-offices in non-member countries and to credit institutions situated in non-member countries whose parent credit institutions have a head-office in the Community should be the subject of bilateral agreement, on the basis of reciprocity, *between the competent authorities of the Member States* and the non-member countries concerned ...

(2) The Commission and the Advisory Committee set up under Article 11 of [the 1977 Directive] ... shall be kept informed of such steps as may be taken in this context and the Commission shall undertake coordination of the above agreements.

It is submitted, however, that despite this changed wording Member States retain jurisdiction to conclude agreements with third countries pertaining to supervision on a consolidated basis, in any event until such time as the provisions of article 8 have not been acted upon by the Commission. In the conclusion and performance of such agreements, Member States must however observe the general principle of Community preference discussed at length in Part Eight, below.

CHAPTER 18

BANKING SECRECY AND THE MONEY LAUNDERING DIRECTIVE: THE ISSUE OF "DOUBLE INCRIMINATION"

1. SCOPE OF THE DISCUSSION

18.1 On 10 June 1991, the Council adopted a Directive "on prevention of the use of the financial system for the purposes of money laundering".[1] Its scope of application includes not only credit institutions but also financial institutions generally, including life insurance companies, and may be extended to other professions and undertakings should this prove necessary. A detailed analysis of this Directive falls outside the scope of this book.[2] Instead, attention will be focused on the interactions or, perhaps, rather the contradictions, that exist between the Money Laundering Directive and the other EC legislation already discussed.

2. GENERAL OUTLINE

18.2 The Money Laundering Directive imposes on banks and other financial institutions a number of obligations in terms of:

— positive identification of (beneficial) customers[3];
— keeping of individual transaction records[4];
— exercising due diligence with regard to any transactions they regard as likely, by their nature, to be related to money laundering[5]; and
— reporting to the authorities "responsible for combating money laundering of the Member State in whose territory the institution forwarding the information is situated", either at the bank's or other financial institution's own initiative, or as a result of a specific request received from such authorities, of information pertaining to suspected cases of money laundering.[6]

These obligations, and in particular the mandatory reporting at the bank's own initiative of "any fact which might be an indication of money laundering" obviously involves a corresponding—and sometimes complete—lifting of banking secrecy on the part of the credit institution concerned.

---

1. Council Directive 91/308/EEC, OJ L166/77 of 28 June 1991.
2. For a detailed analysis, see, eg, Annabelle Ewing, "The Draft EEC Money Laundering Directive: an overview" [1991] JIBL 139; see also, "The EC Money Laundering Directive: an update" [1992] JIBL News S, n. 54.
3. Art. 3.
4. Art. 4.
5. Art. 5.
6. Art. 6.

18.3 However laudable its intentions, the system set in place looks likely to result in years to come in significant clashes with the Second Banking Directive and other accompanying "single market" financial legislation. These inconsistencies and contradictions have two main causes.

First, the lack of uniformity in terms of Community law as regards the definition of money laundering, which is the trigger for the various obligations imposed on banks under the Money Laundering Directive. Article 1 of the directive defines money laundering by reference to certain types of conduct described therein, the common trait of which is the involvement, however indirect, of such conduct with "criminal activity". However, "criminal activity" is defined in the same article as:

a crime specified in Article 3(1)(a) of the Vienna Convention[7] *and any other criminal activity designated as such for the purposes of this directive by each Member State.*

This definition in effect leaves total discretion to each Member State to designate "any other criminal activity," however unrelated to drug offences, as triggering the application of the obligations referred to, including the mandatory own initiative reporting imposed by the directive on credit institutions and other financial institutions. This can create insuperable difficulties where particular conduct, for example having unreported professional income, is listed in Member State A as a criminal activity triggering the obligations imposed by the Money Laundering Directive but is not treated as such in Member State B.

Second, the supervisory authorities of banks and other financial institutions are under an obligation to report to the "authorities responsible for combating money laundering" any suspicion of money laundering activities that has come to their attention in the course of their supervisory functions.[8] It is also up to those authorities—and not to their home country supervisors—that the banks must report, on their own initiative, suspected cases of money laundering. The designation of such authorities is a matter for each Member State individually. In some Member States, such as France, the authorities having responsibility for combating money laundering are the tax authorities.

3. INCONSISTENCIES AND CONTRADICTIONS BETWEEN THE MONEY LAUNDERING DIRECTIVE AND THE FIRST AND SECOND BANKING DIRECTIVES

18.4 The inconsistencies and contradictions which may result from the combination of the provisions of the Money Laundering Directive and the provisions of the First and Second Banking Directives can best be illustrated by an example. Suppose that bank X has its head office in Member State A, where tax offences are listed as a criminal activity triggering the Money Laundering Directive, and has a branch in Member State B, where tax offences are not so listed. The question arises whether the supervisory authorities of Member State A must report to the tax authorities of Member State A (being, it is assumed, the competent authorities for combating money laundering in Member State A) the fact that an on-the-spot inspection of the bank's branch in Member State B has revealed that one or more persons resident in Member State A

---

7. UN Convention against illicit traffic in narcotic drugs and psychotropic substances, opened for signature in Vienna on 19 December 1988.
8. Art. 10.

have deposited what looks suspiciously like the proceeds of an unreported professional activity with the bank's branch in Member State B. If the answer is yes, such a result would, it is submitted, be contrary to the provisions on banking secrecy contained in article 12 of the 1977 Directive. It would appear, therefore, that in the above illustration, and in other similar situations, the reporting can only take place if *both* Member State A and Member State B have designated the same type of activity as a criminal activity triggering the mechanism of the Money Laundering Directive.

It is precisely to attain that result with regard to money laundering proper (that is, drug-related monies) that the original Commission proposal imposed an express obligation on the Member States to criminalise drug-related offences, albeit "according to their national legislation".[9] However, as a result of considerable opposition from the Member States, which insisted that criminal law falls within their exclusive competence, this provision was dropped and instead a statement was made "by the representatives of the governments of the Member States meeting within the Council", at the time of the adoption of the Directive, whereby they undertook to take "all necessary steps by 31 December 1992 at the latest to enact criminal legislation" making (at least) drug offences proper a criminal offence.[10]

However, the lack of uniformity in the Member States in terms of the offences which trigger the obligations imposed on banks and other financial institutions by the Directive, and the fact that the competent authorities to which suspected money laundering must be reported by the banks, either at their own initiative or upon request, are not the home country banking supervisors, but instead "the authorities responsible for combating money laundering of the Member State in whose territory the institution forwarding the information is situated"[11] inevitably results in other difficulties for banking institutions, especially when they operate on a cross-border basis.

In particular, in the reverse situation from that in the illustration just given, where Member State A does not list tax offences as a crime for the purposes of the Directive but Member State B, where the branch of the bank is located, does, there is no doubt that the branch will be required to report suspected tax offences to the national authorities of Member State B responsible for the fight against money laundering.

Under the Directive,[12] if this disclosure is made in good faith by the branch to the authorities of Member State B, it cannot involve the bank in liability of any kind, even if it later proves unfounded. It may be questioned, however, whether the same result will obtain if an action is brought not in the courts of Member State B but, instead, in the courts of Member State A (where the bank in the example given has its head office and where tax offences are not listed as a crime for the purposes of the Directive).

Doubt as to the precise position of the bank may also arise in the case where the bank does not have a branch in Member State B but, instead, provides services on a cross-border basis in Member State B (that is, it has opened an account at its head office in Member State A to a customer resident in Member State B) and it has reason to suspect that the monies deposited by that customer are the proceeds of an unreported professional activity carried out in Member State B. In such a situation, must the bank of Member State A notify this suspected money laundering activity (under the national

9. Art. 2 of the original Commission proposal, document COM (90) 106 final—SYN 254, OJ C106/6 of 28 April 1990.
10. The full text of that statement is published in the OJ together with the Directive.
11. Art. 6.
12. Art. 9.

laws of Member State B) to the authorities of Member State B, even though it does not even have a branch there? If so, and if it is sued for damages in Member State A, will it be able to avail itself of the protection of the Directive even though Member State A does not list tax offences as a crime for the purposes of the Directive?

As can be seen from these examples, which are by no means exhaustive, the Money Laundering Directive has the potential to paralyse to a large extent the proper working of the system put in place by the Second Banking Directive for the supervision of credit institutions. It is to be hoped that Member States will resist the temptation to use its ambiguities to the full in an attempt to regain by the back door some of the supervisory powers they have given up as a result of the Second Banking Directive with regard to EC credit institutions operating in their territory on a cross-border basis.

PART FOUR

THE FREEDOM OF MOVEMENT OF CAPITAL AND CURRENT PAYMENTS

CHAPTER 19

MOVEMENTS OF CAPITAL AND CURRENT PAYMENTS DISTINGUISHED

1. GENERAL REMARKS

19.1 The entry into force of the Capital Movements Directive on 1 July 1990 greatly reduced the importance of the distinction between movements of capital, on the one hand, and current payments, on the other. Although under article 61(2) of the Treaty, the liberalisation of banking services is linked to the progressive liberalisation of the free movement of capital, until the entry into force of the Directive Member States were free to maintain in force exchange regulations which prohibited individuals and undertakings from freely transferring or holding financial assets which were not directly related to the exercise of the fundamental freedoms referred to in article 106 of the Treaty.

The European Court of Justice considered this issue in case *Casati*,[1] where it held that article 67 of the Treaty concerning the freedom of capital movements did not have direct effect, with the consequence that individuals and undertakings could only avail themselves of those provisions to the extent that Council directives had been adopted to implement the provisions of article 67. An exception to this rule existed with regard to article 106 of the Treaty in circumstances where the free movement of capital and of current payments was exercised as a corollary to the implementation of one of the four fundamental freedoms (free movement of goods and persons, freedom of establishment and the freedom to provide services), which freedoms have been in full force since 1 January 1970. Thus, for example, the freedom to provide services involves, as an essential corollary, the right of the beneficiary of the service to pay the provider and to acquire for this purpose the necessary currency.

As will be seen, the effect of the Capital Movements Directive has been to remove the obstacles resulting from the link between most banking services and movements of capital and current payments. Since its entry into force, article 67's lack of direct effect is no longer of any real practical significance.

However, the distinction between movements of capital and current payments remains of some interest, in particular in the context of safeguard provisions.

---

1. Case 203/80 [1981] ECR 2595.

225

2. THE DISTINCTION BETWEEN MOVEMENTS OF CAPITAL AND CURRENT PAYMENTS

19.2 The Treaty is silent on the meaning to be attributed to the term "movements of capital". However, in *Luisi and Carbone* v. *Ministero del Tesoro*[2] the Court of Justice defined it to mean financial operations essentially concerned with the investment of the funds in question.[3] The Court drew a distinction between such operations and "current payments", which it defined in terms of transfers of foreign exchange which constitute the remuneration for a service[4]:

The general scheme of the Treaty shows, and a comparison between Articles 67 and 106 confirms, that current payments are transfers of foreign exchange which constitute the consideration within the context of an underlying transaction, whilst movements of capital are financial operations essentially concerned with the investment of the funds in question rather than remuneration for a service . . .

These definitions, which were reaffirmed by the Court in *Ministère Public* v. *Lambert*,[5] are consistent with the provisions of article 67 itself. Article 67(1) refers to the *investment* of capital and article 67(2) distinguishes between, on the one hand, the movement of capital and, on the other hand, current payments connected therewith.

3. MOVEMENTS OF CAPITAL

19.3 To facilitate its application, the Capital Movements Directive contains in Annex I a classification of capital movements according to the economic nature of the assets and liabilities they concern, denominated either in national currency or in foreign exchange. Although extensive, it is not an exhaustive list of the capital movements referred to in article 1 of the Directive. Therefore, the list is not to be interpreted as restricting the scope of the full liberalisation of capital movements called for by article 1 of the Directive but it provides, in the absence of any definition in the Treaty itself of a capital movement, a very useful guide to the sort of operations which constitute movements of capital.

For there to be a "movement of capital" within the meaning of article 67 of the Treaty, the movement in question must take place between Member States.[6]

2. Joined cases 286/82 and 26/83 [1984] ECR 377.

3. Compare the Court's statement with the observations of the Commission in case 7/78 *R* v. *Thompson* [1978] ECR 2247, at pp. 2263–2264 that "without seeking to define every circumstance in which a movement of capital can take place, it is considered that in many cases a movement of capital will occur when financial sources situated in one country are used to make an investment in another country and the investment is not transferred to the country where those resources were originally situated within a reasonable period". In case 267/86 *Pascal van Eycke* v. *ASPA NV* [1988] ECR 4769, at p. 4793, at point 23, the Court stated that the making of savings deposits was within one of the categories of capital movements in List D of the First Capital Directive.

4. *Ibid.*, at p. 404, point 21.

5. Case 308/86 [1988] ECR 4369, at p. 4389, at point 10.

6. See case 194/84 *Commission* v. *Greece* [1987] ECR 4737, at pp. 4749–4750, at points 6 to 8. In that case, the Court ruled that Greece had failed to fulfil its obligations under art. 52 of its Act of Accession by failing progressively to release funds blocked in Greece belonging to persons resident in other Member States in accordance with the timetable laid down in those provisions. The Greek Government unsuccessfully argued that art. 52 only required funds blocked in Greece and belonging to residents of other Member States to be released solely for use in Greece and not for transfer out of the country.

4. CURRENT PAYMENTS

19.4 Not all transfers of foreign exchange constituting the consideration within the context of an underlying transaction are "current payments" within the meaning of the Treaty. Payments made in the currency of a third country other than the currency of the Member State in which the creditor or beneficiary resides are not covered by the liberalisation of payments provided for by article 106 of the Treaty.[7]

---

7. *Luisi and Carbone* at p. 405, point 28. The same view was expressed by Sir Gordon Slynn A.G. in his Opinion in *Orlandi Italo e Figlio and Others* v. *Ministry of Foreign Trade* [1982] ECR 2147, at p. 2172, referring to C.-D. Ehlermann in Groeben–Boeckh–Thiesing, *EWG-Vertrag Kommentär*, 1974, Vol. I, p. 1383.

CHAPTER 20

FREEDOM OF CAPITAL MOVEMENTS UNDER ARTICLE 67

1. ARTICLE 67 OF THE TREATY

20.1 The abolition, as between Member States, of obstacles to the free movement of capital is one of the activities of the Community envisaged by article 3(c) of the Treaty. Article 8A of the Treaty[1] states that the internal market is to comprise an area without internal frontiers in which *inter alia* the free movement of capital is ensured in accordance with the provisions of the Treaty.

The liberalisation of capital movements both within the Community and between the Community and third countries is the subject of articles 67 to 73 of the Treaty. Because the freedom of capital movements is closely related to the economic, monetary and balance of payments policies of the Member States, these provisions are more restrictive than those which concern the free movement of goods, persons and services. They must also be read in conjunction with articles 104 to 109 of the Treaty which concern economic policy.[2]

Article 67(1) provides that:

During the transitional period and to the extent necessary to ensure the proper functioning of the common market, Member States shall progressively abolish between themselves all restrictions on the movement of capital belonging to persons resident in Member States and any discrimination based on the nationality or on the place of residence of the parties or on the place where such capital is invested.

Unlike article 106(1), the provisions of article 67 were held by the Court of Justice in *Casati*[3] not to have direct effect. In that case the Court recognised that the free movement of capital was one of the fundamental freedoms of the Community and also that the freedom to move certain types of capital was, in practice, a precondition for the effective exercise of the other freedoms granted by the Treaty, in particular the right of establishment. However, it also recognised the close connection between capital movements and the Member States' economic and monetary policies and, accordingly, that complete freedom of movement of capital might undermine the economic policy of a Member State or create an imbalance in its balance of payments situation. It therefore concluded that the obligation contained in article 67(1) to abolish restrictions on movements of capital could not be defined, in relation to a specific category of such movements, in isolation from the Council's assessment under article 69 of the Treaty of

---

1. Added by art. 13 of the Single European Act, [1987] OJ L169/1.
2. The Treaty on European Union replaces the provisions of arts. 67 to 73 and also the provisions of the Treaty on economic and monetary policy with new and substantially different provisions which fall, however, outside the scope of the present edition of this work.
3. Case 203/80 [1981] ECR 2595.

the need to liberalise that category in order to ensure the proper functioning of the common market. However, as already stated, article 67's lack of direct effect is no longer of any real practical significance since the entry into force on 1 July 1990 of the Capital Movements Directive.

2. THE CAPITAL MOVEMENTS DIRECTIVE OF 24 JUNE 1988[4]

20.2 Prior to the entry into force of the Capital Movements Directive on 1 July 1990, the Council's "assessment" of the requirements of the common market referred to by the Court of Justice in *Casati* was reflected in two Directives adopted by the Council, acting under the procedure laid down in article 69 of the Treaty.[5]

The Capital Movements Directive repealed the First Directive with effect from 1 July 1990[6] and, with one minor and perhaps unfortunate qualification,[7] introduced from that date a complete liberalisation of *all* capital movements in the Community, subject only to transitional arrangements for some Member States[8] and specific safeguard provisions to enable Member States to reintroduce restrictions on short-term capital movements for up to six months should monetary or exchange-rate policies be disrupted.[9] Thus certain capital transactions which were previously excluded from liberalisation, such as financial loans and credits, current and deposit account operations and transactions in money market securities, are now subject to the new regime.[10]

4. Directive 88/361 of 24 June 1988, OJ L178/5 of 8 July 1988.

5. Art. 69 of the Treaty provides that "The Council shall, on a proposal from the Commission, which for their purpose shall consult the Monetary Committee provided for in Article 105, issue the necessary directives for the progressive implementation of Article 67, acting unanimously during the first two stages and by a qualified majority thereafter". The First Directive was adopted on 11 May 1960 and the Second, which added to and amended the First, on 18 December 1962. They are now largely of historical interest. All the movements of capital were divided into four lists (A, B, C and D) annexed to the Directives. The liberalisation of the movements of capital specified in Lists A and B was unconditional. The only circumstance in which a Member State might suspend the right to make such movements of capital freely were those laid down in the safeguard provisions contained in arts. 73, 108 and 109 of the Treaty. The liberalisation of the movements specified in List C was conditional in that a Member State was permitted to maintain or to reintroduce any exchange restrictions which were operative on such movements on the date of entry into force of the First Directive, where such free movement of capital might have formed an obstacle to the achievement of the economic objectives of the Member State concerned. In the case of the movements of capital specified in List D, the Directives did not require the Member States to adopt any liberalising measures but merely obliged them to inform the Commission of any amendments to the national provisions governing such movements. See also the amendments made to the First Directive by Directive 85/583 of 20 December 1985, [1985] OJ L372/9 and by Directive 86/566 of 17 November 1986, [1986] OJ L332/22.

6. Art. 9 of the 1988 Directive.

7. See para. 20.4, below.

8. Art. 6(2) authorises Greece, Ireland, Portugal and Spain temporarily to continue to apply or to reintroduce restrictions to the capital movements listed in Annex IV to the Directive, subject to the conditions and time limits laid down in that Annex. Art. 6(3) authorised Belgium and Luxembourg temporarily to continue to operate the dual exchange market system operated by them. This authorisation was justified, in Annex V to the Directive, on the ground that the system "has not had the effect of restricting capital movements"—thus skirting round the contentious issue whether the system was itself a restriction on capital movements—but the authorisation was only valid until 31 December 1992 because of the anomalous nature of the system and in the interests of effective implementation of the Directive and with a view to strengthening the European Monetary System. Until abolition of the system, Belgium and Luxembourg undertook to administer it on the basis of procedures which would continue to ensure the *de facto* free movement of capital on such conditions that the exchange rates ruling on the two markets "show no appreciable and lasting differences". In any event, Belgium and Luxembourg eliminated their two-tier currency market at the beginning of March 1990.

9. Art. 3 of the 1988 Directive. See further below.

10. See Peter Oliver and Jean-Paul Bache, "Free Movement of Capital between the Member States: Recent Developments" (1989) 26 CMLRev. 61, at p. 68.

1. Abolition of restrictions on movements of capital taking place between persons resident in Member States

20.3 The requirement for Member States to abolish restrictions on capital movements between persons resident in Member States is contained in article 1(1) of the Directive. The capital movements which are non-exhaustively listed in Annex I to the Directive in order to facilitate its application are expressed as being taken to cover:

— All the operations necessary for the purposes of capital movements: the conclusion and performance of the transaction and related transfers. Transactions are generally between residents of different Member States but some capital movements, such as the transfer of assets belonging to a person emigrating from one Member State to another, will be carried out by a single person for his own account.

— Operations carried out by any natural or legal person, including operations in respect of the assets or liabilities of Member States or of other public administrations and agencies, subject to the provisions of article 68(3) of the Treaty.[11]

— Access for the economic operator to all the financial techniques available on the market approached for the purpose of carrying out the operation in question. For example, the acquisition of securities and other financial instruments covers not only spot transactions but also all the dealing techniques available such as forward transactions, transactions carrying an option or warrant and swaps. Current and deposit account operations include not only the opening of accounts and placing funds in accounts but also forward foreign exchange transactions.

— Operations to liquidate or assign assets built up, the repatriation of the proceeds of liquidation thereof or the immediate use of such proceeds within the limits of Community obligations.

— Operations to repay credits or loans.

In order to avoid any hidden restriction on capital movements, the Directive expressly states that transfers in respect of capital movements must be made on the same exchange rate conditions as those which govern payments relating to current transactions.[12] The two-tier currency market system which was at one time in force in Belgium and Luxembourg would also have fallen foul of these provisions.

The one minor qualification to the complete liberalisation of capital movements concerns existing national legislation regulating the purchase of secondary residences. Such legislation may be upheld until the Council adopts further provisions pursuant to article 69 of the Treaty.[13] This, at first sight strange, provision was inserted, apparently

---

11. Art. 68(3) contains an important limitation on the free movement of capital. It provides that:
> Loans for the direct or indirect financing of a Member State or its regional or local authorities shall not be issued or placed in other Member States unless the States concerned have reached agreement thereon. This provision shall not preclude the application of Art. 22 of the Protocol on the Statute of the European Investment Bank.

Whether or not a loan is destined for the financing of a Member State or its authorities may be a difficult question to answer in any particular case. The provisions of art. 68(3) do not cover other transactions such as those relating to the financing of the Community institutions under arts. 207 and 208 of the Treaty nor the ability of the European Investment Bank to borrow on the capital market of a Member State in the circumstances envisaged by art. 22 of the Protocol on the Statute of that organisation.

12. Art. 1(2) of the 1988 Directive.

13. Art. 6(4) of the 1988 Directive.

at the request of Denmark, in recognition of the difficulties to which the full liberalisation of capital movements could contribute in the market for second homes, especially in border areas.[14]

2. The recent decision of the Court of Justice in Bachmann v. Belgium[15]

20.4 However, another qualification of potentially greater importance emerges from the recent decision of the Court of Justice in *Bachmann* v. *Belgium*. In that case, the Court was concerned with Belgian tax rules which prevented the deduction for tax purposes of insurance premiums paid to German insurance companies by a German national who had taken up residence in Belgium. The Court held that the Belgian tax rules at issue did not infringe either article 67 or article 106 of the Treaty in circumstances where there was no restriction on the movement of foreign exchange itself.

As observed by Advocate General Mischo, Mr Bachmann did not complain that he had experienced difficulty in acquiring the necessary Deutschmarks in Belgium with which to pay the premiums in Germany but that, in effect, in the absence of the Belgian tax rules in question, more foreign insurers would have been able to sell insurance services in Belgium, with the result that a greater flow of premiums from Belgium to other Member States would have occurred.

The Court apparently followed the Advocate General's Opinion to the effect that the link between the Belgian tax restrictions on the free provision of insurance services and the free movement of capital and current payments was too tenuous and indirect to conclude that article 67 or 106 of the Treaty had been infringed. As a matter of Community law, the need to ensure the cohesion of the Belgian fiscal system justified the prohibition on the deductibility of life insurance premiums paid to foreign (Community) insurers, even though such a prohibition restricted the provision of insurance services on a cross-border basis in Belgium and the free movement of workers.[16]

If the reasoning in *Bachmann* were applied to the banking sector, it could lead to a situation where Member States were able to block the provision of many banking services on a cross-border basis by the introduction of tax measures purportedly justified by the need to ensure the cohesion of their tax systems. For example, a Member State might seek to prohibit any foreign bank from receiving deposits on a cross-border basis on the ground that there is a risk that its customer, being a taxpayer resident in that Member State, may fail to include in his annual tax return the gross interest received in circumstances where interest paid by a local bank is paid net of tax. Such a situation, just at the time when the Second Banking Directive is in force on 1 January 1993, would be unfortunate, to say the least.[17]

In this regard, article 4 of the Capital Movements Directive provides that nothing in the Directive affects the right of Member States to take all requisite measures to prevent

---

14. See Phillippe Vigneron, "La nouvelle directive communautaire relative à la libération des mouvements de capitaux", *Revue de la Banque* (Belgium) 9/1988, p. 7, at p. 11 and also the preamble to the Directive, 7th recital.

15. Case C–204/90, [1992] ECR 249.

16. See also case C–300/90 *Commission* v. *Belgium* [1992] ECR 305.

17. An argument apparently not raised before the Court was whether the Belgian tax rules at issue were not contrary to art. 62 of the Treaty, which requires Member States to refrain from introducing any new restrictions on the freedom to provide services which has in fact been attained at the date of entry into force of the Treaty, except as otherwise provided in the Treaty.

infringement of their laws and regulations *inter alia* in the field of taxation and prudential supervision of financial institutions or to lay down procedures for the declaration of capital movements for purposes of administrative or statistical information. However, the application of such measures and procedures must not have the effect of in any way impeding capital movements which are carried out in accordance with Community law.[18]

3. Capital movements between the Community and third countries

20.5 Capital movements between the Community and third countries are now governed by article 7 of the Directive.[19] It provides that in their treatment of transfers in respect of movements of capital the Member States must endeavour to attain the same degree of liberalisation as that which applies to operations with residents of other Member States, subject to the other provisions of the Directive.[20] However, third countries remain subject to any domestic rules of the Member States or of Community law, in particular any reciprocal conditions concerning operations involving establishment, the provision of financial services and the admission of securities to capital markets.[21]

4. Notification of certain measures regulating bank liquidity

20.6 All measures taken by the Member States to regulate bank liquidity and which have a specific impact on capital transactions carried out by credit institutions with non-residents must be notified to the Commission and also to the Committee of Governors of the Central Banks and the Monetary Committee no later than the date of their entry into force.[22] Such measures may not exceed what is necessary for the purposes of domestic monetary regulation: a matter for consideration by the Committee of Governors of the Central Banks and the Monetary Committee.[23]

5. Examination by the Monetary Committee

20.7 The Directive requires the Monetary Committee to examine at least once a year and to report to the Commission on the situation regarding the free movement of capital as it results from the application of the Directive. The examination encompasses measures concerning the domestic regulation of credit and financial and monetary

18. See further Chap. 22.
19. Under the Treaty on European Union, art. 14, provision is made for the compulsory liberalisation, subject to certain limited exceptions, of the movement of capital and payments between the Community and third countries, by way of insertion into the Treaty of new art. 73a to h. However, these provisions fall outside the scope of the present edition of this book.
20. Art. 7(1). Under art. 70 of the Treaty, the Council, acting on proposals from the Commission, was required to issue directives aimed at the progressive co-ordination of the exchange policies of Member States in respect of the movement of capital between those States and third countries and with a view to attaining "the highest possible" degree of liberalisation. Pursuant to arts. 70 and 103 of the Treaty, the Council adopted on 21 March 1972 Directive 72/156, OJ 1972, p. 296 on the regulation of international capital flows and the neutralisation of their undesirable effects on domestic liquidity. That Directive was repealed with effect from 1 July 1990 by art. 9 of the Capital Movements Directive. The preamble to the Capital Movements Directive recites, in the 9th recital, the provisions of art. 70(1) of the Treaty and is expressed to be based on the provisions of both art. 69 and art. 70.
21. Art. 7(1), second subparagraph.
22. Art. 2, first paragraph, of the 1988 Directive.
23. Art. 2, second paragraph, of the 1988 Directive.

markets which could have a specific impact on international capital movements and on all other aspects of the Directive.[24]

24. Art. 8 of the 1988 Directive.

CHAPTER 21

FREEDOM OF CURRENT PAYMENTS CONNECTED WITH THE MOVEMENT OF GOODS, SERVICES OR CAPITAL AND CERTAIN CAPITAL TRANSFERS UNDER ARTICLE 106

1. ARTICLE 106(1) OF THE TREATY

21.1 Article 106(1) of the Treaty provides amongst other things that:

Each Member State undertakes to authorise, in the currency of the Member State in which the creditor or the beneficiary resides, any payments connected with the movement of goods, services or capital, and any transfers of capital and earnings, to the extent that the movement of goods, services, capital and persons between Member States has been liberalised pursuant to this Treaty.
. . .

The aim of these provisions is to ensure that the necessary monetary transfers may be made both for the liberalisation of movements of capital and for the free movement of goods, services and persons.[1] In contrast to the provisions of article 67 of the Treaty, which concerns capital movements, the provisions of article 106(1) have direct effect.[2]

2. LIBERALISATION OF PAYMENTS CONNECTED WITH THE MOVEMENT OF GOODS, SERVICES AND CAPITAL

21.2 In *Luisi and Carbone*[3] the Court of Justice firmly rejected the arguments of the French and Italian governments that the export of currency by tourists was to be treated not as a payment connected with the provision of services and so governed by article 106 but as a movement of capital governed by article 67.[4] As the Court pointed out[5]:

. . . [T]he freedom to provide services includes the freedom, for the recipients of services, to go to another Member State in order to receive a service there, without being obstructed by restrictions, even in relation to payments, and . . . tourists, persons receiving medical treatment and persons travelling for the purposes of education or business are to be regarded as recipients of services. . . .

Until the entry into force of the Capital Movements Directive, the implications of *Luisi and Carbone* had been far-reaching. Article 106(1) refers not only to payments but also to "any transfer of capital and earnings to the extent that the movement of goods, services . . . and persons between Member States has been liberalised pursuant to this Treaty". The reference to the movement of persons includes the freedom of

1. Case 7/78 *R*. v. *Thompson* [1978] ECR 2247, at p. 2274 at point 24.
2. Joined cases 286/82 and 26/83 *Luisi and Carbone* v. *Ministero del Tesoro* [1984] ECR 377, at p. 404, point 24.
3. Joined cases 286/82 and 26/83 [1984] ECR 377.
4. At p. 387.
5. At pp. 403–404, points 16, 21 and 22 (italics added).

establishment.[6] The reasoning of the Court of Justice implied the complete and unconditional liberalisation not only of payments but also of transfers of capital and earnings connected with the movement of goods, services and persons.[7] Since 1 July 1990, when the Directive entered into force, the Court's decision in *Luisi and Carbone* is of historical interest only insofar as it relates to the admissibility of certain restrictions on the free movement of capital and of payments. However, it remains important insofar as it lays down the principles which must be observed by Member States when they take measures to monitor the transfer of capital and cross-border payments for tax, statistical and other purposes.

3. THE RECENT DECISION OF THE COURT OF JUSTICE IN BACHMANN V. BELGIUM[8]

21.3 Reference has already been made to the recent decision of the Court of Justice in *Bachmann* v. *Belgium*. It will be recalled that the Court held that the Belgian tax rules refusing the deductibility for income tax purposes of premiums paid to foreign insurers were not in breach of article 67 nor of article 106 because the rules in question did not restrict the acquisition of the foreign exchange necessary to pay life insurance premiums to a foreign insurer. The fact that the rules discouraged Belgian taxpayers from "buying" life insurance from insurers established in other Member States, with the result that less money was flowing into the hands of such insurers, was held not to be a restriction on the free movement of capital or payments.[9]

4. THE RIGHT OF MEMBER STATES TO MONITOR TRANSFERS

21.4 Article 106 is not infringed by a provision of national law which requires exporters to have foreign currency payable in respect of their sales paid through a bank and to exchange such currency on the regulated foreign exchange market. Such a provision is concerned solely with the way in which the exporter must receive payment, regardless of whether the payment is expressed in foreign or national currency. It has no effect on the ability of either the importer to make payment in the currency of the State in which the buyer resides or of the importer to receive that payment.[10]

---

6. Arts. 52 to 58 of the Treaty, which contain the rules on the right of establishment, comprises Chap. 2 of Title III of Part Two of the Treaty. Title III concerns the free movement of persons, services and capital.

7. In 1963, the Council had adopted Directive 63/340 of 31 May 1963 [1963–1964] (OJ Spec. Ed. 31) in implementation of art. 106, which was intended to ensure the abolition of all prohibitions on or obtacles to payments for services where the only restriction on the provision of services were those governing such payments. In the light of *Luisi and Carbone*, the importance of the Directive was substantially diminished.

8. Case C–204/90, [1992] ECR 249.

9. See para. 20.4, above.

10. Case 308/86 *Lambert* [1988] ECR 4369, at p. 4391, at points 16 to 19.

CHAPTER 22

LIMITATIONS IMPOSED BY EUROPEAN COMMUNITY LAW ON NATIONAL CONTROL MEASURES IN RESPECT OF TRANSFERS OF FUNDS ABROAD

1. GENERAL REMARKS

22.1 The First Directive of 11 May 1960 implementing article 67 of the Treaty only liberalised unconditionally some movements of capital. In accordance with the Court of Justice's ruling in *Luisi and Carbone*,[1] Member States retained the power to impose controls on transfers of foreign currency in order to verify that the transfers did not in fact constitute movements of capital which had not been liberalised.[2] They also remained entitled to verify the nature and genuineness of the transactions or transfers in question related to the payment of services or of goods[3] and not those related to a non-liberalised transfer.

With the full liberalisation of capital movements brought about by the Capital Movements Directive, the Member States no longer have the power—nor the need—to check whether a transfer falls into the liberalised categories. However, this does not mean that Member States do not have the right to monitor those transfers for other purposes. This continuing right of the Member States is reflected in article 4 of the Directive, which provides that the Directive is without prejudice to the Member States' right to take all requisite measures to prevent infringement of their laws and regulations *inter alia* in the field of taxation and prudential supervision of financial institutions or to laying down procedures for the declaration of capital movements for purposes of administrative or statistical information. However, the application of such measures or procedures is only permitted insofar as they do not have the effect of in any way impeding capital movements carried out in accordance with Community law.

The Court of Justice's ruling in *Luisi and Carbone*, although decided at a time when the old regime was in force, contains important statements of general application with regard to the control measures which Member States remain in certain circumstances entitled to apply.

2. PERMISSIBLE CONTROL MEASURES WHICH MAY BE APPLIED BY THE MEMBER STATES

22.2 National control measures must be kept strictly within the limits imposed by Community law and may not be applied in such a manner as to render the freedoms

---

1. Joined cases 286/82 and 26/83 [1984] ECR 377.
2. *Luisi and Carbone*, at p. 406, point 31.
3. *Ibid.*, at p. 406, point 33.

recognised by the Treaty illusory or to subject the exercise of those freedoms to the discretion of the national authorities.[4]

In *Casati*, the Court of Justice decided that the provisions of article 106[5]:

do not require the Member States to authorise the importation and exportation of bank notes for the performance of commercial transactions, if such transfers are not necessary for the free movement of goods.

The Court pointed out in this regard that "in connection with commercial transactions, that method of transfer which, moreover, is not in conformity with standard practice, cannot be regarded as necessary to ensure such free movement."[6] Commentators pointed out at the time that this reasoning allows the Member States to require payments for commercial transactions to be made by bank transfer only.[7]

In contrast, the general obligation to make all payments by bank transfer in settlement of tourists' expenses appears to be incompatible with Community law. In his Opinion in *Luisi and Carbone*, Advocate General Mancini had asserted that controls authorised in principle[8]:

. . . must take due account of the different risks of fraud which attach to transfers of currency for tourist purposes or business travel, on the one hand, and to those for medical treatment and education, on the other. In the case of tourism, the activity which best lends itself to concealing transfer of capital, a practical solution, being effective and at the same time not excessively rigid, must be based on the amount of foreign currency which those concerned wish to transfer.

The Court clearly followed the Advocate General on this point by holding that the foreign exchange controls which the Member States at that time retained the right to impose might consist in the[9]:

fixing of flat-rate limits below which no verification is carried out and . . . requiring proof, in the case of expenditure exceeding those limits, that the amounts transferred have actually been used in connection with the provision of services, provided however that the flat-rate limits so determined are not such as to affect the normal pattern of the provision of services.

It is for the national court to determine in each individual case whether the controls on transfers of foreign currency which are at issue in proceedings before it are in conformity with the limits thus defined.

This statement reveals another consideration of general application with regard to the control measures which Member States remain entitled to apply today for the tax, statistical and other purposes already referred to. Permissible control measures must be fixed as a function of the normal characteristics of the transactions which are the object of such control measures in such a manner as not to interfere with those transactions. As the Court said in *Casati*[10]:

The administrative measures or penalties must not go beyond what is strictly necessary, the control procedures must not be conceived in such a way as to restrict the freedom required by the Treaty and they must not be accompanied by a penalty which is so disproportionate to the gravity of the infringement that it becomes an obstacle to the exercise of that freedom.

---

4. See *Luisi and Carbone*, at p. 406, point 34 and p. 407, point 37., *Cf.* art. 4, second paragraph of the Capital Movements Directive.
5. Case 203/80 [1981] ECR 2595, at p. 2617, point 24.
6. *Ibid.*
7. See J.V. Louis, "Free Movement of Tourists and Freedom of Payments in the Community: the Luisi and Carbone judgment" [1984] CMLRev.
8. At pp. 419–420.
9. At pp. 406–407, points 35 and 36.
10. [1981] ECR 2595, at p. 2618, at point 27.

If the need for a bank transfer for the payment for the importation of goods bought by a professional—the hypothesis of the *Casati* judgment—is not capable of interfering with the free movement of goods in the Community, because the acquisition of goods for commercial purposes is normally paid for in that way, the same is not true for tourist expenses, which are almost always paid in cash.

The removal of all or most foreign exchange restrictions by Member States in view of the Capital Movements Directive has frequently left intact or been accompanied by the introduction of measures which either require residents wishing to transfer capital abroad to do so via a local bank and/or to inform the national tax authorities of any such transfer.[11]

It is submitted that such monitoring procedures are compatible with Community law so long as they do not make transfers subject to authorisation and so long as they apply only to transfers over a significant level.[12]

3. SAFEGUARD PROVISIONS APPLICABLE TO CAPITAL MOVEMENTS BETWEEN MEMBER STATES

22.3 Where movements of capital lead to disturbances in the functioning of the capital market in any Member State, the State in question may be authorised by the Commission on a temporary basis to take protective measures on terms laid down by the Commission.[13] Any authorisation granted by the Commission is subject to review by the Council, which has the power to revoke or amend the authorisation. In practice, these provisions have been invoked only once.[14] this is because the Treaty contains alternative safeguard provisions in regard to balance of payments difficulties[15] which give the Member States wider room for manoeuvre.[16]

11. See, eg, the statement made by M. Marc-Antoine Autheman, Senior Administrator of the French Treasury, while speaking at a seminar organised by the French Banking Federation on 16 March 1988 on the subject "1992: Quel Droit Bancaire?" *Revue Banque* (France), 16 March 1988, 183: "We desire to be able to continue to insist that in certain circumstances, if not indeed, across the board, transfers destined for abroad must be effected through a financial intermediary [established in France]."

12. See the answer given by Sir Leon Brittan on behalf of the Commission to Written Question 1319/91 by MEP Karel Pinxten, OJ C162/7 of 29 June 1992, concerning the compatibility of a special annual levy imposed by a number of Dutch banks on accounts of non-residents employed in the Netherlands with, *inter alia*, the principle of freedom of capital movements and justified on the basis of a requirement imposed by the Dutch Central Bank that all transactions affecting a non-resident account had to be reported to it: "The main reason for the distinction between resident and non-resident accounts seems to be the notification requirements imposed for non-resident accounts. These notifications do not seem to conflict with Community law, given the provisions in Art. 4 of [the Capital Movements Directive]. However, the Commission is presently studying whether notification procedures can be adapted in such a way as not to hamper cross-border payments." The position is more uncertain with regard to Danish legislation which, it is understood, requires Danish residents wishing to open a personal account abroad to provide details of the account to the Danish tax authorities and to request the foreign bank to provide those authorities upon request with information about foreign assets held by him: see the Commentaire Megret "Le Droit de la CEE", *Editions de l'Université de Bruxelles*, Volume 3, 2nd ed., para. 32, p. 189.

13. Art. 73(1) of the Treaty.

14. By Denmark in 1979 for the sale of certain government bonds to non-residents, see Peter Oliver and Jean-Paul Bache, "Free Movement of Capital between the Member States: Recent Developments" (1989) 26 CMLRev. 61, 71.

15. Arts. 108 and 109.

16. The procedures provided for in art. 73 do not apply to decisions and measures taken pursuant to arts. 107(2), 108 and 109: case 157/85 *Brugnoni and Ruffinengo* v. *Cassa di Risparmio di Genova e Imperia* [1986] ECR 2013, 2031–2032, at points 26 to 28. The case was concerned with art. 108 but the reasoning applies equally to the other safeguard provisions. See the discussion of the case by Peter Oliver and Jean-Paul Bache, fn. 14, above. Note that use has not, in fact, ever been made of art. 107(2).

Member States are also able, on grounds of secrecy or urgency, to take protective measures in the field of capital movements on their own initiative where this proves necessary. In such circumstances, the Member State in question must inform the Commission and the other Member States of such measures no later than the date of their entry into force and must amend or abolish the measures at the Commission's request.[17]

The provisions of article 73 of the Treaty are to some extent reflected in the Capital Movements Directive. Article 3 thereof provides that:

1. Where short-term capital movements of exceptional magnitude impose severe strains on foreign-exchange markets and lead to serious disturbances in the conduct of a Member State's monetary and exchange rate policies, being reflected in particular in substantial variations in domestic liquidity, the Commission may, after consulting the Monetary Committee and the Committee of Governors of the Central Banks, authorise that Member State to take, in respect of the capital movements listed in Annex II, protective measures the conditions and details of which the Commission shall determine.

2. The Member State concerned may itself take the protective measures referred to above, on grounds of urgency, should these measures be necessary. The Commission and the other Member States shall be informed of such measures by the date of their entry into force at the latest. The Commission after consulting the Monetary Committee and the Committee of Governors of the Central Banks, shall decide whether the Member State concerned may continue to apply these measures or whether it should amend or abolish them.

3. The decisions taken by the Commission under paragraphs 1 and 2 may be revoked or amended by the Council acting by a qualified majority.

4. The period of application of protective measures taken pursuant to this Article shall not exceed six months.

5. Before 31 December 1992, the Council shall examine, on the basis of a report from the Commission, after delivery of an opinion by the Monetary Committee and the Committee of Governors of the Central Banks, whether the provisions of this Article remain appropriate, as regards their principle and details, to the requirements which they were intended to satisfy.

However, there are also marked differences between the provisions of article 73 of the Treaty and article 3 of the Directive. In particular:

— Under the Directive, protective measures may only be taken where short-term capital movements of exceptional magnitude occur which impose severe strains on foreign exchange markets and lead to serious disturbances in the conduct of a Member State's monetary and exchange rate policies. Under the Treaty, protective measures can be authorised where a capital movement, whatever its magnitude, leads to disturbances of any nature in the functioning of the capital market in any Member State.

Under the Directive, the Commission, after consulting the Monetary Committee and the Committee of Governors of the Central Banks, has a discretion whether or not to authorise protective measures. Article 3(1) uses the word "may" whereas article 73(1) of the Treaty provides that the Commission "shall" authorise such measures.

— Under the Directive, a Member State is no longer justified in acting on its own initiative without prior reference to the Commission on the ground of secrecy.

— Under the Directive, protective measures may not be applied for longer than a six month period.

— Under the Directive, the only capital movements in respect of which Member

17. Art. 73(2) of the Treaty.

States may be authorised to take protective measures are those listed in Annex II thereto, being operations in securities and other instruments normally dealt in on the money market; operations in current and deposit accounts with financial institutions; certain operations in units of collective investment undertakings; short-term financial loans and credits; personal loans; the physical import and export of securities normally dealt in on the money market and of means of payment; and other short-term operations similar to those just listed. The restrictions which a Member State may apply to these capital movements must be defined and applied in such a way as to cause the least possible hindrance to the free movement of persons, goods and services.

The rationale for the protective measures envisaged by article 3 of the Directive is that disturbances of the kind envisaged might seriously disrupt the conduct of the monetary and exchange-rate policies of the Member States, even in the absence of any appreciable divergence in economic fundamentals.[18]

The safeguard provisions in the Directive do not preclude reliance, in an appropriate case, upon those in article 73 or indeed articles 108 or 109 of the Treaty. It is clear from the different wording of those provisions that they are aimed at different situations.[19]

4. SAFEGUARD PROVISIONS APPLICABLE TO CAPITAL MOVEMENTS BETWEEN THE EC AND THIRD COUNTRIES

22.4 In relation to capital movements between the Community and third countries, the Treaty contains safeguard provisions to cover the situation where continuing differences between the exchange rules of Member States could lead persons resident in one Member State to use the freer transfer facilities within the Community provided for in article 67 to evade the rules of another Member State concerning the movement of capital to or from third countries.[20] In such a situation, the Member State in question may, after consulting the other Member States and the Commission, take appropriate measures to overcome its difficulties.

The Capital Movements Directive authorises limited protective measures. Article 7(2) provides:

Where large-scale short-term capital movements to or from third countries seriously disturb the domestic or external monetary financial situation of the Member States, or of a number of them, or cause serious strains in exchange relations within the Community or between the Community and third countries, Member States shall consult with one another on any measure to be taken to counteract such difficulties. This consultation shall take place within the Committee of Governors of the Central Banks and the Monetary Committee on the initiative of the Commission or of any Member State.

These provisions refer to "large scale" short-term capital movements whereas the provisions of article 3(1) refer to short-term capital movements of exceptional magnitude. They also refer to serious disturbances of the "financial situation" of the Member States whereas in article 3(1) the serious disturbances must be to the conduct of a Member State's monetary and exchange rate policies. However, it is doubtful

---

18. Preamble, 3rd recital.

19. See Phillippe Vigneron, "La nouvelle directive communautaire relative à la libération des mouvements de capitaux", *Revue de la Banque* (Belgium) 9/1988, p. 7 at p. 14.

20. Art. 70(2).

whether these differences in language are intended to reflect any difference in substance in the application of these provisions. The protective measures envisaged by article 7(2) are intended to facilitate the cohesion of the European Monetary System, the smooth operation of the internal market and the progressive achievement of economic and monetary union.[21]

These safeguard provisions in the Directive do not preclude reliance, in an appropriate case, upon those in article 70(2). It is clear from the different wording of those provisions that they are aimed at different situations.

---

21. Preamble, 10th recital.

PART FIVE

THE EUROPEAN COMMUNITY RULES ON COMPETITION AND THEIR IMPACT ON BANKING OPERATIONS

CHAPTER 23

GENERAL PRINCIPLES

1. INTRODUCTION

23.1 The EC rules on competition are contained in articles 85 to 94 of the Treaty which together comprise chapter 1 of Title 1 of Part Three of the Treaty. Part Three deals with the policy of the EC and it is no coincidence that the rules on competition are to be found there, for they are one of the instruments at the disposal of the Commission in its task of bringing about the economic and political objectives of the EC. The Commission's policy towards restrictive practices on the part of undertakings pursues two complementary objectives. First, it enables competition to perform its traditional role in helping improve the allocation of resources, to increase businessmen's capacities for adjustments and to satisfy better the requirements of consumers. Second, it reinforces the unity of the Common Market by eliminating obstacles to trade between Member States.

In examining these practices, the Commission takes account of the intensity of international competition in the Common Market or in a substantial part of it. Accordingly, the objectives of its competition policy beyond those of the domestic policies of Member States which have been developed in the same field and, at the same time, tie in with other Community policies aimed at the attainment of a single market.[1]

Articles 85 and 86 contain the substantive provisions of competition law applicable to both private and public undertakings. Article 90 contains special provisions which affect public undertakings and undertakings to which Member States grant special or exclusive rights. Article 89 imposes on the Commission the duty to ensure the application of the principles laid down in articles 85 and 86 by investigating cases of suspected infringement and by proposing appropriate measures to bring any infringement to an end. In order to give effect to these principles, in 1962 the Council enacted Regulation 17.[2] The Regulation grants the Commission powers not only to ensure the application of the rules on competition but also additional powers not referred to in the Treaty itself.

Under article 87(2)(c) of the Treaty, the Council is empowered to adopt appropriate regulations or directives to define, if need be, in various branches of the economy, the scope of the provisions of articles 85 and 86. The Council can only act upon a proposal by the Commission in this regard. As will be seen, the Commission was at one time considering the use of article 87(2)(c) to delimit the scope of articles 85 and 86 in the banking sector.

---

1. See generally the Reports of the Commission on Competition Policy published annually, also the Bulletin of the European Communities.
2. [1952–1964] OJ Spec. Ed. 87.

Articles 85 and 86 are addressed to undertakings and, unlike other provisions of the Treaty, not to the Member States, and therefore a restriction on competition imposed by a Member State is not capable of falling within the scope of those provisions, at least in the exercise its sovereign functions. However, the Member State cannot, by national provisions, allow undertakings to escape from the requirements of the rules on competition. As early as 1977 the Court of Justice confirmed this approach in *INNO* v. *ATAB*.[3] This case-law was refined in the later *Cognac* cases,[4] *Van Eycke* v. *Aspa*[5] and the *Port of Genoa*[6] case. Here, in the context of article 85, the Court stated that the fact

3. Case 13/77 [1977] ECR 2115. The case concerned the compatibility with Community law of a national measure which enabled private undertakings to escape from the prohibition contained in art. 86 of the Treaty. The principles laid down in that case are just as applicable to a national measure which enables private undertakings to avoid the prohibition contained in art. 85: see at pp. 2144–2145, at points 28–33.

4. Case 123/83, *BNIC* v. *Clair* [1985] ECR 391; case 136/86 *BNIC* v. *Aubert* [1987] ECR 4789. These cases were concerned with agreements restricting competition which were reached between cognac producers and distributors under the auspices and the rules of a semi-state organisation, the Bureau National Interprofessionnel du Cognac. Pursuant to French law, the agreements arrived at within BNIC were subsequently made generally binding by means of ministerial orders. In line with the principles laid down in *INNO* v. *ATAB*, the Court further stated that the fact that the members who attended the BNIC's general meeting, and who negotiated and concluded the agreement, were all appointed by the Minister of Agriculture was not of any consequence. Since the Minister had appointed them on a proposal from the trade organisations directly concerned, they must be regarded as representing those organisations. Also, the fact that the measures decided with the BNIC were intended to prevent the economic collapse of a region dependent on wine production did not mean that they were compatible with art. 85(1). Such considerations might have justified the grant of an exemption under art. 85(3) by the Commission but BNIC had not applied to the Commission for an exemption.

5. Case 267/86 [1988] ECR 4769. The case concerned a Royal Decree in Belgium under which the tax free status (at the hands of the account holder) provided for by the law was restricted to savings account interest earned exclusively on deposits where the rate of interest paid was below certain maxima fixed by the Decree. ASPA, a financial institution, had initially advertised a rate of interest which was in excess of the maximum rate specified in the Decree for the grant of tax free status. Subsequently, the company refused to open a savings account in Mr Van Eycke's name carrying the rate of interest which it had previously advertised. Mr Van Eycke thereupon brought an action against the company in the Belgian courts in which he alleged that the Royal Decree, upon which the company relied to justify its refusal to pay the advertised rate of interest, was contrary to the Community rules on competition in that it was no more than a confirmation of a prior agreement between the banks in Belgium which had the effect of limiting the interest payable on savings accounts. The first question on which the Belgian court requested a ruling from the Court of Justice was intended to determine whether the Royal Decree in issue could be considered as tending to reinforce the effects of a restrictive practice or agreement between the banks on the maximum rates of interest payable on savings accounts. The Court of Justice, in accordance with its previous case-law, held that this would be the case where the national regime limited itself to repeating in whole or in part the provisions of such an agreement in order to make them compulsory or to encourage their application by a system of sanctions. According to the Court of Justice, that was a question to be decided by the national court. The second question for the Court of Justice was whether the Belgian government had not, in the instant case, abolished the sovereign character of its own legislation by transferring to individual persons, namely the representatives of the credit institutions, the responsibility for its interventions in economic life. As was rightly pointed out by the Commission in its *Eighteenth Report on Competition Policy* (point 98), the Court's judgment is indicative on this point of a new development insofar as, in contrast with previous decisions, it extends the category of actions of the Member States which infringe the Treaty. In the Court's view, the purpose of the rules on competition applicable to undertakings is not only restricted where a Member State imposes or encourages restrictive practices which infringe art. 85, or reinforces the effects of such practices but also where the Member State abolishes the sovereign nature of its own legislation by transferring to individuals the responsibility for interventions in economic life. In the judgment in question, the Court held that such was not the case, however. It considered that it resulted from the circumstances of the case indicated in the Royal Decree that the Belgian national authorities had meant to decide themselves the maximum rates of interest payable on the deposit accounts which benefited from tax relief and had not transferred this task to the private sector. According to the Court, the fact that the Royal Decree had been adopted after the taking of concerted action by the competent Belgian authorities and the representatives of the financial institutions concerned was not in itself sufficient to establish that the authorities had abdicated their regulatory task in favour of the institutions concerned.

6. Case C/179/90, judgment of 10 December 1991, not yet published in ECR.

that the relevant agreement had been reached within the framework of, and in accordance with the procedures of, a public body did not make the agreement into a State measure and consequently did not save it from the cartel ban imposed by article 85(1); also, a subsequent act of the authorities could not remove the agreement from the scope of article 85(1). In giving an agreement the force of law, a Member State was enacting a measure likely to deprive the competition rules applicable to business of their practical effectiveness and was thereby breaching its obligations under articles 85, 3(f), and 5 of the EC Treaty.[7]

1. Influence on trade between Member States

23.2 Articles 85 and 86 only apply where the agreement or abuse of the dominant position falling within their respective provisions "may affect trade between Member States". The purpose of this requirement is to draw a boundary between the sphere of the application of the domestic law of the Member States and that of Community law. This particularly critical question of the delineation of the sphere of application of Community law and that of national law was emphasised by the Court of Justice in *Hugin* v. *Commission*.[8] There, the Court of Justice, in annulling the Commission's decision fining Hugin for an infringement of article 86, held that[9]:

The interpretation and application of the condition relating to effects on trade between Member States contained in articles 85 and 86 of the Treaty must be based on the purpose of that condition which is to define, in the context of the law governing competition, the boundary between the areas respectively covered by Community law and the law of the Member States. Thus Community law covers any agreement or any practice which is capable of constituting a threat to the freedom of trade between Member States in a manner which might harm the attainment of the objectives of a single market between the Member States, in particular by partitioning the national markets or affecting the structure of competition within the common market. On the other hand, conduct the effects of which are confined to the territory of a single Member State is governed by the national legal order.

In practice, however, in conducting an investigation under article 85 or 86, the Commission's approach has been first to consider whether competition within the EC has been affected and only then to see whether trade between Member States may be affected. In this way, the requirement has taken on a substantive character which the framers of the Treaty probably never intended it to have.

For the purpose of the rules on competition, the Commission has stated on several occasions that trade is only affected where, as a result of the restriction of competition, it develops in a way which it would not otherwise have done.[10] Trade between Member States will certainly be affected where an agreement or abuse of a dominant position relates to the sale or supply of goods in more than one Member State. But it may also be affected where the agreement or abuse of a dominant position relates solely to one

---

7. Art. 3(f) provides that the activities of the Community are to include the institution of a system ensuring that competition in the common market is not distorted. Art. 5 requires Member States to take all appropriate measures, whether general or particular, to ensure fulfilment of the obligations arising out of the Treaty or resulting from action taken by institutions of the Community; to facilitate the achievement of the Community's tasks; and to abstain from any measure which could jeopardise the attainment of the Treaty's objectives.

8. Case 22/78 [1979] ECR 1869.

9. *Ibid.*, at p. 1899.

10. *Grundig-Consten*, JO 161 of 20 October 1964; case 27/87, *Erauw-Jacquéry* [1988] ECR 1919. The cases cited here and in subsequent fns. are only illustrative of the principles stated in the text of which many examples may be found in the authorities.

Member State.[11] For example, a chain of exclusive dealing contracts in a single Member State may effectively exclude exports from other Member States to the domestic market of the first Member State and so affect trade between Member States.[12] Also, it is not necessary for trade actually to be affected; it is sufficient that trade may be affected in the future.

As the Court of Justice stated in *Van Landewyck* v. *Commission*[13]:

In order that an agreement, decision or concerted practice may effect trade between Member States it must be possible to foresee with a sufficient degree of probability on the basis of a set of objective factors of law or fact that the agreement, decision or concerted practice may have an influence, direct or indirect, actual or potential, on the pattern of trade between Member States. The influence thus foreseeable must give rise to a fear that the realisation of a single market between Member States might be impeded.[14]

2. Services

23.3 At one time, it was considered that the term "trade" in articles 85 and 86 comprised only the movement of goods between Member States.[15] According to one commentator,[16] there was a clear link between the concept of trade between Member States, on the one hand, and the free movement of goods on the other. Trade between Member States, it was said, was one way of bringing about the free movement of goods.

At first, the Commission itself had only applied the rules on competition to undertakings concerned with the supply or processing of goods. However, as Community law has developed, it has become clear that the term "trade" should not be given such a restrictive meaning.[17]

Both the Commission and the Court of Justice have considered the provision of various services in the context of the rules on competition. For example, in the *Gema* case[18] and *BRT* v. *SABAM*[19] the services in issue were those performed by societies for the protection of authors' rights. In *RAI/Unitel*[20] the artistic services of four of La Scala's leading singers were in issue. In the *British Telecommunications* case,[21] the Commission considered the services of message-forwarding agencies. The conditions imposed on exhibitors by the organisers of trade fairs have also attracted the attention

---

11. Case 47/76, *De Norre* v. *NV Brouwerij Concordia* [1977] ECR 65; case 43/69, *Bilger* v. *Jehle* [1970] ECR 127; case 23/67, *Brasserie de Haecht* v. *Wilkin (No. 1)* [1967] ECR 407.

12. Case 47/76, *De Norre* v. *NV Brouwerij Concordia* [1977] ECR 65; case 43/69, *Bilger* v. *Jehle* [1970] ECR 127; case 23/67, *Brasserie de Haecht* v. *Wilkin (No. 1)* [1967] ECR 407.

13. Joined cases 209–215 and 218/78 [1980] ECR 3125, at p. 3274. See also case 99/79, *Lancôme* v. *Etos* [1980] ECR 2511 and case 126/80, *Salonia* v. *Poidomani and Giglio* [1981] ECR 1563.

14. See also case 42/84 *Remia* v. *Commission* [1985] ECR 2545, at p. 2572 at point 22; *Re Roofing Felt Cartel: The Community* v. *Société Coopérative des Asphalteurs Belges (Belasco) and Others*, Commission Decision [1991] 4 CMLR 130; case T–7/89 *Hercules NV* v. *Commission* [1992] 4 CMLR 84.

15. See, eg, the Opinion of A.G. Lagrange in the German language version (the language of the case) of case 13/61, *De Geus* v. *Bosch* [1962] ECR 45.

16. N. Catalano, [1963] *Revue Internationale de Droit Comparé* 269, at pp. 273–274.

17. As a matter of principle, competition and restraints upon competition can exist as much in relation to services as in relation to goods. Art. 90(2) of the Treaty contains special provisions for "undertakings entrusted with the operation of services of general economic interest" and thereby implicitly recognises that services are included within the term "trade". This has also been the view of many commentators, for example, E. Wohlfarth, U. Everling, H.J. Glaesner, R. Sprung, *Die Europäische Wirtschaftsgemeinschaft, Kommentar zum Vertrag*, art. 85, note 4; Gleiss/Hirsch, *Kommentar zum EWG-Kartellrecht* (3rd ed., 1978); Heidelberg; Verlagsgesellschaft Recht und Wirtschaft mbH, p. 82.

18. Case 45/71 [1971] ECR 791.

19. Case 127/73 [1974] ECR 313.

20. OJ L157/39 of 15 June 1978.

21. OJ L360/36 of 21 December 1982.

of both the Commission and Court of Justice.[22] In *Saachi*,[23] the Court of Justice had to consider the services provided by RAI, the Italian state broadcasting corporation, and held that these were within the scope of the rules of the Treaty.

In *Greenwich Film Production* v. *SACEM*[24] the Court of Justice was again concerned with the services performed by a society which managed copyrights. The Court said[25]:

The Court of Justice, in deciding whether trade between Member States may be affected by the abuse of a dominant position in the market in question, has taken the view that it must take into consideration the consequences for the effective competitive structure in the Common Market, adding that there is no reason to distinguish between production intended for sale within the Common Market and that intended for export ... There is no reason to restrict that interpretation to trade in goods and not to apply it to the provision of services such as the management of copyrights.[26]

In the banking context, the Court of Justice accepted, in the important decision in *Züchner* v. *Bayerische Vereinsbank*,[27] that the practice of levying a charge on the transfer of customers' funds from one Member State to another was[28]:

capable, precisely because of the fact that it covers international transactions, of affecting trade between Member States within the meaning of [Article 85], the concept of trade used in that article having a wide scope which includes monetary transactions.

It is now beyond question, therefore, that services in general and banking services in particular are within the scope of the rules on competition.

2. AGREEMENTS BETWEEN UNDERTAKINGS—ARTICLE 85

23.4 Article 85 of the Treaty says that:

(1) The following shall be prohibited as incompatible with the common market: all agreements between undertakings, decisions by associations of undertakings and concerted practices which may affect trade between Member States and which have as their object or effect the prevention, restriction or distortion of competition within the common market, and in particular those which:
  (a) directly or indirectly fix purchase or selling prices or any other trading conditions;
  (b) limit or control production, markets, technical development, or investment;
  (c) share markets or sources of supply;
  (d) apply dissimilar conditions to equivalent transactions with other trading parties, thereby placing them at a competitive disadvantage;
  (e) make the conclusion of contracts subject to acceptance by the other parties of supplementary obligations which, by their nature or according to commercial usage, have no connection with the subject of such contracts.
(2) Any agreements or decisions prohibited pursuant to this Article shall be automatically void.
(3) The provisions of paragraph 1 may, however be declared inapplicable in the case of:
  — any agreement or category of agreements between undertakings;
  — any decision or category of decisions by associations of undertakings;
  — any concerted practice or category of concerted practices;
which contributes to improving the production or distribution of goods or to promoting technical

---

22. *British Telecommunications*, cited in fn. 21 above; *European Machine Tool Exhibitions*, OJ L11/16 of 17 January 1979; *BPICA*, OJ L299/14 of 29 August 1975; *Re Cematex*, OJ L227/26 of 8 October 1971.
23. Case 155/73 [1974] ECR 409.
24. Case 22/79 [1979] ECR 3275.
25. *Ibid.*, p. 3288.
26. See also joined cases 395/87, *Ministère Public* v. *Tournier* and 110/88 & 241–242/88, *Lucazeau* v. *SACEM* [1991] 4 CMLR 248.
27. Case 172/80 [1981] ECR 2021.
28. *Ibid.*, p. 2032.

or economic progress, while allowing consumers a fair share of the resulting benefit, and which does not:

    (a) impose on the undertakings concerned restrictions which are not indispensable to the attainment of these objectives;

    (b) afford such undertakings the possibility of eliminating competition in respect of a substantial part of the products in question.

1. "Undertakings"

23.5 As has been clear from all the Court of Justice's cases on competition since *De Geus* v. *Bosch*,[29] the provisions of article 85 can be directly invoked before national courts by one undertaking against another. The term "undertaking" has been interpreted in the widest possible manner so as to embrace individuals[30] and non-profit making organisations[31] as well as commercial enterprises such as financial institutions.[32] The Commission has stated that the "functional concept of undertaking in article 85(1) covers any activity directed at trade in goods or services irrespective of the legal form of the undertaking and regardless of whether or not it is intended to earn profits".[33] For this purpose it matters not whether the undertakings concerned are situated within or outside the Community.

2. "Agreements . . . decisions . . . and concerted practices"

23.6 Article 85 is only concerned with "agreements between undertakings, decisions by associations of undertakings and concerted practices". Nowhere in the Treaty are the terms "agreements", "decisions", and "concerted practices" defined. Community law has approached the definition of these terms broadly without regard to the position under the laws of the Member States. Hence the fact that the agreement which two or more parties have entered into is no more than a "gentlemen's agreement" will not take it outside the scope of the prohibition contained in article 85(1).[34] Similarly, there is no requirement that a decision made by an association of undertakings should be binding upon the parties to it in order to bring it within article 85(1).[35] Thus a recommendation made by such an association and constituting a faithful expression of the members' intentions to conduct themselves compulsorily on the particular market in conformity with the terms of the recommendation fulfils the necessary conditions for the application of article 85(1).[36]

The term "concerted practice" is intended to cover the situation where an agreement

---

29. Case 13/61 [1962] ECR 45. The judgment was given on the effects of arts. 85 and 86 before the entry into force of Reg. 17. See generally, Jean-Victor Louis, *The Community Legal Order* (Office for Official Publications of the European Communities 1980), point 100. The work is a translation of the original French text, published as *L'Ordre Juridique Communautaire*.

30. Eg, *RAI/Unitel*, cited in fn. 20, above; *Breeders' Rights—maize seed*, OJ L286/23 of 12 October 1978, not challenged on this point on appeal *sub nom.* case 258/78, *Nungesser* v. *Commission* [1982] ECR 2015; case 42/84 *Remia* v. *Commission* [1985] ECR 2545.

31. Joined cases 209–215 and 218/78, *Van Landewyck* v. *Commission* [1980] ECR 3125.

32. See *Züchner* v. *Bayerische Vereinsbank*, cited in fn. 27, above.

33. *Film purchases by Geman television stations* [1989] OJ L284/36, at p. 41.

34. Case 41/69, *ACF Chemiefarma* v. *Commission* [1970] ECR 661; *National Panasonic* [1982] OJ L354/28, at p. 32, [1983] 1 CMLR 497—where the terms of dealer agreements were understood and accepted by the parties although the agreement was not in writing.

35. *German Ceramic Tiles*, JO L10/13 of 13 January 1971; *VVVF*, JO L168/22 of 10 July 1969.

36. *Van Landewyck* v. *Commission*, cited in fn. 31, above; *Re Welded Steel Mesh Cartel: The Community* v. *Trefilunion SA and Others* [1991] 4 CMLR 13.

or decision may be either non-existent or, perhaps, equally important in practice, impossible to prove.[37] For example, factors such as the application of identical prices by undertakings when it is unlikely to occur in the normal conditions of the market and the regular exchange of detailed information on sales may all point towards the existence of a concerted practice where an agreement or decision could not be proved.[38] The notion of a concerted practice is founded upon the concept of informal but conscious co-operation between undertakings operating in a given market. Thus in *Züchner*, the Court of Justice reiterated what it had stated in previous judgments, in particular in *ICI* v. *Commission*,[39] namely that[40]:

a concerted practice within the meaning of Article 85(1) of the Treaty is a form of co-ordination between undertakings which, without having reached the stage where an agreement properly so called has been concluded, knowingly substitutes practical co-operation between them for the risks of competition . . . The criteria of co-ordination and co-operation necessary for the existence of a concerted practice in no way require the working out of an actual plan but must be understood in the light of the concept inherent in the provisions of the Treaty relating to competition, according to which each trader must determine independently the policy which he intends to adopt on the common market and the conditions which he intends to offer to his customers. Although it is correct to say that this requirement of independence does not deprive traders of the right to adapt themselves intellectually to the existing or anticipated conduct of their competitors, it does however strictly preclude any direct or indirect contact between such traders, the object or effect of which is to create conditions of competition which do not correspond to the normal conditions of the market in question, regard being had to the nature of the products or services offered, the size and number of undertakings and the volume of the said market.[41]

3. "Object or effect" of agreement, decision or concerted practice to restrict competition

23.7 An agreement, decision or concerted practice will only be prohibited by article 85(1) if it has as its object or effect the prevention, restriction or distortion of competition.

In conducting an investigation under article 85, the Commission looks first to see whether the object or one of the objects of the agreement is to restrict competition. Only if no such object is revealed will it then be obliged to consider the effect of the agreement.[42] If there is no object to restrict competition then the effects on competition must be shown to be appreciable.[43] There may also be cases where, taken in isolation, an agreement has neither the object nor the effect of restricting competition. Nevertheless that agreement may be one of several agreements which together have the effect of restricting competition.

As the Court of Justice succinctly put it in *Lancôme* v. *Etos*[44]:

. . . in order to decide whether an agreement is to be considered as prohibited by reason of the distortion of competition which is its object or effect, it is necessary to examine the competition

---

37. Case 100/80, etc. *Musique Diffusion Française* [1983] ECR 1825.
38. Eg *BP Kemi-DDSF*, OJ L286/32 of 14 November 1979.
39. Case 48/69 [1972] ECR 619.
40. [1981] ECR 2021, at p. 2031.
41. See also *Hasselblad*, OJ L161/18, at p. 82; [1982] 2 CMLR 233, at p. 249 "for a concerted practice to exist it is sufficient for an independent undertaking knowingly and of its own accord to adjust its behaviour in line with the wishes of another undertaking"; and case T–7/89 *Hercules NV* v. *Commission* [1992] 4 CMLR 84.
42. Cases 56 and 58/64, *Consten and Grundig* v. *Commission* [1966] ECR 299.
43. Case 56/65, *Technique Minière* v. *Maschinenbau Ulm* [1966] ECR 235; case 5/69, *Völk* v. *Vervaecke* [1969] ECR 295.
44. Case 99/79 [1980] ECR 2511, at pp. 2536–2537.

within the actual context in which it would occur in the absence of the agreement in dispute. To that end, it is appropriate to take into account in particular the nature and quantity, limited or otherwise of the products covered by the agreement, the position and importance of the parties on the market for the products concerned and the isolated nature of the disputed agreement or, alternatively, its position in a series of agreements. In that regard, the Court stated in its judgment of 12 December 1967 in Case 23/67 *Brasserie de Haecht I* [1967] ECR 407 that, although not necessarily decisive, the existence of similar contracts is a circumstance which, together with others, is capable of being a factor in the economic and legal context within which the contract must be judged.[45]

Furthermore, the Court appears willing to use the concept of the "rule of reason" in its approach to article 85, that is, certain restrictions on competition do not fall within the prohibition of they are objectively justified by reason of being necessary to market the products or goods in question within the economic structure of the relevant market sectors, or if the overall effect of the restrictions is to promote improved competition.[46]

4. Restriction of competition must occur "within the common market"

23.8 The restrictions of competition which the rules on competition aim to prevent are those which occur "within the common market". This requirement defines the limits of the application of Community law in relation to the law of third countries. Article 85(1) will certainly apply where the object of an agreement is to restrict competition within the Common Market but it also applies where the anti-competitive effect of the agreement is felt within the Common Market. As the Court confirmed in *Ahlström* v. *Commission (Wood Pulp)*[47]:

If the applicability of prohibitions laid down under competition law were made to depend on the place where the agreement, decision or concerted practice was formed, the result would obviously be to give undertakings an easy means of avoiding these provisions. The decisive factor is therefore the place where it is implemented. The producers in this case implemented their pricing agreement within the Common Market. It is immaterial in that respect whether or not they had recourse to subsidiaries, agents, sub-agents or branches within the Community. Accordingly the Community's jurisdiction to apply its competition rules to such conduct is covered by the territorial principle as universally recognised in public international law.

Therefore, an agreement which only restricts competition outside the common market will not be prohibited even if concluded between undertakings situated within it.[48]

Also, an agreement restricting competition which necessitates or results in some positive act of implementation within the Common Market will fall within the prohibition in article 85(1) even if the undertakings which are parties to it are situated in one or more third countries.[49]

45. See also case 234/89, *Stergios Delimitis* v. *Henniger Bräu AG* [1991] ECR I–935.
46. See, eg, case 26/76 *Metro* v. *Commission (No. 1)* [1977] ECR 1875; case 75/84 *Metro* v. *Commission (No. 2)* [1986] ECR 3021 and case 161/84 *Pronuptia de Paris* v. *Schillgalis* [1985] ECR 3933.
47. Case 89/85 [1988] ECR 5193.
48. Eg, *DECA*, JO 173 of 31 October 1964; *Grosfillex-Fillistorf*, JO 58 of 9 April 1964.
49. Eg, *Beecham/Parke, Davis*, OJ L70/11 of 21 March 1979; *Re the French and Taiwanese Mushroom Packers*, OJ L29/36 of 3 February 1975; *Re the Franco-Japanese Ballbearings Agreement*, OJ L343/19 of 21 December 1974; case 22/71, *Béguelin* v. *SAGL* [1971] ECR 949; cases 48 and 49 and 51 to 57/69 [1972] ECR 619 *et seq.*

5. Nullity of agreements and decisions—article 85(2)

23.9 Under article 85(2) it is provided that any agreement or decision prohibited pursuant to article 85(2) shall be "automatically void". In fact, it is not the whole agreement or decision which is thereby made void but only the parts which infringe article 85(1), unless those parts are incapable of being separated from the agreement or decision as a whole.[50] The Court has stated that the question whether the prohibited elements can be separated from the agreement so as to leave the remainder in force is a matter for national law.[51]

Article 85(2) is silent on the position with regard to concerted practices because, by definition, a concerted practice is not capable of being made void. It is simply prohibited under article 85(1).

National courts have no power to apply articles 85(1) and (2) in the absence of a decision by the national authorities under article 88 of the Treaty or the Commission under article 89.[52] However, the national court may rule on the agreement in issue where the conditions for the application of article 85(1) are clearly satisfied and there is scarcely any risk of the Commission taking a different decision, or that the agreement would be the subject of an exemption under article 85(3).[53]

6. Exemption under article 85(3)

23.10 Article 9(1) of Regulation 17 confers exclusively on the Commission the power to declare article 85(1) inapplicable on the basis of article 85(3). Article 85(3) states that article 85(1) may be declared inapplicable by the Commission. Despite the apparent discretion thereby given to the Commission, if the conditions laid down in article 85(3) are satisfied it must grant an exemption.[54] However, the power to determine whether or not those conditions are satisfied rests with the Commission itself.

It will be recalled that one of the conditions for an exemption is that the agreement, decision or concerted practice must contribute to improving the production or distribution of goods.[55] This requirement at first sight appears to narrow the scope for an exemption where the agreement, decision or concerted practice in question relates not to the goods but to services. This apparent discrimination against service industries does not in practice present a problem because of the width of the alternative condition for an exemption, namely that the agreement, decision or concerted practice must contribute to promoting technical or economic progress: that condition is sufficiently wide to include anything which might improve the production or distribution of services.

Exemption under article 85(3) may be granted by the Commission either to individual agreements, decisions and concerted practices notified to it or else on a group basis. In the latter case, exemption does not require the prior notification of the agreement, decision or concerted practice but is automatic, provided that the category

50. Joined cases 56 and 58/64, *Consten and Grundig* v. *Commission* [1966] ECR 299; case 56/65, *LTM* v. *Maschinenbau Ulm* [1966] ECR 235.
51. Case 319/82, *Soc. de Vente de Ciments et Bétons* v. *Kerpen & Kerpen* [1983] ECR 4173.
52. Cases 209/84, etc., *Ministère Public* v. *Asjes (Nouvelles Frontières)* [1986] ECR 1425.
53. Case 234/89 *Delimitis* v. *Henniger Braü AG* [1991] ECR I–935.
54. *Consten and Grundig* v. *Commission*, cited in fn. 42 above.
55. In *Plessey Company plc* v. *General Electric Company plc and Siemens AG* [1992] 4 CMLR 471, the Commission held that an agreement might be exempted under art. 85(3) despite having long-term or permanent effects, not all of which enhance competition, and which outlast the agreement itself.

of agreement, decision or concerted practice into which it falls has been the subject of a Commission regulation granting it exemption.[56] Also, agreements falling within article 4(2) of Regulation 17 are not required to be notified. Broadly speaking, such agreements are of a kind which do not effect exports or imports between Member States and which deal with research and/or development; there may only be two parties to the agreement and both must be from the same Member State.

Under article 15(2) the Commission can only impose a fine where an infringement is committed intentionally or recklessly. The Commission is prepared to impute knowledge of its decisions and those of the Court to the offending party, although the extent of the imputation may depend on the size of the undertaking.[57] Fines may be reduced because of the presence of such factors as the parties' undertaking to promote conditions of competition in the future, because of the brief duration of the infringement and prompt and effective action designed to remedy the infringement.[58]

3. ABUSE OF A DOMINANT POSITION—ARTICLE 86

23.11 Article 86 of the Treaty says that:

Any abuse by one or more undertakings of a dominant position within the common market or in a substantial part of it shall be prohibited as incompatible with the common market in so far as it may affect trade between Member States.

Such abuse may, in particular, consist in:
  (a) directly or indirectly imposing unfair purchase or selling prices or other unfair trading conditions;
  (b) limiting production, markets or technical development to the prejudice of consumers;
  (c) applying dissimilar conditions to equivalent transactions with other trading parties, thereby placing them at a competitive disadvantage;
  (d) making the conclusion of contracts subject to acceptance by the other parties of supplementary obligations which, by their nature or according to common usage, have no connection with the subject of such contracts.

In the years following the creation of the EC, the Commission gave priority to putting into effect the provisions of article 85. Only subsequently did the Commission begin to turn its attention to article 86. Under article 86, a recent decision of the Commission suggests that a dominant position may be held by either a single undertaking or several. The absence of competition between two or more undertakings could indicate the existence of some agreement or concerted practice between them; equally, where those undertakings together hold a dominant position, the absence of competition could indicate that such dominant position is being abused.[59] In such a situation, the

---

56. The Commission's power to grant block exemption by means of a regulation derives from Reg. 19/65 of 2 March 1965, [1965–66], OJ Spec. Ed. 35. The Commission has exercised this power *inter alia* in relation to exclusive distributorship agreements, certain specialisation agreements, certain patent licensing agreements and research and development agreements. However, none of the block exemptions granted to date is likely to have any particular significance in the banking sector.

57. *Nederlandsche Banden-Industrie Michelin* [1981] OJ L353/33, [1982] 1 CMLR 643; case 246/86 *Belasco* v. *Commission* [1989] ECR 2117.

58. Case 26/75, *General Motors Continental NV* v. *Commission* [1975] ECR 1367; case T–7/89 *Hercules NV* v. *Commission* [1992] 4 CMLR 84.

59. See *Italian Flat Glass* [1989] OJ L33/44 and cases T–68/89 and T–77–78/89, *Società Italiana Vetro SpA* v. *Commission* [1992] 5 CMLR 302.

Commission may intervene under either article 85 or 86.[60] The main advantage for the Commission of relying on article 86 is that it becomes unnecessary to prove the existence of the underlying agreement or concerted practice.

1. Dominant position

23.12 The Treaty is silent on the meaning to be attributed to the term "dominant position." In its Memorandum of December 1965 on the *Concentrations of Undertakings in the Common Market*,[61] which contains the first comments of the Commission on the philosophy and concepts of article 86, the Commission stated that an undertaking could be considered as occupying a dominant position if it was "market dominating", that is, if it was able to exert on the operation of the market a substantial and in principle a foreseeable influence. The subject definition of dominant position by the Court of Justice reflects this attitude[62]:

... a position of economic strength enjoyed by an undertaking which enables it to hinder the maintenance of effective competition on the relevant market by allowing it to behave to an appreciable extent independently of its competitors and customers and ultimately of its consumers.

In *BBI/Boosey & Hawkes*[63] the Commission stated that: "besides the ability to behave independently of competitive pressure, [a dominant position] may also involve the ability to exclude existing competition or prevent the entry of newcomers".[64] A very high market share is a clear indication of the existence of a dominant position.[65] However, a company with a very high market share for certain products may not have a dominant position where there are large and effective competing producers and the technical knowledge to produce the goods is not particularly difficult to acquire.[66]

When considering the possibly dominant position of an undertaking, the definition of the market is of fundamental significance. The market must be defined by reference to both product market and the geographic market.[67] As for the product market, the possibilities of competition must be judged in the context of the market comprising the totality of the products or services which, with respect to their characteristics, are particularly suitable for satisfying constant needs and are only to a limited extent interchangeable with other products or services.[68] Interchangeability has two elements, namely, interchangeability in demand and interchangeability in supply. The former reflects the attitude of the product users and the latter that of the product manufacturers. In *Michelin*, the Court held that the replacement market for tyres was independent of the market for tyres for use in new equipment since the demand for

---

60. Case 66/86, *Ahmed Saeed* [1989] ECR 803, where the Court also held that art. 85 did not apply between parent and subsidiary companies which were not economically distinct, although in such a situation art. 86 may apply.
61. Quoted in *Etudes, Série Concurrence*, No. 3, part 3, para. 14; and also in [1966] RTDE 651.
62. Case 322/81, *Michelin* v. *Commission* [1983] ECR 3461; case 311/84 *Télémarketing* [1985] ECR 3261.
63. [1987] OJ L286/36.
64. See also case 30/87, *Bodson* v. *Pompes funèbres des régions liberées SA* [1988] ECR 2479 and case 247/88 *Alsatel* v. *Novosam* [1981] ECR 5987.
65. Case T–30/89 *Hilti AG* v. *Commission* [1992] 4 CMLR 16.
66. *Concentration between Tetra Pak International SA and Alfa Laval* [1992] 4 CMLR M81. See also *Concentration between Aérospatiale and Alenia and De Havilland* [1992] 4 CMLR M2.
67. Case 27/76, *United Brands* v. *Commission* [1978] ECR 207, at p. 270; and see *Società Italiana Vetro SpA* v. *Commission* [1992] 5 CMLR 502.
68. *Europemballage and Continental Can* v. *Commission*, OJ L7/25 of 8 January 1972; case 31/80, *L'Oréal* v. *De Nieuwe AMCK* [1980] ECR 3775, at p. 3793.

replacement tyres was different from the demand for new vehicles which were supplied with new tyres.[69] In *General Motors*,[70] General Motors had a monopoly on the supply of certificates which were required under Belgian law for the importation of motor cars into Belgium; consequently, since it was not possible for any one else to provide that service, the Court held that the relevant market was "applications for general type approval and the issue of certificates of conformity and type shields in Belgium".[71] In *Elopak Italia* v. *Tetra Pak (No. 2)*,[72] the Commission stated that the relevant product market should be defined with reference to a short period of time since, over a long period, the boundaries between various markets shift.

The geographic market comprises the area in which the products or services are marketed and where the conditions of competition are sufficiently homogeneous for the effect of the economic power of the undertaking concerned to be evaluated.[73] The geographic market must be a substantial part of the common market. What qualifies as substantial is a question of fact in each case; in *Bodson* one third of the population in France was considered a substantial part of the common market.

2. "Abuse"

23.13 There is no definition in the Treaty of what constitutes an "abuse" of a dominant position. This was first defined by the Court of Justice in *Hoffmann-La Roche* v. *Commission* as[74]:

... an objective concept relating to the behaviour of an undertaking in a dominant position which is such as to influence the structure of a market where, as a result of the very presence of the undertaking in question, ... the degree of competition is weakened and which, through recourse to methods different from those which condition normal competition in products or services on the basis of the transactions of commercial operators, has the effect of hindering the maintenance of the degree of competition still existing in the market or the growth of that competition.

Anti-competitive activity consists of objectively unjustifiable exclusionary practices, such as:

1. Refusal to supply whether in the particular market in which the supplier is dominant or in an ancillary market.[75] For instance, in *London European Airways* v. *Sabena*[76] the behaviour of Sabena, the Belgian state airline, which had refused to give London European Airways access to its computer reservation system because the latter's policy of low airfares represented a potential threat to Sabena's own passenger traffic was held abusive and

69. See also case 22/78, *Hugin* v. *Commission* [1979] ECR 1869.

70. Case 26/75, *General Motors* v. *Commission* [1975] ECR 1367.

71. This decision has now been followed in case 226/84, *British Leyland* v. *Commission* [1986] ECR 3263 and see also *Hugin*, cited in fn. 69, above.

72. [1992] 4 CMLR 551.

73. *United Brands* v. *Commission*, cited in fn. 67 above; *Concentration between Otto Vessand GmbH & Co. and Gratten plc* [1992] 5 CMLR M49.

74. [1979] ECR 461, at p. 541.

75. *Polaroid/SSI Europe*, Thirteenth Report on Competition Policy (1984); case 311/84 *Centre Belge d'Etudes du Marché-Télémarketing* v. *CLT & IBP* [1985] ECR 3261.

76. 17th Report on Competition Policy (1987), published 1988, p. 86.

contrary to article 86.[77] The later *Magill* case[78] raises the question whether the owner of an intellectual property right who holds a dominant position and who refuses to licence that right for an ancillary market or to exploit it, with the object or effect of stifling competition, will be treated as abusing his dominant position and so as acting contrary to article 86.[79] In contrast, the acquisition of an exclusive licence by a dominant company is not *per se* abusive.[80]

2. Predatory pricing/price discrimination/unfair pricing, which is aimed at weakening competition or eliminating a competitor from the market.[81]

3. Anti-competitive incentives/ancillary obligations in order to secure an increased share of the market in which the supplier is dominant or an ancillary market.[82]

4. Abuse of intellectual property rights.[83]

5. Attempts to widen an existing dominant position by extending it to areas which are objectively unrelated thereto. A case to bear in mind here is the decision in the *TV Guide* case. In that case, the Commission, acting on a complaint from an Irish publisher, rejected attempts by three broadcasting companies to prevent the publication and sale of TV guides in the Irish Republic and in Northern Ireland. The Commission took the view that by so doing the broadcasting companies concerned had abused their dominant position to the detriment of consumers.

6. The Merger Control Regulation[84]—Council Regulation 4964/89 on the control of concentrations between undertakings—the Merger Control Regulation—entered into force on 21 September 1990[85] and is intended to permit the effective and exclusive control by the Community of all concentrations to which it applies from the viewpoint of their effect on the structure of competition in the Community.[86] A concentration within the scope of the Regulation which does not create or strengthen a dominant position as a result

77. Sabena, a Belgian airline, had refused to give to London European Airways, which was operating a new route between the UK and Brussels, access to its Sabre computer reservation system which is used by almost 80% of Belgian travel agents to make their reservations. Sabena had refused access to LEA on the ground that the latter's policy of low airfares represented a potential threat to Sabena's own passenger traffic from Belgium, and because LEA did not intend to grant Sabena the contract for ground handling servicing of its aircraft in Brussels. Following a complaint for abuse of dominant position lodged by LEA with the Commission, Sabena agreed to grant LEA access to its computer reservation system and was fined by the Commission.

78. Case T–69/89 *Radio Telefis Eireann and Others* v. *Commission*, [1991] ECR II–485.

79. In that case, Radio Telefis Eireann refused to publish weekly listings of TV programmes in Northern Ireland and the Irish Republic and sought an injunction against Magill, who planned to do so. The behaviour of RTE was held to be contrary to art. 86.

80. Case T–51/89 *Tetra Pak Rausing SA* v. *Commission* [1990] ECR II–309. The case also confirms that arts. 85 and 86 operate independently of each other so that an exemption under art. 85(3) does not render art. 86 inapplicable.

81. Case 62/86 *AKZO Chemie BV* v. *Commission* [1986] ECR 1503, *Napier Brown/British Sugar*, [1988] OJ L284/41; case 27/76, *United Brands* v. *Commission* [1978] ECR 207; *Elopak Italia Srl* v. *Tetra Pak (No. 2)* [1992] 4 CMLR 551, *B. & I. Line plc* v. *Sealink Harbours and Sealink Stena* [1992] 5 CMLR 255.

82. Case 107/76 *Hoffmann-La Roche* v. *Centrafarm* [1978] ECR 1139; Case T–30/89 *Hilti*, OJ C9/2 of 15 January 1992; *London European/Sabena*, referred to in fn. 76, above.

83. This area is beyond the scope of this book. See, however, the *RTE* case, referred to at fn. 78, above.

84. Council Reg. 4964/89 of 21 December 1989, corrected version published in OJ L257/13 of 21 September 1990.

85. Art. 25(1).

86. Recital 7 and see art. 2, which specifies the matters to be taken into account by the Commission in appraising concentrations within the scope of the Reg. On 28 July 1993 the Commission submitted to the Council a report on the implementation of the Merger Regulation which *inter alia* summarised the

of which effective competition would significantly be impeded in the common market or a substantial part of it will not infringe the Regulation as being incompatible with the common market.[87] Concentrations with a Community dimension are in principle generally subject to the exclusive control of the Commission, subject to review by the Court of Justice,[88] but it may be that national courts, the Court of Final Instance and the Court of Justice will be required to examine the question of the applicability of articles 85 and 86 to such concentrations.[89] Articles 85 and 86 remain applicable to concentrations not falling within the scope of the Merger Control Regulation.

The Regulation applies to all concentrations with a Community dimension. A concentration will be treated as having a Community dimension where the combined aggregate worldwide turnover of all the undertakings concerned is more than 5,000 million ECU and the aggregate Community-wide turnover of each of at least two of the undertakings concerned is more than 250 million ECU, unless each of the undertakings concerned achieves more than two-thirds of its aggregate Community-wide turnover within one and the same Member State. These thresholds are subject to review by the end of 1993.[90] In the case of credit institutions and other financial institutions and of insurance companies, special provision is made,[91] in recognition of the fact that such institutions have no turnover comparable with that of other undertakings. The responsibility for concentrations which fall below these thresholds lies with the competent authorities of the Member States. The thresholds themselves, while considered by the Commission to be too high at present to include in the Community's jurisdiction all concentrations having Community-wide effects, are designed in such a way that mergers between large undertakings which will usually have economic effects throughout the Community fall within the scope of the Regulation.[92]

Concentrations with a Community dimension must be notified to the Commission not more than one week after the conclusion of the agreement or the announcement of the public bid or the acquisition of a controlling interest, whichever is the earliest.[93] In certain circumstances, the Commission is empowered to refer a concentration notified to it but which raises serious competition issues limited solely to a Member State's territory to the competent authorities of the Member State concerned.[94] Also, Member States may request the Commission to take action in relation to a concentration which, although having no Community dimension, creates or strengthens a dominant position as a result of which effective competition would be

---

implementations of the Reg. to that date and proposed to postpone any formal proposal to revise it until, at the latest, the end of 1996: COM(93) 385 final.

87. See art. 2(2) and (3).

88. Art. 21.

89. See the answer of the Council on 21 January 1992 to Written Question 1110/91 of MEP Pierre Bernard-Reymaud, OJ C55/17 of 2 March 1992.

90. Art. 1.

91. Art. 5(3).

92. See p. 4 of the text of the Robert Schuman Lecture given by Sir Leon Brittan on 11 June 1992 at the European University Institute in Florence on "Subsidiarity in the Constitution of the European Community", published in "Europe", Documents no. 1786, 18 June 1992.

93. Art. 4(1).

94. Art. 9.

significantly impeded within the territory of the Member State concerned.[95]

A concentration is deemed to arise where two or more previously independent undertakings merge; or where at least one undertaking or person controlling an undertaking acquires direct or indirect control of the whole or part of at least one other undertaking.[96] However, the Regulation makes express provision for when a concentration is *not* deemed to arise in relation to credit institutions and certain other financial institutions and insurance companies.[97]

Failure to comply with the provisions of the Regulation may lead to the imposition of fines or periodic penalty payments.[98]

4. THE SPECIAL POSITION OF PUBLIC UNDERTAKINGS—ARTICLE 90

23.14 Article 90 of the Treaty recognises that public undertakings in the Member States may be in a special position and makes provision accordingly:

(1) In the case of public undertakings and undertakings to which Member States grant special or exclusive rights, Member States shall neither enact nor maintain in force any measure contrary to the rules laid down in the Treaty, in particular to those rules provided for in Article 7 [laying down the principle of non-discrimination on the grounds of nationality] and Articles 85 to 94.

(2) Undertakings entrusted with the operation of services of a general economic interest or having the character of a revenue- producing monopoly, shall be subject to the rules contained in this Treaty, in particular to the rules on competition, in so far as the application of such rules does not obstruct the performance, in law or in fact, of the particular tasks assigned to them. The development of trade must not be affected to such an extent as would be contrary to the interests of the Community.

(3) The Commission shall ensure the application of the provisions of this Article and shall, where necessary, address appropriate directives or decisions to Member States.

The term "public undertakings" is not defined in the Treaty, but to achieve uniformity of application of the rules on competition throughout the Community, it must be interpreted without reference to whether or not, under the domestic law of a Member State, a particular undertaking is regarded as "public".

Community law does now provide for a definition of public undertaking in Directive 80/723 (adopted pursuant to article 90(3) of the Treaty) on the transparency of financial relations between Member States and public undertakings.[99] Article 2 of the Directive defines a public undertaking as:

any undertaking over which the public authorities may exercise directly or indirectly a dominant influence by virtue of their ownership of it, their financial participation therein, or the rules which govern it.[100]

Article 90 confirms that public undertakings are in general subject to the provisions of the Treaty and in particular to the rules on competition. It is addressed to the Member States and clearly renders it impossible for them to validate what would

95. Art. 22.
96. Art. 3(1).
97. Art. 3(5)(a).
98. Arts. 14 and 15.
99. [1980] OJ L195/35.
100. See *Express Delivery Services in the Netherlands*, [1990] OJ L10/47; case 118/85, *Commission* v. *Italy* [1987] ECR 2599, where a trading arm of the State with no separate personality was held to fall within the definition of public undertaking.

otherwise be anti-competitive behaviour of undertakings by governmental measures or decrees. If this were not the case, distortion of competition would result as between the private and public sectors of a Member State's economy which, in turn, would give a competitive advantage to Member States with a large public sector. Private undertakings are also subject to article 90 to the extent that they are granted special or exclusive rights by a Member State. The interpretation of "special or exclusive rights" has concentrated on the exclusivity aspect of the test.[101]

Article 90(2) deals with, amongst other things, the position of undertakings "entrusted with the operation of services of general economic interest". Undertakings will only be entitled to rely on article 90(2) where the operation of such services is entrusted to them by an act of the public authority.[102] Thus in *Gesellschaft zur Verwertung von Leistungsschutzrechten mbH (GVL)* v. *Commission*,[103] the plaintiff company (the only undertaking for the management of copyright in the former West Germany) contended that it was an undertaking entrusted with the operation of services of general economic interest because of a West German law which provided that management undertakings (such as the company) had to receive official authorisation and were subject to the supervision of the Patent Office. The Court of Justice rejected that contention, holding that the German legislation did not confer the management of copyright on GVL but merely defined in a general manner the rules applying to the activities of companies which intended to undertake the collective exploitation of such rights.[104]

An undertaking of the kind provided for by article 90(2) will not escape the rules on competition unless the application of such rules obstructs the performance of the tasks assigned to it. It is not enough that compliance with the rules on competition would merely make performance of its duties more complicated.[105]

Even though article 90 presupposes the existence of undertakings enjoying special or exclusive rights, it does not thereby follow that all special or exclusive rights are necessarily compatible with the Treaty.[106]

Article 90(3) requires the Commission to ensure the application of the provisions of article 90 and, where necessary, to address appropriate directives or decisions to Member States. In *France* v. *Commission*,[107] the Court was concerned with the validity of certain of the provisions of a Commission Directive adopted under article 90(3) on

101. See case 66/86 *Ahmed Saeed* and case 30/87 *Bodson*, cited in fns. 60 and 64, above.

102. Case 127/73 *BRT* v. *SABAM* [1974] ECR 313; see also case 10/71 *Ministère Public of Luxembourg* v. *Miller* [1971] ECR 723. In *BRT* v. *SABAM* the Court of Justice considered, at p. 318, that it was the duty of the national court to investigate whether an undertaking which invoked before it the provisions of art. 90(2) had in fact been entrusted by a Member State with the operation of a service of general economic interest.

103. Case 7/82 [1983] ECR 483.

104. *Ibid.*, p. 504. In the *GVL* case, the action came directly before the Court of Justice for a declaration that a decision of the Commission adverse to GVL was void. Accordingly, in contrast to *BRT* v. *SABAM*, cited in fn. 102, above, which came before the Court of Justice on a reference for a preliminary ruling from a Belgian court, there was no scope for GVL's status as an undertaking entrusted with the operation of a service of general economic interest to be investigated by a national court.

105. Cases 209/84 etc., *Ministère Public* v. *Asjes* [1986] ECR 1425; case 41/85 *Italy* v. *Commission* [1985] ECR 873.

106. Case C–202/88 *France* v. *Commission* [1991] ECR I–1223. See also case C–353/89 *Commission* v. *Netherlands*, [1991] ECR I–4069 where the Court held, in the context of art. 59 of the Treaty on freedom to provide services, that although cultural policy in a Member State might afford an imperative reason of public interest justifying a restriction on the freedom to provide services, nevertheless by compelling national broadcasting organisations to use the services of a national undertaking for the production of all or part of their broadcasts The Netherlands was exceeding its aim of freedom of speech.

107. Case C–202/88, judgment of 19 March 1991.

competition in the markets in telecommunications terminal equipment.[108] The Directive provided *inter alia* that Member States which had granted special or exclusive rights for the importation, marketing, connection, bringing into service of tele-communications terminal equipment and maintenance of such equipment were to ensure that those rights were withdrawn. While annulling certain of the Directive's provisions, the Court rejected the French government's complaint that the Commission had sought to exercise powers attributed to the Council by articles 87 and 100a of the Treaty. As the Court observed, the purpose of the powers conferred on the Commission by article 90(3) was different and more specific than the powers conferred on the Council by articles 87 and 100a. The possibility that the Council might lay down, in the exercise of a general power conferred on it by other Treaty provisions, rules which included provisions affecting the domain specific to article 90 did not prevent the Commission from exercising the powers which article 90 conferred on it. The Court also ruled that the Commission was entitled, by the Directive,[109] to require the withdrawal of exclusive rights granted by Member States for the importation, marketing, connection, bringing into service of telecommunications terminal equipment and maintenance of such equipment.

5. REGULATION 17

23.15 As already seen, Regulation 17 was enacted by the Council in 1962 to give effect to the principles laid down in articles 85 and 86 and to give the Commission wide powers in relation to the rules on competition. A detailed consideration of Regulation 17 falls outside the scope of this work. However, it is necessary to refer briefly to certain of its provisions. With certain exceptions, the Regulation makes provision for a system of notification to the Commission of agreements, decisions and concerted practices in respect of which the parties seek to be exempted on the basis of article 85(3) from the prohibition in article 85(1).[110]

Article 11 enables the Commission to obtain all information necessary to ensure the application of the principles laid down in articles 85 and 86 from the Member States and from undertakings and associations of undertakings.[111] Failure to supply such information or the supply of incorrect information may result in the imposition of fines and periodic penalty payments. Article 14 gives the Commission wide investigative powers into undertakings and associations of undertakings.[112] The Court has recently held that these administrative procedures must be carried out with respect for fundamental rights, especially the European Convention on Human Rights, and that if the search powers of the Commission are opposed the co-operation of the national

108. Directive 88/301/EEC of 16 May 1988, [1988] OJ L131/73.
109. Art. 2.
110. Arts. 4, 5, 7, 22(1) and 25.
111. See case T–39/90 *SEP* v. *Commission* [1992] 5 CMLR 33.
112. Art. 14 empowers officials authorised by the Commission to examine the books and other records of undertakings and associations of undertakings; to take copies of or extracts from any such books and records; to ask for oral explanations on the spot; and to enter any premises, land and means of transport of undertakings. Community law does, however, recognise a limited doctrine of legal professional privilege whereby the confidentiality of written communications between lawyer and client is protected, provided that they are made for the purpose and in the interests of the client's rights of defence and that they emanate from independent lawyers entitled to practise in a Member State who are not bound to the client by a relationship of employment: case 155/79, *AM & S Europe Ltd.* v. *Commission* [1982] ECR 1575.

authorities is required and national procedural guarantees apply.[113] Information acquired by the Commission as a result of its inquiries and information of the kind covered by the obligation of professional secrecy must not be disclosed by the Commission.[114]

---

113. Joined cases 46/87 & 227/88 *Hoechst AG* v. *Commission* [1989] ECR 2859; case 85/87 *Dow Benelux NV* v. *Commission* [1989] ECR 3137; case 97–99/87 *Dow Chemical Iberica SA* v. *Commission* [1989] ECR 3156.

114. Art. 20. In the exercise of their jurisdiction to apply the Community rules on competition, the authorities in Member States may not use as evidence unpublished information which has been supplied in the replies to requests for information which have been made to undertakings by virtue of art. 11 of Reg. 17: case C–67/91 *Direccion General de Defensa de la Competencia* v. *Associación Española de Banca Privada*, judgment of 16 July 1992.

CHAPTER 24

APPLICABILITY OF THE RULES ON COMPETITION
TO BANKING OPERATIONS

1. THE COMMISSION'S ATTITUDE UNTIL THE ZÜCHNER JUDGMENT
OF 17 JULY 1981

24.1 As long ago as 1973, the Commission had expressed the view that the rules on competition in the Treaty and their implementing regulations were in principle applicable to the banking sector.[1] This viewpoint was reaffirmed by the Commission in 1979.[2] On each of these occasions, however, the Commission had stressed its awareness that "application of the competition rules must take account of the peculiar characteristics of certain industries"[3] and, with regard to the banking sector, must take account of "the peculiar features of the banking industry, which is open to interference from governmental financial and monetary policies, supervision by the central banks, control by national regulatory authorities and exchange control constraints".[4] These are all areas in which the Member States had retained wide powers, now significantly—and increasingly—restricted by the coming into force of the Second Banking Directive and the move towards a single European currency.

Against this background, the Commission stated in 1973 that it was endeavouring to determine whether and, if so, to what extent monetary policy requirements might necessitate the use of article 87(2)(c) to delimit, in the banking sector, the scope of articles 85 and 86 were it to appear that article 85(3) or 90(2) was inapplicable.[5] It will be recalled that article 87(2)(c) empowers the Council, acting on a proposal from the Commission, to define, if need be, the scope of the provisions of articles 85 and 86 in the various branches of the economy.

The view of the Commission in 1973 that the rules on competition were in principle applicable to the banking sector was in marked contrast to the attitude of the banks themselves from the time that Regulation 17 was made.

Amongst other things, the Regulation required undertakings to notify to the Commission by 1 November 1962 all existing agreements between undertakings, decisions by associations of undertakings and concerted practices which infringed article 85(1).[6] At the time, the attitude of most banks was that the majority of banking operations fell outside the scope of the rules on competition because of the role played

1. Second Report on Competition Policy, 1973, published 1974, points 51 to 53.
2. Eighth Report on Competition Policy, 1979, published 1980, points 32 to 37.
3. Second Report on Competition Policy, 1973, published 1974, point 50.
4. Eighth Report on Competition Policy, 1979, published 1980, point 32.
5. Second Report on Competition Policy, 1973, published 1974, point 51.
6. Art. 5 of the Reg. In the case of agreements, decisions and concerted practices to which not more than two undertakings were party, notification had to be made by 1 February 1963.

by those operations in the financial and monetary policy of the Member States.[7] Also, "such agreements, . . . are tolerated, often encouraged and sometimes imposed by the national authorities. . . .". Consequently it would be necessary to make a special Regulation for the banking sector."[8] That attitude explains why the banks in general felt it unnecessary in 1962 to notify to the Commission, in accordance with the provisions of Regulation 17, interbank agreements, decisions by banking associations or concerted practices which existed in the banking sector at the time, even in cases where such agreements, decisions and concerted practices were capable of affecting trade between Member States.

Only one national banking association notified to the Commission at the time the agreements and practices which existed between its members, requesting in the first place negative clearance and, in the alternative, in case the Commission considered that article 85(1) had been infringed, an exemption under article 85(3).[9] However, the Commission did not adopt any position in relation to this request until after the *Züchner* judgment of 17 July 1981.

The failure to notify the vast majority of agreements in the banking sector provoked no reaction from the Commission and the undertakings in question were not in any way penalised—apparently in anticipation of the outcome of the Commission's examination of the possible use of article 87(2)(c) announced in 1973. This examination continued over many years. Thus, in its Eighth Report on Competition Policy published in 1979, the Commission stated that it had[10]:

continued its scrutiny of co-operation agreements between banks in one and the same country. It is seeking to determine which provisions in such agreements may be regarded as the essential adjunct of interest rate decisions and consequently as an instrument of national monetary policies.

2. THE ZÜCHNER JUDGMENT AND ITS CONSEQUENCES[11]

24.2 The facts of *Züchner* are straightforward. On 21 May 1969 Mr Züchner opened a bank account with the Bayerische Vereinsbank in Rosenheim, Federal Republic of Germany, on the bank's standard terms. On 17 July 1979 he drew a cheque on his account in the sum of 10,000 DM in favour of a payee resident in Italy. In respect of this transfer the bank debited his account with a "service charge" of 15 DM, representing 0·15% of the sum transferred. Mr Züchner thereupon sued the bank before the Rosenheim Local Court (Amtsgericht) for repayment of the charge on the grounds that the imposition of such a charge was contrary to the provisions of the Treaty. One of the arguments put forward by Mr Züchner was that the imposition of the charge was incompatible with articles 85 and 86 of the Treaty because it was part of a concerted practice followed by all or most banks both in the Federal Republic of Germany and in other Member States. The Rosenheim Amtsgericht thereupon requested a ruling from the Court of Justice on the following question:

7. See, eg, L. Villaret, "Comment appliquer aux activités bancaires les règles de la concurrence du Traité de la CEE?" (1962) *Revue Banque* (France) p. 511.

8. Ch del Marmol, "L'application des lois anti-trust américaines au réglement de la bourse et aux fusions de banques" (1963) *Revue de la Banque* (Belgium) 675 at 686 (our translation).

9. *Agence Europe*, Bulletin 1577 of 14 June 1963.

10. Point 32. See also the Answer to Written Question 795/76, OJ C94/15 of 18 April 1977.

11. Case 172/80 [1981] ECR 2021.

In transfers of capital and other payments between banks within the Common Market, is the debiting of a general service charge at a rate of 0·15% of the sum transferred a concerted practice which may affect trade, and therefore contrary to Articles 85 and 86 of the EEC Treaty?

The Court of Justice answered the question referred to it by the Amtsgericht as follows[12]:

Parallel conduct in the debiting of a uniform bank charge on transfers by banks from one Member State to another of sums from their customers' funds amounts to a concerted practice prohibited by Article 85(1) of the Treaty if it is established by the national court that such parallel conduct exhibits the features of co-ordination and co-operation characteristic of such a practice and if that practice is capable of significantly affecting conditions of competition in the market for the services connected with such transfer.

In analysing the Court of Justice's decision, it is necessary to consider separately its significance in the general context of the EC rules on competition and in the particular context of the application of those rules to the banking sector. In the general context of the rules on competition the judgment does not develop the law in any way but rather applies the existing law. One interesting feature, however, is that although the Amtsgericht's question asked whether the debiting of the charge was contrary to both article 85 and article 86, the Court of Justice restricted its examination of the question to the provisions of article 85. It did so in view of the fact that the Amtsgericht's question referred only to the existence of a concerted practice as a possible infringement of the rules on competition and that "article 86 deals with the abuse of a dominant position and does not cover the existence of concerted practices, to which solely the provisions of article 85 apply".[13]

However, in the particular context of the application of the rules on competition to the banking sector, the judgment in *Züchner* is undoubtedly a landmark decision.

1. Banks are not undertakings entrusted with the operation of services of general economic interest

24.3 It will be recalled that article 90(2) of the Treaty subjects undertakings entrusted with the operation of services of general economic interest or having the character of a revenue-producing monopoly to the rules contained in the Treaty, in particular to the rules on competition, but only insofar as the application of such rules does not obstruct the performance, in law or in fact, of the particular tasks assigned to them.

In 1962, at the time when the question first arose whether banking agreements and practices which then existed had to be notified to the Commission in accordance with the provisions of Regulation 17, one of the arguments put forward by the banks against notification was that notification was unnecessary because of the provisions of article 90(2)[14]:

Insofar as banks are called upon to play a role in the fulfilment of the economic and monetary policies of the States, they are "undertakings entrusted with the operation of services of general economic interest" within the meaning of article 90(2) . . .; to that extent, therefore, they are only subject to the EEC rules on competition and in particular article 85 "in so far as the application of such rules does not obstruct the performance, in law or in fact, of the particular tasks assigned to them." The provisions of article 90(2), which may have been specially drafted

12. *Ibid.*, at p. 2034.
13. *Ibid.*, point 10. This was also the opinion of A.G. Sir Gordon Slynn: see at p. 2039.
14. L. Villaret, fn. 7, above, at p. 515 (our translation).

with banks in mind, cannot be regarded as applying to every interbank agreement. But it is certain that they apply to those agreements which are both known to the national authorities and regarded by those authorities as necessary to ensure that too much competition does not defeat the fulfilment of the economic and monetary tasks of the banks.

In the course of the oral procedure before the Court of Justice, the Bayerische Vereinsbank appears to have adopted this viewpoint by raising the initial objection that the question of interpretation raised by the national court was without purpose because the Treaty provisions on competition did not apply, at least to a great extent, to banking undertakings. It maintained that by reason of the special nature of the services provided by such undertakings and the vital role which they play in transfers of capital they must be considered as undertakings "entrusted with the operation of services of general economic interest" within the meaning of article 90(2) and so not subject to the rules on competition.[15] However, the Court of Justice unhesitatingly rejected this contention[16]:

Although the transfer of customers' funds from one Member State to another normally performed by banks is an operation which falls within the special tasks of banks, particularly in connection with international movements of capital, that is not sufficient to make them undertakings within the meaning of Article 90(2) of the Treaty unless it can be established that in performing such transfers the banks are operating a service of general economic interest with which they have been entrusted by a measure adopted by the public authorities.

The Court of Justice thereby reaffirmed its position in *BRT* v. *SABAM*[17] where it stated that undertakings which can take advantage of article 90(2) must be strictly defined and that although private undertakings might come within that provision, they must be entrusted with the operation of services of general economic interest by an act of the public authority.[18] A similar line of reasoning was followed by the Commission in its *Eurocheque* decision of 10 December 1984 considered below, to reject the claim that the Eurocheque "package deal agreement" came within the ambit of article 90(2).

2. Banks are not beyond the scope of the rules on competition by reason of the provisions of article 104 *et seq.* of the Treaty concerning economic policy[19]

24.4 Article 104 of the Treaty provides that:

Each Member State shall pursue the economic policy needed to ensure the equilibrium of its overall balance of payments and to maintain confidence in its currency, while taking care to ensure a high level of employment and a stable level of prices.

Also, article 105 provides that:

1. In order to facilitate attainment of the objectives set out in Article 104, Member States shall co-ordinate their economic policies. They shall for this purpose provide for co-operation between their appropriate and administrative departments and between their central banks.

The Commission shall submit to the Council recommendations on how to achieve such co-operation.

2. In order to promote co-ordination of the policies of Member States in the monetary field to the full extent needed for the functioning of the common market, a Monetary Committee with

15. [1981] ECR 2021, at pp. 2029–2030, point 6.
16. *Ibid.*, at p. 2030, point 7. See also the opinion of A.G. Sir Gordon Slynn at pp. 2035–2036.
17. Case 127/73 [1974] ECR 313.
18. Being entrusted with the operation of a service of general economic interest by an act of the public authority will not, of itself, be sufficient to take a bank or a banking organisation outside the scope of the Community rules on competition.
19. The amendments to these provisions brought about by the Treaty on European Union—the Maastricht Agreement—are not considered here since they are not material to the discussion.

advisory status is hereby set up. It shall have the following tasks:—to keep under review the monetary and financial situation of the Member States and of the Community and the general payments system of the Member States and to report regularly thereon to the Council and to the Commission;—to deliver opinions at the request of the Council or of the Commission or on its own initiative, for submission to these institutions. The Member States and the Commission shall each appoint two members of the Monetary Committee.

These provisions, which were relied upon by the Bayerische Vereinsbank before the Court of Justice, had already been invoked in 1962 by the banking sector in support of its contention that notification to the Commission of interbank agreements capable of affecting trade between Member States was unnecessary. At the time, the banking sector maintained that article 104 *et seq.* of the Treaty had to be interpreted in such a way that the co-ordination of the economic and monetary policies of the Member States referred to in those provisions meant that the banks were outside the scope of the rules on competition by reason of the close links between their activities and those policies for the purpose of bringing about the desired co-ordination.

However, the Court of Justice firmly rejected that contention[20]:

As to Article 104 *et seq.* of the Treaty, those provisions in no way have the effect of exempting banks from the competition rules of the Treaty. They appear in chapter 2 of Title II[21] of the Treaty, which concerns "Balance of payments" and are restricted to stipulating that there must be co-ordination between the Member States on economic policy, and to that end, they provide for collaboration between the appropriate national administrative departments and the central banks of the Member States in order to attain the objectives of the Treaty.

3. Equality of treatment of private and public banks under the rules on competition

24.5 The judgment in *Züchner* implicitly rejects the view expressed by some commentators, particularly in France, that banks which have been nationalised might be regarded as undertakings charged by the State with the distribution of credit and, accordingly, undertakings entrusted with services of general economic interest.[22] This wide interpretation of article 90(2) would result in the nationalised commercial banking sector (very large in some Member States, such as France, at least in the 1980s, and Greece) being accorded preferential treatment over the private sector so far as the application to banking undertakings of the rules of competition is concerned.

In 1978, the Commission, in reply to a Written Question in the European Parliament, had already expressed its disagreement with this interpretation of article 90(2) and had affirmed the principle of equal treatment of banking institutions in the private and public sectors.[23] The widespread nationalisation of banks in France, which started in 1981, led the Commission to reaffirm the principle of equal treatment in relation to the rules on competition. In a major speech in London, on 30 November 1981, entitled "Banking in the EEC—the balance between co-operation and competition", Mr. Frans Andriessen, then the EC Commissioner with responsibility for competition, stated[24]:

20. [1981] ECR 2021, at p. 2030, point 8. A.G. Sir Gordon Slynn pointed out in his Opinion, at p. 2036, that "art. 104 *et seq.* seem to do no more than to indicate that some aspects of banking may be of general economic interest. They do not in my opinion go any way to exclude the banks from the rules incorporated in arts. 85 and 86".

21. Presently Chap. 3 of Title II of the Treaty, as amended by the Single European Act of 1986.

22. B. Goldman, *Droit Commercial Européen* (3rd ed., Dalloz), para. 258; B. Goldman, *European Commercial Law* (London, Stevens & Sons; New York, Matthew Bender), para. 372.

23. Answer to Written Question 835/77, OJ C74/10 of 28 March 1978.

24. Stencilled text of the speech, p. 4. A summary of the speech was published in *Agence Europe*, Bulletin 3264 (new series) of 5 December 1981.

Nationalisation (of banks) does not, of course, in itself infringe any provision of the Treaty of Rome. Indeed, article 222 of the Treaty specifically reserves to Member States the power to regulate property rights. However, once an enterprise is nationalised it must, pursuant to article 90, respect all the provisions of the Treaty, notably the rules on competition.

The Commission will certainly ensure that the way in which the nationalisation is implemented or the way in which subsequent state control is exercised does not prejudice Community law with respect to the freedom of movement of capital, the freedom to provide services throughout the EEC, the freedom of establishment and the EEC competition rules . . .

The Commission reaffirmed these views in 1984 as follows[25]:

Among the external factors affecting competition in the banking sector, two kinds of influence come from government in its roles as trustee or owner of the public or nationalised banking sector and as the monetary and regulatory authority.

The first aspect (trustee or owner of the public or nationalised banking sector) points to a need for vigilance to ensure that competition is not distorted by the guarantor role inevitably assumed by the State in such cases. In undertaking risks, public financial institutions should continue to apply general commercial banking principles.

It is precisely in order to avoid the guarantor role inevitably assumed by the State in respect of public sector banking institutions leading to distortions of competition that the Community legislation recently enacted in respect of a bank's own funds requirements has specifically provided that the State's guarantee could not be a substitute for a public sector bank's own funds requirements.[26]

A similar concern of the Commission is reflected in the decision which it took in 1985 with a view to ending the discrimination which existed in Greece against private insurers.[27] Greek legislation imposed an obligation on, *inter alios*, public banks to require their borrowers to use the services of insurance companies in the public sector. It also obliged all publicly owned property to be insured with insurance companies in the public sector. Although the Commission's decision arises in the field of insurance, its reasoning is applicable to the banking field also. By parity of reasoning, it follows that a provision of national law which, for example, obliges public undertakings to use the services of a public sector bank or gives public sector banks the exclusive right to grant public or private undertakings loans subsidised or guaranteed by the State would be open to challenge under Community law.

More recently, the Commission was called upon, in answer to a Written Question in the European Parliament, to reaffirm as follows the principle of equality between public and private credit institutions under the rules on competition.[28]

Article 92 . . . establishes the principle that state aid which is liable to distort competition in intra-Community trade is prohibited. It also lays down certain derogations to that principle. A post office giro institution [not subject to the 1977 Banking Directive] which receives deposits and grants credits is caught by that article. Consequently, where it receives state aid for the pursuit of such activities, that aid must be notified in advance to the Commission in accordance with article 93(3) of the EEC Treaty. The Commission is aware that some post office giro institutions are involved in credit and deposit activities and it is examining this matter and will, where appropriate, apply the provisions of Directive 80/723/EEC on the transparency of financial relations between Member States and public undertakings, as amended by Directive 85/413/EEC.

25. Thirteenth Report on Competition Policy, 1984, published 1985, point 322.
26. See Part Two, above.
27. Commission decision of 24 April 1985, OJ L152/25 of 11 June 1985. See also the Court of Justice's judgment in case C–226/87 *Commission* v. *Greece* [1988] ECR 3611.
28. Commission's answer to Written Question 1975/91 of MEP F. Herman, OJ C55/44 of 2 March 1992.

Also, the Commission has indicated in its annual Report on Competition Policy for 1992, that it[29]:

is currently investigating several complaints against state aid in postal banking services and public credit institutions[30]

and recalled that it[31]:

this year adopted one of the first state aid decisions concerning the banking sector. It applied the principle of the private investor operating in normal market economy conditions to the recapitalization of the Banco di Sicilia and of the Centrale di Risparmio ("Sicilicassa").[32] It initiated proceedings under article 93(2) of the EEC Treaty against Italian tax measures specifically for banks and insurance companies in Trieste.[33]

3. COMPARISON BETWEEN THE ZÜCHNER JUDGMENT AND THE VERBAND DER SACHVERSICHERER JUDGMENT OF 27 JANUARY 1987[34] RELATING TO THE INSURANCE SECTOR

24.6 As was the case with the banks, insurance undertakings had for a long time regarded themselves as falling outside the scope of the Community rules on competition by reason of the particular characteristics of their sector. But as was also the case with the banks, the Commission had since 1973 taken the position that the rules on competition were applicable to the insurance sector just as they applied to any other sector of economic activity.

In 1984, the Commission took its first decision regarding a breach of article 85(1) in the insurance sector. It held that the Verband der Sachversicherer (VdS), the German association of property insurers, had infringed article 85(1) by recommending an increase in premium of between 10% and 30% in June 1980. The VdS had issued this recommendation, which was applied to the end of 1982, in order to stabilise and increase premium rates for industrial fire consequential loss insurance.[35] VdS appealed that decision to the Court of Justice on grounds that were very similar to those relied upon by Bayerische Vereinsbank in the *Züchner* case. By its judgment of 27 January 1987, the Court of Justice dismissed VdS's appeal. In view of the similar arguments advanced in each case, the VdS judgment can, it is submitted, be regarded as a reaffirmation, if any were needed, of the Court of Justice's position taken in the *Züchner* case.

Two arguments advanced by VdS and rejected by the Court are worthy of particular comment. First, VdS had argued that article 85(1) was not applicable in its entirety and without qualification to the insurance industry. It based that argument, as Bayerische Vereinsbank had done in *Züchner*, on article 87(2)(c) by contending that as long as the Council had not adopted rules for the insurance sector pursuant to that article, it had to be assumed that article 85(1) did not apply to the insurance industry. As recalled by the Commission the Court replied that:

29. Twenty-second Report on Competition Policy of 1992, published 1993, point 46.
30. See also point 439 of the Twenty-second Report.
31. Point 47 of the Twenty-second Report.
32. See also point 440 of the Twenty-second Report.
33. See also point 498 of the Twenty-second Report.
34. Case 45/85 [1987] ECR 405.
35. Decision of 5 December 1984, OJ L35 of 7 February 1985—see, further, Fourteenth Report on Competition Policy, 1984, published 1985, point 75.

there was no provision in the EEC Treaty comparable to article 42 (dealing with agriculture) stating that the competition rules were not applicable to insurance or making their application dependent on a Council decision. The Council had not enacted special procedural rules for the insurance industry as it had for parts of the transport sector. It followed that the competition rules including in particular articles 85 and 86 and Regulation 17, were fully applicable to the insurance industry. Allowance could be made for the special features and problems of an industry by the Commission's grant of exemptions under article 85(3).[36]

Second, VdS had further argued that, by prohibiting the premium increase recommendation purely on competition grounds, the Commission had disturbed the delicate balance existing in the Federal Republic of Germany between comprehensive supervision of the insurance industry, separation of the national market by the regulatory requirements and a relaxation of the ordinary competition rules, and had thereby interfered with the conduct of national economic and competition policy. This argument, too, was rejected by the Court. The Commission's decision was directed at a recommendation to increase prices issued by a trade association to its members.

The Commission's decision thus did not impinge upon the general economic policy of the Federal Republic, nor did it adversely affect the effective exercise of supervision over the national insurance industry. While there was nothing to prevent a Member State closely associating competition law and regulation of the insurance industry, despite the different purposes served by them, the enforcement of articles 85 and 86 could not be made subject to the rules of a Member State's regulatory system for an industry.[37]

4. THE CHANGE IN THE COMMISSION'S ATTITUDE SINCE ZÜCHNER

24.7 In the view of the Commission itself, the Court of Justice's decision in *Züchner*[38]:

makes it clear that the banking sector is only exempted from the competition rules to the extent that any anti-competitive conduct by banks is imposed on them by the monetary authorities.

The Court has thus cleared up any remaining doubts about private-sector agreements and concerted practices . . . Where their effects extend beyond national boundaries they must be notified to the Commission with a view to possible exemption under Article 85(3).

It will be recalled that agreements or decisions prohibited pursuant to article 85(1) are automatically void and that, in the absence of notification to the Commission, the undertakings involved are exposed to the risk of heavy fines. In his speech already referred to, Commissioner Andriessen made it clear that, in the light of *Züchner*, the Commission would not hesitate to impose meaningful fines upon guilty banking undertakings in the absence of notification[39]:

. . . the Commission looks favourably at co-operation agreements between banks, especially across Member State frontiers, which make important contributions to economic progress and from which the users of banks' services can derive considerable benefit. However, in order to be able to assess such agreements properly they must be notified to the Commission. Otherwise, no exemption can be granted. Besides, notification is the only way to give the parties immunity from fines.

36. Seventeenth Report on Competition Policy, 1987, published 1988, point 103.
37. Seventeenth Report on Competition Policy, 1987, published 1988, point 103.
38. Eleventh Report on Competition Policy, 1982, published 1983, point 61.
39. Stencilled text of the speech, p. 12. See further for a summary of the speech. *Agence Europe*, Bulletin 3264 (new series) of 5 December 1981.

The same view was strongly reaffirmed by Commissioner Andriessen in May 1984 at a press conference on the subject of the Commission's competition policy[40]:

a dialogue could be opened on certain conditions on the applications of competition regulations in this particular sector, on condition that the banks show willingness and formally notify the Commission of agreements and ententes which link them. In the meantime, the Commission will not abandon existing enquiries and matters which have already been started, but it will delay its decision in order to allow dialogue and to be able to evaluate the banks' willingness.

The result of that enquiry was that "there existed in the majority of the EEC, which consisted of 10 members at the time (Greece having just joined, but Spain and Portugal still not being members) agreements which seemed incompatible with article 85. Talks took place between the Commission and the Banking Federation of the European Community. After these discussions, the national banking associations concerned first of all stated formally that the competition rules applied to the banking sector (which in any case had been settled by the *Züchner* case) and also declared that they had either abandoned their agreements regarding banking services or would notify them to the Commission".[41]

By June 1984, the banking organisations concerned were reported as finalising the formal notification of the agreements they had not abandoned voluntarily.[42] Following these notifications, the Commission was in a position by 1986 to adopt three decisions concerning agreements among Irish, Belgian and Italian banks, to be followed in 1989 by a more far-reaching decision concerning agreements amongst Dutch banks, all of which will be considered below.

40. *Agence Europe*, Bulletin 3866 (new series) of 8 June 1984. See also the Thirteenth Report on Competition Policy, 1984, published 1985, point 69.
41. H. Salmon, "Payment cards and European competition law: an attempt at evaluation" [1990] 1 JIBL 25, at p. 27.
42. *Agence Europe*, Bulletin 3866 (new series), 8 June 1984.

CHAPTER 25

THE EFFECT OF DOMESTIC BANKING AGREEMENTS ON TRADE BETWEEN MEMBER STATES

1. GENERAL REMARKS

25.1 In the banking sector, agreements, decisions and concerted practices most often concern undertakings in a single Member State. It might be thought, therefore, that domestic banking agreements are in general not capable of affecting trade between Member States and so fall outside the scope of the rules on competition. However, any such thought is misconceived because the requirement that there be an effect on trade between Member States will almost certainly be fulfilled, for the reasons stated below. In this regard, it will be recalled that the Commission does not have to show that the restriction on competition created by an agreement between undertakings from the same Member State actually affects trade between Member States in order to bring the agreement within article 85(1); it is sufficient for this purpose to show a potential effect on trade between Member States.

It is submitted that the requirement of an effect on trade between Member States will certainly be fulfilled by domestic banking agreements to which the local subsidiaries or branches of foreign banks are parties. It will also be fulfilled in the case of agreements which concern transfers to and from abroad (for example, commissions on bank transfers and on the collection of cheques) and the financing of external trade (for example documentary credits, export credits and bankers' acceptances). It is also suggested that the position is the same in relation to those banking agreements, much more frequent, which concern the provision of services to both domestic customers and customers resident in other Member States alike.[1] In 1973, the Commission stated that the standard "general terms" recommended by one national banking organisation were subject to the rules on competition because they were applied by its members to all their customers, whether nationals or foreigners.[2]

Also, the Court of Justice has on many occasions held that domestic price-fixing agreements for the whole of the territory of a Member State are, by their very nature,

---

1. In practice, this will almost always be the case for a medium-sized bank and will always be the case for a large bank. Indeed, for a provision of services on a cross-border basis by a bank in Member State A to take place in Member State B it is sufficient that a customer resident in Member State B opens, even of his own initiative and by correspondence, an account with the bank in Member State A: see Part One, above.

2. Second Report on Competition Policy, 1973, published 1974, point 52. The Commission adopted the same view, *inter alia*, in its decision to grant an exemption, on the basis of art. 85(3), to the *Nuovo CEGAM* agreement between Italian insurers, OJ L99/29 of 11 April 1984. The Commission held that the agreement was liable to affect trade between Member States in that the rules of the Nuovo CEGAM Association were applicable to risks situated abroad as well as on Italian territory; affected the coinsurance operations of insurance companies outside Italy; and affected reinsurers outside Italy by preventing members from choosing reinsurers other than those with which the Association was under contract and by imposing contractual restrictions on the latter's activity on the market.

capable of consolidating the isolation of the domestic market from other markets and so capable of hindering the economic integration desired by the Treaty and, at the same time, ensuring that national production is protected. It will be recalled that the Court of Justice in *Züchner* stated unequivocally that the concept of "trade" used in article 85(1) has a wide scope which includes monetary transactions.[3]

The considerations which emerge from that case-law are applicable by analogy to banking agreements which regulate, at the national level, the cost of customer services, including the cost of credit transactions and the interest payable on deposits. In particular, it is considered beyond serious argument that domestic banking agreements on interest rates are capable of affecting the location of lending and borrowing operations within the EC and, accordingly, affect the provision of banking services between Member States. This is especially the case after the coming into force on 1 July 1990 of the 1988 Council Directive which has fully liberalised movements of capital and payments throughout the Community, including movements of private savings.[4] Indeed, pursuant to article 61(2) of the Treaty, the liberalisation of banking services connected with movements of capital is required to be effected in step with the progressive liberalisation of movement of capital.

As a result, the removal as from 1 July 1990 by the 1988 Directive on the restrictions on movements of capital and payments until then permitted by Community law, which restrictions in practice primarily concerned the movement of private savings, has led concomitantly to the full liberalisation of banking services connected with private savings such as, for example, the opening of a savings account by a resident of one Member State on the books of a bank established in another Member State. A good illustration of the direct impact of agreements on credit interest rates on the movement of private savings across national borders and hence on the provision of banking services connected with such savings was described as follows by the Belgian Banking Commission[5]:

In principle, the considerations for establishing the rates of interest on deposits in Belgian francs are the same both in Belgium and abroad. However, technical factors falsify any comparison . . . [for example] foreign intermediaries are not bound by the concerted policy on credit interest rates. In particular, they can freely fix the level of deposits above which rates close to the money market rates may be paid and below which only the agreed rates, considerably lower than the money market rates, can be paid. In these circumstances, foreign credit institutions are able to offer depositors higher rates of interest than can be offered by credit institutions in Belgium. This distortion . . . has resulted in large movements of funds towards banks domiciled in neighbouring countries, in particular towards the Grand Duchy of Luxembourg and The Netherlands . . . Belgian francs deposited with foreign credit intermediaries in fact find their way back to the domestic credit institutions. Most frequently, foreign banks which take the deposits are content to place these assets with banking institutions in Belgium (at rates of interest applicable to interbank deposits) . . .

In general, the decisions taken by the Commission and the positions adopted by it reflect the approach suggested above. However, it is necessary to recall that, in the application to the banking field of the condition that there be an effect on trade between

---

3. [1981] ECR 2021, at p. 2032, point 18.

4. Council Directive 88/361/EEC of 24 June 1988 for the implementation of art. 67 of the Treaty, OJ L178/5 of 8 July 1988, considered in Part Four above.

5. Annual Report 1979–1980 of the Belgian Commission Bancaire, pp. 46–48 (our translation). Even before the entry into force of the Capital Movements Directive, the free movement of private savings out of Belgium was unhindered by any foreign exchange regulations (except for the existence of a two-tier foreign exchange market).

Member States, the Commission's approach has differed from that which emerges from the case-law of the Court of Justice and from the Commission's own case-law in fields other than that of financial services. These differences arise in the area of agreements viewed by the Commission as being of minor importance.

2. THE BANCOMAT AGREEMENT BETWEEN ITALIAN BANKS

25.2 In its decision of 12 December 1986 regarding the Italian Bankers' Association (considered at more length below), the Commission took the view that the Bancomat agreement, being one of the agreements notified by the Italian Bankers' Association, could be granted a negative clearance (ie, was not subject to article 85(1) because it did not affect, in the Commission's view, trade between Member States to any appreciable degree).[6] The Bancomat agreement determines the criteria for the creation in Italy of a system of 24-hour automated teller machines. It provides for certain technical harmonisation as well as for uniform interbank administration of the system (value dates; commissions for each transaction and the apportionment of these commissions between the relevant banks, etc.). The agreement also involves an undertaking on the part of its members not to participate in other organisations of a similar nature in Italy. As commented at the time, "it is of considerable surprise that the inclusion of this provision did not preclude the grant of a negative clearance".[7]

The Commission justified its position by claiming that this exclusivity clause "does not have an appreciable effect on trade between Member States taking into account the fact that possible creation of a competing network in Italy is at present hardly likely so that the restriction has no real practical effect".[8] Yet, as observed at the time, "this begs the question that if the restriction was of no practical effect, then why was it maintained in the agreement?"[9] In any event, is the fact that it is hardly likely that a competing system would emerge not in itself the result of the prohibition imposed on the banks to join such a competing system in the first place?

It is submitted that the Commission's position is hard to reconcile with the doubts later expressed by certain Commission officials, be it in a private capacity, in respect of exclusivity clauses barring banks entering into a contract with one card issuer from entering into a contract with other card issuers[10] and, more generally, with the well-publicised efforts later undertaken by the Commission to promote an open market in the Community for the credit and debit card systems.[11]

6. Decision 87/103, OJ L43/51 of 13 February 1987.
7. M. Dassesse, "EEC Competition law affecting banking: Recent developments and future prospects" [1988] 3 JIBL 105, at p. 110.
8. See p. 57, at §37.
9. M. Dassesse, "EEC Competition law affecting banking: Recent developments and future prospects" [1988] 3 JIBL, 105, at p. 110.
10. H. Salmon, "Payment cards and European competition law . . . " [1990] 1 JIBL 25, at p. 31: "A card issuer . . . might be tempted to ask banks entering into a contract with it to agree not to enter into a contract with other card issuers . . . There is no doubt that European competition law would consider that this constituted a restriction of competition which could not be allowed except if it were clearly justified . . ."
11. See communication of the Commission to the Council, "Europe could play an ace: the new payment cards" of 12 January 1987, Com. 87-754-final; also Recommendation of the Commission of 8 December 1987 on a European Code of Conduct relating to electronic payments, OJ L365/77 of 24 December 1987. See also the Commission's discussion paper "Making payments in the internal market", Com. 90-447-final, 26 September 1990; and the Commission's Working Document "Easier cross-border payments: Breaking down the barriers" SEC(92)621 final of 27 March 1992.

It is suggested that the Commission would be unlikely, in view of these later developments, to grant a negative clearance to an agreement along the lines of the Italian banks Bancomat agreement if it was notified to it today.

3. AGREEMENTS CONCERNING MINIMUM CHARGES FOR SAFE RENTAL AND FOR SAFE-KEEPING SERVICES FOR SECURITIES

25.3 Agreements concerning minimum charges for safe rental and for safe-keeping services for securities were notified to the Commission by the Italian Bankers' Association and by the Dutch Bankers' Association. As pointed out by the Commission itself, these agreements relate directly to conditions to be applied by banks to their customers throughout, respectively, Italy and the Netherlands. They restrict, or even eliminate, the freedom of signatory banks to fix charges. Yet, in both its decision concerning the Italian Bankers' Association[12] and its decision concerning the Dutch Bankers' Association,[13] both considered at more length below, the Commission took the view that these agreements did not come within the ambit of article 85(1) because they did not affect trade between Member States to any appreciable degree.

In the Italian Bankers Association's decision, the Commission's arguments in favour of the grant of negative clearance were as follows[14]:

Although the agreements relate directly to the charges payable by customers and trade may theoretically be affected, the very object of the service is such that the effect cannot be appreciable.

The very fact of depositing articles or securities in a safe or in safe custody is an indication that their owner does not intend to use them for trade; moreover, it is unlikely given Italy's geographical situation, that trade in such services between Italy and the other Member States will develop to any appreciable extent.

In the Dutch Bankers' Association's decision, the justification for the granting of a negative clearance was virtually identical[15]:

These provisions do not appreciably affect trade between Member States since the service has, by its nature, little or no connection with trade between Member States in goods or servics, and since according to the information provided by the parties concerned, insignificant use is made of it by consumers from other Member States. Furthermore, branches of banks from other Member States established in The Netherlands (branches which form an integral part of such banks and which are therefore directly involved in trade in services between Member States) hardly ever offer safes for hire.

While, in all probability, the agreements concerned at present only affect a limited number of individuals (although this may increase in years to come as a result of the liberalisation of capital movements, including those connected with the buying of securities, since the entry into force on 1 July 1990 of the Capital Movements Directive[16]), the position is clearly different when it comes to companies of one Member State holding shares or shares certificates in companies incorporated in other Member States and entrusting these "articles" in safe custody to a local bank.

12. Decision of 12 December 1986, no. 87/103, OJ L43/51 of 13 February 1987.
13. Decision of 19 July 1989, no. 89/112, OJ L253/1 of 30 August 1989.
14. Points 39 and 40.
15. Point 58.
16. Council Directive 88/361/EEC of 24 June 1988 for the implementation of art. 67 of the Treaty, OJ L178/5 of 8 July 1988.

More fundamentally, as a matter of law, the justification of the Commission's decisions is unsatisfactory. As pointed out at the time, the idea that the deposit of articles in a safe or in safe custody in a bank precludes their use in intra-Community trade seems somewhat unrealistic. In line with banking practice, if a foreign institution buys securities in Italy, it is quite likely that it would leave them in the safe custody of an Italian bank. This, moreover, would be quite common where the particular national rules made any transfer of national securities abroad subject to prior authorisation.[17] Additionally, it is submitted that the Commission's line of argument confuses the service provided (safe custody services) and the subject matter of the services (the securities given in safe custody to the bank). Indeed, it is irrelevant, in order to determine whether cartel agreements on safe custody services appreciably affect the trade between Member States in respect of such services, to take into account the fact that the subject matter of these services is unlikely to be used for trade.

Finally, the suggestion that "depositing ... securities ... in safe custody is an indication that their owner does not intend to use them for trade" ignores the possibility that the owner may authorise the bank to use his securities for bond lending activities while keeping them in safe custody. Such activities, however, were less frequent at the time the Italian banks' decision was taken than they are nowadays.

---

17. M. Dassesse, "EEC Competition law: Recent developments and future prospects" [1988] 3 JIBL 105, at p. 111.

CHAPTER 26

RESTRICTIONS ON ACCESS TO THE BANKING SECTOR AND TO FINANCIAL MARKETS: THE SARABEX CASE

26.1 In some Member States, affiliation to a professional organisation of national banks is a prerequisite of entry into the banking sector. In other countries, there is unrestricted entry to the banking sector subject, of course, to registration with the competent supervisory authorities, but participation in certain banking operations, and particularly access to certain financial markets, is confined to members of a professional association, frequently supported by the domestic monetary authorities.

Generally, the requirement of a mandatory affiliation to a professional organisation in order to enter the banking sector or to operate in a given financial market is justified by the need to keep out persons who lack the required financial or professional standing. This aspect of "private" regulation of the banking profession and financial markets undoubtedly meets such need or rather, undoubtedly met such need, at least in certain Member States, until the supervision of credit institutions, including the vetting of their senior managers and main shareholders by the competent supervisory authorities, was introduced on a (minimum) uniform basis throughout the Community as a result of the Second Banking Directive.[1]

26.2 On occasions, however, such requirements have been criticised as being in conflict with EC law in that they result in the creation of a cartel whereby potential competitors in a market may be excluded from that market by being refused membership of the relevant professional organisation. This was the precise cause of the *Sarabex* case, which involved the illegality of "private" restrictions on access to the banking sector and financial markets. The case centred upon the rules governing the operation of the London foreign exchange market. It brought into question the compatibility with the rules on competition of the methods of control of financial markets and institutions in the City of London, which were traditionally based upon consensus and self-regulation under the general supervision of the Bank of England.

Sarabex Limited was a Middle Eastern money-broker with a London branch which at the time dealt in non-scheduled currencies in the London foreign exchange market and which wished to trade in the so-called scheduled currencies (mainly the currencies of Western Europe, North America and Japan). Sarabex complained to the Commission that the conditions of entry to the London foreign exchange broking market prevented it from competing in the scheduled currencies with other brokers already established in that market. Under the rules as they existed, only members of the Foreign Exchange and Currency Deposit Brokers' Association (FECDBA) were allowed to trade in the scheduled currencies. In 1978, there were 16 money-brokers who were members of

---

1. See Part Two, above.

FECDBA.[2] Under arrangements reached under the auspices of the Bank of England between the British Bankers' Association (BBA) and FECDBA, authorised banks using services provided by one or more of the 16 brokers in FECDBA were forbidden to use the services of non-member brokers. This exclusive agreement was notified to the banks by circular in 1967 and reiterated and clarified by a BBA circular in 1975. Also, applicants for FECDBA membership required sponsorship by at least six authorised banks.

Sarabex complained to the Commission in 1978 that the combination of these two rules had the effect of denying entry to FECDBA to new applicants[3]: the authorised banks could never gain sufficient experience of an applicant upon which to base their sponsorship because they were prohibited from using the applicant's services as long as he was not a FECDBA member. Other FECDBA rules prohibited its members from charging rates of commission different from the agreed rates which on average were considerably higher in London than in Frankfurt, Paris or Zurich.[4]

Following discussions with the Commission, the Bank of England agreed to modify the system for admitting broking houses to both the foreign exchange and currency deposit markets and introduced a new structure for commission rates.[5] Under the new rules, an element of exclusivity remained in that, as before, the authorised banks had to use the services of broking houses "recognised" by the Bank of England. However, recognised status under the new rules was granted directly by the Bank of England instead of by FECDBA, under the Bank of England's indirect supervision, as was previously the case. Recognition itself continued to entail an application for membership of FECDBA, which amongst other things became responsible for the day-to-day conduct of the recognised brokers and the investigation of complaints concerning them. Applicants were given the right to be accorded FECDBA membership if both they and the personnel employed by them to conduct annual trading meet certain objective criteria.

In case of refusal of an application for recognition by the Bank of England, a right of appeal was introduced to the Chairman of the Appeals Committee of the City Panel on Mergers and Take Overs.

26.3 The former fixed commission rates have in general become maximum rates. The new structure for commissions has both a maximum and minimum rate for dealings in each currency and so, to quote the Commission, "provides the possibility for competition between broking firms, thereby benefiting those actually engaged in currency transactions".[6] It was made clear by the Commission at the time that its treatment of Sarabex's complaint was intended to state the principle[7]:

that there [should be] no confusion between market regulation by the authorities and regulation by the market participants themselves, whether by way of an agreement or through an association. In the latter case, any action taken by enterprises to restrict competition which may affect interstate trade would come within the scope of the competition rules of the EEC Treaty.

---

2. Eighth Report on Competition Policy, 1978, published 1979, point 36.
3. The question whether Sarabex Ltd, being a branch of a third country institution, had a sufficient interest to pursue such a claim, that is, to rely upon directly applicable provisions of the Treaty, was apparently not raised. See further Part Eight.
4. *Ibid.*
5. *Ibid.*
6. *Ibid.*
7. Speech made by Commissioner Andriessen at a banking conference organised on 30 November and 1 December 1981, stencilled text, p. 10. A summary of the speech was published in *Agence Europe*, Bulletin 3264 (new series) of 5 December 1981.

26.4 The *Sarabex* case and its outcome had important implications for the City of London. It raised the broader question of the compatibility with the rules on competition of the self-regulatory methods commonly used to control London financial markets and institutions. In particular, it had direct relevance for the system of admission and the system of commissions in force in the London Commodity Markets (London Sugar Futures Market; London Cocoa Terminal Market Association Ltd; Coffee Terminal Market Association of London; London Rubber Terminal Market Association Ltd). Following the Commission's intervention, the original Rules and Regulations, as notified to the Commission, were modified in line with the principles already laid down in *Sarabex*.[8]

More recently, the principles laid down in *Sarabex* have been reiterated on two occasions by the Commission. First, when laying down the principles to be observed in terms of membership of payment clearing systems[9] in connection with its recent initiative to facilitate cross-border payments in the Community. Second, when reviewing the rules of the Association of International Bond Dealers, now called the International Securities Markets Association, following their notification to the Commission[10] by the Association in order to seek confirmation of their compatibility with the rules on competition.

---

8. See Fifteenth Report on Competition Policy, 1985, published 1986, point 70.

9. Considered in Chap. 27 below, at para. 27.52. The *Sarabex* principles were also recalled recently by Sir Leon Brittan, Vice-President of the Commission responsible for competition policy and financial institutions, in a lecture on "Competition in Financial Services" delivered at the Centre for European Policy Studies in Brussels on 16 January 1992: see stencilled text, p. 8. See also G. Vernimmen, "Le respect des règles de concurrence dans les services bancaires", ECU (Brussels) (1993), vol. 24/III p. 14, at p. 16.

10. See Chap. 29, below.

CHAPTER 27

BANKING AGREEMENTS WHICH RESTRICT COMPETITION BETWEEN UNDERTAKINGS—THE COMMISSION'S CASE-LAW TO DATE

1. THE "GENERAL TERMS" OF BANKS

27.1 In 1973, the Commission investigated a case concerning the standard "general terms" recommended by one national banking organisation and applied by its members to their customers, whether nationals or foreigners. The association of banks concerned, although challenging the principle of the applicability of article 85 of the Treaty to the banking sector, agreed to amend those clauses in the general terms which, in the original version, were unfavourable, in the Commission's opinion, to the users. The Commission thereupon discontinued the procedure and a formal decision became unnecessary.[1]

In 1973, the Commission was considering the compatibility of the standard general terms of banks with the rules on competition in the context of article 85 alone. However, in view of the subsequent development of Community law and subsequent decisions taken by the Commission, it is pertinent to ask whether, in certain circumstances, the application by banks in a particular Member State to their customers, whether nationals or foreigners, of standard terms would not now constitute an abuse of a dominant position within article 86(a) of the EC Treaty, whereby an abuse may consist in "directly or indirectly imposing . . . unfair trading conditions". The same question arises in respect of the "general regulations" for granting credit facilities operated by banks, certain of whose provisions are often standardised in a given country. In 1992, two Italian courts requested the Court of Justice to give a preliminary ruling concerning the compatibility with the Treaty of regulations and practices whereby banks of a Member State make general use in their relations with customers of contractual arrangements consistent with a measure adopted by all or a significant proportion of such institutions and unilaterally laid down by the relevant professional or trade association.[2] The request of the Italian courts for a preliminary ruling reportedly concerns the compatibility of the measures in question with article 85, *and* article 86.

1. Second Report on Competition Policy, 1972, published 1973, point 52. We understand that the national banking organisation concerned was the Dutch Bankers' Association. The position of the Commission in that case is therefore all the more difficult to reconcile with its latest decision of 19 July 1989, considered below, in as far as such decision states that it does not apply, *inter alia*, to "the general terms and conditions of banking recommended by the 'Dutch Bankers' Association' to its members (as) the Commission reserves its position on such provisions".

2. Case C–79/92 *Credito Italiano* v. *G. Conte*, reference for a preliminary ruling by the Tribunale di Genova, OJ C113/6 of 1 May 1992 and case C–266/92 *G. Semini* v. *Cassa di Risparmio di Alessandria*, reference for a preliminary ruling by the Tribunale di Alessandria, OJ C189/10 of 28 July 1992 (later withdrawn at the parties' request). The association in question in the case is the Italian Bankers' Association. Note also, in the insurance sector, the agreement reportedly made by insurance companies in the Netherlands

2. AGREEMENTS FIXING MINIMUM OR UNIFORM COMMISSION RATES OR UNIFORM VALUE DATES

1. The position before Züchner

27.2 In 1979, the Commission made known the results of an investigation into the compatibility with the rules on competition of the minimum rates of commission uniformly applied in Belgium for cashing travellers' cheques denominated in foreign currencies and in France for cashing Eurocheques drawn on foreign banks.[3] In both cases the Commission, whose investigations resulted from a number of Written Questions in the European Parliament about the relatively high rates of commission applied, indicated that these minimum rates were justified by the high cost to the banks of recovering the cheques in question. However, the Commission expressed no view on the supposed necessity of fixing the minimum rates of commission to be charged on a uniform basis for all the banks concerned.[4]

In *Züchner*, the Court of Justice rejected by implication the argument that the fixing of minimum commissions on a uniform basis is justified under Community law by the relatively high cost to the banks of the transaction in question. The contention of the Bayerische Vereinsbank that[5] "the charge uniformly levied in respect of every transfer above a certain amount represents only a partial contribution towards the total cost of the transfers usually effected" was rejected by the Court of Justice in the following terms[6]:

The fact that the charge in question is justified by the costs involved in all transfers abroad normally effected by banks on behalf of their customers, and that it therefore represents partial reimbursement of such costs, debited uniformly to all those who make use of such service, does not exclude the possibility that parallel conduct in that sphere may, regardless of the motive, result in co-ordination between banks which amounts to a concerted practice within the meaning of Article 85 of the Treaty.

2. The Commission's decisions since Züchner

27.3 As recalled earlier, following the *Züchner* case, the various national banking associations, at the urging of the Commission, formally recognised that EC competition law was applicable to the banking sector and notified to the Commission the agreements and concerted practices which they had not notified previously, and which they wished to keep in force. These notifications took place against the background of the investigation, previously announced by the Commission, following the *Züchner* case, conducted by the Commission in the banking field. The purpose of that investigation was directed at agreements involving commission charged by banks for services rendered (thus excluding agreements on rates of interest, a question which is considered separately later). The Commission's new approach led to the decisions examined below, which represents the first concrete results in the Commission's new approach to the application of article 85 to the banking sector. However, as shall be

not to include the risk of earthquake in their insurance policies, see [Written] Question 1394/92 of MEP A. Metten of 4 June 1992, EP Bulletin, 14 June 1992.

3. Eighth Report on Competition Policy, 1978, published 1979, point 34.

4. See M. Dassesse and S. Isaacs, "UK Implementation of European Banking Law", *Financial Times European Law Letter*, 5 July 1981.

5. [1981] ECR 2021, at p. 2032, point 16.

6. *Ibid.*, point 17.

seen, these decisions address, in effect, ancillary issues, in that they deal with agreements other than those relating to rates of interest, and thus do not deal with the activities that traditionally lie at the heart of the banking industry.

The Eurocheque "package deal agreement" decision of 10 December 1984 and its subsequent review

27.4 The basic aim of the Eurocheque system may be described thus: to provide its users with a means of payment from an affiliated bank on the presentation of a cheque and cheque guarantee card in both their country of origin and abroad. Further, it allows users equally to make purchases abroad directly from the trading sector, which purchases will be covered by the cheque guarantee card. The proper functioning of the system naturally presupposes a multilateral agreement among the various affiliated banks insofar as conditions of payment of cheques at bank counters are concerned as well as the reimbursement to the bank which has cashed the cheque abroad (the payee bank) by the bank where the customer account is held (drawee/issuing bank). The payment by the payee bank may be made, in cash, to the user travelling abroad on the presentation of a Eurocheque or to a trader to whom the user has passed the cheque.

27.5 In 1980, the Eurocheque Community (operating through the auspices of the Eurocheque International Secretariat,[7] based in Brussels and encompassing thousands of banking institutions as its members) concluded the so-called "package deal" agreement. The agreement was entered into for an initial period of five years, with effect from 1 May 1981, with automatic renewals thereafter for successive periods of 12 months. The aim of the agreement was to establish new methods of payment and reimbursement of Eurocheques which were to be called Uniform Eurocheques. The agreement was notified to the Commission on 7 July 1982 (therefore after the *Züchner* judgment of July 1981) even though, as was noted, its provisions had been in force since 1 May 1981. The package deal agreement contains various provisions aimed at the harmonisation of the conditions of payment of Eurocheques and the facilitation of the international clearing of such cheques. They were later supplemented by an agreement relating to automatic cash dispensers. These provisions are of a technical nature and will not be dealt with here. The agreement as notified provided, on the one hand, for a uniform commission of 1·25% of the amount of the cheque, later increased to 1·6% with no minimum, which applied to all uniform Eurocheques paid abroad by an affiliated bank.[8] This commission is not to be deducted from the value of the cheque by the payee bank and therefore difficulties are avoided *vis-à-vis* cheques drawn abroad in favour of the trading sector. The commission is debited to the customer's account by the drawee bank (also referred to as the issuing bank) which transfers this amount to the payee bank through the intermediary of an international clearing centre. The expenses incurred by these international clearing centres (one for each country) are also covered

7. Presently Eurocheque International Co-operative Company. The capital of the company, amounting to 1,800,000 BF, consists of 18 shares each of 100,000 BF subscribed by the national banking associations (or a body close to them) of the 18 countries of the Eurocheque Community. See *Eurocheque Helsinki agreement* decision, referred to below, at point 7.

8. The recent Commission decision on the *Eurocheque Helsinki agreement*, considered below, indicates that, contrary to the Commission's expectation, the "maximum rate only" agreed under the package deal agreement turned out to coincide with a minimum commission as a result of amendments made in 1987 to the original agreement. See the *Eurocheque Helsinki agreement* decision, at points 18 and 22.

by a commission fixed in a uniform manner, but this time individually by each country. This commission is also debited to the customer's account by the drawee bank.

27.6 By its decision of 10 December 1984, the Commission decided that the agreement fell under the prohibition of article 85(1). However, it granted it an exemption for five years, renewable thereafter, from the prohibition on the basis of article 85(3). The exemption was granted with effect from the date of notification (7 July 1982) for an initial period which coincided with the initial duration of the agreement, that is until 30 April 1986. The only condition imposed, by virtue of this decision, was the obligation on banks, insofar as they had not already done so, to inform their customers in exact detail of any costs which could arise as a result of their use of Eurocheques abroad. The Commission, as is usual in such cases, also required Eurocheque International to inform it immediately of any amendment made to the agreement which had been notified to it.

Various considerations arising from this decision merit special attention, in particular in the light of the other decisions granting exemptions which were later taken by the Commission in respect of agreements on bank charges and commission (discussed in detail below).

THE INAPPLICABILITY OF ARTICLE 90(2)

27.7 It appears from the terms of the decision that those persons making the notification had claimed that article 90(2) of the Treaty was applicable (perhaps without too much conviction given the position of the Court in the *Züchner* judgment). This contention was rejected by the Commission in the following terms[9]:

1. The system constitutes a private initiative.
2. The members of the system were not, at any time, entrusted with the operation of a service of general economic interest by a measure adopted by the public authorities.
3. This view cannot be affected by the fact that the system operates with the knowledge and indeed the express approval of the competent authorities in the countries concerned, nor by the fact that in some countries there has been an explicit legal act in favour of the system or part of it.

The Commission went on to state[10]:

Even if the Eurocheque system and its adherents had been entrusted . . . by a group of national public authorities [to put at the disposal of its users an international means of payment] . . . the application of the Community's competition rules to such credit institutions could not, in any way, obstruct the fulfilment of that hypothetical special assignment.

INDISPENSABLE RESTRICTIONS ON COMPETITION PROVIDED FOR IN THE AGREEMENT

27.8 As regards the payment of commission, the Commission made the following points[11]:

When such a service [ie encashment by a bank of a cheque drawn on a bank of another Member State] is provided collectively by all the banks in one country to the customers of banks in other countries, it is indispensable that the terms and conditions for accepting and clearing the cheques concerned be determined in common between the issuing and accepting institutions of the various centres involved.

Within the framework of such an agreement, the common and uniform determination of the

9. Point 29.
10. Point 30.
11. Points 39 and 40.

remuneration for this service . . . is inherent in, and ancillary to, the co-operation between the banks . . . which enables the acceptance and international clearing of cheques drawn abroad. Variations in commissions from one bank to another would imply bilateral negotiations between the 15,000 banks which are parties to the scheme so that each accepting bank (payee bank) may agree with each issuing bank (drawee bank) the remuneration it wishes to receive. Any centralised clearing would thus be made impossible and the cost of processing Eurocheques would substantially increase.

Finally, the Commission stressed that[12]:

This decision does not cover any national agreements between banks . . . whose aim would be to fix the level of commission that individual issuing banks in the country concerned should charge to their customers. National agreements or decisions of that type, which would eliminate residual competition between institutions issuing uniform Eurocheques, could not, in any circumstances, be regarded as indispensable within the meaning of Article 85(3) of the Treaty.

DISTINCTION BETWEEN RELATIONS AMONGST BANKS AND RELATIONS WITH CUSTOMERS

27.9 When justifying its decision to hold article 85(3) applicable in this case, the Commission makes a very fine distinction between, on the one hand, restrictions on competition present in the provisions dealing with relations between banks which are parties to the agreement in the different Member States and, on the other hand, restrictions on competition linking the banks of a particular Member State as regards the rate of remuneration for the costs of the service which has to be recovered from the customer. Restrictions of the first kind are deemed to arise inevitably as a result of the relevant degree of co-operation required to attain the objectives of the agreement. Restrictions of the second kind, to return to the terms of the *Eurocheque* decision,[13] could not, in any circumstances, be regarded as indispensable within the meaning of article 85(3) of the Treaty.

The prohibition on restrictions of competition in the bank's relations with its customers—restrictions which do not appear in the package deal agreement—is explained more fully by paragraphs 42 and 43 of the decision:

42. [The package deal agreement] does not govern relations between the drawee banks and their customers. Scope for competition therefore remains in the relations between each issuing institution and its customers. The extent to which commissions are passed on to customers is left to the discretion of the drawee banks. The commissions may be fixed at a rate higher or lower than that actually paid by the drawee bank via its national clearing centre [to the national clearing centre of] the payee bank abroad. In theory, the drawee bank could decide not to make any charge to the customer at all.

43. However, the above assessment applies only if [the package deal agreement] is not supplemented by national agreements . . . governing relations between banks and their customers on the question of commissions. The customer must be free to approach the credit institution of his choice to open an account and to obtain a cheque book. This freedom of choice of the customer would be illusory if all credit institutions in the same country provided the same service at the same price.

Thus, to quote the words of a member of the Commission's competition service, writing in a private capacity:

in the *Eurocheque* decision, the Commission made an important distinction as regards banking commissions between banks and the relationship banks have with their clients, [a distinction which was] taken up again in other decisions taken in the banking sector and which can be

12. Point 40.
13. *Ibid.*

transposed equally to the payment card sector. As regards interbank relationships, the Commission indicated that it could allow—and this is what it did in the *Eurocheque* case—agreements on interbank commissions (because variable commissions from one bank to another would have implied bilateral negotiations between thousands of banks participating in the system) but on condition that such interbank commissions (which were, in the present case, not fixed commissions but maxima, which already left a margin for competition) would not obligatorily revert to the clients. In effect, if that were the case, such interbank commissions would play the role of minimum commissions, applicable to customers. The Commission stated (in its *Eurocheque* decision) that it would not allow such agreements on banking commissions charged to customers and that these were of a sort which was forbidden by Article 85.

The very fact of admitting or allowing agreements on interbank commissions, although these were only maxima, already constituted an innovation on the part of the Commission, because, this was to allow, for the first time, the possibility of agreements on prices for services.

27.10 With the benefit of hindsight, it would appear that the Commission was overly optimistic in assuming that maximum commissions agreed as between banks would not, as a matter of course, "play the role of minimum commissions applicable to customers"[14] and accepted too easily the argument that agreements on maximum commissions amongst banks were necessary to avoid "bilateral negotiations between thousands of banks participating in the system".[15] This, in any event, appears to be borne out by the difficulties which have to date surrounded the review of the *Eurocheque* decision considered hereafter and by the Commission's adoption on 25 March 1992 of a decision imposing a fine on both Eurocheque International and the Groupement des Cartes Bancaires CB in respect of the so-called *Eurocheque Helsinki agreement* relating to the conditions of payment of Eurocheques in France.[16]

At the time of writing, the review of Eurocheque's application for the renewal of the exemption granted in 1984 is still pending[17] and led in 1990 to the Commission's indicating in a press release to the public that it had sent a statement of objections (*communication de griefs*) to Eurocheque in respect of a revised package deal agreement notified to the Commission.[18] According to the Commission's press release,[19] which in effect echoes a number of complaints addressed to the Commission in the European Parliament regarding the application of the Eurocheque agreement,[20] there are five aspects of the agreement which the Commission believes raise serious

14. H. Salmon "Payment Cards and European Competition Law: an attempt at evaluation" [1990] 1 JIBL 25, at p. 26.

15. *Ibid.*

16. OJ L95/50 of 9 April 1992.

17. The renewal concerns a somewhat modified version of the package deal agreement which was notified to the Commission in 1987. See the *Eurocheque Helsinki agreement* decision, considered at para. 27.34, below, at points 17 and 18, and the Commission press release of September 1990 referred to in fn. 19, below.

18. The renewal, still pending, of the 1984 *Eurocheque* decision should not be confused with the *Eurocheque* decision of 19 December 1988, OJ L36/1 dated 8 February 1989, dealing with the Eurocheque agreements notified to the Commission regarding the production and "finition" of Eurocheques and Eurocards. These agreements, in large part justified by the need for security, benefited from a negative clearance granted by the Commission (for the agreements relating to the production of the cards and cheques) and from the grant of an exemption by the Commission under art. 85(3) (for the agreements relating to the finition of the cheques and cards). The agreements relating to the finition of the cheques and cards were nevertheless amended in certain respects at the Commission's request, in order to remove the possibility of any distortion of competition at the level of the designation of the undertakings made responsible for the finition by the national Eurocheque associations. For more detail, see the Eighteenth General Report on Competition Policy, 1987, published 1988.

19. Commission press release of September 1990, No. 90/765. See also Commission Report to the European Parliament on the application of Community law in 1990.

20. Written Questions 2681/85 of Mr. Roelants du Vivier, OJ C190/25 of 28 July 1986; 865/86 of Mrs. Van Hemeldonck, OJ C60/23 of 9 March 1987; 423/87 of Mr. Dido, OJ C23/33 of 28 January 1988. See also written

doubts about the system and which have not been rectified despite Commission warnings.

The first objection is that too little information is given to customers issuing Eurocheques abroad on the various components of the charges they face. The second objection concerns the modification to the terms and conditions of the interbank commission (paid by the issuer's bank to the foreign bank) which had been exempted in 1984. In particular, Eurocheque is criticised for having applied a minimum commission since 1988. The same problem arises for the interbank commission which is applied to cash withdrawals abroad with the Eurocheque card in ATMs (Automated Teller Machines) the terms and conditions of which were notified to the Commission in 1986. The third objection lies in the fact that two changes to the system exempted in 1984 have been made. On the one hand, the maximum rate of interbank commission is always applied. On the other hand, this interbank commission is systematically charged to the customers.[21] The fourth objection concerns the maximum clearing amount (approximately 340 ECU). Its relatively low level is inconvenient for the customer, since above this amount the Eurocheque is not cleared in the Eurocheque clearing system but processed as an international transfer, usually subject to high commission. The fifth and somewhat different objection concerns the way Eurocheques are accepted in the retail sector in France. This has since led to the Commission's *Eurocheque Helsinki agreement* decision.[22] The Commission has, however, already indicated, as a result of its findings and subsequent proceedings leading to that decision, that it was adamant, as a condition for renewing the exemption of the original package deal agreement, that "Eurocheque clearly state in the so-called 'package deal' agreement . . . that the payee should in principle receive the full amount of the value of Eurocheques".[23] The reason for this determination is that this principle, which the Commission viewed as essential when granting the initial exemption, was in effect set aside as a result of the *Eurocheque Helsinki agreement* in the case of Eurocheques drawn by non-French account holders and presented to French banks for payment.[24] The inordinate—but understandable—delay in bringing the review proceedings to a conclusion means that the whole matter may in any event have to be looked at again soon from a different perspective. Indeed, the Commission has since been apprised of the so-called Europay International project, a grouping of Eurocard and Eurocheque International. Having taken the view that the project does not amount to a "concentration" within the meaning of the Merger Control Regulation, the Commission has further examined it with regard to its compatibility with article 85.

Question 1535/85 of Mr. Dankaert of 17 September 1985, OJ C62/8 of 17 March 1986, at point 3; 2711/85 of Mr. Patterson, of 10 February 1986, OJ C190/25 of 28 July 1986.

21. The Commission will in all likelihood require amendment of these provisions as a condition for renewal of the exemption. This is made clear by the fact that the Commission has since required the deletion of similar provisions during its review of the Eufiserv project (multilateral agreement of the interoperability of the European savings banks' automated teller machines) discussed at para. 28.3, below.

22. OJ L95/50 of 9 April 1992. See para. 27.34, below.

23. See the answer given by Sir Leon Brittan to Written Question 80/91 of MEP Jepsen.

24. As noted by the Commission in its later decision on the *Eurocheque Helsinki agreement* (point 55) "it is not at all clear why a multinational interbank agreement [that is, the package deal agreement] would have been necessary if it had been possible for the paying bank to collect commission [from the holder] on foreign Eurocheques remitted to it for payment. The package deal agreement was justified precisely because the paying bank received no remuneration from the remitter of the Eurocheque but rather received a commission from the issuing bank".

27.11 It is submitted that this press release, reflects to a large extent the more critical approach which the Commission has adopted since the granting of the 1984 Eurocheque exemption towards agreements on interbank commissions. This new approach has been evidenced in the decisions regarding the various national banking associations reviewed below, as well as by various Commission pronouncements indicating that it was looking attentively at agreements on commissions etc. in the field of payment cards.[25]

Italian Bankers' Association decision of 12 September 1986[26]

27.12 The Italian Bankers' Association (ABI) is a non-profit-making association comprising practically all of the credit institutions operating in Italy (banks, savings banks, finance and leasing companies). As a result of the various enquiries into national banking agreements conducted by the Commission after the *Züchner* case, the ABI notified to the Commission in October 1984 almost 20 agreements and recommendations. These agreements and recommendations included the following:

1. agreements concerning relations between banks;
2. agreements and recommendations concerning minimum conditions to apply to customers for remuneration of services rendered;
3. agreements relating to interest rates on loans and deposits.

Following the communication of the statement of objections by the Commission, the ABI stated that it was prepared to abandon various agreements, among which were included the following: agreements concerning the charging of commission for the negotiation and collection of foreign currency travellers' cheques; elimination of certain provisions in the agreement concerning general banking practices, which provisions related to the dealings between the bank and the customer and included, *inter alia*, the fixing of value dates applicable; the fixing of various commissions (commission for transfers by telegraph, telex or telephone; commission on the maximum overdraft; commission concerning requests for data relating to the account; commission payable to foreign banks for information furnished with a view to an audit; charges payable by customers for the administration of ordinary Treasury bonds). The Commission recalled that in its communication of objections it had considered these agreements or provisions to be contrary to article 85(1) and not capable of benefiting from the exemption provided for under article 85(3).

The agreements which remained in force after the Commission's communication of objections were either granted negative clearance or benefited from the granting of an exemption under article 85(3) for a period of 10 years (with effect from the date of notification) expiring on 10 October 1994. Any amendments made to the terms of the agreements exempted by the Commission, especially with regard to value dates and commission rates must however be notified immediately to the Commission so as to ensure that the conditions warranting the exemption are still met. Last but not least, the Commission reserved its position as regards the agreement on interest rates.

25. As to these, see the in-depth analysis of Mr. H. Salmon, Administrator at the Directorate General for Competition, "Payment Cards and European Competition Law: an attempt at evaluation" [1990] 1 JIBL 25, at p. 28 *et seq.*
26. Decision 87/103, OJ L43/51 of 13 February 1987.

AGREEMENTS TO WHICH NEGATIVE CLEARANCE WAS GRANTED

27.13 The agreements to which negative clearance was granted can be divided into two categories.

First, the agreement relating to foreign exchange and non-resident account lire dealings was granted negative clearance on the basis that it did not involve any restrictions on competition. One of the aims of the agreement is that the transfer of non-resident account lire within the banking system should be effected within a maximum period of one day. To that end, the agreement provides that the bank which is responsible for any delay must reimburse any interest paid by the recipient bank. As already stated, this agreement—in its present version—is of a purely technical nature and contains no restriction on competition. Therefore, the grant of negative clearance was entirely justified.

Second, negative clearance was granted to agreements to which article 85(1) was held inapplicable on the basis that they did not affect trade between Member States to any appreciable degree: these agreements concern primarily the RID and RIBA conventions. The former lays down technical procedures for the payment of standing orders (gas, electricity); it fixes the value date applicable between banks (both the paying and payee banks) and the commission for the paying bank and for the company administering the system. The RIBA convention, on the other hand, lays down technical procedures in respect of collection by direct debits and the computerised interbank administration of such debits. Here, too, the agreement provides for commission due and value dates applicable in the event of payment as well as charges payable and value dates applicable in the event of the return of unpaid debits. There is no difficulty in agreeing with the Commission's decision with regard to these agreements. While their provisions do involve restrictions on competition, such restrictions are not capable of affecting trade between Member States to any appreciable degree.

However, the justification for the Commission's decision to grant negative clearance to the Bancomat agreement (involving an undertaking on the part of the member banks not to participate in other organisations of a similar nature, namely Cash Dispenser Systems, in Italy), as well as to agreements concerning minimum charges for renting safes and for safe custody services is less evident, for the reasons given earlier when discussing the applicability in principle of articles 85 and 86 to domestic banking agreements.[27]

AGREEMENTS WITHIN ARTICLE 85(1) BUT FOR WHICH EXEMPTIONS UNDER ARTICLE 85(3) WERE GRANTED

27.14 The agreements within article 85(1) but for which exemptions were granted under article 85(3) are the agreement on the Italian bills and documents collection and acceptance service; the agreement on the service of collecting bank cheques and similar instruments payable in Italy; and interbank agreements on a new, uniform type of lire travellers' cheque.[28]

The basis for the application of article 85(1) was essentially twofold. First, the Commission considered that these agreements fixed the rates of commission to be charged for services rendered by one bank to another and thereby limited the freedom

27. See paras. 25.2 and 25.3, above.
28. See point 41.

of action of the banks involved (the entire banking sector in Italy) and the choices open to their customers. It also considered that the very participation of Italian subsidiaries and branches of foreign banks in the agreement made their penetration of the market more difficult. The restrictions were all the more serious as they could lead to the total elimination of the—limited—competition offered by foreign banks. Therefore, the agreements appreciably restricted competition. Second, in the light of the participation of subsidiaries and branches of foreign banks and the nature of the services, which involved, in particular, payments destined for or having their origin in Italy, there was an appreciable effect on trade between Member States.[29]

27.15 The basis for grant of exemptions under article 85(3) was as follows. The Commission considered that the agreements involved a measure of standardisation and rationalisation of procedures which alone could permit a considerable volume of operations to be dealt with by the various banks involved. They therefore improved the distribution of services and promoted technical progress. The Commission also considered that the agreements benefited the consumer by the provision of a faster and more reliable service. The most sensitive area, despite the fact that the restrictions on competition arising from the agreements involved relations between banks only and not relations between banks and their customers, was the question of the indispensability of the restrictions. The grounds for the Commission's decision on this aspect were similar to those of the *Eurocheque package deal* decision which also concerned restrictions on competition between banks only. According to the Commission[30]:

The restrictions imposed on banks, both on those requesting a service and on those providing it, are indispensable to the proper provision of services covered by the agreements . . .

Where such a service is rendered collectively by all banks to bank customers, it is essential that the procedures for accepting and clearing the cheques and instruments concerned should be determined by mutual agreement between the banks requesting the service and those which, in the various places concerned, are called upon to provide it.[31]

Within the framework of such agreements, the joint and uniform fixing of the remuneration for services (between banks) is inherent in the collaboration between the banks called upon to provide the service.[32]

Despite these matters, the Commission noted that[33]:

the agreements at issue do not afford the signatory banks the possibility of eliminating competition in respect of a substantial part of the services in question.

In effect:

the agreements at issue do not directly govern relations between banks and their customers. A possibility of competition therefore continues to exist at the level of relations between each bank and its customers. The extent to which value dates and commissions are passed on to customers is left to the discretion of the bank which requested the service which makes it only one factor in the ultimate cost of the service rendered to its customers.[34]

It can thus be seen that the grounds for the Commission's decision here and those in the *Eurocheque package deal* decision are virtually identical.

On the other hand, it is submitted that the reasoning here is in contradiction to that adopted by the Commission when it declared article 85(1) inapplicable to the

---

29. See, in particular, point 49.
30. See points 63 and 64.
31. Point 65.
32. Point 66.
33. Point 67.
34. Point 68.

agreements concerning the fixing of minimum charges throughout Italy for the renting of safes and safe custody boxes.[35]

AGREEMENTS IN RELATION TO WHICH THE COMMISSION RESERVED ITS POSITION: AGREEMENTS FIXING INTEREST RATES ON LOANS AND DEPOSITS[36]

27.16 Because of the importance that it has for the overall economic position of banks, this is the most crucial issue for the application of competition law to banking agreements. In this context, the other agreements can be considered to be of only relative, if not of merely symbolic, importance.

It is therefore disappointing that the Commission reserved its position regarding the line to be taken with respect to these agreements following their notification. The reason given was that the Commission considered it necessary "to check the information received and examine the soundness of the arguments put forward in the notification in the light of experience gained over an extended period of time".[37] This point will be returned to later after a discussion of the decisions involving the Belgian Bankers' Association, the Irish Banks Standing Committee and the Dutch Bankers' Association, where the Commission also reserved its position with regard to agreements fixing interest rates.

Belgian Bankers' Association ("ABB") decision of 11 December 1986[38]

27.17 Alone among the banking associations of the Community, the ABB had notified to the Commission on 31 October 1962, in accordance with Regulation 17, a series of restrictive practices entered into by its members. This notification was made with a view to obtaining negative clearance or, in the alternative, an exemption under article 85(1). The notification procedure was finally completed in 1976 following a request for information from the Commission. The notification was not dealt with by the Commission until after the judgment of the Court in the *Züchner* case in 1981.

Within the framework of the inquiry conducted by the Commission after the *Züchner* judgment into national interbank agreements, the ABB sent the Commission texts of the new restrictive practices entered into since 1976, together with details of the amendments made to those already in existence. When the statement of objections was finally sent by the Commission, there were in force 22 conventions, agreements and recommendations (the difference in terminology is of little importance here).

AGREEMENTS TERMINATED BY THE ABB FOLLOWING THE COMMUNICATION OF THE STATEMENT OF OBJECTIONS

27.18 In response to the communication of objections and following subsequent discussions which took place between the ABB and the Commission, several agreements were terminated by the ABB. These included almost all agreements relating to the general provisions regarding charges payable by the customers. In particular, they included the agreements concerning the collection of cheques and bills; the charges for the safe custody of bills; payment of coupons, repayment and other

35. See para. 25.3, above.
36. Points 13 and 18.
37. Points 13 and 18.
38. Decision 87/13, OJ L7/27 of 9 January 1987.

operations relating to securities; the hiring of safes; competition between banks; and international payments and foreign exchange dealings.

It is surprising that the Commission, when it communicated its objections, made clear its intention to prohibit the agreement concerning the hiring of safes and safe custody deposits. This was contrary to its approach in the *Italian Bankers' Association* decision, where it had granted exemptions to such agreements on the grounds that they had no appreciable effect on trade between Member States, taking into account in particular the fixed nature of the subject-matter of the service.[39]

AGREEMENTS REMAINING IN FORCE AND WITH REGARD TO WHICH ARTICLE 85(1) WAS DECLARED INAPPLICABLE

27.19 In its statement of objections, the Commission indicated that it could consider certain agreements as not being in restraint of competition. The following agreements were included here: reduction in the amount of work involved in checking for stops in connection with transactions in securities; promoting the use of cheques; and protection against armed robberies.

AGREEMENTS TO WHICH ARTICLE 85(1) WAS DEEMED APPLICABLE BUT FOR WHICH EXEMPTIONS WERE GRANTED UNDER ARTICLE 85(3)

27.20 Three agreements fall into this category: the convention on transactions in securities; the convention on payments originating abroad; and the convention on the collection of cheques and commercial bills originating abroad and payable in Belgium. The provisions of these agreements relate to the pricing of services in both interbank relations and relations between banks and their customers. The convention on transactions in securities fixes the amount of the rebates (which are based on the commission collected from the institution issuing the securities) that the registrar banks reconvey to the other banks established in Belgium in consideration of their intermediation, on the one part for payment of coupons and securities and on the other part for various other security dealings (exchange/renewal of coupons). The convention on payments originating abroad fixes the maximum amount of the payment commission that may be charged between banks for any international foreign exchange payment transaction originating abroad and transmitted to its beneficiary via a bank established in Belgium. It also provides for a fixed rate of commission which is to be assessed on an *ad valorem* basis. Certain payments are excluded from the scope of the convention, in particular, Eurocheques issued up to the maximum amount accepted for clearing and certain travellers' cheques. The convention on the collection of cheques and commercial bills originating abroad and payable in Belgium no longer contains any schedule of charges and fees. It simply lays down the principle of charging commission and stipulates who is to be liable to pay it. In particular, it provides that the collecting bank may collect commission and costs from the principal. As far as the collection of cheques is concerned, it is provided that the commission is always payable by the principal. In relation to commercial bills, it provides that the commission is to be borne by either the drawee or the principal, depending upon the circumstances.

The basis for the application of article 85(1) was again essentially twofold. First, there was an appreciable effect on trade between Member States:

National pricing agreements covering an entire Member State may have the effect of

---

39. See para. 25.3, above.

consolidating the isolation of a national market, thus hindering the economic interpenetration sought by the Treaty. The restrictive practices notified by the ABB produce their effect throughout Belgium.[40]

. . . [Belgian] branches [of foreign banks] are parties to the agreement. . . . [These branches] constitute direct emanations of those foreign banks and hence participate in trade between Member States.[41]

Second, there was an appreciable restriction on competition:

The convention dealing with transactions in securities and the convention dealing with payments originating abroad restrict the freedom enjoyed by banks in that the conventions provide for a uniform charge for the services rendered between themselves.[42]

27.21 The convention on collection of cheques and commercial bills no longer fixes any rates. Nonetheless, by establishing the principle and procedures for charging a commission the convention restricts competition. In effect, the result is that "the banks agree, on the one hand, not to provide this service free of charge and, on the other hand, which party shall be liable for the commission thus provided for."[43]

The basis for the grant of exemption under article 85(3) was exactly the same as that in the *Italian Bankers' Association* decision: rationalisation of services; indispensable nature of the restrictions on competition (but for which each bank would have to negotiate the levels of commission with hundreds of other banks); benefits for the consumer—more speedy and reliable service; scope for competition—the conventions do not govern the relations between banks and their customers. Competition therefore remains at this level. The convention on the collection of cheques provides most certainly for the charging of commission but does not attempt to determine the amount.

As in the *Italian Bankers' Association* decision, the exemption in the *Belgian Bankers' Association* decision has been granted for a period of 10 years, with effect from 30 May 1986, being the date on which the final version of the three agreements exempted under the decision was notified to the Commission.

FAILURE TO ADOPT A POSITION ON AGREEMENTS CONCERNING INTEREST RATES[44]

27.22 The objections communicated by the Commission to ABB were concerned solely with the agreements relating to commission charged by banks for services provided. Excluded, therefore, were the conventions on accounts and deposits. The Commission reserved its position on the convention, the main provisions of which relate to deposit interest rates.

Irish Banks' Standing Committee ("IBSC") decision of 30 September 1986[45]

27.23 The IBSC comprises four banks, referred to as the Associated Banks, which are the main clearing and retail banks in Ireland. Their market share, according to the Commission's findings, amounted at the time to approximately 38% in terms of credit, and about 43% in terms of private deposits.

---

40. See point 39. The reasoning is wholly consistent with the Court of Justice's reasoning in case 246/86 *Belasco* [1989] ECR 2117.
41. Point 40.
42. Point 44.
43. Point 45.
44. See point 14.
45. Decision 86/507, OJ L295/28 of 30 September 1986.

AGREEMENTS ON COMMISSION AND ON INTEREST RATES

27.24 The agreements existing among the Associated Banks initially included, besides the three "technical" agreements referred to below, an agreement governing the rates of interest on loans and deposits as well as agreements governing commissions payable by customers for services. At the time when these agreements were notified to the Commission, following the inquiries made by the Commission in 1981, a negative clearance was sought for all of them by the IBSC. However, the IBSC indicated to the Commission at the time of notification that its members were re-examining the agreement governing rates of interest for loans and deposits.

Subsequent to the notification, the IBSC informed the Commission that the Associated Banks had voluntarily put an end to the agreement regarding commission for services payable by customers. It further informed the Commission that its members had terminated the agreement governing the rates of interest on loans and deposits. Concomitantly, these agreements on rates of interest were replaced, in substance, by a system whereby each of the Associated Banks freely set its base rate for the granting of loans as long as it did not exceed a maximum rate set by the Central Bank of Ireland; other rates of debit interest, and interest on deposit were set freely as long as they conformed to certain parameters defined by the Central Bank of Ireland.

As in the case of the *Italian Bankers' Association* and the *Belgian Bankers' Association* decisions, the Commission decided to reserve its position regarding the compatibility of these revised arrangements on interest rates with EC competition law. This decision appears to suggest, by implication, that the Commission did not take the view that agreements governing interest rates—whether for loans or deposits—are deemed to be fundamentally different in nature simply because they involve to some extent the monetary authorities, instead of individual banks acting together. This analysis of the implications of the Commission's decision appears to be borne out by later statements of the Commission.[46]

TECHNICAL AGREEMENTS FOR WHICH A NEGATIVE CLEARANCE WAS GRANTED

27.25 The only agreements remaining in force among the Associated Banks by the time the Commission took its decision were an agreement regarding common bank opening hours (to which the unions are also a party); an agreement governing clearing rules, that is rules according to which debits and credits drawn on and for the credit of the banks are settled as between one another; and an agreement relating to a direct debiting scheme. The Commission granted a negative clearance for all three agreements, though for different reasons.

As regards the agreement on opening hours, the Commission affirmed the principle that bank opening hours are an element of competition among banks. However, it took the view that, in this instance, the restriction on competition entailed by the agreement was not significant.[47] One reason advanced by the Commission was that certain banking services are not affected by the agreement but instead are provided on a 24-hour basis by automatic cash dispensers. As regards the clearing rules and debiting scheme, the

---

46. See para. 27.37 and fol., below.
47. A view which the writers find it difficult to share: the effect on competition of unrestricted opening hours has been amply demonstrated in the field of retail services: see, eg, the spate of litigation in recent years in the UK, France and Belgium concerning Sunday opening, culminating in case C–312/89 *Conforama* [1991] ECR 997, case C–322/89 *Marchandise* [1991] ECR 1027 and case C–169/91 *Stoke-on-Trent CC* v. *B & Q plc* [1993] 1 CMLR 426.

Commission was of opinion that they do not have as their object or effect the restriction of competition among the banks concerned. The Commission accordingly took the view that the only three remaining agreements were not caught by the prohibition of article 85(1).

Dutch Banks' decision of 19 July 1989[48]

27.26 The *Dutch Banks'* decision, while showing many points of similarity with the earlier decisions already discussed, nonetheless marks a significant shift in the Commission's original attitude (exemplified by the 1984 *Eurocheque Package Deal* decision) of, as a rule, exempting under article 85(3) agreements on interbank commission (as opposed to agreements on commission charged to the end customers). This shift in emphasis is clear from point 26 of the decision[49]:

The position of the Commission is that only in exceptional cases, where such a necessity is established, may agreements on inter-bank commissions be eligible for exemption under Article 85(3).

It was also recently underlined by Sir Leon Brittan, Vice-President of the Commission then in charge of competition policy:

In this case, we sought the termination of *both* types of agreement and not simply the bank-client type, because the interbank commission agreement was not found to be necessary for the proper functioning of the system.[50]

In effect, the interest of the *Dutch Banks'* decision lies more in the numerous agreements and recommendations that were withdrawn by the parties making the notification, as a result of the Commission's initial statement of objections, than in the agreements—of a limited scope—that were maintained in force and that were either held not to come within the ambit of article 85(1) (and were thus granted a negative clearance) or were granted an exemption under article 85(3). Its interest also lies in the fact that, for the first time, the Commission considered, and opposed, discriminatory bank commissions.

AGREEMENTS WITHDRAWN AS A RESULT OF THE COMMISSION'S INITIAL
STATEMENT OF OBJECTIONS

27.27 According to the decision,[51] various regulations or part thereof were withdrawn voluntarily by the Dutch Bankers' Association (NBV) pursuant to the discussion that took place with the Commission, following their notification. As will be seen, they concern essentially the minimum conditions (mainly minimum commission but also uniform value dates) to be applied by the banks for the various services covered by these regulations[52]:

---

48. Decision 89/512, OJ L253/1 of 30 August 1989.
49. See also H. Salmon, "Payment cards in European Competition Law: an attempt at evaluation", [1990] 1 JIBL, 25, at p. 28: "Thus, it is stressed (by the *Dutch Banks'* decision) that, while agreements on commissions charged to customers could not be exempted, agreements on inter-bank commissions would not get an exemption systematically but in very specific circumstances". This change of emphasis is also stressed by G. Vernimmen in "Le respect des règles de concurrence dans les services bancaires", ECU (Brussels) (1993), Vol. 24/III, p. 14, at p. 15.
50. "Competition in financial services", lecture delivered on 16 January 1992 at the Centre for European Policy Studies in Brussels, stencilled text, p. 7.
51. Point 18.
52. A summary of the relevant provisions of the regulations is set out in the annex to the decision.

— minimum commission on a number of services generally provided in the transfer of payments;
— minimum commission on a number of internal payment services;
— minimum commission in respect of Eurocheques and other guaranteed cheques;
— minimum commission on transactions in foreign banknotes and travellers' cheques;
— minimum commission on foreign transfers;
— minimum commission on services connected with letters of credit, bills of exchange, promissory notes, guarantees and various services concerning securities;
— value dating. This regulation stipulated, for the members of NBV, the day as from which amounts to be debited and credited were to be entered in current accounts, that is, which were to be included in the calculation of debit or credit interest. According to the regulation, amounts to be debited or credited between banks had to be debited or credited in the bank's accounts no later, or earlier, than the date of clearing, but these amounts had to be debited or credited in the bank's customer's current account one or more days later, or earlier, than that date[53];
— minimum rate and margins for the purchase and sale of foreign banknotes and for other foreign exchange transactions, and concertation among banks on the fixing of rates and margins for the purchase of foreign banknotes;
— minimum commission in respect of loans against promissory notes.

Also included in the agreements which were withdrawn was an agreement among the VDB (Association of Foreign Exchange Brokers) and the VWM (Association of Bill Brokers) giving VWM members the exclusive right to act as intermediary for VDB members in connection with foreign exchange transactions.[54]

27.28 However, a recent Written Question to the Commission[55] indicates that a new agreement on charges for various bank services has since been concluded, in mid-1991, between the main Dutch banks and been notified to the Commission by the Dutch Bankers' Association. According to the Written Question, under the agreement the banks charge their customers the full rate consisting of a non-negotiable basic charge and a residual negotiable margin which is allegedly too small to make genuine competition possible. On the basis of this limited information, the agreement would appear to be directly inspired by the recent block exemption for certain categories of agreement in the insurance sector[56] which make a distinction, which it is submitted is unwarranted, between agreements on pure premiums (permitted) and agreements on

53. See the annex to the decision, point 12.
54. The details of this agreement, set out in point 16 of the annex to the decision, bear some similarity to the *Sarabex* case examined earlier.
55. Written Question 196/92 of 10 February 1992 of MEP Janssen Van Raay OJ C235/40 of 14 September 1992.
56. Council Reg. 1934/91 of 31 May 1991, OJ L143/1 of 7 June 1991. A review of the block exemption is contained in the Commission's Twenty-second Report on Competition Policy for 1992, published 1993, points 274 to 288. For a critical review of this approach, see the Report of the E.P. Committee on Economic and Monetary Affairs and Industrial Policy on the application of Community competition policy in the insurance sector of 6 November 1992 (ref. EP 202.750/Fin) at p. 7, para. 9, with regard to "the possible negative implications for competition of encouraging standard policy conditions as a result of the convenience offered by the block excemption". However, the article by G. Vernimmen referred to in fn. 49, above, suggests that the Commission may be inclined to grant exemption to "standard banking clauses" of a

additional commercial premiums (prohibited). It remains to be seen whether the special factors which, in the Commission's view, justified allowing pure premiums in the insurance sector will be found by the Commission also to exist in the banking sector.

OBJECTION BY THE COMMISSION TO CERTAIN REGULATIONS ON THE GROUND OF DISCRIMINATORY PRICING

27.29 Of particular interest is the fact that the *Dutch Banks* decision indicates that the Commission had informed the parties concerned in its statement of objections that the abovementioned regulations were not eligible for exemption under article 85(3), not only because they restricted competition insofar as they prevented the banks from determining independently and individually the price and other conditions applied for services provided to the customers or to other banks but also because the charging of various commissions resulted in discrimination[57]:

22. In particular, different charges were prescribed for comparable banking services in the following cases:
   — In the case of various services, different commissions were prescribed depending on whether the banking services were provided for banks that were members of the association concerned, for banks abroad or for others not members of the relevant association.
   — The commissions that had to be charged to banks abroad and to other non-members (including Dutch banks that were not members) were higher than those charged to members of the association concerned, and those for other non-members were in various cases higher than the commissions charged to banks abroad;
   — in the case of transfers between residents and non-residents, commissions had to be charged, which in most cases were higher than those stipulated for transfers between an account held by a resident in the Netherlands and one held by him in his own name abroad, even though the two banking services were entirely comparable;
   — in the case of commissions charged on transfers between residents and non-residents, provision was made for an exception, to the effect that the commission did not have to be charged if the transfer involved securities transactions carried out via a VDB member. This meant that a VDB member did not have to charge any commission if the transaction was carried out through another VDB member, but did have to charge a commission if the transaction was carried out through a non-member, even though, for the bank concerned, there was no objective difference between the two types of transfer.

23. In the statement of objections, the Commission had informed the parties concerned that the difference between the commission prescribed for transfer between residents' and non-residents' accounts, where both accounts were held with Dutch banks, and the zero rate of commission in effect charged for transfers between residents' accounts could not be attributed to a difference between the operations that had to be carried out for the two types of transfers and could not therefore be accounted for by cost differences.

The only additional operation for a transfer between a resident and a non-resident account, as compared with one between two accounts of a resident was, according to the information provided by the NBV, the notification of the central bank. However, since according to the information provided by the NBV, the cost of the notification of the central bank was only one of a number of costs on the basis of which the commission was prescribed, this single difference could not account for the level of commission prescribed for transfers between residents' and non-residents' accounts.

24. In the statement of objections, the Commission had taken the view that the prescribing of the commissions referred to in paragraphs 22 and 23 meant that banks which were not members of the associations concerned and customers of their suppliers to whom transfers were made, were

---

non-binding nature, along the same lines as those followed for the block exemptions of standard policy conditions in the insurance sector, see at p. 16, point III.

57. Points 22 to 25.

placed directly or indirectly at a disadvantage in competition on the market for the services to be provided by them or the products to be supplied by them, because of the higher costs resulting from the charging of the commissions concerned.

25. Since the parties concerned [did withdraw] all the regulations providing for the above-mentioned differences in commissions, there was no longer any need for the Commission to examine how far the commissions laid down in the regulations might be deemed to be discriminatory or unfair in other respects.

Nevertheless, it appears from recent Written Questions addressed to the Commission that discriminatory bank commission is still applied in the Netherlands, at least in some limited circumstances.[58]

REFUSAL OF THE COMMISSION TO ACCEPT REPLACEMENT OF MINIMUM COMMISSION CHARGED TO CUSTOMERS BY MINIMUM INTERBANK COMMISSION

27.30 Also of particular interest and indicative of the Commission's change of attitude since its 1984 *Eurocheque package deal* decision and later *Italian*, *Belgian* and *Irish Bankers' Associations* decisions, is the Commission's refusal to accept the proposal made, in the written replies to the statement of objections and in discussions with the Commission, that certain minimum commission to be charged to customers pursuant to the regulations (eventually withdrawn) be replaced by minimum commission which banks would charge each other, with any commission chargeable to customers being determined by the banks individually. Indeed, the parties were unable to convince the Commission that such changes would meet the conditions for exemption under article 85(3). They failed to show that such agreements on interbank commission would actually be necessary for the successful implementation of certain forms of co-operation, positive in themselves, between a number of banks. The position of the Commission was that only in the exceptional cases, where such a necessity was established, might agreements on interbank commission be capable of obtaining an exemption under article 85(3).[59]

AGREEMENTS GRANTED A NEGATIVE CLEARANCE

27.31 The agreements granted a negative clearance fall into two categories. First, those which do not appreciably restrict competition[60]; and, second, those which, even though they restrict competition, do not have any appreciable effect on trade between Member States.[61]

Some of the agreements (set out in the annex to the decision) which do not appreciably restrict competition concern such matters as the provision of postage-paid envelopes to customers, the sale of gift vouchers and gifts and bonuses offered as an incentive to savers and are of little importance. Others relate to largely technical matters such as "open-open" telephone lines, dealings by foreign exchange brokers and circulars concerning additional security to be provided by the customer in connection with forward transactions in foreign currencies.

Of more significance is the granting of a negative clearance to the regulation

---

58. See Written Question 1319/91 of MEP Pinxten of 4 July 1991 regarding a "special annual levy on accounts of non-residents employed in the Netherlands", and the answer given by Sir Leon Brittan on 24 January 1992 OJ C162/7 of 29 June 1992. The answer to the question suggests, however, that the commission in question is (now) charged by individual banks and no longer as a result of an industry-wide agreement.
59. Point 26.
60. Points 47 to 57.
61. Points 58 and 59.

concerning the establishment of foreign exchange reference rates, albeit after it had been amended. Under the regulation, as initially notified, both the margins and the middle rates established during the daily fixing by the Foreign Exchange Quotations Committee appointed by the VDB board, had to be applied in foreign exchange transactions by all VDB members.[62] According to the Commission:

The regulation . . . in its [amended] form, no longer restricts competition to any appreciable extent. It results only in the fixing of middle rates which are used as a reference basis . . . In the light of the information provided by the VDB to the Commission, . . . the Commission considers that it can be concluded justifiably that these rates are established by procedures in which competition can play its role . . .

Furthermore, the middle rates determined during the fixing are not mandatory. The banks, bill brokers and other market members are entirely free, in the light of the market situation and the nature of the transaction, to agree on whatever buying and selling rates they want. In so doing, they can choose between various options, such as the application of the middle rates or of more favourable or less favourable buying and selling rates, whether or not coupled with the charging of commissions.[63]

The category of agreements granted a negative clearance, even though they restrict competition, because they do not have any appreciable effect on trade between Member States, includes the uniform conditions applied by the Dutch banks for the hire of safes and an agreement indirectly restricting competition amongst banks in respect of transfers related to fund raising acceptances, by subjecting these transfers to a uniform interbank commission.[64] The reasoning followed by the Commission in respect of this latter agreement is, to all intents and purposes, identical to its reasoning in respect of the uniform conditions for the hire of safes, which reasoning has been analysed—and criticised—when examining the applicability in principle of EC competition law to domestic banking agreements.[65]

For completeness, it should be mentioned that the Dutch Bankers' Association brought an action against the Commission on 2 October 1989, seeking annulment of the Commission's decision "in so far as it finds that the agreement concerning transfers relating to fund-raising acceptances, restricts competition to an appreciable extent".[66] Since the Commission's decision, even though it finds that the agreement appreciably restricts competition, nonetheless grants it a negative clearance on the ground that the restriction of competition does not affect trade between Member States, it may be surmised that the bringing of this action by the Dutch Bankers' Association was not concerned with the implications of the Commission's findings in terms of EC competition law. Indeed, the action was later rejected by the European Court of First Instance, essentially on the ground that the Association lacked any legitimate interest since the Commission's decision was favourable to the plaintiff. It must therefore be assumed that the Association was instead concerned with the possible consequences of those findings in terms of Dutch domestic law. Indeed, these findings could, possibly, provide a ground for action by, say, a consumers' group under Dutch domestic antitrust legislation on the assumption that such domestic antitrust legislation bars agreements appreciably restricting competition in the banking sector.

---

62. Points 31 and 32.
63. Point 49. See, however, the text to fn. 56 above and the parallel there made with the recent block exemption regulation in the insurance sector.
64. Point 56.
65. See para. 25.3, above.
66. Case T–138/89 *NBV and NBB* v. *Commission*, judgment of 17 September 1992.

AGREEMENTS WITHIN THE AMBIT OF ARTICLE 85(1) AND FOR WHICH AN
EXEMPTION WAS GRANTED UNDER ARTICLE 85(3)

27.32 The only agreement which falls into this category is the VDB circulars concerning simplified clearing procedures for cheques denominated in Dutch Guilders and in foreign currencies.[67] In the version notified, the circular concerning cheques in Guilders provided not only for uniform value dates to be applied in relations between the relevant (Dutch) banks but also for uniform value dates to be applied by the banks *vis-à-vis* their customers. Similarly, the circular notified concerning cheques in foreign currencies provided not only for uniform value dates to be applied in relations between the relevant (Dutch) banks but also for the application of uniform value dates by the banks *vis-à-vis* the relevant foreign banks.

After the Commission made it known that, in its opinion, the uniform value dates for customers and foreign banks were not necessary to ensure proper interbank co-operation in clearing cheques, (this being the stated objective of the circulars), these provisions were voluntarily withdrawn by the VDB. The Commission thereafter took the view, with respect to the amended version, that the relevant circulars came within the ambit of article 85(1) since they limited the scope for the banks concerned to agree, bilaterally with one another, more favourable value dates, and that they thereby indirectly restricted competition between the relevant banks for the services concerned.[68] However, the Commission also took the view that the circulars, in their amended version, met the conditions required for an exemption under article 85(3) in that:

— they resulted in an improvement in the payment system[69];
— consumers received a fair share of the improvements thus achieved, since the recipients of cheques were credited more rapidly than would otherwise be the case[70];
— the only restrictions still contained in the circulars, namely the application of uniform value dates between the relevant Dutch banks, "are essential to ensure the reliability and hence the success of the simplified and more rapid clearing method"[71];
— these restrictions did not afford the banks concerned the possibility of eliminating competition in respect of a substantial part of the services in question, since these do not directly govern relations between the banks and their customers and "furthermore, the value dates applied in clearing cheques are not the only area in which competition with regard to cheques takes place. Ultimately, the recipients of cheques have the choice between accepting cheques and other forms of payment".[72]

Accordingly, an exemption was granted to the relevant circulars for a period of 10 years.

67. Points 36 and 37.
68. Point 56.
69. Point 62.
70. Point 63.
71. Point 64.
72. Point 65.

27.33 The decision expressly states that it does not apply to the general terms and conditions of banking, recommended by the NBV to its members; to agreements on interest rates; to agreements concerning co-operation between financial institutions in respect of electronic transactions and bank cards; and to the provisions established by the credit registration office concerning the participation by companies in the credit registration system of that office. The Commission reserved its position on such provisions.[73]

The Commission's decision to reserve its position regarding even the applicability in principle of EC competition law to the general terms and conditions recommended by the NBV to its members appears to contradict the position it adopted almost 30 years ago in this respect.[74] The request for a preliminary ruling recently made by two Italian courts in respect of standard terms and conditions applied by Italian banks pursuant to a recommendation of the Italian Bankers' Association[75] may hopefully lead shortly to clarification of this issue by the Court of Justice.

With regard to agreements on interest rates, the position was the same as that adopted by the Commission in its earlier decisions concerning, respectively, the Italian banks, the Belgian banks and the Irish banks. As will be seen, it is only three years after the *Dutch Banks'* decision that the Commission eventually took a formal stand on this issue.

The decision to reserve the Commission's position in respect of agreements concerning co-operation between financial institutions in the field of electronic transactions and bank cards must, it is submitted, be seen in the context of the Commission's close examination of that sector in terms of competition law, as well as against the background of its efforts to promote better payment systems within the Community.[76]

Finally, the decision to reserve the Commission's position in respect of the provisions concerning the participation by companies in the credit registration system of the Dutch registration office is presumably motivated by the wish not to prejudice the Commission's initiative regarding banking supervision at the Community-wide level.[77]

Eurocheque Helsinki agreement decision of 25 March 1992

27.34 The *Eurocheque Helsinki agreement* decision is distinct from, and should not be confused with, the earlier *Eurocheque package deal agreement* decision and the subsequent review of its renewal, still pending,[78] although its origin would appear to be intrinsically linked to the circumstances surrounding the notification of the Eurocheque package deal agreement. In essence, the facts as set out in the decision are as follows. Apparently unbeknown to the Commission, at the time of the notification of the package deal agreement by Eurocheque International on 7 July 1982 "on behalf of all the members of the Eurocheque Assembly [to which the AFB—French Bankers'

---

73. Point 15.
74. See fn. 1, above.
75. See fn. 2, above.
76. See Part Six, below.
77. See Part Two, above.
78. OJ L95 of 9 April 1992; see also the review of the decision in the Commission's Twenty-second Report on Competition Policy, 1992, published 1993, point 141.

Association belonged, later succeeded to by Groupement des Cartes Bancaires—CB] the AFB had only partially acceded to the package deal agreement".[79] It was later established by the Commission, as a result of requests for information sent to Eurocheque International and to CB, following complaints received by the Commission ever since 1985 regarding the payment of Eurocheques in France, that the French Banks had only agreed to pay Eurocheques drawn on non-French banks "on the same terms as to [their] customers who are Carte Bleue or Visa Card holders"[80] (being the cards issued by the French bank members of CB to their customers). This meant, in practice, that "in respect of purchases paid for by Eurocheques (by tourists visiting France), the [French bank] members of [CB] will charge their affiliated traders a commission which may not be greater than that applicable to payments [made by] Carte Bleue and Eurocard".[81] This arrangement was formalised in an agreement entered into in Helsinki in May 1983 between the French banks and financial institutions, on the one hand, and the Eurocheque International Community on the other. Parallel to the Helsinki agreement, a protocol was signed on 31 July 1984 between the 11 largest French financial institutions laying the principle of interoperability between the three card networks in France which included a clause under which, as from 1 July 1986, the Uniform Eurocheque would no longer be issued with a free of charge guarantee of payment in France but could continue to be issued only for use abroad.[82]

As stated by the Commission in its Statement of Objections to Eurocheque International and CB in respect of the Helsinki agreement, the agreement "had the object and immediate effect in the trading sector of making any competition whatsoever impossible between Eurocheques (in principle free of charge to the payee) and payments by card, which the French banks have on the whole opted for in preference to the Eurocheque System".[83] Another objection was that "this was clearly a price fixing agreement applicable moreover in relation between banks and customers and not only in interbank relations since, through the agreement, the French banks decided, with the approval of the Eurocheque International Community as a whole, to charge their trader customers a commission equal in amount to that which they charge them for payments made by bankcard (French or foreign)".[84] Indeed:

far from having as its object or effect the furtherance of the development of Eurocheques in France, as claimed by [CB], the Helsinki Agreement seems to have had as its object and as its effect the stunting of such development. It can be described as the second aspect of a mechanism set up by French banks to impede potential competition from Eurocheques, the other aspect being the provision in the protocol of 31 July 1984 [between the major French banks on interoperability of the three card networks] which prohibited members of [CB] from issuing Eurocheques for domestic use.[85]

The Commission first noted that there could be no denying that, at the time of its conclusion, the Helsinki agreement was at variance with the package deal agreement, which was based, *inter alia*, on the principle that the Eurocheque is free of charge to its

---

79. Point 23.
80. Point 23.
81. Point 26. A fn to the decision indicates that "the present contract used by CB with retailers applies to payments made by Carte Bleue cards, Visa cards and Eurocard/Master cards".
82. Point 29 and cross reference to point 2. As noted by the decision (point 29) the French Conseil de la Concurrence, by a decision of 11 October 1988, called on CB to abolish this clause.
83. Point 32.
84. Point 32.
85. Point 59.

payee, the costs being borne by the drawer; that this principle was, moreover, one of the grounds for the 1985 decision exempting the package deal agreement; and that it was not at all clear why the package deal agreement would have been necessary if it was possible for the paying bank to collect a commission from the payee on foreign Eurocheques remitted to it for payment.[86] The Commission went on to note that[87]:

> The only category of users—if they could be described as such, but they are, rather, intermediaries in the case in point—to benefit from the Helsinki Agreement is made up of French banks, who are thus paid twice for the same service and are the only banks in the Community to be so remunerated: firstly, by the French traders, as a result of the Helsinki Agreement, and secondly by the foreign banks [the banks of the drawers of Eurocheques] as a result of the Package Deal Agreement,

and concluded, unsurprisingly, that the Helsinki agreement did not benefit users and hence did not qualify for exemption on the basis of article 85(3).

27.35 The Commission also noted, as an "aggravating" factor, that financial profit (being paid twice for the same service) was not the ultimate objective of the Helsinki agreement. The French banks had never claimed that the Helsinki agreement appeared necessary to them because the maximum remuneration provided for by the package deal agreement would have been insufficient to cover their costs. It had first and foremost as its object, and had as its effect, the prevention of the competition that might otherwise have taken place between Eurocheques and bank cards. The agreement, taken together with the provision in the protocol establishing CB which prohibits French banks from issuing Eurocheques for national use, impeded the development of Eurocheques in France.[88] After taking into account various factual elements, including the fact that Eurocheque International itself, as opposed to the French banks represented at Eurocheque level by CB, had not derived any profit from the Helsinki agreement, the Commission held that the agreement constituted during its duration (it was terminated voluntarily, during the proceedings, on 27 May 1991) an infringement of article 85(1); rejected the request made for exemption, following its eventual notification to the Commission on 16 July 1990, for the period between its notification and its later voluntary withdrawal; and imposed a fine of 5,000,000 ECU on CB and a fine of 1,000,000 ECU on Eurocheque International by reason of the infringement of article 85(1). An appeal against the decision was brought by CB and Eurocheque International on 25 May 1992 before the Court of First Instance from which a decision is awaited.

27.36 The Commission's decision is important in that it was the first decision formally rejecting an application for exemption in the banking field and imposing a fine on the undertakings concerned for infringement of article 85(1). However, the principles which it applies to reach that conclusion had already been laid down in its earlier decisions in the banking field which, it will be recalled, had always led to an exemption on the basis of article 85(3) of the agreements in question, as amended.

The *Eurocheque Helsinki Agreement* decision is perhaps most noteworthy in that it indicates the coming of age of EC competition law in the banking field: banking agreements restricting competition are no longer considered, *per se*, as being intrinsically different from agreements restricting competition in other sectors of the services industry. This altogether more critical attitude on the part of the Commission is

---

86. Point 55.
87. Point 70.
88. Point 82.

borne out, *inter alia*, by its recently published Working Document "Easier cross-border payments: breaking down the barriers" which lay at the heart of its recent Recommendation on cross-border payments.

The Commission, when addressing the issue of "interchange fees" in multilateral clearing (or netting) systems, has taken a position far removed from the wholly uncritical attitude it adopted in 1985 in its *Eurocheque package deal* decision with regard to agreements setting uniform charges among banks (as opposed to charges between banks and their customers). Thus, in its 1992 Working Document, it has taken the view that:

[whereas] transaction fees other than those charged by a central body can . . . be the subject of general arrangements between all participants . . . these general arrangements must [nonetheless] leave open the possibility for individual participants to agree on lower interchange fees bilaterally. In other words, a generally agreed fee structure can provide for maximum fees only: it must remain possible to negotiate variations from this maximum, either effected directly through bilateral rebates between participants or through a central mechanism as appropriate. Members of a system with maximum interchange fees are not obliged to offer prices below the maximum. However, the Commission would have to consider individual cases upon their merits to determine whether the absence of prices below the maximum was the result of anti-competitive behaviour.[89]

3. AGREEMENTS ON INTEREST RATES

1. The position before Züchner

27.37 In 1979, the Commission was faced with a Written Question in the European Parliament[90] concerning the compatibility with Community law of a so-called "agreement to harmonise competition", concluded in Belgium between the members of the Concertation Committee, being the consultative body then responsible for changes in the rate of interest paid on bank deposits in Belgium. The presidency of this committee was, at the time, held by the Governor of the National Bank of Belgium—a fact which highlighted the involvement of the domestic monetary authorities in the committee's activities. The Question also asked the Commission to state its view on existing agreements on interest rates in Belgium. The answer shows the attitude of the Commission towards this kind of agreement before the Court of Justice's decision in *Züchner*[91]:

. . . it must be possible for interbank agreements on interest rates to be considered as "monetary policy instruments" of Member States, since they have been established on the initiative of the public authorities and approved by them. The particular case of co-ordination between the financial institutions, established in Belgium, will be examined by the Commission in wider context, in which it is to be determined whether certain interbank agreements are essential for the monetary policy of Member States and should be the subject of special rules pursuant to Article 87(2)(c) of the EEC Treaty.

It appears therefore that the Commission, at the time, was leaning towards the position that the criterion for determining whether an interbank agreement is

---

89. Annex C, "Principles on Competition for credit transfer systems" to the Working document, p. 2, sub. C "interchange fees in multilateral systems". See also G. Vernimmen, in the article referred to in fn. 49 above, at pp. 15–16.
90. Written Question 199/79 by M. Schyns of 6 June 1979, OJ C197/3 of 4 August 1979.
91. OJ C213/6 of 25 August 1979.

compatible with the rules on competition is whether the agreement has been made upon the initiative and with the approval of the national monetary authorities concerned.

2. The Commission's attitude since Züchner

27.38 The change of attitude of the Commission after *Züchner* was highlighted in a speech given by Mr. Andriessen, then EC Commissioner in charge of competition, in November 1981[92]:

After further considering the problem, the Commission is now of the opinion that interest rates should not be governed by interbank agreements, even if they are approved, authorised or promoted by the national authorities competent for economic, financial or monetary matters. Interest rates should either be established individually by banks, freely competing between them, or be regulated directly by the domestic supervisory authorities, if these choose to do so.

When banks regulate the interests between themselves, they seek to impose a ceiling on deposit rates and minimum lending rates and thus avoid the kind of price competition that might lead to a reduction of the differential between these rates. By contrast, the supervisory authorities tend to regulate interest rates by prescribing a permitted range designed to influence the average rate, or to impose minimum deposit rates and maximum lending rates which leaves scope for some competition to the benefit of bank customers and of market efficiency.

In a regime of free competition which already exists in a number of Member States, each individual bank is normally in the best position to balance its books by independently modifying its deposit and lending rates. In other Member States, the monetary authorities may consider it necessary to fix the interest rates in order to control inflation, protect savings, protect the national currency, promote industrial development, etc. Member States are, and should remain, free to choose this way of regulating interest rates, so long as there is no common Community monetary policy. But the Commission considers that it is not compatible with the EEC competition rules for a national authority to have certain of its tasks performed for it by a trade association or a cartel and simply to approve or endorse the decisions or agreements arrived at between the enterprises concerned, whenever trade between Member States may be affected by such actions. Authorities which choose to regulate are, of course, perfectly free to consult and discuss any proposed measures with the interested parties, but the final decision and the responsibility for monitoring and enforcement should rest with the competent authority; they should not result from arrangements between the market participants.

The Commission will endeavour to ensure . . . that there is no confusion between market regulation by the authorities and regulation by the market participants themselves, whether by way of agreement or through an association. In the latter case, any action undertaken by enterprises to restrict competition which may affect inter-state trade would come within the scope of the competition rules of the EEC Treaty.

Notwithstanding the fact that these—on the face of it unequivocal—pronouncements were made as early as November 1981, the Commission nonetheless did not address the question of the compatibility with EC competition law of "private" interest rate agreements in its decisions concerning the Italian banks, the Belgian banks and the Irish banks handed down in 1986, nor in its decision concerning the Dutch banks handed down in July 1989. This is no doubt a silent tribute to the powerful influences which were brought to bear on the Commission's competition service to restrain it from actually carrying out the unambiguous policy announced in 1981 by the then Commissioner in charge of competition. Instead, the Commission reverted in the four aforementioned decisions to the policy of "[reserving] its position on this matter, pending an enquiry as to the relationship between interest rates and monetary policy of

---

92. Stencilled text, p. 8 *et seq*. A summary of the speech was published in *Agence Europe*, Bulletin 3264 (New Series), 5 December 1981.

the individual Member States"[93]—an enquiry which, it will be recalled, first started in 1973.[94]

The necessity for the continuation of such an examination is all the more incomprehensible because the distinction made in 1981 by the Commissioner in charge of competition between, on the one hand, "private" interbank agreements on interest rates—forbidden, as a rule, under article 85(1), even if they are encouraged or approved by the authorities—and, on the other hand, measures regulating interest rates prescribed by the authorities themselves—and, hence, outside the scope of article 85(1) (albeit, even though the Commission did not say so at the time, not necessarily outside the scope of article 5, read in conjunction with article 3(f) and article 85(1)[95]—finds direct support in the latter case-law of the Court of Justice, considered below,[96] and in particular in *Van Eycke* v. *ASPA*[97] which specifically concerned alleged agreements on interest rates.

27.39 It is presumably this last case which has emboldened the Commission, in the person of Sir Leon Brittan, Vice-President of the Commission then in charge of competition policy, to issue a press release on 16 November 1989,[98] indicating that it had:

taken a further step in order to accelerate the application of the competition rules in the banking sector.

. . . (namely) Sir Leon Brittan . . . has now written a letter to the European Banking Federation explaining the Commission's position on interbank agreements concerning interest rates—such agreements restrict competition as do price cartels.

The existence of agreements determining certain interest rates at national level would run counter to the objectives of the completion of the internal market and would make the full gains expected from this process more difficult to achieve. The Commission therefore believes that agreements on interest rates should be avoided or abandoned.

The Commission stresses that its action under Article 85 does not in any way restrict the ability of public authorities to achieve their objectives in the field of monetary policy. The normal use of monetary instruments does not infringe Community competition rules if public authorities do not encourage the constitution of illicit cartels or reinforce their effects.

Eventually, on 24 July 1992, the Commission announced that, following its inquiries, "all the organisations questioned had confirmed that among them no agreements nor recommendations on interest rates exist . . . [nor] did [its] survey indicate the existence of cooperation between banks outside the framework of the associations. If an agreement had been established, it would fall within the prohibition of article 85(1)".[99] The very fact that the Commission decided to launch an investigation into interest rate agreements has, of itself, prompted the termination of such agreements, where they existed, by the national banking associations concerned.

In its Twenty-second Report on Competition Policy for 1992, published in 1993, the Commission stated that[100]:

93. See the Sixteenth Report on Competition Policy, 1986, published 1987, point 58.
94. See the Second Report on Competition Policy, 1973, published 1974, point 51.
95. See, hereafter, "Restrictions on Competition imposed by the national authorities".
96. *Ibid.*
97. Case 267/86 [1989] ECR 2117.
98. Ref. (89)/869 "European Commission calls for termination of interbank agreements on interest rates".
99. Press release I.P. (92)625.
100. Point 44. The statement of objections was reportedly sent to the Luxembourg Banking Association, which later amended its agreement (see the press release referred to in fn. 99, above; also, *Agence Europe* no. 5780 (New Series) of 27/28 July 1992, p. 7; see further the article by G. Vernimmen referred to in fn. 49, above, at p. 17.

It continued its investigation into interest rates [and] concluded its studies of the replies to its requests for information of the previous year. Certain agreements were abandoned or amended as a result, and a statement of objections was sent in one case.

4. POSITION OF THIRD PARTIES AGGRIEVED BY A CARTEL AGREEMENT VOLUNTARILY WITHDRAWN AS A RESULT OF A STATEMENT OF OBJECTIONS BY THE COMMISSION FOLLOWING NOTIFICATION

27.40 The four Commission decisions involving the agreements between the Italian banks, the Belgian banks, the Irish banks and the Dutch banks respectively raise an important question regarding the right of individuals or companies prejudiced by an agreement or concerted practice contrary to EC law to seek redress and, where appropriate, damages in the national courts. The same is true in respect of the interest rate agreements which, as acknowledged by the Commission itself in its Twenty-second Report on Competition Policy, were "voluntarily" amended or withdrawn following its request for information about the agreements.

As already stated, the Commission's approach in the banking sector (in marked contrast to certain other sectors) has been so far to grant an exemption for the agreements from the time when they were notified to it in their amended form, following the Commission's initial statement of objections and ensuing negotiations between the parties making the notification and the Commission, while leaving out of its decisions those (parts of the) agreements which were part of the initial notification and which it found unacceptable (ie, contrary to article 85(1) and not susceptible of an exemption under article 85(3)) as a *quid pro quo* for the willingness of the parties making the notification to withdraw those agreements voluntarily.

A more straightforward approach, and one more in line with the Commission's approach in other sectors as well as with the need to ensure effective application of EC competition law for the benefit of parties prejudiced by anti-competitive agreements, would have been for the Commission to include these provisions in its decision and formally forbid them notwithstanding the fact that they had been voluntarily withdrawn in the course of the discussions following their notification.

27.41 The Commission's present practice makes it unnecessarily difficult for third parties who have been prejudiced by the anti-competitive agreements concerned before the time when they were notified to the Commission and later voluntarily withdrawn to seek damages before the national courts on the ground that these agreements were null and void as being contrary to article 85(1) (and not susceptible of exemption on the basis of article 85(3) by the Commission since, in any event, they were not notified at the time). The Commission's present practice of not formally forbidding the agreements to which it objects, provided they have been voluntarily withdrawn, means that third parties prejudiced by those agreements before their voluntary withdrawal will have to convince the national courts where they seek damages that, had the agreements in question not been voluntarily withdrawn, and had the Commission therefore had to pronounce on their validity, the Commission would have found them to be contrary to article 85(1) and not susceptible of exemption under article 85(3). This places on those parties an unfair burden of proof, which would not be placed upon them if the Commission had included the agreements concerned in its decisions and stated formally, notwithstanding their voluntary withdrawal as a result of the Commission's initial statement of objection, that they were prohibited under article 85(1) and not susceptible of exemption under article 85(3).

27.42 The Commission's competition service has, in the past, sometimes written officially for the benefit of a national court, at the request of a party seeking damages before that court, to confirm that, had the agreements concerned not been voluntarily withdrawn, it would have proposed to the Commissioners formally to prohibit these agreements. However, it is beyond doubt that this *ad hoc* remedy, which the Commission's competition service is in any event under no obligation to provide, falls far short of giving third parties who are prejudiced by an agreement contrary to article 85(1) the same degree of protection as that which would be provided by a formal decision of the Commission to that effect. The situation is exacerbated by the Commission's practice not to publish or make publicly available the full text of agreements which it would have forbidden had they not been voluntarily withdrawn. This, again, makes it unnecessarily difficult for third parties prejudiced by those agreements to seek damages before a national court: they will have to convince the court, by way of circumstantial evidence, that the agreements complained of are the same, in all respects, as the agreements eventually notified to the Commission and later voluntarily withdrawn.

It must, however, be acknowledged that the *Dutch Banks'* decision constitutes in this respect a significant step forward compared with earlier decisions, in that a comprehensive summary of all agreed agreements notified, including those thereafter voluntarily withdrawn, has been included as an annex to the decision. On the other hand, a similar policy has not been followed, at least so far, with regard to those interest rate agreements which were voluntarily withdrawn or amended as a result of the Commission's requests for information.

5. SUGGESTED FUTURE TRENDS IN THE EXEMPTION OF DOMESTIC BANKING AGREEMENTS

1. Interbank co-operation agreements (other than bank alliances) [101]

27.43 The Commission's decisions discussed above and, in particular, the *Dutch Banks* decision of 1989, give a good indication of the way in which its future policy in that field is likely to develop. In particular, it is suggested that the Commission may look with renewed attention in the near future to the question whether certain "interbank co-operation agreements", even though they qualify in principle for exemption on the basis of article 85(3) insofar as they are entered into for the purpose of providing customers with a better service or new facilities, contain certain restrictions on competition which it appears hard to justify as being indispensable to the attainment of the stated objectives of the agreements. The whole field of payment cards networks, automated teller networks, electronic payment networks, etc., merits in this respect, it is submitted, closer examination. [101]

For example, it may be hard to justify, in terms of their necessity to the attainment of the objectives of this type of agreement, clauses whereby undertakings wishing to affiliate themselves to one of these networks are required to charge interest at a

---

101. G. Vernimmen, in the article referred to in fn. 49, above, at p. 16, states that this area is presently the subject of an in-depth examination by the Commission's competition service.

minimum rate on debit balances of their customers or on advances granted in other forms; to pay credit interest, not in excess of a given maximum rate, in respect of credit balances in current accounts or on deposits; to charge an agreed fee, or commission rate, or minimum rate, for the customers when the card is issued to them, or for the use thereof; to refrain from adhering to a competing network; or, in the case of traders accepting payments from customers by way of a (network related) cheque card or terminal, not to give to clients paying by ordinary means the benefit of a discount equivalent to (part of) the commission payable by the retailer to the network in respect of customers using the network related cheques, cards or terminal. As Commissioner Andriessen put it in 1981[102]:

The EEC competition rules do not only apply to directly anti-competitive agreements whose object is clearly the restriction of competition, but also to agreements which have other objects but which incidentally also have the effect of restricting competition. [This can be the case for example] for certain well intended co-operation agreements which, as a side effect, restrict the access of potential new entrants to a particular market segment.

National antitrust authorities, both in France and in the United Kingdom, have taken noted initiatives in their field.[103] Recent Commission initiatives intended to facilitate international payments throughout the Community, especially for private individuals and small and medium enterprises,[104] must logically lead to similar steps, at the Community level being undertaken by the Commission.[105] Indeed, as recently stated by Sir Leon Brittan, it is clear that "a lot of co-operation does not benefit the consumer."[106]

More generally, it is suggested that the group exemption regulation, recently adopted by the Council, concerning co-operation agreements in the insurance sector[107] could usefully be duplicated by the Commission with respect to the banking and financial industry (although it would no doubt need to be substantially amended to take account

102. Stencilled text, p. 11; reported in *Agence Europe*, Bulletin 3264, new series, 5 December 1981.

103. See, in France, the decisions of the French Council for Competition (Conseil de la Concurrence) of 11 October 1988 and 3 May 1989, adopted in the French proceedings against the Group of Bank Cards (Groupement des Cartes Bancaires), French Official Competition Bulletin (*Bulletin Officiel de la Concurrence*) of 15 October 1988 at p. 271 and of 10 May 1989, at p. 137, and in the UK, the recommendations made in 1990 by the Monopolies and Mergers Commission (MMC) in its report on the credit card industry. One of the MMC's recommendations was that "members of credit cards networks should be able to sign up retailers as soon as they join and not have to wait—as National Westminster and Midland Bank did after joining Visa—until they have a large number of card-holding customers. The other recommendation was to allow retailers to give a discount to customers who pay in cash rather than by credit cards" (*Financial Times*, 14 March 1990, p. 10). The Director General of Fair Trading was recently reported as wishing to see similar flexibility extended to the case of debit and charge cards (*Financial Times*, 23 December 1992, p. 6).

104. See Part Six, below.

105. See, in this respect, H. Salmon, "Payment Cards in European Competition Law: an attempt at evaluation" [1990] 1 JIBL 25, at p. 31: "There is no doubt that payment card systems are going to play an increasing role in the future in various Member States of the EEC, as they have already begun to do in the UK and in France. Perhaps this will incite the Commission to consider that it would be the appropriate time for it also to now adopt formal decisions in this sector . . .".

106. "Competition in financial services", lecture delivered on 16 January 1992 at the Centre for European Policy Studies in Brussels, stencilled text, p. 10.

107. Council Reg. 1534/91 of 31 May 1991, OJ L143/1 of 7 June 1991. As pointed out above in the context of the *Dutch Banks'* decision certain provisions of the block exemption look questionable and, it is submitted, should be reappraised by the Commission in the not too distant future once it has gained more insight into the insurance sector.

of the substantial differences that (still) exist between both sectors, notwithstanding the move towards "Bancassurance").[108]

2. Agreements on interest rates

27.44 In the 1985 edition of this book,[109] it was suggested that "here, the availability of an exemption on the basis of article 85(3) is less certain. In some Member States, an argument habitually invoked to justify agreements on the [maximum] rate of interest paid on deposits is the need to maintain at a reasonable level, the costs of funds which the financial institutions derive from these sources and which they use—at least in part—to finance such activities as public housing or investment credits. The wish of the public authorities to keep down the cost of public borrowing is doubtless also a major consideration in some Member States". It is submitted that, in view of the evolution of EC law and of the case-law of the Court of Justice since 1985, whatever value these justifications might have had has been further diminished.

The liberalisation of movements of capital and payments, including those connected with private savings, throughout the Community since 1990 combined with the effective exercise of the freedom of services of "foreign" based EC financial institutions from 1 January 1993 under the Second Banking Directive would, it is submitted, stand in the way of any attempt to impose observance of any such agreements, however socially desirable in any particular Member State, by banks based in other Member States operating on its territory on a cross-border basis. Similarly, they stand in the way of any attempt to prevent or discourage savers in one Member State from moving their savings to better remunerated accounts (in the same or in another EEC currency) with banks or financial institutions in another Member State.

27.45 In the present state of Community law, it is in any event questionable whether objectives such as the provision of low-cost funds for social housing credits or investments credits pursued by way of "private" agreements on interest rates come within the ambit of article 85(3). The developments in the insurance sector, which recently led to the removal of arbitrary restrictions on investments of technical and mathematical reserves imposed on, or voluntarily entered into, by insurance companies in some EC countries is a case in point. There, the view was taken, in our opinion rightly, that these investments restrictions were incompatible with the free movement of capital and with the free provision of insurance services throughout the Community, notwithstanding the fact that one of the justifications that could be advanced for the continuation of these restrictions was that they provided a cheap source of funds for some types of housing credit, or for the national authorities to fund their deficits (for example, by being able to insist on large scale investment of technical and mathematical reserves in government bonds).[110]

Finally, it is submitted that, in the present state of Community law, it is no longer possible to argue that an interbank agreement on interest rates can be exempted pursuant to article 85(3) on the sole ground that such agreement is approved or

108. It must be noted, though, that the Commission has, in some respects, adopted positions in the group exemption for insurance companies which are far more liberal than the positions adopted to date in the banking sector.

109. Page 43.

110. See the Third Non-Life Insurance Directive, 92/49/EEC of 18 June 1992 and the Third Life Assurance Directive, 92/96/EEC of 10 November 1992.

encouraged by the public authorities. The recent case-law of the Court of Justice discussed below[111] put this in our view beyond dispute.

6. RESTRICTIONS ON COMPETITION IMPOSED BY THE NATIONAL AUTHORITIES

27.46 In the absence to date of a common monetary policy for the Community, national measures in that field differ widely between the Member States. It is obvious that certain national monetary measures may directly affect competition between banks both on the domestic market (as in the case of lending restrictions which have the effect of making it difficult for newcomers to expand their share of the market) and on the international market (as in the case of national capital requirements, which have the effect of impeding the ability of banks to compete). This raises the question whether individual Member States have unlimited freedom to take national monetary (and other) measures which unnecessarily impose upon banks some anti-competitive conduct. The imposition of lending restrictions so structured as effectively to exclude competition between banks in that field or the entry and growth of the market share of (foreign) newcomers is a case in point.[112]

Although the Member States have to date retained in large part their wide powers of action in monetary and financial policy, it does not automatically follow that the exercise of the powers of the Member States in those areas (which powers seem likely in any event to shrink rapidly in years to come if the move towards a single European currency is sustained[113]) are subject to no control whatsoever in terms of EC law if they restrict competition among financial institutions. The same position obtains when the measures taken are ostensibly motivated not by reasons of monetary policy but by other objectives which Member States can legitimately pursue under Treaty, such as consumer protection.[114]

Articles 85 and 86 are each addressed to undertakings and, unlike other provisions of the Treaty, not to the Member States. Accordingly, a restriction on competition imposed by a Member State on its banks is not as such capable of falling within the scope of those provisions. However, regard must be had in each case to the justification given by the Member State concerned for the restriction of competition imposed: the Member States cannot, by national provisions, allow undertakings to escape from the

---

111. See hereafter "Restrictions on competition imposed by the national authorities".

112. See the position taken by the Commission regarding the application of turnover criteria in connection with the admission of new entrants to clearing or netting systems, reviewed at para. 27.52, below.

113. See, para. 27.49, below.

114. Reasons for Member States wishing to adopt such measures vary widely and are not necessarily motivated by reasons of monetary policy or of consumer protection. Thus the wish to protect the profitability of a largely inefficient national banking sector (by imposing maximum rates of interest payable on deposits) may be one of the reasons, as will also sometimes be the wish to ensure, again by imposing maximum rates of credit interest payable to customers on deposits rates or on bonds issued by the banks, that the banks do not compete with the public authorities, if these have substantial borrowing requirements, by pushing up the rate of interest that must be offered to the public to induce it to buy government bonds. The statement made in 1981 by Mr. Andriessen, then Commissioner in charge of competition that ". . . supervisory authorities tend to regulate interest rates [*inter alia* by imposing] minimum deposit rates and maximum lending rates" (see Summary in *Agence Europe*, Bulletin 3264, new series of 5 December 1981) cannot therefore be accepted without reservations. In some instances, it is precisely the contrary position which will be obtained. This was the case *inter alia* of the national regulations reviewed by the Court of Justice in *Van Eycke* v. *ASPA* examined hereafter and which made a national tax exemption on interests received by customers from certain types of savings deposits conditional on the rate of interest not exceeding a certain maximum rate.

requirements of the rules on competition. As already seen,[115] this approach was confirmed as early as 1977 by the Court of Justice in the celebrated *INNO* v. *ATAB* case[116] and refined in the two *Cognac* cases and in *Van Eycke* v. *ASPA*.

In its Eleventh Report on Competition Policy for the year 1981, the Commission suggested that the *Züchner* case "made it clear that the banking sector is only exempted from the competition rules to the extent that any anti-competitive conduct by banks is imposed on them by the monetary authorities".[117] As mentioned earlier, the same position was reiterated, in substance, in 1989, in a letter sent by Sir Leon Brittan, Vice-President in charge of competition policy, to the President of the European Banking Federation, regarding interbank agreements on interest rates.

27.47 In the first edition of this book, published in 1985, it was submitted[118] that the Commission's analysis of the *Züchner* judgment was in this respect erroneous because it found no basis either expressly or by implication in the judgment of the Court; and also[119] that in view of the Court's case-law (referring to the *INNO* v. *ATAB* judgment) the distinction made by the Commission was unlikely to be endorsed by the Court, at least in its entirety. The later pronouncements of the Court, first in the two *Cognac* cases and the *Vlaamse Reisbureau* case and, more to the point, in the *Van Eycke* v. *ASPA* case, which directly concerned the banking sector, appears to have borne out those submissions.

Having regard to the Court's case-law, and taking into account the provisions of the Second Banking Directive, which came into force on 1 January 1993, it is submitted that a measure taken by the national authorities which restricts competition amongst banks, including competition in the field of interest rates, can only be upheld—and enforced *vis-à-vis* "foreign" based EC banks operating in the Member State concerned by way of branches or on a cross-border basis—if it can be demonstrated that the measures taken by the authorities:

— actually oblige banks, and not merely permit them, to abstain from competition in certain areas;
— have been taken by the authorities in the exercise of their own regulatory powers, that is, do not simply rubber-stamp an agreement arrived at between private undertakings, or within their trade organisations;
— can be shown to be objectively justified by a goal which the authorities set out to achieve, the pursuit of which is legitimate in terms of EC law, such as consumer protection (in the case of minimum rate on deposits and/or maximum rates on consumer loans) or such as monetary policy objectives, in line with the retained powers of the national competent authorities (as in the case of lending limits imposed on banks generally); and
— can be shown to be proportionate to these objectives.

The application of these criteria, which is fully in line with the general case-law of the Court of Justice, inevitably leads to questioning the validity in terms of EC law of certain national measures which, even though they fulfil the first two conditions, fail to

---

115. Chap. 23, above.
116. Case 13/77 [1977] ECR 2115.
117. Eleventh Report on Competition Policy, point 61.
118. Page 40.
119. Page 42.

meet the third or the fourth one. This is particularly the case since the entry into force of the provisions of the Second Banking Directive.

27.48 For example, in France it appears that national legislation prohibits banks from making interest payments in respect of credit balances held in current accounts. Now that the Second Banking Directive is in force, could a "foreign" EC bank operating by way of a branch in France (and not subject to a similar regulation in its home country) pay interest to the customers of its French branch in respect of the credit balances in current accounts? The answer will, it is suggested, be in the affirmative if the provision is viewed, as a matter of EC law (thus subject to review by the Court of Justice), as a measure designed to ensure the solvency of credit institutions. Indeed, in that case, the authorities of the host country, that is France, have no competence over French branches of banks having their head office in other Member States. On the other hand, the answer will presumably be in the negative if the French legal provision is viewed, again as a matter of EC law, to be a monetary policy measure for which the authorities of the host Member State retain regulatory powers. If, however, the "foreign" EC bank is collecting deposits in France on a cross-border basis (that is, without a local French branch) the answer must, it is submitted, be yes.[120]

The distinction between measures designed to afford protection to the consumer on the one part and measures designed to ensure the solvency of financial institutions on the other part also has far-reaching implications. Thus in certain Member States (for example, reportedly, Italy) legal provisions prohibit banks conducting mortgage credit business from extending loans in excess of a certain percentage of the value of the relevant property. However, in other Member States (for example, the United Kingdom) there are no such restrictions. With the Second Banking Directive now in force, can a United Kingdom bank extend to an Italian borrower mortgage facilities of up to 100% of the value of a building in Italy? The reply to this question would appear to depend on whether the relevant Italian regulation is considered—as a matter of EC law—to be a means to ensure the solvency of Italian banks by preventing the granting of insufficiently guaranteed credit, or else a means to protect borrowers from falling into excessive debt, or else a means to limit, for monetary reasons, the volume of mortgage credit extended.

7. IMPACT OF MOVES TOWARDS A SINGLE EUROPEAN CURRENCY

27.49 Even when a government-imposed measure in the field of interest rates is clearly dictated by the necessities of national monetary policy, such a measure is not *ipso facto* outside the scope of EC law. Indeed, it must be borne in mind that the

---

120. When, on the other hand, the "foreign" EC bank is operating in France by way of a locally-incorporated French subsidiary, the position is different in that the French regulations cannot in any way be viewed in that case as a restriction on the right of "foreign" EC banks to do business in France under the "single licence" created by the Second Banking Directive. Indeed, that "single licence" is not available when the "foreign" EC bank does business in another Member State through a locally-incorporated subsidiary there. This is apparently the situation which arose in France recently when the locally-incorporated subsidiary in France of Barclays Bank offered to its customers a high-interest current account. It is interesting to note that the French Minister of Finance, who insisted that the subsidiary in that case should observe the French regulation prohibiting such accounts, reportedly justified the regulation on the ground that, in its absence, French banks would have to increase the interest rate charged to French borrowers (including commercial credits) to make up for the higher cost of the funds deposited by customers in their current accounts. See further European Report, 1826 of 13 January 1993, p. 5.

freedom of Member States to act in this field looks likely to be progressively restricted in years to come, as a result of the move towards a single European currency set in motion by the Treaty on European Union.

One of the implications of that move is that Member States may no longer fund their public deficit by direct borrowing (from their national central bank) nor by indirect borrowing (by being able, for example, to demand that their local banks or insurance companies should buy large quantities of government bonds).[121] Member States should instead either increase their taxes or cut their spending. On the assumption that these restrictions were already in force, it would be hard to argue that government—imposed measures in the field of interest rates (for example, maximum credit interest payable on banks' bonds to avoid competition with government bonds) can be justified on the ground that they are designed to keep down the cost of public sector borrowing.

For the same reason, the decision by the monetary authorities of a number of Member States to abandon the use of the discount rate as an instrument of monetary policy and to move instead towards open market techniques (ie buying or selling government bonds or treasury certificates in the market to influence its liquidity and hence interest rates) makes it hard to justify, on the ground of the requirements of monetary policy, government imposed measures which restrict competition in the field of interest rates.

8. THE APPLICATION OF ARTICLE 86 TO DOMESTIC BANKING OPERATIONS

27.50 The rules governing the application of article 86, reviewed earlier,[122] need to be considered, in the context of the banking sector, at two levels. First, the level of any large bank or professional grouping, enjoying *de facto* or *de jure* a dominant position in any particular sector of the financial industry. Second, the level of any bank, whatever its size, with regard to certain services which it provides and for which it— necessarily—enjoys a monopoly position.

1. The application of article 86 to any large bank or professional grouping, enjoying *de facto* or *de jure* a dominant position in any particular sector of the financial industry and abusing it

27.51 This is the most obvious situation for the possible application of article 86. Cases where such a dominant position may exist are numerous. For example, large clearing systems at national (or at international) level and large card issuing systems or automated teller networks (the market share of which is increased by existing or proposed "interoperability agreements" which, in effect, turn two or more previously competing networks into, at least in some respect, one large network).

Areas where an abuse of a dominant position can arise include:

— Unfair conditions regarding admission to or exclusion from such a system. An obvious parallel can be made here with the *London European Airways* v. *Sabena* decision taken by the Commission in 1987.[123] In the financial sector,

---

121. See arts. 104 and 104a of the Treaty, as amended by the Treaty on European Union.
122. Chap. 23, above.
123. Seventeenth Report on Competition Policy, 1987, published 1988, point 86.

the reported difficulties at the time surrounding the admission of fund managers to SWIFT, the bank-owned payment and financial messaging system, reportedly because of opposition from banks having a large global custody business which feared that allowing fund managers access to SWIFT would lead to them bypassing the global custodians, is a case in point.[124]

— Attempts to make the provision of the services sought by actual or potential members subject to their agreeing to acquire additional, unrelated services.[125] This would be the case, for example, for an obligation to buy all computer equipments used in connection with, say, the credit card network from the network or its affiliates, even when such an obligation goes beyond what is justified by objective safety or technical standards requirements.[126]

— Attempts to widen an existing dominant position by extending it to areas which are objectively unrelated thereto. A case to bear in mind here is the decision of the Commission in 1988, in the *TV Guide* case.[127] The situation in that case could arise in the financial sector if, say, a stock market authority claimed a monopoly with regard to the sale to the public, or to financial newspapers, of the information which stockbrokers must file with it in respect of off-the-market trades or which the companies whose shares are traded on the market must file with it whenever such information can significantly influence the value of their shares. The question may also be asked whether an abuse of dominant position could arise if the general terms of business recommended by a banking association to all its members in a specific Member State provided that, as a condition for doing business with a bank, the company or individual concerned must agree to do all its financial transactions through that bank or its affiliates. In that situation, the customer who requires a mortgage might, for example, be forced to take out life assurance and insurance for the property from an insurance company or through an insurance broker affiliated to the bank.

27.52 Useful indications of the Commission's present thinking in this field may be gathered from its recent working document "Easier cross-border payments: breaking down the barriers" which constituted the basis for its later Recommendation on cross-border payments. Annex C to the working document sets out the principles which, in the Commission's view, should guide the application of the EC Treaty competition rules to co-operation agreements among banks regarding membership in, and technical, legal and operational aspects of, "systems allowing for clearing, netting and/or settlement of cross-border transfer payments or linking existing transfer networks with each other".

With regard to the membership issue, the Commission takes the view that, as a general rule, co-operation agreements which embrace the majority of credit institutions

---

124. See *Financial Times*, 18 June 1991, p. 24: "Fund managers angry at their exclusion from Swift." It has since been reported that their admission has now been allowed but that they are no longer interested because they have in the meantime decided to develop their own system.

125. See Chap. 23, above.

126. A parallel may usefully be made with the Commission's decision of 19 December 1988 (OJ L36/1 of 8 February 1989) dealing with agreements notified to it regarding the selection of companies entrusted with the production and "finition" of Eurocheques and Eurocards. See fn. 18, above.

127. Decision of 21 December 1988, OJ L78 of 21 March 1989; also Eighteenth Report on Competition Policy, 1988, published 1989, p. 79. See further the article by G. Vernimmen referred to in fn. 49, above, at p. 15, point II.

of one country or which embrace institutions that are likely to process a significant part of payments traffic between different countries either totally or in a given market segment (eg, automated clearing of retail payments; foreign exchange netting) may be considered to provide an "essential facility" and, therefore, "should be open for further membership provided that candidates meet appropriate criteria". The Commission also takes the view that: "When a limited number of institutions set up a payment system, they may be entitled to choose their partners according to their general business strategy and cannot *always* be forced to open their particular agreement to further partners, even of equivalent standing. However, such agreements must not contain clauses which have the effect of preventing individual participants from taking part in other systems." The Commission goes on to stress that "the general requirement of non-exclusivity . . . is not intended to prevent the application of membership criteria . . . which are objectively justified, [such as] the financial standing, the orderly management and the technical capacities of participants". Of particular interest are its additional comments regarding the application of criteria based on volume, which can be especially detrimental for foreign banks applying for membership of a domestic clearing system, (as well as for any bank which, having just been set up, has no existing volume)[128]:

As regards criteria based on volume, it will be legitimate to require that the expected traffic generated by a candidate should not be negligible. But payment systems should wherever possible permit participation by institutions of varying sizes.
. . . Where foreign banks apply for membership in a domestic transfer system, their expected volume may be low in the beginning; in such case, the type of business, the experience and the volume of payment transactions in the country of origin of such banks should be taken into account.
Refusal of membership or exclusion should be subject to an independent review procedure.[129]

2. The application of article 86 to any bank, whatever its size, with regard to certain services which it provides and for which it—necessarily—enjoys a monopoly position

27.53 It is submitted that the possibility of an abuse of a dominant position may also arise at the level of any bank, whatever its size, in respect of certain of its operations. This will be the case, it is submitted, whenever a bank imposes unfair conditions in terms of article 86 for those of its services for which it is in a monopoly position.

One illustration is the payment by a bank of the cheques drawn by its clients on their accounts with the bank, and handed over to a third party beneficiary. Obviously, the only bank that is in a position to pay the cheque to the holder is, eventually, the bank on which it is drawn. Therefore, in line with the case-law of the Court of Justice,[130] the drawee bank must always be viewed as having a dominant position in respect of the payment of the cheques drawn by its own clients. Abusive conditions laid down by it for paying those cheques to the holder thereof (for example by demanding the payment of a

128. In practice, however, the imposition of volume criteria by existing members, who have made sometime very considerable investment in an existing system, as a condition for admission of a new participant, may be explained by the wish to avoid a "free rider" rather than the desire to deprive a competitor of access to an "essential facility".
129. This statement, which obviously echoes the principles laid down in *Sarabex* case reviewed earlier, raises certain question marks in the case of "private" systems: should the contractual arrangements which lay at their basis provide for review of refusal of membership by an outside body?
130. See Case 22/78 *Hugin* v. *Commission* [1979] ECR 1869; case 26/75 *General Motors Continental* v. *Commission* [1975] ECR 1367 and case 226/85 *British Leyland* v. *Commission* [1986] ECR 3263.

fee or commission or, in the case of remittance by post, by delaying payment to the beneficiary even though it has already debited the account of its own client), are capable of being caught by article 86. The question may also be asked whether the same reasoning can be extended, in certain circumstances, to the conditions laid down by the bank (in terms of commission charged) for crediting the account of its client with funds transferred by a third party, via another bank, for the account of the client.

Finally, in considering the application of article 86 to the banking sector, it should be remembered that whereas the prohibition in article 85(1) can be waived by the Commission if it finds that an agreement can be exempted pursuant to article 85(3), no such possibility of exemption exists with respect to an abuse of dominant position prohibited by article 86; and that exemption of an agreement under article 85(3) does not in any way imply exemption from the prohibition on abuse of dominant position contained in article 86. Thus, for example, it is not because, say, a co-operation agreement amongst banks has been exempted from the prohibition of article 85(1), (on the basis of article 85(3)) or even has obtained negative clearance, that the conduct of the venture set up under that agreement (such as a cheque clearing system or the like) cannot be held to be abusive in certain circumstances in terms of article 86 (for example if the joint venture lays down abusive conditions, etc., in terms of entry of members) and be challenged as such in the national courts.[131]

---

131. The relevance of this point becomes more apparent when it is recalled, for instance, that in its recent working document on cross-border payments the Commission stated that even though EC competition law applies to agreements under which clearing or netting systems are set up, "this does not imply that the competition rules will be applicable to all such agreements: indeed, agreements without which the provision of payment services is not conceivable might well not fall under the prohibition in art. 85(1) at all" (see annex C to the working document).

CHAPTER 28

BANKING ALLIANCES AT NATIONAL AND INTERNATIONAL LEVEL

1. CONSORTIUM GROUPS

28.1 In 1973, the Commission indicated that it was considering whether the creation and the operation of banking co-operation groups was compatible with the provisions of article 85(1).[1] The Commission justified its investigation by reference to the anti-competitive effects which, in its view, might flow from co-operation agreements and the creation of joint ventures by parent companies in competition with each other.

In its Eighth Report on Competition Policy, published in 1979, the Commission made known the results of its investigation. The Commission recalled that the activities of the banks belonging to bank groupings such as Abecor, Ebic and Inter Alpha[2]:

are integrated to varying degrees, but they all have the objective of setting up a co-operation arrangement enabling the members in all countries to have access to each other's networks of branches . . . , the establishment of joint branches in non-member countries, the formation of joint subsidiaries specialising in certain lines of business (medium term lending business, hire-purchase or leasing, merchant banking) or, on certain non-European markets, and the joint placing of public and private issues of stocks and shares.

The conclusion reached by the Commission from preliminary soundings was that[3]:

the co-operation within these banking groups is generally rather loose. The banks retain the freedom to extend their own networks of branches individually. There are no reciprocal exclusive arrangements concerning international transactions, but the partner bank has a right of pre-emption over a limited part of them. Joint subsidiaries generally operate as ordinary banks in cooperation and sometimes in competition with the partner banks.

The Commission concluded that there was no need to start proceedings against the relevant agreements, in respect of which there had been no formal applications for a Commission decision nor any complaints. By so doing, it showed a more flexible attitude to joint venture agreements in the banking sector than had previously been the case in relation to cooperation in the manufacturing sector where it had objected to the existence of pre-emption clauses.[4] It was suggested at the time that the Commission's decision not to open "own initiative" proceedings against the relevant agreements could be explained—and justified—by the fact that the experience of recent years had shown

---

1. Second Report on Competition Policy, 1972, published 1973, point 53.
2. Eighth Report on Competition Policy, 1978, published 1979, point 33.
3. *Ibid.*
4. So-called "English clauses" which, according to the Court of Justice's case-law, are capable of having an anti-competitive effect, see case 85/76 *Hoffmann-La Roche* v. *Commission* [1979] ECR 461.

that partner banks had often been disappointed by the results of the co-operation achieved through joint ventures.[5]

28.2 Indeed, in 1983, the Commission recorded that[6]:

... the early 1970s saw the start of a wave of extensive co-operation between banks from different countries. This development apparently did not turn out as well as expected: at any rate, the integration between the banking groups involved did not progress very far. Instead, more and more banks went over to setting up direct foreign subsidiaries.

Even though consortia banks are very much out of fashion at the present time, and have been for some time, it should be borne in mind that any future revival of the concept, possibly under a different name, will need to take account of the requirements of EC competition law, which are likely to be enforced more strictly than they were in the 1970s. This is already evidenced by the Commission's current review of co-operation agreements between European savings banks discussed below.

2. RECENT CO-OPERATION AGREEMENTS AMONG EUROPEAN SAVINGS BANKS

28.3 In preparation for the Single Market, European savings banks have taken various measures to tighten the links between them. According to a Commission press release of 7 June 1991,[7] these steps include classic bilateral co-operation agreements; a multilateral agreement (EUFISERV project) on interoperability of the savings banks' Automated Teller Machines (ATMs); and the foundation of a European Economic Interest Grouping named EGFI (European Group of Financial Institutions). These various steps have been the subject of a review by the Commission.

In relation to the co-operation agreements, a number of bilateral co-operation agreements signed by European savings banks or their national associations have been notified to the Commission. Of these, 10—at the time of the press release—had already been granted a comfort letter (indicating informally their compatibility with EC competition rules). However, these comfort letters were sometimes only granted after the original agreements had been amended at the Commission's request. While stating that it was "in principle in favour of such agreements, which are likely to make life easier for customers of the banks concerned who move from one EC country to another," the Commission felt it useful to identify in its press release some provisions of the agreements which did not seem acceptable and for which amendments were sought. These were provisions:

— not to enter each other's geographical territory;
— not to conclude similar arrangements with other credit institutions in the territory;
— concerning the exclusivity granted to each partner in its home country for dealing in and distributing common products;
— concerning the *a priori* control of the national associations over the bilateral agreements signed by their members.

---

5. M. Dassesse & S. Isaacs, *"Incidences du Droit Communnautaire de la Concurrence sur certains accords bancaires nationaux et transnationaux"*, Cahiers de Droit Européen (1980), p. 527, at p. 533.
6. Thirteenth Report on Competition Policy, 1982, published 1983, point 322.
7. "Competition law and co-operation between European savings banks", ref. 1, P. (91)534. See further the article by G. Vernimmen referred to in fn. 49, above, at p. 16, point V.

28.4 In relation to the conclusion of a multilateral agreement on the interoperability of the savings banks' ATMs, EUFISERV, a Belgian *société coopérative*, was established in 1990 by 11 European national associations of savings banks and the European Savings Banks Group. More than 18,000 ATMs are open to 37 million holders of cards issued by savings banks. The agreement was not formally notified but there was informal contact between the project co-ordinators and the competition services of the Commission. These drew the attention of the savings banks' representatives to the necessity for tariff rules to be in conformity with competition rules. "In particular, [according to the press release] the initial agreement on the interbank commission charged for using ATMs did not specify that the commission provided for was a maximum and that bilateral agreements between savings banks setting lower limits were possible."

In relation to the creation of a European Economic Interest Grouping, EGFI was created in 1990. Savings banks from a number of Member States participate in it. According to the press release, following notification of its rules by EGFI to the Commission, "a comfort letter is likely to be sent soon ... in accordance with the normal application of competition policy in similar cases in other fields".

3. MOVES TOWARDS NATIONAL INTEGRATION AND PRODUCT/ DISTRIBUTION ALLIANCES

28.5 As has been rightly noted[8]:

As banks develop expansion strategies in the run-up to a single financial space, national integration and product distribution alliances have dwarfed the cross-border mergers and acquisitions that attracted the attention of many commentators. The demise of the much debated AMRO/Generale Bank cross-border merger contrasts sharply with the host of national mergers. Banco Bilbao–Viscaya, Bergen Bank/Den Norske Credietbank and Copenhagen Handelsbank/ Den Danske Bank, for example. Whilst any merger involves costs and painful conflicts, former rivals in a given market place clearly prefer to pair with each other, often with the blessing and encouragement of regulatory authorities, rather than with an outsider with a different culture.

The trend observed recently towards national banking mergers, instead of the transnational mergers or alliances that had been expected to take place in the run-up to the single financial market, does not augur well for the private consumers nor for small and medium enterprises who are, and will remain, largely dependent on the national banking industry to serve their needs. The merger of banks which already have a dominant part on their local market can only create local "banking behemoths", which are hardly likely to result in increased competition in the local market. As one observer put it,[9] "Europe's consumers could be the losers if this trend continues unchecked". This trend is all the more worrying since it is also being observed in the insurance industry, which is itself in increasing competition with the banking industry. Indeed, it has been said[10] that perhaps the most meaningful trend in European banking today is the challenge posed to the insurance sector by banks, some of which even have insurance company shareholders that are distributing life and pension products to their vast client base. Faced with the relatively low cost distribution channels keyed to the

8. *Salomon Brothers*, Stock Research—Commercial Banks, September 1990, p. 6.
9. *The Economist*, 31 March 1990, p. 84.
10. *Salomon Brothers*, Stock research—Commercial Banks, September 1990, p. 6. See also *The Economist*, 17 October 1992, p. 81 *ibid.*, 25 September 1993, p. 83 "All aboard for Allfinanz".

banks' existing branch networks and client base, insurance companies are responding by acquiring banks, entering the banking business themselves, or honing their products and selling skills to meet the new threat. The recently abandoned bid for Belgium's second largest bank, BBL, by the Dutch insurance group ING; the stake of 22·3% (eventually cleared in September 1992 by the German Competition Authority) held by Germany's largest insurer, Allianz, in Dresdner Bank, Germany's second largest bank; and the talks in progress at the time of writing for Belgium's largest insurer, Fortis (itself a joint venture of Belgian and Dutch insurers) to acquire Belgium's largest public bank, CGER/ASLK, which is in the process of being privatised, are all pointers in the same direction.

28.6 Some of the agreements concluded in that field and recently notified to the Commission require to be mentioned in the present context. First, a co-operation agreement between the Halifax Building Society and the Bank of Scotland.[11] The purpose of the agreement is the issue of a new credit card to be called the Halifax card and bearing the Visa and Halifax brand names. The agreement was granted a comfort letter by the Commission, but only after Halifax had agreed to limit to five years the period, unlimited originally, during which it covenanted not to promote within its branches any other credit card similar to the Visa card which Bank of Scotland considered might compete with the Halifax card. Second, an agreement between the Halifax Building Society and the Standard Life Insurance Company.[12] Under the agreement, Halifax becomes the "appointed representative", within the meaning of the United Kingdom Financial Services Act, or agent of Standard Life for the purpose of advising on and selling Standard Life's life assurance, pensions, unit trusts and related products. The agreement, as modified, contained two clauses which, in the Commission's opinion, constituted restrictions on competition within article 85(1) and which did not satisfy the conditions for exemption under article 85(3). The clauses prohibited Standard Life from appointing other building societies as its appointed representatives[13] and prohibited commission rebating. At the Commission's request, both clauses were deleted.

In both instances, the question whether the restrictions of competition could affect trade between Member States was not specifically examined. This tends to bear out the comment already made that this condition for the applicability of the rules on competition will, in practice, always be fulfilled when major financial institutions are involved: they can reasonably be expected to have at least some clients resident in other Member States and so a cross-border provision of services in such Member States will *ipso facto* exist.

---

11. See *Agence Europe*, Bulletin 5588 (new series) 14–15 October 1991, p. 12.
12. See Notice pursuant to art. 19(3) of Reg. 17 published in OJ C131/2 of 22 May 1992.
13. Under the so-called polarisation rule, English law requires Halifax, once it has opted to become an "appointed representative" of Standard Life, to be a representative of that company only. It has since been reported that Halifax is to sever "beginning in late 1994 . . . its existing ties with Standard Life . . for whom it acts as exclusive sales agent" and will instead "set up its own insurance company which will sell exclusively to its customers" (*Financial Times*, 4 September 1993, p. 1).

4. "COMMUNITY DIMENSION" CRITERIA—DIFFICULTIES OF APPLICATION OF THE MERGER CONTROL REGULATION—SPECIFIC ISSUES

28.7 The Merger Control Regulation generally was considered in Chapter 22. As there stated, one of the problems of the application of its provisions to credit institutions and other financial institutions is that such institutions have no "turnover" comparable to that of other undertakings. Thus:

Most of the income of a credit institution normally results from interest received on loans and advances. It is therefore necessary to develop particular rules instead of the normal 5 billion and 250 million ECU turnover criteria, in order to apply the thresholds of the Regulation to this sector.[14]

Therefore, article 5(3)(a) of the Regulation provides that, in place of turnover, the following criteria are to be used:

— instead of the 5,000 million ECU threshold for the combined aggregate worldwide turnover of all the undertakings concerned, one-tenth of their total assets;
— instead of the 250 million ECU threshold for the aggregate Community-wide turnover of at least two of the undertakings concerned, one-tenth of total assets multiplied by the ratio between loans and advances to credit institutions and customers in transactions with Community residents and the total sum of those loans and advances;
— instead of having regard to turnover within one and the same Member State, regard must be had to one-tenth of total assets multiplied by the ratio between loans and advances to credit institutions and customers in transactions with residents of that Member State and the total sum of those loans and advances.

28.8 The use of total assets and loans and advances was considered to be more representative of financial activity than other measures of banking output. However:

There are nonetheless problems in ensuring both that these criteria produce a result broadly equivalent in the financial sector to that achieved in other sectors, and also in ensuring the same outcome for different types of financial institutions. Banks, for example, can create credit which appears on their balance sheet. There are certain other types of financial institutions, such as companies principally involved in funds management, credit cards, securities trade or corporate financial advice which are not in this position. Another difficulty is that the calculation of Community and national turnover might produce odd results where the credit activities of the financial institutions in question represent a small proportion of their total assets. This might be the case in respect of certain holding companies.

Further, the calculation of turnover within the Community requires banks and other financial institutions to distinguish financial operations according to the residence of their clients.

In the light of all these factors the Commission and the Council of Ministers have made clear that these provisions may be modified in the light of the comments of regulatory authorities and the market practitioners themselves. Specifically when the Regulation was adopted the Council and Commission stated in a note clarifying the scope of certain articles of the Regulation that they:

"consider that the criterion defined as a proportion of assets should be replaced by a concept of banking income as referred to in Directive 86/635 on the annual accounts and consolidated accounts of banks and other financial institutions, either at the time of entry

14. Lecture by Sir Leon Brittan on "Competition in Financial Services" delivered at the Centre for European Policy Studies in Brussels on 16 January 1992, stencilled text p. 13.

into force of the relevant provisions of that Directive, or at the time of the review of the thresholds."[15]

Indeed, the so far limited experience of the Commission in the field of bank mergers having a Community dimension and, in particular, the difficulties encountered in applying the criteria laid down by the Regulation when examining the Hong Kong and Shanghai Bank/Midland Bank merger, have confirmed the need for a revision of the present criteria.

Thus:

based on banking cases dealt with so far, the [Commission's] Merger Task Force considers that [the present] assets-based system has been poor at tackling such issues as the allocation of turnover by geographical area and the calculation of turnover of credit institutions which either do not lend or advance money, or are widely diversified.[16]

Accordingly, the Commission's Merger Task Force is reported, at the time of writing, as favouring a definition of "Community dimension" of banking concentrations in terms of their banking income, as defined under the 1986 Bank Accounts Directive, rather than in terms of their assets. This approach has reportedly been indorsed by the EC Banking Federation ("ECBF"), in particular because information on income is already compiled under the Bank Accounts Directive.[17] The Merger Task Force is understood to be arguing that this approach allows credit and financial institutions to be treated equally. It would also enable non-lending income to be taken into account, provide a better reflection of these institutions' financial situation and reduce the problem of trying to allocate turnover by country.[18]

With regard to this latter problem, which was particularly complex in the case of the HSBC/Midland Bank merger, the Merger Task Force is reported as having accepted the ECBF's argument that, in the case of banks, income should be allocated according to the location of the product's seller, not the customer, whereas, as a rule, the Regulation seeks to allocate turnover according to the location of the consumer, not the seller, of goods or a service. According to the ECBF, to try to allocate income according to the country of the customer would cause enormous problems, since the raising of finance is often completely separate from the country where it is applied.[19]

As at the time of writing, it is understood that these amendments to the Regulation will be proposed by the Commission to the Council at the same time as it proposes to the Council to lower the Regulation's general thresholds applicable to all economic sectors.[20]

Bank rescue operations

28.9 As already stated, the Regulation makes express provision for when a concentration is *not* deemed to arise in relation to credit institutions and certain other

---

15. *Ibid.*, at pp. 13–14. See also the lecture delivered by Mr. Claus-Dieter Ehlermann, Director-General of DGXV (Competition) on "The application of the EEC rules on competition to credit institutions" in June 1992 to the Annual Meeting of Members of the European Mortgage Federation, Annual Report 1992, p. 35 *et seq.*, at p. 42.

16. The *EC Times*, 19 July 1993, p. 1 *et seq.*

17. *Ibid.*, p. 2.

18. *Ibid.*

19. *Ibid.*

20. *Ibid.* It has since been reported that the Commission unanimously decided not to propose to the Council to change the Regulation and, therefore, to retain the thresholds applicable, yet to plan to discuss the issue within three years: *Agence Europe* 6301 (new series) 29 July 1993, p. 4.

financial institutions and insurance companies. By article 3(5)(a), the Regulation states that a concentration is not deemed to arise where credit institutions or other financial institutions or insurance companies, the normal activities of which include transactions and dealings in securities for their own account or for the account of others, hold on a temporary basis securities which they have acquired in an undertaking with a view to reselling them, provided that:

— they do not exercise voting rights in respect of those securities with a view to determining the competitive behaviour of that undertaking; or
— they exercise such voting rights only with a view to preparing the disposal of all or part of that undertaking or of its assets or the disposal of those securities and that any such disposal takes place within one year of the date of acquisition or any extension of that period granted by the Commission where it can be shown that the disposal was not reasonably possible within the period set.

These provisions in effect acknowledge that credit and financial institutions may, without being caught by the Regulation, acquire a passive, temporary, shareholding in a company in the normal course of their business; or take temporary control of the affairs of a customer, with a view to disposing of the customer's assets within a "reasonable" period of time.

The Commission's recent decision in *Kelt/American Express*[21] illustrates the application of these provisions and indicates the likely limit of their scope. In that case, the Commission considered that there was a merger where there was an operation by which an international banking consortium led by American Express would take control of a company involved in the oil and natural gas sectors, essentially because the consortium had no intention of selling its shareholding within one year.

Definition of relevant market

28.10 As recalled recently by Mr. Ehlermann,[22] the mergers so far notified to the Commission in the banking field have been of limited impact in terms of their effects on competition in the Community. Indeed, all decisions taken to date in this field have been positive, and taken within one month of notification. As a result, in order to minimise the amount of information which must be provided in the notification by the undertakings concerned, the Commission, to quote Mr. Ehlermann:

has been able to forego a precise delimitation of the relevant market and has paid more attention to the categories of activities involved than to the definition of the market affected.[23]

Indeed, a number of the cases notified to the Commission have been concerned with the setting up of joint ventures in third countries.

For example, in *Dresdner Bank/Banque Nationale de Paris*,[24] the Commission considered that the joint services to be offered by the joint ventures in Hungary and Czechoslovakia principally concerned those countries' own respective financial

---

21. M116 of 20 August 1991.
22. In the lecture referred to in fn. 15 above.
23. For a general review, see further B. Sousi-Roubi and Y. Zachmann "Le contrôle communautaire des concentrations bancaires" Revue de Droit bancaire et de la Bourse (1993), p. 77 aid fol.; also, G. Vernimmen, "Le respect des règles de concurrence dans les services bancaires", ECU (Brussels) (1993) III, p. 14 and fn. 1.
24. M.124 of 31 August 1991.

markets which, being outside the Community, made it unnecessary for the Commission to consider the effect on those markets.

In other cases, such as the merger between Kyoma Bank and Saitama Bank[25] and the merger between Crédit Suisse and Swiss Volksbank,[26] the Commission left open the question of a precise definition of the relevant market since, even by taking the narrowest possible definition of the relevant market, the market shares within the Community of the banks involved were clearly negligible.

A similar position has also been adopted more recently by the Commission in the case of the acquisition by Deutsche Bank of the Banco de Madrid. According to the Commission,[27] this operation, which will allow Deutsche Bank to increase its presence in deposit banking in Spain and to expand its network of agencies, will neither create nor strengthen a dominant position in the market in question because Deutsche Bank has only a marginal presence on the Spanish market.

In the case of the merger of HSBC and Midland Bank,[28] the Commission's most significant decision to date, the Commission concluded that, although the notified concentration fell within the scope of the Regulation, it raised no serious doubt as to its compatibility with the common market. This was essentially because the only relevant market identified as affected by the proposed concentration was that of market-making in gilt-edged stocks (United Kingdom government or United Kingdom government-guaranteed stocks denominated in sterling) and, having regard to the structure of that market, the proposed concentration would have no material impact on competition in it. It followed that the concentration would not create or strengthen a dominant position as a result of which competition would be significantly impeded in the common market or a substantial part of it.

Criteria regarding change of control of undertakings

28.11 As already stated, a merger within the meaning of the Regulation presupposes the existence of two or more previously independent undertakings. It therefore came as no surprise that the Commission took the view that the Regulation did not apply to the regrouping in Spain in 1991 of all publicly owned or controlled banks within a single entity. As pointed out by Mr. Ehlermann,[29] this was in effect:

an internal reorganisation of banks which were already controlled by the Spanish State before the regrouping took place. The nature and degree of influence exercised by the Spanish State on each of the banks involved was the same before and after the regrouping. Accordingly, the operation could not come within the ambit of the Regulation.

5. POSSIBLE FUTURE TRENDS

28.12 The present trend towards national rather than transnational banking mergers means that the Commission is unlikely—even if it wished—to be able to exert a significant control on these operations through the Regulation. In this respect, it will be

---

25. M69 of 14 March 1991.
26. M335 of 1 May 1993.
27. See *Agence Europe*, 2 June 1993, no. 5991 (NS), p. 12.
28. M213 of 21 May 1992.
29. In the lecture referred to in fn. 15 above. Our translation.

recalled that, under article 1 of the Regulation,[30] a concentration will not have a Community dimension (and will thus, in principle, be outside the Commission's jurisdiction) when each of the enterprises concerned undertakes more than two thirds of its Community business within a single and the same Member State. In addition, even when a banking merger has a Community dimension in terms of the Regulation, and consequently comes within the Commission's jurisdiction[31], it must be borne in mind that under article 21 an individual Member State retains the right to take "any appropriate measure which complies with Community law" in order to safeguard its other (non competition) "legitimate interests."

Of particular relevance for concentration in the banking sector is no doubt the fact that article 21 expressly recognises as a "legitimate interest" of a Member State the safeguarding of its "prudential rules". It is understood that the minutes of the Council meeting at which the Regulation was adopted state in this regard that[32]: "The Commission considers that . . . the 'prudential rules' extant in the Member States and relating, in particular, to the provision of financial services, may be legitimately invoked, their application generally being given to the national banking regulation organs, stock exchange and insurance companies. They relate, for example, to the integrity of persons, the legality of operations and solvency conditions." These specific prudential criteria however are the subject of minimal efforts at harmonisation, undertaken with a view to ensuring uniform "rules of engagement" within the whole of the Community.[33]

Also, even though article 21 expressly recognises three types of "legitimate interests", it does not preclude Member States from invoking other "legitimate interests", subject, in that case, to the Commission or, in the case of a negative Commission decision, the Court of Justice recognising the public interest invoked as a "legitimate interest". The question may be asked, therefore, whether the "public interest" invoked by a Member State in opposition to an attempted take-over of one of its major clearing banks by a "foreign" EC based competitor, would be recognised as a "legitimate interest" by the Commission or, on appeal, by the Court of Justice.[34]

---

30. Art. 1.

31. See in this regard the Commission's decision relating to the merger between Eurocheque and Eurocard in July 1992. As pointed out by G. Vernimmen, in the article referred to in fn. 23 above, p. 18, this is an instance where the Commission, after it had been apprised of the merger pursuant to the Regulation, took the view that "the combined turnover of the two entities (*which, of course are not credit institutions or financial institutions*) did not reach 5 billion ECU" (our translation, our emphasis).

32. Art. 21(3). See the "Commentary" on the Regulation, Eighteenth Report on Competition Policy, for 1989, published 1990, p. 85.

33. *Ibid. Quaere* in this respect whether a Member State can, since the entry into force of the Second Banking Directive, oppose a takeover of one of "its" banks by a bank of another Member State on the ground that the management or organisation of the predator bank is inadequate. It could presumably be argued that the mutual recognition of supervisory standards brought about by the Directive stands in the way of any such ground of opposition.

34. In particular if the predator were a State-owned or controlled bank of another Member State. Compare reports of the Commission's inquiries about the UK government's policy, at the relevant time, concerning the takeover of UK companies generally by State-owned or controlled (French) companies, European Report 1683, 8 June 1991, p. 10.

6. APPLICATION OF ARTICLE 85

28.13 A clear distinction must be made here between "concentrations" as defined by the Regulation, and other operations which do not come within that definition. It will be recalled[35] that, according to the Regulation itself[36]:

An operation, including the creation of a joint venture, which has as its object or effect the coordination of the competitive behaviour of undertakings which remain independent, shall not constitute a concentration within the meaning of [the Regulation].

Operations such as the creation in the 1970s of consortium banks operating independently of but in collaboration with their shareholders fall outside the scope of the Regulation and exclusively within articles 85 and 86 of the EC Treaty. This is the view taken by the Commission in connection with the Europay International project, which has been held to fall outside the scope of the Regulation (as not being a "concentration" for the Regulation's purposes)[37] but which has nevertheless been examined to determine its compatibility with article 85.

28.14 Having regard to the Commission's policy on competition in other sectors, it may be thought that the Commission would be led to apply these provisions within a relatively short space of time to restructuring operations, including the creation of common subsidiaries, which imply a co-ordination of competitive behaviour on the part of the undertakings concerned and to the taking of cross-shareholdings between banks or, in the light of the convergence of their fields of activity, between banks and insurance companies each time these operations meet the conditions for the application of article 85 or 86. Thus an operation whereby two or more banks jointly decide to make an offer to acquire a competing undertaking with a substantial market share and which is established in another Member State, by agreeing to pursue the activities of the company through a joint subsidiary and to apply provisions equivalent to a market-sharing agreement would, it is submitted, fall fairly and squarely within the scope of application of article 85.[38]

On the other hand, for concentrations falling within the definition of the Regulation,[39] the position is very different. As already pointed out,[40] the Court of Justice's judgment in the *Philip Morris* case has been interpreted by some authors as meaning that article 85 could possibly apply to merger agreements, ie to agreements leading to the *de jure* or *de facto* control of one company by one of its competitors.

28.15 Since article 85 cannot be abrogated by the Regulation, the danger exists therefore that the competitor or an unsuccessful bidder could successfully challenge in the national courts, on the basis of article 85, the validity of a concentration which has been given the go-ahead in accordance with the provisions of the Regulation. Obviously, the same risk exists with respect to article 86, considered below. It is to eliminate that risk, at least as far as article 85 is concerned, that the Regulation provides that Regulation 17 will not apply to a concentration as defined by the Regulation,

35. See Chap. 23, above.
36. Art. 3(2), first paragraph.
37. M241 of 13 July 1992 and see further fn. 31, above.
38. A parallel can be drawn here with the *Irish Distillers* case. See the Eighteenth Report on Competition Policy, 1988, published 1989, point 80.
39. Such as the creation of a joint venture which acts independently, without restrictions of competition between the parent companies, nor between the parent companies and their joint subsidiary. See art. 3(2), second para., of the Reg.
40. See Chap. 23, above.

whether or not such concentration has a Community dimension (ie, irrespective of whether or not it must, under the Regulation, be vetted by the Commission or by the competent national authorities).[41]

28.16 Providing that Regulation 17 is not applicable to concentrations as defined by the Regulation, even if they have no Community dimension, means, in effect, that third parties will probably not be able to challenge a concentration authorised by the national control authorities on the ground that it is contrary to article 85. Indeed, as stated by the Court of Justice in its judgment of 30 April 1986 in *re Asjes and others ("New frontiers")*,[42] national courts have no authority to declare void an agreement or concerted practice on the ground that it is contrary to article 85(1) as long as the rules implementing article 85 have not been adopted pursuant to article 87. It is precisely Regulation 17 which embodies the implementing rules of article 85 contemplated by article 87. As a result, the effect of providing that Regulation 17 will not be applicable to a concentration—whether or not having a Community dimension—as defined by the Merger Control Regulation is in all likelihood to make it impossible for a competitor or an unsuccessful suitor in a hostile take-over battle to challenge on the basis of article 85, before the national courts, a decision taken by the national competition authorities in respect of a concentration as defined by the Regulation.

28.17 If the decision has been taken by the Commission (ie in the case of a concentration having a Community dimension), the only avenue open to the unsuccessful competitor or suitor is to challenge the decision of the Commission directly before the Court of First Instance. Yet, it is only in very exceptional circumstances that the Court may agree to hear such an appeal since the competitor concerned would face the uphill task of demonstrating that the decision challenged is of "direct and individual concern" to him within the meaning of article 173 of the Treaty.[43] True, the Regulation in fact provides for a general right of audience for any natural or legal person "showing a legitimate interest" during the vetting procedure before the Commission. However, the onus will remain with that party if it wants to challenge the Commission's decision to prove that it has sufficient interest to raise such an action under article 173.[44]

7. APPLICATION OF ARTICLE 86

28.18 The position is very different from the situation described above should the competitor or rejected suitor decide to invoke article 86 of the Treaty to challenge a concentration before the national courts. Indeed, as recognised by Sir Leon Brittan, the Commission's Vice-President then in charge of competition himself, in a speech delivered in Cambridge in February 1990, the national courts may, at the request of an aggrieved third party, apply article 86 since that article does not require any

41. See art. 22(2): Regs. Nos. 17 (EEC), 197/68 (EEC), 4056/86 (EEC) and 3975/87 (EEC) do not apply to a concentration as defined in art. 3.
42. Joined cases 209–213/84 [1986] ECR 1425.
43. Art. 173 provides in this respect that: "any natural or legal person may . . . institute proceedings [before the Court of First Instance] against a decision . . . which, although . . . addressed to another person, is of direct and individual concern to the former."
44. See, however, the Council's answer to Written Question 92/C55/29 of MEP P. Bernard Reymond referred to in fn. 46, below.

implementing legislation (contrary to article 85) to be directly effective (and directly applicable by the national courts).[45] Thus, in the words of Sir Leon Brittan[46]:

I cannot, any more than any other honest politician, offer legislative perfection . . . There is no way of completely ruling out litigation probing the Commission's policy . . . [since] articles 85 and 86 apply [or at least may apply] to certain concentrations [covered by the Regulation] and no regulation can abrogate the Treaty and the interpretation placed upon it by the European Court of Justice . . .

In practice, however, it is likely that such individual challenges will be exceptional.

45. Lauterpacht Lecture, stencilled text, p. 25. See also the speech to the EC Chamber of Commerce, New York, 26 March 1990, p. 4.

46. Cambridge speech, p. 25. See, further, the Council's answer to Written Question 92/C55/29 of 5 June 1991 of MEP P. Bernard Reymond, OJ C55/16 of 2 March 1992: ". . . The Council has felt it necessary to specify that the Regulation is only applicable to concentrations, but is aware that national courts, the Court of First Instance and the Court of Justice may be required to examine the question of the applicability of articles 85 and 86 to such concentrations."

CHAPTER 29

THE APPLICATION OF THE RULES ON COMPETITION TO THE EUROMARKETS

1. SELF-REGULATING BODIES

29.1 The first level at which the application of the rules on competition to the Euromarkets must be considered is that of the self-regulating bodies such as, for example, the International Securities Markets Association (ISMA, previously called AIBD) and the International Primary Markets Association (IPMA). These bodies lay down agreed rules for orderly issues and transactions both on the primary and the secondary markets. There is no denying that they have been an important element in ensuring the stability and proper functioning of the markets. Indeed, the absence of institutional control of the markets can only be compensated for by "a competitive discipline beyond which there can be no security for the participants . . .".[1] This feature of the Euro-markets must be borne in mind when assessing the various practices and agreements between participants, of which some might be regarded as anti-competitive in an "institutional" market, but which, in a market based on the self-discipline of the participants, may well be indispensable, or at least be an important factor, in ensuring the stability and proper functioning of the market.

This is a particularly important element when assessing in terms of EC competition law the validity of agreements which affect the timetable for issues and issue syndicates, those which lay down provisions whereby prospective borrowers are sometimes required by the lead bank to refrain from seeking another lead bank for a given period, and those providing for standard commission rates or for agreed uniform issue prices.[2] In this regard, the United Kingdom Office of Fair Trading, after making inquiries in July 1991 into the way underwriting fees are fixed and new bond issues are priced in the international bond market,[3] eventually decided that it had no ground to mount a full restrictive trade practices investigation.[4] This does not mean, however, that all self-regulatory measures at international level should be accepted uncritically. For example, it is questionable whether the restrictions often included in underwriting syndicate agreements whereby financial institutions underwriting the "domestic

---

1. A. Jacquemont, *L'émission des emprunts obligataires, pouvoir bancaire et souveraineté étatique* (1976), p. 63, No. 74 (our translation).
2. Such as the fixed price re-offer mechanism whereby lead managers restrict the price at which other syndicate members can sell bonds, thus avoiding, as in the past, a situation where weaker syndicate members dumped new issues into the market, forcing lead managers to support them at a loss or else face the risk of driving institutional investors from the primary market and, instead, to wait for the price of new issues to fall below the issue price before committing funds. Note also the reports (*Financial Times*, 19 February 1991) that the IPMA's Market Practices Committee agreed that a uniform *force majeure* clause should be used in view of the difficulties experienced at the time of the Gulf War.
3. *Financial Times*, 17 July 1991, p. 1: "UK begins probe of Eurobond markets".
4. *Financial Times*, 11 November 1991, p. 3: "Recession spurs bonds".

tranche" covenant not to sell those securities on other Member States' markets, whereas those institutions underwriting the "Eurotranche" agree not to sell those securities on the domestic market are compatible with Community law.

On the face of it, the application of such restrictions is not objectively justifiable under the rules on competition. On the contrary, they appear, subject to further examination, to be inspired by the wish to protect the market share of the respective financial institutions concerned, without any appreciable resultant benefit for the investors.

29.2 Over the last two years, two important developments have taken place in this respect. The first development concerns the decision of the United Kingdom government to exclude the Euro-markets, largely centred in London, from the most important parts of the Financial Services Act 1986, to which United Kingdom based participants in the Euro-markets would otherwise have been fully subject. In order to avoid driving away the markets from London, a statutory instrument was laid before the United Kingdom Parliament in 1988, allowing the markets to continue operating broadly as they did previously. In order to achieve that result, the AIBD (now the ISMA) was granted designated exchange status, a move which also reportedly allowed "certain primary market practices thought to be under threat from the legislation—such as the price support provided to new issues—to continue, provided that the regulations are incorporated into the [ISMA] rule-book".[5] This designation, in turn, means that what was previously a purely "private" self-regulating body has become, at least as far as the London-based Euro-markets participants are concerned, a statutory self-regulating organisation in that all United Kingdom based participants must—at least as a rule—report their trade to ISMA, or in accordance with the rules of ISMA, in order to satify United Kingdom securities law.[6] It is, however, likely that the present arrangements will need to be reviewed at an early date to take account of the reporting and other requirements introduced by the Investment Services Directive. The second development of significance is that ISMA's board on 20 March 1990 notified to the Commission its statutes and rule-book, which is the basis of ISMA's regulation of the international securities market.

29.3 On 14 December 1991,[7] the Commission indicated that it proposed to take a favourable decision regarding them, after they had been amended at its request in some respects. Thus, at the Commission's request:

— ISMA has amended a statement in its bylaws according to which "the Board is not likely (when assessing whether an applicant has the financial capacity to fulfil its commercial obligations and perform its market activities) to consider that a corporate applicant with less than US$ 1,000,000 or its equivalent in shareholders' funds will have the financial capacity to perform the level of professional market activity expected of a member". According to the Commission,[8] it requested deletion of that statement "because prudential supervision is the responsibility of the regulatory authorities applying either

---

5. *Financial Times*, 10 March 1988, p. 25, "AIBD wins UK legal exemption".

6. *Cf.* "The Creature with two heads", *The Banker*, July 1989, p. 20 *et seq.*, especially p. 21; also, *Financial Times*, 17 June 1990, p. 39.

7. See the Commission's notice pursuant to art. 19(3) of Council Reg. 17, OJ C325/10 of 14 December 1991. No decision was in fact taken by the Commission; instead, a comfort letter was reportedly issued. See *Euromoney*, May 1993, p. 44. References below are to the Commission's notice.

8. See Commission's notice, at point 30.

national or Community legislation. All Community Member States have adopted prudential rules for financial institutions operating within their territory. At Community level, a programme of harmonisation is already under way. It is therefore unnecessary and inappropriate for self regulatory bodies such as ISMA to undertake to impose capital adequacy requirements as a condition, or even a guideline, of membership in as far as this applies to members operating within the European Community." Even though ISMA has deleted the statement at issue as requested by the Commission, one may question whether such a request was objectively justified as a matter of EC law. Recent financial debacles, such as the BCCI affair, suggest that even Community inspired or Community made supervision mechanisms are not infallible. Hence, it is not somewhat presumptuous to insist that a self regulatory body should not impose *more onerous* capital requirements as a guideline for membership than the *minimum* laid down by Community legislation.[9]

— ISMA further agreed "to introduce a requirement that the membership committee must supply reasons for [its] decisions [to reject an application for membership]. The applicant may appeal against the membership committee's decision to the full board. The members of the membership committee may not vote on appeal. A deferral by the membership committee is treated as a rejection for the purposes of filing an appeal".

The amendments requested by the Commission are clearly in line with the long established *Sarabex* principles already discussed.[10]

29.4 The Commission also noted[11] *inter alia* "that there are no numerical limits to the size of ISMA's membership". It further noted, in respect of the rule-making powers of ISMA such as, for example, the right to specify the maximum spread (difference between bid and offer price) on which international securities or various groups of international securities may be traded, the statement of ISMA "that this power ... would not be used to restrict or distort competition" and that its competent committee and sub-committees are obliged, under existing rules, to ensure that such new rules as may be enacted "shall be in the overall interest of improving efficiency and liquidity in the sector concerned and shall not discriminate against any party save to the extent necessary to achieve those objectives".[12] Here too, it is likely that the context in which this decision was reached, and the respective jurisdictions of ISMA and national Member States' authorities will change considerably in the near future, in the run-up to the entry into force of the Investment Services Directive.

9. Especially if the very low levels of minimum start-up capital imposed by the Investment Services Directive are borne in mind.

10. See Chap. 26, above.

11. Commission's notice, OJ C325/15 of 14 December 1991, at point 28.

12. *Ibid.* It is further reported (*Financial Times*, 8 December 1992, "EC throws role of interdealer broker into question") that the Commission had objected to the ISMA rules restricting interdealer brokers (IDBs) to deal with institutions other than market-makers and requiring IDBs to open their broker to inspection to prove they are not breaking the rules. ISMA has now reportedly relaxed these requirements.

2. RULES IMPOSED BY SOME MEMBER STATES ON THE MARKETS

29.5 The second level at which the application of EC competition law to the Euromarkets must be examined concerns the rules which some Member States have sometimes tried to impose on these markets. One example of such rules can be found in the attempts by some domestic monetary authorities to regain control over their respective national currencies whilst discriminating against banks operating in the Euromarkets which are established outside their national territory.

In the 1985 edition of this book, it was stated[13] to that "... at the present time, Deutschmark borrowings must necessarily be led by German banks (because the German monetary authorities will only authorise a DM issue if a German bank participates in the management of the issue syndicate). Similarly, since a protocol agreement concluded ... between [the French] Finance Ministry and the major French banks, Eurofranc borrowings must ... be led by a French bank ... Although the protocol by its terms only affects French banks, in practice it affects the whole international Community since any use of the Eurofranc inevitably requires collaboration with one or more French banks. Again, Euro-issues in Luxembourg francs always have as the lead bank a Luxembourg bank". As commented at the time,[14] "the compulsory reservation of the management or co-management of Euroborrowings issued in the national currency of a Member State to a bank or banks established in that State is hard to reconcile with the fundamental rules of the Treaty; ... it is submitted ... that it is likely to become increasingly difficult to justify the introduction or continuation of such discriminatory measures against undertakings established in other Member States on the ground of the exercise by another Member State of its retained powers in the field of monetary policy or the need of that Member State to safeguard its currency". Since that prediction was made, the 1988 Capital Movements Directive has come into force, as has the Second Banking Directive. So too, will shortly the Investments Services Directive.

29.6 It is probably against the background of these new developments in terms of EC law that the initiatives reportedly taken by the Commission to challenge at least some of these restrictive practices must be viewed. Thus, it is understood that it is as a result of Commission action (presumably following a complaint by aggrieved non-German banks) that the rules in Germany were later relaxed so that non-German banks could co-manage Deutschmark borrowings. It is also against this changed regulatory background that the initiatives more recently taken by some Member States to relax further rules previously in force must be viewed. The move towards a single European currency can only accelerate this trend.

Thus, for instance, the Bundesbank was reported in July 1992 to have announced new rules, with effect from 1 August 1992, for the further liberalisation of the German capital markets by making it easier for foreign companies to issue commercial paper:

The main thrust of the change is the abolition of the two-year minimum maturity requirement for foreign companies. The requirement still applies to banks and other financial institutions. The new Bundesbank regulations have also done away with a number of other inconveniences and expenses involved in issuing DM paper: the requirement to appoint a German paying agent; to use the German clearing system; to list on a German stock exchange; and to use German law.[15]

13. At p. 55.
14. At p. 56.
15. *Financial Times*, 13 July 1992: "Bundesbank guidelines set to give boost to sector."

Also, from 1 August 1992, foreign companies will be able to make DM commercial paper issues without having to set up a special German offshoot and German branches of foreign banks will be able to lead manage issues in Deutschmarks.[16]

It should also be recalled here, even though it does not directly relate to the subject in hand, that the Commission had opposed a few years ago, at least for the future and again as a result of a complaint, restrictions imposed at the initiative of the United Kingdom Government, in connection with the privatisation of government-owned companies, on the percentage of shares that could be offered for sale to non-United Kingdom residents, without omitting from these restrictions persons resident in other Member States.[17] The Commission also opposed similar restrictions imposed at the time by the French Government in connection with the privatisations which took place in France in the 1980s.[18] That these efforts have not been in vain and that indeed a (limited) change of mentality has taken place since then in the Member States would appear to be borne out by the conditions recently announced by the French Government in connection with its privatisation drive: intended restrictions on foreign investors to a maximum 20% shareholding in the companies in question will reportedly only apply to investors outside the Community.[19] The same is true, reportedly after some prodding by the Commission, of recent Portuguese privatisation plans.[20]

16. *Financial Times*, 6 July 1992: "Germany eases CP issuance."

17. See *Agence Europe*, Bulletin 5063 (new series) 24–25 July 1989, p. 10 which reported that the Commission had considered as acceptable "the revised modalities for the [privatisation] of Rolls Royce regarding the one aspect which was contested: the shares . . . which may be purchased by non-British citizens. In principle, any limits of this kind are banned within the EEC. However, the Commission took account of the fact that Rolls Royce played an important role in the military security of the country. The percentage which had first of all been established by the British Government (15%) was too low; now the Government has accepted bringing this up to 29·5% and the Commission feels this is reasonable. This does not constitute a precedent: the general rule remains that there should be no differentiation between EEC citizens". Indeed, the justification for the increased limit on the ground of "the important role played by Rolls Royce in the military security of the country", always a feeble one, cannot be relied upon in respect of privatisation of "non-strategic" industries that took place before *Rolls Royce I* and which were subject to similar restrictions. See, also, the Commission's answer of 28 May 1990 to Written Question 1047/89 of MEP J. Ford, OJ C233/4 of 17 September 1990, regarding the restriction on the sending of prospectuses by the UK Government to UK residents only.

18. See Written Question 1224/86 of MEP Metten, OJ C91/13 of 6 April 1987.

19. *Financial Times*, 2 July 1993.

20. Following the Portuguese Government's agreement "in principle" not to apply a clause limiting foreign ownership, see European Report, 1993. The Commission has also reported that it is watching privatisation in Germany (Treuhand privatisation programme), in Italy (EFIM) and Belgium (GGER and OCCH), see Memorandum 28/93 of 17 June 1993 "Competition policy—six months of Commission activities", p. 9.

PART SIX

CONSUMER PROTECTION IN THE FIELD OF FINANCIAL SERVICES

CHAPTER 30

THE CONSUMER AND THE SINGLE MARKET

INTRODUCTION

30.1 Elsewhere in this book consideration is given to some of the implications for EC credit institutions that will flow from the creation in the EC of a single market in the field of banking and financial services. However, most of these implications relate to the institutions themselves which undertake what might loosely be termed "the business of banking". This Part considers various ways in which the consumer of banking services in the EC will also benefit from the creation of that single market, not least because of the greater choice that will result as a consequence of the inevitable increase in competition in the banking and financial services sector.

When the Commission embarked on its programme aimed at achieving the objective of a single market in the field of banking and financial services by the end of 1992, it envisaged that the removal of economic barriers within the EC and the progress achieved in the field of monetary and banking co-operation would lead to an increase in cross-border purchases of goods and services and greater mobility for individuals, particularly workers, tourists and pensioners. Furthermore, it envisaged that this increase in cross-border purchases and the free movement of individuals and products would lead to an increase in the number of cross-border financial transactions and the number of operators carrying out such transactions. Consequently, the Commission formed the view that a more efficient system for transferring funds would need to be a key part of the single market in the field of banking and financial services.

In its determination to improve the efficiency of the funds transfer system operating within the EC the Commission also sought to ensure a high degree of consumer protection within such payment system. In order to achieve this stated aim, the Council has, at the time of writing, passed two Directives[1] regulating consumer credit agreements and the Commission has published five important texts[2] on the cross-border

---

1. Council Directive of 22 December 1986 for the approximation of the laws, regulations and administrative provisions of the Member States concerning consumer credit and Council Directive of 22 February 1990 amending the former.

2. Commission Recommendation of 8 December 1987 on a European Code of Conduct relating to electronic payments (87/598/ECC); Commission Recommendation of 14 February 1990 on transparency of banking conditions relating to cross-border financial transactions (90/109/EEC); the Green Paper on making payments in the internal market—COM(90)477 final, published on 26 September 1990. The Green Paper has, to a certain extent, been superseded by a working document published by the Commission in March 1992 entitled "Easier cross-border payments: breaking down the barriers"; Commission Recommendation of 17 November 1988 regarding payment systems and in particular the relationship between cardholder and card issuer (88/590/EEC); and the communication from the Commission to the European Council entitled "Europe could play an ace: the new payment cards" published on 12 January 1987 (Com(86)754 Final). Each of these texts, including the working document, is considered in detail below.

transfer of funds and on payment cards, the latter with particular reference to the important relationship between the cardholder and the card issuer. The Council Directives and texts published by the Commission can be conveniently discussed under three headings: transfer of funds between Member States; credit cards; and consumer credit.

A. TRANSFER OF FUNDS BETWEEN MEMBER STATES

Introduction

30.2 The aim of the Commission in the area of cross-border funds transfer has been to identify areas in which cross-border payment systems can be improved while ensuring that the customer is given sufficient information in advance about the cost and time needed for effecting such transactions. The Commission's policy has been to encourage the development of an interoperable payment system within the EC in order that payment devices issued in one Member State could be used in other Member States. There are three texts dealing with the transfer of funds between Member States: (i) the Recommendation on a European Code of Conduct relating to electronic payments[3]; (ii) the Recommendation on transparency of banking conditions relating to cross-border financial transactions[4]; and (iii) the Green Paper on making payments in the internal market.[5] Each of these will now be considered separately.

(i) Recommendation on a European Code of Conduct relating to electronic payment[6] (the "Code")

Purpose of the Code

30.3 The Code attempts to foster the development of compatible electronic payment systems within the EC by providing a number of general principles to be observed both by those who bring card payment systems into operation and also those who make use of such systems. It lays down general principles concerning contracts for the use of cards, the scale of charges to be applied to such cards, interoperability of cards issued, electronic payment terminals, data protection and security and fair access to payment systems.

Scope of the Code

30.4 The Code applies to payment cards incorporating a magnetic strip or microcircuit used to effect payment transactions at an electronic payment terminal or a point-of-sale terminal. Therefore it does not cover the growing area of company specific cards (eg, store cards) which are not used as described above, payments by cheque supported by bank guarantee cards, payments by cards using mechanical processes (eg, invoice slips) or cards serving purposes other than direct or deferred payment for goods or services (eg, cash point cards). The Code deals with the three important relationships

3. Fn. 2, above.
4. *Ibid.*
5. *Ibid.*
6. 87/598/EEC of 8 December 1987.

which may arise in relation to payment cards namely relations between card issuers and traders, traders and consumers and consumers and card issuers. It lays down the following general principles:

(a) *Contracts*. Contracts concluded by card issuers with traders or with consumers are required to be in writing and must set out in detail the general and specific conditions of the agreement including any scale of charges and the conditions specific to termination of the contract. Such contracts are required to be drawn up in the official language(s) of the Member State in which the contract is concluded and all its conditions are required to be freely negotiable and clearly stipulated in the contract.

(b) *Interoperability*. The Commission recommended that by 31 December 1992 cards and card readers used in various systems operated throughout the EC should have been opened up by means of reciprocity agreements so that traders and consumers would be able to join the various network(s) or contract with the card issuer(s) of their choice with each terminal being able to process all cards issued within the EC. Many such reciprocity agreements have, at the time of writing, already been entered into and more will undoubtedly follow, making it possible for consumers to use electronic payment cards in terminals throughout the EC. In addition, traders and the banking industry (representing card issuers) are currently working on a draft code of practice which will reflect the principles set out in the Code. The Commission's mediating role in the negotiations on the draft code of practice will enable it more readily to determine whether, on the basis of the code of practice ultimately adopted by the traders and the banking industry, there is a need to review the recommendations set out in the Code.

(c) *Equipment*. The Code provides that electronic payment terminals be able to register, control and transmit payments and may be integrated into a point-of-sale terminal. It also provides that traders must be free to choose which point-of-sale terminal they will install, being at liberty either to rent or purchase such equipment, and be able, if they wish, to install a single, multicard terminal.

(d) *Data protection and security*. The Code provides that an order given by means of a payment card shall be irrevocable and may not be countermanded. The Code also states that the information transmitted, at the time of payment, to the trader's bank and subsequently to the issuer must not in any circumstances prejudice the protection of privacy. It also provides that contracts must not restrict the trader's freedom of operation or freedom to compete.

Any problems that arise in connection with the protection of information about security are required to be openly acknowledged and cleared at whatever stage in the contract between the relevant parties.

(e) *Fair access to the system*. Irrespective of its economic size, all service establishments are required to be allowed fair access to the system of electronic payments and a trader may be refused access for a legitimate reason only.

Also, the Code provides for fair competition in respect of services offered from different Member States by stressing that there must be no unwarranted difference in the remuneration for services concerning transactions within one Member State and the remuneration for the same services concerning cross-border transactions with other Member States, especially in border regions where such conflicts are likely to be acute.

(f) *Relations between issuers and traders*. In order to promote mutual access among different card systems, contracts between card issuers and traders are required to contain no exclusive trading clause requiring the trader to operate only the system in respect of which he has concluded an agreement. Contracts with traders are required to admit effective competition between various issuers and compulsory provisions must be limited strictly to technical requirements for ensuring that the system functions properly.

(g) *Relations between issuers and consumers*. Cardholders are required to take all reasonable precautions to ensure the safety of the card issued and to observe the special conditions especially those regarding loss or theft in the contract which they have signed.

(h) *Relations between traders and consumers*. Traders are required to display, in a fully visible manner, the signs of the card issuing companies to which they are affiliated and they shall be obliged to accept such cards.

It should be noted that the Code is not binding. However, the Commission recommends that its principles be adopted by all operators of electronic payment systems within the EC. Some of its requirements (eg the requirement that the conditions of contracts concluded by issuers with consumers be freely negotiable) may prove difficult to comply with in certain Member States. For example, in the United Kingdom, as is now common in other Member States, contracts between card issuers and consumers are in standard form and not usually the subject of any negotiation. Standardisation is particularly important in those jurisdictions, like the United Kingdom, which are subject to detailed (and highly technical) consumer credit legislation governing the form and content of contracts between card issuers and consumers. Changes to the standard contract may have the effect of rendering the contract unenforceable by the card issuer.

(ii) Recommendation on the transparency of banking conditions relating to cross-border financial transactions[7] (the "Transparency Recommendation")

30.5 In the preamble to the Transparency Recommendation, the Commission envisages that the system for cross-border transfers of funds is likely to be more complex than any transfer of funds system because one or more intermediary institutions are likely to be involved. Also, different clearing arrangements are likely to apply in countries not having the same currency and in such cases an exchange transaction must take place in order to complete any funds transfer. The Commission has expressed the concern that the complexity inherent in an EC-wide (and hence international) funds transfer system would significantly add to the cost and time needed for cross-border financial transactions and it is therefore of the view that persons undertaking such transactions should be clearly informed in advance of the cost and time needed to execute such transactions. The Commission aims to encourage institutions undertaking cross-border financial transactions to estimate their costs more accurately and give the customer sufficient information of the prices charged for such transactions. However, the Commission is reluctant to pass legislation setting out rules relating solely to cross-border transactions, preferring instead to make

7. 90/109/EEC of 14 February 1990.

recommendations enabling competent authorities in the various Member States to secure, on a voluntary basis, the co-operation of the institutions concerned to bring about a change of behaviour and devise new structures which would reduce the cost of cross-border transfers under the conditions of free competition. The Commission's recommendations are contained in the Transparency Recommendation in the form of six principles which, when taken together, are designed to provide a customer with sufficient information regarding the terms and costs of cross-border transactions. The principles also identify the invoicing rules to be observed by institutions undertaking such transactions. Member States are required to ensure that institutions which undertake cross-border financial transactions apply the principles set out in the Transparency Recommendation.

30.6 The six principles set out in the Transparency Recommendation apply to all categories of customer and to all institutions being legal persons, in particular credit institutions and postal services, providing facilities for effecting or facilitating cross-border transfers including branches of such institutions. The principles are:

(1) Each institution is required to bring to the attention of its customers easily understandable and readily available information concerning cross-border financial transactions.

The Commission suggests three methods of applying this principle:

(a) by a notice or some other permanent form of information drawing attention to the cost of, and time needed for, all cross-border financial transactions and encouraging customers to seek further information; or

(b) by standarised information in the form of a notice, booklet or brochure specifying the amount or, where appropriate, the percentage of commission fees and charges applied by the institution in respect of each transaction that may be invoiced either to the transferor or the transferee where a cross-border financial transaction is undertaken, as well as, if necessary, the provisions relating to the value dates; or

(c) by information of a more specific nature in the form of a booklet, brochure or some other appropriate means given to the transferor, if he so requests, regarding the procedures applied by the institution in executing his orders, together with an estimate from intermediary banks of expected charges and time needed, having due regard to the various procedures.

(2) In the statement relating to a cross-border financial transaction, the institution is required to inform its customer in detail of the commission fees and charges it is invoicing and of the exchange rate it has applied.

The Commission suggests that this principle could be complied with by clearly specifying in a statement or some other document given to the customer, regardless of whether he is the transferor or the transferee, informing him of (a) the exchange rate applied in converting the amount of foreign currency, (b) the amount of the commission fee or fees applied or invoiced by the institution, (c) the list and amount of any taxes payable, (d) the nature and amount of the charges payable by the customer, and (e) the nature and amount of any additional invoice.

(3) The transferor's institution is required to inform its customer when the customer gives his order that (a) the commission fees and charges it imposes for transmitting the order may either remain payable by the transferor or be

345

invoiced to the transferee, and (b) that any commission fees and charges invoiced by the transferee's institution to its customer when it places the funds at the transferee's disposal may either remain payable by the transferee or be invoiced to the transferor. However, this requirement is without prejudice to the transferor's ability to choose other ways of apportioning commission fees and charges. Furthermore, where the transferor has specifically instructed his institution to ensure that the transferee is credited with the exact amount shown on the transfer order, it is recommended that the institution apply a method of transfer which will make it possible to achieve this result and that, before undertaking the transfer operation, it informs the transferor of the additional amount which will be invoiced to him.

The Commission suggests that this principle could be applied by making available to the transferor who wanted the transferee to be credited with an exact amount prior information based on the flat rate calculation or an estimate that could take account of the average of the commission fees and charges applied by institutions in the country of the transferee where information permitting a more accurate calculation was not available. If the amount estimated was smaller than the amount of commission fees and charges actually payable, the difference could be invoiced only to the transferor.

(4) In the absence of instructions to the contrary and except in cases of *force majeure*, each intermediary institution is required to deal with a transfer order within two working days of receipt of the funds specified in the order. Alternatively, it is required to give notification of its refusal to execute the order or of any foreseeable delay to the institution issuing the order and, where different, to the transferor's institution. In the event of any delay in executing his/her order, it is recommended that the transferor should be able to obtain a refund of part of the costs of the transfer.

(5) The transferee's institution is required to fulfil its obligations arising from a transfer order not later than the working day following receipt of the funds specified in the order unless the order stipulates a later date of execution. If the transferee's institution is unable to execute the order within the time indicated, it is required as soon as possible to inform the institution issuing the order and, where different, the transferor's institution of the reasons for its failure to execute the order or for the delay in execution.

(6) Any institution participating in a cross-border financial transaction is required to be capable of dealing rapidly with complaints lodged by the transferor or the transferee in connection with the execution of the transaction or with the statement relating to it. If no action is taken on a complaint or no answer received within three months it is provided that the complainants may refer the matter to one of the Member State's bodies competent to deal with complaints from users. Member States were recommended to notify the Commission not later than 30 September 1990 of the names and addresses of such bodies. The list and addresses of such national bodies should be available on request from any institution undertaking cross-border financial transactions.

The Commission suggests that this principle may be applied by entrusting the task of dealing with complaints to bodies independent of the parties concerned and forming part of:

(a) the public sector (eg a ministerial department);

(b) a contract committee comprising bank representatives and users.

European banking industry guidelines on customer information relating to cross-border remote payments

30.7 The European banking industry has also recognised the need for improvement in the quality of information made available to customers in respect of cross-border payments and has produced a set of guidelines (the "Guidelines") for its members. At this juncture it should be noted that the move to greater transparency is planned as a two stage development:

(i) greater transparency in relation to remote payments (ie where the sender and the beneficiary are in separate countries);

(ii) greater transparency relating to face-to-face payments.

The Guidelines cover the former case, but it is intended that the EC banking industry should develop its ideas regarding transparency with respect to face-to-face payments by using the Guidelines as a model.

The Commission has been monitoring the implementation of the Guidelines and will recommend changes where it feels these are necessary.

The Guidelines were produced by the three EC credit sector associations, (that is EBF, the European Savings Bank Group and the Association of Co-operative Banks of the EC) ("ECSAs"). The purpose of the Guidelines is:

To provide guidance to the associations member organisations in issuing recommendations to member banks in relation to the production of brochures and other literature for information from the customers on cross-border remote payment.

30.8 A cardinal feature of the Guidelines is the commitment to make information available to help customers to understand the various transfer methods which they can use so that they may chose which cross-border remote payment method is best suited to their needs. Essentially, the guidelines require banks to provide the following information:

(i) the complete range of payment services available. The manner in which the list of services is to be provided is left to the discretion of each bank;

(ii) the principal features of each type of service offered. The Guidelines recommend that banks ensure that the information is presented in a readily understandable form and in a way which will enable customers to compare the services on offer;

(iii) the time each method of payment will take in normal circumstances. The Guidelines recognise that it will not always be possible for the bank to know exactly when the transfer will be credited to the beneficiary's account. Consequently the timetable drawn up by the banks is intended to be read as covering a transfer under normal circumstances;

(iv) all charges including the basis of the exchange rate applied;

(v) the value dating arrangements;

(vi) how to obtain more information (eg, the way in which the customer can obtain more information including tariffs and exchange rates in effect). The Guidelines suggest that such information could consist of notices in branches or an indication of how the relevant person may be contacted;

(vii) warnings about particular payment methods where relevant;

(viii) complaints and redress procedures.

At the time of writing most of the major banks in the various Member States have produced brochures that conform with the Guidelines and those which have not are in the process of finalising such literature.

(iii) The Green Paper on making payments in the internal market (the "Green Paper")[8]

30.9 In the Green Paper, which was published on 26 September 1990, the Commission sought to identify the key administrative, political and economic obstacles to be overcome in order to achieve efficient payment systems within the Community. The Green Paper stressed the need for efficient payment systems for the efficient operation of any integrated economic system and noted that, in general, such systems exist within each Member State but are not efficiently connected with each other, so that cross-border payments are slower, more expensive and less reliable than those effected within a single Member State. It proposed a framework for improvements to be made to the existing methods for cross-border payments (ie, cash transactions, bank transfers, cheques and payment cards).

In the Green Paper the Commission identified[9] the main problem with effecting cross-border payments by cash as being the risk of loss arising from adverse exchange rate movements. This risk would obviously be eliminated in the event that full monetary union were to be achieved in the EC. The Commission's aspiration of achieving the goal of monetary union is evidenced in the Green Paper in which the Commission stated its belief that such union should enable cash transactions between different countries to be made free of any commission or other charge.

The Green Paper suggested[10] that the present elaborate and slow system of effecting cross-border transfers through correspondent banks should be improved by creating an institution formally to link the various automated clearing houses which exist in most Member States to handle domestic credit and debit transfers. It proposed that the new institution would carry out the same function as clearing houses in individual countries and could be the first step towards a single EC clearing house.

The Commission noted[11] that most cross-border payments are presently made using Eurocheques and recognised the Eurocheque system as a useful means of effecting cross-border payments, but it highlighted the fact that this system was restricted to low-value payments. The Commission suggested that the Eurocheque system be extended to higher-value payments and that other types of cheques used within the various Member States be standardised so as to enable them to benefit from the same methods of electronic handling throughout the EC. The Commission's suggestion was acted upon, in part, on 1 March 1992 when the Eurocheque Association increased the value of the Eurocheque clearing limit to 1,000 ECU.

Finally, the Green Paper made a few suggestions[12] for improving interoperability. In particular, it encouraged organisers of card systems to co-operate and open their

8. Com(90)477 Final, published on 26 September 1990.
9. *Ibid.*, paras. 27–32.
10. *Ibid.*, paras. 33–64.
11. *Ibid.*, paras. 33–64: see Annex 2 for a more detailed treatment of Eurocheques.
12. *Ibid.*, paras. 72–80.

networks and terminals to each other in order to accept each other's cards in their payment processes.

The cross-border payments paper

30.10 The Green Paper did not suggest definitive solutions to the problems it identified but rather guidelines and aims at generating a debate between banks, central banks, the representatives of national payment systems and users. The Commission suggested that, following discussion of the proposals contained in the Green Paper, there should be created a payments systems co-ordinating group representing banks and clearing houses which would analyse the proposals and consider responses thereto and the best means to implement them. This group was established in April 1991 and its membership comprises both central and commercial bankers. The group, which was named the Payment Systems Technical Development Group and was chaired by a representative from the Commission, drew up a report in January 1992 which, together with a similar report drawn up by the Payment Systems Users' Liaison Group (whose members comprise bankers and representatives of card users, ie, both consumers and traders) formed the basis of a working paper produced by the Commission in March 1992 entitled "Easier Cross Border Payments: Breaking Down the Barriers"[13] (the "cross-border payments paper"). The aim of the cross-border payments paper is two-fold:

(i) to help the banking industry develop more efficient payment systems; and
(ii) to improve the user's ability to insist on a better service.

30.11 The cross-border payments paper reviewed developments which had occurred to equal the transparency, speed, reliability and cost of the retail cross-border payments systems, the development of which was encouraged in the Green Paper, with those of domestic systems. The cross-border payments paper recommended that "a continuing programme of work is needed in a range of areas."[14] The areas that were perceived to be in need of improvement were:

(a) transparency for users;
(b) the end of double charging;
(c) foreign exchange transactions; and
(d) complaints and redress.

The Commission recognised that great progress had been made towards the development of efficient payment systems, but it also recognised that a considerable amount of work was still needed to be done.

The Commission's recommendations and resolutions

1. Transparency

(A) THE FIVE POINT USER'S CHARTER

30.12 In the cross-border payments paper, the Commission stated that immediate action could be taken to improve the transparency of payment systems:

---

13. Commission Information No. P(92)17, 25 March 1992.
14. *Ibid.*, p. 2.

Users have a right to receive full information about the various possibilities open to them for sending funds across frontiers.[15]

The European Credit Associations ("ECA") had recognised this point and had circulated guidelines on customer information amongst their members with the intention that these should be implemented by 31 December 1992. The Commission responded to the ECA's guidelines by publishing the five point user's charter,[16] the aim of which was to set out "in a clear and usable form the information to which users are entitled."[17] The five points are:

(i) the bank must inform the user of the most appropriate payment system available;

(ii) the user must be given in advance full information regarding the total cost of the payment;

(iii) the user must have the option of paying all charges so that the beneficiary received the full amount;

(iv) cross-border payments should be accelerated, the objective being the same time delay and reliability as for domestic payments by stage 3 of EMU; and

(v) the user should have access to a redress procedure at least equivalent to that existing for domestic payments.

Essentially the five point user's charter sets out a framework for the establishment of a high quality service which would be in the best interests of banks' customers. In December 1992 the Commission initiated an independent study of the service being provided on the High Street in the various Member States. The results of this study are expected to be published early in 1994 and will determine, to a large extent, whether or not further action will be required, including possible legislation.

(B) DOUBLE CHARGES

30.13 In relation to the making of remote cross-border payments the problem of double charging was highlighted by the Commission. The originator of a cross-border payment may want to pay in full for the cost of transferring a specified sum but may be unable to ensure that the beneficiary will be fully credited. The beneficiary may be charged at his end on receiving the transferred money. Notwithstanding the recommendations laid down by the Transparency Recommendation[18] which, *inter alia*, covered double charges, the practice continued to occur. The Commission therefore recommended, in the cross-border payments paper, that banks should at least provide their customers with an estimate of the total charges.[19]

The Transparency Recommendation had suggested that where the originator had specifically instructed his bank to ensure that the beneficiary is credited with the exact amount shown on the transfer order, the bank should apply a mode of transfer which makes it possible to achieve this result.[20] Regardless of this recommendation the Commission indicated that, if the abuse of double charging persisted it would consider taking appropriate counter-measures. At the time of writing it is understood that the

---

15. *Ibid.*, p. 2.
16. *Ibid.*, Annex B.
17. *Ibid.*, p. 2.
18. Fn. 7, above.
19. Fn. 13 above, at p. 4.
20. Fn. 7 above, principle 3(2).

Commission will review the market position on double charging during the summer of 1994. In the event that the results of that review prove unsatisfactory, binding legislation will be proposed. The self-regulatory approach is likely to continue however if the results of the review prove satisfactory. The problem of double charging is also currently being examined by the Payment Systems Users' Liaison Group (the "Users' Group"). Banks in the Member States have been asked to revert to the Commission with ideas on how they will prevent the abuse of double charging. According to the Commission, the way forward is still one of the "soft" law approach. However, it may well transpire that the Users' Group will have to recommend binding legislation to eliminate the problem.

(c) OVER-THE-COUNTER FOREIGN EXCHANGE TRANSACTIONS

30.14 Given the intense competition between banks and *bureaux de change* in the buying and selling of foreign currency, the Commission recommended, in the cross-border payments paper, that the customer should receive full and clear information as to exchange rates and commission charges.[21]

The Commission opined that there should be a binding obligation on all banks, *bureaux de change* and others who offer cash foreign exchange services to display all elements of the transaction over and above the exchange rate (if appropriate) very clearly and prominently so that there are no "surprise" charges.[22] The purpose of this recommendation is to produce a uniformly high level of transparency in foreign exchange transactions across the whole of the EC. The Commission considered this a matter for urgent discussion.[23] At the time of writing, the Commission is engaged in discussion with governmental representatives of the Member States. In 1992 there were two such meetings, from which it appeared that the majority of the Member States had implemented transparency legislation dealing with over-the-counter foreign exchange transactions. The Commission therefore considers that there is no need, at this stage, for further Community level legislation.

(d) COMPLAINTS AND REDRESS PROCEDURES

30.15 In the Transparency Recommendation the Commission recommended that any institution participating in cross-border financial transactions should be capable of dealing rapidly with complaints lodged by the transferor or the transferee in connection with the execution of transactions or with the statement relating to it.[24] Also, the Commission recommended that where no action was taken on a complaint or no answer was received within three months, the complainant should be able to refer the matter to one of the Member State's bodies competent to deal with the complaint.[25] Originally this recommendation was limited to transfers. In the cross-border payments paper the Commission recommended that the complaints procedure should be extended to cover all forms of cross-border payments.[26]

The Commission also noted that business users were not eligible to use the existing procedure in all Member States and therefore recommended that the complaints and

---

21. Fn. 13 above, at p. 5.
22. *Ibid.*
23. *Ibid.*
24. *Ibid.*
25. *Ibid.*, principle 6(2).
26. Fn. 13 above, at p. 6.

redress schemes should be extended to cover them.[27] The Commission planned to examine the way in which to do this. The result of this examination revealed that most Member States have extended their complaints and redress procedures to cover small business users. In the United Kingdom, for example, the ombudsman is now authorised to investigate complaints by small business users up to a financial limit of £1 million. Similar provisions apply in other Member States and it therefore appears unlikely that the Commission will issue a directive on this matter.

2. *Integration of payment systems*

(A) CROSS-BORDER LINKS BETWEEN NATIONAL AUTOMATED CLEARING HOUSES

30.16 In the area of cross-border links between national automated clearing houses the cross-border payments paper follows on from recommendations made in the Green Paper which stressed the need for efficient payment systems in order to facilitate the efficient operation of an integrated economic system.[28] In the cross-border payments paper the commission reported that the Payment Systems Technical Development Group (the "Technical Group")[29] had examined, *inter alia*, ways in which cross-border payment could be improved. In particular, the Technical Group concentrated upon the possibility of linking Automated Clearing Houses ("ACHs"). The Commission offered its support to national ACH associations to link across borders with other ACHs or equivalent systems[30] and by the summer of 1992 there had been many initiatives to provide workable improvements to cross-frontier payment systems; for example, Telegiro (the postal banks transfer system), TIPAnet (the Co-operative Banks cross-European link up) and Eufiserv (the European Saving Banks ATM linkage). In the United Kingdom BACS (the Bankers' Automated Clearing Services) is currently preparing a feasibility study with the EBF aimed at examining a possible link up between the ACHs of the United Kingdom, Germany, Holland and Belgium. The study's brief is to analysis the scope, time scale and cost of such a link up with a view to producing a pilot scheme. At the time of writing, the study remains in draft form, and it is expected to be published early in 1994.

(B) DIRECT DEBITING

30.17 Another aspect of improved cross-border co-ordination is the improvement of the direct debiting technique (ie, where a creditor initiates a debit on the debtor's accounts, based on a prior written agreement of the debtor). In its cross-border payments paper the Commission considered this method to be a promising means of improving the efficiency of retail cross-border payments systems.[31] The Commission has expressed interest in supporting service providers and users in determining what specific further measures may be required in this area.

---

27. See p. 6 of the cross-border payments paper, fn. 13, above.
28. See para. 30.9, above.
29. See para. 30.10, above.
30. Fn. 13 above, at p. 8.
31. *Ibid.*, p. 8.

3. Interoperability of payment cards

30.18 In the cross-border payments paper, the Commission reported that, as regards payment cards, the situation was satisfactory. The Technical Group did not recommend the need for any improvements.[32]

Interoperability of payments cards was seen to be making good progress with particularly widespread access to ATMs. Progress was reported also to have been made in the area of debit cards used for automated payments at the point of sale. Finally, work on European standards for machine readable cards ("IC cards") was reported to be under way with special consideration being given to the possibilities offered by the technique of prepaid cards.

Conclusion

30.19 By far the most important development in the sphere of cross-border transfers of funds within the Community has been the publication of the cross-border payments paper, which emphasises the Commission's role as a catalyst for change. The Commission has not been slow to identify many of the underlying problems and thereafter to identify the appropriate bodies perceived capable of proffering solutions. By acting as a catalyst for change considerable progress has been made by the Commission (together with the help of the various bodies identified earlier in this Chapter) in developing cross-border payment systems and improving such areas as transparency, interoperability, co-ordination of systems and consumer protection. However, notwithstanding these meritorious achievements, the Commission continues to seek the development and introduction of new and better cross-border payment systems which will provide even higher standards of speed and reliability in the field of electronic processing practice.

B. CREDIT CARDS

Introduction

30.20 In a communication from the Commission to the Council entitled "Europe could play ace: the new payment cards",[33] the Commission encouraged the interoperability of payment cards at the same time as the completion of the Single Market in the field of banking and financial services. The objective is that cards issued in one Member State should be capable of being used by the cardholder in each of the other Member States. In this text, the Commission indicates that its policy in this area is to encourage compatibility and connection between card systems and card processors while also ensuring that the consumer is adequately protected. The issue of adequacy of consumer protection for cardholders is specifically addressed in the Recommendation concerning payment systems to which we now turn.

---

32. *Ibid.*, p. 9.
33. Com(86)754 Final, published on 12 January 1987.

Recommendation regarding payment systems and in particular the relationship between cardholder and card issuer[34] **(the "Payment Systems Recommendation")**

30.21 The objective of the Payment Systems Recommendation was to establish minimum rules of protection for consumers in this area and to ensure that contracts concluded between card issuers and cardholders include the minimum rules. The Payment Systems Recommendation sets out detailed provisions in accordance with which issuers of payment devices and system providers should conduct their activities. The provisions were required to be complied with not later than 17 November 1989.

The detailed provisions set out in the Payment Systems Recommendation apply only to the following operations:

(a) electronic payment involving the use of a card, in particular at point of sale;
(b) the withdrawing of banknotes, the depositing of banknotes and cheques, and connected operations, at electronic devices such as cash dispensing machines and automated teller machines;
(c) non-electronic payment by card, including processes for which a signature is required and a voucher is produced, but not including cards whose sole function is to guarantee payment made by cheque; and
(d) electronic payment effected by a member of the public without the use of a card, such as home banking.

30.22 The provisions set out in the Payment Systems Recommendation are as follows:

1. Each issuer is required to draw up full and fair terms of contract in writing to govern the issuing and use of the payment devices he issues. The terms of such contract must be expressed in simple language, in a form which is easy to read and in a language which is ordinarily used for such purpose in the region where the terms of contract are offered.
2. The terms of contract must specify the basis of calculation of the amount of the charges, if any, which the contracting holder must pay to the issuer and must also specify when the debiting or crediting of operations will be done and, for those operations which lead to invoicing of the contracting cardholder, the period of time within which this will be done.
3. The terms of contract must not be altered except by agreement between the parties. However, such agreement is deemed to exist where the issuer proposes an amendment to the contract terms and, the contracting holder having received notice thereof, continues to make use of the payment device.
4. The terms of contract are required to put the contracting holder under an obligation *vis-à-vis* the issuer:
   (i) to take all reasonable steps to keep safe the payment device and the means which enable it to be used, eg a personal identification number (PIN) or code;
   (ii) to notify the issuer or a central agency without undue delay after becoming aware of any of the following events or occurrences:
      — the loss or theft or copying of the payment devised or of the means which enable it to be used;

34. 88/590/EEC of 17 November 1988.

354

— the recording on the contracting holder's account of any unauthorised transaction;

— any error or other irregularity in the maintaining of that account by the issuer;

(iii) not to record on any payment device the contracting holder's PIN or code, if any, nor to record those things on anything which he usually keeps or carries with the payment device, particularly if they are likely to be lost or stolen or copied together; and

(iv) not to countermand an order which he has given by means of his payments device.

5. Provided that the contracting holder complies with 4(i), (ii) and (iv) above and does not act fraudulently or with extreme negligence and terms of the contract must state that he shall not after notification be liable for damage arising from such use.

6. The terms of the contract must put the issuer under an obligation not to disclose the contracting holder's PIN or similar confidential data to anyone except the contracting holder.

7. No payment device must be despatched to a member of the public except in response to an application from such person and the contract between the issuer and the contracting holder is deemed to be concluded at the time when the applicant receives the payment device and a copy of the terms of the contract accepted by him.

8. Issuers must keep internal records which are sufficiently substantial to enable operations regarding the use of a payment device to be traced and errors rectified and where a dispute arises regarding liability for an unauthorised electronic fund transfer, the burden of proof is on the issuer to show that the operation was accurately recorded and accurately entered into accounts and was not affected by the technical breakdown or other deficiency.

9. The contracting holder, if he so requests, must be supplied with a record of each of his operations, instantaneously or shortly after he has completed it; however, in the case of payment at point of sale the till receipt supplied by the retailer at the time of purchase and containing the references to the payment device must satisfy the requirements of this provision.

10. The contracting holder is liable to the issuer for:

(i) the non-execution or defective execution of the contracting holder's operations even if an operation is initiated at electronic devices which are not under the issuer's direct or exclusive control;

(ii) operations not authorised by the contracting holder.

However, the issuer's liability is limited as follows:

(a) in the case of non-execution or defective execution of an operation, the amount of the liability is limited to the amount of the unexecuted or defectively executed operation;

(b) in the case of an unauthorised operation, the amount of liability extends to the sum required to restore the contracting holder to the position he was in before the unauthorised operation took place.

11. Any further financial consequences, and, in particular, questions concerning the extent of the damage for which compensation is to be paid must be

governed by the law applicable to the contract concluded between the issuer and the contracting holder.

12. (i) Each issuer must provide means whereby his customers may at any time of the day or night notify the loss, theft or copying of their payments devices.

   (ii) Once the contracting holder has notified the issuer or a central agency, as required by paragraph 4(iii), the contracting holder must not thereafter be liable; but this provision does not apply if the contracting holder acted with extreme negligence or fraudulently.

  (iii) The contracting holder must bear the loss sustained, up to the time of notification, in consequence of the loss, theft or copying of the payment device, but only up to the equivalent of 160 ECU for each event, except where he acted with extreme negligence or fraudulently.

  (iv) The issuer, upon receipt of notification, is under an obligation, even if the contracting holder acted with extreme negligence or fraudulently, to take all action open to him to stop any further use of the payment device.

The response of the banking industry to the Payment Systems Recommendation

30.23 In response to the Commission's Payment Systems Recommendation, a code of good conduct (the "Code of Good Conduct") has been drawn up and agreed by the EBF, the EEC Savings Bank Group and the EEC Association of Co-operative Banks in consultation with Visa, Eurocard and Eurocheque. It has been observed by the Commission[35] that, although the Code of Good Conduct was a step in the right direction, it does not allow for the protection of the consumer to the extent envisaged by the Payment Systems Recommendation. For instance, it states that the cardholder should take all appropriate steps to keep the card safe, whereas the Commission's recommendation requires the cardholder to take all reasonable steps to keep the card safe. Also, the Code of Good Conduct states that the issuer shall not be responsible for losses to the cardholder arising as a result of a system malfunction not directly within the control of the issuer, whereas in the Commission's recommendation the cardholder is not to be held responsible for such loss provided he did not act fraudulently or negligently and, in the case of loss of the card, he gave prompt notice to the issuer of such loss.[36] The Commission is reported to have sent a "firm but courteous" letter to the three main banking associations requesting them to bring their contractual provisions concerning electronic payment systems into line with those contained in the Payment Systems Recommendation and has stated that, unless that is done, it may consider submitting a more constraining instrument (a regulation or directive) to the Council on the subject. Such course of action does not appear, at the time of writing, imminent. It is submitted that legislation will only be proposed in the event that the Commission concludes that an unacceptable level of implementation has been achieved. A recent study commissioned by a Dutch consumer group indicates that, in the northern Member States, implementation of the Payment Systems Recommendation is almost total. However the position in the southern Member States appears much less satisfactory. This situation naturally begs the question as to what the Commission will

---

35. See "Consumers Electronic Payment: Banks should conform to the Commission's Recommendations by November at the latest—Second Anniversary of its Adoption", published in *Agence Europe*, Bulletin 5316 of Wednesday, 29 August 1990.

36. *Ibid.*

consider to be a "reasonable" level of implementation in relation to its Payment Systems Recommendation.

C. CONSUMER CREDIT

Introduction

30.24 In the field of consumer credit, the move towards a single market in the field of banking financial services has been marked by the passing of two Council Directives on the approximation of the laws, regulations and administrative provisions of Member States concerning consumer credit. The first is Directive 87/102/EEC adopted on 22 December 1986[37] (the "First Consumer Credit Directive") which was amended by Directive 90/88 adopted on 22 February 1990[38] (the "Second Consumer Credit Directive") (together the "Consumer Credit Directives"). In the preamble to the First Consumer Credit Directive, it was noted that wide differences existed in the laws of the Member States which resulted in the distortion of competition between grantors of credit and unequal consumer protection in the various Member States. The Consumer Credit Directives aim to provide a degree of harmonisation in the laws of Member States and thereby contribute to the establishment of a common market in consumer credit and the setting of common minimum standards of consumer protection in that market.

30.25 The First Consumer Credit Directive lays down common rules covering the procedure for making consumer credit agreements, advertising, the contents of credit agreements and the relationship between the consumer and the creditor. This Directive was required to be implemented by Member States by 1 January 1990. Previously, there was distortion of competition between creditors in different Member States because some had to comply with regulatory requirements while others did not. The United Kingdom and Germany were notable for their strict regulatory requirements in the area of consumer credit. The comprehensive approach introduced by the First Consumer Credit Directive should reduce many of the irregularities.

An important issue which was not resolved by the First Consumer Credit Directive was a uniform method of calculating the true cost of credit made available to a consumer. The European Parliament insisted that the EC should have such a uniform method and that it should be expressed as a percentage on the basis of one year, that is, an annual percentage rate of the charge for credit. However during the early stages of the Council's working party's discussions on this issue only two Member States, namely the Netherlands and the United Kingdom, had adopted (in the case of the United Kingdom) or were proposing to adopt (in the case of the Netherlands) specific rules on the cost of credit calculation. The other Member States were, at best, lukewarm on the issue and at worst positively hostile.[39] Consequently a temporary compromise was agreed whilst the debate was vigorously pursued by the Commission. The compromise was that Member States which had adopted specific rules on the matter would continue

37. Directive 87/102: OJ L42 of 12 February 1987.
38. Directive 90/88: OJ L61 of 10 March 1990.
39. For a more detailed account of the positions which previously existed in various Member States and the attitude of those States to a uniform method of calculating the cost of credit see E. P. Latham, "The EEC Consumer Credit Directive", *The Law Society Gazette*, 18 November 1987, p. 3331.

to apply them and Member States which had not were obliged to "... require the total cost of the credit to the consumer to be indicated" either as one figure or item by item.

The Commission's determination to introduce a uniform method for calculating the true cost of credit can be seen from the wording of what one might term the "compromise" article in the First Consumer Credit Directive, namely article 5 which reads as follows:

> By way of derogation from Articles 3 and 4(2), *and pending a decision on the introduction of an EEC method or methods of calculating the annual percentage rate of charge* [emphasis added] those Member States which, at the time of notification of this Directive, do not require the annual percentage rate of charge to be shown or which do not have an established method for its calculation, shall at least require the total cost of credit to the consumer to be indicated.

30.26 The Commission finally succeeded in its aim with the adoption of the Second Consumer Credit Directive which aimed to introduce, as from 1 January 1993, a uniform method of calculating the annual percentage rate ("APR") of charge being the rate which, over the year, equalises the present values of the prospective or actual commitments (loans, repayments and charges) of the lender and the borrower. The rate is required to be calculated on the basis of a mathematical formula which is set out in Annex II to the First Consumer Credit Directive, as amended by the Second Consumer Credit Directive. The objective of the Second Consumer Credit Directive is to make offers of credit more transparent and to provide better information for the consumer.

When taken together the Consumer Credit Directives represent significant progress for consumers in the EC in the sense that consumers seeking credit will be able to compare more fully the various offers of credit being made throughout the EC and, in particular, the contractual terms of such offers.

The scope of the Consumer Credit Directives

30.27 The regulatory requirements of the Consumer Credit Directives only apply to agreements whereby a creditor grants or promises to grant a consumer credit in the form of a deferred payment, a loan or other similar financial accommodation.[40] The definition of "credit agreement" set out in article 1(2) of the First Consumer Credit Directive is therefore much clearer than earlier EC definitions and the new definition contains an important second paragraph,[41] the purpose of which is to clarify that an agreement for the provision of a service or utility on a continuing basis, for which the consumer is entitled to make periodical payments for as long as the service or utility is provided, is not a credit agreement within the meaning of the First Consumer Credit Directive. As E. P. Latham, principal administrator to the Commission of the EC Directorate-General 11 (which includes consumer protection) at the relevant time, pointed out "... the most important consequence of adding the second paragraph [to article 1(2)(c)] was that all Member States immediately agreed that genuine credit for the provision of services must be covered by the Directive; and the consequence of that step was that the basic aim, that the Directive should apply to every type of consumer credit, was attained, subject to proper exceptions [set out in article 2]".[42]

A creditor is defined in the First Consumer Credit Directive as a natural or legal person who grants credit in the course of a trade, business or profession or a group of

---

40. Directive 87/102, art. 1(2)(c).
41. *Ibid.*, second para.
42. Fn. 39 above, at p. 3332.

such persons[43]; and a consumer is defined as a natural person who, in a transaction covered by the Consumer Credit Directives, acts outside his trade or profession,[44] that is to say that the consumer is one who borrows for the purpose of his own consumption or the requirements of those of his family or other dependants.[45]

Excluded agreements

30.28 The regulatory requirements set out in the Consumer Credit Directives do not apply to the following agreements[46]:

(a) Credit agreements or agreements promising to grant credit:
  (i) intended primarily for the purpose of acquiring or retaining property rights in land or in an existing or projected building; or
  (ii) intended for the purpose of renovating or improving[47] a building as such.

(b) Hiring agreements, except where these provide that the title will pass ultimately to the hirer.

  Where an agreement for hire contains provisions pursuant to which it can be changed, with the result that the object "hired" will become the property of the "hirer," the agreement ceases to be exempt and will be construed as a credit agreement for the purposes of the Consumer Credit Directives. As E. P. Latham has rightly pointed out,[48] a number of Member States are likely to experience difficulty in applying this exemption since it will be unclear, under the relevant national law, when an agreement ceases to be a hiring agreement by virtue of the title in the hired property passing to the hirer.[49]

(c) Credit granted or made available without payment of interest or any other charge.

(d) Credit agreements under which no interest is charged provided the consumer agrees to repay the credit in a single payment.

  American Express cards, Diners Club and Diners International cards would clearly fall into this category.

(e) Credit in the form of advances on a current account granted by a credit institution or financial institution other than a credit card account. Agreements within this category are subject to less stringent requirements.[50]

  This category would apply to an overdraft on an account with a bank or other financial institution and requires the information set out in article 6 of the First

---

43. Directive 87/102, art. 1(2)(a).
44. *Ibid.*
45. The definition of consumer in the First Consumer Credit Directive is identical to that set out in the "Door-to-door Sales Directive" (see OJ L372 of 31 December 1985, p. 31), Council Directive 85/577/EEC of 20 December 1985, and reflects the description of the consumer contained in art. 13 of the Brussels Convention on Jurisdiction and the Enforcement of Judgments in Civil and Commercial Matters 1968.
46. Directive 87/102, art. 2.
47. The terms "renovating" and "improving" are not defined in the Consumer Credit Directives and will be defined by national laws.
48. Fn. 39 above, at p. 3334.
49. *Ibid.*, p. 3334, where Latham expresses his opinion that the text (of art. 2) would have been better left in the Commission's original wording, which simply referred to "hiring agreements" and therefore would have left it for national courts to determine whether a particular agreement was for mere hiring or for credit.
50. See art. 6 of the First Consumer Credit Directive which requires that the consumer under such an agreement shall be informed before the agreement is concluded of the credit limit, if any, the APR, the charges applicable from the time the agreement is concluded, the conditions under which these may be amended and the procedure for terminating the agreement. This information must be confirmed in writing.

Consumer Credit Directive[51] to be given to the customer concerning overdraft agreements. Article 6 stipulates that, although the information may be given orally in the first instance, it must be confirmed by the bank or other financial institution in writing.

(f) Credit agreements involving amounts less than 200 ECUs or more than 20,000 ECUs.

(g) Credit agreements under which the consumer is required to repay the credit either within a period not exceeding three months or by a maximum number of four payments within a period not exceeding 12 months.

30.29 Article 2(3) of the First Consumer Credit Directive also exempts credit agreements or agreements promising to grant credit, secured by a mortgage on immovable property, insofar as these are not already excluded, from all of the regulatory requirements of the Directive, except for the requirements relating to misleading advertising. Accordingly, the rules concerning credit advertisements and about offers of credit apply to credits and promises of credit secured by a mortgage on land.

Member States are given the discretion to exempt from some of the regulatory requirements set out in the Consumer Credit Directives credit agreements in the form of an authentic act signed before a notary or judge.[52] In addition, a Member State may, in consultation with the Commission, exempt from the application of the First Consumer Credit Directive certain types of credit which (i) are granted at rates of charge below those prevailing in the market, and (ii) are not offered to the public generally.[53] This possible exemption would cover loans made, for example, by social security authorities or like bodies and loans granted by educational authorities.

Advertisements

30.30 The First Consumer Credit Directive[54] requires that offers of credit displayed on business premises and any credit advertisements which carry an indication of an interest rate or which state any figures relating to the cost of the credit must also specify the APR. This can be done by means of a representative example even though other means are practicable. However, it should be noted that article 3 is expressed to be "without prejudice to the rules and principles applicable to unfair advertising and therefore in no way detracts from the rules set out in the misleading advertising Directive".[55]

Formalities of a credit agreement

30.31 All credit agreements regulated by the First Consumer Credit Directive are required to be made in writing and the consumer must be given a copy of the written agreement.[56] There are no exceptions to the requirement that a credit agreement must

---

51. *Ibid.*
52. France sought to secure an automatic exemption for such cases but this policy was not followed by the other Member States which, as a consequence, will have to pass national legislation in order to achieve the necessary exemption: see Latham, fn. 39, above.
53. See the First Consumer Credit Directive, art. 2(2).
54. *Ibid.*, art. 3.
55. Directive 84/450/EEC of 10 September 1984.
56. See art. 4(1) of the First Consumer Credit Directive.

be made in writing (other than in relation to bank overdrafts which must be confirmed in writing[57]), which emphasises the importance the Commission placed on this issue. In practice making a credit agreement in writing is a condition precedent to the existence of such an agreement. It is much more than merely a matter of best evidence. The written credit agreement must also contain the following information[58]:

(a) A statement of the APR which is the total of all the costs, including interest and other charges, which the consumer has to pay for the credit, expressed as an annual percentage of the amount of the credit granted and calculated in accordance with a specified formula.

(b) A statement of the conditions under which the APR may be amended.

(c) A statement of the amount, number and frequency of dates of the payments which the consumer must make to repay the credit including the payments for interest and other charges. It is also required that the total amount of these payments should be indicated wherever possible.

(d) A statement of the cost of certain items payable by the consumer but which are excluded from the total cost of credit. These include default charges and charges payable whether the transaction is paid for in cash or by credit.

Where it is not possible to state the APR (for example, because the period of borrowing is not known at the time the credit agreement is entered into), it is provided that the consumer shall be given adequate information in the written agreement, which information shall include the credit limit, if any, the annual rate of interest, the charges applicable from the time the agreement is concluded and the conditions under which these may be amended and the procedure for terminating the agreement.

30.32 The First Consumer Credit Directive[59] also provides that the written credit agreement shall further include the other essential terms of the contract. It does not set out such essential terms (since the Member States could not agree on what are "essential" terms) but contains, by way of illustration, a list of terms[60] which Member States may require to be included in the written credit agreement as being essential. They include where relevant:

(i) a description of the goods or services covered by the agreement;

(ii) the cash price and the price payable under the credit agreement;

(iii) the amount of the deposit, if any, the number and amount of instalments and the dates on which they fall due, or the method of ascertaining any of these if unknown at the time the agreement is concluded;

(iv) an indication that the consumer will be entitled, as provided in article 8, to a reduction if he repays early;

(v) the owner of the goods (if ownership does not pass immediately to the consumer) and the terms on which the consumer becomes the owner of them;

(vi) a description of the security required, if any;

(vii) the cooling off period, if any;

(viii) an indication of the insurance required, if any, and, when the choice of insurer is not left to the consumer, an indication of the cost thereof;

---

57. Fn. 50, above.
58. See art. 4(2) of the First Consumer Credit Directive.
59. *Ibid.*, art. 4(3).
60. See Annex 1 of the Second Consumer Credit Directive.

    (ix) the amount of the credit limit, if any; and

    (x) the terms of repayment or the means of determining them.

As already indicated in relation to credit granted by credit establishments in the form of an overdraft on a current account, the consumer is to be informed of the credit limit, if any, the annual rate of interest, other charges, the conditions in which the interest or charges may be amended and the procedure for terminating the agreement.[61] Furthermore, the First Consumer Credit Directive[62] provides that Member States are to specify the conditions under which goods bought on credit or on hire purchase may be repossessed. The Directive[63] also requires that the consumer be given the rights to make any repayment of credit if he/she wishes to do so and where the consumer so chooses, the Directive provides that the consumer shall be entitled to an equitable reduction in the total cost of the credit.

Calculation of the annual percentage rate ("APR")

30.33 The APR is required to be calculated in accordance with the mathematical formula set out in Annex II to the First Consumer Credit Directive, as amended by the Second Consumer Credit Directive, and four examples of the method of calculation are given in Annex II by way of illustration. The APR is required to be calculated at the time the credit agreement is concluded (except, of course, where it is quoted in the context of an advertisement) and the calculation shall be made on the assumption that the credit agreement is valid for the period agreed and that the creditor and the consumer fulfil their obligations under the terms and on the dates agreed.[64]

In calculating the APR, the First Consumer Credit Directive permits the following assumptions may be made where necessary[65]:

    (i) if the contract does not specify a credit limit, the amount of credit granted shall be equal to the amount fixed by the relevant Member State without exceeding a figure equivalent to 2,000 ECUs;

    (ii) if there is no fixed timetable for repayment and one cannot be deduced from the terms of the agreement and the means for repaying the credit granted, the duration of the credit shall be deemed to be one year;

    (iii) unless otherwise specified, where the contract provides for more than one repayment date, the credit will be made available and the repayments made at the earliest time provided for in the agreement;

    (iv) where the credit agreement contains a clause allowing variation in the rate of interest and the amount of other charges contained in the APR but such variations are unquantifiable at the time when the APR is calculated, it is provided that the APR shall be calculated on the assumption that the interest and other charges remain fixed and will apply until the end of the credit agreement.[66]

61. See fn. 50, above.
62. See art. 7.
63. *Ibid.*, art. 8.
64. See art. 1a of Directive 87/102, as amended by art. 1(2) of Directive 90/88.
65. Directive 87/102, art. 1a(4).
66. *Ibid.*, art. 1a(7).

Breach of contract by the supplier

30.34 In certain circumstances[67] where, in order to buy goods or obtain services, the consumer enters into a credit agreement with a person other than the supplier and the goods or services covered by the credit agreement are not supplied, or are supplied only in part, or are not in conformity with the contract for supply of them, the consumer is allowed to pursue remedies against the grantor of the credit provided that:

(i) the grantor of the credit and the supplier of the goods or services have a pre-existing agreement pursuant to which credit is made available by that grantor of credit to customers of that supplier for the acquisition of goods or services from that supplier and the consumer obtains his or her credit pursuant to that pre-existing agreement; and

(ii) the consumer has pursued his remedies against the supplier but has failed to obtain the satisfaction to which he is entitled.

The Directive provides that the national laws of Member States shall determine to what extent and under what conditions these remedies shall be exercisable. However, these remedies are not available where the individual transaction in question is for an amount less than the equivalent of 200 ECUs.[68]

Authorisation of creditors

30.35 Member States are required to ensure that persons offering credit or offering to arrange credit agreements obtain official authorisation to do so either specifically or as suppliers of goods and services. Alternatively Member States may (a) ensure that such persons are subject to inspection or monitoring of their activities by an institution, or (b) establish appropriate bodies to receive complaints or provide relevant information regarding credit agreements.[69] However, Member States may provide that such authorisation shall not be required where persons offering or arranging credit agreements are credit institutions within the definition of article 1 of the First Banking Directive, and are authorised in accordance with the provisions of that Directive.[70]

Implementation of the Consumer Credit Directives

30.36 The deadline for implementing the First Consumer Credit Directive was 1 January 1990, and 31 December 1992 in the case of the Second Consumer Credit Directive. The First Consumer Credit Directive permits Member States to adopt more stringent measures to protect consumers and the Consumer Credit Act 1974 in the United Kingdom is notable for its imposition of stricter regulatory requirements on grantors of credit to consumers.[71]

67. *Ibid.*, art. 11(2).
68. *Ibid.*, art. 11(3).
69. *Ibid.*, art. 12(1).
70. *Ibid.*, art. 12(2).
71. For instance, its requirements apply to consumer hire agreements (Consumer Credit Act 1974, s. 15), and consumers are defined to include partnerships and other unincorporated associations (see the definition of "individual" in s. 189(1)). Also, where the credit has been used by the consumer to purchase goods or services from a supplier, the 1974 Act provides that the creditor and supplier shall be jointly and severally liable for any breach of contract or misrepresentation by the supplier (see s. 75—the amount of the credit must be £15,000 or less and more than £50). Under the UK system the consumer does not have to exhaust his/her remedies against the supplier before proceeding against the creditor.

Therefore, although the Consumer Credit Directives remove some of the distortions in competition between creditors in different Member States, because of the more stringent regulatory requirements in some Member States, some element of distortion will remain.

CHAPTER 31

DEPOSIT GUARANTEE SCHEMES

INTRODUCTION

31.1 Most Member States have recognised for some time that an important element in any formal structure for the supervision of credit institutions is an effective deposit guarantee scheme to protect depositors against the risk of a credit institution failure. The recent collapse of BCCI[1] once again graphically illustrated the hardship which depositors and others[2] suffer whenever a credit institution fails. The collapse also prompted the Commission to bring forward proposals for an EC deposit protection scheme[3] which had been on the Commission's agenda, in one form or another, since January 1986.[4]

Whilst one of the principal aims of the new supervisory regime established in the EC in respect of credit institutions is to create a stable financial system, as we indicated in earlier chapters of this book, numerous difficulties and inconsistencies lie in the existing supervisory structure. It remains to be seen whether the regime will achieve this important aim. In addition, a fundamental principle lying at the core of banking supervision is the protection of depositors' cash and, therefore, the maintenance of confidence in the banking sector. Consequently, although the aim of the Community supervisory structure is to maintain soundness in the single market in banking and financial services, both in general and specific terms, the recent moves towards implementation of an EC-wide deposit guarantee scheme could be viewed as a pragmatic acknowledgement that EC credit institutions will continue to fail and that depositors prejudiced by such failures should be compensated.

31.2 Deposit guarantee schemes generally serve the dual purposes of providing protection for depositors of credit institutions as well as contributing to the stability of the banking system as a whole. It is argued by those in favour of such schemes that depositors, particularly those who do not have the level of financial knowledge required properly to discriminate between sound and unsound banks, are protected in the event of a financial crisis befalling an institution. At the same time, the banking system is

---

1. For an interesting account of the collapse of BCCI see Dale, "Bank Regulation after BCCI" [1993] 1 JIBL 8. Comprehensive accounts of the collapse can also be found in the report which followed the inquiry by Bingham L.J. into the supervision of BCCI (London): HMSO, October 1992, and the report to the Senate Committee on Foreign Relations from Senator John Kerry and from Senator Hank Brown, 30 September 1992.

2. Because of the nature of BCCI's depositor base many individuals, not directly connected to BCCI as either depositors or investors/shareholders, suffered as a consequence of its failure, eg, the poll tax payers of certain local authorities which had made large deposits with BCCI.

3. Proposal for a Council Directive on Deposit Guarantee Schemes: Com(92)188 Final.

4. See the Proposal for a Council Directive on the Co-ordination of Laws, Regulations and Administrative Provisions relating to the Reorganisation and Winding-up of Credit Institutions: Com(85)356 Final.

protected from the risk of a general run on banks which are in a relatively sound condition but which may be the subject of unfounded rumours or simply caught up in a lack of confidence in the banking system as a whole brought on by the failure of a small number of banks. One of the main arguments postulated by opponents of deposit guarantee schemes is that they put a premium on sloppy banking and penalise good banking.

31.3 Deposit guarantee schemes are a relatively recent phenomenon, perhaps reflecting the change in the ratio of capital to assets required of banks. A hundred years ago, when there was little or no liquidity in bank assets and a very strong culture of relationship banking, capital/asset ratios were appreciably higher and far easier to calculate. The current ratio of 8% which applies in most western countries[5] is very low in historical terms and presupposes the existence of a lender of last resort and, inevitably, greater state intervention or support in the banking sector.

Whilst most western countries now accept the need for deposit guarantee schemes, the nature and extent of the protection which depositors should enjoy is the subject of considerable debate. At the time of writing, the majority of Member States have implemented some form of national deposit protection scheme. Eight Member States have schemes where membership is compulsory[6] and three operate voluntary schemes.[7] Only Greece has yet to implement any sort of deposit protection scheme.[8]

EC PROPOSALS ON DEPOSIT GUARANTEE SCHEMES

31.4 The Commission first referred formally to the need for a deposit guarantee scheme in the EC in January 1986 in a proposed Directive on the co-ordination of laws, regulations and administrative provisions relating to the reorganisation and winding-up of credit institutions.[9] That proposal envisaged that depositors' interests would be safeguarded by existing guarantee schemes operating within the various Member States, without discrimination between branches of national or non-national EC credit institutions or between deposits placed within the national territory or in a branch established in another Member State where no scheme existed. It also proposed that Member States ensure that their deposit protection schemes cover the deposits of branches of institutions having their head offices in other Member States.[10] As a transitional measure, pending the implementation of a scheme in all Member States, it was proposed that existing schemes be extended to cover deposits received by branches set up in other Member States which had no deposit guarantee scheme.[11] The proposal, which mostly dealt with the reorganisation and winding up of credit institutions, was amended by the Commission and resubmitted to the Council in January 1988[12] but has not subsequently been accepted by the Council. Those provisions of the proposal dealing with deposit guarantee schemes have now been superseded by subsequent proposals.

---

5. The exceptions to this general rule are considered in Chap. 15: see especially para. 15.25.
6. Namely, Belgium, Denmark, France, Ireland, Luxembourg, the Netherlands, Portugal and the UK.
7. Namely, Germany, Spain and Italy.
8. At the time of writing although the Portuguese scheme has been finalised its provisions are not legally binding.
9. Proposal 85/C356/10.
10. *Ibid.*, art. 16(1).
11. *Ibid.*, art. 16(2).
12. As proposal 88/C36/01. The provisions dealing with deposit guarantee schemes were not amended.

31.5 The next step towards a single deposit protection scheme in the EC came with the publication in 1987 of a recommendation concerning the introduction of deposit guarantee schemes in the EC.[13] At the time of its publication, six Member States had no deposit guarantee sheme[14] and those Member States which did operate schemes did so on a "host country" basis; that is, such schemes protected deposits made within the Member State, including deposits made at branches of credit institutions authorised in other Member States, but not deposits made outside the Member State at branches of credit institutions authorised in the Member State. The Council recommended that the existing schemes be extended to cover deposits received by credit institutions at branches established in host countries in which no scheme existed. It noted that the common requirement that branches of credit institutions authorised in other Member States must join the deposit protection scheme of the host country would maintain, at the EC level, the disparities between the various schemes which already existed at national level. In the Council's opinion such a requirement was likely to prejudice the proper functioning of the European internal market. However, it felt that more evidence and experience from the operation of the schemes operating in the various Member States was required before an EC-wide directive could be proposed. Accordingly, the Commission recommended that Member States which already operated deposit protection schemes[15] should verify that in the event of a winding-up of a credit institution revealing insufficient assets, those schemes comply with four basic requirements:

(i) guarantee compensation for depositors not possessing the means properly to assess the financial policies of credit institutions to which they had entrusted their deposits;

(ii) cover for depositors of all authorised credit institutions, including the depositors of branches of credit institutions, that have their head offices in other Member States;

(iii) distinguish sufficiently clearly between intervention prior to winding-up and compensation after winding-up;

(iv) clearly set out the criteria for compensation and the formalities to be completed in order to receive compensation.

The Commission recommended that Member States which already had plans for introducing deposit protection schemes[16] should ensure that the schemes comply with the above conditions, and that they were in place by not later than 31 December 1988. It also recommended that Member States which had not drawn up plans for deposit protection schemes[17] should do so (and ensure that the proposed scheme complied, at least, with the above conditions) and have them in place by not later than 1 January 1990.

13. Recommendation 87/63/EEC of 22 December 1986.
14. Namely, Denmark, Greece, Ireland, Italy, Luxembourg and Portugal.
15. Namely, Belgium, Germany, Spain, France, the Netherlands and the UK.
16. Namely, Italy, Ireland and Portugal.
17. Namely, Denmark, Greece and Luxembourg.

THE MOVE TOWARDS IMPLEMENTATION OF A BINDING DEPOSIT GUARANTEE SCHEME IN THE EC

31.6 The first move by the Commission towards the implementation of binding legislation on deposit guarantee schemes came in April 1992 when it issued a proposal for a Council Directive on the subject (the "Proposed Deposit Guarantee Directive").[18] At that time, notwithstanding the recommendations of the Commission referred to above, only 10 Member States had deposit guarantee schemes in place which accorded with the Commission's recommendation of December 1986.[19] The Proposed Deposit Guarantee Directive noted that under the single banking licence regime, which was to apply from 1 January 1993, the solvency of branches of credit institutions will be monitored by the competent authorities of the home Member States. Consequently, it was the Commission's view that all branches of a credit institution should belong to a single guarantee scheme which, logically, should be the scheme operating in the Member State where the head office of the credit institution is situated, because of the link between supervision of a branch's solvency and its membership of a deposit guarantee scheme. The proposal also noted that unequal conditions of competition may arise due to the disparities in compensation under the various schemes operating throughout the EC. Problems were noted to arise, for example, where a branch situate in one Member State belongs to a deposit protection scheme of its home country which provides less protection than the scheme operating in the Member State where the branch is situate.[20] To overcome that problem, the Commission proposed that such branches should be permitted to join the host country scheme in order to offer their depositors the same deposit protection as that offered to depositors of host country credit institutions.

31.7 The importance which the Commission attaches to the issue of deposit protection, in the context of the freedom of establishment and the freedom to provide services given to credit institutions pursuant to the Second Banking Directive can be seen from the wording of the second recital in the Proposed Deposit Guarantee Directive which reads:

Whereas, at the same time as restrictions on their [credit institutions'] activities are eliminated, consideration should be given to the situation which might arise if a credit institution that has branches in other Member States suffers a financial crisis; whereas it is indispensable to ensure a harmonised minimum level of deposit protection wherever in the Community deposits are located; whereas such deposit protection *is as essential as the prudential rules for the completion of the single banking market.* (emphasis added)

The words in emphasis might be considered a little surprising in the light of the elaborate supervisory structure which now operates in the EC banking sector and they

18. Proposal 92/C163/05, now amended by Amended Proposal 93/C178/14, submitted by the Commission on 7 June 1993. See para. 31.10, below.

19. Portugal and Greece being the two countries without a deposit guarantee scheme in place.

20. A potential of unequal conditions of competition arises in the converse situation, *viz.* where the branch competing in the host country belongs to a scheme in its home country which provides higher protection than schemes operating in the host country. However, that is less likely to lead to a problem in practice because (a) the number of foreign branches will be relatively small compared to the number of branches of the host country's credit institutions; (b) depositors in the host country are, on the whole, likely to feel more comfortable with their own credit institutions and unlikely therefore to change to a foreign institution solely because its scheme affords higher deposit protection; and (c) as noted by the Parliament's Legal Affairs and Citizens' Rights Committee in a draft report of 28 January 1993, credit institutions are unlikely to advertise themselves as being safe in the event of insolvency.

should be read in light of the proximity of the collapse of BCCI. As already indicated, it was the collapse of BCCI that prompted the Commission to bring forward the Proposed Deposit Guarantee Directive. In the light of the public outcry that followed the collapse of BCCI it is hardly surprising that the Commission saw fit to highlight, in the preamble to the Proposed Deposit Guarantee Directive, the importance of deposit protection in the event of a credit institution failure.

31.8 The main provisions of the Proposed Deposit Guarantee Directive, as amended by the Amended Proposal[21] (the "Amended Proposal"), are as follows:

1. Each Member State must ensure that it introduces one or more deposit guarantee schemes on its territory and, subject to certain exceptions contained in article 2 of the Amended Proposal, no credit institution authorised in that Member State may accept deposits unless it is a member of one of those schemes. The schemes must also cover the depositors of branches set up by those credit institutions in other Member States. Deposit guarantee schemes are therefore proposed to be administered on a home country basis. Credit institutions may be exempted if they belong to a scheme which protects the credit institution (with particular regard to its liquid assets and solvency) in a manner equivalent to that provided by the relevant authorised scheme or schemes.[22]

2. A branch of a credit institution authorised in another Member State may apply to join the scheme covering similar institutions in the host Member State.

3. Member States may stipulate that branches established by credit institutions with their head offices outside the EC must join a deposit guarantee scheme in that Member State.

4. The minimum level of deposit protection is 20,000 ECUs for the aggregate deposits of each depositor. Member States may limit the guarantee to a specified percentage of deposits. However, the percentage must equal or exceed 90% of the aggregate deposits until the amount to be paid under the guarantee reaches 20,000 ECUs. Member States are, however, permitted to limit the deposit protection to 15,000 ECUs for a transitional period of up to five years. Thus, the Proposed Deposit Guarantee Directive allows the principle of co-responsibility in a scheme if a Member State so wishes.

5. Certain specified depositors may be excluded from the scheme. These are, in summary, large institutions quite capable of evaluating for themselves the creditworthiness of a credit institution; directors, shareholders and other persons closely associated with the credit institution; and deposits for which the depositor has, on an individual basis, obtained from the credit institution rates or concessions which have helped to aggravate the financial situation of that credit institution.[23] This principle is in keeping with the usual objective of deposit guarantee schemes to protect small depositors who are unable properly to evaluate the creditworthiness of the credit institution.

---

21. Amended proposal for a Council Directive on deposit guarantee schemes COM(93) final-SYN 415, OJ C163 of 30 June 1993.
22. See art. 2(1) of the Amended Proposal.
23. As was the case with the collapse of BCCI; see Dale, fn. 1, above.

6. The deposit guarantee applies to the aggregate deposits of a depositor placed with the same credit institution irrespective of the number of deposits, currency or location within the EC.

7. The protection is extended to each beneficial owner of a deposit and each owner's interest is to be treated separately. Thus, if a credit institution collapses, joint depositors and beneficiaries of a deposit held on trust each receive separate payments, up to the maximum amount guaranteed by the scheme, according to the extent of their interest in the deposit. Joint depositors are assumed to have equal interests unless special provisions apply. A beneficiary's interest in a deposit subject to a trust will depend upon the terms of the trust.[24]

8. Credit institutions must provide depositors with sufficient information to enable them to identify the deposit guarantee scheme in which the institution and its branches take part within the EC, in order clearly to indicate the coverage available under the relevant scheme or schemes. In addition, information must be made available, upon first request, regarding "the conditions for compensation and the formalities which must be fulfilled in order to obtain compensation".[25]

9. Payments pursuant to a scheme are to be made within three months of the date on which the deposit becomes unavailable, or of any earlier finding by a court or other relevant authority that payment has ceased. A deposit is defined as being unavailable if the credit institution is experiencing a financial crisis and is unable to repay under the legal and contractual conditions applicable to the repayment. It is not necessary for a judicial or administrative authority to declare the suspension of payments; it is sufficient for the suspension actually to last for 10 consecutive days, after which the deposit is deemed to be unavailable.

10. Credit institutions which fail to comply with the relevant deposit protection scheme requirements may have penalties imposed upon them by the home supervisor in order to secure compliance. Continuing failure to comply may lead to an exclusion from the scheme.[26]

11. The proposed date for Member States to bring into force the necessary laws, regulations and administrative provisions to comply with the Proposed Deposit Guarantee Directive is 5 January 1994.

12. After the transitional period, referred to at provision 4 above, where the level and/or scope of cover offered by the host Member State deposit guarantee scheme exceeds that provided in the Member State where the relevant credit institution is authorised, the host Member State shall ensure that there is an officially recognised deposit guarantee scheme which a branch of a credit institution may join voluntarily in order to increase depositor protection to the levels set in the host Member State and so offer the same level of protection as local credit institutions. Branches of third country credit institutions may also be required to join the deposit guarantee scheme of a host Member State.

---

24. The treatment of joint accounts and trust accounts poses complex issues in the context of deposit protection: see, eg, Penn, *Banking Supervision* (Butterworths) (1987), pp. 122–124, where the position in the UK under the Banking Act 1987 is considered.
25. Art. 6(1) of the Amended Proposal.
26. *Ibid.*, art. 2(3).

THE CURRENT POSITION

31.9 The Council of Ministers adopted a common position on the Proposed Deposit Guarantee Directive (as amended by the Amended Proposal) on 25 October 1993 and that common position was put forward to the European Parliament on 11 November 1993 for its second reading under the new co-decision procedure introduced by the Maastricht Treaty. At the time of writing the European Parliament has yet to give its opinion (it has three months so to do) on whether to accept, reject or propose further amendments to the proposed Directive.

CONCLUSION

31.10 The Proposed Deposit Guarantee Directive conforms with the approach taken in other EC banking measures in the area of banking supervision, in that it stipulates certain minimum standards and leaves the setting of standards to the home regulator. This approach, in the context of deposit protection in a single Community banking market, is fraught with difficulties and will undoubtedly lead to competitive inequality because banks in countries which offer a high level of deposit protection will attempt to attract deposits by advertising that fact to both existing and prospective depositors in Member States offering lower levels of protection. This competitive distortion is covered, to a certain extent, by the "topping-up provision" contained in article 2 of the Proposed Deposit Guarantee Directive which provides that a branch of a credit institution authorised in another Member State may apply voluntarily to join the deposit protection scheme operating in the host Member State. However, although a distortion of competitive conditions may have been provided for in the case of establishment, given that credit institutions can, pursuant to the Second Banking Directive, offer banking services across national borders, there is nothing contained in the Proposed Deposit Guarantee Directive or the Amended Proposal to prevent a credit institution in one Member State making it known in another Member State that it offers a higher degree of deposit protection than that offered by "local" credit institutions, in order to attract cross border deposits. Any attempt by the Commission to limit the ability of credit institutions to attract deposits in such a way would be a clear breach of the Treaty.[27]

31.11 Another criticism of the Proposed Deposit Guarantee Directive is that it fails to distinguish, in terms of the protection offered, between strong and weak credit institutions. In the United Kingdom, for example, the Bank of England identifies capital requirements for each credit institution under its supervision using target and trigger risk asset ratios. Therefore, as we have already indicated in an earlier chapter of this book, the 8% minimum standard is the minimum trigger risk asset ratio (but even this is increased in the case of certain banks), but the target ratio is set on an individual basis at a level which the Bank of England deems appropriate in particular circumstances. The majority of banks authorised by the Bank of England are understood to have target ratios significantly in excess of the 8% minimum which undoubtedly reflects, at least in part, the risk which the Bank of England attaches to the credit institution in question. It could be argued that the level of deposit protection

---

27. See Tony Shea, "European Banking in the 1990s", *Butterworths Journal of International Banking and Financial Law*, January 1993, p. 8.

provided by credit institutions should also be addressed on a case-by-case basis if regulators like the Bank of England, which apply the capital adequacy rules, to a certain extent, on a case-by-case basis, are to be consistent in their approach. However, all the indications are that this will not, at least in the short to medium term, be the case. Consequently, competitive advantages will be obtained by banks in those Member States which operate high levels of deposit protection, and those advantages will be available to all credit institutions authorised in those Member States notwithstanding the risk to depositors who place their deposits with the weaker credit institutions in those States.

PART SEVEN

PRESENTATION OF BANKS' ACCOUNTS

CHAPTER 32

PRESENTATION OF BANKS' ACCOUNTS

INTRODUCTION

32.1 Pursuant to article 54(3)(g) of the Treaty, which requires the co-ordination of national laws relating to company safeguards protecting the interests of shareholders, employees and third parties, the Commission embarked on an important programme aimed at the harmonisation of certain national company laws of Member States. The programme included two major directives: (i) the Fourth Council Directive of 25 July 1978[1] (the "Fourth Company Law Directive") on the annual accounts of certain types of companies, being public or private companies limited by shares or guarantee and similar companies in other Member States which, in general terms, set forth the format to be used for group accounts (amended to reflect minority interests); and (ii) the Seventh Council Directive of 13 June 1983[2] ("the Seventh Company Law Directive") on consolidated accounts which redefined general accounting principles for companies. When taken together these two Directives had a fundamental impact throughout Member States with regard to the principles of preparation of consolidated accounts (group accounts), the important definition of "subsidiary" in the context of group accounting treatment and the requirement that a company's accounts give "a true and fair view".

Credit and other financial institutions were specifically excluded from the scope of the Fourth Company Law Directive because of their special characteristics as deposit-taking institutions and, for the same reason, the Seventh Company Law Directive provided for derogations for credit institutions. However, in order to put credit and other financial institutions onto the same footing as other companies insofar as the presentation and consolidation of annual accounts is concerned the Council adopted, on 8 December 1986, a Directive on the annual accounts and consolidated accounts of credit and other financial institutions[3] (hereafter referred to as the Bank Accounts Directive).

The Bank Accounts Directive required implementation into national laws of Member States by 31 December 1990. It then gave a period of grace to credit institutions which were required to comply with its provisions not later than the accounting period beginning on or after 1 January 1993. However, because of its

---

1. Fourth Company Law Directive, OJ L222/11 of 14 August 1978.
2. Seventh Company Law Directive, OJ L193/1 of 18 September 1983.
3. Bank Accounts Directive, OJ L372/1 of 31 December 1986.

complex and highly technical nature a number of Member States failed to implement the Directive by its required deadline.[4]

1. THE PURPOSE OF THE BANK ACCOUNTS DIRECTIVE

32.2 The purpose of the Bank Accounts Directive was to harmonise the presentation of the annual accounts of credit and other financial institutions. The harmonisation achieved by the Bank Accounts Directive covers the layout, terminology and nomenclature of the balance sheet and the profit and loss accounts; the valuation rules; the contents of the notes on the accounts; the provisions related to consolidated accounts; and the rules concerning publication and auditing. Such harmonisation was important not only to enable proper comparisons to be made of the accounts of credit and financial institutions, of which an increasing number are operating, and will continue to operate, across national frontiers, but also because aspects of the provisions governing annual accounts inevitably have an impact on other areas of co-ordination in the banking sector, in particular the requirements for authorisation and the indicators used for supervisory purposes which is considered in greater detail in Chapters 10 and 17.

As emphasised in its recitals, the Bank Accounts Directive had to be drafted "in the framework of rules devised for undertakings generally" and, consequently, its terms render credit and financial institutions subject to most of the provisions laid down in the Fourth and Seventh Company Law Directives.

It should be noted however that, as a practical matter, the Bank Accounts Directive only addresses the specific problems relating to the annual accounts of credit institutions which are excepted from the ambit of the Fourth and Seventh Company Law Directives. The Bank Accounts Directive does not establish an independent and separate set of rules which are intended to stand beside the general accounting rules applicable to all other companies. It must be read in conjunction with the provisions set out in the Fourth and Seventh Company Law Directives to which Directives it frequently makes cross-references whenever the applicable provisions are identical.

A further point which should be noted is that the Bank Accounts Directive only lays down the minimum disclosure requirements. Member States are free to authorise or require the disclosure of further information in the annual accounts over and above that required by the Bank Accounts Directive.[5]

---

4. The UK response towards implementation of the Bank Accounts Directive has been, *inter alia*, the passing of subordinate legislation. The principal response came with the publication of the Companies Act 1985 (Bank Accounts) Regulations 1991 (SI 1991/2705), which came into force on 2 December 1991. These regs., which effectively implemented the Bank Accounts Directive in relation to the majority of banking companies in the UK, amended Sched. 9 of the Companies Act 1985 by making special provisions to the accounts treatment of banking companies. The regs. also introduced a new s. 255 into the Companies Act 1985 requiring UK banks to prepare their individual accounts in accordance with Sched. 9. Interestingly, the building society industry in the UK was treated separately and implementation was achieved pursuant to the Building Societies Accounts and Related Provisions Regulations 1992 (SI 1992/359), which came into force on 1 January 1993. The impact of the implementation in the UK of the Bank Accounts Directive on both the banking and the building society sectors is considered in an interesting article by Harry Venet: see "Banks and Building Societies: Coming into Line", *Accountancy*, October 1992, p. 112.

5. See art. 2(6) of the Fourth Company Law Directive applicable to credit and financial institutions by virtue of art. 1 of the Bank Accounts Directive.

2. THE SCOPE OF APPLICATION OF THE BANK ACCOUNTS DIRECTIVE

32.3 The measures prescribed by the Bank Accounts Directive apply to all credit institutions within the meaning of article 1 of the First Banking Directive[6] where such institutions are companies or firms within the meaning of article 58(2) of the Treaty (namely, companies or firms constituted under civil or commercial law and other legal persons governed by public or private law, save for those which are non-profit-making). Consequently, the Bank Accounts Directive covers a wider range of local institutions than the Fourth Company Law Directive which applies only to public or private companies limited by shares or guarantees and similar institutions throughout the EC.[7] The Bank Accounts Directive also applies to financial institutions having one of the legal forms referred to in article 1(1) of the Fourth Company Law Directive (being public or private companies limited by shares or guarantees) but which institutions are not subject to that Directive.

32.4 Certain credit institutions[8] specific to Greece, Ireland and the United Kingdom are excluded from the Bank Accounts Directive and Member States are free to exclude from the Directive credit institutions listed in article 2(2)[9] and 2(4)(a)[10] of the First Banking Directive. Member States are also permitted to lay down rules derogating from the Bank Accounts Directive in the case of:

(i) credit institutions which receive deposits, or other repayable funds from the public and grant credits for its own account, but which are not companies of the types listed in article 1(1) of the Fourth Company Law Directive where

6. OJ L322/30 of 17 December 1977. In the UK the general categories of institution falling within the scope of the Bank Accounts Directive are: (i) institutions authorised under the Banking Act 1987; (ii) building societies; and (iii) other financial institutions. It should also be noted that the Directive applies not only to UK banking institutions which are special category companies under the Companies Act 1985, but also to all forms of credit institution as defined by the First Banking Co-Ordination Directive which are "companies or firms" as defined by art. 58 of the EEC Treaty. For a detailed analysis of the scope of the Bank Accounts Directive in the UK see the Consultative Document issued by the Department of Trade and Industry (July 1990).

7. There are a number of additional deposit-taking institutions and categories of institutions covered by the Bank Accounts Directive, some of which may be exempted from compliance by the relevant Member State by virtue of art. 2(2). The categories of institutions which may be exempted are set out in art. 2(2) of the Bank Accounts Directive and those relevant to the UK include: credit unions; municipal banks; friendly societies; and industrial and provident societies, all of which have been exempted from the requirements of the Directive in the UK.

8. The ETEBA (National Investment Bank for Industrial Development) and the Investment Bank, both in Greece, Industrial and Provident Societies in Ireland and Friendly Societies and Industrial and Provident Societies in the UK.

9. These are central banks of Member States, Post Office giro institutions and other specified institutions in various Member States. In the UK they include the following bodies: the Bank of England; Post Office giro institutions; National Savings Bank; Crown Agents for Overseas Governments and Administrations; Crown Agents Financial Services Limited; Loan Societies; school banks; local authorities; and any other body which by virtue of any enactment has power to issue a precept to a local authority in England or Wales or a requisition to a local authority in Scotland.

10. These are institutions of Member States which, as defined in art. 2(4)(a) of the First Banking Co-Ordination Directive, are affiliated to a central body of a State in which they are established provided that (i) the commitments of the central body and affiliated institutions are joint and several liabilities or the commitments of the affiliated institutions are entirely guaranteed by the central body; (ii) the central body and its affiliated institutions are subject to consolidated accounts including an annual report drawn up, audited and published in accordance with the Bank Accounts Directive; and (iii) the management of the central body is empowered to issue instructions to the management of the affiliated institutions.

such derogating rules are necessary because of such institutions legal form[11]; and

(ii) specialised credit institutions, where derogating rules are necessary because of the special nature of the institutions' business.[12]

However, such derogating rules may only provide for adaptations to the layout, nomenclature, terminology and content of items in the balance sheet and profit and loss account. Such rules may not have the effect of permitting the institutions to which they apply to provide less information in the annual accounts than other institutions subject to the Directive. Member States are required to inform the Commission of the derogating rules so provided and of the credit institutions affected thereby within six months of the end of 1993 and such derogations shall be reviewed within ten years of notification of the Directive.

3. GENERAL PROVISIONS REGARDING THE BALANCE SHEET AND THE PROFIT AND LOSS ACCOUNT

A. Layout of the balance sheet

32.5 The present structure and contents of balance sheets of credit institutions differ between Member States. The Bank Accounts Directive sets out provisions (contained in article 4) for the balance sheets of all credit institutions throughout the EC to have the same layout, nomenclature and terminology. Certain derogations from article 4 are permitted, however, if either the legal form or the special nature of the business of the credit institution renders it necessary and provided that any such derogations may not have the effect of permitting institutions to which they apply to provide less information in their annual accounts than other institutions subject to this Directive.[13] Article 4 lists all the items (assets, liabilities and off-balance sheet items) which must be disclosed in the balance sheet pursuant to a specific nomenclature.

(a) Asset items

32.6 The following asset items are required to be disclosed:

(i) cash in hand, including balances with central banks and post office banks;
(ii) treasury bills and other bills eligible for refinancing with central banks;
(iii) loans and advances to credit institutions;
(iv) loans and advances to customers;
(v) debts securities including fixed income securities;
(vi) shares and other variable yield securities;
(vii) participating interests;
(viii) shares in affiliated undertakings;
(ix) intangible assets;
(x) tangible assets;
(xi) unpaid subscribed capital;
(xii) own shares;

11. The Bank Accounts Directive, art. 2(4)(a).
12. *Ibid.*, art. 2(4)(b).
13. *Ibid.*, art. 2(4).

(xiii) other assets;
(xiv) subscribed capital called but not paid;
 (xv) pre-payments and accrued income; and
(xvi) loss for the financial year.

(b) Liabilities items

32.7 The following liabilities items are required to be disclosed:

  (i) amounts owed to credit institutions;
 (ii) amounts owed to customers;
(iii) debts evidenced by certificates;
(iv) other liabilities;
 (v) accruals and deferred income;
(vi) provisions for liabilities and charges;
(vii) profits for the financial year;
(viii) subordinated liabilities;
 (ix) subscribed capital;
  (x) shared premium accounts;
 (xi) reserves;
(xii) revaluation reserve;
(xiii) profit or loss brought forward; and
(xiv) profit or loss for the financial year.

(c) Off-balance sheet items

32.8 Both the contingent liabilities and commitments which could give rise to a risk are required to be disclosed under the heading "off-balance sheet items".

In addition to listing the assets, liabilities and off-balance sheet items specified above, the Bank Accounts Directive also requires certain sub-items of those items to be shown separately. For example, claims, whether or not evidenced by certificates, on affiliated undertakings or undertakings with which a credit institution is linked by virtue of a participating interest which claims are included in asset items (ii), (iii), (iv) and (v) or liabilities items (i), (ii), (iii) and (viii) are required to be shown separately.[14] However, Member States are given a discretion to permit the disclosure of such information in the notes on the accounts.[15]

32.9 The Bank Accounts Directive also allows some flexibility in the manner in which the required information is specified in the balance sheet of the credit institution in question in that it gives Member States a discretion to permit the disclosure of certain items under different headings (for example, the national laws of Member States may prescribe that certain items falling under asset item (ii) be shown under asset items (iii) and (iv))[16] or under different categories (for example, the national laws of Member States may provide for asset item (xvi) to be included under liabilities item (xiv)[17] or for liabilities item (vii) to be included under liabilities item (xiv))[18] or in other parts of the

---

14. *Ibid.*, art. 5. See also art. 6.
15. *Ibid.*, art. 7.
16. *Ibid.*, art. 4, Assets item 2(b).
17. *Ibid.*, art. 4, Assets item 14.
18. *Ibid.*, art. 4, Liabilities item 7.

accounts (for example, the national laws of Member States may provide formation expenses or goodwill which fall within asset items (ix) to be disclosed in the accounts).[19]

Certain items (for example gold bullion) are not explicitly covered by the Bank Accounts Directive and the treatment of such items remains at the discretion of the Member States. Furthermore, the Directive authorises the introduction of new items provided that their contents are not covered by any of the items prescribed by the layouts.[20]

32.10 Although the Fourth Company Law Directive gives a certain degree of relief to small and medium sized companies by allowing Member States to permit such companies to draw up abridged balance sheets which have less extensive disclosure requirements, no such relief is given in the Bank Accounts Directive presumably because of the "particular" risks associated with banks and the business of banking and the need to maintain "confidence" in the banking sector.[21]

B. Sale and repurchase transactions

32.11 Article 12 of the Bank Accounts Directive makes specific provisions regarding sale and repurchase transactions which are defined as transactions which involve the transfer by a credit institution or customer (the "transferor") to another credit institution or customer (the "transferee") of assets, such as bills, debts or transferable securities subject to an agreement that the same assets will subsequently be transferred back to the transferor at a specified price. The transaction will only be regarded as a genuine sale and repurchase transaction if the transferee undertakes to return the assets specified or to be specified by the transferor. If, however, the transferee is merely entitled to return the assets at the purchase price or for a different amount agreed in advance on a date specified, or to be specified, the transaction is deemed to be a sale with an option to repurchase. In the case of a genuine sale and repurchase transaction, the asset transferred shall continue to appear in the transferor's balance sheet with the purchase price received by the transferor shown as an amount owed to the transferee. In addition, the value of the assets transferred is required to be disclosed in a note in the transferor's accounts. The transferee is not entitled to show the assets transferred in his balance sheet and the purchase price paid by the transferee is required to be shown as an amount owed by the transferor.

Where the transaction is deemed to be a sale with an option to repurchase, the transferor shall not be entitled to show the assets transferred in his balance sheet and those items shall be shown as assets in the transferee's balance sheet. The transferor is required to enter under off-balance sheet item 2 an amount equal to the price agreed in the event of repurchase.

32.12 Article 12(6) of the Bank Accounts Directive clarifies the meaning of "sale and repurchase transactions" somewhat by providing that forward exchange transactions, options, transactions involving the issue of debt securities with a commitment to repurchase all or part of the issue before maturity or any similar transactions shall not be regarded as sale and repurchase transactions.

---

19. *Ibid.*, art. 4, Assets item 9.
20. *Ibid.*, art. 1 adopting art. 4(1) of the Fourth Company Law Directive.
21. See respectively the 15th and 17th recitals in the preamble to the Bank Accounts Directive.

C. Layout of the profit and loss account

32.13 The Bank Accounts Directive sets out two alternative layouts of the profit and loss accounts of credit institutions. It provides a vertical layout and a horizontal layout. Member States are given a discretion as to which layout shall apply. Both layouts may be selected, in which case the Member State may permit credit institutions to select the layout to be adopted.[22] Whichever layout is adopted, the following items are required to be specified[23]:

    (i) interest receivable and similar income;
    (ii) interest payable and similar charges;
    (iii) income from securities;
    (iv) commission receivable;
    (v) commission payable;
    (vi) net profit or net loss on financial operations;
    (vii) other operating income;
    (viii) general administrative expenses;
    (ix) value adjustments in respect of asset items (ix) and (x);
    (x) other operating charges;
    (xi) value adjustments in respect of loans and advances and provisions for contingent liabilities for commitments;
    (xii) value readjustments in respect of loans and advances and provisions for contingent liabilities and for commitments;
    (xiii) value adjustments in respect of transferable securities held as financial fixed assets, participating interests and shares in affiliated undertakings;
    (xiv) value readjustments in respect of transferable securities held as financial fixed assets, participating interests and shares in affiliated undertakings;
    (xv) tax on profit or loss on ordinary activities;
    (xvi) profit or loss on ordinary activities after tax;
    (xvii) extraordinary income;
    (xviii) extraordinary charges;
    (xix) extraordinary profit or loss;
    (xx) tax on extraordinary profit or loss;
    (xxi) extraordinary profit or loss after tax;
    (xxii) other taxes not shown in the preceding items; and
    (xxiii) profit or loss for the financial year.

Where the vertical layout is adopted, the above items are required to be listed without classification. However, on the horizontal layout the above items are classified under the headings "charges" and "income".

32.14 The Bank Accounts Directive also provides that certain sub-items falling within the items specified above must be shown separately. For instance, under item (i), interest arising from fixed income securities is required to be shown separately and under item (iii) income from shares and other variable yield securities, from participating interest and from shares in affiliated undertakings is required to be shown separately. It should be noted that where certain sub-items which are an item of the profit and loss account are required to be shown separately, Member States are not in

22. *Ibid.*, art. 26.
23. See art. 27.

this instance given the discretion to permit such sub-items to be specified in the notes on the accounts.

Small and medium sized credit institutions are not allowed to draw up simplified profit and loss accounts as are small and medium sized companies under the Fourth Company Law Directive.

4. VALUATION RULES

32.15 The valuation rules set out in the Bank Accounts Directive relating to credit institutions loans and advances, debt securities, shares and other variable yield securities which are not held as financial fixed assets draw heavily from the valuation rules prescribed in the Fourth Company Law Directive.[24] However, the Bank Accounts Directive adapts those rules to the specific requirements of credit institutions. For example, where the terms "financial fixed assets" is used in article 7 of the Fourth Company Law Directive, the Bank Accounts Directive provides that the term shall, in the case of credit institutions, be taken to mean participating interests, shares in affiliated undertakings and securities intended for use on a continuing basis in the normal course of the undertaking's activities.[25] The Bank Accounts Directive also provides specific rules for the valuation of debt securities held as financial fixed assets and also for the valuation of tangible and intangible assets.

As already indicated[26] the system of valuation laid down by the Bank Accounts Directive is not inflexible and allows Member States to adopt derogatory rules in various instances.[27]

5. CONTENTS OF THE NOTES ON THE ACCOUNTS

32.16 The Bank Accounts Directive[28] adopts the rules specified in article 43(1) of the Fourth Company Law Directive dealing with notes on the accounts. It also requires credit institutions to disclose other information relating to subordinated liabilities and also certain specified information in case of the information required under article 43(1)(6) and (8) of the Fourth Company Law Directive. By article 41(2) of the Bank Accounts Directive, Member States are required to prescribe the rules requiring credit institutions to give certain additional information in the notes on their accounts. Such information includes the value of leasing transactions apportioned between the relevant balance sheet items and the charges paid on account of subordinated liabilities by a credit institution in the year under review.

6. CONSOLIDATED ACCOUNTS

32.17 The Bank Accounts Directive[29] adopts the rules specified in the Seventh Company Law Directive regarding the drawing up of consolidated accounts and

---

24. See art. 37(1) of the Bank Accounts Directive.
25. *Ibid.*, art. 35(2).
26. See para. 32.5, above.
27. See art. 37(2) of the Bank Accounts Directive.
28. *Ibid.*, art. 40(1).
29. *Ibid.*, art. 42.

consolidated annual reports for credit institutions subject to certain limits, conditions and adaptations. However, it should be noted that the Bank Accounts Directive has not adopted the exemption laid down in the Seventh Company Law Directive whereby parent undertakings are not bound by the consolidation requirements if the undertakings to be consolidated do not together exceed a certain size. This is another illustration of the desire to subject as many credit institutions as possible to equivalent provisions.

7. PUBLICATION

32.18 Article 44 of the Bank Accounts Directive provides that the duly approved annual accounts of credit institutions together with the annual reports and reports by the auditors shall be published as required by national law. Where the credit institution is of a type not required by its national law to publish its annual accounts or reports, it must at least make them available to the public at its registered office or in the absence of a registered office, at its principal place of business and it must be possible to obtain copies of such documents on request. Member States are given the discretion to exempt the annual reports from publication provided that they are made available to the public at the company's registered office.

The same rules apply to the consolidated accounts and related reports. The annual accounts and consolidated accounts are required to be published in every Member State in which credit institutions have branches and such Member States may require that those documents be published in the official language of the Member State.

8. CONCLUSION

32.19 The Bank Accounts Directive must be read in conjunction with the First and Second Consolidated Supervision Directives, which are considered in detail elsewhere in this book,[30] and the Directive on the obligations of branches of credit institutions regarding the publication of annual accounting documents in order fully to appreciate the impact of EC law on the accounts of credit institutions. When viewed together these three Directives contain provisions not only important to credit institutions, but also to creditors and debtors of such institutions and the general public. Together with the provisions set out in the Own Funds Directive[31] and the Solvency Ratio Directive,[32] they will provide a significant source of information on the strength and soundness of credit institutions which will be relevant not only to national bank regulators in light of the new rules relating to consolidated supervison.[33] In addition, on the pure accounting front, the co-ordination and uniformity of procedures and publication will improve comparability of the records of credit institutions operating across national borders and thereby aid freedom of choice on the part of the consumer of such services.

30. See Chap. 10.
31. See Chap. 14.
32. See Chap. 15.
33. A discussion of the importance of this information to national regulators is considered at para. 10.32, above.

PART EIGHT

THE POSITION OF NON-EC BANKS AND THEIR SUBSIDIARIES

CHAPTER 33

THE POSITION OF NON-EC CREDIT INSTITUTIONS

1. GENERAL REMARKS

33.1 The position of non-EC credit institutions under Community law must be viewed from three different angles. It is necessary to consider the conditions under which a credit institution based outside the Community may:

— provide services in the Community from that outside base;
— open a branch in one or more Member States and, from that branch, open a "secondary" branch or provide services in other Member States;
— incorporate or acquire an existing banking subsidiary in a Member State which may itself open branches and provide services in other Member States.

These issues are, generally, loosely put under the heading of "problems of reciprocity". However, as will be seen, the issue of reciprocity proper is a much narrower one.

The "problems of reciprocity" cut across more or less the whole field of Community legislation directly or indirectly relating to the operations in the Community of non-EC credit institutions. It arises *inter alia* in the context of the Investment Services Directive (whose reciprocity provisions are identical to those of the Second Banking Directive), the Capital Movements Directive and the Directives on Banking Supervision and Money Laundering. It is proposed to discuss the reciprocity issue here only in the context of the provisions of the Second Banking Directive.

2. DEFINITION OF NON-EC BASED CREDIT INSTITUTIONS

33.2 In Chapter 1, consideration was given generally to the persons who are able to benefit from the right of establishment conferred by article 52 of the Treaty.

As far as credit institutions are concerned, however, the possibilities for taking advantage of the right of establishment are more limited. Although, under the company law of some Member States such as the United Kingdom, Ireland and the Netherlands, it is accepted that a company incorporated under their respective laws and having its registered office there may have its "head office"[1] in another Member State, the company law of other civil law Member States does not accept the existence of a "registered office" distinct from the place of location of the "head office". Under the Second Banking Directive, in one of its recitals, it is provided that a Member State

---

1. We leave here outside consideration the question what the content of the term "head office" is *for the purposes of the Second Banking Directive*. It is submitted that it coincides in effect with the terms "*siège social*", ie, the place of highest control and management as the term is understood in civil law countries.

"must require that the head office [of a credit institution] be situated in the same Member State as its registered office".[2] In effect, this requirement precludes a Member State from granting a "single licence" to a credit institution having its registered office on its territory, in accordance with its national laws, unless the head office of that institution is located there too.

If the head office is located in another Member State, it is the latter Member State which has jurisdiction as the "home" Member State, to issue the single licence to the credit institution concerned (while insisting that its registered office be moved to the same place as its head office).

If the head office is located outside the Community, that credit institution cannot be granted a single licence by the Member State where it has its registered office, nor—obviously—by the third country in which the head office is located. Hence, it will not be an EC-based credit institution and will not be able to avail itself of the provisions of the Second Banking Directive. The BCCI affair must obviously be kept in mind when examining the implications of the above principles.

2. See recital 8. A similar requirement has been introduced in other EC financial legislation, including the recently adopted Investment Services Directive.

CHAPTER 34

THE PROVISION OF SERVICES WITHIN THE COMMUNITY BY A NON-EC BASED CREDIT INSTITUTION FROM A HEAD OFFICE OR BRANCH OUTSIDE THE COMMUNITY

34.1 The conditions under which a non-EC based credit institution may provide services within the EC from a head office or branch outside the EC are not covered by the First Banking Directive nor by the Second Banking Directive. The First Banking Directive only addresses the position of non-EC based credit institutions having branches in the Community. The Second Banking Directive only addresses the position of non-EC based credit institutions having subsidiaries in the Community. In other words, as far as Community law is concerned, third country credit institutions have no right to provide cross-border services within the Community from their home base.

As stated by Commissioner Bangemann[1]:

> Under Article 58 of the EC Treaty, companies or firms formed in accordance with the laws of a Member State and having their registered office, central administration or principal place of business within the Community are free to provide services in the other Member States as provided for in Article 59 of the Treaty. . . .
>
> Companies or firms which are established outside the Community and which have not set up a subsidiary in a Member State satisfying the conditions of Article 58 are not free to provide services under Article 59. The possibility for such companies or firms to do business in a Member State depends solely on the law of the Member State concerned or on any international conventions which it has signed.

In practice, it is principally[2] in the field of large ticket international transactions that the provision of banking services within the Community from a fixed base outside the Community takes place. Since these activities are not governed by either the First or Second Banking Directive, they remain governed by the bilateral relationships between the individual Member State concerned and the third country where the non-EC credit institution is based or, in the absence of a bilateral treaty, by the national laws only of the individual Member State.

34.2 However, in exercising their powers in this field, the Member States must obey the general principle of Community preference, according to which a non-EC based credit institution must not be accorded more favourable treatment than that accorded to an EC based credit institution, even if such advantageous treatment flows from a

---

1. Answer of 6 November 1991 to Written Question 92/C20/48 of MEP Alex Smith, OJ C20/25 of 27 January 1992. See also Commission's report dated 22 June 1992 on "the treatment accorded in third countries to Community credit institutions and insurance companies" (Document XV/4005/92—EN. Report by the Commission to the Council), at p. 5: ". . . the provisions of art. 9 [of the Second Banking Directive reviewed below] do not apply to branches *or the provision of cross-border services [in the Community by third country credit institutions].*" Emphasis added.

2. Though by no means only: witness the provision of financial services to private individuals resident in the Community (often on the own initiative of the customer) by financial institutions operating from a third country. *In practice*, however, these services are largely unregulated and likely to continue to be so.

bilateral agreement between the Member State and third country concerned. If Member States were allowed to give more favourable treatment to non-EC nationals than to Community nationals, they would in effect be able to discriminate against Community nationals, which discrimination is prohibited by Community law.[3] In the banking field, the general principle of Community preference is expressly recalled, *inter alia*, by the First Banking Directive when dealing with the position of third country branches in the individual Member States[4] but it is equally valid when determining the conditions under which an individual Member State may allow the direct provision of financial services on its territory[5] by a credit institution based outside the Community.

The implications for the provision of services in the Community by credit institutions based (and operating from) outside the Community of the current Uruguay Round negotiations within the GATT framework and of the bilateral treaties in existence between a number of Member States and third countries, is discussed separately later.[6]

3. For a recent illustration of this principle, which is of general application, in the field of taxation see O. Thommes, "EC Tax Scene: US–German Tax Treaty under examination by the EC Commission", Intertax 1990/12, p. 605.
4. See art. 9.1 of the 1977 First Banking Directive reviewed below.
5. It is important to recall that a service will be provided by a third country credit institution "on the territory" of a Member State whenever it is provided (even by correspondence or as a result of a visit made by the customer of his own initiative, to the credit institution in the third country concerned) to a customer resident in the territory of that Member State.
6. See below.

CHAPTER 35

THE CONDITIONS UNDER WHICH A NON-EC BASED CREDIT INSTITUTION MAY OPEN A BRANCH IN A MEMBER STATE AND, FROM IT, OPEN A SECONDARY BRANCH OR PROVIDE SERVICES IN OTHER MEMBER STATES

1. INAPPLICABILITY OF THE RECIPROCITY PROVISIONS OF THE SECOND BANKING DIRECTIVE

35.1 The reciprocity provisions of the Second Banking Directive cover subsidiaries, not branches. The direct branches of non-EC banks are not "undertakings" and so are not eligible for the single banking licence. Thus the establishment of a branch in one Member State does not have the same implications as the establishment of a subsidiary. Even if a third country failed the reciprocity test so that its banks could not set up Community subsidiaries, expansion through branches would still be possible in Member States that permitted it.[1]

2. NO EUROPEAN PASSPORT

35.2 The position under Community law of the branches of non-EC based credit institutions is, in effect, the same as that of credit institutions based outside the Community and providing services therein: third country credit institutions do not have an "EC right" to open a branch in the Community, authorisation to do so being solely a matter for the individual Member States in the exercise of their discretion. Also, a branch of a third country credit institution established in a Member State has, under Community law, no right to open a "secondary" branch in another Member State nor any right to provide cross-border services in another Member State.[2] It may only do so if so allowed by both the Member State where the branch is established and the Member State where the service is provided (that is, where the recipient of the service is established), under their respective national laws. The result is "that the branches [of third country institutions] simply do not have a European passport."[3] Therefore, the treatment of these branches in the Community is solely a matter for the Member State (or Member States) concerned, without prejudice to bilateral agreements that may be

---

1. George S. Zavvos, "Banking Integration in 1992—Legal Issues and Policy Implications", *Harvard International Law Journal*, 1990 Vol. 31, No. 2, p. 463, at p. 491.
2. It will be recalled that a cross-border service will be provided whenever the branch opens an account to a client resident in another Member State, even at the client's own initiative.
3. Comments made by Sir Leon Brittan, Vice-President of the Commission then in charge of competition and financial institutions, in the European Parliament on the occasion of the first reading of the Large Exposure Directive, EP Report, 11 May 1992, at p. 62, col. 94.

in force between an individual Member State and the third country concerned but subject always to the principle of Community preference.

3. THE PRINCIPLE OF COMMUNITY PREFERENCE AND ITS IMPLICATIONS FOR THIRD COUNTRY CREDIT INSTITUTIONS

35.3 The general principle of Community preference is expressly recalled by article 9(1) of the First Banking Directive:

> Member States shall not apply to branches of credit institutions having their head office outside the Community, when commencing or carrying on their business, provisions which result in more favourable treatment than those accorded to branches of credit institutions having their head office in the Community.

By article 9(2), the Member State concerned is required to notify the Commission and the Banking Advisory Committee of any such authorisation, once granted.

The practical implications of the Community preference principle recalled by article 9(1) of the First Banking Directive are bound to come increasingly to the fore as a result of the substantial—and still increasing—body of EC regulations which is—or will shortly—become applicable to EC credit institutions but not to third country branches operating in the Community: in particular, the Own Funds Directive, the Credit Ratios Directive, the Large Exposure Directive, the Capital Adequacy Directive, the Investment Services Directive and the Consolidated Supervision Directive. None of these (will) apply to third country branches in the Community. Indeed, since these branches have no European passport, "it is difficult to see the justification for Community harmonisation as far as they are concerned".[4]

35.4 The concern on the part of some Member States and no doubt on the part of some EC credit institutions is that a situation may arise where third country branches, although not in theory entitled to provide services on a cross-border basis in the Community under Community law, will in practice continue to do so[5] without being subject to the same or equivalent regulatory requirements to those imposed on EC credit institutions. This concern has been repeatedly expressed in the European Parliament at the time of the reading of the Second Banking Directive and later EC credit institutions legislation. It has resulted in certain political initiatives and commitments which are discussed separately later.[6]

---

4. Comments made by Sir Leon Brittan, Vice-President of the Commission then in charge of competition and financial institutions, on the occasion of the first reading of the Large Exposure Directive in the European Parliament to justify the Commission's objection to an amendment making the Large Exposure Directive applicable to third country branches in the Community: EP Report, 11 May 1992, at p. 62, col. 94.

5. One fails to see how it could be otherwise, short of a revolution in banking in Europe. A situation is hard to imagine where third country branches, sometimes established for more than 100 years in a Member State, are suddenly forbidden from lending to or receiving deposits from customers established in other Member States. Also, the activities of correspondent banking always include an element of cross-border provision of services, as where Bank A in, say, the US, is the US $ correspondent of Bank B in, say, the UK.

6. See para. 35.7, below.

4. COMMUNITY POWER TO CONCLUDE AGREEMENTS WITH THIRD COUNTRIES FOR THE PROVISION OF CROSS-BORDER SERVICES AND THE OPENING OF BRANCHES BY CREDIT INSTITUTIONS

35.5 The right to provide cross-border services, such as the granting of credits to, or the receipt of deposits from, clients resident in Member States other than the one in which they are established could be granted to third country branches in the Community by the Council in the exercise of its powers under the second paragraph of article 59(2) of the Treaty.[7] To date, however, no use has been made of those provisions.

Under the First Banking Directive, the Community has the power to conclude agreements with non-Member States regarding the opening of branches throughout the Community by a credit institution having its head office outside the Community. Article 9(3) of the Directive provides:

Without prejudice to [article 9(1)], the *Community* may, through agreements concluded *in accordance with the Treaty* with one or more third countries, agree to apply provisions which, *on the basis of the principle of reciprocity*, accord to branches of a credit institution having its head office outside the Community identical treatment throughout the territory of the Community.

At first sight, article 9(3) appears to mirror, in relation to the extension of the freedom of establishment to third country branches, the approach taken in relation to the extension of the freedom to provide services to third country credit institutions provided for in article 59(2) of the Treaty. However, unlike article 59(2) of the Treaty, article 9(3) of the Directive specifically links such extension to the principle of reciprocity. Given the current Uruguay Round negotiations, this distinction may in practice be more apparent than real: it seems likely that the application of article 59(2) would also involve consideration of the reciprocal opportunities available to Community banks in the third country in question.

35.6 According to Clarotti, article 9(3) is "the embryo of a common Community policy towards the setting up of branches by banks from non-Member States" in the Community. In accordance with the general principles of Community law, the grant of this right to the Community implies:

a corollary under the Treaty, which is the giving up by the Member States of their corresponding powers. In other words, if the Community can conclude agreements with non-Member States in a particular field, the Member States lose the right of concluding bilateral agreements of the same type relating to the same subject matter.[8]

The Community has so far not exercised the power given to it to conduct a common policy with regard to the setting up of branches in the Community by credit institutions from non-Member States, nor, consequently, has the Commission received a mandate from the Council to that effect. It is therefore arguable that Member States retain their own powers in this field, subject to the principle of Community preference, until such time as the Community does exercise that power.[9]

The position may perhaps be different if, acting pursuant to the declarations which

7. See Chap. 2.
8. Paolo Clarotti, "The Harmonisation of Legislation relating to Credit Institutions" [1982] CMLRev. 245, at p. 263.
9. A parallel can no doubt be drawn here with the judgment of the Court of Justice of 31 March 1971 in *re European Road Transports Agreement*, Case No. 22/70, [1971] ECR 263. See also the Court's opinion of 19 March 1993 given pursuant to art. 228(1) of the Treaty concerning the Community's competence to conclude ILO Convention no. 170 OJ C109/1 of 19 April 1993. Also, P. Vigneron and A. Smith "Le Fondement de la

are understood to be contained in the minutes of the Council meeting at which the Second Banking Directive was adopted,[10] the Commission were to recommend the introduction of common arrangements relating to third country branches. Zavvos, after noting that the Community has exclusive powers to negotiate with third countries on matters relating to market access, either by way of branches under the First Banking Directive or by way of acquisition or incorporation of a local subsidiary under the Second Banking Directive, raises the question whether Member States are still empowered to invoke their own reciprocity clauses and thus block the first establishment of non-EC banks.[11] It is submitted that the answer to this question, both in relation to branches and in relation to acquisitions and the incorporation of subsidiaries, must be yes, so long as the Community has not actually used the powers granted to it or, at least, has not initiated preparatory moves in this field.[12]

The view has even been expressed recently by certain Commission officials speaking in a private capacity that, in accordance with the principle of subsidiarity which has found renewed favour following adoption of the Maastricht Agreement, the treatment of third country branches in the Community is best dealt with at Member State level. This view is probably excessive: subsidiarity or not, it is not for the Member States to set aside the principle of Community preference enshrined in article 9(3) of the First Banking Directive.

5. CIRCUMSTANCES SURROUNDING THE ADOPTION OF THE SECOND BANKING DIRECTIVE

35.7 These are of interest in relation to the possible future application of article 59(2) of the Treaty and article 9(3) of the First Banking Directive. As already pointed out on several occasions, the Second Banking Directive does not deal with the treatment of the branches in the Community of credit institutions based in third countries. In fact, the only reference made in the Directive to such branches is in recital 19 and then only to state that:

. . . the procedures established in Directive 77/780/EEC . . . with regard to the authorisation of branches of credit institutions authorised in third countries will continue to apply to such institutions

and that:

those branches will not enjoy the freedom to provide services under the second paragraph of article 59 of the Treaty or the freedom of establishment in Member States other than those in which they are established.

The definition of the expression "branch" in the Second Banking Directive is restricted to the branches of a credit institution having its head office in another Member State. It therefore excludes the branches within the Community of credit

---

Compétence communautaire en matière de commerce international de services", Cahiers de droit européen (1992) p. 51 and fn. 1.

10. As to these, see below at para. 35.7.

11. "Banking integration in 1992: legal issues and policy implications", *Harvard International Law Journal*, Vol. 35, No. 2, p. 463, at p. 493, and fn. 169 thereto.

12. It is submitted that the Commission's current involvement in the Uruguay Round negotiations relating, *inter alia*, to the liberalisation of financial services (currently not covered by GATT), does not presently affect that conclusion.

institutions having their head office outside it.[13] Thus article 23 of the Second Banking Directive, which enshrines the acquired rights of branches established in a Member State before the date of entry into force of the Directive, does not apply to the branches of third country credit institutions.

However, the fact that the Second Banking Directive does not cover the position of branches within the Community of credit institutions based in third countries does not mean that the issue was not raised during the legislative process which led to its eventual adoption. The issue arose acutely in March 1989 during the first reading of the draft Directive in the European Parliament. The Parliament, following the lead from its *rapporteur*, MEP Georgios Saridakis, adopted a series of amendments which aimed at imposing a minimum Community-wide co-ordination of rules designed principally to deal with the capital requirements of such branches, in particular minimum initial capital, endowment capital and solvency ratio requirements. The Commission did not take up these amendments. Indeed, in his speech during the debate in the Parliament, Sir Leon Brittan, while noting that the amendments were not held out as being concerned with the issue of reciprocity, explained that they were unnecessary and unworkable, that they ran counter to current international trends concerning consolidated supervision and that they might involve some Member States having to adopt a stricter approach than they did at the time.

35.8 The next relevant development occurred at the time of the Council's adoption of a common position. The common position made express reference in recital 19 (corresponding to recital 17 of the original proposal) to the fact that such branches would not enjoy the freedom to provide services under the second paragraph of article 59 of the Treaty nor the freedom of establishment in Member States other than those in which they were established. This statement was presumably inserted at the time to appease the European Parliament but it was insufficient to prevent the Parliament from readopting essentially the same amendments at the second reading stage in November 1989.

Eventually a compromise was reached: the Commission, while refusing to accept the Parliament's amendments, undertook to prepare a report reviewing the treatment of third country branches prior to the entry into force of the Second Banking Directive on 1 January 1993. Should "clear" examples of distortion of competition be identified in it, the Commission stated that remedial measures including, "if necessary," legislation would be proposed. Since then, concern for the more favourable treatment that may be enjoyed by third country branches in the Community, as a result of their exclusion from the scope of EC financial regulations, has re-emerged periodically, and most recently on the occasion of the first reading of the Large Exposures Directive in the European Parliament.[14]

35.9 In view of these matters, it is significant that although the text of the Second Banking Directive, as adopted by the Council on 15 December 1989, contains no substantive amendment to the previous common position, it is understood that certain declarations on the treatment of third country branches are contained in the Council minutes agreed upon at the time of the Directive's adoption. These are understood to have been inserted at the instigation of some Member States which remained concerned, despite the terms of recital 19 and the general principles of Community law,

13. See arts. 1(1) and 3 of the Second Banking Directive in conjunction with art. 1 of the First Banking Directive.

14. See EP Report, 11 May 1992, p. 62, col. 94.

that certain other Member States would continue to seek to grant more favourable treatment to third country branches.

The substance of these declarations is understood to be to the effect that:

1. the provisions of the Second Banking Directive will not apply to third country branches, the regulation of which is to be left to the discretion of the Member States;

2. article 9 of the First Banking Directive will continue to apply in this respect and the Commission is obliged to propose measures—involving, if necessary, proceedings for infringement under article 169 of the Treaty—to ensure compliance by the Member States with the provisions of article 9;

3. within six months of the entry into force of the Second Banking Directive, and periodically thereafter, the Commission will report to the Banking Advisory Committee on the application of article 9 of the First Banking Directive and may seek to introduce common arrangements relating to third country branches in the Community.[15]

Therefore, it appears that the European Parliament was in the end successful in securing at least the possibility of future action in relation to third country branches along the lines proposed in its amendments. The Commission's initial commitment to monitor the treatment of such branches may even have been extended by the declarations in the Council minutes. This is because there is to be more than a single report; the reports will be additional to that prepared for the Parliament; they will cover the situation *after* the entry into force of the Second Banking Directive; they are understood to involve a more comprehensive review; and they are to be supplied to the national representatives on the Banking Advisory Committee.

---

15. As at the time of writing, however, no such report has been published by the Commission.

CHAPTER 36

THE CONDITIONS UNDER WHICH A NON-EC BASED CREDIT INSTITUTION MAY INCORPORATE AN EC BANKING SUBSIDIARY OR ACQUIRE AN EXISTING EC BANK WHICH MAY THEN OPEN BRANCHES AND PROVIDE SERVICES THROUGHOUT THE EUROPEAN COMMUNITY UNDER THE SINGLE BANKING LICENCE: THE "RECIPROCITY" ISSUE PROPER

1. BACKGROUND AND JUSTIFICATION FOR THE "RECIPROCITY" PROVISIONS

36.1 The issue of reciprocity in the strict sense only concerns the conditions under which a non-EC based credit institution may incorporate or acquire an existing banking subsidiary in the Community. In fact, the Second Banking Directive never uses the word "reciprocity."[1] Even though the concept of reciprocity appears in the Treaty itself,[2] the idea of having recourse to *unilateral* measures, in order to palliate the absence of reciprocity in a third country, had never previously been applied in Community law.

The concept was first introduced in article 7 of the Commission's original proposal:

. . .

(5) The Commission shall, within three months of receiving the information provided for in paragraphs 2 and 3 [namely, the request for authorisation of a third country undertaking addressed to the competent authorities of a Member State in respect of the incorporation or the acquisition of a local banking subsidiary] examine whether all credit institutions of the Community enjoy reciprocal treatment in particular regarding the establishment of subsidiaries or the acquisition of participation in credit institutions in the third country in question.

(6) If the Commission finds that reciprocity is not ensured, it may [require the competent authorities of the Member State which have received the application to suspend their decision].

The technical justification for the inclusion of such provisions follows directly from the liberal approach taken by the Treaty in granting the right of establishment and the freedom to provide services to any company "based" (that is, incorporated) in the Community, even if it is wholly controlled by non-EC interests. As a result of this approach, the single licence created under the Second Banking Directive can be

---

1. See Philippe Vigneron and Aubrey Smith, "The Concept of Reciprocity in Community Legislation: The Example of the Second Banking Directive", *Journal of International Banking Law*, (1990), p. 181, at p. 183.

2. See art. 238(1): "The Community may conclude with a third state . . . agreements establishing an association involving reciprocal rights. . . ."

enjoyed by *any credit* institution based in a Member State. As a result, the adoption of the Second Banking Directive renders immediately obsolete the national reciprocity provisions which exist in some Member States under which the incorporation or acquisition of a local banking subsidiary by a third country credit institution is made conditional upon reciprocal treatment being granted to that Member State's credit institutions in the third country concerned. As Smits observes:

the Commission . . . proposed to insert a reciprocity clause in the Second Banking Directive in order to ensure that the benefits of the internal market are not reaped by third country nationals while EC citizens and companies would be denied the benefit of operating in the third country. [Indeed, in the absence of such a Community-wide reciprocity clause,] enterprises from third countries [could] circumvent any current reciprocity practices undertaken by a single Member State through the establishment of a legal entity in another, more liberal Member State. Once established in [that other] Member State, a third country company [incorporated locally] can branch out to the State which had originally sought to limit the entry of foreigners into its market to its own nationals being able to enter the relevant third country market.[3]

And Clarotti points out that:

article 7 has caused much ink to flow and has been highly controversial, not only in the countries most concerned, such as the United States and Japan, but even in some countries of the Community which are very opposed to the image of the Community as that of "fortress Europe" and to all measures which might prejudice the policy of openness towards external markets which has characterised the Community for several years.[4]

This explains why article 9 of the text finally adopted by the Council (corresponding with article 7 of the original proposal) differs in several respects from the Commission's original text.[5]

36.2 Article 9 of the Directive distinguishes two stages in terms of the "reciprocity" expected by the Community from third countries as a condition for allowing undertakings based in those countries to incorporate or acquire a local credit institution in one of the Member States. These are, first, the "no national treatment" stage, governed by article 9(4); and, second, the "no comparable market access" stage, governed by article 9(3).

The conditions governing those two stages have been commented upon by the Commission in its report dated 23 June 1992 to the Council regarding "the treatment accorded in third countries to Community credit institutions and insurance companies",[6] which Report was drawn up by the Commission pursuant to article 9(2) of the Directive. The Report covers the position of EC financial institutions (banks and insurance) in third countries and the treatment of third country financial institutions in the Community from the point of view of market access.[7]

---

3. "Banking Regulation in a European Perspective, Legal Issues of European Integration" 1989/1, 61, at p. 74. Also, J. Van Dijk and M. Van Empel "Reciprocity", Banking and EC Law, at p. 16: "As long as there would remain at least one Member State which would not impose reciprocity, those requirements in other Member States would of course lose much of their substance as entry into the Internal Banking Market would be possible through the loophole of that one Member State."

4. "La Seconde Directive de Coordination en matière d'établissements de crédit," [1989] *Revue du Marché Commun.* No. 330, 453, at p. 457.

5. For a consideration of the successive texts presented by the Commission and the checkered history of the reciprocity clause during the adoption process of the Second Banking Directive, see in particular P. Vigneron and A. Smith, fn. 1, above, at p. 183.

6. "Treatment accorded in third countries to Community credit institutions and insurance companies— report by the Commission to the Council", document XV/4005/92–EN of 23 June 1992.

7. It should be noted that the 1992 Commission's report, just mentioned, is distinct from the report, not yet published, which was delivered by the Commission to the European Parliament before 1 January 1993

2. INFORMATION PROCEDURES DESIGNED TO TRIGGER THE "RECIPROCITY" PROVISIONS

36.3 The activation of the two stages distinguished by article 9 depends on a prior information procedure. Article 9(1) and (2) provides two separate procedures for collection of the information which may lead to an eventual finding that either the "no national treatment" or the "no effective market access" stage has been reached.

The first procedure is a specific information procedure provided for by article 9(1) whereby:

The Member States shall inform the Commission of any general difficulties encountered by their credit institutions in establishing themselves or carrying on banking activities in a third country.

The second procedure lays down on the Commission the duty to check periodically whether the "no national treatment" stage or the "no comparable market access" stage has been reached in one or more third countries. Article 9(2) says:

Initially no later than six months before the application of this Directive, and thereafter periodically, the Commission shall draw up a report examining the treatment accorded to Community credit institutions in third countries, in the terms referred to in paragraphs 3 and 4 [that is, comparable market access and national treatment respectively] as regards establishment and the carrying on of banking activities and the acquisition of holdings in third country credit institutions. The Commission shall submit those reports to the Council, together with any appropriate proposals.

In addition to these specific procedures, the Directive provides in article 8 for a general information procedure. Under those provisions, the competent authorities of the Member States must inform the Commission of any authorisation granted to a direct or indirect subsidiary of a non-EC undertaking, together with the group structure, and also whenever a non-EC undertaking acquires a holding in a Community credit institution such that the latter becomes its subsidiary.

36.4 As pointed out by Clarotti,[8] the obligation to notify the Commission of authorisations *granted* to subsidiaries of non-EC undertakings effectively adds nothing because in any event all new authorisations must be notified to the Commission in accordance with article 3(1) of the First Banking Directive. The text of article 8 constitutes a substantial change from the Commission's original proposal, which would have required it to be informed, as a matter of routine, of all *requests* by non-EC undertakings for authorisation or acquisition of shareholdings and not of all authorisations actually granted.

Under article 9(5), whenever it appears to the Commission that either the "no national treatment" stage or the "no comparable market access" stage has been reached in a particular third country, it must be notified by the Member States, at *its* request:

(a) of any request for the authorisation of a direct or indirect subsidiary one or more parent undertakings of which are governed by the laws of the third country in question;
(b) whenever [the competent authorities of the Member States] are informed in accordance with article 11 . . . that such an undertaking proposes to acquire a holding in a Community credit

---

following the concern there expressed that third country branches may enjoy more favourable treatment than EC institutions as a result of the exclusion—in principle—of third country institutions from the scope of application of EC financial legislation. See para. 35.9 and fn. 15, above.

8. "La Seconde Directive de Coordination en matière d'établissements de crédit" [1989] *Revue du Marché Commun*. No. 330, 453 at p. 457.

institution [authorized by those competent authorities] such that the latter would become its subsidiary.

This obligation to provide information to the Commission in advance lapses whenever an agreement is reached by the Community with the third country concerned or when the sanctions that can be applied (in the absence of "national treatment" only) by the Community pending a successful outcome of the negotiations[9] cease to apply.[10]

3. THE "NO NATIONAL TREATMENT" STAGE

1. Meaning of the concept

36.5 According to article 9(4):

Whenever it appears to the Commission ... that Community credit institutions in a third country do not receive national treatment offering the same competitive opportunities as are available to domestic credit institutions and that the conditions of effective market access are not fulfilled, the Commission may initiate negotiations in order to remedy the situation. ...

The concept of "national treatment" is not defined by the Directive. However, it is a concept well-known in the Treaty[11] and in the context of various international agreements such as the GATT and the OECD. The reference in article 9(4) to "the same competitive opportunities" underlines the Community's concern that EC banks obtain not only *de jure* but also *de facto* national treatment abroad.

36.6 This concern has since been officially reflected by the Commission. In its report to the Council,[12] it states:

... *de jure* national treatment ... is not the only criterion to assess whether national treatment is granted in effect. Thus, any other official requirement or instruction which, although formally not discriminatory, distorts competitive opportunities in favour of domestic institutions, or which adversely affects the ability of foreign financial institutions to enter and compete effectively in the market as compared with their domestic counterparts, would also constitute a denial of national treatment, unless the measures providing for such a treatment may be properly justified for prudential reasons. This is the concept of *de facto* national treatment, which requires that countries, in the exercise of their regulatory activity, should not do so in such a way that disadvantages foreign institutions.

In addition to the concept of "national treatment offering the same competitive opportunities", article 9(4) establishes an *additional* criterion: the concept of "effective market access." Such a concept cannot be delinked in article 9(4) from the application of a *de facto* national treatment standard, and gives particular emphasis to the concept of right of establishment: foreign countries should not impose restrictions on the establishment which would deny them in effect access to the market. There are many examples of such restrictive regulations, which even if applied formally in a no-discriminatory manner, imply a denial of "*effective market access*": quotas on new entrance or application of economic needs tests, unreasonably and disproportionately high standards for entry, discretionary powers exercised in a manner which results in a denial of right of establishment, restrictive practices conducted by self-regulatory organizations.[13]

Difficulties may also arise with regard to the exact scope of the generally recognised exceptions to the national treatment rule.

9. See below.
10. Art. 9(4), last para.
11. See, eg, arts. 7, 52(2), 60(2) and 221.
12. P. 6.
13. Emphasis in Commission's report.

It has been suggested, for example, that since the granting of foreign exchange authorisations and import/export licences constitutes the exercise of official authority, the question whether or not to delegate such public authority to foreign banks is not a matter for national treatment.[14] However, that suggestion cannot, it is submitted, be accepted. While it is, perhaps, "a matter of course that the reasons permitting discrimination based on nationality which are valid between the Member States should also be valid between the EC itself and non-EC countries,"[15] such a suggestion extends the scope of the exercise of official authority beyond generally accepted limits.

2. Ambiguities in the concept

36.7 There are numerous and perhaps inevitable ambiguities in the concept of "national treatment with the same competitive opportunities." In particular, there are at least six glaring ambiguities which can be identified.

First, there is no escaping the fact that, "by adding qualificatory subordinates [("offering the same competitive opportunities")] the European legislator has without doubt made the concept [of national treatment] much harder to handle".[16] These uncertainties are compounded by the fact that the same "qualificatory subordinates" have been used to define not only the "no national treatment" stage but also the "no comparable market access" stage.

Second, the Second Banking Directive does not give the benefit of the single licence to branches of third country banks but exclusively to the subsidiaries of such banks formed under the laws of a Member State. It does not state, however, in the context of determining whether Community banks operating in third countries are being accorded national treatment, whether this requirement is only valid for EC banks wishing to establish themselves in the third country in the same way, that is, by the creation or acquisition of local subsidiaries, or whether it extends also to establishment through branches. On the contrary, all the indications in the context of article 9 are that the establishment of an EC bank in a third country concerns as much establishment by means of a locally incorporated subsidiary as directly by means of a branch.[17]

Third, if, as appears to be the case, article 9 must be taken to cover the establishment of an EC bank in a third country as much by the creation of a locally incorporated subsidiary as by means of a branch, there is a plain imbalance in this approach in that third countries are required to give EC banks the right to establish themselves in the territory of the third country concerned by means of branches and subsidiaries whereas the Community affords third country banks no such possibility of establishing themselves by these two means throughout its territory but, on the contrary, subjects

14. See Sooman Park, "The treatment of non-EEC banks under EEC banking directives and problems of the principle of reciprocity. The viewpont of a lawyer from a non-EEC country", *Journal of International Banking Law* (1990), p. 413, at p. 417.

15. *Ibid.*, at p. 418.

16. Philippe Vigneron and Aubrey Smith, "The concept of reciprocity in Community legislation: The Example of the Second Banking Directive", *Journal of International Banking Law* (1990), 181, at p. 184.

17. See in this regard the observations of Sooman Park at p. 417. See, further, Michael Gruson and Wolfgang Feuring, "The New Banking Law of the European Economic Community". *The International Lawyer*, (1991), Vol. 25, no. 1, p. 1 *et seq.*, at p. 20: "It is important to note in this connection that the Second Banking Directive does not guarantee non-EC credit institutions 'effective market access' or reciprocal treatment with respect to the establishment or regulation of branches in the EC, nor does it obligate the Member States to grant licences to subsidiaries of non-EC banks or to permit non-EC persons to acquire banks in its territory. It is not clear what effect a Member State's denial of effective market entry to non-EC banks would have on the Commission's rights under art. 9."

them to the discretionary requirements of each Member State in relation to the establishment of branches.[18]

Fourth, so long as the Community is unable to offer a single Community-wide treatment to a third country bank wishing to establish itself in the Community by means of branches but only 12 different national treatments, the question arises by reference to which of these national treatments is a comparison to be made of the treatment given to Community banks by the third country concerned when they wish to establish themselves in the territory of that third country by means of branches. Is it to be by reference to the most liberal national regime or the most restrictive or by some other criterion?[19]

36.8 The same comment may be made in relation to establishment by means of the setting up of a locally incorporated subsidiary. It cannot be stressed enough that the approach of the Second Banking Directive has been to achieve the *minimum* degree of harmonisation necessary to permit the creation of the single licence. In consequence, it does not in any way reduce the ability of a Member State to impose conditions for the creation or acquisition of a locally incorporated bank which are stricter than those imposed by the Directive. In other words, it is not because the Community is satisfied that a particular third country is giving Community banks establishing themselves within its territory national treatment (or even comparable market access) that a Member State is required to authorise the setting up or acquisition of a local bank in its territory by an undertaking based in that third country. The only thing which the Member State concerned may not do, if it refuses to authorise such setting up or acquisition, is thereafter to prevent a subsidiary set up by the foreign group in another more welcoming Member State from opening a branch or from providing its services in its territory pursuant to the Second Banking Directive.

Fifth, as Key has commented[20]:

---

18. This imbalance is also present in the Commission's report itself. Indeed, when defining the scope of its review of the treatment of EC credit institutions in third countries, the report states the following (at p. 4):

> Art. 9 of the Second Banking Directive relates to establishment of a commercial presence in the form of a subsidiary (including by acquisition) and to the conditions governing the operations of that commercial presence, once it has been established. In other words, the provisions of art. 9 do not apply to branches and provision of cross-border services. The Commission's Report to the Council does not therefore cover the treatment which other countries apply to cross-border services.

It is submitted that, logically, the last sentence should have read: "the Commission's Report to the Council does not therefore cover the treatment which other countries apply to cross-border services *or to branches of EC credit institutions on their territory.*"

19. The Commission's report acknowledges this ambiguity. Indeed, after using the term "Community regime" to describe "the Community's liberal policy with regard to market access for third country credit institutions, in particular through the single licence system which allows an EC credit institution to carry out throughout the whole Community all the activities subject to mutual recognition" (see p. 7), it goes on to add, in a footnote, that the "Community regime" is "determined by a combination of the legislation of both the Community and individual Member States" (p. 7, fn. 2). As pointed out by Michael Gruson and Wolfgang Feuring ("The New Banking Law of the European Economic Community" *The International Lawyer*, (1991) Vol. 25, no. 1, p. 1 *et seq.* at p. 22), the reverse situation can obtain, in the case of certain third countries, such as the United States: "a reciprocity or even a national treatment test [by the Commission] would have to look, in the case of a national bank, to US federal law and, in the case of State-chartered banks, to the State in which the institution seeking authorisation in the EC is chartered. Therefore, a retaliatory response under art. 9.4 could only extend to national banks or to banks from the particular State in question. Applications by New York banks or by national banks cannot be suspended because a particular State X discriminates against EC banks."

20. Sidney Key, "Is National Treatment Still Viable: US Policy in Theory and Practice", *Journal of International Banking Law* (1990), p. 365, at p. 370.

direct branches of foreign banks, unlike subsidiaries, are an integral part of the foreign parent banks and are not separately incorporated in the host country. Therefore, even under a policy of national treatment, host country rules designed for separately incorporated entities cannot be literally applied to branches . . . [Indeed] as applied to direct branches of foreign banks, even the policy of national treatment involves some reliance on home country rules and enforcement procedures.

Sixthly, the determination of the country of origin may give rise to substantial problems. It may not always be clear which is the country of origin of a (third country) bank or of its holding company when the bank in question is established in several countries (witness the recent BCCI saga). Even by adopting the test of the country where the greatest amount of deposits is to be found, the identification of the country of origin may be difficult to apply in practice to establishments which also provide non-banking services.[21]

3. Procedure for negotiation and the imposition of sanctions

36.9 According to article 9(4), when the Commission finds that the "no national treatment" stage exists in a third country, it may initiate negotiations in order to remedy the situation.[22] It may also be decided at any time and in addition to initiating negotiations in accordance with the procedure laid down in article 22, that the competent authorities of the Member States must limit or suspend their decisions regarding requests pending at the time of the decision, or future requests for authorisation of a local banking subsidiary, and the acquisition of holdings by undertakings established in the third country concerned. These requests, it will be recalled, must be notified to the Commission by the competent authorities of the Member States, at the Commission's request, once the Commission decides to open negotiations.[23] The duration of these measures may not exceed three months unless they are prorogued by the Council, acting by a qualified majority, at the Commission's request.

4. Respect for vested rights

36.10 The last paragraph of article 9(4) expressly provides that the measures just referred to may not apply to the setting up of subsidiaries by credit institutions or their subsidiaries already duly authorised in the Community or to the acquisition of holdings in existing Community credit institutions by such third country institutions or their subsidiaries.

These provisions acknowledge the benefit of the rights already acquired by groups established in third countries which have set up or acquired a banking subsidiary in a Member State before the entry into force of the Directive on 1 January 1993. The time (between the adoption of the Directive on 15 December 1989 and its entry into force) which non-EC groups therefore have had within which to establish themselves in the Community before the test of Community reciprocity becomes applicable to them is

21. See Hal S. Scott, "La notion de réciprocité dans la proposition de Deuxième Directive de Coordination Bancaire" [1989] *Revue du Marché Commun.* No. 323, 45, at p. 49.
22. The Commission's report notes in this respect (see p. 5): "it will be noted that the authority of the Commission to enter into negotiations with third countries under art. 9.4 does not require a separate mandate from the Council of Ministers."
23. Art. 9(5).

thus extremely long. This provision is a good illustration of the different viewpoints which had to be reconciled within the Council. Had the Community wished to apply the test of Community reciprocity with full vigour, it would have laid down a much earlier date for the entry into force of these provisions than for the other provisions of the Directive.

However, even though the Commission's report goes to great lengths to stress that "[article 9(4)] explicitly confirms that any . . . suspension or limitation cannot apply to subsidiaries already established . . .",[24] many questions remain unanswered concerning the extent of these rights and precisely who may benefit from them. For example, are they accorded to the subsidiary or to the foreign group which holds the shares? This is an important question where there is a change in the main shareholder. What is the position where a non-banking subsidiary of a foreign group which was established in the Community before 1 January 1993 seeks, at the present time, to extend its activities into the banking field? What is the position where a banking subsidiary established in the Community before 1 January 1993 seeks, at the present time, to carry out in other Member States, whether through a branch or the provision of cross-border services, banking activities included in the list of agreed activities which it did not previously carry on? What if the list of agreed activities annexed to the Directive were to be extended? Would banking subsidiaries of foreign groups established in the Community before 1 January 1993 be able to take advantage of the extended list as part of their vested rights even though the extension took place after that date? What would be the position of the banking subsidiary of a foreign group[25] established in the Community before 1 January 1993 if the foreign group were taken over by a group, from another third country[26] which did not satisfy the reciprocity test?[27]

5. Possible conflict between sanctions imposed at Community level and the international obligations of certain Member States

36.11 A complicated and potentially highly contentious issue which has arisen in the context of the reciprocity provisions introduced by the Second Banking Directive is the fact that the "suspension and limitation procedure" introduced by the Directive may conflict with the international commitments of certain Member States, either as members of the OECD (to which the Community as such is not a party) or under bilateral agreements with third countries such as the treaties of Friendship, Commerce and Navigation (FCN) concluded by the United States of America with most Member States.

This issue, the examination of which falls outside the scope of this book, is also

---

24. At p. 5.
25. According to Professor Hal S. Scott, reporting the comments made by leading EC officials during a conference in Brussels in 1988, only the persons who were owners of the banks before 1 January 1993 and not the banks themselves would obtain the benefit of vested rights: see "La notion de réciprocité dans la proposition de Deuxième Directive de Coordination Bancaire" [1989] *Revue du Marché Commun.* No. 323, pp. 45 and 48 and note 16.
26. It is assumed that such group fulfils all conditions of good repute etc. required of the large shareholders of any credit institutions authorised under Community law.
27. As Philippe Vigneron and Aubrey Smith have observed, withdrawal or suspension of authorisation would have the consequence that an EC company would be discriminated against following a change in the nationality of its shareholders. See "The Concept of Reciprocity: The Example of the Second Banking Directive", *Journal of International Banking Law* (1990), p. 181, at p. 184.

complicated by the distinction that must be made, in terms of article 234 of the Treaty,[28] between agreements concluded by the Member States with third countries before their accession to the Treaty (which is the case for all FCN Treaties between the United States and Member States) and those concluded after that date (which is the case for the OECD Code adopted in 1960 and, therefore, for subsequent decisions of the OECD pertaining to the Code).[29]

4. THE "NO COMPARABLE MARKET ACCESS" STAGE

36.12 According to article 9(3):

Whenever it appears to the Commission ... that a third country is not granting Community credit institutions effective market access *comparable* to that granted by the Community to credit institutions from that third country, the Commission may submit proposals to the Council for the appropriate mandate for negotiation with a view to obtaining comparable competitive opportunities for Community credit institutions. The Council shall decide by a qualified majority.

1. The meaning of the concept

36.13 According to the Commission's report[30]:

Application of article 9(3) is intended to deal with problems *outside* the scope of article 9(4). Article 9(3) represents an objective: that Community credit institutions may establish themselves and carry on their activities in third countries with a comparable degree of facility and freedom as is enjoyed by third country credit institutions in the Community. This is reflected in the different wording of article 9(3) which refers to *comparable* effective market access. Therefore, article 9(3) addresses restrictions arising from non-discriminatory regulations, applying in the same form both to domestic and foreign firms and not disadvantaging foreign firms as compared with domestic ones. In particular, article 9(3) was designed to deal with restrictions resulting from differences of regulatory regimes between the Community and its trading partners, which may pose problems to Community firms as regards access to these markets.

 ... For the Community, the basis for comparison is the opportunities offered by the "single licence" or "single passport" ... adopted for banks ... as well as the ability to engage in a wide range of activities and the free circulation of a wide variety of financial products. Other examples are restrictions to the introduction of new financial products or services, or a rigid regulation of the investment of the assets of financial institutions.

 Article 9(3) is a reflexion of the Community's liberal policy with regard to market access for third countries, in particular through the single licence system which allows an EC credit institution to carry throughout the whole Community all the activities subject to mutual recognition among the Member States of the Community, which include securities activities; ...

28. Art. 234 reads in part: "the rights and obligations arising from agreements concluded before the entry into force of this Treaty between one or more Member States on the one hand, and one or more third countries on the other, shall not be affected by the provisions of this Treaty ..."

29. For an extensive review of this issue from a US perspective, see *inter alia* Michael J. Leventin, "The Treatment of US Financial Services in Post-1992 Europe" (1990) *Harvard International Law Journal*, vol. 31, p. 507. Also Joël P. Trachtman, "Recent Initiatives in International Financial Regulations", *Northwestern Journal of International Law and Business*, (1991), p. 241 *et seq.*; Geert Wils, "The Concept of Reciprocity in EC Law" [1991] CMLRev., Vol. 28, p. 245. The issue of possible conflict between the general principle of Community preference and the FCN Treaties concluded by various Member States with the USA has recently come to the fore as a result of Germany's proposed intention (since reportedly abandoned) to sign a bilateral agreement with the USA to exempt US firms from Community-mandated countersanctions regarding access to public procurement contracts in the telecommunications sector in Germany, on the ground that such sanctions would be in breach of the FCN Treaty between the USA and Germany (eg, European Report 1874 of 10 July 1993, p. 5).

30. At p. 7 and fn. 2. Emphasis in the report.

that "Community regime" [which is determined by a combination of the legislation of both the Community and the individual Member States] thus constitutes a standard against which the performance of other countries can be examined.

2. Negotiations to remedy a "no comparable market access" situation

36.14 The position which obtains when "comparable market access" is not granted (article 9(3)) is quite different from that which obtains when "national treatment" is denied (article 9(4)). As already indicated, when "national treatment" is lacking, the Commission can itself initiate negotiations. In addition to initiating negotiations, it may be decided at any time, in accordance with the procedure laid down in article 22(2), that Member States must limit or suspend their decision regarding requests for authorisations pending at the moment of the decision, as well as future requests.

However, the position is different when the Commission finds that no "comparable market access" is granted. First, the Commission is not empowered itself to initiate negotiations to remedy that situation. Instead, it may only submit proposals to the Council for the appropriate mandate for negotiations with a view to obtaining comparable competitive opportunities for Community credit institutions. The Council must decide by a qualified majority. Second, there is no provision in the Directive to direct the Member States to limit or suspend their decisions regarding requests for authorisation pending at the time or future requests for authorisation, either pending the outcome of the negotiations or in retaliation if negotiations fail. In other words, to quote the Commission's report[31]:

Article 9(3) establishes a procedure for addressing cases where a third country does not provide effective market access comparable to that granted by the Community. This procedure consists of the *option* for the Commission to submit proposals to the Council for the appropriate mandate for negotiations with a view to obtaining such comparable competitive opportunities for Community credit institutions. The Community acknowledges that its own standard of access cannot be imposed on others. The Community thus accepts implicitly that the achievement of "comparable competitive opportunities" should be the subject of negotiations, but article 9(3) does not provide for sanctions if the objective is not obtained.

5. THE POSITION OF EUROPEAN ECONOMIC AREA COUNTRIES

36.15 As a result of the European Economic Area Agreement, the reciprocity procedures discussed above do not apply to credit institutions authorised by countries which are to become members of the European Economic Area (in effect the present EFTA Member States except Switzerland and, provisionally, Liechtenstein). The EEA countries, by the very fact of adhering to the EEA Agreement, have accepted the so-called "*acquis communautaire*", that is, the existing body of Community legislation, including Community legislation covering financial institutions. Thus, credit institutions authorised by the competent authorities of EEA countries will enjoy the full benefit of the single licence in terms of their operations in the EC and, *vice versa*, credit institutions authorised by Member States of the EC will see their single licence under the Second Banking Directive extended to cover the EEA countries.

A specific procedure, the review of which falls outside the scope of this book, is provided for by the EEA Agreement to cover the situation which may arise if the

31. Emphasis in report.

Community applies the "suspension and limitation" procedure already discussed (article 9(4) of the Second Banking Directive) to credit institutions of a specific third country, so as to ensure that the effect of such a procedure cannot be circumvented by credit institutions from that third country setting up or acquiring a credit institution in an EEA country (which, in turn, can then operate freely in the Community). That procedure also covers the reverse situation, where one or more EEA countries refuses access to their market to credit institutions established in a third country while the Community itself does not apply its own "suspension and limitation" procedure to that third country.

These arrangements look destined to have a very short existence since several EEA countries have already formally applied to become full members of the Community, or indicated their intention to do so shortly.

36.16 It is, however, worth noting that the coming into force of the EEA Agreement may, in effect, result for third country credit institutions in an extension of the deadline set by the Second Banking Directive for the coming into force of the reciprocity procedures. The EEA Agreement provides for the vested rights in terms of a single licence to operate in the Community market, for credit institutions authorised by EEA countries (including a locally-incorporated subsidiary of a credit institution based in a third country) prior to 1 January 1994, being the revised date when the EEA is scheduled to come into force if the ratification process is completed on time.[32]

6. LIMITS ON THE COMMUNITY'S POWERS IN THE FIELD OF RECIPROCITY RESULTING FROM INTERNATIONAL COMMITMENTS TO WHICH IT IS A PARTY

36.17 According to article 9(6), measures taken pursuant to the provisions of article 9 must comply with the Community's obligations under any bilateral or multilateral agreement governing the taking up and pursuit of the business of credit institutions. Such a provision, which was not included in the original proposal and which was not discussed at length in the Council, is rather unusual in a Community Directive and was introduced "in the hope of reassuring anyone who was worried about the insertion of the principle of reciprocity into the Directive."[33] At the international level, such a provision adds nothing to the Community's obligations under international agreements to which it is a party. However, at the internal level, within the Community itself, the inclusion of the provisions may have consequences which were—perhaps—not foreseen by its draftsmen.

36.18 It is generally accepted that international agreements, such as the GATT impose obligations on the Community as such in its dealings with third countries which are parties to those agreements but that, on the other hand, these obligations do not have direct effect in its internal legal order.[34] In other words, a person may not rely in

---

32. See art. 129(3) of the EEA Agreement which stipulated 1 January 1993 as the scheduled date of entry. This has obviously been put back as a result of the Swiss no vote in their referendum in December 1992.

33. Vigneron and Smith, "The Concept of Reciprocity in Community Legislation: The Example of the Second Banking Directive", *Journal of International Banking Law* (1990), p. 181, at p. 189; also, by the same authors, "Le Fondement de la Compétence communautaire en matière de commerce international de services." Cahiers de droit européen (1992), p. 51 and fn. 1.

34. See case 21–24/72, *International Fruit Company*, [1972] ECR 1219; also case 70/87 *Fediol* v. *Commission*, [1989] ECR 1781.

proceedings before national courts in the Community upon the Community's international obligations as a ground for the inapplicability to him of a particular measure which is in conflict with those international obligations. In principle, therefore, in a case where a Member State suspends a request for authorisation made by a third country undertaking pursuant to a decision to that effect taken by the Community, that undertaking cannot challenge the suspension by alleging that the Community's decision which underlay it was contrary to its international obligations.

The general position just described may perhaps be modified by the provisions of article 9(6). The question arises whether, in the example just given, the undertaking might not be able successfully to challenge the suspension on the ground of its incompatibility with the Community's international obligations by alleging that the suspension was incompatible with the Directive itself since the Directive only authorises suspension within the limits of the Community's international obligations. As Vigneron and Smith write[35]:

It might be asked whether this provision . . . simply has a declaratory value or whether it could have the effect of introducing the Community's international obligations within Community law. In the second case, it would have the consequences of henceforth making these obligations subject not only to the International Court in The Hague but also the European Court of Justice.

For the time being, the effect of article 9(6) is only of theoretical interest. This is because the Community is not at the present time a party to any international agreement concerning the free provision of services and the freedom of establishment in the financial sector, although the position would be different were the Uruguay Round of negotiations currently under way within the GATT framework to result in the conclusion of a general agreement on trade in financial services.

7. THE REMAINING POWERS OF MEMBER STATES IN THE RECIPROCITY FIELD

36.19 As already pointed out, the term "Community regime" used in the Commission's report to describe the Community's policy towards third country credit institutions is ambiguous. It covers not only rules laid down at EC level but also, to a very significant extent, the manner in which the individual Member States exercise their—so far unfettered—powers[36] with regard to three matters. First, the provision of cross-border services by a credit institution established in a third country on their territory. Second, the grant or refusal of authorisation for the opening of a third country branch on their territory. Third, the refusal to grant authorisation to a third country credit institution wishing to incorporate or acquire a local credit institution, even if the Community is satisfied that the third country concerned grants full national treatment or even comparable market access to Community credit institutions operating there.

In relation to the last of these matters, the Commission's report acknowledges[37] "the concern . . . expressed about restrictions to market access . . . which could arise from the application of reciprocity provisions existing in Member States' legislations". Hence when the Commission's report states[38] that:

---

35. "The concept of reciprocity in Community legislation: The Example of the Second Banking Directive", *Journal of International Banking Law* (1990) p. 181, at p. 189.

36. Subject, of course, to their possible obligations under bilateral agreements with the third country concerned.

37. At p. 15.

38. At p. 15.

in any event, as part of its negotiating offer in the Uruguay Round, the Community has declared that it is ready not to apply these powers to signatories of the General Agreement on Trade and Services subject to adequate market access commitments being made by other countries,

it is unclear whether this declaration applies exclusively to the "suspension and limitation" procedure covered by article 9(4) (in which case it can only lead to a situation where Member States are bound to suspend or limit authorisations but never forced to grant authorisation), or whether it also encompasses the (so far) retained powers of the Member States.

36.20 It is submitted that until the position is clarified the Community's "reciprocity policy" will, of necessity, remain unbalanced in that it necessarily leaves the Community to require third countries to grant more (for example, in terms of branch access) than the Community itself can deliver in terms of Community law. It is probably reasonable to expect that, in case of successful conclusion of the Uruguay Round negotiations, Member States would, in fact, agree not to refuse authorisation to a third country credit institution to acquire or open a local subsidiary if the Community itself sees no reason to apply the "suspension and limitation" procedure. There is, however, apparently little likelihood that Member States will agree to waive their present discretionary powers in terms of authorising the opening of a branch of a third country credit institution on their territory. Indeed, according to pronouncements recently made by EC officials, albeit in a private capacity, the view taken by the Commission is apparently that, in accordance with the principle of "subsidiarity", the regime applicable to the opening of branches by third country institutions in the Community is best dealt with at national level rather than at Community level.

8. CONCLUSION

36.21 The reciprocity provisions of the Second Directive illustrate most clearly the political will on the part of the Member States to arrive at a compromise acceptable to all of them and at the same time to give a strong base for their negotiations with third countries, whether bilateral or multilateral as in the framework of the GATT.[39] They also illustrate the absence of any political will to lay down a precise set of legal rules.

The greatest uncertainty is in the manner in which the provisions will be applied in the future, should the need arise, and the interpretation which the Court of Justice will place on them.

Precisely because of their ambiguity, the reciprocity provisions of the Directive have speeded up the establishment within the Community, by the creation or acquisition of local banks, of foreign groups not previously established there which wished to do so before the entry into force of the Directive. The fact that the Community legislator did not provide for an earlier date for the entry into force of the reciprocity provisions than for the other provisions of the Directive reflects the need to reconcile divergent views within the Council.

36.22 The approach finally adopted has led to a paradoxical result. Most of the banks from developed countries have been established in the Community, sometimes for a

39. *Cf.* Bevis Longstreth and Thomas Kelly, "EEC Banking: Interpreting the Reciprocity Standard", *International Financial Law Review*, June 1990, at p. 9: ". . . EEC officials intend to pursue an active strategy of negotiations (using the ambiguities in the Directive's reciprocity language as a source of bargaining power) to persuade the US and other nations to liberalise their banking regime."

very long time, before the entry into force of the Directive. In those circumstances, it is probable that the impact of the reciprocity provisions will be most felt by banks from less developed countries which have not been in a position (nor perhaps have had the need) to establish a bank within the Community before the entry into force of the Directive. As one commentator has pointed out,[40] many developing countries are strongly protectionist of their financial market to prevent foreign domination. The question has been asked whether it is reasonable on the part of the Commission to require a country, such as, for example, Mexico, to authorise the banks of each Member State to establish themselves there under conditions of national treatment as a prerequisite for a Mexican bank being able to establish itself in the Community. This problem may perhaps be solved by the grant of an exemption: the Commission has indicated in the past its desire to act in this way.[41] But questions remain as to which developing countries would be exempted and by the application of what criteria.[42]

It is nevertheless necessary to state that, even before they came into force, the reciprocity provisions of the Second Banking Directive have had a positive effect by introducing a sense of greater urgency in the developed countries into the sometimes longstanding discussion of their internal policies for the liberalisation of their financial markets. This is the explanation for the fact that certain American and Japanese bankers see positive aspects in the European requirement of reciprocal treatment: they see it as a possible basis for applying pressure for the deregulation of their own national markets.[43]

Indeed, it may be thought that the proposals—recently renewed but so far unsuccessful—for reform of the American banking system would not have been advanced in so pressing a way and would have been less far-reaching had it not been for the pressure brought to bear by the Community in the course of the past few years on the United States to abolish or limit the application of certain rules which, in the eyes of the Community, constitute a source of discrimination against European banks.[44]

40. Hal S. Scott, "La notion de reciprocite dans la proposition de Deuxieme Directive de Coordination Bancaire", [1989] *Revue du Marché Commun*. No 323, p. 45 at p. 48.

41. *European Community News*, 20 October 1988, p. 4.

42. With regard to Mexico, now a member of NAFTA, attention should be drawn to the fact that in the area of *inter alia* financial services, "the benefits of NAFTA [are] limited to companies which are majority owned/controlled by NAFTA nationals", a situation which has been viewed as "a very important and unjustified discrimination against Community owned/controlled subsidiaries in North America" *Agence Europe* 5991 (new series) of 2 June 1993, p. 11.

43. Hal Scott, above, p. 51 and note 39 thereto, quoting D. Weatherstone, President of J.P. Morgan & Co.: "Happily for those of us who think change in our market is long overdue, the integration of European financial markets may also directly increase the pressure for reform in the US . . . and other non-Member States . . . through demands for reciprocity."

44. For the most recent review of those barriers as seen by the Commission, at the time of writing, see the Commission's "Report on United States Trade and Investment Services—Problems of doing business with the US" (1993) p. 64 and fn. 1.

APPENDICES

* Appendices A, C, D, E, F and K are reprinted from *The Amsterdam Financial Series*, edited by Martijn van Empel and Patrick Pearson, with the permission of Kluwer Law and Taxation Publishers, Deventer, The Netherlands.

FIRST COUNCIL DIRECTIVE[*] 77/780/EEC OF 12 DECEMBER 1977

on the co-ordination of laws, regulations and administrative provisions relating to the taking up and pursuit of the business of credit institutions[**]

THE COUNCIL OF THE EUROPEAN COMMUNITIES,

Having regard to the Treaty establishing the European Economic Community, and in particular Article 57 thereof,

Having regard to the proposal from the Commission,

Having regard to the opinion of the European Parliament,[1]

Having regard to the opinion of the Economic and Social Committee,[2]

Whereas, pursuant to the Treaty, any discriminatory treatment with regard to establishment and to the provision of services, based either on nationality or on the fact that an undertaking is not established in the Member States where the services are provided, is prohibited from the end of the transitional period;

Whereas, in order to make it easier to take up and pursue the business of credit institutions, it is necessary to eliminate the most obstructive differences between the laws of the Member States as regards the rules to which these institutions are subject;

Whereas, however, given the extent of these differences, the conditions required for a common market for credit institutions cannot be created by means of a single Directive; whereas it is therefore necessary to proceed by successive stages; whereas the result of this process should be to provide for overall supervision of a credit institution operating in several Member States by the competent authorities in the Member State where it has its head office, in consultation, as appropriate, with the competent authorities of the other Member States concerned;

Whereas measures to co-ordinate credit institutions must, both in order to protect savings and to create equal conditions of competition between these institutions, apply to all of them; whereas due regard must be had, where applicable, to the objective differences in their statutes and their proper aims as laid down by national laws;

Whereas the scope of those measures should therefore be as broad as possible, covering all institutions whose business is to receive repayable funds from the public whether in the form of deposits or in other forms such as the continuing issue of bonds and other comparable securities and to grant credits for their own account; whereas exceptions must be provided for in the case of certain credit institutions to which this Directive cannot apply;

Whereas the provisions of the Directive shall not prejudice the application of national laws which provide for special supplementary authorizations permitting credit institutions to carry on specific activities or undertake specific kinds of operations;

Whereas the same system of supervision cannot always be applied to all types of credit institution; whereas provision should therefore be made for application of this Directive to be deferred in the case of certain groups or types of credit institutions to which its immediate application might cause technical problems; whereas more specific provisions for such institutions may prove necessary in the future; whereas these specific provisions should nonetheless be based on a number of common principles;

Whereas the eventual aim is to introduce uniform authorization requirements throughout the

---

[*] OJ 1977, L322/30.

[**] This Directive has been amended by Directive 85/345/EEC, by Directive 86/524/EEC and by Directive 89/646/EEC.

1. OJ No C128, 9 June 1975, p. 25.

2. OJ No C263, 17 November 1975, p. 25.

Community for comparable types of credit institution; whereas at the initial stage it is necessary, however, to specify only certain minimum requirements to be imposed by all Member States;

Whereas this aim can be achieved only if the particularly wide discretionary powers which certain supervisory authorities have for authorizing credit establishments are progressively reduced; whereas the requirement that a programme of operations must be produced should therefore be seen merely as a factor enabling the competent authorities to decide on the basis of more precise information using objective criteria;

Whereas the purpose of co-ordination is to achieve a system whereby credit institutions having their head office in one of the Member States are exempt from any national authorization requirement when setting up branches in other Member States;

Whereas a measure of flexibility may nonetheless be possible in the initial stage as regards the requirements on the legal form of credit institutions and the protection of banking names;

Whereas equivalent financial requirements for credit institutions will be necessary to ensure similar safeguards for savers and fair conditions of competition between comparable groups of credit institutions; whereas, pending further co-ordination, appropriate structural ratios should be formulated that will make it possible within the framework of co-operation between national authorities to observe, in accordance with standard methods, the position of comparable types of credit institutions; whereas this procedure should help to bring about the gradual approximation of the systems of co-efficients established and applied by the Member States; whereas it is necessary, however, to make a distinction between co-efficients intended to ensure the sound management of credit institutions and those established for the purposes of economic and monetary policy; whereas, for the purpose of formulating structural ratios and of more general co-operation between supervisory authorities, standardization of the layout of credit institutions' accounts will have to begin as soon as possible.

Whereas the rules governing branches of credit institutions having their head office outside the Community should be analogous in all Member States; whereas it is important at the present time to provide that such rules may not be more favourable than those for branches of institutions from another Member State; whereas it should be specified that the Community may conclude agreements with third countries providing for the application of rules which accord such branches the same treatment throughout its territory, account being taken of the principle of reciprocity;

Whereas the examination of problems connected with matters covered by Council Directives on the business of credit institutions requires co-operation between the competent authorities and the Commission within an Advisory Committee, particularly when conducted with a view to closer co-ordination;

Whereas the establishment of an Advisory Committee of the competent authorities of the Member States does not rule out other forms of co-operation between authorities which supervise the taking up and pursuit of the business of credit institutions and, in particular, co-operation within the Contact Committee set up between the banking supervisory authorities,

HAS ADOPTED THIS DIRECTIVE

TITLE I: DEFINITIONS AND SCOPE

Article 1

For the purposes of this Directive:

— "credit institution" means an undertaking whose business is to receive deposits or other repayable funds from the public and to grant credits for its own account,
— "authorization" means an instrument issued in any form by the authorities by which the right to carry on the business of a credit institution is granted,
— "branch" means a place of business which forms a legally dependent part of a credit institution and which conducts directly all or some of the operations inherent in the business of credit institutions; any number of branches set up in the same Member State by a credit institution having its head office in another Member State shall be regarded as a single branch, without prejudice to Article 4(1),
— "own funds" means the credit institution's own capital, including items which may be treated as capital under national rules.

414

Article 2

1. This Directive shall apply to the taking up and pursuit of the business of credit institutions.
2. It shall not apply to:

— the central banks of Member States,
— post office giro institutions,
— in Belgium, the communal savings bank (*"caisses d'épargne communales—gemeentelijke spaarkassen"*), the *"Institut de Réescompte et de Garantie—Herdiscontering- en Waarborginstituut"*, the *"Société nationale d'Investissement—Nationale Investerings-maatschappij"*, the regional development companies (*"Sociétés de développement régional—gewestelijke ontwikkelingsmaatschappijen"*), the *"Société nationale du Logement—Nationale Maatschappij voor de Huisvesting"* and its authorized companies and the *"Société nationale terrienne—Nationale Landmaatschappij"* and its authorized companies,
— in Denmark, the *"Dansk Eksportfinansieringsfond"* and *"Danmarks Skibskreditfond"*,
— in Germany, the *"Kreditanstalt für Wiederaufbau"*, undertakings which are recognized under the *"Wohnungsgemeinnützigkeitsgesetz"* (non-profit housing law) as bodies of state housing policy and are not mainly engaged in banking transactions and undertakings recognized under that law as non-profit housing undertakings,
— in France, the *"Caisse des Dépôts et Consignations"*, the *"Crédit Foncier"* and the *"Crédit National"*,
— in Ireland, credit unions,
— in Italy, the *"Cassa Depositi e Prestiti"*,
— in the Netherlands, the *"NV Export-Financieringsmaatschappij"*, the *"Nederlandse Financieringsmaatschappij voor Ontwikkelingslanden NV"*, the *"Nederlandse Investeringsbank voor Ontwikkelingslanden NV"* the *"Nationale Investeringsbank NV"*, the *"NV Bank van Nederlandse Gemeenten"*, the *"Nederlandse Waterschapsbank NV"*, the *"Financieringsmaatschappij Industrieel Garantiefonds Amsterdam NV"*, the *"Financieringsmaatschappij Industrieel Garantiefonds 's Gravenhage NV"*, the *"NV Noordelijke Ontwikkelings Maatschappij"*, the *"NV Industriebank Limburgs Instituut voor ontwikkeling en financiering"* and the *"Overijsselse Ontwikkelingsmaatschappij NV"*,
— in the United Kingdom, the National Savings Bank, the Commonwealth Development Finance Company Ltd, the Agricultural Mortgage Corporation Ltd, the Scottish Agricultural Securities Corporation Ltd, the Crown Agents for overseas governments and administrations, credit unions, and municipal banks.

3. The Council, acting on a proposal from the Commission, which, for this purpose, shall consult the Committee referred to in Article 11 (hereinafter referred to as "the Advisory Committee") shall decide on any amendments to the list in paragraph 2.
4. (a) Credit institutions existing in the same Member State at the time of the notification of this Directive and permanently affiliated at that time to a central body which supervises them and which is established in that same Member State, may be exempted from the requirements listed in the first, second and third indents of the first subparagraph of Article 3(2), the second subparagraph of Article 3(2), Article 3(4) and Article 6, if, no later than the date when the national authorities take the measures necessary to translate this Directive into national law, that law provides that:

— the commitments of the central body and affiliated institutions are joint and several liabilities or the commitments of its affiliated institutions are entirely guaranteed by the central body,
— the solvency and liquidity of the central body and of all the affiliated institutions are monitored as a whole on the basis of consolidated accounts,
— the management of the central body is empowered to issue instructions to the management of the affiliated institutions.

(b) Credit institutions operating locally which are affiliated, subsequent to notification of this Directive, to a central body within the meaning of subparagraph (a) may benefit from the conditions laid down in subparagraph (a) if they constitute normal additions to the network belonging to that central body.

(c) In the case of credit institutions other than those which are set up in areas newly reclaimed from the sea or have resulted from scission or mergers of existing institutions dependent or answerable to the central body, the Council, acting on a proposal from the Commission, which shall, for this purpose, consult the Advisory Committee, may lay down additional rules for the application of subparagraph (b) including the repeal of exemptions provided for in subparagraph (a), where it is of the opinion that the affiliation of new institutions benefiting from the arrangements laid down in subparagraph (b) might have an adverse effect on competition. The Council shall decide by a qualified majority.

5. Member States may defer in whole or in part the application of this Directive to certain types or groups of credit institutions where such immediate application would cause technical problems which cannot be overcome in the short-term. The problems may result either from the fact that these institutions are subject to supervision by an authority different from that normally responsible for the supervision of banks, or from the fact that they are subject to a special system of supervision. In any event, such deferment cannot be justified by the public law statutes, by the smallness of size or by the limited scope of activity of the particular institutions concerned.

Deferment can apply only to groups or types of institutions already existing at the time of notification of this Directive.

6. Pursuant to paragraph 5, a Member State may decide to defer application of this Directive for a maximum period of five years from the notification thereof and, after consulting the Advisory Committee, may extend deferment once only for a maximum period of three years.

The Member State shall inform the Commission of its decision and the reasons therefor not later than six months following the notification of this Directive. It shall also notify the Commission of any extension or repeal of this decision. The Commission shall publish any decision regarding deferment in the *Official Journal of the European Communities*.

Not later than seven years following the notification of this Directive, the Commission shall, after consulting the Advisory Committee, submit a report to the Council on the situation regarding deferment. Where appropriate, the Commission shall submit to the Council, not later than six months following the submission of its report, proposals for either the inclusion of the institutions in question in the list in paragraph 2 or for the authorization of a further extension of deferment. The Council shall act on these proposals not later than six months after their submission.[3]

TITLE II. CREDIT INSTITUTIONS HAVING THEIR HEAD OFFICE IN A MEMBER STATE AND THEIR BRANCHES IN OTHER MEMBER STATES

Article 3

1. Member States shall require credit institutions subject to this Directive to obtain authorization before commencing their activities. They shall lay down the requirements for such authorization subject to paragraphs 2, 3 and 4 and notify them to both the Commission and the Advisory Committee.

2. Without prejudice to other conditions of general application laid down by national laws, the competent authorities shall grant authorization only when the following conditions are complied with:

— the credit institution must possess separate own funds,
— the credit institution must possess adequate minimum own funds,
— there shall be at least two persons who effectively direct the business of the credit institution.

Moreover, the authorities concerned shall not grant authorization if the persons referred to in the third indent of the first subparagraph are not of sufficiently good repute or lack sufficient experience to perform such duties.

3. (a) The provisions referred to in paragraphs 1 and 2 may not require the application for authorization to be examined in terms of the economic needs of the market.

3. See Directive 86/137/EEC.

(b) Where the laws, regulations or administrative provisions of a Member State provide, at the time of notification of the present Directive, that the economic needs of the market shall be a condition of authorization and where technical or structural difficulties in its banking system do not allow it to give up the criterion within the period laid down in Article 14(1), the State in question may continue to apply the criterion for a period of seven years from notification.

It shall notify its decision and the reasons therefor to the Commission within six months of notification.

(c) Within six years of the notification of this Directive the Commission shall submit to the Council, after consulting the Advisory Committee, a report on the application of the criterion of economic need. If appropriate, the Commission shall submit to the Council proposals to terminate the application of that criterion. The period referred to in subparagraph (b) shall be extended for one further period of five years, unless, in the meantime, the Council, acting unanimously on proposals from the Commission, adopts a Decision to terminate the application of that criterion.

(d) The criterion of economic need shall be applied only on the basis of general predetermined criteria, published and notified to both the Commission and the Advisory Committee and aimed at promoting:

— security of savings,
— higher productivity in the banking system,
— greater uniformity of competition between the various banking networks,
— a broader range of banking services in relation to population and economic activity.

Specification of the above objectives shall be determined within the Advisory Committee, which shall begin its work as from its initial meetings.

4. Member States shall also require applications for authorization to be accompanied by a programme of operations setting out *inter alia* the types of business envisaged and the structural organization of the institution.

5. The Advisory Committee shall examine the content given by the competent authorities to requirements listed in paragraph 2, any other requirements which the Member States apply and the information which must be included in the programme of operations, and shall, where appropriate, make suggestions to the Commission with a view to a more detailed co-ordination.

6. Reasons shall be given whenever an authorization is refused and the applicant shall be notified thereof within six months of receipt of the application or, should the latter be incomplete, within six months of the applicant's sending the information required for the decision. A decision shall, in any case, be taken within 12 months of the receipt of the application.

7. Every authorization shall be notified to the Commission. Each credit institution shall be entered in a list which the Commission shall publish in the *Official Journal of the European Communities* and shall keep up to date.[4]

Article 4

1. Member States may make the commencement of business in their territory by branches of credit institutions covered by this Directive which have their head office in another Member State subject to authorization according to the law and procedure applicable to credit institutions established on their territory.

2. However, authorization may not be refused to a branch of a credit institution on the sole ground that it is established in another Member State in a legal form which is not allowed in the case of a credit institution carrying out similar activities in the host country. This provision shall not apply, however, to credit institutions which possess no separate own funds.

3. The competent authorities shall inform the Commission of any authorizations which they grant to the branches referred to in paragraph 1.

4. This Article shall not affect the rules applied by Member States to branches set up on their territory by credit institutions which have their head office there. Notwithstanding the second part of the third indent of Article 1, the laws of Member States requiring a separate authorization for each branch of a credit institution having its head office in their territory shall apply equally to the branches of credit institutions the head offices of which are in other Member States.

4. The tenth edition of this list was published in OJ 1990, C107/1.

Article 5

For the purpose of exercising their activities, credit institutions to which this Directive applies may, notwithstanding any provisions concerning the use of the words "bank", "saving bank" or other banking names which may exist in the host Member State, use throughout the territory of the Community the same name as they use in the Member States in which their head office is situated. In the event of there being any danger of confusion, the host Member State may, for the purposes of clarification, require that the name be accompanied by certain explanatory particulars.

Article 6

1. Pending subsequent co-ordination, the competent authorities shall, for the purposes of observation and, if necessary, in addition to such co-efficients as may be applied by them, establish ratios between the various assets and/or liabilities of credit institutions with a view to monitoring their solvency and liquidity and the other measures which may serve to ensure that savings are protected.

To this end, the Advisory Committee shall decide on the content of the various factors of the observation ratios referred to in the first subparagraph and lay down the method to be applied in calculating them.

Where appropriate, the Advisory Committee shall be guided by technical consultations between the supervisory authorities of the categories of institutions concerned.

2. The observation ratios established in pursuance of paragraph 1 shall be calculated at least every six months.

3. The Advisory Committee shall examine the results of analyses carried out by the supervisory authorities referred to in the third subparagraph of paragraph 1 on the basis of the calculations referred to in paragraph 2.

4. The Advisory Committee may make suggestions to the Commission with a view to co-ordinating the co-efficients applicable in the Member States.

Article 7

1. The competent authorities of the Member States concerned shall collaborate closely in order to supervise the activities of credit institutions operating, in particular by having established branches there, in one or more Member States other than that in which their head offices are situated. They shall supply one another with all information concerning the management and ownership of such credit institutions that is likely to facilitate their supervision and the examination of the conditions for their authorization and all information likely to facilitate the monitoring of their liquidity and solvency.

2. The competent authorities may also, for the purposes and within the meaning of Article 6, lay down ratios applicable to the branches referred to in this Article by reference to the factors laid down in Article 6.

3. The Advisory Committee shall take account of the adjustments necessitated by the specific situation of the branches in relation to national regulations.

Article 8

1. The competent authorities may withdraw the authorization issued to a credit institution subject to this Directive or to a branch authorized under Article 4 only where such an institution or branch:

   (a) does not make use of the authorization within 12 months, expressly renounces the authorization or has ceased to engage in business for more than six months, if the Member State concerned has made no provision for the authorization to lapse in such cases;
   (b) has obtained the authorization through false statements or any other irregular means;
   (c) no longer fulfils the conditions under which authorization was granted, with the exception of those in respect of own funds;
   (d) no longer possesses sufficient own funds or can no longer be relied upon to fulfil its

obligations towards its creditors, and in particular no longer provides security for the assets entrusted to it;

(e) falls within one of the other cases where national law provides for withdrawal of authorization.

2. In addition, the authorization issued to a branch under Article 4 shall be withdrawn if the competent authority of the country in which the credit institution which established the branch has its head office has withdrawn authorization from the institution.

3. Member States which grant the authorizations referred to in Articles 3(1) and 4(1) only if, economically, the market situation requires it may not invoke the disappearance of such a need as grounds for withdrawing such authorizations.

4. Before withdrawal from a branch of an authorization granted under Article 4, the competent authority of the Member State in which its head office is situated shall be consulted. Where immediate action is called for, notification may take the place of such consultation. The same procedure shall be followed, by analogy, in cases of withdrawal of authorization from a credit institution which has branches in other Member States.

5. Reasons must be given for any withdrawal of authorization and those concerned informed thereof; such withdrawal shall be notified to the Commission.

TITLE III. BRANCHES OF CREDIT INSTITUTIONS HAVING THEIR HEAD OFFICES OUTSIDE THE COMMUNITY

Article 9

1. Member States shall not apply to branches of credit institutions having their head office outside the Community, when commencing or carrying on their business, provisions which result in more favourable treatment than that accorded to branches of credit institutions having their head office in the Community.

2. The competent authorities shall notify the Commission and the Advisory Committee of all authorizations for branches granted to credit institutions having their head office outside the Community.

3. Without prejudice to paragraph 1, the Community may, through agreements concluded in accordance with the Treaty with one or more third countries, agree to apply provisions which, on the basis of the principle of reciprocity, accord to branches of a credit institution having its head office outside the Community identical treatment throughout the territory of the Community.

TITLE IV. GENERAL AND TRANSITIONAL PROVISIONS

Article 10

1. Credit institutions subject to this Directive, which took up their business in accordance with the provisions of the Member States in which they have their head offices before the entry into force of the provisions implementing this Directive shall be deemed to be authorized. They shall be subject to the provisions of this Directive concerning the carrying on of the business of credit institutions and to the requirements set out in the first and third indents of the first subparagraph and in the second subparagraph of Article 3(2).

Member States may allow credit institutions which at the time of notification of this Directive do not comply with the requirement laid down in the third indent of the first subparagraph of Article 3(2), no more than five years in which to do so.

Member States may decide that undertakings which do not fulfil the requirements set out in the first indent of the first subparagraph of Article 3(2) and which are in existence at the time this Directive enters into force may continue to carry on their business. They may exempt such undertakings from complying with the requirement contained in the third indent of the first subparagraph of Article 3(2).

2. All the credit institutions referred to in paragraph 1 shall be given in the list referred to in Article 3(7).

3. If a credit institution deemed to be authorized under paragraph 1 has not undergone any authorization procedure prior to commencing business, a prohibition on the carrying on of its business shall take the place of withdrawal of authorization.

Subject to the first subparagraph, Article 8 shall apply by analogy.

4. By way of derogation from paragraph 1, credit institutions established in a Member State without having undergone an authorization procedure in that Member State prior to commencing business may be required to obtain authorization from the competent authorities of the Member State concerned in accordance with the provisions implementing this Directive. Such institutions may be required to comply with the requirement in the second indent of Article 3(2) and with such other conditions of general application as may be laid down by the Member State concerned.

Article 11

1. An "Advisory Committee of the Competent Authorities of the Member States of the European Economic Community" shall be set up alongside the Commission.

2. The tasks of the Advisory Committee shall be to assist the Commission in ensuring the proper implementation of both this Directive and Council Directive 73/183/EEC of 28 June 1973 on the abolition of restrictions on freedom of establishment and freedom to provide services in respect of self-employed activities of banks and other financial institutions[5] in so far as it relates to credit institutions. Further it shall carry out the other tasks prescribed by this Directive and shall assist the Commission in the preparation of new proposals to the Council concerning further co-ordination in the sphere of credit institutions.

3. The Advisory Committee shall not concern itself with concrete problems relating to individual credit institutions.

4. The Advisory Committee shall be composed of not more than three representatives from each Member State and from the Commission. These representatives may be accompanied by advisers from time to time and subject to the prior agreement of the Committee. The Committee may also invite qualified persons and experts to participate in its meetings. The secretariat shall be provided by the Commission.

5. The first meeting of the Advisory Committee shall be convened by the Commission under the chairmanship of one of its representatives. The Advisory Committee shall then adopt its rules of procedure and shall elect a chairman from among the representatives of Member States. Thereafter it shall meet at regular intervals and whenever the situation demands. The Commission may ask the Committee to hold an emergency meeting if it considers that the situation so requires.

6. The Advisory Committee's discussions and the outcome thereof shall be confidential except when the Committee decides otherwise.

Article 12

1. Member States shall ensure that all persons now or in the past employed by the competent authorities are bound by the obligation of professional secrecy. This means that any confidential information which they may receive in the course of their duties may not be divulged to any person or authority except by virtue of provisions laid down by law.

2. Paragraph 1 shall not, however, preclude communications between the competent authorities of the various Member States, as provided for in this Directive. Information thus exchanged shall be covered by the obligation of professional secrecy applying to the persons now or in the past employed by the competent authorities receiving the information.

3. Without prejudice to cases covered by criminal law, the authorities receiving such information shall use it only to examine the conditions for the taking up and pursuit of the business of credit institutions, to facilitate monitoring of the liquidity and solvency of these institutions or when the decisions of the competent authority are the subject of an administrative appeal or in court proceedings initiated pursuant to Article 13.

5. OJ No L194, 16 July 1973, p. 1.

Article 13

Member States shall ensure that decisions taken in respect of a credit institution in pursuance of laws, regulations and administrative provisions adopted in accordance with this Directive may be subject to the right to apply to the courts. The same shall apply where no decision is taken within six months of its submission in respect of an application for authorization which contains all the information required under the provisions in force.

TITLE V. FINAL PROVISIONS

Article 14

1. Member States shall bring into force the measures necessary to comply with this Directive within 24 months of its notification and shall forthwith inform the Commission thereof.

2. As from the notification of this Directive, Member States shall communicate to the Commission the texts of the main laws, regulations and administrative provisions which they adopt in the field covered by this Directive.

Article 15

This Directive is addressed to the Member States.

Done at Brussels, 12 December 1977.

For the Council
The President
A. HUMBLET

COUNCIL DIRECTIVE 92/30/EEC OF 6 APRIL 1992

on the supervision of credit institutions on a consolidated basis

THE COMMISSION OF THE EUROPEAN COMMUNITIES,

Having regard to the Treaty establishing the European Economic Community, and in particular the first and third sentences of Article 57(2) thereof,

Having regard to the proposal from the Commission,

In co-operation with the European Parliament,[1]

Having regard to the opinion of the Economic and Social Committee,[2]

Whereas Council Directive 83/350/EEC of 13 June 1983 on the supervision of credit institutions on a consolidated basis[3] established the necessary framework for the introduction of supervision of credit institutions on a consolidated basis; whereas, following the transposition of that Directive into the national law of the Member States, the principle of supervision on a consolidated basis is now applied throughout the Community;

Whereas, in order to be effective, supervision on a consolidated basis must be applied to all banking groups, including those the parent undertakings of which are not credit institutions; whereas the competent authorities must hold the necessary legal instruments to be able to exercise such supervision;

Whereas, in the case of groups with diversified activities the parent undertakings of which control at least one credit institution subsidiary, the competent authorities must be able to assess the financial situation of a credit institution in such a group; whereas, pending subsequent co-ordination, the Member States may lay down appropriate methods of consolidation for the achievement of the objective of this Directive; whereas the competent authorities must at least have the means of obtaining from all undertakings within a group the information necessary for the performance of their function; whereas co-operation between the authorities responsible for the supervision of different financial sectors must be established in the case of groups of undertakings carrying on a range of financial activities;

Whereas rules limiting the risks taken by a credit institution on the mixed-activity holding company of which it is a subsidiary, as well as those taken on the other subsidiaries of the same mixed-activity holding company, can be particularly useful; whereas it would, however, appear to be preferable to settle this question in a more systematic manner in the framework of a future Directive on the limitation of large exposures;

Whereas the Member States can, furthermore, refuse or withdraw banking authorization in the case of certain group structures considered inappropriate for carrying on banking activities, in particular because such structures could not be supervised effectively; whereas in this respect the competent authorities have the powers mentioned in Article 8(1)(c) of the First Council Directive (77/780/EEC) of 12 December 1977 on the co-ordination of the laws, regulations and administrative provisions relating to the taking up and pursuit of the business of credit institutions[4] and in Articles 5 and 11 of the Second Council Directive (89/646/EEC) of 15 December 1989 on the co-ordination of laws, regulations and administrative provisions relating

---

1. OJ No C326, 16 December 1991, p. 106, and OJ No C94, 13 April 1992.
2. OJ No C102, 18 April 1991, p. 19.
3. OJ No L193, 18 July 1983, p. 18.
4. OJ No L322, 17 December 1977, p. 30. Directive as last amended by Directive 89/646/EEC (OJ No L386, 30 December 1989, p. 1).

to the taking up and pursuit of the business of credit institutions,[5] in order to ensure the sound and prudent management of credit institutions;

Whereas the Member States can equally apply appropriate supervision techniques to groups with structures not covered by this Directive; whereas, if such structures become common, this Directive should be extended to cover them;

Whereas supervision on a consolidated basis must take in all activities defined in the Annex to Directive 89/646/EEC; whereas all undertakings principally engaged in such activities must therefore be included in supervision on a consolidated basis; whereas, as a result, the definition of a financial institution given in Directive 83/350/EEC must be widened to cover such activities;

Whereas, regarding the consolidation of financial institutions involved in activities principally subject to market risks and subject to particular rules of supervision, the co-ordination of the methods for the consolidated supervision of market risks is possible in the framework of Community harmonization of capital adequacy of investment firms and credit institutions, for which the Commission has introduced a proposal for a Directive; whereas such harmonization concerns, *inter alia*, the conditions which must be applied when offsetting opposing positions in the group and the case where these financial institutions are subject to specific supervisory rules regarding their financial stability; whereas this implies that, until the future Directive on capital adequacy to cover market risks is brought into effect, the competent authorities shall include in consolidated supervision financial institutions which are principally exposed to market risks, in accordance with methods determined by those authorities in the light of the particular nature of the risks involved;

Whereas, following the adoption of Council Directive 86/635/EEC of 8 December 1986 on the annual accounts and consolidated accounts of banks and other financial institutions,[6] which, together with the Seventh Council Directive (83/349/EEC) of 13 June 1983 on consolidated accounts,[7] established the rules of consolidation applicable to consolidated accounts published by credit institutions, it is now possible to define more precisely the methods to be used in prudential supervision exercised on a consolidated basis;

Whereas this Directive is fully in keeping with the objectives defined in the Single European Act; whereas it will, in particular, ensure the homogeneous application throughout the Community of prudential rules established by other Community legislation, which must be observed on a consolidated basis; whereas this Directive is, in particular, necessary for the correct application of Council Directive 89/299/EEC of 17 April 1989 on the own funds of credit institutions[8];

Whereas supervision of credit institutions on a consolidated basis must be aimed at, in particular, protecting the interests of the depositors of the said institutions and at ensuring the stability of the financial system;

Whereas it is desirable that agreement should be reached, on the basis of reciprocity, between the Community and third countries with a view to allowing the practical exercise of consolidated supervision over the largest possible geographical area;

Whereas the amendments to be made to Directive 83/350/EEC are so considerable that it is preferable that it be wholly replaced by this Directive,

HAS ADOPTED THIS DIRECTIVE:

Article 1

Definitions

For the purposes of this Directive:

— *credit institution* shall mean a credit institution within the meaning of the first indent of Article 1 of Directive 77/780/EEC, or any private or public undertaking which

---

5. OJ No L386, 30 December 1989, p. 1.
6. OJ No L372, 31 December 1986, p. 1.
7. OJ No L193, 18 July 1983, p. 1. Directive as last amended by Directive 90/605/EEC (OJ No L317, 16 November 1990, p. 60).
8. OJ No L124, 5 May 1989, p. 16.

corresponds to the definition in the first indent of Article 1 of Directive 77/780/EEC and has been authorized in a third country,
— *financial institution* shall mean an undertaking, other than a credit institution, the principal activity of which is to acquire holdings or to carry on one or more of the activities referred to in numbers 2 to 12 of the list appearing in the Annex to Directive 89/646/EEC,
— *financial holding company* shall mean a financial institution the subsidiary undertakings of which are either exclusively or mainly credit institutions or financial institutions, one at least of such subsidiaries being a credit institution,
— *mixed-activity holding company* shall mean a parent undertaking, other than a financial holding company or a credit institution, the subsidiaries of which include at least one credit institution,
— *ancillary banking services* undertaking shall mean an undertaking the principal activity of which consists in owning or managing property, managing data-processing services, or any other similar activity which is ancillary to the principal activity of one or more credit institution,
— *participation* shall mean the ownership, direct or indirect, of 20% or more of the voting rights or capital of an undertaking,
— *parent undertaking* shall mean a parent undertaking within the meaning of Article 1(1) of the Directive 83/349/EEC and any undertaking which, in the opinion of the competent authorities, effectively exercises a dominant influence over another undertaking,
— *subsidiary* shall mean a subsidiary undertaking within the meaning of Article 1(1) of Directive 83/349/EEC and any undertaking over which, in the opinion of the competent authorities, a parent undertaking effectively exercises a dominant influence. All subsidiaries of subsidiary undertakings shall also be considered subsidiaries of the undertaking that is their original parent,
— *competent authorities* shall mean the national authorities which are empowered by law or regulation to supervise credit institutions.

Article 2

Scope

This Directive shall apply to credit institutions that have obtained the authorization referred to in Article 3 of Directive 77/780/EEC, financial holding companies and mixed-activity holding companies which have their head offices in the Community.

The institutions permanently excluded by Article 2 of Directive 77/780/EEC, with the exception, however, of the Member States' central banks, shall be treated as financial institutions for the purposes of this Directive.

Article 3

Supervision on a consolidated basis of credit institutions

1. Every credit institution which has a credit institution or a financial institution as a subsidiary or which holds a participation in such institutions shall be subject, to the extent and in the manner prescribed in Article 5, to supervision on the basis of its consolidated financial situation. Such supervision shall be exercised at least in the areas referred to in paragraphs 5 and 6.

2. Every credit institution the parent undertaking of which is a financial holding company shall be subject, to the extent and in the manner prescribed in Article 5, to supervision on the basis of the consolidated financial situation of that financial holding company. Such supervision shall be exercised at least in the areas referred to in paragraphs 5 and 6. The consolidation of the financial situation of the financial holding company shall not in any way imply that the competent authorities are required to play a supervisory role in relation to the financial holding company standing alone.

3. The Member States or the competent authorities responsible for exercising supervision on a consolidated basis pursuant to Article 4 may decide in the cases listed below that a credit institution, financial institution or auxiliary banking services undertaking which is a subsidiary or in which a participation is held need not be included in the consolidation:

— if the undertaking that should be included is situated in a third country where there are legal impediments to the transfer of the necessary information,

— if, in the opinion of the competent authorities, the undertaking that should be included is of negligible interest only with respect to the objectives of monitoring credit institutions and in all cases if the balance sheet total of the undertaking that should be included is less than the smaller of the following two amounts: ECU 10 million or 1% of the balance sheet total of the parent undertaking or the undertaking that holds the participation. If several undertakings meet the above criteria, they must nevertheless be included in the consolidation where collectively they are of non-negligible interest with respect to the aforementioned objectives, or

— if, in the opinion of the competent authorities responsible for exercising supervision on a consolidated basis, the consolidation of the financial situation of the undertaking that should be included would be inappropriate or misleading as far as the objectives of the supervision of credit institutions are concerned.

4. When the competent authorities of a Member State do not include a credit institution subsidiary in supervision on a consolidated basis under one of the cases provided for in the second and third indents of paragraph 3, the competent authorities of the Member State in which that credit institution subsidiary is situated may ask the parent undertaking for information which may facilitate their supervision of that credit institution.

5. Supervision of solvency, and of the adequacy of own funds to cover market risks and control of large exposures, as governed by the relevant Community acts in force, shall be exercised on a consolidated basis in accordance with this Directive. Member States shall adopt any measures necessary, where appropriate, to include financial holding companies in consolidated supervision, in accordance with paragraph 2.

Compliance with the limits set in Article 12(1) and (2) of Directive 89/646/EEC shall be supervised and controlled on the basis of the consolidated or sub-consolidated financial situation of the credit institution.

6. The competent authorities shall ensure that, in all the undertakings included in the scope of the supervision on a consolidated basis that is exercised over a credit institution in implementation of paragraphs 1 and 2, there are adequate internal control mechanisms for the production of any data and information which would be relevant for the purposes of supervision on a consolidated basis.

7. Without prejudice to specific provisions contained in other Directives, Member States may waive application, on an individual or sub-consolidated basis, of the rules laid down in paragraph 5 to a credit institution that, as a parent undertaking, is subject to supervision on a consolidated basis, and to any subsidiary of such a credit institution which is subject to their authorization and supervision and is included in the supervision on a consolidated basis of the credit institution which is the parent company. The same exemption option shall be allowed where the parent undertaking is a financial holding company which has its head office in the same Member State as the credit institution, provided that it is subject to the same supervision as that exercised over credit institutions, and in particular the standards laid down in paragraph 5.

In both cases, steps must be taken to ensure that capital is distributed adequately within the banking group.

If the competent authorities do apply those rules individually to such credit institutions, they may, for the purpose of calculating own funds, make use of the provision in the last subparagraph of Article 2(1) of Directive 89/299/EEC.

8. Where a credit institution the parent of which is a credit institution has been authorized and is situated in another Member State, the competent authorities which granted that authorization shall apply the rules laid down in paragraph 5 to that institution on an individual or, when appropriate, a sub-consolidated basis.

9. Notwithstanding the requirements of paragraph 8, the competent authorities responsible for authorizing the subsidiary of a parent undertaking which is a credit institution may, by bilateral agreement, delegate their responsibility for supervision to the competent authorities which authorized and supervise the parent undertaking. The Commission must be kept informed of the existence and content of such agreements. It shall forward such information to the competent authorities of the other Member States and to the Banking Advisory Committee.

10. Member States shall provide that their competent authorities responsible for exercising

supervision on a consolidated basis may ask the subsidiaries of a credit institution or a financial holding company which are not included within the scope of supervision on a consolidated basis for the information referred to in Article 6. In such a case, the procedures for transmitting and verifying the information laid down in that Article shall apply.

Article 4

Competent authorities responsible for exercising supervision on a consolidated basis

1. Where a parent undertaking is a credit institution, supervision on a consolidated basis shall be exercised by the competent authorities that authorized it under Article 3 of Directive 77/780/EEC.

2. Where the parent of a credit institution is a financial holding company, supervision on a consolidated basis shall be exercised by the competent authorities which authorized that credit institution under Article 3 of Directive 77/780/EEC.

However, where credit institutions authorized in two or more Member States have as their parent the same financial holding company, supervision on a consolidated basis shall be exercised by the competent authorities of the credit institution authorized in the Member State in which the financial holding company was set up.

If no credit institution subsidiary has been authorized in the Member State in which the financial holding company was set up, the competent authorities of the Member States concerned (including those of the Member State in which the financial holding company was set up) shall seek to reach agreement as to who amongst them will exercise supervision on a consolidated basis. In the absence of such agreement, supervision on a consolidated basis shall be exercised by the competent authorities that authorized the credit institution with the greatest balance sheet total; if that figure is the same, supervision on a consolidated basis shall be exercised by the competent authorities which first gave the authorization referred to in Article 3 of Directive 77/780/EEC.

3. The competent authorities concerned may by common agreement waive the rules laid down in the first and second subparagraphs of paragraph 2.

4. The agreements referred to in the third subparagraph of paragraph 2 and in paragraph 3 shall provide for procedures for co-operation and for the transmission of information such that the objectives of this Directive may be achieved.

5. Where Member States have more than one competent authority for the prudential supervision of credit institutions and financial institutions, Member States shall take the requisite measures to organize co-ordination between such authorities.

Article 5

Form and extent of consolidation

1. The competent authorities responsible for exercising supervision on a consolidated basis must, for the purposes of supervision, require full consolidation of all the credit institutions and financial institutions which are subsidiaries of a parent undertaking.

However, proportional consolidation may be prescribed where, in the opinion of the competent authorities, the liability of a parent undertaking holding a share of the capital is limited to that share of the capital because of the liability of the other shareholders or members whose solvency is satisfactory. The liability of the other shareholders and members must be clearly established, if necessary by means of formal, signed commitments.

2. The competent authorities responsible for carrying out supervision on a consolidated basis must, in order to do so, require the proportional consolidation of participations in credit institutions and financial institutions managed by an undertaking included in the consolidation together with one or more undertakings not included in the consolidation, where those undertakings' liability is limited to the share of the capital they hold.

3. In the case of participations or capital ties other than those referred to in paragraphs 1 and 2, the competent authorities shall determine whether and how consolidation is to be carried out. In particular, they may permit or require use of the equity method. That method shall not, however, constitute inclusion of the undertakings concerned in supervision on a consolidated basis.

427

4. Without prejudice to paragraphs 1, 2 and 3, the competent authorities shall determine whether and how consolidation is to be carried out in the following cases:

— where, in the opinion of the competent authorities, a credit institution exercises a significant influence over one or more credit institutions or financial institutions, but without holding a participation or other capital ties in these institutions,
— where two or more credit institutions or financial institutions are placed under single management other than pursuant to a contract or clauses of their memoranda or articles of association.
— where two or more credit institutions or financial institutions have administrative, management or supervisory bodies with the same persons constituting a majority.

In particular, the competent authorities may permit, or require use of, the method provided for in Article 12 of Directive 83/349/EEC. That method shall not, however, constitute inclusion of the undertakings concerned in consolidated supervision.

5. Where consolidated supervision is required pursuant to Article 3(1) and (2), ancillary banking services undertakings shall be included in consolidations in the cases, and in accordance with the methods, laid down in paragraphs 1 to 4, of this Article.

Article 6

Information to be supplied by mixed-activity holding companies and their subsidiaries

1. Pending further co-ordination of consolidation methods, Member States shall provide that, where the parent undertaking of one or more credit institutions is a mixed-activity holding company, the competent authorities responsible for the authorization and supervision of those credit institutions shall, by approaching the mixed-activity holding company and its subsidiaries either directly or via credit institution subsidiaries, require them to supply any information which would be relevant for the purposes of supervising the credit institution subsidiaries.

2. Member States shall provide that their competent authorities may carry out, or have carried out by external inspectors, on-the-spot inspections to verify information received from mixed-activity holding companies and their subsidiaries. If the mixed-activity holding company or one of its subsidiaries is an insurance undertaking, the procedure laid down in Article 7(4) may also be used. If a mixed-activity holding company or one of its subsidiaries is situated in a Member State other than that in which the credit institution subsidiary is situated, on-the-spot verification of information shall be carried out in accordance with the procedure laid down in Article 7(7).

Article 7

Measures to facilitate the application of this Directive

1. Member States shall take the necessary steps to ensure that there are no legal impediments preventing the undertakings included within the scope of supervision on a consolidated basis, mixed-activity holding companies and their subsidiaries, or subsidiaries of the kind covered in Article 3(10), from exchanging amongst themselves any information which would be relevant for the purposes of supervision in accordance with this Directive.

2. Where a parent undertaking and any of its subsidiaries that are credit institutions are situated in different Member States, the competent authorities of each Member State shall communicate to each other all relevant information which may allow or aid the exercise of supervision on a consolidated basis.

Where the competent authorities of the Member State in which a parent undertaking is situated do not themselves exercise supervision on a consolidated basis pursuant to Article 4, they may be invited by the competent authorities responsible for exercising such supervision to ask the parent undertaking for any information which would be relevant for the purposes of supervision on a consolidated basis and to transmit it to these authorities.

3. Member States shall authorize the exchange between their competent authorities of the information referred to in paragraph 2, on the understanding that, in the case of financial holding companies, financial institutions or ancillary banking services undertakings, the collection or

possession of information shall not in any way imply that the competent authorities are required to play a supervisory role in relation to those institutions or undertakings standing alone.

Similarly, Member States shall authorize their competent authorities to exchange the information referred to in Article 6 on the understanding that the collection or possession of information does not in any way imply that the competent authorities play a supervisory role in relation to the mixed-activity holding company and those of its subsidiaries which are not credit institutions, or to subsidiaries of the kind covered in Article 3(10).

4. Where a credit institution, financial holding company or a mixed-activity holding company controls one or more subsidiaries which are insurance companies or other undertakings providing investment services which are subject to authorization, the competent authorities and the authorities entrusted with the public task of supervising insurance undertakings or those other undertakings providing investment services shall co-operate closely. Without prejudice to their respective responsibilities, those authorities shall provide one another with any information likely to simplify their task and to allow supervision of the activity and overall financial situation of the undertakings they supervise.

5. Information received pursuant to this Directive and in particular any exchange of information between competent authorities which is provided for in this Directive shall be subject to the obligation of professional secrecy defined in Article 12 of Directive 77/780/EEC.

6. The competent authorities responsible for supervision on a consolidated basis shall establish lists of the financial holding companies referred to in Article 3(2). Those lists shall be communicated to the competent authorities of the other Member States and to the Commission.

7. Where, in applying this Directive, the competent authorities of one Member State wish in specific cases to verify the information concerning a credit institution, a financial holding company, a financial institution, an ancillary banking services undertaking, a mixed-activity holding company, a subsidiary of the kind covered in Article 6 or a subsidiary of the kind covered in Article 3(10), situated in another Member State, they must ask the competent authorities of that other Member State to have that verification carried out. The authorities which receive such a request must, within the framework of their competence, act upon it either by carrying out the verification themselves, by allowing the authorities who made the request to carry it out, or by allowing an auditor or expert to carry it out.

8. Without prejudice to their provisions of criminal law, Member States shall ensure that penalties or measures aimed at ending observed breaches or the causes of such breaches may be imposed on financial holding companies and mixed-activity holding companies, or their effective managers, that infringe laws, regulations or administrative provisions enacted to implement this Directive. In certain cases, such measures may require the intervention of the courts. The competent authorities shall co-operate closely to ensure that the abovementioned penalties or measures produce the desired results, especially when the central administration or main establishment of a financial holding company or of a mixed-activity holding company is not located at its head office.

Article 8

Third countries

1. The Commission may submit proposals to the Council, either at the request of a Member State or on its own initiative, for the negotiation of agreements with one or more third countries regarding the means of exercising supervision on a consolidated basis over:

— credit institutions the parent undertakings of which have their head offices situated in a third country, and
— credit institutions situated in third countries the parent undertakings of which, whether credit institutions or financial holding companies, have their head offices in the Community.

2. The agreements referred to in paragraph 1 shall in particular seek to ensure both:

— that the competent authorities of the Member States are able to obtain the information necessary for the supervision, on the basis of their consolidated financial situations, of credit institutions or financial holding companies situated in the Community and which have as subsidiaries credit institutions or financial institutions situated outside the Community, or which hold participations in such institutions,

— that the competent authorities of third countries are able to obtain the information necessary for the supervision of parent undertakings the head offices of which are situated within their territories and which have as subsidiaries credit institutions or financial institutions situated in one or more Member States, or which hold participations in such institutions.

3. The Commission and the Advisory Committee set up under Article 11 of Directive 77/780/EEC shall examine the outcome of the negotiations referred to in paragraph 1 and the resulting situation.

Article 9

Final provisions

1. Member States shall bring into force the laws, regulations and administrative provisions necessary to comply with this Directive before 1 January 1993. They shall forthwith inform the Commission thereof.

When Member States adopt the abovementioned measures, the measures shall contain a reference to this Directive or be accompanied by such reference on the occasion of their official publication. The methods of making such a reference shall be laid down by the Member States.

2. Notwithstanding the provisions of Article 3(5) and until the future Directive on capital adequacy to cover market risks is brought into effect, the competent authorities shall include in consolidated supervision financial institutions which are principally exposed to market risks in accordance with methods to be determined by those authorities in the light of the particular nature of the risks involved.

3. Member States shall communicate to the Commission the texts of the main provisions of internal law which they adopt in the field governed by this Directive.

Article 10

1. Directive 83/350/EEC is hereby repealed with effect from 1 January 1993.

2. In the following provisions, the words "Directive 83/350/EEC" shall be replaced by "Directive 92/350/EEC":

— Article 5 of Directive 89/299/EEC,
— Articles 12(5), 13(3) and 15(2) and the fifth indent of the first subparagraph of Article 18(2) of Directive 89/646/EEC,
— Article 3(3) of Directive 89/647/EEC.

3. In Article 1, point 5, of Directive 89/646/EEC and the first indent of Article 2(1) of Directive 89/647/EEC, the definition of competent authorities shall be replaced by the following: "the national authorities which are empowered by law or regulation to supervise credit institutions."

Article 11

This Directive is addressed to the Member States.

Done at Luxembourg, 6 April 1992.

For the Council
The President
JOÃO PINHEIRO

COUNCIL DIRECTIVE* 89/299/EEC OF 17 APRIL 1989

on the own funds of credit institutions

THE COUNCIL OF THE EUROPEAN COMMUNITIES,

Having regard to the Treaty establishing the European Economic Community, and in particular the first and third sentences of Article 57(2) thereof,

Having regard to the proposal from the Commission,[1]

In co-operation with the European Parliament,[2]

Having regard to the opinion of the Economic and Social Committee,[3]

Whereas common basic standards for the own funds of credit institutions are a key factor in the creation of an internal market in the banking sector since own funds serve to ensure the continuity of credit institutions and to protect savings; whereas such harmonization will strengthen the supervision of credit institutions and contribute to further co-ordination in the banking sector, in particular the supervision of major risks and solvency ratios;

Whereas such standards must apply to all credit institutions authorized in the Community:

Whereas the own funds of a credit institution can serve to absorb losses which are not matched by a sufficient volume of profits; whereas the own funds also serve as an important yardstick for the competent authorities, in particular for the assessment of the solvency of credit institutions and for other prudential purposes;

Whereas credit institutions in a common banking market engage in direct competition with each other, and the definitions and standards pertaining to own funds must therefore be equivalent; whereas, to that end, the criteria for determining the composition of own funds must not be left solely to Member States; whereas the adoption of common basic standards will be in the best interests of the Community in that it will prevent distortions of competition and will strengthen the Community banking system;

Whereas the definition laid down in this Directive provides for a maximum of items and qualifying amounts, leaving it to the discretion of each Member State to use all or some of such items or to adopt lower ceilings for the qualifying amounts;

Whereas this Directive specifies the qualifying criteria for certain own funds items, and the Member States remain free to apply more stringent provisions;

Whereas at the initial stage common basic standards are defined in broad terms in order to encompass all the items making up own funds in the different Member States;

Whereas, according to the nature of the items making up own funds, this Directive distinguishes between, on the one hand, items contituting original own funds and, on the other, those constituting additional own funds;

Whereas it is recognized that due to the special nature of the fund for general banking risks, this item is to be included provisionally in own funds without limit; whereas, however, a decision on its final treatment will have to be taken as soon as possible after the implementation of the Directive; whereas that decision will have to take into account the results of discussions in international fora;

Whereas, to reflect the fact that items constituting additional own funds are not the same nature as those constituting original own funds, the amount of the former included in own funds

* OJ 1989, L124/16.
1. OJ No C243, 27 September 1986, p. 4 and OJ No. C32, 5 February 1988, p. 2.
2. OJ No C246, 14 September 1987, p. 72 and OJ No. C96, 17 April 1989.
3. OJ No C180, 8 July 1987, p. 51.

must not exceed the original own funds, whereas, moreover, the amount of certain items of additional own funds included must not exceed one-half of the original own funds;

Whereas, in order to avoid distortions of competition, public credit institutions must not include in their own funds guarantees granted them by the Member States or local authorities; whereas, however, the Kingdom of Belgium should be granted a transitional period up to 31 December 1994 in order to permit the institutions concerned to adjust to the new conditions by reforming their statutes;

Whereas whenever in the course of supervision it is necessary to determine the amount of the consolidated own funds of a group of credit institutions, that calculation shall be effected in accordance with Council Directive 83/350/EEC of 13 June 1983 on the supervision of credit institutions on a consolidated basis[4]; whereas that Directive leaves the Member States scope to interpret the technical details of its application, and that scope should be in keeping with the spirit of this Directive; whereas the former Directive is currently being revised to achieve greater harmonization;

Whereas the precise accounting technique to be used for the calculation of own funds must take account of the provisions of Council Directive 86/635/EEC of 8 December 1986 on the annual accounts and consolidated accounts of banks and other financial institutions,[5] which incorporates certain adaptations of the provisions of Council Directive 83/349/EEC of 13 June 1983 based on Article 54(3)(g) of the Treaty on consolidated accounts,[6] whereas pending transposition of the provisions of the abovementioned Directives into the national laws of the Member States, the use of a specific accounting technique for the calculation of own funds should be left to the discretion of the Member States;

Whereas this Directive forms part of the wider international effort to bring about approximation of the rules in force in major countries regarding the adequacy of own funds;

Whereas measures to comply with the definitions in this Directive must be adopted no later than the date of entry into force of the measures implementing the future directive harmonizing solvency ratios;

Whereas the Commission will draw up a report and periodically examine this Directive with the aim of tightening its provisions and thus achieving greater convergence on a common definition of own funds; whereas such convergence will allow the alignment of Community credit institution's own funds;

Whereas it will probably be necessary to make certain technical and terminological adjustments to the directive to take account of the rapid development of financial markets; whereas pending submission by the Commission of a proposal which takes account of the special characteristics of the banking sector and which permits the introduction of a more suitable procedure for the implementation of this Directive, the Council reserves the right to take such measures.

HAS ADOPTED THIS DIRECTIVE:

Article 1. Scope

1. Wherever a Member State lays down by law, regulation or administrative action a provision in implementation of Community legislation concerning the prudential supervision of an operative credit institution which uses the term or refers to the concept of own funds, it shall bring this term or concept into line with the definition given in the following Articles.

2. For the purposes of this Directive, "credit institutions" shall mean the institutions to which Directive 77/780/EEC,[7] as last amended by Directive 86/524/EEC,[8] applies.

Article 2. General principles

1. Subject to the limits imposed in Article 6, the unconsolidated own funds of credit institutions shall consist of the following items:

4. OJ No L193, 18 July 1983, p. 18.
5. OJ No L372, 31 December 1986, p. 1.
6. OJ No L193, 18 July 1983, p. 1.
7. OJ No L322, 17 December 1977, p. 30.
8. OJ No L309, 4 November 1986, p. 15.

(1) capital within the meaning of Article 22 of Directive 86/635/EEC, in so far as it has been paid up, plus share premium accounts but excluding cumulative preferential shares;

(2) reserves within the meaning of Article 23 of Directive 86/635/EEC and profits and losses brought forward as a result of the application of the final profit or loss. The Member States may permit inclusion of interim profits before a formal decision has been taken only if these profits have been verified by persons responsible for the auditing of the accounts and if it is proved to the satisfaction of the competent authorities that the amount thereof has been evaluated in accordance with the principles set out in Directive 86/635/EEC and is net of any foreseeable charge or dividend;

(3) revaluation reserves within the meaning of Article 33 of Council Directive 78/660/EEC of 25 July 1978 based on Article 54(3)(g) of the Treaty on the annual accounts of certain types of companies,[9] as last amended by Directive 84/569/EEC[10];

(4) funds for general banking risks within the meaning of Article 38 of Directive 86/635/EEC;

(5) value adjustments within the meaning of Article 37(2) of Directive 86/635/EEC;

(6) other items within the meaning of Article 3;

(7) the commitments of the members of credit institutions set up as co-operative societies and the joint and several commitments of the borrowers of certain institutions organized as funds, as referred to in Article 4(1);

(8) fixed-term cumulative preferential shares and subordinated loan capital as referred to in Article 4(3).

The following items shall be deducted in accordance with Article 6:

(9) own shares at book value held by a credit institution;

(10) intangible assets within the meaning of Article 4(9) ("assets") of Directive 86/635/EEC;

(11) material losses of the current financial year;

(12) holdings in other credit and financial institutions amounting to more than 10% of their capital, subordinated claims and the instruments referred to in Article 3 which a credit institution holds in respect of credit and financial institutions in which it has holdings exceeding 10% of the capital in each case.

   Where shares in another credit or financial institution are held temporarily for the purposes of a financial assistance operation designed to reorganize and save that institution, the supervisory authority may waive this provision;

(13) holdings in other credit and financial institutions of up to 10% of their capital, the subordinated claims and the instruments referred to in Article 3 which a credit institution holds in respect of credit and financial institutions other than those referred to in point 12 in respect of the amount of the total of such holdings, subordinated claims and instruments which exceed 10% of that credit institution's own funds calculated before the deduction of items 12 and 13.

Pending subsequent co-ordination of the provisions on consolidation, Member States may provide that, for the calculation of unconsolidated own funds, parent companies subject to supervision on a consolidated basis need not deduct their holdings in other credit institutions or financial institutions which are included in the consolidation. This provision shall apply to all the prudential rules harmonized by Community acts.

2. The concept of own funds as defined in points 1 to 8 of paragraph 1 embodies a maximum number of items and amounts. The use of those items and the fixing of lower ceilings, and the deduction of items other than those listed in items 9 to 13 of paragraph 1 shall be left to the discretion of the Member States. Member States shall nevertheless be obliged to consider increased convergence with a view to a common definition of own funds.

To that end, the Commission shall, not more than three years after the date referred to in Article 9(1), submit a report to the European Parliament and to the Council on the application of

9. OJ No L222, 14 August 1978, p. 11.
10. OJ No L314, 4 December 1984, p. 28.

this Directive, accompanied, where appropriate, by such proposals for amendment as it shall deem necessary. Within five years of the date referred to in Article 9(1), the Council shall, acting by qualified majority on a proposal from the Commission, in co-operation with the European Parliament and after consultation of the Economic and Social Committee, examine the definition of own funds with a view to the uniform application of the common definition.

3. The items listed in points 1 to 5 must be available to a credit institution for unrestricted and immediate use to cover risks or losses as soon as these occur. The amount must be net of any foreseeable tax charge at the moment of its calculation or be suitably adjusted in so far as such tax charges reduce the amount up to which these items may be applied to cover risks or losses.

Article 3. Other items referred to in Article 2(1)(6)

1. The concept of own funds used by a Member State may include other items provided that, whatever their legal or accounting designations might be, they have the following characteristics:

   (a) they are freely available to the credit institution to cover normal banking risks where revenue or capital losses have not yet been identified;
   (b) their existence is disclosed in internal accounting records;
   (c) their amount is determined by the management of the credit institution, verified by independent auditors, made known to the competent authorities and placed under the supervision of the latter. With regard to verification, internal auditing may be considered as provisionally meeting the aforementioned requirements until such time as the Community provisions making external auditing mandatory have been implemented.

2. Securities of indeterminate duration and other instruments that fulfil the following conditions may also be accepted as other items:

   (a) they may not be reimbursed on the bearer's initiative or without the prior agreement of the supervisory authority;
   (b) the debt agreement must provide for the credit institution to have the option of deferring the payment of interest on the debt;
   (c) the lender's claims on the credit institution must be wholly subordinated to those of all non-subordinated creditors;
   (d) the documents governing the issue of the securities must provide for debt and unpaid interest to be such as to absorb losses, whilst leaving the credit institution in a position to continue trading;
   (e) only fully paid-up amounts shall be taken into account.

To these may be added cumulative preferential shares other than those referred to in Article 2(1)(8).

Article 4

1. The commitments of the members of credit institutions set up as co-operative societies referred to in Article 2(1)(7), shall comprise those societies' uncalled capital, together with the legal commitments of the members of those co-operative societies to make additional non-refundable payments should the credit institution incur a loss, in which case it must be possible to demand those payments without delay.

The joint and several commitments of borrowers in the case of credit institutions organized as funds shall be treated in the same way as the preceding items.

All such items may be included in own funds in so far as they are counted as the own funds of institutions of this category under national law.

2. Member States shall not include in the own funds of public credit institutions guarantees which they or their local authorities extend to such entities.

However, the Kingdom of Belgium shall be exempt from this obligation until 31 December 1994.

3. Member States or the competent authorities may include fixed-term cumulative preferential shares referred to in Article 2(1)(8) and subordinated loan capital referred to in that provision in own funds, if binding agreements exist under which, in the event of the bankruptcy or liquidation of the credit institution, they rank after the claims of all other creditors and are not to be repaid until all other debts outstanding at the time have been settled.

Subordinated loan capital must also fulfil the following criteria:

(a) only fully paid-up funds may be taken into account;

(b) the loans involved must have an original maturity of at least five years, after which they may be repaid; if the maturity of the debt is not fixed, they shall be repayable only subject to five years' notice unless the loans are no longer considered as own funds or unless the prior consent of the competent authorities is specifically required for early repayment. The competent authorities may grant permission for the early repayment of such loans provided the request is made at the initiative of the issuer and the solvency of the credit institution in question is not affected;

(c) the extent to which they may rank as own funds must be gradually reduced during at least the last five years before the repayment date;

(d) the loan agreement must not include any clause providing that in specified circumstances, other than the winding up of the credit institution, the debt will become repayable before the agreed repayment date.

Article 5

Until further co-ordination of the provisions on consolidation, the following rules shall apply.

1. Where the calculation is to be made on a consolidated basis, the consolidated amounts relating to the items listed under Article 2(1) shall be used in accordance with the rules laid down in Directive 83/350/EEC. Moreover, the following may, when they are credit ("negative") items, be regarded as consolidated reserves for the calculation of own funds:

— any minority interests within the meaning of Article 21 of Directive 83/349/EEC, where the global integration method is used,

— the first consolidation difference within the meaning of Articles 19, 30 and 31 of Directive 83/349/EEC,

— the translation differences included in consolidated reserves in accordance with Article 39(6) of Directive 86/635/EEC,

— any difference resulting from the inclusion of certain participating interests in accordance with the method prescribed in Article 33 of Directive 83/349/EEC.

2. Where the above are debit ("positive") items, they must be deducted in the calculation of consolidated own funds.

Article 6. Deductions and limits

1. The items referred to in Article 2(1), points 3 and 5 to 8, shall be subject to the following limits:

(a) the total of items 3 and 5 to 8 may not exceed a maximum of 100% of items 1 plus 2 minus 9, 10 and 11;

(b) the total of items 7 and 8 may not exceed a maximum of 50% of items 1 plus 2 minus 9, 10, and 11;

(c) the total of items 12 and 13 shall be deducted from the total of all items.

2. The item referred to in Article 2(1)(4) shall constitute a separate category. Provisionally, it shall be included in own funds without limit, but shall not be included when the basis of the limit for the items referred to in points 3 and 5 to 8 is fixed. Within six months of the implementation of this Directive the Commission shall, in accordance with the procedure provided for in Article 8, propose the final treatment for this item either in original own funds or in additional own funds.

3. The limits referred to in paragraph 1 must be complied with as from the date of the entry into force of the implementing measures for the Council Directive on a solvency ratio for credit institutions and by 1 January 1993 at the latest.

Credit institutions exceeding those limits must gradually reduce the extent to which the items referred to in Article 2(1), points 3 and 5 to 8, are taken into account so that they comply with those limits before the aforementioned date.

4. The competent authorities may authorize credit institutions to exceed the limit laid down in paragraph 1 in temporary and exceptional circumstances.

Article 7

Compliance with the conditions laid down in Articles 2 to 6 must be proved to the satisfaction of the competent authorities.

Article 8

Without prejudice to the report referred to in Article 2(2), second sub-paragraph, technical adaptions deemed to be necessary to this Directive to:

- clarify the definitions to ensure uniform application of the said Directive throughout the Community,
- clarify the definitions to take account, in implementing the said Directive, of developments on the financial markets,
- bring the terminology and wording of the definitions into line with that of subsequent acts concerning credit institutions and related areas,

shall be adopted by the Council acting by a qualified majority on a Commission proposal.

Article 9

1. Member States shall bring into force the laws, regulations and administrative provisions necessary for them to comply with this Directive no later than the date laid down for the entry into force of the implementing measures of the Council Directive on a solvency ratio for credit institutions, and by 1 January 1993 at the latest. They shall forthwith inform the Commission thereof.

2. Member States shall communicate to the Commission the texts of the main provisions of national law which they adopt in the field governed by this Directive.

3. The communication referred to in paragraph 2 must also include a statement, accompanied by an explanatory text, notifying the Commission of the specific provisions adopted and the items selected by the Member States' respective competent authorities as comprising own funds.

Article 10

This Directive is addressed to the Member States.

Done at Luxembourg, 17 April 1989.

For the Council
The President
C. SOLCHAGA CATALAN

SECOND COUNCIL DIRECTIVE* 89/646/EEC OF 15 DECEMBER 1989

on the co-ordination of laws, regulations and administrative provisions relating to the taking up and pursuit of the business of credit institutions and amending Directive 77/780/EEC as corrected**

THE COUNCIL OF THE EUROPEAN COMMUNITIES,

Having regard to the Treaty establishing the European Economic Community, and in particular the first and third sentences of Article 57(2) thereof,

Having regard to the proposal from the Commission,[1]

In co-operation with the European Parliament,[2]

Having regard to the opinion of the Economic and Social Committee,[3]

Whereas this Directive is to constitute the essential instrument for the achievement of the internal market, a course determined by the Single European Act and set out in timetable form in the Commission's White Paper, from the point of view of both the freedom of establishment and the freedom to provide financial services, in the field of credit institutions;

Whereas this Directive will join the body of Community legislation already enacted, in particular the first Council Directive 77/780/EEC of 12 December 1977 on the co-ordination of laws, regulations and administrative provisions relating to the taking up and pursuit of the business of credit institutions,[4] as last amended by Directive 86/524/EEC,[5] Council Directive 83/350/EEC of 13 June 1983 on the supervision of credit institutions on a consolidated basis,[6] Council Directive 86/635/EEC of 8 December 1986 on the annual and consolidated accounts of banks and other financial institutions[7] and Council Directive 89/299/EEC of 17 April 1989 on the own funds of credit institutions[8];

Whereas the Commission has adopted recommendations 87/62/EEC on large exposures of credit institutions[9] and 87/63/EEC concerning the introduction of deposit-guarantee schemes[10];

Whereas the approach which has been adopted is to achieve only the essential harmonization necessary and sufficient to secure the mutual recognition of authorization and of prudential supervision systems, making possible the granting of a single licence recognized throughout the Community and the application of the principle of home Member State prudential supervision;

Whereas, in this context, this Directive can be implemented only simultaneously with specific Community legislation dealing with the additional harmonization of technical matters relating to own funds and solvency ratios;

---

* OJ 1989, L386/1.
** OJ 1990, L83/128 and OJ 1990, L158/87.
1. OJ No C84, 31 March 1988, p. 1.
2. OJ No C96, 17 April 1989, p. 33 and Decision of 22 November 1989.
3. OJ No C318, 17 December 1988, p. 42.
4. OJ No L322, 17 December 1977, p. 30.
5. OJ No L309, 4 November 1986, p. 15.
6. OJ No L193, 18 July 1983, p. 18.
7. OJ No L372, 31 December 1986, p. 1.
8. OJ No L124, 5 May 1989, p. 16.
9. OJ No L33, 4 February 1987, p. 10.
10. OJ No L33, 4 February 1987, p. 16.

Whereas, moreover, the harmonization of the conditions relating to the reorganization and winding-up of credit institutions is also proceeding;

Whereas the arrangements necessary for the supervision of the liquidity, market, interest-rate and foreign-exchange risks run by credit institutions will also have to be harmonized;

Whereas the principles of mutual recognition and of home Member State control require the competent authorities of each Member State not to grant authorization or to withdraw it where factors such as the activities programme, the geographical distribution or the activities actually carried on make it quite clear that a credit institution has opted for the legal system of one Member State for the purpose of evading the stricter standards in force in another Member State in which it intends to carry on or carries on the greater part of its activities; whereas, for the purposes of this Directive, a credit institution shall be deemed to be situated in the Member State in which it has its registered office; whereas the Member States must require that the head office be situated in the same Member State as the registered office;

Whereas the home Member State may also establish rules stricter than those laid down in Articles 4, 5, 11, 12 and 16 for institutions authorized by its competent authorities;

Whereas responsibility for supervising the financial soundness of a credit institution, and in particular its solvency, will rest with the competent authorities of its home Member State; whereas the host Member State's competent authorities will retain responsibility for the supervision of liquidity and monetary policy; whereas the supervision of market risk must be the subject of close co-operation between the competent authorities of the home and host Member States;

Whereas the harmonization of certain financial and investment services will be effected, where the need exists, by specific Community instruments, with the intention, in particular, of protecting consumers and investors; whereas the Commission has proposed measures for the harmonization of mortgage credit in order, *inter alia*, to allow mutual recognition of the financial techniques peculiar to that sphere;

Whereas, by virtue of mutual recognition, the approach chosen permits credit institutions authorized in their home Member States to carry on, throughout the Community, any or all of the activities listed in the Annex by establishing branches or by providing services;

Whereas the carrying-on of activities not listed in the Annex shall enjoy the right of establishment and the freedom to provide services under the general provisions of the Treaty;

Whereas it is appropriate, however, to extend mutual recognition to the activities listed in the Annex when they are carried on by financial institutions which are subsidiaries of credit institutions, provided that such subsidiaries are covered by the consolidated supervision of their parent undertakings and meet certain strict conditions;

Whereas the host Member State may, in connection with the exercise of the right of establishment and the freedom to provide services, require compliance with specific provisions of its own national laws or regulations on the part of institutions not authorized as credit institutions in their home Member States and with regard to activities not listed in the Annex provided that, on the one hand, such provisions are compatible with Community law and are intended to protect the general good and that, on the other hand, such institutions or such activities are not subject to equivalent rules under the legislation or regulations of their home Member States;

Whereas the Member States must ensure that there are no obstacles to carrying on activities receiving mutual recognition in the same manner as in the home Member State, as long as the latter do not conflict with legal provisions protecting the general good in the host Member State;

Whereas the abolition of the authorization requirement with respect to the branches of Community credit institutions once the harmonization in progress has been completed necessitates the abolition of endowment capital; whereas Article 6(2) constitutes a first transitional step in this direction, but does not, however, affect the Kingdom of Spain or the Portuguese Republic, as provided for in the Act concerning the conditions of those States' accession to the Community;

Whereas there is a necessary link between the objective of this Directive and the liberalization of capital movements being brought about by the other Community legislation; whereas in any case the measures regarding the liberalization of banking services must be in harmony with the measures liberalizing capital movements; whereas where the Member States may, by virtue of Council Directive 88/361/EEC of 24 June 1988 for the implementation of Article 67 of the

Treaty,[11] invoke safeguard clauses in respect of capital movements, they may suspend the provision of banking services to the extent necessary for the implementation of the abovementioned safeguard clauses;

Whereas the procedures established in Directive 77/780/EEC, in particular with regard to the authorization of branches of credit institutions authorized in third countries, will continue to apply to such institutions; whereas those branches will not enjoy the freedom to provide services under the second paragraph of Article 59 of the Treaty or the freedom of establishment in Member States other than those in which they are established; whereas, however, requests for the authorization of subsidiaries or of the acquisition of holdings made by undertakings governed by the laws of third countries are subject to a procedure intended to ensure that Community credit institutions receive reciprocal treatment in the third countries in question;

Whereas the authorizations granted to credit institutions by the competent national authorities pursuant to this Directive will have Community-wide, and no longer merely nationwide, application, and whereas existing reciprocity clauses will henceforth have no effect; whereas a flexible procedure is therefore needed to make it possible to assess reciprocity on a Community basis; whereas the aim of this procedure is not to close the Community's financial markets but rather, as the Community intends to keep its financial markets open to the rest of the world, to improve the liberalization of the global financial markets in other third countries; whereas, to that end, this Directive provides for procedures for negotiating with third countries and, as a last resort, for the possibility of taking measures involving the suspension of new applications for authorization or the restriction of new authorizations;

Whereas the smooth operation of the internal banking market will require not only legal rules but also close and regular co-operation between the competent authorities of the Member States; whereas for the consideration of problems concerning individual credit institutions the Contact Committee set up between the banking supervisory authorities, referred to in the final recital of Directive 77/780/EEC, remains the most appropriate forum; whereas that Committee is a suitable body for the mutual exchange of information provided for in Article 7 of that Directive;

Whereas that mutual information procedure will not in any case replace the bilateral collaboration established by Article 7 of Directive 77/780/EEC; whereas the competent host Member State authorities can, without prejudice to their powers of control proper, continue either, in an emergency, on their own initiative or following the initiative of the competent home Member State authorities to verify that the activities of a credit institution established within their territories comply with the relevant laws and with the principles of sound administrative and accounting procedures and adequate internal control;

Whereas technical modifications to the detailed rules laid down in this Directive may from time to time be necessary to take account of new developments in the banking sector; whereas the Commission shall accordingly make such modifications as are necessary, after consulting the Banking Advisory Committee, within the limits of the implementing powers conferred on the Commission by the Treaty; whereas that Committee shall act as a "Regulatory" Committee, according to the rules of procedure laid down in Article 2, procedure III, variant (b), of Council Decision 87/373/EEC of 13 July 1987 laying down the procedures for the exercise of implementing powers conferred on the Commission,[12]

HAS ADOPTED THIS DIRECTIVE:

TITLE I. DEFINITIONS AND SCOPE

Article 1

For the purposes of this Directive:

1. "credit institution" shall mean a credit institution as defined in the first indent of Article 1 of Directive 77/780/EEC;

2. "authorization" shall mean authorization as defined in the second indent of Article 1 of Directive 77/780/EEC;

11. OJ No L178, 8 July 1988, p. 5.
12. OJ No L197, 18 July 1987, p. 33.

3. "branch" shall mean a place of business which forms a legally dependent part of a credit institution and which carries out directly all or some of the transactions inherent in the business of credit institutions; any number of places of business set up in the same Member State by a credit institution with headquarters in another Member State shall be regarded as a single branch;

4. "own funds" shall mean own funds as defined in Directive 89/299/EEC;

5. "competent authorities" shall mean competent authorities as defined in Article 1 of Directive 83/350/EEC;

6. "financial institution" shall mean an undertaking other than a credit institution the principal activity of which is to acquire holdings or to carry on one or more of the activities listed in points 2 to 12 in the Annex;

7. "home Member State" shall mean the Member State in which a credit institution has been authorized in accordance with Article 3 of Directive 77/780/EEC;

8. "host Member State" shall mean the Member State in which a credit institution has a branch or in which it provides services;

9. "control" shall mean the relationship between a parent undertaking and a subsidiary, as defined in Article 1 of Directive 83/349/EEC,[13] or a similar relationship between any natural or legal person and an undertaking;

10. "qualifying holding" shall mean a direct or indirect holding in an undertaking which represents 10% or more of the capital or of the voting rights or which makes it possible to exercise a significant influence over the management of the undertaking in which a holding subsists.

For the purposes of this definition, in the context of Articles 5 and 11 and of the other levels of holding referred to in Article 11, the voting rights referred to in Article 7 of Directive 88/627/EEC[14] shall be taken into consideration;

11. "initial capital" shall mean capital as defined in Article 2(1)(1) and (2) of Directive 89/299/EEC;

12. "parent undertakings" shall mean a parent undertaking as defined in Articles 1 and 2 of Directive 83/349/EEC;

13. "subsidiary" shall mean a subsidiary undertaking as defined in Articles 1 and 2 of Directive 83/349/EEC; any subsidiary of a subsidiary undertaking shall also be regarded as a subsidiary of the parent undertaking which is at the head of those undertakings;

14. "solvency ratio" shall mean the solvency coefficient of credit institutions calculated in accordance with Directive 89/647/EEC.[15]

Article 2

1. This Directive shall apply to all credit institutions.

2. It shall not apply to the institutions referred to in Article 2(2) of Directive 77/780/EEC.

3. A credit institution which, as defined in Article 2(4)(a) of Directive 77/780/EEC, is affiliated to a central body in the same Member State may be exempted from the provisions of Articles 4, 10 and 12 of this Directive provided that, without prejudice to the application of those provisions to the central body, the whole as constituted by the central body together with its affiliated institutions is subject to the abovementioned provisions on a consolidated basis.

In cases of exemption, Articles 6 and 18 to 21 shall apply to the whole as constituted by the central body together with its affiliated institutions.

Article 3

The Member States shall prohibit persons or undertakings that are not credit institutions from carrying on the business of taking deposits or other repayable funds from the public. This prohibition shall not apply to the taking of deposits or other funds repayable by a Member State or by a Member State's regional or local authorities or by public international bodies of which one or more Member States are members or to cases expressly covered by national or Community legislation, provided that those activities are subject to regulations and controls intended to protect depositors and investors and applicable to those cases.

13. OJ No L193, 18 July 1983, p. 1.
14. OJ No L348, 17 December 1988, p. 62.
15. See OJ 1989, L386/14.

TITLE II. HARMONIZATION OF AUTHORIZATION CONDITIONS

Article 4

1. The competent authorities shall not grant authorization in cases where initial capital is less than ECU 5 million.

2. The Member States shall, however, have the option of granting authorization to particular categories of credit institutions the initial capital of which is less than that prescribed in paragraph 1. In such cases:

    (a) the initial capital shall not be less than ECU 1 million;

    (b) the Member States concerned must notify the Commission of their reasons for making use of the option provided for in this paragraph;

    (c) when the list referred to in Article 3(7) of Directive 77/780/EEC is published, the name of each credit institution that does not have the minimum capital prescribed in paragraph 1 shall be annotated to that effect;

    (d) within five years of the date referred to in Article 24(1), the Commission shall draw up a report on the application of this paragraph in the Member States, for the attention of the Banking Advisory Committee referred to in Article 11 of Directive 77/780/EEC.

Article 5

The competent authorities shall not grant authorization for the taking-up of the business of credit institutions before they have been informed of the identities of the shareholders or members, whether direct or indirect, natural or legal persons, that have qualifying holdings, and of the amounts of those holdings.

The competent authorities shall refuse authorization if, taking into account the need to ensure the sound and prudent management of a credit institution, they are not satisfied as to the suitability of the abovementioned shareholders or members.

Article 6

1. Host Member States may no longer require authorization, as provided for in Article 4 of Directive 77/780/EEC, or endowment capital for branches of credit institutions authorized in other Member States. The establishment and supervision of such branches shall be effected as prescribed in Articles 13, 19 and 21 of this Directive.

2. Until the entry into force of the provisions implementing paragraph 1, host Member States may not, as a condition of the authorization of branches of credit institutions, authorized in other Member States, require initial endowment capital exceeding 50% of the initial capital required by national rules for the authorization of credit institutions of the same nature.

3. Credit institutions shall be entitled to the free use of the funds no longer required pursuant to paragraphs 1 and 2.

Article 7

There must be prior consultation with the competent authorities of the other Member State involved on the authorization of a credit institution which is:

    — a subsidiary of a credit institution authorized in another Member State, or

    — a subsidiary of the parent undertaking of a credit institution authorized in another Member State, or

    — controlled by the same persons, whether natural or legal, as control a credit institution authorized in another Member State.

TITLE III. RELATIONS WITH THIRD COUNTRIES

Article 8

The competent authorities of the Member States shall inform the Commission:

    (a) of any authorization of a direct or indirect subsidiary one or more parent undertakings of which are governed by the laws of a third country. The Commission shall inform the Banking Advisory Committee accordingly;

   (b) whenever such a parent undertaking acquires a holding in a Community credit institution such that the latter would become its subsidiary. The Commission shall inform the Banking Advisory Committee accordingly.

When authorization is granted to the direct or indirect subsidiary of one or more parent undertakings governed by the law of third countries, the structure of the group shall be specified in the notification which the competent authorities shall address to the Commission in accordance with Article 3(7) of Directive 77/780/EEC.

Article 9

1. The Member States shall inform the Commission of any general difficulties encountered by their credit institutions in establishing themselves or carrying on banking activities in a third country.

2. Initially no later than six months before the application of this Directive and thereafter periodically, the Commission shall draw up a report examining the treatment accorded to Community credit institutions in third countries, in the terms referred to in paragraphs 3 and 4, as regards establishment and the carrying-on of banking activities, and the acquisition of holdings in third-country credit institutions. The Commission shall submit those reports to the Council, together with any appropriate proposals.

3. Whenever it appears to the Commission, either on the basis of the reports referred to in paragraph 2 or on the basis of other information, that a third country is not granting Community credit institutions effective market access comparable to that granted by the Community to credit institutions from that third country, the Commission may submit proposals to the Council for the appropriate mandate for negotiation with a view to obtaining comparable competitive opportunities for Community credit institutions. The Council shall decide by a qualified majority.

4. Whenever it appears to the Commission, either on the basis of the reports referred to in paragraph 2 or on the basis of other information that Community credit institutions in a third country do not receive national treatment offering the same competitive opportunities as are available to domestic credit institutions and the conditions of effective market access are not fulfilled, the Commission may initiate negotiations in order to remedy the situation.

In the circumstances described in the first subparagraph, it may also be decided at any time, and in addition to initiating negotiations, in accordance with the procedure laid down in Article 22(2), that the competent authorities of the Member States must limit or suspend their decisions regarding requests pending at the moment of the decision or future requests for authorizations and the acquisition of holdings by direct or indirect parent undertakings governed by the laws of the third country in question. The duration of the measures referred to may not exceed three months.

Before the end of that three-month period, and in the light of the results of the negotiations, the Council may, acting on a proposal from the Commission, decide by a qualified majority whether the measures shall be continued.

Such limitations or suspension may not apply to the setting up of subsidiaries by credit institutions or their subsidiaries duly authorized in the Community, or to the acquisition of holdings in Community credit institutions by such institutions or subsidiaries.

5. Whenever it appears to the Commission that one of the situations described in paragraphs 3 and 4 obtains, the Member States shall inform it at its request:

   (a) of any request for the authorization of a direct or indirect subsidiary one or more parent undertakings of which are governed by the laws of the third country in question;

   (b) whenever they are informed in accordance with Article 11 that such an undertaking proposes to acquire a holding in a Community credit institution such that the latter would become its subsidiary.

This obligation to provide information shall lapse whenever an agreement is reached with the third country referred to in paragraph 3 or 4 or when the measures referred to in the second and third subparagraphs of paragraph 4 cease to apply.

6. Measures taken pursuant to this Article shall comply with the Community's obligations

under any international agreements, bilateral or multilateral, governing the taking-up and pursuit of the business of credit institutions.

TITLE IV. HARMONIZATION OF THE CONDITIONS GOVERNING PURSUIT OF THE BUSINESS OF CREDIT INSTITUTIONS

Article 10

1. A credit institution's own funds may not fall below the amount of initial capital required pursuant to Article 4 at the time of its authorization.

2. The Member States may decide that credit institutions already in existence when the Directive is implemented, the own funds of which do not attain the levels prescribed for initial capital in Article 4, may continue to carry on their activities. In that event, their own funds may not fall below the highest level reached after the date of the notification of this Directive.

3. If control of a credit institution falling within the category referred to in paragraph 2 is taken by a natural or legal person other than the person who controlled the institution previously, the own funds of that institution must attain at least the level prescribed for initial capital in Article 4.

4. However, in certain specific circumstances and with the consent of the competent authorities, where there is a merger of two or more credit institutions falling within the category referred to in paragraph 2, the own funds of the institution resulting from the merger may not fall below the total own funds of the merged institutions at the time of the merger, as long as the appropriate levels pursuant to Article 4 have not been attained.

5. However, if, in the cases referred to in paragraphs 1, 2 and 4, the own funds should be reduced, the competent authorities may, where the circumstances justify it, allow an institution a limited period in which to rectify its situation or cease its activities.

Article 11

1. The Member States shall require any natural or legal person who proposes to acquire, directly or indirectly, a qualifying holding in a credit institution first to inform the competent authorities, telling them of the size of the intended holding. Such a person must likewise inform the competent authorities if he proposes to increase his qualifying holdings so that the proportion of the voting rights or of the capital held by him would reach or exceed 20%, 33% or 50% or so that the credit institution would become his subsidiary.

Without prejudice to the provisions of paragraph 2 the competent authorities shall have a maximum of three months from the date of the notification provided for in the first subparagraph to oppose such a plan if, in view of the need to ensure sound and prudent management of the credit institution, they are not satisfied as to the suitability of the person referred to in the first subparagraph. If they do not oppose the plan referred to in the first subparagraph, they may fix a maximum period for its implementation.

2. If the acquirer of the holdings referred to in paragraph 1 is a credit institution authorized in another Member State or the parent undertaking of a credit institution authorized in another Member State or a natural or legal person controlling a credit institution authorized in another Member State and if, as a result of that acquisition, the institution in which the acquirer proposes to acquire a holding would become a subsidiary or subject to the control of the acquirer, the assessment of the acquisition must be the subject of the prior consultation referred to in Article 7.

3. The Member States shall require any natural or legal person who proposes to dispose, directly or indirectly, of a qualifying holding in a credit institution first to inform the competent authorities, telling them of the size of his intended holding. Such a person must likewise inform the competent authorities if he proposes to reduce his qualifying holding so that the proportion of the voting rights or of the capital held by him would fall below 20%, 33% or 50% or so that the credit institution would cease to be his subsidiary.

4. On becoming aware of them, credit institutions shall inform the competent authorities of any acquisitions or disposals of holdings in their capital that cause holdings to exceed or fall below one of the thresholds referred to in paragraphs 1 and 3.

They shall also, at least once a year, inform them of the names of shareholders and members possessing qualifying holdings and the sizes of such holdings as shown, for example, by the information received at the annual general meetings of shareholders and members or as a result of compliance with the regulations relating to companies listed on stock exchanges.

5. The Member States shall require that, where the influence exercised by the persons referred to in paragraph 1 is likely to operate to the detriment of the prudent and sound management of the institution, the competent authorities shall take appropriate measures to put an end to that situation. Such measures may consist for example in injunctions, sanctions against directors and managers, or the suspension of the exercise of the voting rights attaching to the shares held by the shareholders or members in question.

Similar measures shall apply to natural or legal persons failing to comply with the obligation to provide prior information, as laid down in paragraph 1. If a holding is acquired despite the opposition of the competent authorities, the Member States shall, regardless of any other sanctions to be adopted, provide either for exercise of the corresponding voting rights to be suspended, or for the nullity of votes cast or for the possibility of their annulment.

Article 12

1. No credit institution may have a qualifying holding the amount of which exceeds 15% of its own funds in an undertaking which is neither a credit institution, nor a financial institution, nor an undertaking carrying on an activity referred to in the second subparagraph of Article 43(2)(f) of Directive 86/635/EEC.

2. The total amount of a credit institution's qualifying holdings in undertakings other than credit institutions, financial institutions or undertakings carying on activities referred to in the second subparagraph of Article 43(2)(f) of Directive 86/635/EEC may not exceed 60% of its own funds.

3. The Member States need not apply the limits laid down in paragraphs 1 and 2 to holdings in insurance companies as defined in Directive 73/239/EEC,[16] as last amended by Directive 88/357/EEC,[17] and Directive 79/267/EEC,[18] as last amended by the Act of Accession of 1985.

4. Shares held temporarily during a financial reconstruction or rescue operation or during the normal course of underwriting or in an institution's own name or behalf of others shall not be counted as qualifying holdings for the purpose of calculating the limits laid down in paragraphs 1 and 2. Shares which are not financial fixed assets as defined in Article 35(2) of Directive 86/635/EEC shall not be included.

5. The limits laid down in paragraphs 1 and 2 may be exceeded only in exceptional circumstances. In such cases, however, the competent authorities shall require a credit institution either to increase its own funds or to take other equivalent measures.

6. Compliance with the limits laid down in paragraphs 1 and 2 shall be ensured by means of supervision and monitoring on a consolidated basis in accordance with Directive 83/350/EEC.

7. Credit institutions which, on the date of entry into force of the provisions implementing this Directive, exceed the limits laid down in paragraphs 1 and 2 shall have a period of 10 years from that date in which to comply with them.

8. The Member States may provide that the competent authorities shall not apply the limits laid down in paragraph 1 and 2 if they provide that 100% of the amounts by which a credit institution's qualifying holdings exceed those limits must be covered by own funds and that the latter shall not be included in the calculation of the solvency ratio. If both the limits laid down in paragraphs 1 and 2 are exceeded, the amount to be covered by own funds shall be the greater of the excess amounts.

Article 13

1. The prudential supervision of a credit institution, including that of the activities it carries on in accordance with Article 18, shall be the responsibility of the competent authorities of the home Member State, without prejudice to those provisions of this Directive which give responsibility to the authorities of the host Member State.

2. Home Member State competent authorities shall require that every credit institution have sound administrative and accounting procedures and adequate internal control mechanisms.

16. OJ No L228, 16 August 1973, p. 3.
17. OJ No L172, 4 July 1988, p. 1.
18. OJ No L63, 13 March 1979, p. 1.

3. Paragraphs 1 and 2 shall not prevent supervision on a consolidated basis pursuant to Directive 83/350/EEC.

Article 14

1. In Article 7(1) of Directive 77/780/EEC, the end of the second sentence is hereby replaced by the following: "and all information likely to facilitate the monitoring of such institutions, in particular with regard to liquidity, solvency, deposit guarantees, the limiting of large exposures, administrative and accounting procedures and internal control mechanisms."

2. Host Member States shall retain responsibility in co-operation with the competent authorities of the home Member State for the supervision of the liquidity of the branches of credit institutions pending further co-ordination. Without prejudice to the measures necessary for the reinforcement of the European Monetary System, host Member States shall retain complete responsibility for the measures resulting from the implementation of their monetary policies. Such measures may not provide for the discriminatory or restrictive treatment based on the fact that a credit institution is authorized in another Member State.

3. Without prejudice to further co-ordination of the measures designed to supervise the risks arising out of open positions on markets, where such risks result from transactions carried out on the financial markets of other Member States, the competent authorities of the latter shall collaborate with the competent authorities of the home Member State to ensure that the institutions concerned take steps to cover those risks.

Article 15

1. Host Member States shall provide that, where a credit institution authorized in another Member State carries on its activities through a branch, the competent authorities of the home Member State may, after having first informed the competent authorities of the host Member State, carry out themselves or through the intermediary of persons they appoint for that purpose on-the-spot verification of the information referred to in Article 7(1) of Directive 77/780/EEC.

2. The competent authorities of the home Member State may also, for purposes of the verification of branches, have recourse to one of the other procedures laid down in Article 5(4) of Directive 83/350/EEC.

3. This Article shall not affect the right of the competent authorities of the host Member State to carry out, in the discharge of their responsibilities under this Directive, on-the-spot verifications of branches established within their territory.

Article 16

Article 12 of Directive 77/780/EEC is hereby replaced by the following:

"Article 12

1. The Member States shall provide that all persons working or who have worked for the competent authorities, as well as auditors or experts acting on behalf of the competent authorities, shall be bound by the obligation of professional secrecy. This means that no confidential information which they may receive in the course of their duties may be divulged to any person or authority whatsoever, except in summary or collective form, such that individual institutions cannot be identified, without prejudice to cases covered by criminal law.

Nevertheless, where a credit institution has been declared bankrupt or is being compulsorily wound up, confidential information which does not concern third parties involved in attempts to rescue that credit institution may be divulged in civil or commercial proceedings.

2. Paragraph 1 shall not prevent the competent authorities of the various Member States from exchanging information in accordance with the Directives applicable to credit institutions. That information shall be subject to the conditions of professional secrecy indicated in paragraph 1.

3. Member States may conclude co-operation agreements, providing for exchanges of information, with the competent authorities of third countries only if the information

disclosed is subject to guarantees of professional secrecy at least equivalent to those referred to in this Article.

4. Competent authorities receiving confidential information under paragraphs 1 or 2 may use it only in the course of their duties:

— to check that the conditions governing the taking-up of the business of credit institutions are met and to facilitate monitoring, on a non-consolidated or consolidated basis, of the conduct of such business, especially with regard to the monitoring of liquidity, solvency, large exposures, and administrative and accounting procedures and internal control mechanisms, or
— to impose sanctions, or
— in an administrative appeal against a decision of the competent authority, or
— in court proceedings initiated pursuant to Article 15 or to special provisions provided for in the Directives adopted in the field of credit institutions.

5. Paragraphs 1 and 4 shall not preclude the exchange of information within a Member State, where there are two or more competent authorities in the same Member State, or between Member States, between competent authorities and:

— authorities entrusted with the public duty of supervising other financial organizations and insurance companies and the authorities responsible for the supervision of financial markets,
— bodies involved in the liquidation and bankruptcy of credit institutions and in other similar procedures,
— persons responsible for carrying out statutory audits of the accounts of credit institutions and other financial institutions,

in the discharge of their supervisory functions, and the disclosure to bodies which administer deposit-guarantee schemes of information necessary to the exercise of their functions. The information received shall be subject to the conditions of professional secrecy indicated in paragraph 1.

6. Nor shall the provisions of this Article preclude a competent authority from disclosing to those central banks which do not supervise credit institutions individually such information as they may need to act as monetary authorities. Information received in this context shall be subject to the conditions of professional secrecy indicated in paragraph 1.

7. In addition, notwithstanding the provisions referred to in paragraphs 1 and 4, the Member States may, by virtue of provisions laid down by law, authorize the disclosure of certain information to other departments of their central government administrations responsible for legislation on the supervision of credit institutions, financial institutions, investment services and insurance companies and to inspectors acting on behalf of those departments.

However, such disclosures may be made only where necessary for reasons of prudential control.

However, the Member States shall provide that information received under paragraphs 2 and 5 and that obtained by means of the on-the-spot verification referred to in Article 15(1) and (2) of Directive 89/646/EEC[19] may never be disclosed in the cases referred to in this paragraph except with the express consent of the competent authorities which disclosed the information or of the competent authorities of the Member State in which on-the-spot verification was carried out.''

Article 17

Without prejudice to the procedures for the withdrawal of authorizations and the provisions of criminal law, the Member States shall provide that their respective competent authorities may, as against credit institutions or those who effectively control the business of credit institutions which breach laws, regulations or administrative provisions concerning the supervision or pursuit of their activities, adopt or impose in respect of them penalties or measures aimed specifically at ending observed breaches or the causes of such breaches.

19. OJ No L386, 30 December 1989, p. 1.

TITLE V. PROVISIONS RELATING TO THE FREEDOM OF ESTABLISHMENT AND THE FREEDOM TO PROVIDE SERVICES

Article 18

1. The Member States shall provide that the activities listed in the Annex may be carried on within their territories, in accordance with Articles 19 to 21, either by the establishment of a branch or by way of the provision of services, by any credit institution authorized and supervised by the competent authorities of another Member State, in accordance with this Directive, provided that such activities are covered by the authorization.

2. The Member States shall also provide that the activities listed in the Annex may be carried on within their territories, in accordance with Articles 19 to 21, either by the establishment of a branch or by way of the provision of services, by any financial institution from another Member State, whether a subsidiary of a credit institution or the jointly-owned subsidiary of two or more credit institutions, the memorandum and articles of association of which permit the carrying on of those activities and which fulfils each of the following conditions:

— the parent undertaking or undertakings must be authorized as credit institutions in the Member State by the law of which the subsidiary is governed,
— the activities in question must actually be carried on within the territory of the same Member State,
— the parent undertaking or undertakings must hold 90% or more of the voting rights attaching to shares in the capital of the subsidiary,
— the parent undertaking or undertakings must satisfy the competent authorities regarding the prudent management of the subsidiary and must have declared, with the consent of the relevant home Member State competent authorities, that they jointly and severally guarantee the commitments entered into by the subsidiary,
— the subsidiary must be effectively included, for the activities in question in particular, in the consolidated supervision of the parent undertaking, or of each of the parent undertakings, in accordance with Directive 83/350/EEC, in particular for the calculation of the solvency ratio, for the control of large exposures and for purposes of the limitation of holdings provided for in Article 12 of this Directive.

Compliance with these conditions must be verified by the competent authorities of the home Member State and the latter must supply the subsidiary with a certificate of compliance with which must form part of the notification referred to in Articles 19 and 20.

The competent authorities of the home Member State shall ensure the supervision of the subsidiary in accordance with Articles 10(1), 11, 13, 14(1), 15 and 17 of this Directive and Articles 7(1) and 12 of Directive 77/780/EEC.

The provisions mentioned in this paragraph shall be applicable to subsidiaries, subject to the necessary modifications. In particular, the words "credit institution" should be read as "financial institution fulfilling the conditions laid down in Article 18(2)" and the word "authorization" as "memorandum and articles of association."

The second paragraph of Article 19(3) shall read:

"The home Member State competent authorities shall also communicate the amount of own funds of the subsidiary financial institution and the consolidated solvency ratio of the credit institution which is its parent undertaking."

If a financial institution eligible under this paragraph should cease to fulfil any of the conditions imposed, the home Member State shall notify the competent authorities of the host Member State and the activities carried on by that institution in the host Member State shall become subject to the legislation of the host Member State.

Article 19

1. A credit institution wishing to establish a branch within the territory of another Member State shall notify the competent authorities of its home Member State.

2. The Member State shall require every credit institution wishing to establish a branch in another Member State to provide the following information when effecting the notification referred to in paragraph 1:

(a) the Member State within the territory of which it plans to establish a branch;
(b) a programme of operations setting out *inter alia* the types of business envisaged and the structural organization of the branch;
(c) the address in the host Member State from which documents may be obtained;
(d) the names of those responsible for the management of the branch.

3. Unless the competent authorities of the home Member State have reason to doubt the adequacy of the administrative structure or the financial situation of the credit institution, taking into account the activities envisaged, they shall within three months of receipt of the information referred to in paragraph 2 communicate that information to the competent authorities of the host Member State and shall inform the institution concerned accordingly.

The home Member State competent authorities shall also communicate the amount of own funds and the solvency ratio of the credit institution and, pending subsequent co-ordination, details of any deposit-guarantee scheme which is intended to ensure the protection of depositors in the branch.

Where the competent authorities of the home Member State refuse to communicate the information referred to in paragraph 2 to the competent authorities of the host Member State, they shall give reasons for their refusal to the institution concerned within three months of receipt of all the information. That refusal or failure to reply shall be subject to a right to apply to the courts in the home Member State.

4. Before the branch of a credit institution commences its activities the competent authorities of the host Member State shall, within two months of receiving the information mentioned in paragraph 3, prepare for the supervision of the credit institution in accordance with Article 21 and if necessary indicate the conditions under which, in the interest of the general good, those activities must be carried on in the host Member State.

5. On receipt of a communication from the competent authorities of the host Member State, or in the event of the expiry of the period provided for in paragraph 4 without receipt of any communication from the latter, the branch may be established and commence its activities.

6. In the event of a change in any of the particulars communicated pursuant to paragraph 2(b), (c) or (d) or in the deposit-guarantee scheme referred to in paragraph 3 a credit institution shall give written notice of the change in question to the competent authorities of the home and host Member States at least one month before making the change so as to enable the competent authorities of the home Member State to take a decision pursuant to paragraph 3 and the competent authorities of the host Member State to take a decision on the change pursuant to paragraph 4.

Article 20

1. Any credit institution wishing to exercise the freedom to provide services by carrying on its activities within the territory of another Member State for the first time shall notify the competent authorities of the home Member State of the activities on the list in the Annex which it intends to carry on.

2. The competent authorities of the home Member State shall, within one month of receipt of the notification mentioned in paragraph 1, send the notification to the competent authorities of the host Member State.

Article 21

1. Host Member States may, for statistical purposes, require that all credit institutions having branches within their territories shall report periodically on their activities in those host Member States to the competent authorities of those host Member States.

In discharging the responsibilities imposed on them in Article 14(2) and (3), host Member States may require that branches of credit institutions from other Member States provide the same information as they require from national credit institutions for that purpose.

2. Where the competent authorities of a host Member State ascertain that an institution having a branch or providing services within its territory is not complying with the legal provisions adopted in that State pursuant to the provisions of this Directive involving powers of the host Member State competent authorities, those authorities shall require the institution concerned to put an end to that irregular situation.

3. If the institution concerned fails to take the necessary steps, the competent authorities of the host Member State shall inform the competent authorities of the home Member State accordingly. The competent authorities of the home Member State shall, at the earliest opportunity, take all appropriate measures to ensure that the institution concerned puts an end to that irregular situation. The nature of those measures shall be communicated to the competent authorities of the host Member State.

4. If, despite the measures taken by the home Member State or because such measures prove inadequate or are not available in the Member State in question, the institution persists in violating the legal rules referred to in paragraph 2 in force in the host Member State, the latter State may, after informing the competent authorities of the home Member State, take appropriate measures to prevent or to punish further irregularities and, insofar as is necessary, to prevent that institution from initiating further transactions within its territory. The Member States shall ensure that within their territories it is possible to serve the legal documents necessary for these measures on credit institutions.

5. The foregoing provisions shall not affect the power of host Member States to take appropriate measures to prevent or to punish irregularities committed within their territories which are contrary to the legal rules they have adopted in the interest of the general good. This shall include the possibility of preventing offending institutions from initiating any further transactions within their territories.

6. Any measure adopted pursuant to paragraphs 3, 4 and 5 involving penalties or restrictions on the exercise of the freedom to provide services must be properly justified and communicated to the institution concerned. Every such measure shall be subject to a right of appeal to the courts in the Member State the authorities of which adopted it.

7. Before following the procedure provided for in paragraphs 2 to 4, the competent authorities of the host Member State may, in emergencies, take any precautionary measures necessary to protect the interests of depositors, investors and others to whom services are provided. The Commission and the competent authorities of the other Member States concerned must be informed of such measures at the earliest opportunity.

The Commission may, after consulting the competent authorities of the Member States concerned, decide that the Member State in question must amend or abolish those measures.

8. Host Member States may exercise the powers conferred on them under this Directive by taking appropriate measures to prevent or punish irregularities committed within their territories. This shall include the possibility of preventing institutions from initiating further transactions within their territories.

9. In the event of the withdrawal of authorization the competent authorities of the host Member State shall be informed and shall take appropriate measures to prevent the institution concerned from initiating further transactions within its territory and to safeguard the interests of depositors. Every two years the Commission shall submit a report on such cases as to the Banking Advisory Committee.

10. The Member States shall inform the Commission of the number and type of cases in which there has been a refusal pursuant to Article 19 or in which measures have been taken in accordance with paragraph 4. Every two years the Commission shall submit a report on such cases to the Banking Advisory Committee.

11. Nothing in this Article shall prevent credit institutions with head offices in other Member States from advertising their services through all available means of communication in the host Member State, subject to any rules governing the form and the content of such advertising adopted in the interest of the general good.

TITLE VI. FINAL PROVISIONS

Article 22

1. The technical adaptations to be made to this Directive in the following areas shall be adopted in accordance with the procedure laid down in paragraph 2:

— expansion of the content of the list referred to in Article 18 and set out in the Annex or adaptation of the terminology used in that list to take account of developments on financial markets,

— alteration of the amount of initial capital prescribed in Article 4 to take account of developments in the economic and monetary field,

— the areas in which the competent authorities must exchange information as listed in Article 7(1) Directive 77/780/EEC,

— clarification of the definitions in order to ensure uniform application of this Directive throughout the Community,

— clarification of the definitions in order to take account in the implementation of this Directive of developments on financial markets,

— the alignment of terminology on and the framing of definitions in accordance with subsequent acts on credit institutions and related matters.

2. The Commission shall be assisted by a committee composed of representatives of the Member States and chaired by a representative of the Commission.

The Commission representative shall submit to the committee a draft of the measures to be taken. The committee shall deliver its opinion on the draft within a time limit which the chairman may lay down according to the urgency of the matter. The opinion shall be delivered by the majority laid down in Article 148(2) of the Treaty in the case of decisions which the Council is required to adopt on a proposal from the Commission. The votes of the representatives of the Member States in the committee shall be weighted in the manner set out in that Article. The chairman shall not vote.

The Commission shall adopt the measures envisaged if they are in accordance with the opinion of the committee.

If the measures envisaged are not in accordance with the opinion of the committee, or if no opinion is delivered, the Commission shall, without delay, submit to the Council a proposal concerning the measures to be taken. The Council shall act by a qualified majority.

If the Council does not act within three months of the referral to it the Commission shall adopt the measures proposed, unless the Council has decided against those measures by a simple majority.

Article 23

1. Branches which have commenced their activities, in accordance with the provisions in force in their host Member States, before the entry into force of the provisions adopted in implementation of this Directive shall be presumed to have been subject to the procedure laid down in Article 19(1) to (5). They shall be governed, from the date of that entry into force, by Articles 15, 18, 19(6) and 21. They shall benefit pursuant to Article 6(3).

2. Article 20 shall not affect rights acquired by credit institutions providing services before the entry into force of the provisions adopted in implementation of this Directive.

Article 24

1. Subject to paragraph 2, the Member States shall bring into force the laws, regulations and administrative provisions necessary for them to comply with this Directive by the later of the two dates laid down for the adoption of measures to comply with Directives 89/299/EEC and 89/647/EEC and at the latest by 1 January 1993. They shall forthwith inform the Commission thereof.

2. The Member States shall adopt the measures necessary for them to comply with Article 6(2) by 1 January 1990.

3. The Member States shall communicate to the Commission the texts of the main provisions of national law which they adopt in the field covered by this Directive.

Article 25

This Directive is addressed to the Member States.

Done at Brussels, 15 December 1989.

For the Council
The President
P. BÉRÉGOVOY

ANNEX. LIST OF ACTIVITIES SUBJECT TO MUTUAL RECOGNITION

1. Acceptance of deposits and other repayable funds from the public
2. Lending[1]
3. Financial leasing
4. Money transmission services
5. Issuing and administering means of payment (e.g., credit cards, travellers' cheques and bankers' drafts)
6. Guarantees and commitments
7. Trading for own account or for account of customers in:
   (a) money market instruments (cheques, bills, CDs, etc.);
   (b) foreign exchange;
   (c) financial futures and options;
   (d) exchange and interest rate instruments;
   (e) transferable securities.
8. Participation in securities issues and the provision of services related to such issues.
9. Advice to undertakings on capital structure, industrial strategy and related questions and advice and services relating to mergers and the purchase of undertakings
10. Money broking
11. Portfolio management and advice
12. Safekeeping and administration of securities
13. Credit reference services
14. Safe custody services

---

1. Including *inter alia*;
   — consumer credit,
   — mortgage credit,
   — factoring, with or without recourse,
   — financing of commercial transactions (including forfaiting).

COUNCIL DIRECTIVE* 89/647/EEC OF 18 DECEMBER 1989

on a solvency ratio for credit institutions

THE COUNCIL OF THE EUROPEAN COMMUNITIES,

Having regard to the Treaty establishing the European Economic Community, and in particular the first and third sentences of Article 57(2) thereof,

Having regard to the proposal from the Commission,[1]

In co-operation with the European Parliament,[2]

Having regard to the opinion of the Economic and Social Committee,[3]

Whereas this Directive is the outcome of work carried out by the Banking Advisory Committee, which, pursuant to Article 6(4) of Council Directive 77/780/EEC of 12 December 1977 on the co-ordination of laws, regulations and administrative provisions relating to the taking up and pursuit of the business of credit institutions,[4] as last amended by Directive 89/646/EEC,[5] is responsible for making suggestions to the Commission with a view to co-ordinating the coefficients applicable in the Member States;

Whereas the establishment of an appropriate solvency ratio plays a central role in supervision of credit institutions;

Whereas a ratio which weights assets and off-balance-sheet items according to the degree of credit risk is a particularly useful measure of solvency;

Whereas the development of common standards for own funds in relation to assets and off-balance-sheet items exposed to credit risk is, accordingly, an essential aspect of the harmonization necessary for the achievement of the mutual recognition of supervision techniques and thus the completion of the internal banking market;

Whereas, in that respect, this Directive must be considered in conjunction with other specific instruments also harmonizing the fundamental techniques of the supervision of credit institutions;

Whereas this Directive must also be seen as complementary to Directive 89/646/EEC, which lays out the broader framework of which this Directive is an integral part;

Whereas, in a common banking market, institutions are required to enter into direct competition with one another and whereas the adoption of common solvency standards in the form of a minimum ratio will prevent distortions of competition and strengthen the Community banking system;

Whereas this Directive provides for different weightings to be given to guarantees issued by different financial institutions; whereas the Commission accordingly undertakes to examine whether the Directive taken as a whole significantly distorts competition between credit institutions and insurance companies and, in the light of that examination, to consider whether any remedial measures are justified;

Whereas the minimum ratio provided for in this Directive reinforces the capital of credit institutions in the Community; whereas a level of 8% has been adopted following a statistical survey of capital requirements in force at the beginning of 1988;

---

* OJ 1989, L386/14.
1. OJ No C135, 25 May 1988, p. 2.
2. OJ No C96, 17 April, 1984, p. 86 and OJ No C304, 4 December 1984.
3. OJ No C337, 31 December 1988, p. 8.
4. OJ No L322, 17 December 1977, p. 30.
5. *See* OJ 1989, L386/1.

Whereas measurement of and allowance for interest-rate, foreign-exchange and other market risks are also of great importance in the supervision of credit institutions; whereas the Commission will accordingly, in co-operation with the competent authorities of the Member States and all other bodies working towards similar ends, continue to study the techniques available; whereas it will then make appropriate proposals for the further harmonization of supervision rules relating to those risks; whereas in so doing it will keep a special watch on the possible interaction between the various banking risks and consequently pay particular attention to the consistency of the various proposals;

Whereas, in making proposals for rules for the supervision of investment services and the adequacy of the capital of entities operating in that area, the Commission will ensure that equivalent requirements are applied in respect of the level of own funds, if the same type of business is transacted and identical risks are assumed;

Whereas the specific accounting technique to be used for the calculation of solvency ratios must take account of the provisions of Council Directive 86/635/EEC of 8 December 1986 on the annual accounts and consolidated accounts of banks and other financial institutions,[6] which incorporates certain adaptations of the provisions of Council Directive 83/349/EEC,[7] as amended by the Act of Accession of Spain and Portugal; whereas, pending transposition of the provisions of those Directives into the national laws of the Member States, the use of specific accounting techniques for the calculation of solvency ratios should be left to the discretion of the Member States;

Whereas the application of a 20% weighting to credit institutions' holdings of mortgage bonds may unsettle a national financial market on which such instruments play a preponderant role; whereas, in this case, provisional measures are taken to apply a 10% risk weighting;

Whereas technical modifications to the detailed rules laid down in this Directive may from time to time be necessary to take account of new developments in the banking sector; whereas the Commission will accordingly make such modifications as are necessary, after consulting the Banking Advisory Committee, within the limits of the implementing powers conferred on the Commission by the provisions of the Treaty; whereas that Committee will act as a "Regulatory" Committee, according to the rules of procedure laid down in Article 2, procedure III, variant (b), of Council Decision 87/373/EEC of 13 July 1987 laying down the procedures for the exercise of implementing powers conferred on the Commission,[8]

HAS ADOPTED THIS DIRECTIVE:

SCOPE AND DEFINITIONS

Article 1

1. This Directive shall apply to credit institutions as defined the first indent of Article 1 of Directive 77/780/EEC.

2. Notwithstanding paragraph 1, the Member States need not apply this Directive to credit institutions listed in Article 2(2) of Directive 77/780/EEC.

3. A credit institution which, as defined in Article 2(4)(a) of Directive 77/780/EEC, is affiliated to a central body in the same Member State, may be exempted from the provisions of this Directive, provided that all such affiliated credit institutions and their central bodies are included in consolidated solvency ratios in accordance with this Directive.

4. Exceptionally, and pending further harmonization of the prudential rules relating to credit, interest-rate and market risks, the Member States may exclude from the scope of this Directive any credit institution specializing in the inter-bank and public-debt markets and fulfilling, together with the central bank, the institutional function of banking-system liquidity regulator, provided that:

— the sum of its asset and off-balance-sheet items included in the 50% and 100% weightings, calculated in accordance with Article 6, must not normally exceed 10% of

6. OJ No L372, 31 December 1986, p. 1.
7. OJ No L193, 18 July 1983, p. 18.
8. OJ No L197, 18 July 1987, p. 33.

total assets and off-balance-sheet items and shall not in any event exceed 15% before application of the weightings,

— its main activity consists of acting as intermediary between the central bank of its Member State and the banking system,

— the competent authority applies adequate systems of supervision and control of its credit, interest-rate and market risks.

The Member States shall inform the Commission of the exemptions granted, in order to ensure that they do not result in distortions of competition. Within three years of the adoption of this Directive, the Commission shall submit to the Council a report together, where necessary, with any proposals it may consider appropriate.

Article 2

1. For the purposes of this Directive:

— "competent authorities" shall mean the authorities defined in the fifth indent of Article 1 of Council Directive 83/350/EEC,

— "Zone A" shall comprise all the Member States and all other countries which are full members of the Organization for Economic Co-operation and Development (OECD) and those countries which have concluded special lending arrangements with the International Monetary Fund (IMF) associated with the Fund's General Arrangements to Borrow (GAB),

— "Zone B" shall comprise all countries not in Zone A,

— "Zone A credit institutions" shall mean all credit institutions authorized in the Member States, in accordance with Article 3 of Directive 77/780/EEC, including their branches in third countries, and all private and public undertakings covered by the definition in the first indent of Article 1 of Directive 77/780/EEC and authorized in other Zone A countries, including their branches,

— "Zone B credit institutions" shall mean all private and public undertakings authorized outside Zone A covered by the definition in the first indent of Article 1 of Directive 77/780/EEC, including their branches within the Community,

— "non-bank sector" shall mean all borrowers other than credit institutions as defined in the fourth and fifth indents, central governments and central banks, regional governments and local authorities, the European Communities, the European Investment Bank and multilateral development banks as defined in the seventh indent,

— "multilateral development banks" shall mean the International Bank for Reconstruction and Development, the International Finance Corporation, the Inter-American Development Bank, the Asian Development Bank, the African Development Bank, the Council of Europe Resettlement Fund, the Nordic Investment Bank and the Caribbean Development Bank,

— "full-risk", "medium-risk", "medium/low-risk" and "low-risk" off-balance-sheet items shall mean the items described in Article 6(2) and listed in Annex I.

2. For the purposes of Article 6(1)(b), the competent authorities may include within the concept of regional governments and local authorities non-commercial administrative bodies responsible to regional governments or local authorities, and those non-commercial undertakings owned by central governments, regional governments, local authorities or authorities which, in the view of the competent authorities, exercise the same responsibilities as regional and local authorities.

Article 3

General principles

1. The solvency ratio referred to in paragraphs 2 to 7 expresses own funds, as defined in Article 4, as a proportion of total assets and off-balance-sheet items, risk-adjusted in accordance with Article 5.

2. The solvency ratios of credit institutions which are neither parent undertakings as defined in

455

Article 1 of Directive 83/349/EEC nor subsidiaries of such undertakings shall be calculated on an individual basis.

3. The solvency ratios of credit institutions which are parent undertakings shall be calculated on a consolidated basis in accordance with the methods laid down in this Directive and in Directives 83/350/EEC and 86/635/EEC.[9]

4. The competent authorities responsible for authorizing and supervising a parent undertaking which is a credit institution may also require the calculation of a subconsolidated or unconsolidated ratio in respect of that parent undertaking and of any of its subsidiaries which are subject to authorization and supervision by them. Where such monitoring of the satisfactory allocation of capital within a banking group is not carried out, other measures must be taken to attain that end.

5. Where the subsidiary of a parent undertaking has been authorized and is situated in another Member State, the competent authorities which granted that authorization shall require the calculation of a subconsolidated or unconsolidated ratio.

6. Notwithstanding paragraph 5, the competent authorities responsible for authorizing the subsidiary of a parent undertaking situated in another Member State may, by way of a bilateral agreement, delegate their responsibility for supervising solvency to the competent authorities which have authorized and which supervise the parent undertaking so that they assume responsibility for supervising the subsidiary in accordance with this Directive. The Commission shall be kept informed of the existence and content of such agreements. It shall forward such information to the other authorities and to the Banking Advisory Committee.

7. Without prejudice to credit institutions' compliance with the requirements of paragraphs 2 to 6, the competent authorities shall ensure that ratios are calculated not less than twice each year, either by credit institutions themselves, which shall communicate the results and any component data required to the competent authorities, or by the competent authorities, using data supplied by the credit institutions.

8. The valuation of assets and off-balance-sheet items shall be effected in accordance with Directive 86/635/EEC. Pending implementation of the provisions of that Directive, valuation shall be left to the discretion of the Member States.

Article 4

The numerator: own funds

Own funds as defined in Directive 89/299/EEC[10] shall form the numerator of the solvency ratio.

Article 5

The denominator: risk-adjusted assets and off-balance-sheet items

1. Degrees of credit risk, expressed as percentage weightings, shall be assigned to asset items in accordance with Articles 6 and 7, and exceptionally Articles 8 and 11. The balance-sheet value of each asset shall then be multiplied by the relevant weighting to produce a risk-adjusted value.

2. In the case of the off-balance-sheet items listed in Annex I, a two-stage calculation as prescribed in Article 6(2) shall be used.

3. In the case of the interest-rate- and foreign-exchange-related off-balance-sheet items referred to in Article 6(3), the potential costs of replacing contracts in the event of counterparty default shall be calculated by means of one of the two methods set out in Annex II. Those costs shall be multiplied by the relevant counterparty weightings in Article 6(1), except that the 100% weightings as provided for these shall be replaced by 50% weightings to produce risk-adjusted values.

4. The total of the risk-adjusted values of the assets and off-balance-sheet items mentioned in paragraphs 2 and 3 shall be the denominator of the solvency ratio.

9. OJ No L372, 31 December 1986, p. 1.
10. OJ No L124, 5 May 1989, p. 16.

Article 6

Risk weightings

1. The following weightings shall be applied to the various categories of asset items, although the competent authorities may fix higher weightings as they see fit:

(a) Zero weighting

    1. cash in hand and equivalent items;

    2. asset items constituting claims on Zone A central governments and central banks;

    3. asset items constituting claims on the European Communities;

    4. asset items constituting claims carrying the explicit guarantees of Zone A central governments and central banks;

    5. asset items constituting claims on Zone B central governments and central banks, denominated and funded in the national currencies of the borrowers;

    6. asset items constituting claims carrying the explicit guarantees of Zone B central governments and central banks, denominated and funded in the national currency common to the guarantor and the borrower;

    7. asset items secured, to the satisfaction of the competent authorities, by collateral in the form of Zone A central government or central bank securities, or securities issued by the European Communities, or by cash deposits placed with the lending institution or by certificates of deposit or similar instruments issued by and lodged with the latter;

(b) 20% weighting

    1. asset items constituting claims on the European Investment Bank (EIB);

    2. asset items constituting claims on multilateral development banks;

    3. asset items constituting claims carrying the explicit guarantee of the European Investment Bank (EIB);

    4. asset items constituting claims carrying the explicit guarantees of multilateral development banks;

    5. asset items constituting claims on Zone A regional governments or local authorities, subject to Article 7;

    6. asset items constituting claims carrying the explicit guarantees of Zone A regional governments or local authorities, subject to Article 7;

    7. asset items constituting claims on Zone A credit institutions but not constituting such institutions' own funds as defined in Directive 89/299/EEC;

    8. asset items constituting claims, with a maturity of one year or less, on Zone B credit institutions, other than securities issued by such institutions which are recognized as components of their own funds;

    9. asset items carrying the explicit guarantees of Zone A credit institutions;

    10. asset items constituting claims with a maturity of one year or less, carrying the explicit guarantees of Zone B credit institutions;

    11. asset items secured, to the satisfaction of the competent authorities, by collateral in the form of securities issued by the EIB or by multilateral development banks;

    12. cash items in the process of collection;

(c) 50% weighting

    1. loans fully and completely secured, to the satisfaction of the competent authorities, by mortgages on residential property which is or will be occupied or let by the borrower;

    2. prepayments and accrued income: these assets shall be subject to the weighting corresponding to the counterparty where a credit institution is able to determine it in accordance with Directive 86/635/EEC. Otherwise, where it is unable to determine the contraparty, it shall apply a flat-rate weighting of 50%;

(d) 100% weighting

    1. asset items constituting claims on Zone B central governments and central banks except where denominated and funded in the national currency of the borrower;

    2. asset items constituting claims on Zone B regional governments or local authorities;

    3. asset items constituting claims with a maturity of more than one year on Zone B credit institutions;

    4. asset items constituting claims on the Zone A or Zone B non-bank sectors;

5. tangible assets within the meaning of assets as listed in Article 4(10) of Directive 86/635/EEC;

6. holdings of shares, participations and other components of the own funds of other credit institutions which are not deducted from the own funds of the lending institutions;

7. all other assets except where deducted from own funds.

2. The following treatment shall apply to off-balance-sheet items other than those covered in paragraph 3. They shall first be grouped according to the risk groupings set out in Annex I. The full value of the full-risk items shall be taken into account, 50% of the value of the medium-risk items and 20% of the medium/low-risk items, while the value of the low-risk items shall be set at zero. The second stage shall be to multiply the off-balance-sheet values, adjusted as described above, by the weightings attributable to the relevant counterparties, in accordance with the treatment of asset items prescribed in paragraph 1 and Article 7. In the case of asset sale and repurchase agreements and outright forward purchases, the weightings shall be those attaching to the assets in question and not to the counterparties to the transactions.

3. The methods set out in Annex II shall be applied to the interest-rate and foreign-exchange risks listed in Annex III.

4. Where off-balance-sheet items carry explicit guarantees, they shall be weighted as if they had been incurred on behalf of the guarantor rather than the counterparty. Where the potential exposure arising from off-balance-sheet transactions is fully and completely secured, to the satisfaction of the competent authorities, by any of the asset items recognized as collateral in paragraph 1(a)(7) or (b)(11), weightings of 0% or 20% shall apply, depending on the collateral in question.

5. Where asset and off-balance-sheet items are given a lower weighting because of the existence of explicit guarantees or collateral acceptable to the competent authorities, the lower weighting shall apply only to that part which is guaranteed or which is fully covered by the collateral.

Article 7

1. Notwithstanding the requirements of Article 6(1)(b), the Member States may fix a weighting of 0% for their own regional governments and local authorities if there is no difference in risk between claims on the latter and claims on their central governments because of the revenue-raising powers of the regional governments and local authorities and the existence of specific institutional arrangements the effect of which is to reduce the chances of default by the latter. A zero weighting fixed in accordance with these criteria shall apply to claims on and off-balance-sheet items incurred on behalf of the regional governments and local authorities in question and claims on others and off-balance-sheet items incurred on behalf of others and guaranteed by those regional governments and local authorities.

2. The Member States shall notify the Commission if they believe a zero weighting to be justified according to the criteria laid down in paragraph 1. The Commission shall circulate that information. Other Member States may offer the credit institutions under the supervision of their competent authorities the possibility of applying a zero weighting where they undertake business with the regional governments or local authorities in question or where they hold claims guaranteed by the latter.

Article 8

1. The Member States may apply a weighting of 20% to asset items which are secured, to the satisfaction of the competent authorities concerned, by collateral in the form of securities issued by Zone A regional governments or local authorities, by deposits placed with Zone A credit institutions other than the lending institution, or by certificates of deposit of similar instruments issued by those credit institutions.

2. The Member States may apply a weighting of 10% to claims on institutions specializing in the inter-bank and public-debt markets in their home Member States and subject to close supervision by the competent authorities where those asset items are fully and completely secured, to the satisfaction of the competent authorities of the home Member States, by a combination of asset items mentioned in Article 6(1)(a) and (b) recognized by the latter as constituting adequate collateral.

3. The Member States shall notify the Commission of any provisions adopted pursuant to paragraphs 1 and 2 and of the grounds for such provisions. The Commission shall forward that information to the Member States. The Commission shall periodically examine the implications of those provisions in order to ensure that they do not result in any distortions of competition. Within three years of the adoption of this Directive, the Commission shall submit to the Council a report together, where necessary, with any proposals it may consider appropriate.

Article 9

1. The technical adaptions to be made to this Directive in the following areas shall be adopted in accordance with the procedure laid down in paragraph 2:

— a temporary reduction in the minimum ratio prescribed in Article 10 or the weightings prescribed in Article 6 in order to take account of specific circumstances,
— the definition of "Zone A" in Article 2,
— the definition of "multilateral development banks" in Article 2,
— amendment of the definitions of the assets listed in Article 6 in order to take account of developments on financial markets,
— the lists and classification of off-balance-sheet items in Annexes I and III and their treatment in the calculation of the ratio as described in Articles 5, 6 and 7 and Annex II,
— clarification of the definitions in order to ensure uniform application of this Directive throughout the Community,
— clarification of the definitions in order to take account in the implementation of this Directive of developments on financial markets,
— the alignment of terminology on and the framing of definitions in accordance with subsequent acts on credit institutions and related matters.

2. The Commission shall be assisted by a committee composed of representatives of the Member States and chaired by a representative of the Commission.

The Commission representative shall submit to the committee a draft of the measures to be taken. The committee shall deliver its opinion on the draft within a time limit which the chairman may lay down according to the urgency of the matter. The opinion shall be delivered by the majority laid down in Article 148(2) of the Treaty in the case of decisions which the Council is required to adopt on a proposal from the Commission. The votes of the representatives of the Member States in the committee shall be weighted in the manner set out in that Article. The chairman shall not vote.

The Commission shall adopt the measures envisaged if they are in accordance with the opinion of the committee.

If the measures envisaged are not in accordance with the opinion of the committee, or if no opinion is delivered, the Commission shall, without delay, submit to the Council a proposal concerning the measures to be taken. The Council shall act by a qualified majority.

If the Council does not act within three months of the referral to it the Commission shall adopt the measures proposed, unless the Council has decided against those measures by a simple majority.

Article 10

1. With effect from 1 January 1993 credit institutions shall be required permanently to maintain the ratio defined in Article 3 at a level of at least 8%.

2. Notwithstanding paragraph 1, the competent authorities may prescribe higher minimum ratios as they consider appropriate.

3. If the ratio falls below 8% the competent authorities shall ensure that the credit institution in question takes appropriate measures to restore the ratio to the agreed minimum as quickly as possible.

Article 11

1. A credit institution the minimum ratio of which has not reached the 8% prescribed in Article 10(1) by the date prescribed in Article 12(1) must gradually approach that level by successive

stages. It may not allow the ratio to fall below the level reached before that objective has been attained. Any fluctuation should be temporary and the competent authorities should be apprised of the reasons for it.

2. For not more than five years after the date prescribed in Article 10(1) the Member States may fix a weighting of 10% for the bonds defined in Article 22(4) of Council Directive 85/611/EEC on the co-ordination of laws, regulations and administrative provisions relating to undertakings for collective investment in transferable securities (UCITS),[11] as amended by Directive 88/220/EEC,[12] and maintain it for credit institutions when and if they consider it necessary, to avoid grave disturbances in the operation of their markets. Such exceptions shall be reported to the Commission.

3. For not more than seven years after 1 January 1993, Article 10(1) shall not apply to the Agricultural Bank of Greece. However, the latter must approach the level prescribed in Article 10(1) by successive stages according to the method described in paragraph 1.

4. By derogation from Article 6(1)(c)(1), until 1 January 1996 Germany, Denmark and Greece may apply a weighting of 50% to assets which are entirely and completely secured to the satisfaction of the competent authorities concerned, by mortgages on completed residential property, on offices or on multi-purpose commercial premises, situated within the territories of those three Member States provided that the sum borrowed does not exceed 60% of the value of the property in question, calculated on the basis of rigorous assessment criteria laid down in statutory or regulatory provisions.

5. Member States may apply a 50% weighting to property leasing transactions concluded within ten years of the date laid down in Article 12(1) and concerning assets for business use situated in the country of the head office and governed by statutory provisions whereby the lessor retains full ownership of the rented asset until the tenant exercises his option to purchase.

Article 12

1. The Member States shall adopt the measures necessary for them to comply with the provisions of this Directive by 1 January 1991 at the latest.

2. The Member States shall communicate to the Commission the texts of the main laws, regulations and administrative provisions which they adopt in the field covered by this Directive.

Article 13

This Directive is addressed to the Member States.

Done at Brussels, 18 December 1989.

For the Council
The President
P. BÉRÉGOVOY

ANNEX I. CLASSIFICATION OF OFF-BALANCE-SHEET ITEMS

Full risk

— Guarantees having the character of credit substitutes,
— Acceptances,
— Endorsements on bills not bearing the name of another credit institution,
— Transactions with recourse,
— Irrevocable standby letters of credit having the character of credit substitutes,
— Asset sale and repurchase agreements as defined in Articles 12(1) and (2) of Directive 86/635/EEC, if these agreements are treated as off-balance-sheet items pending application of Directive 86/635/EEC,
— Assets purchased under outright forward purchase agreements,

11. OJ No L375, 31 December 1985, p. 3.
12. OJ No L100, 19 April 1988, p. 31.

— Forward forward deposits,
— The unpaid portion of partly-paid shares and securities,
— Other items also carrying full risk.

Medium risk

— Documentary credits issued and confirmed (see also medium/low risk),
— Warranties and indemnities (including tender, performance, customs and tax bonds) and guarantees not having the character of credit substitutes,
— Asset sale and repurchase agreements as defined in Article 12(3) and (5) of Directive 86/635/EEC,
— Irrevocable standby letters of credit not having the character of credit substitutes,
— Undrawn credit facilities (agreements to lend, purchase securities, provide guarantees or acceptance facilities) with an original maturity of more than one year,
— Note issuance facilities (NIFs) and revolving underwriting facilities (RUFs),
— Other items also carrying medium risk.

Medium/low risk

— Documentary credits in which underlying shipment acts as collateral and other self-liquidating transactions,
— Other items also carrying medium/low risk.

Low risk

— Undrawn credit facilities (agreements to lend, purchase securities. provide guarantees or acceptance facilities) with an original maturity of up to and including one year or which may be cancelled unconditionally at any time without notice,
— Other items also carrying low risk.

The Member States undertake to inform the Commission as soon as they have agreed to include a new off-blance-sheet item in any of the last indents under each category of risk. Such items will be definitively classified at Community level once the procedure laid down in Article 9 has been completed.

ANNEX II. THE TREATMENT OF OFF-BALANCE-SHEET ITEMS CONCERNING INTEREST AND FOREIGN-EXCHANGE RATES

Subject to the consent of their supervisory authorities, credit institutions may choose one of the methods set out below to measure the risks associated with the transactions listed in Annex III. Interest-rate and foreign-exchange contracts traded on recognized exchanges where they are subject to daily margin requirements and foreign-exchange contracts with an original maturity of 14 calendar days or less are excluded.

Where there is a separate bilateral contract for novation, recognized by the national supervisory authorities, between a credit institution and its counterparty under which any obligation to each other to deliver payments in their common currency on a given date are automatically amalgamated with other similar obligations due on the same date, the single net amount fixed by such novation is weighted, rather than the gross amounts involved.

Method 1: the "marking to market" approach

Step (a): by attaching current market values to contracts (marking to market) the current replacement cost of all contracts with positive values is obtained.
Step (b): to obtain a figure for potential future credit exposure,[13] the notional principal amounts or values underlying an institution's aggregate books are multiplied by the following percentages:

---

13. Except in the case of single-currency "floating/floating interest rate swaps" in which only the current replacement cost will be calculated.

Residual maturity	Interest-rate contracts	Foreign-exchange contracts
One year or less	0%	1%
More than one year	0.5%	5%

Step (c): the sum of current replacement cost and potential future credit exposure is multiplied by the risk weightings allocated to the relevant counterparties in Article 6.

Method 2: the "original exposure" approach

Step (a): the notional principle amount of each instrument is multiplied by the percentages given below:

Original maturity[1]	Interest-rate contracts	Foreign-exchange contracts
One year or less	0.5%	2%
More than one year but not exceeding two years	1%	5%
Additional allowance for each additional year	1%	3%

1. In the case of interest-rate contracts, credit institutions may, subject to the consent of their supervisory authorities, choose either original or residual maturity.

Step (b): the original exposure thus obtained is multiplied by the risk weightings allocated to the relevant counterparties in Article 6.

ANNEX III. TYPES OF OFF-BALANCE ITEMS CONCERNING INTEREST RATES AND FOREIGN EXCHANGE

Interest-rate contracts

— Single-currency interest rate swaps
— Basis swaps
— Forward-rate agreements
— Interest-rate futures
— Interest-rate options purchased
— Other contracts of a similar nature

Foreign-exchange contracts

— Cross-currency interest-rate swaps
— Forward foreign-exchange contracts
— Currency futures
— Currency options purchased
— Other contracts of a similar nature

COUNCIL DIRECTIVE* 91/308/EEC OF 10 JUNE 1991

on prevention of the use of the financial system for the purpose of money laundering

THE COUNCIL OF THE EUROPEAN COMMUNITIES,

Having regard to the Treaty establishing the European Economic Community, and in particular Article 57(2), first and third sentences, and Article 100a thereof,

Having regard to the proposal from the Commission,[1]

In co-operation with the European Parliament,[2]

Having regard to the opinion of the Economic and Social Committee,[3]

Whereas when credit and financial institutions are used to launder proceeds from criminal activities (hereinafter referred to as "money laundering"), the soundness and stability of the institution concerned and confidence in the financial system as a whole could be seriously jeopardized, thereby losing the trust of the public;

Whereas lack of Community action against money laundering could lead Member States, for the purpose of protecting their financial systems, to adopt measures which could be inconsistent with completion of the single market; whereas, in order to facilitate their criminal activities, launderers could try to take advantage of the freedom of capital movement and freedom to supply financial services which the integrated financial area involves, if certain co-ordinating measures are not adopted at Community level;

Whereas money laundering has an evident influence on the rise of organized crime in general and drug trafficking in particular; whereas there is more and more awareness that combating money laundering is one of the most effective means of opposing this form of criminal activity, which constitutes a particular threat to Member States' societies;

Whereas money laundering must be combated mainly by penal means and within the framework of international co-operation among judicial and law enforcement authorities, as has been undertaken, in the field of drugs, by the United Nations Convention Against Illicit Traffic in Narcotic Drugs and Psychotropic Substances, adopted on 19 December 1988 in Vienna (hereinafter referred to as the "Vienna Convention") and more generally in relation to all criminal activities, by the Council of Europe Convention on laundering, tracing, seizure and confiscation of proceeds of crime, opened for signature on 8 November 1990 in Strasbourg;

Whereas a penal approach should, however, not be the only way to combat money laundering, since the financial system can play a highly effective role; whereas reference must be made in this context to the recommendation of the Council of Europe of 27 June 1980 and to the declaration of principles adopted in December 1988 in Basle by the banking supervisory authorities of the Group of Ten, both of which constitute major steps towards preventing the use of the financial system for money laundering;

Whereas money laundering is usually carried out in an international context so that the criminal origin of the funds can be better disguised; whereas measures exclusively adopted at a national level, without taking account of international co-ordination and co-operation, would have very limited effects;

Whereas any measures adopted by the Community in this field should be consistent with other action undertaken in other international fora; whereas in this respect any Community action

---

* OJ 1991, L166/77.
1. OJ No C106, 28 April 1990, p. 6: and OJ No C319, 19 December 1990, p. 9.
2. OJ No C324, 24 December 1990, p. 264; and OJ No C129, 20 May 1991.
3. OJ No C332, 31 December 1990, p. 86.

should take particular account of the recommendations adopted by the financial action task force on money laundering, set up in July 1989 by the Paris summit of the seven most developed countries;

Whereas the European Parliament has requested, in several resolutions, the establishment of a global Community programme to combat drug trafficking, including provisions on prevention of money laundering;

Whereas for the purposes of this Directive the definition of money laundering is taken from that adopted in the Vienna Convention; whereas, however, since money laundering occurs not only in relation to the proceeds of drug-related offences but also in relation to the proceeds of other criminal activities (such as organized crime and terrorism), the Member States should, within the meaning of their legislation, extend the effects of the Directive to include the proceeds of such activities, to the extent that they are likely to result in laundering operations justifying sanctions on that basis;

Whereas prohibition of money laundering in Member States' legislation backed by appropriate measures and penalties is a necessary condition for combating this phenomenon;

Whereas ensuring that credit and financial institutions require identification of their customers when entering into business relations or conducting transactions, exceeding certain thresholds, are necessary to avoid launderers' taking advantage of anonymity to carry out their criminal activities; whereas such provisions must also be extended, as far as possible, to any beneficial owners;

Whereas credit and financial institutions must keep for at least five years copies or references of the identification documents required as well as supporting evidence and records consisting of documents relating to transactions or copies thereof similarly admissible in court proceedings under the applicable national legislation for use as evidence in any investigation into money laundering;

Whereas ensuring that credit and financial institutions examine with special attention any transaction which they regard as particularly likely, by its nature, to be related to money laundering is necessary in order to preserve the soundness and integrity of the financial system as well as to contribute to combating this phenomenon; whereas to this end they should pay special attention to transactions with third countries which do not apply comparable standards against money laundering to those established by the Community or to other equivalent standards set out by international fora and endorsed by the Community;

Whereas, for those purposes, Member States may ask credit and financial institutions to record in writing the results of the examination they are required to carry out and to ensure that those results are available to the authorities responsible for efforts to eliminate money laundering;

Whereas preventing the financial system from being used for money laundering is a task which cannot be carried out by the authorities responsible for combating this phenomenon without the co-operation of credit and financial institutions and their supervisory authorities; whereas banking secrecy must be lifted in such cases; whereas a mandatory system of reporting suspicious transactions which ensures that information is transmitted to the abovementioned authorities without alerting the customers concerned, is the most effective way to accomplish such co-operation; whereas a special protection clause is necessary to exempt credit and financial institutions, their employees and their directors from responsibility for breaching restrictions on disclosure of information;

Whereas the information received by the authorities pursuant to this Directive may be used only in connection with combating money laundering; whereas Member States may nevertheless provide that this information may be used for other purposes;

Whereas establishment by credit and financial institutions of procedures of internal control and training programmes in this field are complementary provisions without which the other measures contained in this Directive could become ineffective;

Whereas, since money laundering can be carried out not only through credit and financial institutions but also through other types of professions and categories of undertakings, Member States must extend the provisions of this Directive in whole or in part, to include those professions and undertakings whose activities are particularly likely to be used for money laundering purposes;

Whereas it is important that the Member States should take particular care to ensure that co-ordinated action is taken in the Community where there are strong grounds for believing that professions or activities the conditions governing the pursuit of which have been harmonized at Community level are being used for laundering money;

Whereas the effectiveness of efforts to eliminate money laundering is particularly dependent on the close co-ordination and harmonization of national implementing measures; whereas such co-ordination and harmonization which is being carried out in various international bodies requires, in the Community context, co-operation between Member States and the Commission in the framework of a contact committee;

Whereas it is for each Member State to adopt appropriate measures and to penalize infringement of such measures in an appropriate manner to ensure full application of this Directive.

HAS ADOPTED THIS DIRECTIVE:

Article 1

For the purpose of this Directive:

— "credit institution" means a credit institution, as defined as in the first indent of Article 1 of Directive 77/780/EEC,[4] as last amended by Directive 89/646/EEC,[5] and includes branches within the meaning of the third indent of that Article and located in the Community, of credit institutions having their head offices outside the Community,

— "financial institution" means an undertaking other than a credit institution whose principal activity is to carry out one or more of the operations included in numbers 2 to 12 and number 14 of the list annexed to Directive 89/646/EEC, or an insurance company duly authorized in accordance with Directive 79/267/EEC,[6] as last amended by Directive 90/619/EEC,[7] in so far as it carries out activities covered by that Directive; this definition includes branches located in the Community of financial institutions whose head offices are outside the Community,

— "money laundering" means the following conduct when committed intentionally:

— the conversion or transfer of property, knowing that such property is derived from criminal activity or from an act of participation in such activity, for the purpose of concealing or disguising the illicit origin of the property or of assisting any person who is involved in the commission of such activity to evade the legal consequences of his action,

— the concealment or disguise of the true nature, source, location, disposition, movement, rights with respect to, or ownership of property, knowing that such property is derived from criminal activity or from an act of participation in such activity,

— the acquisition, possession or use of property, knowing, at the time of receipt, that such property was derived from criminal activity or from an act of participation in such activity,

— participation in, association to commit, attempts to commit and aiding, abetting, facilitating and counselling the commission of any of the actions mentioned in the foregoing paragraphs.

Knowledge, intent or purpose required as an element of the abovementioned activities may be inferred from objective factual circumstances.

Money laundering shall be regarded as such even where the activities which generated the property to be laundered were perpetrated in the territory of another Member State or in that of a third country.

— "property" means assets of every kind, whether corporeal or incorporeal, movable or immovable, tangible or intangible, and legal documents or instruments evidencing title to or interests in such assets.

4. OJ No L322, 17 December 1977, p. 30.
5. OJ No L386, 30 December 1989, p. 1.
6. OJ No L63, 13 March 1979, p. 1.
7. OJ No L330, 29 November 1990, p. 50.

— "criminal activity" means a crime specified in Article 3(1)(a) of the Vienna Convention and any other criminal activity designated as such for the purposes of this Directive by each Member State.

— "competent authorities" means the national authorities empowered by law or regulation to supervise credit or financial institutions.

Article 2

Member States shall ensure that money laundering as defined in this Directive is prohibited.

Article 3

1. Member States shall ensure that credit and financial institutions require identification of their customers by means of supporting evidence when entering into business relations, particularly when opening an account or savings account, or when offering safe custody facilities.

2. The identification requirement shall also apply for any transaction with customers other than those referred to in paragraph 1, involving a sum amounting to ECU 15,000 or more, whether the transaction is carried out in a single operation or in several operations which seem to be linked. Where the sum is not known at the time when the transaction is undertaken, the institution concerned shall proceed with identification as soon as it is apprised of the sum and establishes that the threshold has been reached.

3. By way of derogation from paragraphs 1 and 2, the identification requirements with regard to insurance policies written by insurance undertakings within the meaning of Directive 79/267/EEC, where they perform activities which fall within the scope of that Directive shall not be required where the periodic premium amount or amounts to be paid in any given year does or do not exceed ECU 1,000 or where a single premium is paid amounting to ECU 2,500 or less. If the periodic premium amount or amounts to be paid in any given year is or are increased so as to exceed the ECU 1,000 threshold, identification shall be required.

4. Member States may provide that the identification requirement is not compulsory for insurance policies in respect of pension schemes taken out by virtue of a contract of employment or the insured's occupation, provided that such policies contain no surrender clause and may not be used as collateral for a loan.

5. In the event of doubt as to whether the customers referred to in the above paragraphs are acting on their own behalf, or where it is certain that they are not acting on their own behalf, the credit and financial institutions shall take reasonable measures to obtain information as to the real identity of the persons on whose behalf those customers are acting.

6. Credit and financial institutions shall carry out such identification, even where the amount of the transaction is lower than the threshold laid down, wherever there is suspicion of money laundering.

7. Credit and financial institutions shall not be subject to the identification requirements provided for in this Article where the customer is also a credit or financial institution covered by this Directive.

8. Member States may provide that the identification requirements regarding transactions referred to in paragraphs 3 and 4 are fulfilled when it is established that the payment for the transaction is to be debited from an account opened in the customer's name with a credit institution subject to this Directive according to the requirements of paragraph 1.

Article 4

Member States shall ensure that credit and financial institutions keep the following for use as evidence in any investigation into money laundering:

— in the case of identification, a copy or the references of the evidence required, for a period of at least five years after the relationship with their customer has ended,

— in the case of transactions, the supporting evidence and records, consisting of the original documents or copies admissible in court proceedings under the applicable national legislation for a period of at least five years following execution of the transactions.

Article 5

Member States shall ensure that credit and financial institutions examine with special attention any transaction which they regard as particularly likely, by its nature, to be related to money laundering.

Article 6

Member States shall ensure that credit and financial institutions and their directors and employees co-operate fully with the authorities responsible for combating money laundering:

— by informing those authorities, on their own initiative, of any fact which might be an indication of money laundering,
— by furnishing those authorities, at their request, with all necessary information, in accordance with the procedures established by the applicable legislation.

The information referred to in the first paragraph shall be forwarded to the authorities responsible for combating money laundering of the Member State in whose territory the institution forwarding the information is situated. The person or persons designated by the credit and financial institutions in accordance with the procedures provided for in Article 11(1) shall normally forward the information.

Information supplied to the authorities in accordance with the first paragraph may be used only in connection with the combating of money laundering. However, Member States may provide that such information may also be used for other purposes.

Article 7

Member States shall ensure that credit and financial institutions refrain from carrying out transactions which they know or suspect to be related to money laundering until they have apprised the authorities referred to in Article 6. Those authorities may, under conditions determined by their national legislation, give instructions not to execute the operation. Where such a transaction is suspected of giving rise to money laundering and where to refrain in such manner is impossible or is likely to frustrate efforts to pursue the beneficiaries of a suspected money-laundering operation, the institutions concerned shall apprise the authorities immediately afterwards.

Article 8

Credit and financial institutions and their directors and employees shall not disclose to the customer concerned nor to other third persons that information has been transmitted to the authorities in accordance with Articles 6 and 7 or that a money laundering investigation is being carried out.

Article 9

The disclosure in good faith to the authorities responsible for combating money laundering by an employee or director of a credit or financial institution of the information referred to in Articles 6 and 7 shall not constitute a breach of any restriction on disclosure of information imposed by contract or by any legislative, regulatory or administrative provision, and shall not involve the credit or financial institution, its directors or employees in liability of any kind.

Article 10

Member States shall ensure that if, in the course of inspections carried out in credit or financial institutions by the competent authorities, or in any other way, those authorities discover facts that could constitute evidence of money laundering, they inform the authorities responsible for combating money laundering.

Article 11

Member States shall ensure that credit and financial institutions:

1. establish adequate procedures of internal control and communication in order to forestall and prevent operations related to money laundering,
2. take appropriate measures so that their employees are aware of the provisions contained in this Directive. These measures shall include participation of their relevant employees in special training programmes to help them recognize operations which may be related to money laundering as well as to instruct them as to how to proceed in such cases.

Article 12

Member States shall ensure that the provisions of this Directive are extended in whole or in part to professions and to categories of undertakings, other than the credit and financial institutions referred to in Article 1, which engage in activities which are particularly likely to be used for money-laundering purposes.

Article 13

1. A contact committee (hereinafter referred to as "the Committee") shall be set up under the aegis of the Commission. Its function shall be:
   (a) without prejudice to Articles 169 and 170 of the Treaty, to facilitate harmonized implementation of this Directive through regular consultation on any practical problems arising from its application and on which exchanges of view are deemed useful;
   (b) to facilitate consultation between the Member States on the more stringent or additional conditions and obligations which they may lay down at national level;
   (c) to advise the Commission, if necessary, on any supplements or amendments to be made to this Directive or on any adjustments deemed necessary, in particular to harmonize the effects of Article 12;
   (d) to examine whether a profession or a category of undertaking should be included in the scope of Article 12 where it has been established that such profession or category of undertaking has been used in a Member State for money laundering.
2. It shall not be the function of the Committee to appraise the merits of decisions taken by the competent authorities in individual cases.
3. The Committee shall be composed of persons appointed by the Member States and of representatives of the Commission. The secretariat shall be provided by the Commission. The chairman shall be a representative of the Commission. It shall be convened by its chairman, either on his own initiative or at the request of the delegation of a Member State.

Article 14

Each Member State shall take appropriate measures to ensure full application of all the provisions of this Directive and shall in particular determine the penalties to be applied for infringement of the measures adopted pursuant to this Directive.

Article 15

The Member States may adopt or retain in force stricter provisions in the field covered by this Directive to prevent money laundering.

Article 16

1. Member States shall bring into force the laws, regulations and administrative decisions necessary to comply with this Directive before 1 January 1993 at the latest.
2. Where Member States adopt these measures, they shall contain a reference to this Directive or shall be accompanied by such reference on the occasion of their official publication. The methods of making such a reference shall be laid down by the Member States.
3. Member States shall communicate to the Commission the text of the main provisions of national law which they adopt in the field governed by this Directive.

Article 17

One year after 1 January 1993, whenever necessary and at least at three yearly intervals thereafter, the Commission shall draw up a report on the implementation of this Directive and submit it to the European Parliament and the Council.

Article 18

This Directive is addressed to the Member States.

Done at Luxembourg, 10 June 1991.

> *For the Council*
> *The President*
> J . C . JUNCKER

STATEMENT BY THE REPRESENTATIVES OF THE GOVERNMENTS OF THE MEMBER STATES MEETING WITHIN THE COUNCIL

The representatives of the Governments of the Member States, meeting within the Council,

Recalling that the Member States signed the United Nations Convention against illicit traffic in narcotic drugs and psychotropic substances, adopted on 19 December 1988 in Vienna;

Recalling also that most Member States have already signed the Council of Europe Convention on laundering, tracing, seizure and confiscation of proceeds of crime on 8 November 1990 in Strasbourg;

Conscious of the fact that the description of money laundering contained in Article 1 of Council Directive 91/308/EEC derives its wording from the relevant provisions of the aforementioned Conventions;

Hereby undertake to take all necessary steps by 31 December 1992 at the latest to enact criminal legislation enabling them to comply with their obligations under the aforementioned instruments.

PROPOSAL FOR A COUNCIL DIRECTIVE ON DEPOSIT-GUARANTEE SCHEMES

(92/C163/05) COM(92) 188 final—SYN 415
(Submitted by the Commission on 14 April 1992)

THE COUNCIL OF THE EUROPEAN COMMUNITIES,

Having regard to the Treaty establishing the European Economic Community, and in particular the first and third sentences of Article 57(2) thereof,

Having regard to the proposal from the Commission,

In co-operation with the European Parliament,

Having regard to the opinion of the Economic and Social Committee,

Whereas, in accordance with the objectives of the Treaty, the harmonious development of the activities of credit institutions throughout the Community should be promoted through the elimination of any restrictions on freedom of establishment and the freedom to provide services while increasing the stability of the banking system and the protection of savers;

Whereas, at the same time as restrictions on their activities are eliminated, consideration should be given to the situation which might arise if a credit institution that has branches in other Member States suffers a financial crisis; whereas it is indispensable to ensure a harmonized minimum level of deposit protection wherever in the Community deposits are located; whereas such deposit protection is as essential as the prudential rules for the completion of the single banking market;

Whereas, in the event of the closure of an insolvent credit institution, the depositors of branches situated in a Member State other than that where the credit institution has its head office must be protected by a guarantee scheme, in the same way as all the institution's other depositors;

Whereas the cost to credit institutions of participating in a guarantee scheme bears no relation to the cost that would result from a massive withdrawal of bank deposits not only from a credit institution in difficulties but also from healthy institutions following a loss of depositor confidence in the solidity of the banking system;

Whereas only ten Member States have a guarantee scheme in accordance with Commission Recommendation 87/63/EEC of 22 December 1986 concerning the introduction of deposit-guarantee schemes in the Community[1]; whereas this situation may prove prejudicial to the proper functioning of the Single Market;

Whereas the Second Directive 89/646/EEC,[2] as amended by Directive 92/30/EEC,[3] provides for a system for authorizing and supervising credit institutions which will enter into force on 1 January 1993;

Whereas branches will no longer require authorization in host Member States, because they will be granted a single authorization valid throughout the Community, and their solvency will be monitored by the competent authorities of the home Member State; whereas this situation justifies all branches, set up in the Community, of the same credit institution in belonging to a single guarantee scheme; whereas this scheme can only be the one which exists, for this category of institution, in the state where the head office is situated, in particular because of the link which exists between supervision of a branch's solvency and its membership of a deposit-guarantee scheme;

1. OJ No L33, 4 February 1987, p. 16.
2. OJ No L386, 30 December 1989, p. 1.
3. OJ No L110, 28 April 1992, p. 52.

Whereas harmonization must be confined to the elements necessary and sufficient to ensure, within a very short period, a payment under the guarantee calculated on the basis of a harmonized minimum level;

Whereas, for economic reasons, it is undesirable to introduce throughout the Community a very high level of protection which is liable to encourage the reckless management of institutions; whereas, in addition, in the event of a serious claim, contributions to the funding of the scheme could become too burdensome for the member institutions;

Whereas, however, the harmonized guarantee level must not be too low in order not to leave too great a number of deposits outside the minimum protection threshold; whereas in the absence of statistics on the amount and distribution of deposits in Community credit institutions, it seemed reasonable to take as a basis the median guarantee offered by the national systems; whereas that amount is ECU 15,000;

Whereas in the six Member States which are above that median level, the guarantee schemes offer depositors a coverage of their deposits which is higher; whereas it does not seem appropriate to require that these schemes, certain of which have been introduced only recently pursuant to Recommendation 87/63/EEC, be amended on this point;

Whereas the retention in the Community of schemes providing coverage of deposits which is higher than the harmonized minimum may lead on the same territory to disparities in compensation which are prejudicial to depositors and unequal conditions of competition between national institutions and the branches of institutions of other Member States; whereas, in order to counteract these disadvantages, branches should be authorized to join the host country scheme so that they can offer their depositors the same guarantees as those offered by the scheme of the country where they are located;

Whereas, in order to speed up payments under the guarantee, the initiation of insolvency proceedings should not be awaited, unless the latter take place within 10 days of the deposits becoming unavailable because a credit institution finds it impossible to comply with the obligation of refunding them in accordance with the legal and contractual provisions applicable to them;

Whereas a number of Member States have deposit-protection schemes under the responsibility of professional organizations; whereas other Member States have schemes set up and administered on a statutory basis and whereas some schemes, although set up on a contractual basis are partly administered on a statutory basis; whereas this variety of status poses a problem only with regard to compulsory membership of and exclusion from the scheme; whereas it is therefore necessary to take steps to limit the powers of schemes in this area;

Whereas one of the objectives of the harmonized minimum protection laid down by the Directive is to ensure depositor protection up to a certain amount, while excluding from such protection only deposits of other credit institutions and claims which are the subject of special conditions such as subordinated deposits; whereas it should, however, be possible for each Member State to limit such protection to depositors who are unable to evaluate the financial policy of the institutions to which they entrust their deposits, by enabling certain categories of depositors or of deposit to be excluded from the guarantee;

Whereas the principle of a harmonized minimum limit per depositor and not per deposit has been retained; whereas it is therefore appropriate to take into consideration the deposits made by depositors who either are not mentioned as holders of the account or are not the sole holders; whereas the limit must therefore be applied to each identifiable depositor; whereas the same does not apply to collective investments in transferable securities made via financial institutions and subject to special protection rules which do not exist for the abovementioned deposits;

Whereas in compliance with the Directives governing the admission of credit institutions having their head office in third countries, and in particular Article 9(1) of Council Directive 77/780/EEC,[4] as last amended by Directive 89/646/EEC, Member States are to decide whether and on what conditions to admit the branches of such credit institutions to operate on their territory; whereas such branches will not benefit from the free provision of services by virtue of Article 59, second paragraph of the Treaty, nor from freedom of establishment in Member States other than the one in which they are established; whereas accordingly a Member State admitting such branches may decide to oblige or permit such branches access to the guarantee system in place on their territory; whereas, however, it is appropriate that such branches should be required

---

4. OJ No L322, 17 December 1977, p. 30.

to inform their depositors of whether or not they belong to any guarantee system and of the extent and limits of any such guarantees;

Whereas depositor information is an essential element in their protection and must therefore also be the subject of a minimum number of binding provisions;

Whereas deposit protection is an essential element in the completion of the Internal Market and an indispensable supplement to the system of supervision of credit institutions on account of the solidarity it creates between all the institutions in a given financial market in the event of one of them failing,

HAS ADOPTED THIS DIRECTIVE:

Article 1

1. For the purpose of this Directive, the following definitions shall apply:

deposit: credit balances which result from funds left in accounts or from temporary situations deriving from normal banking transactions and which the credit institution must repay under the legal and contractual conditions applicable, and claims for which negotiable certificates have been issued by a credit institution;

joint account: an account opened in the name of two or more persons or over which two or more persons have rights that may operate against the signature of one or more of those persons;

unavailable deposit: a deposit which a credit institution experiencing a financial crisis is unable to repay under the legal and contractual conditions applicable to such repayment.

This suspension of payments need not necessarily be declared or decided by a judicial or administrative authority; it is sufficient for it actually to last for 10 consecutive days.

At the end of that period, the deposit shall be deemed to be unavailable.

2. The following shall be excluded from any repayment by the guarantee schemes:

— the obligations towards other credit institutions,

— subordinated loans in respect of which there exist binding agreements whereby such loans are not to be repaid until after settlement of all other debts in the event of the bankruptcy or liquidation of the credit institution.

Article 2

1. Each Member State shall ensure that on its territory one or more deposit-guarantee schemes are introduced in which all credit institutions authorized in that Member State under Article 3 of Directive 77/780/EEC must take part. The schemes shall cover the depositors of branches set up by such institutions in other Member States.

2. A branch of a credit institution authorized in another Member State may apply to join voluntarily the scheme covering the category of institution to which it belongs in the Member State in which it is established in order to supplement the guarantee which its depositors already enjoy by virtue of their obligatory coverage by the scheme referred to in paragraph 1.

Member States shall ensure that objective conditions relating to the membership of these branches form part of all deposit-guarantee schemes.

3. If one of the credit institutions required by paragraph 1 to take part in the scheme or one of the branches granted voluntary membership under paragraph 2 does not comply with the obligations incumbent on it as a member of the deposit-guarantee scheme, the supervisory authority which issued the authorization shall be notified, and, in co-operation with the managers of the guarantee scheme, shall take all appropriate measures, including the imposition of penalties, to secure compliance by the credit institution with its obligations.

After taking all the measures necessary to secure compliance by the credit institution, or branch thereof, with its obligations and after noting the decisions taken by the supervisory authority (for example reorganization or withdrawal of the authorization), the guarantee scheme may exclude the credit institution or branch. In that case, the guarantee covering the institution's depositors shall be maintained for twelve months from the date of exclusion.

Article 3

1. Subject to Article 9(1) of Directive 77/780/EEC, Member States may stipulate that the branches established by credit institutions with their head office outside the Community must join a deposit-guarantee scheme in operation on their territory.

2. In any event, the managers of foreign branches shall provide their depositors with information enabling them:

— either to identify the guarantee scheme to which the branch belongs and to be aware of the limits or ceilings which exist in that scheme,

— or to note the absence of any such guarantee.

3. The information referred to in paragraph 2 shall be made available in the official language(s) of the Member State in which the branch is established and shall be drafted in a clear and comprehensible form.

Article 4

1. The deposit-guarantee schemes shall stipulate that the aggregate deposits of a given depositor must be covered up to ECU 15,000 in the event of a financial crisis in a credit institution rendering deposits unavailable.

2. Member States may provide that certain depositors or deposits shall be excluded from the guarantee or shall be granted a lower level of guarantee. The exceptions are listed in the Annex.

3. This Article shall not preclude the retention or adoption of provisions which offer a higher guarantee ceiling.

4. Member States may limit the guarantee provided for in paragraph 1 or that referred to in paragraph 3 to a specified percentage of the deposits. However, the percentage guaranteed must equal or exceed 90% of the aggregate deposits until the amount to be paid under the guarantee reaches ECU 15,000.

Article 5

1. The limits referred to in Article 4(1), (3) and (4) shall apply to the aggregate deposits placed with the same credit institution irrespective of the number of deposits, the currency and the location within the Community.

2. The share of each depositor in a joint account shall be taken into account in calculating the limits provided for in Article 4(1), (3) and (4).

In the absence of special provisions, the account shall be divided equally between the depositors.

3. Where an account holder is not the beneficial owner of the sums held in the account, it is the beneficial owner who shall be covered by the guarantee. If there are several beneficial owners, the share of each owner shall be taken into account in calculating the limits provided for in Article 4(1), (3) and (4).

This provision shall not apply to collective investments in transferable securities.

Article 6

1. Member States shall ensure that the managers of the credit institution provide depositors with the information necessary for them to identify the deposit-guarantee scheme in which the institution and its branches take part within the Community. The limits or ceilings applicable under the deposit-guarantee scheme shall be indicated in a readily-comprehensible manner.

2. The information provided for in paragraph 1 shall be available in the official language(s) of the Member State in which the branch is established and the guarantee limits or ceilings and the level of payments shall be expressed in ecus and in national currency.

Article 7

1. Payments under the guarantee provided for in Articles 4 and 5 shall be effected within three months of the date on which the deposit becomes unavailable, or of a court or other authority finding that payment has ceased if this has occurred prior to that date.

2. For justified reasons, relating solely to certain depositors or certain deposits, the guarantee scheme may request the supervisory authority for an extension of the time limit. Such extension may not exceed three months.

3. The time limits referred to in paragraphs 1 and 2 may not be invoked by the guarantee scheme in order to deny the benefit of the guarantee to a depositor who, due to absence or for any other justified reason, has been unable to assert his claim to a payment under the guarantee in time.

4. The documents relating to the conditions and formalities to be fulfilled in order to benefit from a payment under the guarantee referred to in paragraph 1 shall be drawn up in detail in the official language(s) of the Member State in which the guaranteed deposit is located.

5. Payment under the guarantee shall be effected in the national currency of the Member State in which the guaranteed deposit is located or in ecus irrespective of the currency in which the deposits are denominated.

Article 8

1. Member States shall bring into force the laws, regulations and administrative provisions necessary to comply with this Directive by 1 January 1994. They shall forthwith inform the Commission thereof.

When Member States adopt these provisions, these shall contain a reference to this Directive or shall be accompanied by such reference at the time of their official publication. The procedure for such reference shall be adopted by Member States.

2. Member States shall communicate to the Commission the text of the main laws, regulations and administrative decisions which they adopt in the field governed by this Directive.

Article 9

This Directive is addressed to the Member States.

ANNEX. LIST OF DEPOSITS REFERRED TO IN ARTICLE 4(2)

1. Deposits of financial institutions within the meaning of Article 1(6) of Directive 89/646/EEC.

2. Deposits of insurance companies.

3. Deposits of the government and central administrative authorities.

4. Deposits of provincial, regional, local or municipal authorities.

5. Deposits of undertakings for collective investment in transferable securities.

6. Deposits of pension or retirement funds.

7. Deposits of directors, managers, members personally liable, holders of at least 5% of the capital of the credit institution, members of the external auditing bodies and depositors with similar status in subsidiaries.

8. Deposits of close relatives and third parties acting on behalf of the depositors referred to at point 7.

9. Non-nominative deposits.

10. Deposits for which the depositor has, on an individual basis, obtained from the credit institution rates and financial concessions which have helped to aggravate the financial situation of that credit institution.

11. Debt securities issued by the credit institution.

AMENDED PROPOSAL FOR A COUNCIL DIRECTIVE ON DEPOSIT-GUARANTEE SCHEMES[1]

(93/C 178/14) COM(93) 235 final—SYN 415
(Submitted by the Commission pursuant to Article 149(3) of the EEC Treaty
on 7 June 1993)

Initial Proposal	Amended Proposal

THE COUNCIL OF THE EUROPEAN COMMUNITIES,

Unchanged

Having regard to the Treaty establishing the European Economic Community, and in particular the first and third sentences of Article 57(2) thereof,
    Having regard to the proposal from the Commission,
    In co-operation with the European Parliament,
    Having regard to the opinion of the Economic and Social Committee,

First to tenth recital unchanged

Tenth recital

Whereas, however, the harmonized guarantee level must not be too low in order not to leave too great a number of deposits outside the minimum protection threshold; whereas in the absence of statistics on the amount and distribution of deposits in Community credit institutions, it seemed reasonable to take as a basis the median guarantee offered by the national systems; whereas that amount is ECU 15,000;

Tenth recital

Whereas, however, the harmonized guarantee level must not be too low in order not to leave too great a number of depositors outside the minimum protection threshold; whereas it seems reasonable to take as a basis an amount of ECU 20,000 as the harmonized guarantee level;

1. OJ No C 163, 30 June 1992, p. 6.

Eleventh recital

Whereas in the six Member States which are above that median level, the guarantee schemes offer depositors a coverage of their deposits which is higher; whereas it does not seem appropriate to require that these schemes, certain of which have been introduced only recently pursuant to Recommendation 87/63/EEC, be amended on this point;

Eleventh recital

Whereas some Member States offer depositors a coverage of their deposits which is higher; whereas it does not seem appropriate to require that these schemes, certain of which have been introduced only recently pursuant to Recommendation 87/63/EEC, be amended on this point:

Recital 14a (new)

Whereas harmonization of deposit-guarantee schemes in the Community must under no circumstances jeopardize schemes based on the protection of institutions, particularly as they have demonstrated their efficiency; whereas some Member States may accept that institutions participating in such schemes, which pursue a slightly different protection goal, satisfy the Directive's objectives;

The other recitals are unchanged

HAS ADOPTED THIS DIRECTIVE: Unchanged

Article 1

1. For the purpose of this Directive, the following definitions shall apply:

Article 1

1. For the purpose of this Directive the following definitions shall apply:
Credit institution: an undertaking whose business is to receive deposits or other repayable funds from the public and to grant credits for its own account.
Branch: a place of business which forms a legally dependent part of a credit institution and which conducts directly all or some of the operations inherent in the business of credit institutions; any number of branches set up in the same Member State by a credit institution having its head office in another Member State shall be regarded as a single branch;

Deposit: credit balances which result from funds left in accounts or from temporary situations deriving from normal banking transactions and which the credit institution must repay under the legal and contractual conditions applicable, and claims for which negotiable certificates have been issued by a credit institution;

Deposit: credit balances which result from funds left in accounts or from temporary situations deriving from normal banking transactions and which the credit institution must repay under the legal and contractual conditions applicable, and claims for which negotiable certificates have been issued by a credit institution, with the exception of bonds which satisfy the conditions of Article 22(4) of Directive 88/220/EEC concerning undertakings for collective investment in transferable securities (UCITS);

The other definitions are unchanged

2. The following shall be excluded from any repayment by the guarantee schemes:

— the obligations towards other credit institutions,

— subordinated loans in respect of which there exist binding agreements whereby such loans are not to be repaid until after settlement of all other debts in the event of the bankruptcy or liquidation of the credit institution.

2. The following shall be excluded from any repayment by the guarantee schemes;

— subject to the provisions of Article 5(3), the obligations towards other credit institutions,

— subordinated loans in respect of which there exist binding agreements whereby such loans are not to be repaid until after settlement of all other debts in the event of the bankruptcy or liquidation of the credit institution.

Article 2

1. Each Member State shall ensure that on its territory one or more deposit-guarantee schemes are introduced in which all credit institutions authorized in that Member State under Article 3 of Directive 77/780/EEC must take part. The schemes shall cover the depositors of branches set up by such institutions in other Member States.

Article 2

1. Each Member State shall ensure that on its territory one or more deposit-guarantee schemes are introduced. With the exception of the cases referred to in the following subparagraph, no institution authorized in that Member State under Article 3 of Directive 77/780/EEC may accept deposits unless it is a member of one of these schemes. The schemes shall cover the depositors of branches set up by such institutions in other Member States.

Nevertheless, Member States may exempt a credit institution from taking part in a deposit-guarantee scheme if that institution belongs to a scheme which protects the credit institution itself and in particular guarantees its liquid assets and its solvency, provided that:

— such protection is recognized as equivalent to that provided by the authorized scheme or schemes, and

— the protection concerned is not that granted to a public credit institution by Member States themselves or by their local authorities.

Paragraph 2 is unchanged

3. If one of the credit institutions required by paragraph 1 to take part in the scheme or one of the branches granted voluntary membership under paragraph 2 does not comply with the obligations incumbent on it as a member of the deposit-guarantee scheme, the supervisory authority which issued the authorization shall be notified.

3. If one of the credit institutions required by the first subparagraph of paragraph 1 to take part in the scheme or one of the branches granted voluntary membership under paragraph 2 does not comply with the obligations incumbent on it as a member of the deposit-guarantee scheme, the supervisory authority which issued the authorization shall be notified and, in co-operation with the managers of the guarantee scheme, shall take all appropriate measures, including the imposition of penalties, to secure compliance by the credit institution with its obligations.

After taking all the measures necessary to secure compliance by the credit institution, or branch thereof, with its obligations and after noting the decisions taken by the supervisory authority (for example reorganization or withdrawal of the authorization), the guarantee scheme may exclude the credit institution or branch.

In that case, the guarantee covering the institution's depositors shall be maintained for 12 months.

If, as a result of these measures compliance by the credit institution, or branch thereof, with their obligations is not secured, the managers of the guarantee scheme may exclude the credit institution or branch, where national law authorizes such exclusion and with the explicit consent of the supervisory authority.

In that case, the guarantee covering the deposits with that institution, or branch thereof, which were placed no later than one month after the date of exclusion, shall be maintained for 12 months from the date of exclusion.

Article 3

1. Subject to Article 9(1) of Directive 77/780/EEC, Member States may stipulate that the branches established by credit institutions with their head office outside the Community must join a deposit-guarantee scheme in operation on their territory.

Article 3

1. Subject to Article 9(1) of Directive 77/780/EEC, Member States shall ensure that the branches established by credit institutions with their head office outside the Community receive coverage equivalent to that applicable in the Member State concerned under the terms of a guarantee scheme to which their parent institution belongs.

Failing this, Member States may stipulate that the branches established by credit institutions with their head office outside the Community must join a deposit-guarantee scheme in operation on their territory.

Paragraphs 2 and 3 and unchanged

Article 4

1. The deposit-guarantee schemes shall stipulate that the aggregate deposits of a given depositor must be covered up to ECU 15,000 in the event of a financial crisis in a credit institution rendering deposits unavailable.

Article 4

1. The deposit-guarantee schemes shall stipulate that the aggregate deposits of a given depositor must be covered up to ECU 20,000 in the event of a financial crisis in a credit institution rendering deposits unavailable.

Paragraph 2 is unchanged

3. This Article shall not preclude the retention or adoption of provisions which offer a higher guarantee ceiling.

3. This Article shall not preclude the retention or adoption of provisions which offer more comprehensive cover for depositors, in particular by extending the categories of investors protected by the guarantee or raising the maximum level of compensation, nor shall it preclude the adoption of provisions stipulating that certain deposits of vital importance such as pension funds must be guaranteed in their entirety.

4. Member States may limit the guarantee provided for in paragraph 1 or that referred to in paragraph 3 to a specified percentage of the deposits. However, the percentage guaranteed must equal or exceed 90% of the aggregate deposits until the amount to be paid under the guarantee reaches ECU 15,000.

4. Member States may limit the guarantee provided for in paragraph 1 or that referred to in paragraph 3 to a specified percentage of the deposits. However, the percentage guaranteed must equal or exceed 90% of the aggregate deposits until the amount to be paid under the guarantee reaches ECU 20,000.

Paragraph 5 (new)

5. No later than five years after the date mentioned in Article 8(1), the Commission shall present a report to the Council on the application of this Article, accompanied if necessary by proposals which in particular take account of changes in the banking sector and in the economic and monetary situation in the Community.

Article 5 is unchanged

Article 6

1. Member States shall ensure that the managers of the credit institution provide depositors with the information necessary for them to identify the deposit-guarantee scheme in which the institution and its branches take part within the Community. The limits or ceilings applicable under the deposit-guarantee scheme shall be indicated in a readily-comprehensible manner.

Article 6

1. Member States shall ensure that the managers of the credit institution provide depositors with the information necessary for them to identify the deposit-guarantee scheme in which the institution and its branches take part within the Community. The amount of coverage under the deposit guarantee shall be made available to depositors.

Information shall also be given at first request on the conditions for compensation and the formalities which must be fulfilled in order to obtain compensation.

Paragraph 2 is unchanged

Articles 7 to 9 are unchanged

The Annex is unchanged

COUNCIL DIRECTIVE 93/22/EEC OF 10 MAY 1993

on investment services in the securities field

THE COUNCIL OF THE EUROPEAN COMMUNITIES,

Having regard to the Treaty establishing the European Economic Community, and in particular Article 57(2) thereof,

Having regard to the proposal from the Commission,[1]

In co-operation with the European Parliament,[2]

Having regard to the opinion of the Economic and Social Committee,[3]

Whereas this Directive constitutes an instrument essential to the achievement of the internal market, a course determined by the Single European Act and set out in timetable form in the Commission's White Paper, from the point of view both of the right of establishment and of the freedom to provide financial services, in the field of investment firms;

Whereas firms that provide the investment services covered by this Directive must be subject to authorization by their home Member States in order to protect investors and the stability of the financial system;

Whereas the approach adopted is to effect only the essential harmonization necessary and sufficient to secure the mutual recognition of authorization and of prudential supervision systems, making possible the grant of a single authorization valid throughout the Community and the application of the principle of home Member State supervision; whereas, by virtue of mutual recognition, investment firms authorized in their home Member States may carry on any or all of the services covered by this Directive for which they have received authorization throughout the Community by establishing branches or under the freedom to provide services;

Whereas the principles of mutual recognition and of home Member State supervision require that the Member States' competent authorities should not grant or should withdraw authorization where factors such as the content of programmes of operations, the geographical distribution or the activities actually carried on indicate clearly that an investment firm has opted for the legal system of one Member State for the purpose of evading the stricter standards in force in another Member State within the territory of which it intends to carry on or does carry on the greater part of its activities; whereas, for the purposes of this Directive, an investment firm which is a legal person must be authorized in the Member State in which it has its registered office; whereas an investment firm which is not a legal person must be authorized in the Member State in which it has its head office; whereas, in addition, Member States must require that an investment firm's head office must always be situated in its home Member State and that it actually operates there;

Whereas it is necessary, for the protection of investors, to guarantee the internal supervision of every firm, either by means of two-man management or, where that is not required by this Directive, by other mechanisms that ensure an equivalent result;

Whereas in order to guarantee fair competition, it must be ensured that investment firms that are not credit institutions have the same freedom to create branches and provide services across frontiers as is provided for by the Second Council Directive (89/646/EEC) of 15 December 1989

---

1. OJ No C43, 22 February 1989, p. 7; and OJ No C42, 22 February 1990, p. 7.
2. OJ No C304, 4 December 1989, p. 39; and OJ No C115, 26 April 1993.
3. OJ No C298, 27 November 1989, p. 6.

on the co-ordination of laws, regulations and administrative provisions relating to the taking up and pursuit of the business of credit institutions[4];

Whereas an investment firm should not be able to invoke this Directive in order to carry out spot or forward exchange transactions other than as services connected with the provision of investment services; whereas, therefore, the use of a branch solely for such foreign-exchange transactions would constitute misuse of the machinery of this Directive;

Whereas an investment firm authorized in its home Member State may carry on business throughout the Community by whatever means it deems appropriate; whereas, to that end it may, if it deems it necessary, retain tied agents to receive and transmit orders for its account and under its full and unconditional responsibility; whereas, in these circumstances, such agents' business must be regarded as that of the firm; whereas, moreover, this Directive does not prevent a home Member State from making the status of such agents subject to special requirements; whereas should the investment firm carry on cross-border business, the host Member State must treat those agents as being the firm itself; whereas, moreover, the door-to-door selling of transferable securities should not be covered by this Directive and the regulation thereof should remain a matter for national provisions;

Whereas "transferable securities" means those classes of securities which are normally dealt in on the capital market, such as government securities, shares in companies, negotiable securities giving the right to acquire shares by subscription or exchange, depositary receipts, bonds issued as part of a series, index warrants and securities giving the right to acquire such bonds by subscription;

Whereas "money-market instruments" means those classes of instruments which are normally dealt in on the money market such as treasury bills, certificates of deposit and commercial paper;

Whereas the very wide definitions of transferable securities and money-market instruments included in this Directive are valid only for this Directive and consequently in no way affect the various definitions of financial instruments used in national legislation for other purposes such as taxation; whereas, furthermore, the definition of transferable securities covers negotiable instruments only; whereas, consequently, shares and other securities equivalent to shares issued by bodies such as building societies and industrial and provident societies, ownership of which cannot in practice be transferred except by the issuing body's buying them back, are not covered by this definition;

Whereas "instrument equivalent to a financial-futures contract" means a contract which is settled by a payment in cash calculated by reference to fluctuations in interest or exchange rates, the value of any instrument listed in Section B of the Annex or an index of any such instruments;

Whereas, for the purposes of this Directive, the business of the reception and transmission of orders also includes bringing together two or more investors thereby bringing about a transaction between those investors;

Whereas no provision in this Directive affects the Community provisions or, failing such, the national provisions regulating public offers of the instruments covered by this Directive; whereas the same applies to the marketing and distribution of such instruments;

Whereas Member States retain full responsibility for implementing their own monetary-policy measures, without prejudice to the measures necessary to strengthen the European Monetary System;

Whereas it is necessary to exclude insurance undertakings the activities of which are subject to appropriate monitoring by the competent prudential-supervision authorities and which are co-ordinated at Community level and undertakings carrying out reinsurance and retrocession activities;

Whereas undertakings which do not provide services for third parties but the business of which consists in providing investment services solely for their parent undertakings, for their subsidiaries, or for other subsidiaries of their parent undertakings should not be covered by this Directive;

Whereas the purpose of this Directive is to cover undertakings the normal business of which is to provide third parties with investment services on a professional basis; whereas its scope should not therefore cover any person with a different professional activity (eg, a barrister or solicitor)

---

4. OJ No L386, 30 December 1989, p. 1. Directive as last amended by Directive 92/30/EEC (OJ No L110, 28 April 1992, p. 52).

who provides investment services only on an incidental basis in the course of that other professional activity, provided that that activity is regulated and the relevant rules do not prohibit the provision, on an incidental basis, of investment services; whereas it is also necessary for the same reason to exclude from the scope of this Directive persons who provide investment services only for producers or users of commodities to the extent necessary for transactions in such products where such transactions constitute their main business;

Whereas firms which provide investment services consisting exclusively in the administration of employee-participation schemes and which therefore do not provide investment services for third parties should not be covered by this Directive;

Whereas it is necessary to exclude from the scope of this Directive central banks and other bodies performing similar functions as well as public bodies charged with or intervening in the management of the public debt, which concept covers the investment thereof; whereas, in particular, this exclusion does not cover bodies that are partly or wholly State-owned the role of which is commercial or linked to the acquisition of holdings;

Whereas it is necessary to exclude from the scope of this Directive any firms or persons whose business consists only of receiving and transmitting orders to certain counterparties and who do not hold funds or securities belonging to their clients; whereas, therefore, they will not enjoy the right of establishment and freedom to provide services under the conditions laid down in this Directive, being subject, when they wish to operate in another Member State, to the relevant provisions adopted by that State;

Whereas it is necessary to exclude from the scope of this Directive collective investment undertakings whether or not co-ordinated at Community level, and the depositaries or managers of such undertakings, since they are subject to specific rules directly adapted to their activities;

Whereas, where associations created by a Member State's pension funds to permit the management of their assets confine themselves to such management and do not provide investment services for third parties, and where the pension funds are themselves subject to the control of the authorities charged with monitoring insurance undertakings, it does not appear to be necessary to subject such associations to the conditions for taking up business and for operation imposed by this Directive;

Whereas this Directive should not apply to "agenti di cambio" as defined by Italian law since they belong to a category the authorization of which is not to be renewed, their activities are confined to the national territory and they do not give rise to a risk of the distortion of competition;

Whereas the rights conferred on investment firms by this Directive are without prejudice to the right of Member States, central banks and other national bodies performing similar functions to choose their counterparties on the basis of objective, non-discriminatory criteria;

Whereas responsibility for supervising the financial soundness of an investment firm will rest with the competent authorities of its home Member State pursuant to Council Directive 93/6/EEC of 15 March 1993 on the capital adequacy of investment firms and credit institutions,[5] which co-ordinates the rules applicable to market risk;

Whereas a home Member State may, as a general rule, establish rules stricter than those laid down in this Directive, in particular as regards authorization conditions, prudential requirements and the rules of reporting and transparency;

Whereas the carrying on of activities not covered by this Directive is governed by the general provisions of the Treaty on the right of establishment and the freedom to provide services;

Whereas in order to protect investors an investor's ownership and other similar rights in respect of securities and his rights in respect of funds entrusted to a firm should in particular be protected by being kept distinct from those of the firm; whereas this principle does not, however, prevent a firm from doing business in its name but on behalf of the investor, where that is required by the very nature of the transaction and the investor is in agreement, for example stock lending;

Whereas the procedures for the authorization of branches of investment firms authorized in third countries will continue to apply to such firms; whereas those branches will not enjoy the freedom to provide services under the second paragraph of Article 59 of the Treaty or the right of establishment in Member States other than those in which they are established; whereas, however, requests for the authorization of subsidiaries or of the acquisition of holdings by

5. OJ No L141, 11 June 1993, p. 27.

undertakings governed by the laws of third countries are subject to a procedure intended to ensure that Community investment firms receive reciprocal treatment in the third countries in question;

Whereas the authorizations granted to investment firms by the competent national authorities pursuant to this Directive will have Community-wide, and no longer merely nationwide application, and existing reciprocity clauses will henceforth have no effect; whereas a flexible procedure is therefore needed to make it possible to assess reciprocity on a Community basis; whereas the aim of this procedure is not to close the Community's financial markets but rather, as the Community intends to keep its financial markets open to the rest of the world, to improve the liberalization of the global financial markets in third countries; whereas, to that end, this Directive provides for procedures for negotiating with third countries and, as a last resort, for the possibility of taking measures involving the suspension of new applications for authorization and the restriction of new authorizations;

Whereas one of the objectives of this Directive is to protect investors; whereas it is therefore appropriate to take account of the different requirements for protection of various categories of investors and of their levels of professional expertise;

Whereas the Member States must ensure that there are no obstacles to prevent activities that receive mutual recognition from being carried on in the same manner as in the home Member State, as long as they do not conflict with laws and regulations protecting the general good in force in the host Member State;

Whereas a Member State may not limit the right of investors habitually resident or established in that Member State to avail themselves of any investment service provided by an investment firm covered by this Directive situated outside that Member State and acting outwith that Member State;

Whereas in certain Member States clearing and settlement functions may be performed by bodies separate from the markets on which transactions are effected; whereas, accordingly, any reference in this Directive to access to and membership of regulated markets should be read as including references to access to and membership of bodies performing clearing and settlement functions for regulated markets;

Whereas each Member State must ensure that within its territory, treatment of all investment firms authorized in any Member State and likewise all financial instruments listed on the Member States' regulated markets is non-discriminatory; whereas investment firms must all have the same opportunities of joining or having access to regulated markets; whereas, regardless of the manner in which transactions are at present organized in the Member States, it is therefore important, subject to the conditions imposed by this Directive, to abolish the technical and legal restrictions on access to the regulated markets within the framework of this Directive;

Whereas some Member States authorize credit institutions to become members of their regulated markets only indirectly, by setting up specialized subsidiaries; whereas the opportunity which this Directive gives credit institutions of becoming members of regulated markets directly without having to set up specialized subsidiaries constitutes a significant reform for those Member States and all its consequences should be reassessed in the light of the development of the financial markets; whereas, in view of those factors, the report which the Commission will submit to the Council on this matter no later than 31 December 1998 will have to take account of all the factors necessary for the Council to be able to reassess the consequences for those Member States, and in particular the danger of conflicts of interest and the level of protection afforded to investors;

Whereas it is of the greatest importance that the harmonization of compensation systems be brought into effect on the same date as this Directive; whereas, moreover, until the date on which a Directive harmonizing compensation systems is brought into effect, host Member States will be able to impose application of their compensation systems on investment firms including credit institutions authorized by other Member States, where the home Member States have no compensation systems or where their systems do not offer equivalent levels of protection;

Whereas the structure of regulated markets must continue to be governed by national law, without thereby forming an obstacle to the liberalization of access to the regulated markets of host Member States for investment firms authorized to provide the services concerned in their home Member States; whereas, pursuant to that principle, the law of the Federal Republic of Germany and the law of the Netherlands govern the activities *Kursmakler* and *hoekmannen* respectively so as to ensure that they do not exercise their functions in parallel with other functions; whereas it should be noted that *Kursmakler* and *hoekmannen* may not provide services in other Member States; whereas no one, whatever his home Member State, may claim to act as a *Kursmakler* or a *hoekman* without being subject to the same rules on incompatibility as result from the status of *Kursmakler* or *hoekman*;

Whereas it should be noted that this Directive cannot affect the measures taken pursuant to Council Directive 79/279/EEC of 5 March 1979 co-ordinating the conditions for the admission of securities to official stock-exchanging listing[6];

Whereas the stability and sound operation of the financial system and the protection of investors presuppose that a host Member State has the right and responsibility both to prevent and to penalize any action within its territory by investment firms contrary to the rules of conduct and other legal or regulatory provisions it has adopted in the interest of the general good and to take action in emergencies; whereas, moreover, the competent authorities of the host Member State must, in discharging their responsibilities, be able to count on the closest co-operation with the competent authorities of the home Member State, particularly as regards business carried on under the freedom to provide services; whereas the competent authorities of the home Member State are entitled to be informed by the competent authorities of the host Member State of any measures involving penalties on an investment firm or restrictions on its activities which the latter have taken *vis-à-vis* the investment firms which the former have authorized so as to be able to perform their function of prudential supervision efficiently; whereas to that end co-operation between the competent authorities of home and host Member States must be ensured;

Whereas, with the two-fold aim of protecting investors and ensuring the smooth operation of the markets in transferable securities, it is necessary to ensure that transparency of transactions is achieved and that the rules laid down for that purpose in this Directive for regulated markets apply both to investment firms and to credit institutions when they operate on the market;

Whereas examination of the problems arising in the areas covered by the Council Directives on investment services and securities, as regards both the application of existing measures and the possibility of closer co-ordination in the future, requires co-operation between national authorities and the Commission within a committee; whereas the establishment of such a committee does not rule out other forms of co-operation between supervisory authorities in this field;

Whereas technical amendments to the detailed rules laid down in this Directive may from time to time be necessary to take account of new developments in the investment-services sector; whereas the Commission will make such amendments as are necessary, after referring the matter to the committee to be set up in the securities-markets field,

HAS ADOPTED THIS DIRECTIVE:

TITLE I. DEFINITIONS AND SCOPE

Article 1

For the purposes of this Directive:

1. *Investment service* shall mean any of the services listed in Section A of the Annex relating to any of the instruments listed in Section B of the Annex that are provided for a third party;

2. *Investment firm* shall mean any legal person the regular occupation or business of which is the provision of investment services for third parties on a professional basis.

For the purposes of this Directive, Member States may include as investment firms undertakings which are not legal persons if:

— their legal status ensures a level of protection for third parties' interests equivalent to that afforded by legal persons, and
— they are subject to equivalent prudential supervision appropriate to their legal form.

However, where such natural persons provide services involving the holding of third parties' funds or transferable securities, they may be considered as investment firms for the purposes of

6. OJ No L66, 16 March 1979, p. 21. Directive last amended by the Act of Accession of Spain and Portugal.

this Directive only if, without prejudice to the other requirements imposed in this Directive and in Directive 93/6/EEC, they comply with the following conditions:

- the ownership rights of third parties in instruments and funds belonging to them must be safeguarded, especially in the event of the insolvency of a firm or of its proprietors, seizure, set-off or any other action by creditors of the firm or of its proprietors,
- an investment firm must be subject to rules designed to monitor the firm's solvency and that of its proprietors,
- an investment firm's annual accounts must be audited by one or more persons empowered, under national law, to audit accounts,
- where a firm has only one proprietor, he must make provision for the protection of investors in the event of the firm's cessation of business following his death, his incapacity or any other such event.

No later than 31 December 1997 the Commission shall report on the application of the second and third subparagraphs of this point and, if appropriate, propose their amendment or deletion.

Where a person provides one of the services referred to in Section A(1)(a) of the Annex and where that activity is carried on solely for the account of and under the full and unconditional responsibility of an investment firm, that activity shall be regarded as the activity not of that person but of the investment firm itself;

3. *Credit institution* shall mean a credit institution as defined in the first indent of Article 1 of Directive 77/780/EEC[7] with the exception of the institutions referred to in Article 2(2) thereof;

4. *Transferable securities* shall mean:

- shares in companies and other securities equivalent to shares in companies,
- bonds and other forms of securitized debt

which are negotiable on the capital market and

- any other securities normally dealt in giving the right to acquire any such transferable securities by subscription or exchange or giving rise to a cash settlement

excluding instruments of payment;

5. *Money-market instruments* shall mean those classes of instruments which are normally dealt in on the money market;

5. *Home Member State* shall mean:

(a) where the investment firm is a natural person, the Member State in which his head office is situated;

(b) where the investment firm is a legal person, the Member State in which its registered office is situated or, if under its national law it has no registered office, the Member State in which its head office is situated;

(c) in the case of a market, the Member State in which the registered office of the body which provides trading facilities is situated or, if under its national law it has no registered office, the Member State in which that body's head office is situated;

7. *Host Member State* shall mean the Member State in which an investment firm has a branch or provides services;

8. *Branch* shall mean a place of business which is a part of an investment firm, which has no legal personality and which provides investment services for which the investment firm has been authorized; all the places of business set up in the same Member State by an investment firm with headquarters in another Member State shall be regarded as a single branch;

9. *Competent authorities* shall mean the authorities which each Member State designates under Article 22;

10. *Qualifying holding* shall mean any direct or indirect holding in an investment firm which represents 10% or more of the capital or of the voting rights or which makes it possible to exercise a significant influence over the management of the investment firm in which that holding subsists.

For the purposes of this definition, in the context of Articles 4 and 9 and of the other levels of

7. OJ No L322, 17 December 1977, p. 30. Directive last amended by Directive 89/646/EEC (OJ No L386, 30 December 1989, p. 1).

holding referred to in Article 9, the voting rights referred to in Article 7 of Directive 88/627/EEC[8] shall be taken into account;

11. *Parent undertaking* shall mean a parent undertaking as defined in Articles 1 and 2 of Directive 83/349/EEC[9];

12. *Subsidiary* shall mean a subsidiary undertaking as defined in Articles 1 and 2 of Directive 83/349/EEC; any subsidiary of a subsidiary undertaking shall also be regarded as a subsidiary of the parent undertaking which is the ultimate parent of those undertakings;

13. *Regulated market* shall mean a market for the instruments listed in Section B of the Annex which:

— appears on the list provided for in Article 16 drawn up by the Member State which is the home Member State as defined in Article 1(6)(c),
— functions regularly,
— is characterized by the fact that regulations issued or approved by the competent authorities define the conditions for the operation of the market, the conditions for access to the market and, where Directive 79/279/EEC is applicable, the conditions governing admission to listing imposed in that Directive and, where that Directive is not applicable, the conditions that must be satisfied by a financial instrument before it can effectively be dealt in on the market,
— requires compliance with all the reporting and transparency requirements laid down pursuant to Articles 20 and 21;

14. *Control* shall mean control as defined in Article 1 of Directive 83/349/EEC.

Article 2

1. This Directive shall apply to all investment firms. Only paragraph 4 of this Article and Articles 8(2), 10, 11, 12, first paragraph, 14(3) and (4), 15, 19 and 20, however, shall apply to credit institutions the authorization of which, under Directives 77/780/EEC and 89/646/EEC, covers one or more of the investment services listed in Section A of the Annex to this Directive.

2. This Directive shall not apply to:

(a) insurance undertakings as defined in Article 1 of Directive 73/239/EEC[10] or Article 1 of Directive 79/267/EEC[11] or undertakings carrying on the reinsurance and retrocession activities referred to in Directive 64/225/EEC[12];

(b) firms which provide investment services exclusively for their parent undertakings, for their subsidiaries or for other subsidiaries of their parent undertakings;

(c) persons providing an investment service where that service is provided in an incidental manner in the course of a professional activity and that activity is regulated by legal or regulatory provisions or a code of ethics governing the profession which do not exclude the provision of that service;

(d) firms that provide investment services consisting exclusively in the administration of employee-participation schemes;

(e) firms that provide investment services that consist in providing both the services referred to in (b) and those referred to in (d);

(f) the central banks of Member States and other national bodies performing similar functions and other public bodies charged with or intervening in the management of the public debt;

(g) firms

— which may not hold clients' funds or securities and which for that reason may not at any time place themselves in debit with their clients, and

8. OJ No L348, 17 December 1988, p. 62.

9. OJ No L193, 18 July 1983, p. 1. Directive last amended by Directive 90/605/EEC (OJ No L317, 16 November 1990, p. 60).

10. OJ No L228, 16 August 1973, p. 3. Directive last amended by Directive 90/619/EEC (OJ No L330, 29 November 1990, p. 50).

11. OJ No L63, 13 March 1979, p. 1. Directive last amended by Directive 90/618/EEC (OJ No L330, 29 November 1990, p. 44).

12. OJ No 56, 4 April 1964, p. 878/64.

— which may not provide any investment service except the reception and transmission of orders in transferable securities and units in collective investment undertakings, and

— which in the course of providing that service may transmit orders only to
  (i) investment firms authorized in accordance with this Directive;
  (ii) credit institutions authorized in accordance with Directives 77/780/EEC and 89/646/EEC;
  (iii) branches of investment firms or of credit institutions which are authorized in a third country and which are subject to and comply with prudential rules considered by the competent authorities as at least as stringent as those laid down in this Directive, in Directive 89/646/EEC or in Directive 93/6/EEC;
  (iv) collective investment undertakings authorized under the law of a Member State to market units to the public and to the managers of such undertakings;
  (v) investment companies with fixed capital, as defined in Article 15(4) of Directive 77/91/EEC,[13] the securities of which are listed or dealt in on a regulated market in a Member State;

— the activities of which are governed at national level by rules or by a code of ethics;

(h) collective investment undertakings whether co-ordinated at Community level or not and the depositaries and managers of such undertakings;

(i) persons whose main business is trading in commodities amongst themselves or with producers or professional users of such products and who provide investment services only for such producers and professional users to the extent necessary for their main business;

(j) firms that provide investment services consisting exclusively in dealing for their own account on financial-futures or options markets or which deal for the accounts of other members of those markets or make prices for them and which are guaranteed by clearing members of the same markets. Responsibility for ensuring the performance of contracts entered into by such firms must be assumed by clearing members of the same markets;

(k) associations set up by Danish pension funds with the sole aim of managing the assets of pension funds that are members of those associations;

(l) "agenti di cambio" whose activities and functions are governed by Italian Royal Decree No 222 of 7 March 1925 and subsequent provisions amending it, and who are authorized to carry on their activities under Article 19 of Italian Law No 1 of 2 January 1991.

3. No later than 31 December 1998 and at regular intervals thereafter the Commission shall report on the application of paragraph 2 in conjunction with Section A of the Annex and shall, where appropriate, propose amendments to the definition of the exclusions and the services covered in the light of the operation of this Directive.

4. The rights conferred by this Directive shall not extend to the provision of services as counterparty to the State, the central bank or other Member State national bodies performing similar functions in the pursuit of the monetary, exchange-rate, public-debt and reserves management policies of the Member State concerned.

TITLE II. CONDITIONS FOR TAKING UP BUSINESS

Article 3

1. Each Member State shall make access to the business of investment firms subject to authorization for investment firms of which it is the home Member State. Such authorization shall be granted by the home Member State's competent authorities designated in accordance with Article 22. The authorization shall specify the investment services referred to in Section A of the Annex which the undertaking is authorized to provide. The authorization may also cover one or more of the non-core services referred to in Section C of the Annex. Authorization within the meaning of this Directive may in no case be granted for services covered only by Section C of the Annex.

---

13. OJ No L26, 30 January 1977, p. 1. Directive last amended by the Act of Accession of Spain and Portugal.

2. Each Member State shall require that:

— any investment firm which is a legal person and which, under its national law, has a registered office shall have its head office in the same Member State as its registered office,

— any other investment firm shall have its head office in the Member State which issued its authorization and in which it actually carries on its business.

3. Without prejudice to other conditions of general application laid down by national law, the competent authorities shall not grant authorization unless:

— an investment firm has sufficient initial capital in accordance with the rules laid down in Directive 93/6/EEC having regard to the nature of the investment service in question,

— the persons who effectively direct the business of an investment firm are of sufficiently good repute and are sufficiently experienced.

The direction of a firm's business must be decided by at least two persons meeting the above conditions. Where an appropriate arrangement ensures that the same result will be achieved, however, particularly in the cases provided for in the last indent of the third subparagraph of Article 1(2), the competent authorities may grant authorization to investment firms which are natural persons or, taking account of the nature and volume of their activities, to investment firms which are legal persons where such firms are managed by single natural persons in accordance with their articles of association and national laws.

4. Member States shall also require that every application for authorization be accompanied by a programme of operations setting out *inter alia* the types of business envisaged and the organizational structure of the investment firm concerned.

5. An applicant shall be informed within six months of the submission of a complete application whether or not authorization has been granted. Reasons shall be given whenever an authorization is refused.

6. An investment firm may commence business as soon as authorization has been granted.

7. The competent authorities may withdraw the authorization issued to an investment firm subject to this Directive only where that investment firm:

(a) does not make use of the authorization within 12 months, expressly renounces the authorization or ceased to provide investment services more than six months previously unless the Member State concerned has provided for authorization to lapse in such cases;

(b) has obtained the authorization by making false statements or by any other irregular means;

(c) no longer fulfils the conditions under which authorization was granted;

(d) no longer complies with Directive 93/6/EEC;

(e) has seriously and systematically infringed the provisions adopted pursuant to Articles 10 or 11; or

(f) falls within any of the cases where national law provides for withdrawal.

Article 4

The competent authorities shall not grant authorization to take up the business of investment firms until they have been informed of the identities of the shareholders or members, whether direct or indirect, natural or legal persons, that have qualifying holdings and of the amounts of those holdings.

The competent authorities shall refuse authorization if, taking into account the need to ensure the sound and prudent management of an investment firm, they are not satisfied as to the suitability of the aforementioned shareholders or members.

Article 5

In the case of branches of investment firms that have registered offices outwith the Community and are commencing or carrying on business, the Member States shall not apply provisions that result in treatment more favourable than that accorded to branches of investment firms that have registered offices in Member States.

Article 6

The competent authorities of the other Member State involved shall be consulted beforehand on the authorization of any investment firm which is:

— a subsidiary of an investment firm or credit institution authorized in another Member State,

— a subsidiary of the parent undertaking of an investment firm or credit institution authorized in another Member State, or

— controlled by the same natural or legal persons as control an investment firm or credit institution authorized in another Member State.

TITLE III. RELATIONS WITH THIRD COUNTRIES

Article 7

1. The competent authorities of the Member States shall inform the Commission:
    (a) of the authorization of any firm which is the direct or indirect subsidiary of a parent undertaking governed by the law of a third country;
    (b) whenever such a parent undertaking acquires a holding in a Community investment firm such that the latter would become its subsidiary.

In both cases the Commission shall inform the Council until such time as a committee on transferable securities is set up by the Council acting on a proposal from the Commission.

When authorization is granted to any firm which is the direct or indirect subsidiary of a parent undertaking governed by the law of a third country, the competent authorities shall specify the structure of the group in the notification which they address to the Commission.

2. The Member States shall inform the Commission of any general difficulties which their investment firms encounter in establishing themselves or providing investment services in any third country.

3. Initially no later than six months before this Directive is brought into effect and thereafter periodically the Commission shall draw up a report examining the treatment accorded to Community investment firms in third countries, in the terms referred to in paragraphs 4 and 5, as regards establishment, the carrying on of investment services activities and the acquisition of holdings in third-country investment firms. The Commission shall submit those reports to the Council together with any appropriate proposals.

4. Whenever it appears to the Commission, either on the basis of the reports provided for in paragraph 3 or on the basis of other information, that a third country does not grant Community investment firms effective market access comparable to that granted by the Community to investment firms from that third country, the Commission may submit proposals to the Council for an appropriate mandate for negotiation with a view to obtaining comparable competitive opportunities for Community investment firms. The Council shall act by a qualified majority.

5. Whenever it appears to the Commission, either on the basis of the reports referred to in paragraph 3 or on the basis of other information, that Community investment firms in a third country are not granted national treatment affording the same competitive opportunities as are available to domestic investment firms and that the conditions of effective market access are not fulfilled, the Commission may initiate negotiations in order to remedy the situation.

In the circumstances described in the first subparagraph it may also be decided, at any time and in addition to the initiation of negotiations, in accordance with the procedure to be laid down in the Directive by which the Council will set up the committee referred to in paragraph 1, that the competent authorities of the Member States must limit or suspend their decisions regarding requests pending or future requests for authorization and the acquisition of holdings by direct or indirect parent undertakings governed by the law of the third country in question. The duration of such measures may not exceed three months.

Before the end of that three-month period and in the light of the results of the negotiations the Council may, acting on a proposal from the Commission, decide by a qualified majority whether the measures shall be continued.

Such limitations or suspensions may not be applied to the setting up of subsidiaries by investment firms duly authorized in the Community or by their subsidiaries, or to the acquisition of holdings in Community investment firms by such firms or subsidiaries.

6. Whenever it appears to the Commission that one of the situations described in paragraphs 4 and 5 obtains, the Member States shall inform it at its request:

(a) of any application for the authorization of any firm which is the direct or indirect subsidiary of a parent undertaking governed by the law of the third country in question;

(b) whenever they are informed in accordance with Article 10 that such a parent undertaking proposes to acquire a holding in a Community investment firm such that the latter would become its subsidiary.

This obligation to provide information shall lapse whenever agreement is reached with the third country referred to in paragraph 4 or 5 or when the measures referred to in the second and third subparagraphs of paragraph 5 cease to apply.

7. Measures taken under this Article shall comply with the Community's obligations under any international agreements, bilateral or multilateral, governing the taking up or pursuit of the business of investment firms.

TITLE IV. OPERATING CONDITIONS

Article 8

1. The competent authorities of the home Member States shall require that an investment firm which they have authorized comply at all times with the conditions imposed in Article 3(3).

2. The competent authorities of the home Member State shall require that an investment firm which they have authorized comply with the rules laid down in Directive 93/6/EEC.

3. The prudential supervision of an investment firm shall be the responsibility of the competent authorities of the home Member State whether the investment firm establishes a branch or provides services in another Member State or not, without prejudice to those provisions of this Directive which give responsibility to the authorities of the host Member State.

Article 9

1. Member States shall require any person who proposes to acquire, directly or indirectly, a qualifying holding in an investment firm first to inform the competent authorities, telling them of the size of his intended holding. Such a person shall likewise inform the competent authorities if he proposes to increase his qualifying holding so that the proportion of the voting rights or of the capital that he holds would reach or exceed 20, 33, or 50% or so that the investment firm would become his subsidiary.

Without prejudice to paragraph 2, the competent authorities shall have up to three months from the date of the notification provided for in the first subparagraph to oppose such a plan if in view of the need to ensure sound and prudent management of the investment firm, they are not satisfied as to the suitability of the person referred to in the first subparagraph. If they do not oppose the plan, they may fix a deadline for its implementation.

2. If the acquirier of the holding referred to in paragraph 1 is an investment firm authorized in another Member State or the parent undertaking of an investment firm authorized in another Member State or a person controlling an investment firm authorized in another Member State and if, as a result of that acquisition, the firm in which the acquirier proposes to acquire a holding would become the acquirier's subsidiary or come under his control, the assessment of the acquisition must be the subject of the prior consultation provided for in Article 6.

3. Member States shall require any person who proposes to dispose, directly or indirectly, of a qualifying holding in an investment firm first to inform the competent authorities telling them of the size of his holding. Such a person shall likewise inform the competent authorities if he proposes to reduce his qualifying holding so that the proportion of the voting rights or of the capital held by him would fall below 20, 33 or 50% or so that the investment firm would cease to be his subsidiary.

4. On becoming aware of them, investment firms shall inform the competent authorities of any acquisitions or disposals of holding in their capital that cause holdings to exceed or fall below any of the thresholds referred to in paragraphs 1 and 3.

At least once a year they shall also inform the competent authorities of the names of shareholders and members possessing qualifying holdings and the sizes of such holdings as shown, for example, by the information received at annual general meetings of shareholders and members or as a result of compliance with the regulations applicable to companies listed on stock exchanges.

5. Member States shall require that, where the influence exercised by the persons referred to in paragraph 1 is likely to be prejudicial to the sound and prudent management of an investment firm, the competent authorities take appropriate measures to put an end to that situation. Such measures may consist, for example, in injunctions, sanctions against directors and those responsible for management or suspension of the exercise of the voting rights attaching to the shares held by the shareholders or members in question.

Similar measures shall apply to persons failing to comply with the obligation to provide prior information imposed in paragraph 1. If a holding is acquired despite the opposition of the competent authorities, the Member States shall, regardless of any other sanctions to be adopted, provide either for exercise of the corresponding voting rights to be suspended, for the nullity of the votes cast or for the possibility of their annulment.

Article 10

Each home Member State shall draw up prudential rules which investment firms shall observe at all times. In particular, such rules shall require that each investment firm:

— have sound administrative and accounting procedures, control and safeguard arrangements for electronic data processing, and adequate internal control mechanisms including, in particular, rules for personal transactions by its employees,

— make adequate arrangements for instruments belonging to investors with a view to safeguarding the latter's ownership rights, especially in the event of the investment firm's instruments for its own account except with the investors' express consent,

— make adequate arrangements for funds belonging to investors with a view to safeguarding the latter's rights and, except in the case of credit institutions, preventing the investment firm's using investors' funds for its own account,

— arrange for records to be kept of transactions executed which shall at least be sufficient to enable the home Member State's authorities to monitor compliance with the prudential rules which they are responsible for applying; such records shall be retained for periods to be laid down by the competent authorities,

— be structured and organized in such a way as to minimize the risk of clients' interests being prejudiced by conflicts of interest between the firm and its clients or between one of its clients and another. Nevertheless, where a branch is set up the organizational arrangements may not conflict with the rules of conduct laid down by the host Member State to cover conflicts of interest.

Article 11

1. Member States shall draw up rules of conduct which investment firms shall observe at all times. Such rules must implement at least the principles set out in the following indents and must be applied in such a way as to take account of the professional nature of the person for whom the service is provided. The Member States shall also apply these rules where appropriate to the non-core services listed in Section C of the Annex. These principles shall ensure that an investment firm:

— acts honestly and fairly in conducting its business activities in the best interests of its clients and the integrity of the market,

— acts with due skill, care and diligence, in the best interests of its clients and the integrity of the market,

— has and employs effectively the resources and procedures that are necessary for the proper performance of its business activities,

— seeks from its clients information regarding their financial situations, investment experience and objectives as regards the services requested,

— makes adequate disclosure of relevant material information in its dealings with its clients,

— tries to avoid conflicts of interests and, when they cannot be avoided, ensures that its clients are fairly treated, and

— complies with all regulatory requirements applicable to the conduct of its business activities so as to promote the best interests of its clients and the integrity of the market.

2. Without prejudice to any decisions to be taken in the context of the harmonization of the rules of conduct, their implementation and the supervision of compliance with them shall remain the responsibility of the Member State in which a service is provided.

3. Where an investment firm executes an order, for the purposes of applying the rules referred to in paragraph 1 the professional nature of the investor shall be assessed with respect to the investor from whom the order originates, regardless of whether the order was placed directly by the investor himself or indirectly through an investment firm providing the service referred to in Section A(1)(a) of the Annex.

Article 12

Before doing business with them, a firm shall inform investors which compensation fund or equivalent protection will apply in respect of the transactions envizaged, what cover is offered by whichever system applies, or if there is no fund or compensation.

The Council notes the Commission's statement to the effect that it will submit proposals on the harmonization of compensation systems covering transactions by investment firms by 31 July 1993 at the latest. The Council will act on those proposals within the shortest possible time with the aim of bringing the systems proposed into effect on the same date as this Directive.

Article 13

This Directive shall not prevent investment firms authorized in other Member States from advertizing their services through all available means of communication in their host Member States, subject to any rules governing the form and the content of such advertizing adopted in the interest of the general good.

TITLE V. THE RIGHT OF ESTABLISHMENT AND THE FREEDOM TO PROVIDE SERVICES

Article 14

1. Member States shall ensure that investment services and the other services listed in Section C of the Annex may be provided within their territories in accordance with Articles 17, 18 and 19 either by the establishment of a branch or under the freedom to provide services by any investment firm authorized and supervised by the competent authorities of another Member State in accordance with this Directive, provided that such services are covered by the authorization.

This Directive shall not affect the powers of host Member States in respect of the units of collective investment undertakings to which Directive 85/611/EEC[14] does not apply.

2. Member States may not make the establishment of a branch or the provision of services referred to in paragraph 1 subject to any authorization requirement, to any requirement to provide endowment capital or to any other measure having equivalent effect.

3. A Member State may require that transactions relating to the services referred to in paragraph 1 must, where they satisfy all the following criteria, be carried out on a regulated market:

— the investor must be habitually resident or established in that Member State,

— the investment firm must carry out such transactions through a main establishment, through a branch situated in that Member State or under the freedom to provide services in that Member State,

14. OJ No L375, 31 December 1985, p. 3. Directive last amended by Directive 88/220/EEC (OJ No L100, 19 April 1988, p. 31).

— the transaction must involve an instrument dealt in on a regulated market in that Member State.

4. Where a Member State applies paragraph 3 it shall give investors habitually resident or established in that Member State the right not to comply with the obligation imposed in paragraph 3 and have the transactions referred to in paragraph 3 carried out away from a regulated market. Member States may make the exercise of this right subject to express authorization, taking into account investors' differing needs for protection and in particular the ability of professional and institutional investors to act in their own best interests. It must in any case be possible for such authorization to be given in conditions that do not jeopardize the prompt execution of investors' orders.

5. The Commission shall report on the operation of paragraphs 3 and 4 not later than 31 December 1998 and shall, if appropriate, propose amendments thereto.

Article 15

1. Without prejudice to the exercise of the right of establishment or the freedom to provide services referred to in Article 14, host Member States shall ensure that investment firms which are authorized by the competent authorities of their home Member States to provide the services referred to in Section A(1)(b) and (2) of the Annex can, either directly or indirectly, become members of or have access to the regulated markets in their host Member States where similar services are provided and also become members of or have access to the clearing and settlement systems which are provided for the members of such regulated markets there.

Member States shall abolish any national rules or laws or rules of regulated markets which limit the number of persons allowed access thereto. If, by virtue of its legal structure or its technical capacity, access to a regulated market is limited, the Member State concerned shall ensure that its structure and capacity are regularly adjusted.

2. Membership of or access to a regulated market shall be conditional on investment firms' complying with capital adequacy requirements and home Member States' supervizing such compliance in accordance with Directive 93/6/EEC.

Host Member States shall be entitled to impose additional capital requirements only in respect of matters not covered by that Directive.

Access to a regulated market, admission to membership thereof and continued access or membership shall be subject to compliance with the rules of the regulated market in relation to the constitution and administration of the regulated market and to compliance with the rules relating to transactions on the market, with the professional standards imposed on staff operating on and in conjunction with the market, and with the rules and procedures for clearing and settlement. The detailed arrangements for implementing these rules and procedures may be adapted as appropriate, *inter alia* to ensure fulfilment of the ensuing obligations, provided, however, that Article 28 is complied with.

3. In order to meet the obligation imposed in paragraph 1, host Member States shall offer the investment firms referred to in that paragraph the choice of becoming members of or of having access to their regulated markets either:

— directly, by setting up branches in the host Member States, or
— indirectly, by setting up subsidiaries in the host Member States or by acquiring firms in the host Member States that are already members of their regulated markets or already have access thereto.

However, those Member States which, when this Directive is adopted, apply laws which do not permit credit institutions to become members of or have access to regulated markets unless they have specialized subsidiaries may continue until 31 December 1996 to apply the same obligation in a non-discriminatory way to credit institutions from other Member States for purposes of access to those regulated markets.

The Kingdom of Spain, the Hellenic Republic and the Portuguese Republic may extend that period until 31 December 1999. One year before that date the Commission shall draw up a report, taking into account the experience acquired in applying this Article and shall if appropriate, submit a proposal. The Council may, acting by qualified majority on the basis of that proposal, decide to review those arrangements.

4. Subject to paragraphs 1, 2 and 2, where the regulated market of the host Member State operates without any requirement for a physical presence the investment firms referred to in paragraph 1 may become members of or have access to it on the same basis without having to be established in the host Member State. In order to enable their investment firms to become members of or have access to host Member States' regulated markets in accordance with this paragraph home Member States shall allow those host Member States' regulated markets to provide appropriate facilities within the home Member States' territories.

5. This Article shall not affect the Member States' right to authorize or prohibit the creation of new markets within their territories.

6. This Article shall have no effect:

— in the Federal Republic of Germany, on the regulation of the activities of *Kursmakler*, or
— in the Netherlands, on the regulation of the activities of *hoekmannen*.

Article 16

For the purposes of mutual recognition and the application of this Directive, it shall be for each Member State to draw up a list of the regulated markets for which it is the home Member State and which comply with its regulations, and to forward that list for information, together with the relevant rules of procedures and operation of those regulated markets, to the other Member States and the Commission. A similar communication shall be effected in respect of each change to the aforementioned list or rules. The Commission shall publish the lists of regulated markets and updates thereto in the *Official Journal of the European Communities* at least once a year.

No later than 31 December 1996 the Commission shall report on the information thus received and, where appropriate, propose amendments to the definition of regulated market for the purposes of this Directive.

Article 17

1. In addition to meeting the conditions imposed in Article 3, any investment firm wishing to establish a branch within the territory of another Member State shall notify the competent authorities of its home Member State.

2. Member States shall require every investment firm wishing to establish a branch within the territory of another Member State to provide the following information when effecting the notification provided for in paragraph 1:
    (a) the Member State within the territory of which it plans to establish a branch;
    (b) a programme of operations setting out *inter alia* the types of business envisaged and the organizational structure of the branch;
    (c) the address in the host Member State from which documents may be obtained;
    (d) the names of those responsible for the management of the branch.

3. Unless the competent authorities of the home Member State have reason to doubt the adequacy of the administrative structure or the financial situation of an investment firm, taking into account the activities envisaged, they shall, within three months of receiving all the information referred to in paragraph 2, communicate that information to the competent authorities of the host Member State and shall inform the investment firm concerned accordingly.

They shall also communicate details of any compensation scheme intended to protect the branch's investors.

Where the competent authorities of the home Member State refuse to communicate the information referred to in paragraph 2 to the competent authorities of the host Member State, they shall give reasons for their refusal to the investment firm concerned within three months of receiving all the information. That refusal or failure to reply shall be subject to the right to apply to the courts in the home Member States.

4. Before the branch of an investment firm commences business the competent authorities of the host Member State shall, within two months of receiving the information referred to in paragraph 3, prepare for the supervision of the investment firm in accordance with Article 19 and, if necessary, indicate the conditions, including the rules of conduct, under which, in the interest of the general good, that business must be carried on in the host Member State.

5. On receipt of a communication from the competent authorities of the host Member State or

on the expiry of the period provided for in paragraph 4 without receipt of any communication from those authorities, the branch may be established and commence business.

6. In the event of a change in any of the particulars communicated in accordance with paragraph 2(b), (c) or (d), an investment firm shall give written notice of that change to the competent authorities of the home and host Member States at least one month before implementing the change so that the competent authorities of the home Member State may take a decision on the change under paragraph 3 and the competent authorities of the host Member State may do so under paragraph 4.

7. In the event of a change in the particulars communicated in accordance with the second subparagraph of paragraph 3, the authorities of the home Member State shall inform the authorities of the host Member State accordingly.

Article 18

1. Any investment firm wishing to carry on business within the territory of another Member State for the first time under the freedom to provide services shall communicate the following information to the competent authorities of its home Member State:

— the Member State in which it intends to operate,
— a programme of operations stating in particular the investment service or services which it intends to provide.

2. The competent authorities of the home Member State shall, within one month of receiving the information referred to in paragraph 1, forward it to the competent authorities of the host Member State. The investment firm may then start to provide the investment service or services in question in the host Member State.

Where appropriate, the competent authorities of the host Member State shall, on receipt of the information referred to in paragraph 1, indicate to the investment firm the conditions, including the rules of conduct, with which, in the interest of the general good, the providers of the investment services in question must comply in the host Member State.

3. Should the content of the information communicated in accordance with the second indent of paragraph 1 be amended, the investment firm shall give notice of the amendment in writing to the competent authorities of the home Member State and of the host Member State before implementing the change, so that the competent authorities of the host Member State may, if necessary, inform the firm of any change or addition to be made to the information communicated under paragraph 2.

Article 19

1. Host Member States may, for statistical purposes, require all investment firms with branches within their territories to report periodically on their activities in those host Member States to the competent authorities of those host Member States.

In discharging their reponsibilities in the conduct of monetary policy, without prejudice to the measures necessary for the strengthening of the European Monetary System, host Member States may within their territories require all branches of investment firms originating in other Member States to provide the same particulars as national investment firms for that purpose.

2. In discharging their responsibilities under this Directive, host Member States may require branches of investment firms to provide the same particulars as national firms for that purpose.

Host Member States may require investment firms carrying on business within their territories under the freedom to provide services to provide the information necessary for the monitoring of their compliance with the standards set by the host Member State that apply to them, although those requirements may not be more stringent than those which the same Member State imposes on established firms for the monitoring of their compliance with the same standards.

3. Where the competent authorities of a host Member State ascertain that an investment firm that has a branch or provides services within its territory is in breach of the legal or regulatory provisions adopted in that State pursuant to those provisions of this Directive which confer powers on the host Member State's competent authorities, those authorities shall require the investment firm concerned to put an end to its irregular situation.

4. If the investment firm concerned fails to take the necessary steps, the competent authorities

of the host Member State shall inform the competent authorities of the home Member State accordingly. The latter shall, at the earliest opportunity, take all appropriate measures to ensure that the investment firm concerned puts an end to its irregular situation. The nature of those measures shall be communicated to the competent authorities of the host Member State.

5. If, despite the measures taken by the home Member State or because such measures prove inadequate or are not available in the State in question, the investment firm persists in violating the legal or regulatory provisions referred to in paragraph 2 in force in the host Member State, the latter may, after informing the competent authorities of the home Member State, take appropriate measures to prevent or to penalize further irregularities and, in so far as necessary, to prevent that investment firm from initiating any further transactions within its territory. The Member States shall ensure that within their territories it is possible to serve the legal documents necessary for those measures on investment firms.

6. The foregoing provisions shall not affect the powers of host Member States to take appropriate measures to prevent or to penalize irregularities committed within their territories which are contrary to the rules of conduct introduced pursuant to Article 11 as well as to other legal or regulatory provisions adopted in the interest of the general good. This shall include the possibility of preventing offending investment firms from initiating any further transactions within their territories.

7. Any measure adopted pursuant to paragraphs 4, 5 or 6 involving penalties or restrictions on the activities of an investment firm must be properly justified and communicated to the investment firm concerned. Every such measure shall be subject to the right to apply to the courts in the Member State which adopted it.

8. Before following the procedure laid down in paragraphs 3, 4 or 5 the competent authorities of the host Member State may, in emergencies, take any precautionary measures necessary to protect the interests of investors and others for whom services are provided. The Commission and the competent authorities of the other Member States concerned must be informed of such measures at the earliest opportunity.

After consulting the competent authorities of the Member States concerned, the Commission may decide that the Member State in question must amend or abolish those measures.

9. In the event of the withdrawal of authorization, the competent authorities of the host Member State shall be informed and shall take appropriate measures to prevent the investment firm concerned from initiating any further transactions within its territory and to safeguard investors' interests. Every two years the Commission shall submit a report on such cases to the committee set up at a later stage in the securities field.

10. The Member States shall inform the Commission of the number and type of cases in which there have been refusals pursuant to Article 17 or measures have been taken in accordance with paragraph 5. Every two years the Commission shall submit a report on such cases to the committee set up at a later date in the securities field.

Article 20

1. In order to ensure that the authorities responsible for the markets and for supervision have access to the information necessary for the performance of their duties, home Member States shall at least require:
   (a) without prejudice to steps taken in implementation of Article 10, that investment firms keep at the disposal of the authorities for at least five years the relevant data on transactions relating to the services referred to in Article 14(1) which they have carried out in instruments dealt in on a regulated market, whether such transactions were carried out on a regulated market or not;
   (b) that investment firms report to competent authorities in their home Member States all the transactions referred to in (a) where those transactions cover:
   — shares or other instruments giving access to capital,
   — bonds and other forms of securitized debt,
   — standardized forward contracts relating to shares or
   — standardized options on shares.

Such reports must be made available to the relevant authority at the earliest opportunity. The time limit shall be fixed by that authority. It may be extended to the end of the following working day where operational or practical reasons so dictate but in no circumstances may it exceed that limit.

Such reports must, in particular, include details of the names and numbers of the instruments bought or sold, the dates and times of the transactions, the transaction prices and means of identifying the investment firms concerned.

Home Member States may provide that the obligation imposed in (b) shall, in the case of bonds and other forms of securitized debt, apply only to aggregated transactions in the same instrument.

2. Where an investment firm carries out a transaction on a regulated market in its host Member State, the home Member State may waive its own requirements as regards reporting if the investment firm is subject to equivalent requirements to report the transaction in question to the authorities in charge of that market.

3. Member States shall provide that the report referred to in paragraph 1(b) shall be made either by the investment firm itself or by a trade-matching system, or through stock-exchange authorities or those of another regulated market.

4. Member States shall ensure that the information available in accordance with this Article is also available for the proper application of Article 23.

5. Each Member State may, in a non-discriminatory manner, adopt or maintain provisions more stringent in the field governed by this Article with regard to substance and form in respect of the conservation and reporting of data relating to transactions:

— carried out on a regulated market of which it is the home Member State or
— carried out by investment firms of which it is the home Member State.

Article 21

1. In order to enable investors to assess at any time the terms of a transaction they are considering and to verify afterwards the conditions in which it has been carried out, each competent authority shall, for each of the regulated markets which it has entered on the list provided for in Article 16, take measures to provide investors with the information referred to in paragraph 2. In accordance with the requirements imposed in paragraph 2, the competent authorities shall determine the form in which and the precise time within which the information is to be provided, as well as the means by which it is to be made available, having regard to the nature, size and needs of the market concerned and of the investors operating on that market.

2. The competent authorities shall require for each instrument at least:

(a) publication at the start of each day's trading on the market of the weighted average price, the highest and the lowest prices and the volume dealt in on the regulated market in question for the whole of the preceding day's trading;

(b) in addition, for continuous order-driven and quote-driven markets, publication:

— at the end of each hour's trading on the market, of the weighted average price and the volume dealt in on the regulated market in question for a six-hour trading period ending so as to leave two hours' trading on the market before publication, and
— every 20 minutes, of the weighted average price and the highest and lowest prices on the regulated market in question for a two-hour trading period ending so as to leave one hour's trading on the market before publication.

Where investors have prior access to information on the prices and quantities for which transactions may be undertaken:

(i) such information shall be available at all times during market trading hours;
(ii) the terms announced for a given price and quantity shall be terms on which it is possible for an investor to carry out such a transaction.

The competent authorities may delay or suspend publication where that proves to be justified by exceptional market conditions or, in the case of small markets, to preserve the anonymity of firms and investors. The competent authorities may apply special provisions in the case of exceptional transactions that are very large in scale compared with average transactions in the security in question on that market and in the case of highly illiquid securities defined by means of objective criteria and made public. The competent authorities may also apply more flexible provisions, particularly as regards publication deadlines, for transactions concerning bonds and other forms of securitized debt.

3. In the field governed by this Article each Member State may adopt or maintain more

stringent provisions or additional provisions with regard to the substance and form in which information must be made available to investors concerning transactions carried out on regulated markets of which it is the home Member State, provided that those provisions apply regardless of the Member State in which the issuer of the financial instrument is located or of the Member State on the regulated market of which the instrument was listed for the first time.

4. The Commission shall report on the application of this Article no later than 31 December 1977; the Council may, on a proposal from the Commission, decide by a qualified majority to amend this Article.

TITLE VI. AUTHORITIES RESPONSIBLE FOR AUTHORIZATION AND SUPERVISION

Article 22

1. Member States shall designate the competent authorities which are to carry out the duties provided for in this Directive. They shall inform the Commission thereof, indicating any division of those duties.

2. The authorities referred to in paragraph 1 must be either public authorities, bodies recognized by national law or bodies recognized by public authorities expressly empowered for that purpose by national law.

3. The authorities concerned must have all the powers necessary for the performance of their functions.

Article 23

1. Where there are two or more competent authorities in the same Member State, they shall collaborate closely in supervising the activities of investment firms operating in that Member State.

2. Member States shall ensure that such collaboration takes place between such competent authorities and the public authorities responsible for the supervision of financial markets, credit and other financial institutions and insurance undertakings, as regards the entities which those authorities supervise.

3. Where, through the provision of services or by the establishment of branches, an investment firm operates in one or more Member States other than its home Member State the competent authorities of all the Member States concerned shall collaborate closely in order more effectively to discharge their respective responsibilities in the area covered by this Directive.

They shall supply one another on request with all the information concerning the management and ownership of such investment firms that is likely to facilitate their supervision and all information likely to facilitate the monitoring of such firms. In particular, the authorities of the home Member State shall co-operate to ensure that the authorities of the host Member State collect the particulars referred to in Article 19(2).

In so far as it is necessary for the purpose of exercising their powers of supervision, the competent authorities of the home Member State shall be informed by the competent authorities of the host Member State of any measures taken by the host Member State pursuant to Article 19(6) which involve penalties imposed on an investment firm or restrictions on an investment firm's activities.

Article 24

1. Each host Member State shall ensure that, where an investment firm authorized in another Member State carries on business within its territory through a branch, the competent authorities of the home Member State may, after informing the competent authorities of the host Member State, themselves or through the intermediary of persons they instruct for the purpose carry out on-the-spot verification of the information referred to in Article 23(3).

2. The competent authorities of the home Member State may also ask the competent authorities of the host Member State to have such verification carried out. Authorities which receive such requests must, within the framework of their powers, act upon them by carrying out

the verifications themselves, by allowing the authorities who have requested them to carry them out or by allowing auditors or experts to do so.

3. This Article shall not affect the right of the competent authorities of a host Member State, in discharging their responsibilties under this Directive, to carry out on-the-spot verifications of branches established within their territory.

Article 25

1. Member States shall provide that all persons who work or who have worked for the competent authorities, as well as auditors and experts instructed by the competent authorities, shall be bound by the obligation of professional secrecy. Accordingly no confidential information which they may receive in the course of their duties may be divulged to any person or authority whatsoever, save in summary or aggregate form such that individual investment firms cannot be identified, without prejudice to cases covered by criminal law.

Nevertheless, where an investment firm has been declared bankrupt or is being compulsorily wound up, confidential information which does not concern third parties involved in attempts to rescue that investment firm may be divulged in civil or commercial proceedings.

2. Paragraph 1 shall not prevent the competent authorities of different Member States from exchanging information in accordance with this Directive or other Directives applicable to investment firms. That information shall be subject to the conditions of professional secrecy imposed in paragraph 1.

3. Member States may conclude co-operation agreements providing for exchanges of information with the competent authorities of third countries only if the information disclosed is covered by guarantees of professional secrecy at least equivalent to those provided for in this Article.

4. Competent authorities receiving confidential information under paragraph 1 or 2 may use it only in the course of their duties:

— to check that the conditions governing the taking up of the business of investment firms are met and to facilitate the monitoring, on a non-consolidated or consolidated basis, of the conduct of that business, especially with regard to the capital adequacy requirements imposed in Directive 93/6/EEC, administrative and accounting procedures and internal-control mechanisms,

— to impose sanctions,

— in administrative appeals against decisions by the competent authorities, or

— in court proceedings initiated under Article 26.

5. Paragraphs 1 and 4 shall not preclude the exchange of information:
   (a) within a Member State, where there are two or more competent authorities, or
   (b) within a Member State or between Member States, between competent authorities and
      — authorities responsible for the supervision of credit institutions, other financial organizations and insurance undertakings and the authorities responsible for the supervision of financial markets,
      — bodies responsible for the liquidation and bankruptcy of investment firms and other similar procedures and
      — persons responsible for carrying out statutory audits of the accounts of investment firms and other financial institutions,
      — in the performance of their supervisory functions, or the disclosure to bodies which administer compensation schemes of information necessary for the performance of their functions. Such information shall be subject to the conditions of professional secrecy imposed in paragraph 1.

6. This Article shall not prevent a competent authority from disclosing to those central banks which do not supervise credit institutions or investment firms individually such information as they may need to act as monetary authorities. Information received in this context shall be subject to the conditions of professional secrecy imposed in paragraph 1.

7. This Article shall not prevent the competent authorities from communicating the information referred to in paragraphs 1 to 4 to a clearing house or other similar body recognized under national law for the provision of clearing or settlement services for one of their Member

State's markets if they consider that it is necessary to communicate the information in order to ensure the proper functioning of those bodies in relation to defaults or potential defaults by market participants. The information received shall be subject to the conditions of professional secrecy imposed in paragraph 1. The Member States shall, however, ensure that information received under paragraph 2 may not be disclosed in the circumstances referred to in this paragraph without the express consent of the competent authorities which disclosed it.

8. In addition, notwithstanding the provisions referred to in paragraphs 1 and 4, Member States may, by virtue of provisions laid down by law, authorize the disclosure of certain information to other departments of their central government administrations responsible for legislation on the supervision of credit institutions, financial institutions, investment firms and insurance undertakings and to inspectors instructed by those departments.

Such disclosures may, however, be made only where necessary for reasons of prudential control.

Member States shall, however, provide that information received under paragraphs 2 and 5 and that obtained by means of the on-the-spot verifications referred to in Article 24 may never be disclosed in the cases referred to in this paragraph except with the express consent of the competent authorities which disclosed the information or of the competent authorities of the Member State in which the on-the-spot verification was carried out.

9. If, at the time of the adoption of this Directive, a Member State provides for the exchange of information between authorities in order to check compliance with the laws on prudential supervision, on the organization, operation and conduct of commercial companies and on the regulation of financial markets, that Member State may continue to authorize the forwarding of such information pending co-ordination of all the provisions governing the exchange of information between authorities for the entire financial sector but not in any case after 1 July 1996.

Member States shall, however, ensure that, where information comes from another Member State, it may not be disclosed in the circumstances referred to in the first subparagraph without the express consent of the competent authorities which disclosed it and it may be used only for the purposes for which those authorities gave their agreement.

The Council shall effect the co-ordination referred to in the first subparagraph on the basis of a Commission proposal. The Council notes the Commission's statement to the effect that it will submit proposals by 31 July 1993 at the latest. The Council will act on those proposals within the shortest possible time with the intention of bringing the rules proposed into effect on the same date as this Directive.

Article 26

Member States shall ensure that decisions taken in respect of an investment firm under laws, regulations and administrative provisions adopted in accordance with this Directive are subject to the right to apply to the courts; the same shall apply where no decision is taken within six months of its submission in respect of an application for authorization which provides all the information required under the provisions in force.

Article 27

Without prejudice to the procedures for the withdrawal of authorization or to the provisions of criminal law, Member States shall provide that their respective competent authorities may, with regard to investment firms or those who effectively control the business of such firms that infringe laws, regulations or administrative provisions concerning the supervision or carrying on of their activities, adopt or impose in respect of them measures or penalties aimed specifically at ending observed breaches or the causes of such breaches.

Article 28

Member States shall ensure that this Directive is implemented without discrimination.

TITLE VII. FINAL PROVISIONS

Article 29

Pending the adoption of a further Directive laying down provisions adapting this Directive to technical progress in the areas specified below, the Council shall, in accordance with Decision 87/373/EEC,[15] acting by a qualified majority on a proposal from the Commission, adopt any adaptations which may be necessary, as follows:

- expansion of the list in Section C of the Annex,
- adaptation of the terminology of the lists in the Annex to take account of developments on financial markets,
- the areas in which the competent authorities must exchange information as listed in Article 23;
- clarification of the definitions in order to ensure uniform application of this Directive in the Community,
- clarification of the definitions in order to take account in the implementation of this Directive of developments on financial markets,
- the alignment of terminology and the framing of definitions in accordance with subsequent measures on investment firms and related matters,
- the other tasks provided for in Article 7(5).

Article 30

1. Investment firms already authorized in their home Member States to provide investment services before 31 December 1995 shall be deemed to be so authorized for the purpose of this Directive, if the laws of those Member States provide that to take up such activities they must comply with conditions equivalent to those imposed in Articles 3(3) and 4.

2. Investment firms which are already carrying on business on 31 December 1995 and are not included among those referred to in paragraph 1 may continue their activities provided that, no later than 31 December 1996 and pursuant to the provisions of their home Member States, they obtain authorization to continue such activities in accordance with the provisions adopted in implementation of this Directive.

Only the grant of such authorization shall enable such firms to qualify under the provisions of this Directive on the right of establishment and the freedom to provide services.

3. Where before the date of the adoption of this Directive investment firms have commenced business in other Member States either through branches or under the freedom to provide services, the authorities of each home Member State shall, between 1 July and 31 December 1995, communicate, for the purposes of Articles 17(1) and (2) and 18, to the authorities of each of the other Member States concerned the list of firms that comply with this Directive and operate in those States, indicating the business carried on.

4. Natural persons authorized in a Member State on the date of the adoption of this Directive to offer investment services shall be deemed to be authorized under this Directive, provided that they fulfil the requirements imposed in Article 1(2), second subparagraph, second indent, and third subparagraph, all four indents.

Article 31

No later than 1 July 1995 Member States shall adopt the laws, regulations and administrative provisions necessary for them to comply with this Directive.

These provisions shall enter into force no later than 31 December 1995. The Member States shall forthwith inform the Commission thereof.

15. OJ No L197, 18 July 1987, p. 33.

When Member States adopt the provisions referred to in the first paragraph they shall include a reference to this Directive or accompany them with such a reference on the occasion of their official publication. The manner in which such references are to be made shall be laid down by the Member States.

Article 32

This Directive is addressed to the Member States.

Done at Brussels, 10 May 1993.

For the Council
The President
N. HELVEG PETERSEN

ANNEX

SECTION A: SERVICES

1. (a) Reception and transmission, on behalf of investors, of orders in relation to one or more of the instruments listed in Section B.
     (b) Execution of such orders other than for own account.
2. Dealing in any of the instruments listed in Section B for own account.
3. Managing portfolios of investments in accordance with mandates given by investors on a discriminatory, client-by-client basis where such portfolios include one or more of the instruments listed in Section B.
4. Underwriting in respect of issues of any of the instruments listed in Section B and/or the placing of such issues.

SECTION B: INSTRUMENTS

1. (a) Transferable securities.
     (b) Units in collective investment undertakings.
2. Money-market instruments.
3. Financial-futures contracts, including equivalent cash-settled instruments.
4. Forward interest-rate agreements (FRAs).
5. Interest-rate, currency and equity swaps.
6. Options to acquire or dispose of any instruments falling within this section of the Annex, including equivalent cash-settled instruments. This category includes in particular options on currency and on interest rates.

SECTION C: NON-CORE SERVICES

1. Safekeeping and administration in relation to one or more of the instruments listed in Section B.
2. Safe custody services.
3. Granting credits or loans to an investor to allow him to carry out a transaction in one or more of the instruments listed in Section B, where the firm granting the credit or loan is involved in the transaction.
4. Advice to undertakings on capital structure, industrial strategy and related matters and advice and service relating to mergers and the purchase of undertakings.
5. Services related to underwriting.
6. Investment advice concerning one or more of the instruments listed in Section B.
7. Foreign-exchange services where these are connected with the provision of investment services.

COUNCIL DIRECTIVE 93/6/EEC OF 15 MARCH 1993

on the capital adequacy of investments firms and credit institutions

THE COUNCIL OF THE EUROPEAN COMMUNITIES,

Having regard to the Treaty establishing the European Economic Community, and in particular the first and third sentences of Article 57(2) thereof,

Having regard to the proposal from the Commission,[1]

In co-operation with the European Parliament,[2]

Having regard to the opinion of the Economic and Social Committee,[3]

Whereas the main objective of Council Directive 93/22/EEC of 10 May 1993 on investment services in the securities field[4] is to allow investment firms authorized by the competent authorities of their home Member States and supervised by the same authorities to establish branches and provide services freely in other Member States; whereas that Directive accordingly provides for the co-ordination of the rules governing the authorization and pursuit of the business of investment firms;

Whereas that Directive does not, however, establish common standards for the own funds of investment firms nor indeed does it establish the amounts of the initial capital of such firms; whereas it does not establish a common framework for monitoring the risks incurred by the same firms; whereas it refers, in several of its provisions, to another Community initiative, the objective of which would be precisely to adopt co-ordinated measures in those fields;

Whereas the approach that has been adopted is to effect only the essential harmonization that is necessary and sufficient to secure the mutual recognition of authorization and of prudential supervision systems; whereas the adoption of measures to co-ordinate the definition of the own funds of investment firms, the establishment of the amounts of their initial capital and the establishment of a common framework for monitoring the risks incurred by investment firms are essential aspects of the harmonization necessary for the achievement of mutual recognition within the framework of the internal financial market;

Whereas it is appropriate to establish different amounts of initial capital depending on the range of activities that investment firms are authorized to undertake;

Whereas existing investment firms should be permitted, under certain conditions, to continue their business even if they do not comply with the minimum amount of initial capital fixed for new firms;

Whereas the Member States may also establish rules stricter than those provided for in this Directive;

Whereas this Directive forms part of the wider international effort to bring about approximation of the rules in force regarding the supervision of investment firms and credit institutions (hereinafter referred to collectively as "institutions");

Whereas common basic standards for the own funds of institutions are a key feature in an internal market in the investment services sector, since own funds serve to ensure the continuity of institutions and to protect investors;

Whereas in a common financial market, institutions, whether they are investment firms or credit institutions, engage in direct competition with one another;

1. OJ No C152, 21 June 1990, p. 6; and OJ No C50, 25 February 1992, p. 5.
2. OJ No C326, 16 December 1991, p. 89; and OJ No C337, 21 December 1992, p. 114.
3. OJ No C69, 18 March 1991, p. 1.
4. See Appendix H, *supra*.

Whereas it is therefore desirable to achieve equality in the treatment of credit institutions and investment firms;

Whereas, as regards credit institutions, common standards are already established for the supervision and monitoring of credit risks in Council Directive 89/647/EEC of 18 December 1989 on a solvency ratio for credit institutions[5];

Whereas it is necessary to develop common standards for market risks incurred by credit institutions and provide a complementary framework for the supervision of the risks incurred by institutions, in particular market risks, and more especially position risks, counterparty/settlement risk and foreign-exchange risks;

Whereas it is necessary to introduce the concept of a "trading book" comprising positions in securities and other financial instruments which are held for trading purposes and are subject mainly to market risks and exposures relating to certain financial services provided to customers;

Whereas it is desirable that institutions with negligible trading-book business, in both absolute and relative terms, should be able to apply Directive 89/647/EEC, rather than the requirements imposed in Annexes I and II to this Directive;

Whereas it is important that monitoring of settlement/delivery risks should take account of the existence of systems offering adequate protection that reduces that risk;

Whereas, in any case, institutions must comply with this Directive as regards the coverage of the foreign-exchange risks on their overall business; whereas lower capital requirements should be imposed for positions in closely correlated currencies, whether statistically confirmed or arising out of binding intergovernmental agreements, with a view in particular to the creation of the European Monetary Union;

Whereas the existence, in all institutions, of internal systems for monitoring and controlling interest-rate risks on all of their business is a particularly important way of minimizing such risks; whereas, consequently, such systems must be subject to overview by the competent authorities;

Whereas Council Directive 92/121/EEC of 21 December 1992 on the monitoring and control of large exposures of credit institutions[6] is not aimed at establishing common rules for monitoring large exposures in activities which are principally subject to market risks; whereas that Directive makes reference to another Community initiative intended to adopt the requisite co-ordination of methods in that field;

Whereas it is necessary to adopt common rules for the monitoring and control of large exposures incurred by investment firms;

Whereas the own funds of credit institutions have already been defined in Council Directive 89/299/EEC of 17 April 1989 on the own funds of credit institutions[7];

Whereas the basis for the definition of the own funds of institutions should be that definition;

Whereas, however, there are reasons why for the purposes of this Directive the definition of the own funds of institutions may differ from that in the aforementioned Directive in order to take account of the particular characteristics of the activities carried on by those institutions which mainly involve market risks;

Whereas Council Directive 92/30/EEC of 6 April 1992 on the supervision of credit institutions on a consolidated basis[8] states the principle of consolidation; whereas it does not establish common rules for the consolidation of financial institutions which are involved in activities principally subject to market risks; whereas that Directive makes reference to another Community initiative intended to adopt co-ordinated measures in that field;

Whereas Directive 92/30/EEC does not apply to groups which include one or more investment firms but no credit institutions; whereas it was, however, felt desirable to provide a common framework for the introduction of the supervision of investment firms on a consolidated basis;

Whereas technical adaptations to the detailed rules laid down in this Directive may from time to time be necessary to take account of new developments in the investment services field; whereas the Commission will accordingly propose such adaptations as are necessary;

Whereas the Council should, at a later stage, adopt provision for the adaptation of this

5. OJ No L386, 30 December 1989, p. 14. Directive as amended by Directive 92/30/EEC (OJ No L110, 28 April 1992, p. 52).

6. OJ No L29, 5 February 1993, p. 1.

7. OJ No L124, 5 May 1989, p. 16. Directive as last amended by Directive 92/30/EEC (OJ No L110, 24 September 1992, p. 52).

8. OJ No L110, 28 April 1992, p. 52.

Directive to technical progress in accordance with Council Decision 87/373/EEC of 13 July 1987 laying down the procedures for the exercise of implementing powers conferred on the Commission[9]; whereas meanwhile the Council itself, on a proposal from the Commission, should carry out such adaptations;

Whereas provision should be made for the review of this Directive within three years of the date of its application in the light of experience, developments on financial markets and work in international fora of regulatory authorities; whereas that review should also include the possible review of the list of areas that may be subject to technical adjustment;

Whereas this Directive and Directive 93/22/EEC on investment services in the securities field are so closely interrelated that their entry into force on different dates could lead to the distortion of competition,

HAS ADOPTED THIS DIRECTIVE

Article 1

1. Member States shall apply the requirements of this Directive to investment firms and credit institutions as defined in Article 2.

2. A Member State may impose additional or more stringent requirements on the investment firms and credit institutions that it has authorized.

DEFINITIONS

Article 2

For the purposes of this Directive:

1. *Credit institutions* shall mean all institutions that satisfy the definition in the first indent of Article 1 of the First Council Directive (77/780/EEC) of 12 December 1977 on the co-ordination of laws, regulations and administrative provisions relating to the taking up and pursuit of the business of credit institutions[10] which are subject to the requirements imposed by Directive 89/647/EEC;

2. *Investment firms* shall mean all institutions that satisfy the definition in point 2 of Article 1 of Directive 93/22/EEC, which are subject to the requirements imposed by the same Directive, excluding:

— credit institutions,
— local firms as defined in 20, and
— firms which only receive and transmit orders from investors without holding money or securities belonging to their clients and which for that reason may not at any time place themselves in debit with their clients;

3. *Institutions* shall mean credit institutions and investment firms;

4. *Recognized third-country investment firms* shall mean firms which, if they were established within the Community, would be covered by the definition of investment firm in 2, which are authorized in a third country and which are subject to and comply with prudential rules considered by the competent authorities as at least as stringent as those laid down in this Directive;

5. *Financial instruments* shall mean the instruments listed in Section B of the Annex to Directive 93/22/EEC;

6. *The trading book* of an institution shall consist of:

(a) its proprietary positions in financial instruments which are held for resale and/or which are taken on by the institution with the intention of benefiting in the short term from actual and/or expected differences between their buying and selling prices, or from other

9. OJ No L197, 18 July 1987, p. 33.
10. OJ No L322, 17 December 1977, p. 30. Directive as amended by Directive 89/646/EEC (OJ No L386, 30 December 1989, p. 1).

price or interest-rate variations, and positions in financial instruments arising from matched principal broking, or positions taken in order to hedge other elements of the trading book;

(b) the exposures due to the unsettled transactions, free deliveries and over-the-counter (OTC) derivative instruments referred to in paragraphs 1, 2, 3 and 5 of Annex II, the exposures due to repurchase agreements and securities lending which are based on securities included in the trading book as defined in (a) referred to in paragraph 4 of Annex II, those exposures due to reverse repurchase agreements and securities-borrowing transactions described in the same paragraph, provided the competent authorities so approve, which meet either the conditions (i), (ii), (iii) and (v) or conditions (iv) and (v) as follows:

    (i) the exposures are marked to market daily following the procedures laid down in Annex II;

    (ii) the collateral is adjusted in order to take account of material changes in the value of the securities involved in the agreement or transaction in question, according to a rule acceptable to the component authorities;

    (iii) the agreement or transaction provides for the claims of the institution to be automatically and immediately offset against the claims of its counter-party in the event of the latter's defaulting;

    (iv) the agreement or transaction in question is an interprofessional one;

    (v) such agreements and transactions are confined to their accepted and appropriate use and artificial transactions, especially those not of a short-term nature, are excluded; and

(c) those exposures in the form of fees, commission, interest, dividends and margin on exchange-traded derivatives which are directly related to the items included in the trading book referred to in paragraph 6 of Annex II.

Particular items shall be included in or excluded from the trading book in accordance with objective procedures including, where appropriate, accounting standards in the institution concerned, such procedures and their consistent implementation being subject to review by the competent authorities;

7. *Parent undertaking, subsidiary undertaking* and *financial institution* shall be defined in accordance with Article 1 of Directive 92/30/EEC;

8. *Financial holding company* shall mean a financial institution the subsidiary undertakings of which are either exclusively or mainly credit institutions, investment firms or other financial institutions, one of which at least is a credit institution or an investment firm;

9. *Risk weightings* shall mean the degrees of credit risk applicable to the relevant counter-parties under Directive 89/647/EEC. However, assets constituting claims on and other exposures to investment firms or recognized third-country investment firms and exposures incurred to recognized clearing houses and exchanges shall be assigned the same weighting as that assigned where the relevant counterparty is a credit institution;

10. *Over-the-counter (OTC) derivative instruments* shall mean the interest-rate and foreign-exchange contracts referred to in Annex II to Directive 89/647/EEC and off-balance-sheet contracts based on equities, provided that no such contracts are traded on recognized exchanges where they are subject to daily margin requirements and, in the case of foreign-exchange contracts, that every such contract has an original maturity of more than 14 calendar days;

11. *Regulated market* shall mean a market that satisfies the definition given in Article 1(13) of Directive 93/22/EEC;

12. *Qualifying items* shall mean long and short positions in the assets referred to in Article 6(1)(b) of Directive 89/647/EEC and in debt instruments issued by investment firms or by recognized third-country investment firms. It shall also mean long and short positions in debt instruments provided that such instruments meet the following conditions: such instruments must firstly be listed on at least one regulated market in a Member State or on a stock exchange in a third country provided that that exchange is recognized by the competent authorities of the relevant Member State; and secondly both be considered by the institution concerned to be sufficiently liquid and, because of the solvency of the issuer, be subject to a degree of default risk

which is comparable to or lower than that of the assets referred to in Article 6(1)(b) of Directive 89/647/EEC; the manner in which the instruments are assessed shall be subject to scrutiny by the competent authorities, which shall overturn the judgment of the institution if they consider that the instruments concerned are subject to too high a degree of default risk to be qualifying items.

Notwithstanding the foregoing and pending further co-ordination, the competent authorities shall have the discretion to recognize as qualifying items instruments which are sufficiently liquid and which, because of the solvency of the issuer, are subject to a degree of default risk which is comparable to or lower than that of the assets referred to in Article 6(1)(b) and Directive 89/647/EEC. The default risk associated with such instruments must have been evaluated at such a level by at least two credit-rating agencies recognized by the competent authorities or by only one such credit-rating agency so long as they are not rated below such a level by any other credit-rating agency recognized by the competent authorities.

The competent authorities may, however, waive the condition imposed in the preceding sentence if they judge it inappropriate in the light of, for example, the characteristics of the market, the issuer, the issue, or some combination of those characteristics.

Furthermore, the competent authorities shall require the institutions to apply the maximum weighting shown in Table 1 in paragraph 14 of Annex I to instruments which show a particular risk because of the insufficient solvency of the issuer or liquidity.

The competent authorities of each Member State shall regularly provide the Council and the Commission with information concerning the methods used to evaluate the qualifying items, in particular the methods used to assess the degree of liquidity of the issue and the solvency of the issuer;

13. *Central government items* shall mean long and short positions in the assets referred to in Article 6(1)(a) of Directive 89/647/EEC and those assigned a weighting of 0% in Article 7 of the same Directive;

14. *Convertible* shall mean a security which, at the option of the holder, can be exchanged for another security, usually the equity of the issuer;

15. *Warrant* shall mean an instrument which gives the holder the right to purchase a number of shares of common stock or bonds at a stipulated price until the warrant's expiry date. They may be settled by the delivery of the securities themselves or their equivalent in cash;

16. *Covered warrant* shall mean an instrument issued by an entity other than the issuer of the underlying instrument which gives the holder the right to purchase a number of shares of common stock or bonds at a stipulated price or a right to secure a profit or avoid a loss by reference to fluctuations in an index relating to any of the financial instruments listed in Section B of the Annex to Directive 93/22/EEC until the warrant's expiry date;

17. *Repurchase agreement* and *reverse repurchase agreement* shall mean any agreement in which an institution or its counter-party transfers securities or guaranteed rights relating to title to securities where that guarantee is issued by a recognized exchange which holds the rights to the securities and the agreement does not allow an institution to transfer or pledge a particular security to more than one counter-party at one time, subject to a commitment to repurchase them (or substituted securities of the same description) at a specified price on a future date specified, or to be specified, by the transferor, being a repurchase agreement for the institution selling the securities and a reverse repurchase agreement for the institution buying them.

A reverse repurchase agreement shall be considered an interprofessional transaction when the counter-party is subject to prudential co-ordination at Community level or is a Zone A credit institution as defined in Directive 89/647/EEC or is a recognized third-country investment firm or when the agreement is concluded with a recognized clearing house or exchange;

18. *Securities lending* and *securities borrowing* shall mean any transaction in which an institution or its counter-party transfers securities against appropriate collateral subject to a commitment that the borrower will return equivalent securities at some future date or when requested to do so by the transferor, being securities lending for the institution transferring the securities and securities borrowing for the institution to which they are transferred.

Securities borrowing shall be considered an interprofessional transaction when the counterparty is subject to prudential co-ordination at Community level or is a Zone A credit institution as defined in Directive 89/647/EEC or is a recognized third-country investment firm or when the transaction is concluded with a recognized clearing house or exchange;

19. *Clearing member* shall mean a member of the exchange or the clearing house which has a direct contractual relationship with the central counterparty (market guarantor); non-clearing members must have their trades routed through a clearing member;

20. *Local firm* shall mean a firm dealing only for its own account on a financial-futures or options exchange or for the accounts of or making a price to other members of the same exchange and guaranteed by a clearing member of the same exchange. Responsibility for ensuring the performance of contracts entered into by such a firm must be assumed by a clearing member of the same exchange, and such contracts must be taken into account in the calculation of the clearing member's overall capital requirements so long as the local firm's positions are entirely separate from those of the clearing member;

21. *Delta* shall mean the expected change in an option price as a proportion of a small change in the price of the instrument underlying the option;

22. For the purposes of paragraph 4 of Annex I, *long position* shall mean a position in which an institution has fixed the interest rate it will receive at some time in the future, and *short position* shall mean a position in which it has fixed the interest rate it will pay at some time in the future;

23. *Own funds* shall mean own funds as defined in Directive 89/299/EEC. This definition may, however, be amended in the circumstances described in Annex V;

24. *Initial capital* shall mean items 1 and 2 of Article 2(1) of Directive 89/299/EEC;

25. *Original own funds* shall mean the sum of items 1, 2 and 4, less the sum of items 9, 10 and 11 of Article 2(1) of Directive 89/299/EEC;

26. *Capital* shall mean own funds;

27. *Modified duration* shall be calculated using the formula set out in paragraph 26 of Annex I.

INITIAL CAPITAL

Article 3

1. Investment firms which hold clients' money and/or securities and which offer one or more of the following services shall have initial capital of ECU 125,000:

— the reception and transmission of investors' orders for financial instruments,
— the execution of investors' orders for financial instruments,
— the management of individual portfolios of investments in financial instruments,

provided that they do not deal in any financial instruments for their own account or underwrite issues of financial instruments on a firm commitment basis.

The holding of non-trading-book positions in financial instruments in order to invest own funds shall not be considered as dealing for the purposes set out in the first paragraph or for the purposes of paragraph 2.

The competent authorities may, however, allow an investment firm which executes investors' orders for financial instruments to hold such instruments for its own account if:

— such positions arise only as a result of the firm's failure to match investors' orders precisely,
— the total market value of all such positions is subject to a ceiling of 15% of the firm's initial capital,
— the firm meets the requirements imposed in Articles 4 and 5, and
— such positions are incidental and provisional in nature and strictly limited to the time required to carry out the transaction in question.

2. Member States may reduce the amount referred to in paragraph 1 to ECU 50,000 where a firm is not authorized to hold clients' money or securities, to deal for its own account, or to underwrite issues on a firm commitment basis.

3. All other investment firms shall have initial capital of ECU 730,000.

4. The firms referred to in the second and third indents of Article 2(2) shall have initial capital of ECU 50,000 in so far as they benefit from freedom of establishment or provide services under Articles 14 or 15 of Directive 93/22/EEC.

5. Notwithstanding paragraphs 1 to 4, Member States may continue the authorization of investment firms and firms covered by paragraph 4 in existence before this Directive is applied the

own funds of which are less than the initial capital levels specified for them in paragraphs 1 to 4. The own funds of such firms shall not fall below the highest reference level calculated after the date of notification of this Directive. That reference level shall be the average daily level of own funds calculated over a six-month period preceding the date of calculation. It shall be calculated every six months in respect of the corresponding preceding period.

6. If control of a firm covered by paragraph 5 is taken by a natural or legal person other than the person who controlled it previously, the own funds of that firm must attain at least the level specified for it in paragraphs 1 to 4, except in the following situations:

(i) in the case of the first transfer by inheritance after the application of this Directive, subject to the competent authorities' approval, for not more than 10 years after that transfer;

(ii) in the case of a change in the composition of a partnership, as long as at least one of the partners at the date of the application of this Directive remains in the partnership, for not more than 10 years after the date of the application of this Directive.

7. In certain specific circumstances and with the consent of the competent authorities, however, in the event of a merger of two or more investment firms and/or firms covered by paragraph 4, the own funds of the firm produced by the merger need not attain the level specified in paragraphs 1 to 4. Nevertheless, during any period when the levels specified in paragraphs 1 to 4 have not been attained, the own funds of the new firm may not fall below the merged firms' total own funds at the time of the merger.

8. The own funds of investment firms and firms covered by paragraph 4 may not fall below the level specified in paragraphs 1 to 5 and 7. If they do, however, the competent authorities may, where the circumstances justify it, allow such firms a limited period in which to rectify their situations or cease their activities.

PROVISIONS AGAINST RISKS

Article 4

1. The competent authorities shall require institutions to provide own funds which are always more than or equal to the sum of:

(i) the capital requirements, calculated in accordance with Annexes, I, II and VI, for their trading-book business;

(ii) the capital requirements, calculated in accordance with Annex III, for all of their business activities;

(iii) the capital requirements imposed in Directive 89/647/EEC for all of their business activities, excluding both their trading-book business and their illiquid assets if they are deducted from own funds under paragraph 2(d) of Annex V;

(iv) the capital requirements imposed in paragraph 2.

Irrespective of the amount of the capital requirement referred to in (i) to (iv) the own-funds requirement for investment firms shall never be less than the amount prescribed in Annex IV.

2. The competent authorities shall require institutions to cover the risks arising in connection with business that is outside the scope of both this Directive and Directive 89/647/EEC and considered to be similar to the risks covered by those Directives by adequate own funds.

3. If the own funds held by an institution fall below the amount of the own funds requirement imposed in paragraph 1, the competent authorities shall ensure that the institution in question takes appropriate measures to rectify its situation as quickly as possible.

4. The competent authorities shall require institutions to set up systems to monitor and control the interest-rate risk on all of their business, and those systems shall be subject to overview by the competent authorities.

5. Institutions shall be required to satisfy their competent authorities that they employ systems which can calculate their financial positions with reasonable accuracy at any time.

6. Notwithstanding paragraph 1, the competent authorities may allow institutions to calculate the capital requirements for their trading-book business in accordance with Directive 89/647/EEC rather than in accordance with Annexes I and II to this Directive provided that:

(i) the trading-book business of such institutions does not normally exceed 5% of their total business;

(ii) their total trading-book positions do not normally exceed ECU 15 million; and

(iii) the trading-book business of such institutions never exceeds 6% of their total business and their total trading-book positions never exceed ECU 20 million.

7. In order to calculate the proportion that trading-book business bears to total business as in paragraph 6(i) and (iii), the competent authorities may refer either to the size of the combined on- and off-balance-sheet business, to the profit and loss account or to the own funds of the institutions in question, or to a combination of those measurements. When the size of on- and off-balance-sheet business is assessed, debt instruments shall be valued at their market prices or their principal values, equities at their market prices and derivatives according to the nominal or market values of the instruments underlying them. Long positions and short positions shall be summed regardless of their signs.

8. If an institution should happen for more than a short period to exceed either or both of the limits imposed in paragraph 6(i) and (ii) or to exceed either or both of the limits imposed in paragraph 6(iii), it shall be required to meet the requirements imposed in Article 4(1)(i) rather than those of Directive 89/647/EEC in respect of its trading-book business and to notify the competent authority.

MONITORING AND CONTROL OF LARGE EXPOSURES

Article 5

1. Institutions shall monitor and control their large exposures in accordance with Directive 92/121/EEC.

2. Notwithstanding paragraph 1, those institutions which calculate the capital requirements for their trading-book business in accordance with Annexes I and II shall monitor and control their large exposures in accordance with Directive 92/121/EEC subject to the modifications laid down in Annex VI to this Directive.

VALUATION OF POSITIONS FOR REPORTING PURPOSES

Article 6

1. Institutions shall mark to market their trading books on a daily basis unless they are subject to Article 4(6).

2. In the absence of readily available market prices, for example in the case of dealing in new issues on the primary markets, the competent authorities may waive the requirement imposed in paragraph 1 and require institutions to use alternative methods of valuation provided that those methods are sufficiently prudent and have been approved by competent authorities.

SUPERVISION ON A CONSOLIDATED BASIS

Article 7

General principles

1. The capital requirements imposed in Articles 4 and 5 for institutions which are neither parent undertakings nor subsidiaries of such undertakings shall be applied on a solo basis.

2. The requirements imposed in Articles 4 and 5 for:

— any institution which has a credit institution within the meaning of Directive 92/30/EEC, an investment firm or another financial institution as a subsidiary or which holds a participation in such an entity, and

— any institution the parent undertaking of which is a financial holding company shall be applied on a consolidated basis in accordance with the methods laid down in the abovementioned Directive and in paragraphs 7 to 14 of this Article.

3. When a group covered by paragraph 2 does not include a credit institution, Directive 92/30/EEC shall apply, subject to the following adaptations:

— *financial holding company* shall mean a financial institution the subsidiary undertakings of which are either exclusively or mainly investment firms or other financial institutions one at least of which is an investment firm,

— *mixed-activity holding company* shall mean a parent undertaking, other than a financial holding company or an investment firm, the subsidiaries of which include at least one investment firm,

— *competent authorities* shall mean the national authorities which are empowered by law or regulation to supervise investment firms,

— every reference to credit institutions shall be replaced by a reference to investment firms,

— the second subparagraph of Article 3(5) of Directive 92/30/EEC shall not apply,

— in Articles 4(1) and (2) and 7(5) of Directive 92/30/EEC each reference to Directive 77/780/EEC shall be replaced by a reference to Directive 93/22/EEC,

— for the purposes of Articles 3(9) and 8(3) of Directive 92/30/EEC the references to the Banking Advisory Committee shall be substituted by references to the Council and the Commission,

— the first sentence of Article 7(4) of Directive 92/30/EEC shall be replaced by the following:

"Where an investment firm, a financial holding company or a mixed-activity holding company controls one or more subsidiaries which are insurance companies, the competent authorities and the authorities entrusted with the public task of supervising insurance undertakings shall co-operate closely."

4. The competent authorities required or mandated to exercise supervision of groups covered by paragraph 3 on a consolidated basis may, pending further co-ordination on the supervision of such groups on a consolidated basis and where the circumstances justify it, waive that obligation provided that each investment firm in such a group:

(i) uses the definition of own funds given in paragraph 9 of Annex V;

(ii) meets the requirements imposed in Articles 4 and 5 on a solo basis;

(iii) sets up systems to monitor and control the sources of capital and funding of all other financial institutions within the group.

5. The competent authorities shall require investment firms in a group which has been granted the waiver provided for in paragraph 4 to notify them of those risks, including those associated with the composition and sources of their capital and funding, which could undermine their financial positions. If the competent authorities then consider that the financial positions of those investment firms is not adequately protected, they shall require them to take measures including, if necessary, limitations on the transfer of capital from such firms to group entities.

6. Where the competent authorities waive the obligation of supervision on a consolidated basis provided for in paragraph 4 they shall take other appropriate measures to monitor the risks, namely large exposures, of the whole group, including any undertakings not located in a Member State.

7. Member States may waive the application of the requirements imposed in Articles 4 and 5, on an individual or subconsolidated basis, to an institution which, as a parent undertaking, is subject to supervision on a consolidated basis, and to any subsidiary of such an institution which is subject to their authorization and supervision and is included in the supervision on a consolidated basis of the institution which is its parent company.

The same right of waiver shall be granted where the parent undertaking is a financial holding company which has its head office in the same Member State as the institution, provided that it is subject to the same supervision as that exercised over credit institutions or investment firms, and in particular the requirements imposed in Articles 4 and 5.

In both cases, if the right of waiver is exercised measures must be taken to ensure the satisfactory allocation of own funds within the group.

8. Where an institution the parent undertaking of which is an institution has been authorized

and is situated in another Member State, the competent authorities which granted that authorization shall apply the rules laid down in Articles 4 and 5 to that institution on a individual or, where appropriate, a subconsolidated basis.

9. Notwithstanding paragraph 8, the competent authorities responsible for authorizing the subsidiary of a parent undertaking which is an institution may, by a bilateral agreement, delegate their responsibility for supervising the subsidiary's capital adequacy and large exposures to the competent authorities which authorized and supervise the parent undertaking. The Commission must be kept informed of the existence and content of such agreements. It shall forward such information to the competent authorities of the other Member States and to the Banking Advisory Committee and to the Council, except in the case of groups covered by paragraph 3.

Calculating the consolidated requirements

10. Where the rights of waiver provided for in paragraphs 7 and 9 are not exercised, the competent authorities may, for the purpose of calculating the capital requirements set out in Annex I and the exposures to clients set out in Annex VI on a consolidated basis, permit net positions in the trading book of one institution to offset positions in the trading book of another institution according to the rules set out in Annexes I and VI respectively.

In addition, they may allow foreign-exchange positions subject to Annex III in one institution to offset foreign-exchange positions subject to Annex III in another institution in accordance with the rules set out in Annex III.

11. The competent authorities may also permit offsetting of the trading book and of the foreign-exchange positions of undertakings located in third countries, subject to the simultaneous fulfilment of the following conditions:

(i) those undertakings have been authorized in a third country and either satisfy the definition of credit institution given in the first indent of Article 1 of Directive 77/780/EEC or are recognized third-country investment firms;
(ii) such undertakings comply, on a solo basis, with capital adequacy rules equivalent to those laid down in this Directive;
(iii) no regulations exist in the countries in question which might significantly affect the transfer of funds within the group.

12. The competent authorities may also allow the offsetting provided for in paragraph 10 between institutions within a group that have been authorized in the Member State in question, provided that:

(i) there is a satisfactory allocation of capital within the group;
(ii) the regulatory, legal or contractual framework in which the institutions operate is such as to guarantee mutual financial support within the group.

13. Furthermore, the competent authorities may allow the offsetting provided for in paragraph 10 between institutions within a group that fulfil the conditions imposed in paragraph 12 and any institution included in the same group which has been authorized in another Member State provided that that institution is obliged to fulfil the capital requirements imposed in Articles 4 and 5 on a solo basis.

Definition of consolidated own funds

14. In the calculation of own funds on a consolidated basis Article 5 of Directive 89/299/EEC shall apply.

15. The competent authorities responsible for exercising supervision on a consolidated basis may recognize the validity of the specific own-funds definitions applicable to the institutions concerned under Annex V in the calculation of their consolidated own funds.

REPORTING REQUIREMENTS

Article 8

1. Member States shall require that investment firms and credit institutions provide the competent authorities of their home Member States with all the information necessary for the

assessment of their compliance with the rules adopted in accordance with this Directive. Member States shall also ensure that institutions' internal control mechanisms and administrative and accounting procedures permit the verification of their compliance with such rules at all times.

2. Investment firms shall be obliged to report to the competent authorities in the manner specified by the latter at least once every month in the case of firms covered by Article 3(3), at least once every three months in the case of firms covered by Article 3(1) and at least once every six months in the case of firms covered by Article 3(2).

3. Notwithstanding paragraph 2, investment firms covered by Article 3(1) and (3) shall be required to provide the information on a consolidated or subconsolidated basis only once every six months.

4. Credit institutions shall be obliged to report in the manner specified by the competent authorities as often as they are obliged to report under Directive 89/647/EEC.

5. The competent authorities shall oblige institutions to report to them immediately any case in which their counterparties in repurchase and reverse repurchase agreements or securities-lending and securities-borrowing transactions default on their obligations. The Commission shall report to the Council on such cases and their implications for the treatment of such agreements and transactions in this Directive not more than three years after the date referred to in Article 12. Such reports shall also describe the way that institutions meet those of conditions (i) to (v) in Article 2(6)(b) that apply to them, in particular that referred to in condition (v). Furthermore it shall give details of any changes in the relative volume of institutions' traditional lending and their lending through reverse repurchase agreements and securities-borrowing transactions. If the Commission concludes on the basis of this report and other information that further safeguards are needed to prevent abuse it shall make appropriate proposals.

COMPETENT AUTHORITIES

Article 9

1. Member States shall designate the authorities which are to carry out the duties provided for in this Directive. They shall inform the Commission thereof, indicating any division of duties.

2. The authorities referred to in paragraph 1 must be public authorities or bodies officially recognized by national law or by public authorities as part of the supervisory system in operation in the Member State concerned.

3. The authorities concerned must be granted all the powers necessary for the performance of their tasks, and in particular that of overseeing the constitution of trading books.

4. The competent authorities of the various Member States shall collaborate closely in the performance of the duties provided for in this Directive, particularly when investment services are provided on a services basis or through the establishment of branches in one or more Member States. They shall on request supply one another with all information likely to facilitate the supervision of the capital adequacy of investment firms and credit institutions, in particular the verification of their compliance with the rules laid down in this Directive. Any exchange of information between competent authorities which is provided for in this Directive in respect of investment firms shall be subject to the obligation of professional secrecy imposed in Article 25 of Directive 93/22/EEC and, as regards credit institutions, to the obligation imposed in Article 12 of Directive 77/780/EEC, as amended by Directive 89/646/EEC.

Article 10

Pending adoption of a further Directive laying down provisions for adapting this Directive to technical progress in the areas specified below, the Council shall, acting by qualified majority on a proposal from the Commission, in accordance with Decision 87/373/EEC, adopt those adaptations which may be necessary, as follows:

— clarification of the definitions in Article 2 in order to ensure uniform application of this Directive throughout the Community,
— clarification of the definitions in Article 2 to take account of developments on financial markets,

— alteration of the amounts of initial capital prescribed in Article 3 and the amount referred to in Article 4(6) to take account of developments in the economic and monetary field,

— the alignment of terminology on and the framing of definitions in accordance with subsequent acts on institutions and related matters.

TRANSITIONAL PROVISIONS

Article 11

1. Member States may authorize investment firms subject to Article 30(1) of Directive 93/22/EEC the own funds of which are on the day of the application of this Directive lower than the levels specified in Article 3(1) to (3) of this Directive. Thereafter, however, the own funds of such investment firms must fulfil the conditions laid down in Article 3(5) to (8) of this Directive.

2. Notwithstanding paragraph 14 of Annex I, Member States may set a specific-risk requirement for any bonds assigned a weighting of 10% under Article 11(2) of Directive 89/647/EEC equal to half the specific-risk requirement for a qualifying item with the same residual maturity as such a bond.

FINAL PROVISIONS

Article 12

1. Member States shall bring into force the laws, regulations and administrative provisions necessary for them to comply with this Directive by the date fixed in the second paragraph of Article 31 of Directive 93/22/EEC. They shall forthwith inform the Commission thereof.

When Member States adopt these provisions they shall include a reference to this Directive or add such a reference on the occasion of their official publication. The manner in which such references are to be made shall be laid down by the Member States.

2. Member States shall communicate to the Commission the main provisions of national law which they adopt in the field covered by this Directive.

Article 13

The Commission shall as soon as possible submit to the Council proposals for capital requirements in respect of commodities trading, commodity derivatives and units of collective-investment undertakings.

The Council shall decide on the Commission's proposals no later than six months before the date of application of this Directive.

REVIEW CLAUSE

Article 14

Within three years of the date referred to in Article 12, acting on a proposal from the Commission, the Council shall examine and, if necessary, revise this Directive in the light of the experience acquired in applying it, taking into account market innovation and, in particular, developments in international fora of regulatory authorities.

Article 15

This Directive is addressed to the Member States.

Done at Brussels, 15 March 1993.

For the Council
The President
M. JELVED

ANNEX I. POSITION RISK

INTRODUCTION

Netting

1. The excess of an institution's long (short) positions over its short (long) positions in the same equity, debt and convertible issues and identical financial futures, options, warrants and covered warrants shall be its net position in each of those different instruments. In calculating the net position the competent authorities shall allow positions in derivative instruments to be treated, as laid down in paragraphs 4 to 7, as positions in the underlying (or notional) security or securities. Institutions' holdings of their own debt instruments shall be disregarded in calculating specific risk under paragraph 14.

2. No netting shall be allowed between a convertible and an offsetting position in the instrument underlying it, unless the competent authorities adopt an approach under which the likelihood of a particular convertible's being converted is taken into account or have a capital requirement to cover any loss which conversion might entail.

3. All net positions, irrespective of their signs, must be converted on a daily basis into the institution's reporting currency at the prevailing spot exchange rate before their aggregation.

Particular instruments

4. Interest-rate futures, forward-rate agreements (FRAs) and forward commitments to buy or sell debt instruments shall be treated as combinations of long and short positions. Thus a long interest-rate futures position shall be treated as a combination of a borrowing maturing on the delivery date of the futures contract and a holding of an asset with maturity date equal to that of the instrument or notional position underlying the futures contract in question. Similarly a sold FRA will be treated as a long position with a maturity date equal to the settlement date plus the contract period, and a short position with maturity equal to the settlement date. Both the borrowing and the asset holding shall be included in the Central government column of Table 1 in paragraph 14 in order to calculate the capital required against specific risk for interest-rate futures and FRAs. A forward commitment to buy a debt instrument shall be treated as a combination of a borrowing maturing on the delivery date and a long (spot) position in the debt instrument itself. The borrowing shall be included in the Central government column of Table 1 for purposes of specific risk, and the debt instrument under whichever column is appropriate for it in the same table. The competent authorities may allow the capital requirement for an exchange-traded future to be equal to the margin required by the exchange if they are fully satisfied that it provides an accurate measure of the risk associated with the future and that the method used to calculate the margin is equivalent to the method of calculation set out in the remainder of this Annex.

5. Options on interest rates, debt instruments, equities, equity indices, financial futures, swaps and foreign currencies shall be treated as if they were positions equal in value to the amount of the underlying instrument to which the option refers, multiplied by its delta for the purposes of this Annex. The latter positions may be netted off against any offsetting positions in the identical underlying securities or derivatives. The delta used shall be that of the exchange concerned, that calculated by the competent authorities or, where that is not available or for OTC options, that calculated by the institution itself, subject to the competent authorities' being satisfied that the model used by the institution is reasonable.

However, the competent authorities may also prescribe that institutions calculate their deltas using a methodology specified by the competent authorities.

The competent authorities shall require that the other risks, apart from the dealt risk, associated with options are safeguarded against. The competent authorities may allow the requirement against a written exchange-traded option to be equal to the margin required by the exchange if they are fully satisfied that it provides an accurate measure of the risk associated with the option and that the method used to calculate the margin is equivalent to the method of calculation set out in the remainder of this Annex for such options. In addition they may allow the requirement on a bought exchange-traded or OTC option to be the same as that for the instrument underlying it, subject to the constraint that the resulting requirement does not exceed the market value of the option. The requirement against a written OTC option shall be set in relation to the instrument underlying it.

6. Warrants and covered warrants shall be treated in the same way as options under paragraph 5.

7. Swaps shall be treated for interest-rate risk purposes on the same basis as on-balance-sheet instruments. Thus an interest-rate swap under which an institution receives floating-rate interest and pays fixed-rate interest shall be treated as equivalent to a long position in a floating-rate instrument of maturity equivalent to the period until the next interest fixing and a short position in a fixed-rate instrument with the same maturity as the swap itself.

8. However, institutions which mark to market and manage the interest-rate risk on the derivative instruments covered in paragraphs 4 to 7 on a discounted-cash-flow basis may use sensitivity models to calculate the positions referred to above and may use them for any bond which is amortized over its residual life rather than via one final repayment of principal. Both the model and its use by the institution must be approved by the competent authorities. These models should generate positions which have the same sensitivity to interest-rate changes as the underlying cash flows. This sensitivity must be assessed with reference to independent movements in sample rates across the yield curve, with at least one sensitivity point in each of the maturity bands set out in Table 2 of paragraph 18. The positions shall be included in the calculation of capital requirements according to the provisions laid down in paragraphs 15 to 30.

9. Institutions which do not use models under paragraph 8 may instead, with the approval of the competent authorities, treat as fully offsetting any positions in derivative instruments covered in paragraphs 4 to 7 which meet the following conditions at least:

(i) the positions are of the same value and denominated in the same currency;
(ii) the reference rate (for floating-rate positions) or coupon (for fixed-rate positions) is closely matched;
(iii) the next interest-fixing date or, for fixed coupon positions, residual maturity corresponds with the following limits:

— less than one month hence; same day,
— between one month and one year hence: within seven days,
— over one year hence: within 30 days.

10. The transferor of securities or guaranteed rights relating to title to securities in a repurchase agreement and the lender of securities in a securities lending shall include these securities in the calculation of its capital requirement under this Annex provided that such securities meet the criteria laid down in Article 2(6)(a).

11. Position in units of collective-investment undertakings shall be subject to the capital requirements of Directive 89/647/EEC rather than to position-risk requirements under this Annex.

Specific and general risks

12. The position risk on a traded debt instrument or equity (or debt or equity derivative) shall be divided into two components in order to calculate the capital required against it. The first shall be its specific-risk component—this is the risk of a price change in the instrument concerned due to factors related to its issuer or, in the case of a derivative, the issuer of the underlying instrument. The second component shall cover its general risk—this is the risk of a price change in the instrument due (in the case of a traded debt instrument or debt derivative) to a change in the level of interest rates or (in the case of an equity or equity derivative) to a broad equity-market movement unrelated to any specific attributes of individual securities.

13. The institution shall classify its net positions according to the currency in which they are denominated and shall calculate the capital requirement for general and specific risk in each individual currency separately.

Specific risk

14. The institution shall assign its net positions, as calculated in accordance with paragraph 1, to the appropriate categories in Table 1 on the basis of their residual maturities and then multiply them by the weightings shown. It shall sum its weighted positions (regardless of whether they are long or short) in order to calculate its capital requirement against specific risk.

Table 1

Central government items	Qualifying items			Other items
	Up to 6 months	Over 6 and up to 24 months	Over 24 months	
0.00%	0.25%	1.00%	1.60%	8.00%

General risk

(a) *Maturity-based*

15. The procedure for calculating capital requirements against general risk involves two basic steps. First, all positions shall be weighted according to maturity (as explained in paragraph 16), in order to compute the amount of capital required against them. Second, allowance shall be made for this requirement to be reduced when a weighted position is held alongside an opposite weighted position within the same maturity band. A reduction in the requirement shall also be allowed when the opposite weighted positions fall into different maturity bands, with the size of this reduction depending both on whether the two positions fall into the same zone, or not, and on the particular zones they fall into. There are three zones (groups of maturity bands) altogether.

16. The institution shall assign its net positions to the appropriate maturity bands in column 2 or 3, as appropriate, in Table 2 appearing in paragraph 18. It shall do so on the basis of residual maturity in the case of fixed-rate instruments and on the basis of the period until the interest rate is next set in the case of instruments on which the interest rate is variable before final maturity. It shall also distinguish between debt instruments with a coupon of 3% or more and those with a coupon of less than 3% and thus allocate them to column 2 or column 3 in Table 2. It shall then multiply each of them by the weighting for the maturity band in question in column 4 in Table 2.

17. It shall then work out the sum of the weighted long positions and the sum of the weighted short positions in each maturity band. The amount of the former which are matched by the latter in a given maturity band shall be the matched weighted position in that band, while the residual long or short position shall be the unmatched weighted position for the same band. The total of the matched weighted positions in all bands shall then be calculated.

18. The institution shall compute the totals of the unmatched weighted long positions for the bands included in each of the zones in Table 2 in order to derive the unmatched weighted long position for each zone. Similarly the sum of the unmatched weighted short positions for each band in a particular zone shall be summed to compute the unmatched weighted short position for that zone. That part of the unmatched weighted long position for a given zone that is matched by the unmatched weighted short position for the same zone shall be the matched weighted position for that zone. That part of the unmatched weighted long or unmatched weighted short position for a zone that cannot be thus matched shall be the unmatched weighted position for that zone.

521

Table 2

Zone	Maturity band		Weighting (in %)	Assumed interest rate change (in %)
(1)	Coupon of 3% or more	Coupon of less than 3%	(4)	(5)
	(2)	(3)		
One	$0 \leq$ 1 month	$0 \leq 1$ month	0.00	—
	$> 1 \leq$ 3 months	$> 1 \leq 3$ months	0.20	1.00
	$> 3 \leq$ 6 months	$> 3 \leq 6$ months	0.40	1.00
	$> 6 \leq$ 12 months	$> 6 \leq 12$ months	0.70	1.00
Two	$> 1 \leq$ 2 years	$> 1.0 \leq$ 1.9 years	1.25	0.90
	$> 2 \leq$ 3 years	$> 1.9 \leq$ 2.8 years	1.75	0.80
	$> 3 \leq$ 4 years	$> 2.8 \leq$ 3.6 years	2.25	0.75
Three	$> 4 \leq$ 5 years	$> 3.6 \leq$ 4.3 years	2.75	0.75
	$> 5 \leq$ 7 years	$> 4.3 \leq$ 5.7 years	3.25	0.70
	$> 7 \leq$ 10 years	$> 5.7 \leq$ 7.3 years	3.75	0.65
	$> 10 \leq$ 15 years	$> 7.3 \leq$ 9.3 years	4.50	0.60
	$> 15 \leq$ 20 years	$> 9.3 \leq$ 10.6 years	5.25	0.60
	$\leq$ 20 years	$> 10.6 \leq$ 12.0 years	6.00	0.60
		$> 12.0 \leq$ 20.0 years	8.00	0.60
		$\leq$ 20 years	12.50	0.60

19. The amount of the unmatched weighted long (short) position in zone one which is matched by the unmatched weighted short (long) position in zone two shall then be computed. This shall be referred to in paragraph 23 as the matched weighted position between zones one and two. The same calculation shall then be undertaken with regard to that part of the unmatched weighted position in zone two which is left over and the unmatched weighted position in zone three in order to calculate the matched weighted position between zones two and three.

20. The institution may, if it wishes, reverse the order in paragraph 19 so as to calculate the matched weighted position between zones two and three before working out that between zones one and two.

21. The remainder of the unmatched weighted position in zone one shall then be matched with what remains of that for zone three after the latter's matching with zone two in order to derive the matched weighted position between zones one and three.

22. Residual positions, following the three separate matching calculations in paragraphs 19, 20 and 21, shall be summed.

23. The institution's capital requirement shall be calculated as the sum of:

    (a) 10% of the sum of the matched weighted positions in all maturity bands;

    (b) 40% of the matched weighted position in zone one;

    (c) 30% of the matched weighted position in zone two;

    (d) 30% of the matched weighted position in zone three;

    (e) 40% of the matched weighted position between zones one and two and between zones two and three (see paragraph 19);

    (f) 150% of the matched weighted position between zones one and three;

    (g) 100% of the residual unmatched weighted positions.

(b) *Duration based*

24. The competent authorities in a Member State may allow institutions in general or on an individual basis to use a system for calculating the capital requirement for the general risk on traded debt instruments which reflects duration instead of the system set out in paragraphs 15 to 23, provided that the institution does so on a consistent basis.

25. Under such a system the institution shall take the market value of each fixed-rate instrument and thence calculate its yield to maturity, which is implied discount rate for that instrument. In the case of floating-rate instruments, the institution shall take the market value of

each instrument and thence calculate its yield on the assumption that the principal is due when the interest rate can next be changed.

26. The institution shall then calculate the modified duration of each debt instrument on the basis of the following formula:

$$\text{modified duration} = \frac{\text{duration (D)}}{(1 + r)}, \text{ where:}$$

$$D = \frac{\displaystyle\sum_{t=1}^{m} \frac{t\,C_t}{(1 + r)^t}}{\displaystyle\sum_{t=1}^{m} \frac{C_t}{(1 + r)^t}}$$

where:

r = yield to maturity (see paragraph 25),

C_t = cash payment in time t,

m = total maturity (see paragraph 25).

27. The institution shall then allocate each debt instrument to the appropriate zone in Table 3. It shall do so on the basis of the modified duration of each instrument.

Table 3

Zone	Modified duration (in years)	Assumed interest (change in %)
(1)	(2)	(3)
One	$> \ 0 \leq 1.0$	1.0
Two	$> 1.0 \leq 3.6$	0.85
Three	> 3.6	0.7

28. The institution shall then calculate the duration-weighted position for each instrument by multiplying its market price by its modified duration and by the assumed interest-rate change for an instrument with that particular modified duration (see column 3 in Table 3).

29. The institution shall work out its duration-weighted long and its duration-weighted short positions within each zone. The amount of the former which are matched by the latter within each zone shall be the matched duration-weighted position for that zone.

The institution shall then calculate the unmatched duration-weighted positions for each zone. It shall then follow the procedures laid down for unmatched weighted positions in paragraphs 19 to 22.

30. The institution's capital requirement shall then be calculated as the sum of:

(a) 2% of the matched duration-weighted position for each zone;
(b) 40% of the matched duration-weighted positions between zones one and two and between zones two and three;
(c) 150% of the matched duration-weighted position between zones one and three;
(d) 100% of the residual unmatched duration-weighted positions.

31. The institution shall sum all its net long positions and all its net short positions in accordance with paragraph 1. The sum of the two figures shall be its overall gross position. The difference between them shall be its overall net position.

Specific risk

32. It shall multiply its overall gross position by 4% in order to calculate its capital requirement against specific risk.

33. Notwithstanding paragraph 32, the competent authorities may allow the capital requirement against specific risk to be 2% rather than 4% for those portfolios of equities that an institution holds which meet the following conditions:

(i) the equities shall not be those of issuers which have issued traded debt instruments that currently attract an 8% requirement in Table 1 appearing in paragraph 14;

(ii) the equities must be adjudged highly liquid by the competent authorities according to objective criteria;

(iii) no individual position shall comprise more than 5% of the value of the institution's whole equity portfolio. However, the competent authorities may authorize individual positions of up to 10% provided that the total of such positions does not exceed 50% of the portfolio.

General risk

34. Its capital requirement against general risk shall be its overall net position multiplied by 8%.

Stock-index futures

35. Stock-index futures, the delta-weighted equivalents of options in stock-index futures and stock indices collectively referred to hereafter as "stock-index futures", may be broken down into positions in each of their constituent equities. These positions may be treated as underlying positions in the equities in question; therefore, subject to the approval of the competent authorities, they may be netted against opposite positions in the underlying equities themselves.

36. The competent authorities shall ensure that any institution which has netted off its positions in one or more of the equities constituting a stock-index future against one or more positions in the stock-index future itself has adequate capital to cover the risk of loss caused by the future's values not moving fully in line with that of its constituent equities; they shall also do this when an institution holds opposite positions in stock-index futures which are not identical in respect of either their maturity or their composition or both.

37. Notwithstanding paragraphs 35 and 36, stock-index futures which are exchange traded and—in the opinion of the competent authorities—represent broadly diversified indices shall attract a capital requirement against general risk of 8%, but no capital requirement against specific risk. Such stock-index futures shall be included in the calculation of the overall net position in paragraph 31, but disregarded in the calculation of the overall gross position in the same paragraph.

38. If a stock-index future is not broken down into its underlying positions, it shall be treated as if it were an individual equity. However, the specific risk on this individual equity can be ignored if the stock-index future in question is exchange traded and, in the opinion of the competent authorities, represents a broadly diversified index.

UNDERWRITING

39. In the case of the underwriting of debt and equity instruments, the competent authorities may allow an institution to use the following procedure in calculating its capital requirements. Firstly, it shall calculate the net positions by deducting the underwriting positions which are subscribed or sub-underwritten by third parties on the basis of formal agreements; secondly, it shall reduce the net positions by the following reduction factors:

— working day 0: 100%
— working day 1: 90%
— working days 2 to 3: 75%
— working day 4: 50%
— working day 5: 25%
— after working day 5: 0%.

Working day zero shall be the working day on which the institution becomes unconditionally committed to accepting a known quantity of securities at an agreed price.

Thirdly, it shall calculate its capital requirements using the reduced underwriting positions. The competent authorities shall ensure that the institution holds sufficient capital against the risk of loss which exists between the time of the initial commitment and working day 1.

ANNEX II. SETTLEMENT AND COUNTER-PARTY RISK

SETTLEMENT/DELIVERY RISK

1. In the case of transactions in which debt instruments and equities (excluding repurchase and reverse repurchase agreements and securities lending and securities borrowing) are unsettled after their due delivery dates, an institution must calculate the price difference to which it is exposed. This is the difference between the agreed settlement price for the debt instrument or equity in question and its current market value, where the difference could involve a loss for the institution. It must multiply this difference by the appropriate factor in column A of the table appearing in paragraph 2 in order to calculate its capital requirement.

2. Notwithstanding paragraph 1, an institution may, at the discretion of its competent authorities, calculate its capital requirements by multiplying the agreed settlement price of every transaction which is unsettled between 5 and 45 working days after its due date by the appropriate factor in column B of the table below. As from 46 working days after the due date it shall take the requirement to be 100% of the price difference to which it is exposed as in column A.

Number of working days after due settlement date	Column A (%)	Column B (%)
5–15	8	0.5
16–30	50	4.0
31–45	75	9.0
46 or more	100	see paragraph 2

COUNTER-PARTY RISK

Free deliveries

3.1 An institution shall be required to hold capital against counter-party risk if:

(i) it has paid for securities before receiving them or it has delivered securities before receiving payment for them; and

(ii) in the case of cross-border transactions, one day or more has elapsed since it made that payment or delivery.

3.2 The capital requirement shall be 8% of the value of the securities or cash owed to the institution multiplied by the risk weighting applicable to the relevant counter-party.

Repurchase and reverse repurchase agreements and securities lending and borrowing

4.1 In the case of repurchase agreements and securities lending based on securities included in the trading book the institution shall calculate the difference between the market value of the securities and the amount borrowed by the institution or the market value of the collateral, where that difference is positive. In the case of reverse repurchase agreements and securities borrowing the institution shall calculate the difference between the amount the institution has lent or the market value of the collateral and the market value of the securities it has received, where that difference is positive.

The competent authorities shall take measures to ensure that the excess collateral given is acceptable.

Furthermore, the competent authorities may allow institutions not to include the amount of excess collateral in the calculations described in the first two sentences of this paragraph if the amount of excess collateral is guaranteed in such a way that the transferor is always assured that the excess collateral will be returned to it in the event of defaults of its counter-party.

Accrued interest shall be included in calculating the market value of amounts lent or borrowed and collateral.

4.2 The capital requirement shall be 8% of the figure produced in accordance with paragraph 4.1, multiplied by the risk weighting applicable to the relevant counter-party.

OTC derivative instruments

5. In order to calculate the capital requirement on their OTC derivative instruments, institutions shall apply Annex II to Directive 89/647/EEC in the case of interest-rate and exchange-rate contracts; bought OTC equity options and covered warrants shall be subject to the treatment accorded to exchange-rate contracts in Annex II to Directive 89/647/EEC.

The risk weightings to be applied to the relevant counter-parties shall be determined in accordance with Article 2(9) of this Directive.

OTHER

6. The capital requirements of Directive 89/647/EEC shall apply to those exposures in the form of fees, commission, interest, dividends and margin in exchange-traded futures or options contracts which are neither covered in this Annex or Annex I nor deducted from own funds under paragraph 2(d) of Annex V and which are directly related to the items included in the trading book.

The risk weightings to be applied to the relevant counter-parties shall be determined in accordance with Article 2(9) of this Directive.

ANNEX III. FOREIGN-EXCHANGE RISK

1. If an institution's overall net foreign-exchange position, calculated in accordance with the procedure set out below, exceeds 2% of its total own funds, it shall multiply the excess by 8% in order to calculate its own-funds requirement against foreign-exchange risk.

2. A two-stage calculation shall be used.

3.1 Firstly, the institution's net open position in each currency (including the reporting currency) shall be calculated. This position shall consist of the sum of the following elements (positive or negative):

— the net spot position (i.e. all asset items less all liability items, including accrued interest, in the currency in question),

— the net forward position (i.e. all amounts to be received less all amounts to be paid under forward exchange transactions, including currency futures and the principal on currency swaps not included in the spot position),

— irrevocable guarantees (and similar instruments) that are certain to be called,

— net future income/expenses not yet accrued but already fully hedged (at the discretion of the reporting institution and with the prior consent of the competent authorities, net future income/expenses not yet entered in accounting records but already fully hedged by forward foreign exchange transactions may be included here). Such discretion must be exercised on a consistent basis,

— the net delta (or delta-based) equivalent of the total book of foreign-currency options,

— the market value of other (i.e. non-foreign-currency) options,

— any positions which an institution has deliberately taken in order to hedge against the adverse effect of the exchange rate on its capital ratio may be excluded from the calculation of net open currency positions. Such positions should be of a non-trading or structural nature and their exclusion, and any variation of the terms of their exclusion, shall require the consent of the competent authorities. The same treatment subject to the same conditions as above may be applied to positions which an institution has which relate to items that are already deducted in the calculation of own funds.

3.2 The competent authorities shall have the discretion to allow institutions to use the net present value when calculating the net open position in each currency.

4. Secondly, net short and long positions in each currency other than the reporting currency shall be converted at spot rates into the reporting currency. They shall then be summed separately to form the total of the net short positions an the total of the net long positions respectively. The higher of these two totals shall be the institution's overall net foreign-exchange position.

5. Notwithstanding paragraphs 1 to 4 and pending further co-ordination, the competent authorities may prescribe or allow institutions to use alternative procedures for the purposes of this Annex.

6. First, the competent authorities may allow institutions to provide lower capital requirements against positions in closely correlated currencies than those which would result from applying paragraphs 1 to 4 to them. The competent authorities may deem a pair of currencies to be closely correlated only if the likelihood of a loss—calculated on the basis of daily exchange-rate data for the preceding three or five years—occurring on equal and opposite positions in such currencies over the following 10 working days, which is 4% or less of the value of the matched position in question (valued in terms of the reporting currency) has a probability of at least 99%, when an observation period of three years is used, or 95%, when an observation period of five years is used. The own-funds requirement on the matched position in two closely correlated currencies shall be 4% multiplied by the value of the matched position. The capital requirement on unmatched positions in closely correlated currencies, and all positions in other currencies, shall be 8%, multiplied by the higher of the sum of the net short or the net long positions in those currencies after the removal of matched positions in closely correlated currencies.

7. Secondly, the competent authorities may allow institutions to apply an alternative method to those outlined in paragraphs 1 to 6 for the purposes of this Annex. The capital requirement produced by this method must be sufficient:

(i) to exceed the losses, if any, that would have occurred in at least 95% of the rolling 10-working-day periods over the preceding five years, or, alternatively, in at least 99% of the rolling 10-working-day periods over the preceding three years, had the institution begun each such period with its current positions;

(ii) on the basis of an analysis of exchange-rate movements during all the rolling 10-working-day periods over the preceding five years, to exceed the likely loss over the following 10-working-day holding period 95% or more of the time, or, alternatively, to exceed the likely loss 99% or more of the time where the analysis of exchange-rate movements covers only the preceding three years; or

(iii) irrespective of the size of (i) or (ii) to exceed 2% of the net open position as measured in paragraph 4.

8. Thirdly, the competent authorities may allow institutions to remove positions in any currency which is subject to a legally binding intergovernmental agreement to limit its variation relative to other currencies covered by the same agreement from whichever of the methods described in paragraphs 1 to 7 that they apply. Institutions shall calculate their matched positions in such currencies and subject them to a capital requirement no lower than half of the maximum permissible variation laid down in the intergovernmental agreement in question in respect of the currencies concerned. Unmatched positions in those currencies shall be treated in the same way as other currencies.

Notwithstanding the first paragraph, the competent authorities may allow the capital requirement on the matched positions in currencies of Member States participating in the second stage of the European monetary union to be 1.6%, multiplied by the value of such matched positions.

9. The competent authorities shall notify the Council and Commission of the methods, if any, that they are prescribing or allowing in respect of paragraphs 6 to 8.

10. The Commission shall report to the Council on the methods referred to in paragraph 9 and, where necessary and with due regard to international developments, shall propose a more harmonized treatment of foreign-exchange risk.

11. Net positions in composite currencies may be broken down into the component currencies according to the quotas in force.

ANNEX IV. OTHER RISKS

Investment firms shall be required to hold own funds equivalent to one quarter of their preceding year's fixed overheads. The competent authorities may adjust that requirement in the event of a material change in a firm's business since the preceding year. Where a firm has not completed a year's business, including the day it starts up, the requirement shall be a quarter of the fixed overheads figure projected in its business plan unless an adjustment to that plan is required by the authorities.

ANNEX V. OWN FUNDS

1. The own funds of investment firms and credit institutions shall be defined in accordance with Directive 89/299/EEC.

For the purposes of this Directive, however, investment firms which do not have one of the legal forms referred to in Article 1(1) of the Fourth Council Directive 78/660/EEC of 25 July 1978 based on Article 54(3)(g) of the Treaty on the annual accounts of certain types of companies[11] shall nevertheless be deemed to fall within the scope of Council Directive 86/635/EEC of 8 December 1986 on the annual accounts and consolidated accounts of banks and other financial institutions.[12]

2. Notwithstanding paragraph 1, the competent authorities may permit those institutions which are obliged to meet the own-funds requirements laid down in Annexes I, II, III, IV and VI to use an alternative definition when meeting those requirements only. No part of the own funds thus provided may be used simultaneously to meet other own-funds requirements. This alternative definition shall include the following items (a), (b) and (c) less item (d), the deduction of that item being left to the discretion of the competent authorities:

(a) own funds as defined in Directive 89/299/EEC excluding only items (12) and (13) of Article 2(1) of the same Directive for those investment firms which are required to deduct item (d) of this paragraph from the total of items (a), (b) and (c) of this paragraph;

(b) an institution's net trading-book profits net of any foreseeable charges or dividends, less net losses on its other business provided that none of those amounts has already been included in item (a) of this paragraph under item 2 or 11 of Article 2(1) of Directive 89/299/EEC;

(c) subordinated loan capital and/or the items referred to in paragraphs 5, subject to the conditions set out in paragraphs 3 to 7;

(d) illiquid assets as defined in paragraph 8.

3. The subordinated loan capital referred to in paragraph 2(c) shall have an initial maturity of at least two years. It shall be fully paid up and the loan agreement shall not include any clause providing that in specified circumstances other than the winding up of the institution the debt will become repayable before the agreed repayment date, unless the competent authorities approve the repayment. Neither the principal nor the interest on such subordinated loan capital may be repaid if such repayment would mean that the own funds of the institution in question would then amount to less than 100% of the institution's overall requirements.

11. OJ No L222, 14 August 1978, p. 11. Directive as last amended by Directive 90/605/EEC (OJ No L317, 16 November 1990, p. 60).

12. OJ No L372, 31 December 1986, p. 1.

In addition, an institution shall notify the competent authorities of all repayments on such subordinated loan capital as soon as its own funds fall below 120% of its overall requirements.

4. The subordinated loan capital referred to in paragraph 2(c) may not exceed a maximum of 150% of the original own funds left to meet the requirements laid down in Annexes I, II, III, IV and VI and may approach that maximum only in particular circumstances acceptable to the relevant authorities.

5. The competent authorities may permit institutions to replace the subordinated loan capital referred to in paragraphs 3 and 4 with items 3 and 5 to 8 of Article 8(1) of Directive 89/299/EEC.

6. The competent authorities may permit investment firms to exceed the ceiling for subordinated loan capital prescribed in paragraph 4 if they judge it prudentially adequate and provided that the total of such subordinated loan capital and the items referred to in paragraph 5 does not exceed 200% of the original own funds left to meet the requirements imposed in Annexes I, II, III, IV and VI, or 250% of the same amount where investment firms deduct item (2)(d) referred to in paragraph 2 when calculating own funds.

7. The competent authorities may permit the ceiling for subordinated loan capital prescribed in paragraph 4 to be exceeded by a credit institution if they judge it prudentially adequate and provided that the total of such subordinated loan capital and the items referred to in paragraph 5 does not exceed 250% of the original own funds left to meet the requirements imposed in Annexes, I, II, III and VI.

8. Illiquid assets include:

— tangible fixed assets (except to the extent that land and buildings may be allowed to count against the loans which they are securing),
— holdings in, including subordinated claims on, credit or financial institutions which may be included in the own funds of such institutions, unless they have been deducted from items 12 and 13 of Article 2(1) of Directive 89/299/EEC or under paragraph 9(iv) of this Annex.

   Where shares in a credit or financial institution are held temporarily for the purpose of a financial assistance operation designed to reorganize and save that institution, the competent authorities may waive this provision. They may also waive it in respect of those shares which are included in the investment firms's trading book,
— holdings and other investments, in undertakings other than credit institutions and other financial institutions, which are not readily marketable,
— deficiencies in subsidiaries,
— deposits made, other than those which are available for repayment within 90 days, and also excluding payments in connection with margined futures or options contracts,
— loans and other amounts due, other than those due to be repaid within 90 days,
— physical stocks, unless they are subject to the capital requirements imposed in Article 4(2) and provided that such requirements are not less stringent than those imposed in Article 4(1)(iii).

9. Those investment firms included in a group subject to the waiver described in Article 7(4) shall calculate their own funds in accordance with paragraphs 1 to 8 subject to the following modifications:

   (i) the illiquid assets referred to in paragraph 2(d) shall be deducted;
  (ii) the exclusion referred to in paragraph 2(a) shall not cover those components of items 12 and 13 of Article 2(1) of Directive 89/299/EEC which an investment firm holds in respect of undertakings included in the scope of consolidation as defined in Article 7(2) of this Directive;
 (iii) the limits referred to in Article 6(1)(a) and (b) of Directive 89/299/EEC shall be calculated with reference to the original own funds less those components of items 12 and 13 of Article 2(1) of Directive 89/299/EEC described in (ii) which are elements of the original own funds of the undertakings in question;
 (iv) those components of items 12 and 13 of Article 2(1) of Directive 89/299/EEC referred to in (iii) shall be deducted from the original own funds rather than from the total of all items as prescribed in Article 6(1)(c) of the same Directive for the purposes, in particular, of paragraphs 4 to 7 of this Annex.

529

ANNEX VI. LARGE EXPOSURES

1. Institutions referred to in Article 5(2) shall monitor and control their exposures to individual clients and groups of connected clients as defined in Directive 92/121/EEC, subject to the following modifications.

2. The exposures to individual clients which arise on the trading book shall be calculated by summing the following items (i), (ii) and (iii):

   (i) the excess—where positive—of an institution's long positions over it short positions in all the financial instruments issued by the client in question (the net position in each of the different instruments being calculated according to the methods laid down in Annex I);

   (ii) in the case of the underwriting of a debt or an equity instrument, the institution's exposure shall be its net exposure (which is calculated by deducting those underwriting positions which are subscribed or sub-underwritten by third parties on the basis of a formal agreement) reduced by the factors set out in paragraph 39 of Annex I.

     Pending further co-ordination, the competent authorities shall require institutions to set up systems to monitor and control their underwriting exposures between the time of the initial commitment and working day one in the light of the nature of the risks incurred in the markets in question;

   (iii) the exposures due to the transactions, agreements and contracts referred to in Annex II with the client in question, such exposures being calculated in the manner laid down in that Annex, without application of the weightings for counter-party risk.

3. Thereafter, the exposures to groups of connected clients on the trading book shall be calculated by summing the exposure to individual clients in a group, as calculated in paragraph 2.

4. The overall exposures to individual clients or groups of connected clients shall be calculated by summing the exposures which arise on the trading book and the exposures which arise on the non-trading book, taking into account Article 4(6) to (12) of Directive 92/121/EEC. In order to calculate the exposure on the non-trading book, institutions shall take the exposure arising from assets which are deducted from their own funds by virtue of paragraph 2(d) of Annex V to be zero.

5. Institutions' overall exposures to individual clients and groups of connected clients calculated in accordance with paragraph 4 shall be reported in accordance with Article 3 of Directive 92/121/EEC.

6. That sum of the exposures to an individual client or group of connected clients shall be limited in accordance with Article 4 of Directive 92/121/EEC subject to the transitional provisions of Article 6 of the same Directive.

7. Notwithstanding paragraph 6 the competent authorities may allow assets constituting claims and other exposures on investment firms, on recognized third-country investment firms and recognized clearing houses and exchanges in financial instruments to be subject to the same treatment accorded to those on credit institutions in Article 4(7)(i), (9) and (10) of Directive 92/121/EEC.

8. The competent authorities may authorize the limits laid down in Article 4 of Directive 92/121/EEC to be exceeded subject to the following conditions being met simultaneously:

   1. the exposure on the non-trading book to the client or group of clients in question does not exceed the limits laid down in Directive 92/121/EEC, calculated with reference to own funds as defined in Directive 89/299/EEC, so that the excess arises entirely on the trading book;

   2. the firm meets an additional capital requirement on the excess in respect of the limits laid down in Article 4(1) and (2) of Directive 92/121/EEC. This shall be calculated by selecting those components of the total trading exposure to the client or group of clients in question which attract the highest specific-risk requirements in Annex I and/or requirements in Annex II, the sum of which equals the amount of the excess referred to in 1; where the excess has not persisted for more than 10 days, the additional capital requirement shall be 200% of the requirements referred to in the previous sentence, on these components.

     As from 10 days after the excess has occurred, the components of the excess, selected in accordance with the above criteria, shall be allocated to the appropriate line in column 1 of the table below in ascending order of specific-risk requirements in Annex I and/or requirements in Annex II. The institution shall then meet an additional capital requirement equal to the sum of the specific-risk requirements in Annex I and/or the Annex II requirements on these components multiplied by the corresponding factors in column 2;

Table

Excess over the limits *(on the basis of a percentage of own funds)*	Factors
(1)	(2)
Up to 40%	200%
From 40% to 60%	300%
From 60% to 80%	400%
From 80% to 100%	500%
From 100% to 250%	600%
Over 250%	900%

3. where 10 days or less has elapsed since the excess occurred, the trading-book exposure to the client or group of connected clients in question must not exceed 500% of the institution's own funds;
4. any excesses which have persisted for more than 10 days must not, in aggregate, exceed 600% of the institution's own funds;
5. institutions must report to the competent authorities every three months all cases where the limits laid down in Article 4(1) and (2) of Directive 92/121/EEC have been exceeded during the preceding three months. In each case in which the limits have been exceeded the amount of the excess and the name of the client concerned must be reported.

9. The competent authorities shall establish procedures, of which they shall notify the Council and the Commission, to prevent institutions from deliberately avoiding the additional capital requirements that they would otherwise incur on exposures exceeding the limits laid down in Article 4(1) and (2) of Directive 92/121/EEC once those exposures have been maintained for more than 10 days, by means of temporarily transferring the exposures in question to another company, whether within the same group or not, and/or by undertaking artificial transactions to close out the exposure during the 10-day period and create a new exposure. Institutions shall maintain systems which ensure that any transfer which has this effect is immediately reported to the competent authorities.

10. The competent authorities may permit those institutions which are allowed to use the alternative definition of own funds under paragraph 2 of Annex V to use that definition for the purposes of paragraphs 5, 6 and 8 of this Annex provided that the institutions concerned are required, in addition, to meet all of the obligations set out in Articles 3 and 4 of Directive 92/121/EEC, in respect of the exposures which arise outside their trading books by using own funds as defined in Directive 89/299/EEC.

COUNCIL DIRECTIVE* 88/361/EEC OF 24 JUNE 1988

for the implementation of Article 67 of the Treaty

THE COUNCIL OF THE EUROPEAN COMMUNITIES,

Having regard to the Treaty establishing the European Economic Community, and in particular Articles 69 and 70(1) thereof,

Having regard to the proposal from the Commission, submitted following consultation with the Monetary Committee,[1]

Having regard to the opinion of the European Parliament,[2]

Whereas Article 8a of the Treaty stipulates that the internal market shall comprise an area without internal frontiers in which the free movement of capital is ensured, without prejudice to the other provisions of the Treaty;

Whereas Member States should be able to take the requisite measures to regulate bank liquidity; whereas these measures should be restricted to this purpose;

Whereas Member States should, if necessary, be able to take measures to restrict, temporarily and within the framework of appropriate Community procedures, short-term capital movements which, even where there is no appreciable divergence in economic fundamentals, might seriously disrupt the conduct of their monetary and exchange-rate policies;

Whereas, in the interests of transparency, it is advisable to indicate the scope, in accordance with the arrangements laid down in this Directive, of the transitional measures adopted for the benefit of the Kingdom of Spain and the Portuguese Republic by the 1985 Act of Accession in the field of capital movements;

Whereas the Kingdom of Spain and the Portuguese Republic may, under the terms of Articles 61 to 66 and 222 to 232 respectively of the 1985 Act of Accession, postpone the liberalization of certain capital movements in derogation from the obligations set out in the First Council Directive of 11 May 1960 for the implementation of Article 67 of the Treaty,[3] as last amended by Directive 86/566/EEC[4]; whereas Directive 86/566/EEC also provides for transitional arrangements to be applied for the benefit of those two Member States in respect of their obligations to liberalize capital movements; whereas it is appropriate for those two Member States to be able to postpone the application of the new liberalization obligations resulting from this Directive;

Whereas the Hellenic Republic and Ireland are faced, albeit to differing degrees, with difficult balance-of-payments situations and high-levels of external indebtedness; whereas the immediate and complete liberalization of capital movements by those two Member States would make it more difficult for them to continue to apply the measures they have taken to improve their external positions and to reinforce the capacity of their financial systems to adapt to the requirements of an integrated financial market in the Community; whereas it is appropriate, in accordance with Article 8c of the Treaty, to grant to those two Member States, in the light of their specific circumstances, further time in which to comply with the obligations arising from this Directive;

Whereas, since the full liberalization of capital movements could in some Member States, and

---

* OJ 1988, L178/5.
1. OJ No C26, 1 February 1988, p. 1.
2. Opinion delivered on 17 June 1988.
3. OJ No 43, 12 July 1960, p. 921/60.
4. OJ No L332, 26 November 1986, p. 22.

especially in border areas, contribute to difficulties in the market for secondary residences; whereas existing national legislation regulating these purchases should not be affected by the entry into effect of this Directive;

Whereas advantage should be taken of the period adopted for bringing this Directive into effect in order to enable the Commission to submit proposals designed to eliminate or reduce risks of distortion, tax evasion and tax avoidance resulting from the diversity of national systems for taxation and to permit the Council to take a position on such proposals;

Whereas, in accordance with Article 70(1) of the Treaty, the Community shall endeavour to attain the highest possible degree of liberalization in respect of the movement of capital between its residents and those of third countries;

Whereas, large-scale short-term capital movements to or from third countries may seriously disturb the monetary or financial situation of Member States or cause serious stresses on the exchange markets; whereas such developments may prove harmful for the cohesion of the European Monetary System, for the smooth operation of the internal market and for the progressive achievement of economic and monetary union; whereas it is therefore appropriate to create the requisite conditions for concerted action by Member States should this prove necessary;

Whereas this Directive replaces Council Directive 72/156/EEC of 21 March 1972 on regulating international capital flows and neutralizing their undesirable effects on domestic liquidity[5]; whereas Directive 72/156/EEC should accordingly be repealed,

HAS ADOPTED THIS DIRECTIVE:

Article 1

1. Without prejudice to the following provisions, Member States shall abolish restrictions on movements of capital taking place between persons resident in Member States. To facilitate application of this Directive, capital movements shall be classified in accordance with the Nomenclature in Annex 1.

2. Transfers in respect of capital movements shall be made on the same exchange rate conditions as those governing payments relating to current transactions.

Article 2

Member States shall notify the Committee of Governors of the Central Banks, the Monetary Committee and the Commission, by the date of their entry into force at the latest, of measures to regulate bank liquidity which have a specific impact on capital transactions carried out by credit institutions with non-residents.

Such measures shall be confined to what is necessary for the purposes of domestic monetary regulation. The Monetary Committee and the Committee of Governors of the Central Banks shall provide the Commission with opinions on this subject.

Article 3

1. Where short-term capital movements of exceptional magnitude impose severe strains on foreign-exchange markets and lead to serious disturbances in the conduct of a Member State's monetary and exchange rate policies, being reflected in particular in substantial variations in domestic liquidity, the Commission may, after consulting the Monetary Committee and the Committee of Governors of the Central Banks, authorize that Member State to take, in respect of the capital movements listed in Annex II, protective measures the conditions and details of which the Commission shall determine.

2. The Member State concerned may itself take the protective measures referred to above, on grounds of urgency, should these measures be necessary. The Commission and the other Member States shall be informed of such measures by the date of their entry into force at the latest. The Commission, after consulting the Monetary Committee and the Committee of Governors of the Central Banks, shall decide whether the Member State concerned may continue to apply these measures or whether it should amend or abolish them.

5. OJ No L91, 18 April 1972, p. 13.

3. The decisions taken by the Commission under paragraphs 1 and 2 may be revoked or amended by the Council acting by a qualified majority.

4. The period of application of protective measures taken pursuant to this Article shall not exceed six months.

5. Before 31 December 1992, the Council shall examine, on the basis of a report from the Commission, after delivery of an opinion by the Monetary Committee and the Committee of Governors of the Central Banks whether the provisions of this Article remain appropriate, as regards their principle and details, to the requirements which they were intended to satisfy.

Article 4

This Directive shall be without prejudice to the right of Member States to take all requisite measures to prevent infringements of their laws and regulations, *inter alia* in the field of taxation and prudential supervision of financial institutions, or to lay down procedures for the declaration of capital movements for purposes of administrative or statistical information.

Application of those measures and procedures may not have the effect of impeding capital movements carried out in accordance with Community law.

Article 5

For the Kingdom of Spain and the Portuguese Republic, the scope, in accordance with the Nomenclature of capital movements contained in Annex I, of the provisions of the 1985 Act of Accession in the field of capital movements shall be as indicated in Annex III.

Article 6

1. Member States shall take the measures necessary to comply with this Directive no later than 1 July 1990. They shall forthwith inform the Commission thereof. They shall also make known, by the date of their entry into force at the latest, any new measure or any amendment made to the provisions governing the capital movements listed in Annex 1.

2. The Kingdom of Spain and the Portuguese Republic, without prejudice for these two Member States to Articles 61 to 66 and 222 to 232 of the 1985 Act of Accession, and the Hellenic Republic and Ireland may temporarily continue to apply restrictions to the capital movements listed in Annex IV, subject to the conditions and time limits laid down in that Annex.

If, before expiry of the time limit set for the liberalization of the capital movements referred to in Lists III and IV of Annex IV, the Portuguese Republic or the Hellenic Republic considers that it is unable to proceed with liberalization, in particular because of difficulties as regards its balance of payments or because the national financial system is insufficiently adapted, the Commission, at the request of one or other of these Member States, shall in collaboration with the Monetary Committee, review the economic and financial situation of the Member State concerned. On the basis of the outcome of this review, the Commission shall propose to the Council an extension of the time limit set for liberalization of all or part of the capital movements referred to. This extension may not exceed three years. The Council shall act in accordance with the procedure laid down in Article 69 of the Treaty.

3. The Kingdom of Belgium and the Grand Duchy of Luxembourg may temporarily continue to operate the dual exchange market under the conditions and for the periods laid down in Annex V.

4. Existing national legislation regulating purchases of secondary residences may be upheld until the Council adopts further provisions in this area in accordance with Article 69 of the Treaty. This provision does not affect the applicability of other provisions of Community law.

5. The Commission shall submit to the Council, by 31 December 1988, proposals aimed at eliminating or reducing risks of distortion, tax evasion and tax avoidance linked to the diversity of national systems for the taxation of savings and for controlling the application of these systems.

The Council shall take a position on these Commission proposals by 30 June 1989. Any tax provisions of a Community nature shall, in accordance with the Treaty, be adopted unanimously.

Article 7

1. In their treatment of transfers in respect of movements of capital to or from third countries, the Member States shall endeavour to attain the same degree of liberalization as that which applies to operations with residents of other Member States, subject to the other provisions of this Directive.

The provisions of the preceding subparagraph shall not prejudice the application to third countries of domestic rules or Community law, particularly any reciprocal conditions, concerning operations involving establishment, the provisions of financial services and the admission of securities to capital markets.

2. Where large-scale short-term capital movements to or from third countries seriously disturb the domestic or external monetary or financial situation of the Member States, or of a number of them, or cause serious strains in exchange relations within the Community or between the Community and third countries, Member States shall consult with one another on any measure to be taken to counteract such difficulties. This consultation shall take place within the Committee of Governors of the Central Banks and the Monetary Committee on the initiative of the Commission or of any Member State.

Article 8

At least once a year the Monetary Committee shall examine the situation regarding free movement of capital as it results from the application of this Directive. The examination shall cover measures concerning the domestic regulation of credit and financial and monetary markets which could have a specific impact on international capital movements and on all other aspects of this Directive. The Committee shall report to the Commission on the outcome of this examination.

Article 9

The First Directive of 11 May 1960 and Directive 72/156/EEC shall be repealed with effect from 1 July 1990.

Article 10

This Directive is addressed to the Member States.

Done at Luxembourg, 24 June 1988.

For the Council
The President
M. BANGEMANN

ANNEX I. NOMENCLATURE OF THE CAPITAL MOVEMENTS REFERRED TO IN ARTICLE 1 OF THE DIRECTIVE

In this Nomenclature, capital movements are classified according to the economic nature of the assets and liabilities they concern, denominated either in national currency or in foreign exchange.

The capital movements listed in this Nomenclature are taken to cover:

— all the operations necessary for the purposes of capital movements: conclusion and performance of the transaction and related transfers. The transaction is generally between residents of different Member States although some capital movements are carried out by a single person for his own account (e.g. transfers of assets belonging to emigrants),

— operations carried out by any natural or legal person,[6] including operations in respect of the assets or liabilities of Member States or of other public administrations and agencies, subject to the provisions of Article 68(3) of the Treaty,

6. See Explanatory Notes, pp. 540–542.

— access for the economic operator to all the financial techniques available on the market approached for the purpose of carrying out the operation in question. For example, the concept of acquisition of securities and other financial instruments covers not only spot transactions but also all the dealing techniques available: forward transactions, transactions carrying an option or warrant, swaps against other assets, etc. Similarly, the concept of operations in current and deposit accounts with financial institutions, includes not only the opening and placing of funds on accounts but also forward foreign exchange transactions, irrespective of whether these are intended to cover an exchange risk or to take an open foreign exchange position,

— operations to liquidate or assign assets built up, repatriation of the proceeds of liquidation thereof[6] or immediate use of such proceeds within the limits of Community obligations,

— operations to repay credits or loans.

This Nomenclature is not an exhaustive list for the notion of capital movements—whence a heading XIII—F. "Other capital movements—Miscellaneous". It should not therefore be interpreted as restricting the scope of the principle of full liberalization of capital movements as referred to in Article 1 of the Directive.

I. DIRECT INVESTMENTS[7]

1. Establishment and extension of branches or new undertakings belonging solely to the person providing the capital, and the acquisition in full of existing undertakings.
2. Participation in new or existing undertakings with a view to establishing or maintaining lasting economic links.
3. Long-term loans with a view to establishing or maintaining lasting economic links.
4. Reinvestment of profits with a view to maintaining lasting economic links.

A—Direct investments on national territory by non-residents[7]

B—Direct investments abroad by residents[7]

II. INVESTMENTS IN REAL ESTATE (NOT INCLUDED UNDER I)[7]

A—Investments in real estate on national territory by non-residents

B—Investments in real estate abroad by residents

III. OPERATIONS IN SECURITIES NORMALLY DEALT IN ON THE CAPITAL MARKET (NOT INCLUDED UNDER I, IV and V)

(a) Shares and other securities of a participating nature.[7]
(b) Bonds.[7]

A—Transactions in securities on the capital market

1. Acquisition by non-residents of domestic securities dealt in on a stock exchange.[7]
2. Acquisition by residents of foreign securities dealt in on a stock exchange.
3. Acquisition by non-residents of domestic securities not dealt in on a stock exchange.[8]
4. Acquisition by residents of foreign securities not dealt in on a stock exchange.

7. *Ibid.*
8. *Ibid.*

B—Admission of securities to the capital market[8]

(i) Introduction on a stock exchange.[8]
(ii) Issue and placing on a capital market.[8]
    1. Admission of domestic securities to a foreign capital market.
    2. Admission of foreign securities to the domestic capital market.

IV. OPERATIONS IN UNITS OF COLLECTIVE INVESTMENT UNDERTAKINGS[8]

(a) Units of undertakings for collective investment in securities normally dealt in on the capital market (shares, other equities and bonds).
(b) Units of undertakings for collective investment in securities or instruments normally dealt in on the money market.
(c) Units of undertakings for collective investment in other assets.

A—Transactions in units of collective investment undertakings

1. Acquisition by non-residents of units of national undertakings dealt in on a stock exchange.
2. Acquisition by residents of units of foreign undertakings dealt in on a stock exchange.
3. Acquisition by non-residents of units of national undertakings not dealt in on a stock exchange.
4. Acquisition by residents of units of foreign undertakings not dealt in on a stock exchange.

B—Admission of units of collective investment undertakings to the capital market

(i) Introduction on a stock exchange.
(ii) Issue and placing on a capital market.

    1. Admission of units of national collective investment undertakings to a foreign capital market.
    2. Admission of units of foreign collective investment undertakings to the domestic capital market.

V. OPERATIONS IN SECURITIES AND OTHER INSTRUMENTS NORMALLY DEALT IN ON THE MONEY MARKET[9]

A—Transactions in securities and other instruments on the money market

1. Acquisition by non-residents of domestic money market securities and instruments.
2. Acquisition by residents of foreign money market securities and instruments.

B—Admission of securities and other instruments to the money market

(i) Introduction on a recognized money market.[9]
(ii) Issue and placing on a recognized money market.

    1. Admission of domestic securities and instruments to a foreign money market.
    2. Admission of foreign securities and instruments to the domestic money market.

9. *Ibid.*

VI. OPERATIONS IN CURRENT AND DEPOSIT ACCOUNTS WITH FINANCIAL INSTITUTIONS[9]

A—Operations carried out by non-residents with domestic financial institutions

B—Operations carried out by residents with foreign financial institutions

VII. CREDITS RELATED TO COMMERCIAL TRANSACTIONS OR TO THE PROVISION OF SERVICES IN WHICH A RESIDENT IS PARTICIPATING[10]

1. Short-term (less than one year).
2. Medium-term (from one to five years).
3. Long-term (five years or more).

A—Credits granted by non-residents to residents

B—Credits granted by residents to non-residents

VIII. FINANCIAL LOANS AND CREDITS (NOT INCLUDED UNDER I, VII AND XI)[10]

1. Short-term (less than one year).
2. Medium-term (from one to five years).
3. Long-term (five years or more).

A—Loans and credits granted by non-residents to residents

B—Loans and credits granted by residents to non-residents

IX. SURETIES, OTHER GUARANTEES AND RIGHTS OF PLEDGE

A—Granted by non-residents to residents

B—Granted by residents to non-residents

X. TRANSFERS IN PERFORMANCE OF INSURANCE CONTRACTS

A. Premiums and payments in respect of life assurance

1. Contracts concluded between domestic life assurance companies and non-residents.
2. Contracts concluded between foreign life assurance companies and residents.

B—Premiums and payments in respect of credit insurance

1. Contracts concluded between domestic credit insurance companies and non-residents.
2. Contracts concluded between foreign credit insurance companies and residents.

C—Other transfers of capital in respect of insurance contracts

10. *Ibid.*

XI. PERSONAL CAPITAL MOVEMENTS

A—Loans

B—Gifts and endowments

C—Dowries

D—Inheritances and legacies

E—Settlement of debts by immigrants in their previous country of residence

F—Transfers of assets constituted by residents, in the event of emigration, at the time of their installation or during their period of stay abroad

G—Transfers, during their period of stay, of immigrants' savings to their previous country of residence

XII. PHYSICAL IMPORT AND EXPORT OF FINANCIAL ASSETS

A—Securities

B—Means of payment of every kind

XIII. OTHER CAPITAL MOVEMENTS

A—Death duties

B—Damages (where these can be considered as capital)

C—Refunds in the case of cancellation of contracts and refunds of uncalled-for payments (where these can be considered as capital)

D—Authors' royalties; patents, designs, trade marks and inventions (assignments and transfers arising out of such assignments)

E—Transfers of the monies required for the provision of services (not included under VI)

F—Miscellaneous

EXPLANATORY NOTES

For the purposes of this Nomenclature and the Directive only, the following expressions have the meanings assigned to them respectively:

Direct investments

Investments of all kinds by natural persons or commercial, industrial or financial undertakings, and which serve to establish or to maintain lasting and direct links between the person providing the capital and the entrepreneur to whom or the undertaking to which the capital is made available in order to carry on an economic activity. This concept must therefore be understood in its widest sense.

The undertakings mentioned under I–1 of the Nomenclature include legally independent undertakings (wholly-owned subsidiaries) and branches.

As regards those undertakings mentioned under I–2 of the Nomenclature which have the status of companies limited by shares, there is participation in the nature of direct investment where the block of shares held by a natural person of another undertaking or any other holder enables the shareholder, either pursuant to the provisions of national laws relating to companies limited by shares or otherwise, to participate effectively in the management of the company or in its control.

Long-term loans of a participating nature, mentioned under I–3 of the Nomenclature, means loans for a period of more than five years which are made for the purpose of establishing or maintaining lasting economic links. The main examples which may be cited are loans granted by a company to its subsidiaries or to companies in which it has a share and loans linked with a profit-sharing arrangement. Loans granted by financial institutions with a view to establishing or maintaining lasting economic links are also included under this heading.

Investments in real estate

Purchases of buildings and land and the construction of buildings by private persons for gain or personal use. This category also includes rights of usufruct, easements and building rights.

Introduction on a stock exchange or on a recognized money market

Access—in accordance with a specified procedure—for securities and other negotiable instruments to dealings, whether controlled officially or unofficially, on an officially recognized stock exchange or in an officially recognized segment of the money market.

Securities dealt in on a stock exchange (quoted or unquoted)

Securities the dealings in which are controlled by regulations, the prices for which are regularly published, either by official stock exchanges (quoted securities) or by other bodies attached to a stock exchange e.g. committees of banks (unquoted securities).

Issue of securities and other negotiable instruments

Sale by way of an offer to the public.

Placing of securities and other negotiable instruments

The direct sale of securities by the issuer or by the consortium which the issuer has instructed to sell them, with no offer being made to the public.

Domestic or foreign securities and other instruments

Securities according to the country in which the issuer has his principal place of business. Acquisition by residents of domestic securities and other instruments issued on a foreign market ranks as the acquisition of foreign securities.

Shares and other securities of a participating nature

Including rights to subscribe to new issues of shares.

Bonds

Negotiable securities with a maturity of two years or more from issue for which the interest rate and the terms for the repayment of the principal and the payment of interest are determined at the time of issue.

Collective investment undertakings

Undertakings:

- the object of which is the collective investment in transferable securities or other assets of the capital they raise and which operate on the principle of risk-spreading, and
- the units of which are, at the request of holders, under the legal, contractual or statutory conditions governing them, repurchased or redeemed, directly or indirectly, out of those undertakings' assets. Action taken by a collective investment undertaking to ensure that the stock exchange value of its units does not significantly vary from their net asset value shall be regarded as equivalent to such repurchase or redemption.

Such undertakings may be constituted according to law either under the law of contract (as common funds managed by management companies) or trust law (as unit trusts) or under statute (as investment companies).

For the purposes of the Directive, "common funds" shall also include unit trusts.

Securities and other instruments normally dealt in on the money market

Treasury bills and other negotiable bills, certificates of deposit, bankers' acceptances, commercial paper and other like instruments.

Credit related to commercial transactions or to the provision of services

Contractual trade credits (advances or payments by instalment in respect of work in progress or on order and extended payment terms, whether or not involving subscription to a commercial bill) and their financing by credits provided by credit institutions. This category also includes factoring operations.

Financial loans and credits

Financing of every kind granted by financial institutions, including financing related to commercial transactions or to the provision of services in which no resident is participating.

This category also includes mortgage loans, consumer credit and financial leasing, as well as back-up facilities and other note-issuance facilities.

Residents or non-residents

Natural and legal persons according to the definitions laid down in the exchange control regulations in force in each Member State.

Proceeds of liquidation (of investments, securities, etc.)

Proceeds of sale including any capital appreciation, amount of repayments, proceeds of execution of judgments, etc.

Natural or legal persons

As defined by the national rules.

Financial institutions

Banks, savings banks and institutions specializing in the provision of short-term, medium-term and long-term credit, and insurance companies, building societies, investment companies and other institutions of like character.

Credit institutions

Banks, savings banks and institutions specializing in the provision of short-term, medium-term and long-term credit.

ANNEX II. LIST OF OPERATIONS REFERRED TO IN ARTICLE 3 OF THE DIRECTIVE

Nature of operation	Heading
Operations in securities and other instruments normally dealt in on the money market	V
Operations in current and deposit accounts with financial institutions	VI
Operations in units of collective investment undertakings — undertakings for investment in securities normally dealt in on the money market	IV–A and B–(c)
Financial loans and credits — short-term	VIII–A and B–1
Personal capital movements — loans	XI–A
Physical import and export of financial assets — securities normally dealt in on the money market — means of payment	XII
Other capital movements: Miscellaneous — short-term operations similar to those listed above	XIII–F

The restrictions which Member States may apply to the capital movements listed above must be defined and applied in such a way as to cause the least possible hindrance to the free movement of persons, goods and services.

ANNEX III. REFERRED TO IN ARTICLE 5 OF THE DIRECTIVE

Scope of the provisions of the 1985 Act of Accession relating to capital movements, in accordance with the Nomenclature of capital movements set out in the Annex to the Directive

Articles of the Act of Accession (dates of expiry of transitional provisions)	Nature of operation	Heading

(a) Provisions concerning the Kingdom of Spain

Article 62 (31.12.1990)	Direct investments abroad by residents	I–B
Article 63 (31.12.1990)	Investments in real estate abroad by residents	II–B
Article 64 (31.12.1988)	Operations in securities normally dealt in on the capital market. — Acquisition by residents of foreign securities dealt in on a stock exchange. — excluding bonds issued on a foreign market and denominated in national currency	 III–A–2

Articles of the Act of Accession (dates of expiry of transitional provisions)	Nature of operation	Heading
	Operations in units of collective investment undertakings — Acquisition by residents of units of collective investment undertakings dealt in on a stock exchange — excluding units of undertakings taking the form of common funds	IV–A–2

(b) Provisions concerning the Portuguese Republic

Articles	Nature of operation	Heading
Article 222 (31.12.1989)	Direct investments on national territory by non-residents	I–A
Article 224 (31.12.1992)	Direct investments abroad by residents	I–B
Articles 225 and 226 (31.12.1990)	Investments in real estate on national territory by non-residents	II–A
Article 227 (31.12.1992)	Investments in real estate abroad by residents	II–B
Article 228 (31.12.1990)	Personal capital movements (i) for the purpose of applying the higher amounts specified in Article 228(2):	
	— Dowries	XI–C
	— Inheritances and legacies	XI–D
	— Transfers of assets built up by residents in case of emigration at the time of their installation or during their period of stay abroad	XI–F
	(ii) for the purpose of applying the lower amounts specified in Article 228(2):	
	— Gifts and endowments	XI–B
	— Settlement of debts by immigrants in their previous country of residence	XI–E
	— Transfers of immigrants' savings to their previous country of residence during their period of stay	XI–G
Article 229 (31.12.1990)	Operations in securities normally dealt in on the capital market — Acquisition by residents of foreign securities dealt in on a stock exchange excluding bonds issued on a foreign market and denominated in national currency	III–A–2
	Operations in units of collective investment undertakings — Acquisition by residents of units of foreign collective investment undertakings dealt in on a stock exchange excluding units of undertakings taking the form of common funds	IV–A–2

ANNEX IV. REFERRED TO IN ARTICLE 6(2) OF THE DIRECTIVE

I. The Portuguese Republic may continue to apply or reintroduce, until 31 December 1990, restrictions existing on the date of notification of the Directive on capital movements given in List I below:

List I

Nature of operation	Heading
Operations in units of collective investment undertakings	
— Acquisition by residents of units of foreign collective investment undertakings dealt in on a stock exchange—undertakings subject to Directive 85/611/EEC[11] and taking the form of common funds	IV–A–2 (a)
— Acquisition by residents of units of foreign collective investment undertakings not dealt in on a stock exchange—undertakings subject to Directive 85/611/EEC[11]	IV–A–4 (a)

II. The Kingdom of Spain and the Portuguese Republic may continue to apply or reintroduce, until 31 December 1990 and 31 December 1992 respectively, restrictions existing on the date of notification of the Directive on capital movements given in List II below:

List II

Nature of operation	Heading
Operations in securities normally dealt in on the capital market	
— Acquisition by residents of foreign securities dealt in on a stock exchange—bonds issued on a foreign market and denominated in national currency	III–A–2 (b)
— Acquisition by residents (non-residents) of foreign (domestic) securities not dealt in on a stock exchange	III–A–3 and 4
— Admission of securities to the capital market—where they are dealt in on or in the process of introduction to a stock exchange in a Member State	III–B–1 and 2
Operations in units of collective investment undertakings	
— Acquisition by residents of units of foreign collective investment undertakings dealt in on a stock exchange—undertakings not subject to Directive 85/611/EEC[12] and taking the form of common funds	IV–A–2
— Acquisition by residents (non-residents) of units of foreign (domestic) collective investment undertakings not dealt in on a stock exchange—undertakings not subject to Directive 85/611/EEC[13] and the sole object of which is the acquisition of assets that have been liberalized	IV–A–3 and 4
— Admission to the capital market of units of collective investment undertakings—undertakings subject to Directive 85/611/EEC[13]	IV–B–1 and 2 (a)
— Credits related to commercial transactions or to the provision of services in which a resident is participating	VII–A and B–3
— Long-term credits	

11. Council Directive 85/611/EEC on the co-ordination of laws, regulations and administrative provisions relating to undertakings for collective investments in transferable securities (UCITS) (OJ No L375, 31 December 1985, p. 3).

12. See footnote to List I.

13. See footnote to List I.

III. The Hellenic Republic, the Kingdom of Spain, Ireland and the Portuguese Republic may, until 31 December 1992, continue to apply or reintroduce restrictions existing at the date of notification of the Directive on capital movements given in List III below:

List III

Nature of operation	Heading
Operations in securities dealt in on the capital market	
— Admission of securities to the capital market	III–B–1 and 2
— where they are not dealt in on or in the process of introduction to a stock exchange in a Member State	
Operations in units of collective investment undertakings	
— Admission to the capital market of units of collective investment undertakings—undertakings not subject to Directive 85/611/EEC[14] and the sole object of which is the acquisition of assets that have been liberalized	IV–B–1 and 2
Financial loans and credits	VIII–A, B–2 and 3
— medium-term and long-term	

IV. The Hellenic Republic, the Kingdom of Spain, Ireland and the Portuguese Republic may, until 31 December 1992, defer liberalization of the capital movements given in List IV below:

List IV

Nature of operation	Heading
Operations in securities and other instruments normally dealt in on the money market	V
Operations in current and deposit accounts with financial institutions	VI
Operations in units of collective investment undertakings	IV–A and B (c)
— undertakings for investment in securities or instruments normally dealt in on the money market	
Financial loans and credits	VIII–A and B–1
— short term	
Personal capital movements	XI–A
— loans	
Physical import and export of financial assets	XII
— securities normally dealt in on the money market	
— means of payment	
Other capital movements: Miscellaneous	XIII–F

14. See footnote to List I.

ANNEX V

Since the dual exchange market system, as operated by the Kingdom of Belgium and the Grand Duchy of Luxembourg, has not had the effect of restricting capital movements but nevertheless constitutes an anomaly in the EMS and should therefore be brought to an end in the interests of effective implementation of the Directive and with a view to strengthening the European Monetary System, these two Member States undertake to abolish it by 31 December 1992. They also undertake to administer the system, until such time as it is abolished, on the basis of procedures which will still ensure the *de facto* free movement of capital on such conditions that the exchange rates ruling on the two markets show no appreciable and lasting differences.

ARTICLE 73 OF THE TREATY ON EUROPEAN UNION

Article 73

1. If movements of capital lead to disturbances in the functioning of the capital market in any Member State, the Commission shall, after consulting the Monetary Committee, authorize that State to take *protective* measures in the field of capital movements, the conditions and details of which the Commission shall determine.

The Council may, acting by a qualified majority, revoke this authorization or amend the conditions or details thereof.

2. A Member State which is in difficulties may, however, on grounds of secrecy or urgency, take the measures mentioned above, where this proves necessary, on its own initiative. The Commission and the other Member State shall be informed of such measures by the date of their entry into force at the latest. In this event the Commission may, after consulting the Monetary Committee, decide that the State concerned shall amend or abolish the measures.

Article 73a[1]

As from 1 January 1994, Articles 67 to 73 shall be replaced by Articles 73b, c, d, e, f and g.

Article 73b[1]

1. Within the framework of the provisions set out in this Chapter, all restrictions on the movement of capital between Member States and between Member States and third countries shall be prohibited.

2. Within the framework of the provisions set out in this Chapter, all restrictions on payments between Member States and between Member States and third countries shall be prohibited.

Article 73c[1]

1. The provisions of Article 73b shall be without prejudice to the application to third countries of any restrictions which exist on 31 December 1993 under national or Community law adopted in respect of the movement of capital to or from third countries involving direct investment—including in real estate—, establishment, the provision of financial services or the admission of securities to capital markets.

2. Whilst endeavouring to achieve the objective of free movement of capital between Member States and third countries to the greatest extent possible and without prejudice to the other Chapters of this Treaty, the Council may, acting by a qualified majority on a proposal from the Commission, adopt measures on the movement of capital to or from third countries involving direct investment—including investment in real estate—, establishment, the provision of financial services or the admission of securities to capital markets. Unanimity shall be required for measures under this paragraph which constitute a step back in Community law as regards the liberalization of the movement of capital to or from third countries.

1. Articles 73a to 73h as inserted by G(15) TEU.

Article 73d[1]

   1. The provision of Article 73b shall be without prejudice to the right of Member States:

     (a) to apply the relevant provisions of their tax law which distinguish between tax-payers who are not in the same situation with regard to their place of residence or with regard to the place where their capital is invested;

     (b) to take all requisite measures to prevent infringements of national law and regulations, in particular in the field of taxation and the prudential supervision of financial institutions, or to lay down procedures for the declaration of capital movements for purposes of administrative or statistical information, or to take measures which are justified on grounds of public policy or public security.

   2. The provisions of this Chapter shall be without prejudice to the applicability of restrictions on the right of establishment which are compatible with this Treaty.

   3. The measures and procedures referred to in paragraphs 1 and 2 shall not constitute a means of arbitrary discrimination or a disguised restriction on the free movement of capital and payments as defined in Article 73b.

Article 73e[1]

By way of derogation from Article 73b, Member States which, on 31 December 1993, enjoy a derogation on the basis of existing Community law, shall be entitled to maintain, until 31 December 1995 at the latest, restrictions on movements of capital authorized by such derogations as exist on that date.

Article 73f[1]

Where, in exceptional circumstances, movements of capital to or from third countries cause, or threaten to cause, serious difficulties for the operation of economic and monetary union, the Council, acting by a qualified majority on a proposal from the Commission and after consulting the ECB, may take safeguard measures with regard to third countries for a period not exceeding six months if such measures are strictly necessary.

Article 73g[1]

   1. If, in the cases envisaged in Article 228a, action by the Community is deemed necessary, the Council may, in accordance with the procedure provided for in Article 228a, take the necessary urgent measures on the movement of capital and on payments as regards the third countries concerned.

   2. Without prejudice to Article 224 and as long as the Council has not taken measures pursuant to paragraph 1, a Member State may, for serious political reasons and on grounds of urgency, take unilateral measures against a third country with regard to capital movements and payments. The Commission and the other Member States shall be informed of such measures by the date of their entry into force at the latest.

   The Council may, acting by a qualified majority on a proposal from the Commission, decide that the Member State concerned shall amend or abolish such measures. The President of the Council shall inform the European Parliament of any such decision taken by the Council.

Article 73h[1]

Until 1 January 1994, the following provisions shall be applicable:

   (1) Each Member State undertakes to authorize, in the currency of the Member State in which the creditor or the beneficiary resides, any payments connected with the movement of goods, services or capital, and any transfers of capital and earnings, to the extent that the movement of goods, services, capital and persons between Member States has been liberalized pursuant to this Treaty.

   The Member States declare their readiness to undertake the liberalization of payments beyond the extent provided in the preceding subparagraph, in so far as their economic situation in general and the state of their balance of payments in particular so permit.

(2) In so far as movements of goods, services and capital are limited only by restrictions on payments connected therewith, these restrictions shall be progressively abolished by applying, *mutatis mutandis*, the provisions of this Chapter and the Chapters relating to the abolition of quantitative restrictions and to the liberalization of services.

(3) Member States undertake not to introduce between themselves any new restrictions on transfers connected with the invisible transactions listed in Annex III to this Treaty.

The progressive abolition of existing restrictions shall be effected in accordance with the provisions of Articles 63 to 65, in so far as such abolition is not governed by the provisions contained in paragraphs 1 and 2 or by the other provisions of this Chapter.

(4) If need be, Member States shall consult each other on the measures to be taken to enable the payments and transfers mentioned in this Article to be effected; such measures shall not prejudice the attainment of the objectives set out in this Treaty.

COUNCIL DIRECTIVE 92/121/EEC OF 21 DECEMBER 1992

on the monitoring and control of large exposures of credit institutions

THE COUNCIL OF THE EUROPEAN COMMUNITIES,

Having regard to the Treaty establishing the European Economic Community, and in particular the first and third sentences of Article 57(2) thereof,

Having regard to the proposal from the Commission,[1]

In co-operation with the European Parliament,[2]

Having regard to the opinion of the Economic and Social Committee,[3]

Whereas this Directive comes within the framework of the aims set out in the Commission's White Paper on completing the internal market;

Whereas the essential rules for monitoring large exposures of credit institutions should be harmonized; whereas Member States should still be able to adopt provisions more stringent than those provided for by this Directive;

Whereas this Directive has been the subject of consultation with the Banking Advisory Committee, which, under Article 6(4) of Council Directive 77/780/EEC of 12 December 1977 on the co-ordination of laws, regulations and administrative provisions relating to the taking-up and pursuit of the business of credit institutions,[4] is responsible for making suggestions to the Commission with a view to co-ordinating the co-efficients applicable in the Member States;

Whereas the monitoring and control of a credit institution's exposures is an integral part of its supervision; whereas an excessive concentration of exposures to a single client or group of connected clients may result in an unacceptable risk of loss; whereas such a situation may be considered prejudicial to the solvency of a credit institution;

Whereas common guidelines for monitoring and controlling credit institutions' large exposures were initially introduced by Commission recommendation 87/62/EEC[5]; whereas that instrument was chosen because it permitted the gradual adjustment of existing systems and the establishment of new systems without dislocating the Community's banking system; whereas, now that that first phase is over, a binding instrument applicable to all Community credit institutions should be adopted;

Whereas in a unified banking market credit institutions are engaged in direct competition with one another and monitoring requirements throughout the Community should therefore be equivalent; whereas, to that end, the criteria applied to determining the concentration of exposures must be the subject of legally binding rules at Community level and cannot be left entirely to the discretion of the Member States; whereas the adoption of common rules will therefore best serve the Community's interests, since it will prevent differences in the conditions of competition, while strengthening the Community's banking system;

Whereas, for the precise accounting technique to be used for the assessment of exposures

1. OJ No C 123, 9 May 1991, p. 18 and OJ No C 175, 11 July 1992, p. 4.
2. OJ No C 150, 15 June 1992, p. 74 and OJ No C 337, 21 December 1992.
3. OJ No C 339, 31 December 1991, p. 35.
4. OJ No L 322, 17 December 1977, p. 30. Directive last amended by Directive 89/646/EEC (OJ No L 386, 30 December 1989, p. 1).
5. OJ No L 33, 4 February 1987, p. 10.

reference is made to Council Directive 86/635/EEC of 8 December 1986 on the annual accounts and consolidated accounts of banks and other financial institutions[6];

Whereas Council Directive 89/647/EEC of 18 December 1989 on a solvency ratio for credit institutions[7] includes a list of credit risks which may be incurred by credit institutions; whereas that list should therefore be used for the definition of exposures for the purposes of this Directive; whereas it is not, however, appropriate to refer on principle to the weightings or degrees of risk laid down in that Directive; whereas those weightings and degrees of risk were devised for the purpose of establishing a general solvency requirement to cover the credit risk of credit institutions; whereas, in the context of the regulation of large exposures, the aim is to limit the maximum loss that a credit institution may incur through any single client or group of connected clients; whereas it is therefore appropriate to adopt a prudent approach in which, as a general rule, account is taken of the nominal value of exposures, but no weightings or degrees of risk are applied;

Whereas, when a credit institution incurs an exposure to its own parent undertaking or to other subsidiaries of its parent undertaking, particular prudence is necessary; whereas the management of exposures incurred by credit institutions must by [sic] carried out in a fully autonomous manner, in accordance with the principles of sound banking management, without regard to any considerations other than those principles; whereas the Second Council Directive 89/646/EEC of 15 December 1989 on the co-ordination of laws, regulations and administrative provisions relating to the taking up and pursuit of the business of credit institutions[8] requires that where the influence exercised by persons directly or indirectly holding a qualifying participation in a credit institution is likely to operate to the detriment of the sound and prudent management of that institution, the competent authorities shall take appropriate measures to put an end to that situation; whereas, in the field of large exposures, specific standards should also be laid down for exposures incurred by a credit institution to its own group and in such cases more stringent restrictions are justified than for other exposures; whereas more stringent restrictions need not, however, be applied where the parent undertaking is a financial holding company or a credit institution or where the other subsidiaries are either credit or financial institutions or undertakings offering ancillary banking services, provided that all such undertakings are covered by the supervision of the credit institution on a consolidated basis; whereas in such cases the consolidated monitoring of the group of undertaking allows for an adequate level of supervision, and does not require the imposition of more stringent limits on exposure; whereas under this approach banking groups will also be encouraged to organize their structures in such a way as to allow consolidated monitoring, which is desirable because a more comprehensive level of monitoring is possible;

Whereas, in order to ensure harmonious application of this Directive, Member States should be allowed to provide for the two-stage application of the new limits; whereas, for smaller credit institutions, a longer transitional period may be warranted inasmuch as too rapid an application of the 25% rule could reduce their lending activity too abruptly;

Whereas implementing powers of the same type as those which the Council reserved for itself in Directive 89/299/EEC on the own funds of credit institutions[9] were granted to the Commission in Directive 89/646/EEC;

Whereas, taking account of the specific characteristics of the sector in question, it is appropriate to give the Committee set up by Article 22 of Directive 89/646/EEC the role of assisting the Commission in exercising the powers conferred on it under the procedure laid down in Article 2 (Procedure III, Variant (b)) of Council Decision 87/373/EEC of 13 July 1987 laying down the procedures for the exercise of implementing powers conferred on the Commission[10];

Whereas, with regard to the monitoring of large exposures concerning activities which are principally exposed to market risks, the necessary co-ordination of monitoring methods can be ensured under a Community act on the capital adequacy of investment firms and credit institutions; whereas that implies that until Community legislation on the aforementioned large

6. OJ No L 372, 31 December 1986, p. 1.
7. OJ No L 386, 30 December 1989, p. 14.
8. OJ No L 386, 30 December 1989, p. 1. Directive amended by Directive 92/30/EEC (OJ No L 110, 28 April 1992, p. 52).
9. OJ No L 124, 5 May 1989, p. 16.
10. OJ No L 197, 18 July 1987, p. 33.

exposures is adopted the monitoring of large exposures relating to activities which are principally exposed to market risks, such as the trading portfolio, underwriting commitments for the issue of securities and claims related to the settlement of securities transactions may be left to the competent authorities of each Member State,

HAS ADOPTED THIS DIRECTIVE:

Article 1

Definitions

For the purposes of this Directive:

(a) *credit institution* shall mean a credit institution as defined in the first indent of Article 1 of Directive 77/780/EEC, including such a credit institution's branches in third countries, and any private or public undertaking, including its branches, which satisfies the definition in the first indent of Article 1 of Directive 77/780/EEC and which has been authorized in a third country;

(b) *competent authorities* shall mean the competent authorities as defined in the ninth indent of Article 1 of Council Directive 92/30/EEC of 6 April 1992 on the supervision of credit institutions on a consolidated basis[11];

(c) *parent undertaking* shall mean a parent undertaking as defined in the seventh indent of Article 1 of Directive 92/30/EEC;

(d) *subsidiary undertaking* shall mean a subsidiary undertaking as defined in the eighth indent of Article 1 of Directive 92/30/EEC;

(e) *financial holding company* shall mean a financial holding company as defined in the third indent of Article 1 of Directive 92/30/EEC;

(f) *financial institution* shall mean a financial institution as defined in the second indent of Article 1 of Directive 92/30/EEC;

(g) *ancillary banking-services undertaking* shall mean an undertaking as defined in the fifth indent of Article 1 of Directive 92/30/EEC;

(h) *exposures* shall mean the assets and off-balance-sheet items referred to in Article 6 of Directive 89/647/EEC and in Annexes I and III thereto, without application of the weightings or degrees of risk there provided for; the risks referred to in the aforementioned Annex III must be calculated in accordance with one of the methods set out in Annex II to that Directive, without application of the weightings for counter-party risk; all elements entirely covered by own funds may, with the agreement of the competent authorities, be excluded from the definition of exposures provided that such own funds are not included in the calculation of the solvency ratio or of other monitoring ratios provided for in Community acts; exposures shall not include:

— in the case of foreign exchange transactions, exposures incurred in the ordinary course of settlement during the 48 hours following payment, or

— in the case of transactions for the purchase or sale of securities, exposures incurred in the ordinary course of settlement during the five working days following payment or delivery of the securities, whichever is the earlier;

(i) *Zone A* shall mean the zone referred to in the second indent of Article 2(1) of Directive 89/647/EEC;

(j) *Zone B* shall mean the zone referred to in the third indent of Article 2(1) of Directive 89/647/EEC;

(k) *own funds* shall mean the own funds of a credit institution as defined in Directive 89/299/EEC;

(l) *control* shall mean the relationship between a parent undertaking and a subsidiary, as defined in Article 1 of Directive 83/349/EEC, or a similar relationship between any natural or legal person and an undertaking;

(m) *group of connected clients* shall mean:

11. OJ No L 110, 28 April 1992, p. 52.

> — two or more natural or legal persons who, unless it is shown otherwise, constitute a single risk because one of them, directly or indirectly, has control over the other or others, or
> — two or more natural or legal persons between whom there is no relationship of control as defined in the first indent but who are to be regarded as constituting a single risk because they are so interconnected that, if one of them were to experience financial problems, the other or all of the others would be likely to encounter repayment difficulties.

Article 2

Scope

This Directive shall apply to credit institutions which have obtained the authorization referred to in Article 3 of Directive 77/780/EEC.

Member States need not, however, apply this Directive to:

(a) the institutions listed in Article 2(2) of Directive 77/780/EEC, or

(b) the institutions in the same Member State which, as defined in Article 2(4)(a) of Directive 77/780/EEC, are affiliated to a central body established in that Member State, provided that, without prejudice to the application of this Directive to the central body, the whole as constituted by the central body and its affiliated institutions is subject to global monitoring.

Article 3

Reporting of large exposures

1. A credit institution's exposure to a client or group of connected clients shall be considered a large exposure where its value is equal to or exceeds 10% of its own funds.

2. A credit institution shall report every large exposure within the meaning of paragraph 1 to the competent authorities. Member States shall provide that that reporting is to be carried out, at their discretion, in accordance with one of the following two methods:

> — reporting of all large exposures at least once a year, combined with reporting during the year of all new large exposures and any increases in existing large exposures of at least 20% with respect to the previous communication,
> — reporting of all large exposures at least four times a year.

3. Exposures exempted under Article 4(7)(a), (b), (c), (d), (f), (g) and (h) need not, however, be reported as laid down in paragraph 2. The reporting frequency laid down in the second indent of paragraph 2 may be reduced to twice a year for the exposures referred to in Article 4(7)(e) and (i) to (s), (8), (9) and (10).

4. The competent authorities shall require that every credit institution have sound administrative and accounting procedures and adequate internal control mechanisms for the purpose of identifying and recording all large exposures and subsequent changes to them, as defined and required by this Directive, and for that of monitoring those exposures in the light of each credit institution's own exposure policies.

Where a credit institution invokes paragraph 3, it shall keep a record of the grounds advanced for at least one year after the event giving rise to the dispensation, so that the competent authorities may establish whether it is justified.

Article 4

Limits on large exposures

1. A credit institution may not incur an exposure to a client or group of connected clients the value of which exceeds 25% of its own funds.

2. Where that client or group of connected clients is the parent undertaking or subsidiary of the credit institution and/or one or more subsidiaries of that parent undertaking, the percentage laid

down in paragraph 1 shall be reduced to 20%. Member States may, however, exempt the exposures incurred to such clients from the 20% limit if they provide for specific monitoring of such exposures by other measures or procedures. They shall inform the Commission and the Banking Advisory Committee of the content of such measures or procedures.

3. A credit institution may not incur large exposures which in total exceed 800% of its own funds.

4. Member States may impose limits more stringent than those laid down in paragraphs 1, 2 and 3.

5. A credit institution shall at all times comply with the limits laid down in paragraphs 1, 2 and 3 in respect of its exposures. If in an exceptional case exposures exceed those limits, that fact must be reported without delay to the competent authorities which may, where the circumstances warrant it, allow the credit institution a limited period of time in which to comply with the limits.

6. Member States may fully or partially exempt from the application of paragraphs 1, 2 and 3 exposures incurred by a credit institution to its parent undertaking, to other subsidiaries of that parent undertaking or to its own subsidiaries, in so far as those undertakings are covered by the supervision on a consolidated basis to which the credit institution itself is subject, in accordance with Directive 92/30/EEC or with equivalent standards in force in a third country.

7. Member States may fully or partially exempt the following exposures from the application of paragraphs 1, 2 and 3:

(a) asset items constituting claims on Zone A central governments or central banks;

(b) asset items constituting claims on the European Communities;

(c) asset items constituting claims carrying the explicit guarantees of Zone A central governments or central banks or of the European Communities;

(d) other exposures attributable to, or guaranteed by, Zone A central governments or central banks or the European Communities;

(e) asset items constituting claims on and other exposures to Zone B central governments or central banks which are denominated and, where applicable, funded in the national currencies of the borrowers;

(f) asset items and other exposures secured, to the satisfaction of the competent authorities, by collateral in the form of Zone A central government or central bank securities, or securities issued by the European Communities or by Member State regional or local authorities for which Article 7 of Directive 89/647/EEC lays down a zero weighting for solvency purposes;

(g) asset items and other exposures secured, to the satisfaction of the competent authorities, by collateral in the form of cash deposits placed with the lending institution or with a credit institution which is the parent undertaking or a subsidiary of the lending institution;

(h) asset items and other exposures secured, to the satisfaction of the competent authorities, by collateral in the form of certificates of deposit issued by the lending institution or by a credit institution which is the parent undertaking or a subsidiary of the lending institution and lodged with either of them;

(i) asset items constituting claims on and other exposures to credit institutions, with a maturity of one year or less, but not constituting such institutions' own funds as defined in Directive 89/299/EEC;

(j) asset items constituting claims on and other exposures to those institutions which are not credit institutions but which fulfil the conditions referred to in Article 8(2) of Directive 89/647/EEC, with a maturity of one year or less, and secured in accordance with the same paragraph;

(k) bills of trade and other similar bills, with a maturity of one year or less, bearing the signatures of other credit institutions;

(l) debt securities as defined in Article 22(4) of Directive 85/611/EEC[12];

(m) pending subsequent coordination, holdings in the insurance companies referred to in Article 12(3) of Directive 89/646/EEC up to 40% of the own funds of the credit institution acquiring such a holding;

12. OJ No L 375, 31 December 1985, p. 3. Directive as amended by Directive 88/220/EEC (OJ No L 100, 19 April 1988, p. 31).

(n) asset items constituting claims on regional or central credit institutions with which the lending institution is associated in a network in accordance with legal or statutory provisions and which are responsible, under those provisions, for cash-clearing operations within the network;

(o) exposures secured, to the satisfaction of the competent authorities, by collateral in the form of securities other than those referred to in (f) provided that those securities are not issued by the credit institution itself, its parent company or one of their subsidiaries, or by the client or group of connected clients in question. The securities used as collateral must be valued at market price, have a value that exceeds the exposures guaranteed and be either traded on a stock exchange or effectively negotiable and regularly quoted on a market operated under the auspices of recognized professional operators and allowing, to the satisfaction of the competent authorities of the Member State of origin of the credit institution, for the establishment of an objective price such that the excess value of the securities may be verified at any time. The excess value required shall be 100%; it shall, however, be 150% in the case of shares and 50% in the case of debt securities issued by credit institutions, Member State regional or local authorities other than those referred to in Article 7 of Directive 89/647/EEC, and in the case of debt securities issued by the European Investment Bank and multilateral development banks as defined in Article 2 of Directive 89/647/EEC. Securities used as collateral may not constitute credit institutions' own funds as defined in Directive 89/229/EEC;

(p) loans secured, to the satisfaction of the competent authorities, by mortgages on residential property and leasing transactions under which the lessor retains full ownership of the residential property leased for as long as the lessee has not exercised his option to purchase, in both cases up to 50% of the value of the residential property concerned. The value of the property shall be calculated, to the satisfaction of the competent authorities, on the basis of strict valuation standards laid down by law, regulation or administrative provisions. Valuation shall be carried out at least once a year. For the purposes of this subparagraph residential property shall mean a residence to be occupied or let by the borrower;

(q) 50% of the medium/low-risk off-balance-sheet items referred to in Annex I to Directive 89/647/EEC;

(r) subject to the competent authorities' agreement, guarantees other than loan guarantees which have a legal or regulatory basis and are given for their members by mutual guarantee schemes possessing the status of credit institutions as defined in Article 1(a), subject to a weighting of 20% of their amount.

Member States shall inform the Commission of the use they make of this option in order to ensure that it does not result in distortions of competition. Within five years of the adoption of this Directive, the Commission shall submit to the Council a report accompanied, if necessary, by appropriate proposals;

(s) the low-risk off-balance-sheet items referred to in Annex I to Directive 89/647/EEC, to the extent that an agreement has been concluded with the client or group of connected clients under which the exposure may be incurred only if it has been ascertained that it will not cause the limits applicable under paragraphs 1, 2 and 3 to be exceeded.

8. For the purposes of paragraphs 1, 2 and 3, Member States may apply a weighting of 20% to asset items constituting claims on Member State regional and local authorities and to other exposures to or guaranteed by such authorities; subject to the conditions laid down in Article 7 of Directive 89/647/EEC, however, Member States may reduce that rate to 0%.

9. For the purposes of paragraphs 1, 2 and 3, Member States may apply a weighting of 20% to asset items constituting claims on and other exposures to credit institutions with a maturity of more than one but not more than three years and a weighting of 50% to asset items constituting claims on credit institutions with a maturity of more than three years, provided that the latter are represented by debt instruments that were issued by a credit institution and that those debt instruments are, in the opinion of the competent authorities, effectively negotiable on a market made up of professional operators and are subject to daily quotation on that market, or the issue of which was authorized by the competent authorities of the Member State of origin of the issuing

credit institution. In no case may any of these items constitute own funds within the meaning of Directive 89/299/EEC.

10. By way of derogation from paragraphs 7(i) and 9, Member States may apply a weighting of 20% to asset items constituting claims on and other exposures to credit institutions, regardless of their maturity.

11. Where an exposure to a client is guaranteed by a third party, or by collateral in the form of securities issued by a third party under the conditions laid down in paragraph 7(o), Member States may:

— treat the exposure as having been incurred to the third party rather than to the client, if the exposure is directly and unconditionally guaranteed by that third party, to the satisfaction of the competent authorities,

— treat the exposure as having been incurred to the third party rather than to the client, if the exposure defined in paragraph 7(o) is guaranteed by collateral under the conditions there laid down.

12. Within five years of the date referred to in Article 8(1), the Council shall, on the basis of a report from the Commission, examine the treatment of interbank exposures provided for in paragraphs 7(i), 9 and 10. The Council shall decide on any changes to be made on a proposal from the Commission.

Article 5

Supervision on a consolidated or unconsolidated basis

1. If the credit institution is neither a parent undertaking nor a subsidiary, compliance with the obligations imposed in Articles 3 and 4 or in any other Community provision applicable to this area shall be monitored on an unconsolidated basis.

2. In the other cases, compliance with the obligations imposed in Articles 3 and 4 or in any other Community provision applicable to this area shall be monitored on a consolidated basis in accordance with Directive 92/30/EEC.

3. Member States may waive monitoring on an individual or subconsolidated basis of compliance with the obligations imposed in Articles 3 and 4 or in any other Community provision applicable to this area by a credit institution which, as a parent undertaking, is subject to monitoring on a consolidated basis and by any subsidiary of such a credit institution which is subject to their authorization and supervision and is covered by monitoring on a consolidated basis.

Member States may also waive such monitoring where the parent undertaking is a financial holding company established in the same Member State as the credit institution, provided that that company is subject to the same monitoring as credit institutions.

In the cases referred to in the first and second subparagraphs measures must be taken to ensure the satisfactory allocation of risks within the group.

4. Where a credit institution the parent undertaking of which is a credit institution has been authorized and has its registered office in another Member State, the competent authorities which granted that authorization shall require compliance with the obligations imposed in Articles 3 and 4 or in any other Community provision applicable to this area on an individual basis or, when appropriate, a subconsolidated basis.

5. Notwithstanding paragraph 4, the competent authorities responsible for authorizing the subsidiary of a parent undertaking which is a credit institution which has been authorized by and has its registered office in another Member State may, by way of bilateral agreement, transfer responsibility for monitoring compliance with the obligations imposed in Articles 3 and 4 or in any other Community provision applicable to this area to the competent authorities which have authorized and which monitor the parent undertaking. The Commission and the Banking Advisory Committee shall be kept informed of the existence and content of such agreements.

Article 6

Transitional provisions relating to exposures in excess of the limits

1. If, when this Directive is published in the *Official Journal of the European Communities*, a

credit institution has already incurred an exposure or exposures exceeding either the large exposure limit or the aggregate large exposure limit laid down in this Directive, the competent authorities shall require the credit institution concerned to take steps to have that exposure or those exposures brought within the limits laid down in this Directive.

2. The process of having such an exposure or exposures brought within authorized limits shall be devised, adopted, implemented and completed within the period which the competent authorities consider consistent with the principle of sound administration and fair competition. The competent authorities shall inform the Commission and the Banking Advisory Committee of the schedule for the general process adopted.

3. A credit institution may not take any measure which would cause the exposures referred to in paragraph 1 to exceed their level on the date of the publication of this Directive in the *Official Journal of the European Communities*.

4. The period applicable under paragraph 2 shall expire no later than 31 December 2001. Exposures with a longer maturity, for which the lending institution is bound to observe the contractual terms, may be continued until their maturity.

5. Until 31 December 1998, Member States may increase the limit laid down in Article 4(1) to 40% and the limit laid down in Article 4(2) to 30%. In such cases and subject to paragraphs 1 to 4, the time limit for bringing the exposures existing at the end of this period within the limits laid down in Article 4 shall expire on 31 December 2001.

6. In the case of credit institutions the own funds of which, as defined in Article 2(1) of Directive 89/299/EEC, do not exceed ECU 7 million, and only in the case of such institutions, Member States may extend the time limits laid down in paragraph 5 by five years. Member States that avail themselves of the option provided for in this paragraph shall take steps to prevent distortions of competition and shall inform the Commission and the Banking Advisory Committee thereof.

7. In the cases referred to in paragraphs 5 and 6, an exposure may be considered a large exposure if its value is equal to or exceeds 13% of own funds.

8. Until 31 December 2001 Member States may substitute a frequency of at least twice a year for the frequency of notification of large exposures referred to in the second indent of Article 3(2).

9. Member States may fully or partially exempt from the application of Article 4(1), (2) and (3) exposures incurred by a credit institution consisting of mortgage loans as defined in Article 11(4) of Directive 89/647/EEC concluded within eight years of the date laid down in Article 8(1) of this Directive, as well as property leasing transactions as defined in Article 11(5) of Directive 89/647/EEC concluded within eight years of the date laid down in Article 8(1) of this Directive, in both cases up to 50% of the value of the property concerned.

10. Without prejudice to paragraph 4, Portugal may, until 31 December 1998, fully or partially exempt from the application of Article 4(1) and (3) exposures incurred by a credit institution to Electricidade de Portugal (EDP) and Petrogal.

Article 7

Subsequent amendments

1. Technical amendments to the following points shall be adopted in accordance with the procedure laid down in paragraph 2:

— the clarification of definitions to take account of developments on financial markets,
— the clarification of definitions to ensure the uniform application of this Directive,
— the alignment of the terminology and of the wording of the definitions on those in subsequent instruments concerning credit institutions and related matters,
— the clarification of the exemptions provided for in Article 4(5) to (10).

2. The Commission shall be assisted by the committee provided for in the first subparagraph of Article 22(2) of Directive 89/646/EEC.

The Commission representative shall submit to the committee a draft of the measures to be taken. The committee shall deliver its opinion on that draft within a time limit which the chairman may lay down according to the urgency of the matter. The opinion shall be delivered by the majority laid down in Article 148(2) of the Treaty in the case of decisions which the Council is required to adopt on a proposal from the Commission. The votes of the Member States' representatives on the committee shall be weighted as laid down in that Article. The chairman shall not vote.

The Commission shall adopt the measures envisaged if they are in accordance with the committee's opinion.

If the measures envisaged are not in accordance with the committee's opinion, or if no opinion is delivered, the Commission shall, without delay, submit to the Council a proposal concerning the measures to be taken. The Council shall act by a qualified majority.

If the Council does not act within three months of the referral to it the Commission shall adopt the measures proposed unless the Council has decided against those measures by a simple majority.

Article 8

Final provisions

1. Member States shall bring into force the laws, regulations and administrative provisions necessary to comply with this Directive by 1 January 1994. They shall forthwith inform the Commission thereof.

When Member States adopt these measures, they shall include a reference to this Directive or be accompanied by such a reference on the occasion of their official publication. The manner in which such a reference is to be made shall be laid down by the Member States.

2. Member States shall communicate to the Commission the texts of the main provisions of national law which they adopt in the field governed by this Directive.

3. Pending Community legislation on the monitoring on a consolidated or non-consolidated basis of large exposures concerning activities which are principally exposed to market risks the Member States shall deal with such large exposures in accordance with methods which they shall determine, having regard to the particular nature of the risks involved.

Article 9

This Directive is addressed to the Member States.

Done at Brussels, 21 December 1992.

For the Council
The President
D. HURD

INDEX